FUNCTION name [(parameters)][STATIC]	Establish a function. (End FUNCTION.)	
GET #filenum [,recordnumber]	Reads data from a random number is not specified, the *next* record is read.	
GOSUB linelabel	Begins execution of a subroutine. The RETURN statement returns from the subroutine.	46
GOTO linelabel	Branches to the specified line label.	139
IF condition THEN statement(s) [ELSE statement(s)]	Performs the statement(s) following THEN when the condition evaluates *true*. Performs the statements following the ELSE (if included) when the condition evaluates *false*.	104

IF condition THEN
  [statement(s)]
[ELSEIF condition THEN
  statement(s)]
[ELSE
  statement(s)]
END IF
	Block IF statement.	109

INPUT [;] ["prompt";] variable [,variable2,...]	Inputs data from the keyboard. If a prompt is included, it prints before the input occurs.	39
INPUT #filenum, variable [,variable2,...]	Reads data from a sequential data file.	12
KILL "filename"	Deletes a file from disk.	416
[LET] variable = expression	Evaluates the expression and assigns the result to the variable.	12
LINE [(XStart, YStart)]—(XEnd, YEnd) [,[ColorAttribute] [,B[F]]]	Draws a line in medium or high resolution graphics modes.	451
LINE INPUT [;] ["prompt";] stringvariable	Inputs all characters (limit 255) typed at the keyboard. Accepts all characters including commas and colons, until ENTER is pressed.	196
LOCATE row, column [,cursor]	Places the cursor at the row and column position specified. The optional cursor parameter controls the visibility of the cursor.	181
LPRINT items to print	Prints data on the printer. Items are separated by commas or semicolons.	12
LPRINT USING "stringliteral"; items to print LPRINT USING stringvariable; items to print	Prints data on the printer, according to the format specified in the string literal or variable.	84
MID$(stringvariable, start position, number of characters) = stringexpression	Replaces part of a string variable with the string expression.	187
NAME "old filename" AS "new filename"	Renames a disk file.	416
NEXT [loop index]	Terminates a FOR...NEXT loop.	258
ON ERROR GOTO line label	Enables program error trapping and specifies the line label of the error handling routine.	525
OPEN mode, #filenum, "filename"	Opens a sequential data file. Mode must be "I" for input files or "O" for output files.	362

ALTERNATE EDITION

QuickBASIC
and
QBASIC
Using
Modular
Structure
with
Visual Basic

JULIA CASE BRADLEY
Mt. San Antonio College

Irwin
McGraw-Hill

Boston, Massachusetts   Burr Ridge, Illinios   Dubuque, Iowa
Madison, Wisconsin   New York, New York   San Francisco, California   St. Louis, Missouri

Irwin/McGraw-Hill

A Division of The **McGraw·Hill** *Companies*

Irwin Book Team

Sponsoring editor: Associate editor: *Garrett Glanz*
Project editor: *Gladys True*
Production supervisor: *Dina L. Treadaway*
Assistant manager, graphics: *Charlene R. Breeden*
Coordinator, graphics & desktop services: *Keri Kunst*
Designer: *Keith McPherson*
Compositor: *Times Mirror Higher Education Group, Inc., Imaging Group*
Printer: Quebecor Printing/Dubuque was printer and binder.

Library of Congress Cataloging-in-Publication Data

Bradley, Julia Case.
    QuickBASIC and QBASIC using modular structure with Visual Basic/
Julia Case Bradley.—Alternate ed.
      p.   cm.
    Includes index.
    ISBN: 0–256–20797–6
    1. Microsoft QuickBASIC. 2. QBasic (Computer program language)
3. BASIC (Computer program language) I. Title.
QA76.73.B3B726   1996
005.265—dc20   95–35898

Printed in the United States of America
  3 4 5 6 7 8 9 QPD QPD 9 0 9

Contents

5 Structured Programming 135

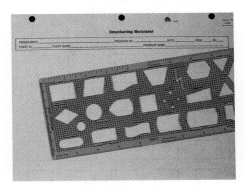

6 Report Design and Subtotals 147

7 Data Validation and Interactive Programs 177

8 Text Graphics, Color, and Sound 217

9 Menus 235

10 Additional Control Structures and Numeric Functions 257

11 Single-Dimension Arrays 293

12   Advanced Array Handling   323

13   Sequential Data Files   357

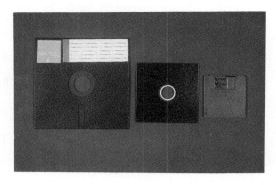

14   Random Data Files   381

15   Additional File Handling Concepts   413

16   Pixel Graphics   441

Appendixes   475

Preface

This textbook is intended for use in an introductory course in BASIC, which assumes no prior knowledge of computers or programming. The fundamentals of programming are taught in a style consistent with current thinking in the computing field. The student programmer will learn good techniques from the start, rather than having to alter habits that are already formed.

Structured Programming

The primary feature of the text is the development of well-structured, modular programs. Program modules are implemented with subroutines by the early introduction of the GOSUB statement. Appearing throughout the text are complete example programs that are models of good programming style—meaningful variable names; complete remarks including a dictionary of variable names, program mainline and subroutines; clear, consistent indentation; and control structures limited to the three "proper" constructs—sequence, selection, and iteration. The students are *not* taught to program with the GOTO statement at all.

Microsoft's QuickBASIC and QBASIC

The dialects of BASIC chosen are QuickBASIC and QBASIC, from the Microsoft Corporation. Release 4.0 and 4.5 of QuickBASIC are covered along with QBASIC. The selection of QB was made for several important reasons. The BASIC from Microsoft

1. is the leading BASIC in the marketplace.
2. is an excellent learning and teaching tool, since it identifies syntax errors in a statement as it is typed.
3. integrates a program editor, pull-down menus, and powerful debugger into an easy-to-use programming environment. The debugger provides for single-stepping program execution, watching the values in any program variables, conditionally stopping program execution, displaying the contents of variables or conditions, and even changing the value of a variable during execution.
4. has added state-of-the-art constructs to the language to make BASIC a truly structured language.
5. includes multi-line, block IF...THEN...ELSE statements.
6. provides exceptional loop control to implement DO WHILE and DO UNTIL with either pretest or posttest.
7. includes an excellent CASE structure implementation.
8. allows for user-defined variable types, which can define a data structure to be used as a record description for data files.

Extensive Appendixes

The inclusion of necessary reference material in the appendixes will do away with the need for most additional, supplementary material generally needed in programming courses. By limiting the discussion to QB, the text can cover the system commands necessary to operate in this environment. The appendixes include:

1. The operating environment, including keyboard and mouse interfaces, menus and dialog boxes
2. Entering and editing code with the smart program editor
3. Debugging techniques and the QB debugger
4. Reference to BASIC statements
5. Discussion and examples of methods to control the special functions of printers
6. Answers to the many feedback questions interspersed throughout the text
7. A list of the reserved words in QB
8. The ASCII code
9. Error trapping
10. Writing programs with subprograms and functions
11. Converting programs written in BASICA or GW-BASIC to QB

Interactive Program Style

The programming emphasis is on interactive program style using menus, good screen design, and input data validation. The INPUT statement is the first method covered for entering data into programs. Not until students are accustomed to interactive programs are the READ and DATA statements covered. Since the majority of software implemented on microcomputers is interactive, it makes sense to learn programming in this manner.

Data File Handling

This text goes well beyond most in the area of data file handling. Chapter 13 covers file concepts and gives extensive coverage of sequential files, including creation, retrieval, and appending data. Chapter 14 covers random data files and shows examples of random and sequential retrieval, updating, and reporting. In chapter 15, indexed files are discussed, and a complete example is included illustrating the creation and maintenance of an indexed file. Sequential file updates are also covered in chapter 15.

Graphics

The currently hot topic of graphics is well-covered. Chapter 8 introduces text graphics, which can be used on any computer. Chapter 16 introduces pixel graphics for black-and-white as well as color monitors and includes a discussion of the rapidly-changing "standards" for graphics.

Complete Chapter Summaries

At the conclusion of each chapter is a comprehensive list of topics covered in the chapter. During extensive classroom testing of the manuscript, this was one of the most popular features. Although a few of the more advanced students read *only* the summary, most students used the summaries to review the material, for reference to look up topics and terms, and to study for exams. Professors found them a concise source of exam questions.

Program Planning with Flowcharts, Pseudocode, and Hierarchy Charts

The important topic of program planning is covered completely using the three most popular planning tools. Although the trend in the industry is toward dropping the use of flowcharts and switching to either pseudocode or hierarchy charts (or a combination of the two), many students benefit from the visual presentation of program logic afforded by flowcharts. By including all three methods, the student can select the method most beneficial to him or her—and the professor has the choice of methods to use in class.

Significant Changes   (Improvements) in the traditional sequence of topics

1. *Early coverage of subroutines.* Early (chapter 2) programs are broken into modules using subroutines. Throughout the text programs are written in a modular style, stressing the concept of good module design.

2. *Coverage of looping before selection.* The concept of conditions is presented in the context of controlling loop execution rather than selecting alternate courses of action. The student can easily grasp simple program loops without the necessity of the IF...THEN and IF...THEN...ELSE. With this order of topics, programs can be more meaningful sooner.

3. *Usage of the DO and LOOP statements for most program loops.* Until chapter 10, all program loops are formed with DO and LOOP. The FOR/NEXT is introduced just before array handling, mainly as an aid to subscript manipulation. Any loop that must be terminated early is always coded with DO...LOOP, and *never* does execution branch out of a loop with a GOTO or IF...THEN branch.

4. *Early coverage of PRINT USING and LPRINT USING.* The first programs involving program loops (chapter 3) also include formatting the output with (L)PRINT USING. In this way, the student programmer can create pleasing, properly aligned output.

5. *Early coverage of structured programming guidelines.* The first program examples are coded in a consistent, structured style without giving the complete rationale. Then, as soon as the student has learned enough to understand the terms (chapter 5), a complete coverage of structured programming and top-down programming is presented. This is far superior to having either a late chapter (after the student has developed a programming style) or an early chapter (before the student can understand the terms) devoted to structured programming concepts.

Numerous Examples and Programming Exercises   Each chapter has one complete programming example, showing the program planning, program coding, and output. Additionally, many smaller examples are included throughout the text.

Feedback Questions and Exercises   Interspersed at appropriate points are thought-provoking questions and exercises to test student learning. Answers are found in appendix E.

BASIC Statements and Functions Boxed   As each new statement or function is introduced, it is enclosed in a box with its general form. It is also explained and illustrated with examples that clearly demonstrate its use. These boxes serve as a source of easy reference for the student.

Coverage of Output Report Design   A rare topic for BASIC programming textbooks is planning reports. The use of printer spacing charts is covered, along with multiple page output.

Flexibility of Use   This text is ideally suited for the variety of programming courses currently being taught (and those being considered). That "one-semester course in BASIC" is far from standardized, and many colleges and universities are now offering a second semester of BASIC programming. In many cases, BASIC is introduced in a computer concepts course, and in others, the programming is in an independent course.

The coverage of this text is actually more comprehensive than that of most one-semester courses. This gives the professor some latitude in the selection of topics. Here are some possible variations, using parts of the material presented.

1. *Short course for students with no background.* Spend two or three hours on chapter 1 to give the student an understanding of the hardware and software concepts. Leave out the material on data files and sorting. The course would terminate with chapter 12.

2. *Concept courses that include BASIC.* Skip chapter 1 (which covers the fundamentals being more completely covered). Use chapters 2, 3, 4, 5, 9, FOR/NEXT from 10, and 11.

3. *One-semester (or quarter) course that has a prerequisite.* Skip chapter 1.

4. *File-oriented course.* Cover chapter 14 (random files) early. Some successful courses cover this material before chapter 4, which allows programs to have data file input even before the introduction of selection (IF-THEN).

5. *Advanced course.* The concepts in chapter 7 (interactive programming, screen formatting, data validation) are often taught in a second BASIC course. Also, sequential updates and indexing random files (chapter 15) are topics often found in second semester programming courses. Graphics (chapters 8 and 16) are good topics for an advanced class. Some of the materials in the Appendixes make ideal lessons for an advanced course. Error trapping (appendix I) and subprograms and functions (appendix G) are generally considered advanced topics, as well as controlling printer functions (appendix H).

6. *Mathematically oriented course.* Cover chapter 10 after chapter 2. Chapter 10 includes the FOR-NEXT statements, functions, and the DEF FN statement. Appendix G subprograms and functions, should also be covered early.

Supplementary Materials   This text is part of a complete package of course materials.

1. *Instructor's Manual.* Includes chapter outlines, teaching suggestions, and test questions.

2. *Instructor's Disks.* A set of two disks, which include working solutions to many of the programming exercises, and all of the programming assignments.

3. *TestPak.* Available to instructors, this computerized version of the test questions in the Instructor's Manual can be used to print tests or quiz students.

Acknowledgments

I would like to express my appreciation to the many people who have contributed to the successful completion of this text. Most especially, I want to thank my colleagues and the students of Mt. San Antonio College who helped class test the material in the text and greatly influenced the final form of the manuscript. A special "thank you" goes to David M. Harris of the Toronto School of Business, for his many helpful suggestions. This text could not have come out on schedule without the hours of dedicated service of Anna Gonzales. I am also grateful to the reviewers who gave constructive criticism and many valuable suggestions.

William E. Burkhardt—Carl Sandburg College
Curtis R. Bring—Moorhead State University
Anita Gilmer—Shawnee State University

1

Introduction to Computers and BASIC

REM Statement
CLS Statement
PRINT and LPRINT
  Statements
END Statement

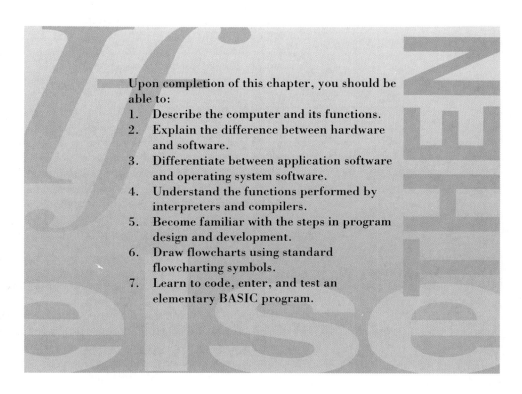

Upon completion of this chapter, you should be able to:
1. Describe the computer and its functions.
2. Explain the difference between hardware and software.
3. Differentiate between application software and operating system software.
4. Understand the functions performed by interpreters and compilers.
5. Become familiar with the steps in program design and development.
6. Draw flowcharts using standard flowcharting symbols.
7. Learn to code, enter, and test an elementary BASIC program.

The Computer

IBM-AT. An IBM AT computer.

The computer, like a typewriter or calculator, is a tool for solving problems. Once mastered, it can be made to perform marvelous feats on command. Without mastery, it can be like a typewriter or calculator in the hands of a child who has not learned its use—its great potential goes to waste.

Many things must operate together for a computer to do any useful work. Assume you have just purchased a powerful, flexible, accurate, obedient robot. You want the robot to work for you—perhaps scrub the floor, fix the car, wash the dishes, or do your math homework.

This robot will do anything you ask, but it doesn't know *how* to do anything for itself. It has no common sense. If you tell the robot to change the spark plugs in the car, it won't know that first it must open the hood. If you remember to tell it to open the hood, you had better be sure to place the steps in the correct sequence. Otherwise, it will attempt to change the spark plugs and *then* open the hood. (At this point, hope that the robot is not strong enough to carry out the task, gets stuck, and sends a message saying, "Not able to carry out the task.")

In many ways a computer is similar to that obedient, dumb robot. It must be told each step to carry out. Additionally, each step must be carried out in the correct sequence. The computer is not smart enough to know when steps are out of sequence, so it simply follows directions as long as it possibly can. Sometimes the results will not be what you expected, but you can be sure that the computer followed directions exactly.

Did you instruct the robot to remove the spark plugs with a wrench? Did you tell it to check the gap? Exactly how do you think it will replace the old plugs with the new plugs? If it hasn't been told these things, it will either stop or do something strange and unexpected. In either case, the results can be frustrating.

When writing instructions for the computer to solve a problem, you must be certain to compute the result *before* printing it. Since the computer doesn't know the difference, it will do only and exactly what you ask. Depending on your frame of mind, sometimes the results of computer processing can be uproariously funny or infuriating. Frankly, some people get so frustrated with the level of detail required that computer programming would be better left to someone else.

Hardware and Software

In our robot story, you could say that you had a powerful robot (the hardware), but without the proper instructions (the software), the robot would not be much help. The same is true for the computer. The computer itself—the circuitry, the case, the keyboard, the screen—are called the *hardware*. While the computer has tremendous power and flexibility, it absolutely *must* have instructions in order to carry out any useful work. Those instructions are the *software,* or the **computer programs.** Computer programs can be thought of as the instructions necessary to convert inputs into outputs.

Laptop computer. This portable lap-top computer from Hewlett-Packard can be carried around and used anywhere.

TI with graphics on screen. This microcomputer from Texas Instruments is targeted at the business market.

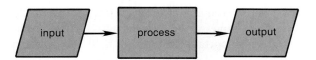

The entire purpose of computer **processing** is to produce some type of **output** (e.g., a report, a computation, a sorted list, a graph). Output may be generated on a screen, a printer, a plotter, a speaker, or some other output device. In order to produce output, there must be processing of the input data. The input to the program may come from the keyboard, from magnetic disk or tape, from a microphone, or from some type of reader such as a bar code reader or scanner. The processing may be arithmetic computations or rearranging, reorganizing, or reformatting data.

The primary goal of this text is to present a method of writing computer software—turning inputs into useful outputs. A basic knowledge of computer hardware is helpful when writing computer instructions.

Hardware

Note the block diagram of a computer. The computer can be seen as a group of components working together. The following sections explain the various components.

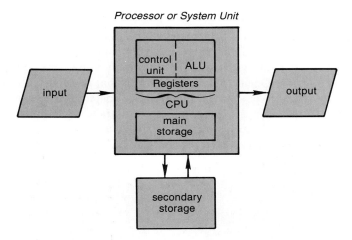

Processor

The main unit of the computer is often called the *processor* or *system unit*. In the block diagram, the two primary components of the processor are the *CPU* (*Central Processing Unit*) and the *main storage* of the computer.

The CPU, sometimes called the "brain" of the computer, does the actual manipulation of the data. One part of the CPU, called the *ALU* (*Arithmetic and Logic Unit*), does all computations and logical operations. Logical operations include such things as determining that one number is greater than another, that one name follows another, or that a condition is *true* or *false*.

Another part of the CPU is the control unit. It is the control unit that controls and coordinates the execution of instructions. The control unit and the ALU working together carry out the instructions of the computer program.

There are several types of processors available in the microcomputer market. The IBM PC/AT/PS2 and their compatibles are the processors referred to in this text.

Main Storage

The main storage of the computer can have many different names. The words *storage* and *memory* are used interchangeably when referring to the computer. Main storage may be called *primary storage, internal storage, temporary storage,* or *RAM* (*Random Access Memory*).

When a computer is executing a program, main storage must hold the program as well as some of the data being operated upon. For this reason, the size of main storage is important. In order to hold a large program, a computer must have a sufficient amount of memory.

Computers are sold with varying amounts of main storage, and often additional memory may be added. Memory size is generally stated in terms of the number of characters that can be stored, where one character equals one letter of the alphabet, one digit of a number, or one of the special symbols such as $, %, *.

In computer terms, the amount of storage needed to hold one character is called a **byte.** A group of 1024 bytes is referred to as one **K** (*k*ilobyte). As a rough guide to computer storage, remember that 1 K holds about one thousand characters, which would be approximately two-thirds of a double-spaced, typewritten page of data. One thousand K bytes, approximately one million bytes, is called one MB (megabyte).

Typical main storage sizes:

640K bytes—approximately 640,000 characters
1MB—one megabyte—approximately 1 million characters

Since the entire program and its data must fit into main storage, the computer's memory may be a limiting factor when developing computer programs.

Volatility

As a general rule, you don't need to know how a computer works in order to use one, just as you don't need to understand all of the systems of a car in order to drive. But there are a few pieces of information that will make life easier for you.

One helpful fact to know is that most computer memory is *volatile;* that is, when the power source is removed, the contents of the storage are lost. Any program or data stored in the computer's main storage is gone when the computer is turned off or a power failure occurs. This phenomenon has been the source of many curses and tears by computer users.

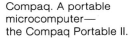

Compaq. A portable microcomputer— the Compaq Portable II.

Secondary or Auxiliary Storage

Fortunately, there is storage that is nonvolatile—that does *not* lose its memory when the power goes off. This is the type of memory used for long-term storage of data files and programs—the media used to store programs when they are *not* being executed. This is called *secondary storage, auxiliary storage, external storage* (or memory), or sometimes *long-term storage.*

The two most common forms of secondary storage are magnetic disk and magnetic tape. Within these two groups, the types are further broken down into small disks, large disks, hard-surface disks, floppy disks, and cassette tapes of various sizes and shapes. As a BASIC programmer for a personal computer, the storage media you will most likely see is the **floppy disk** (**diskette**) and the **hard disk.** Disks must be formatted before they can be used.

Since it is likely that you will be handling diskettes for storage of programs and data, a few words about the care of diskettes are in order.

1. The data is stored magnetically, similar to audio tapes. A magnetic field (magnet, power supply, TV screen, etc.) can erase or scramble your data.
2. *Anything* on the surface of the diskette can ruin the data, and maybe even the read/write heads in the disk drive. This means no fingerprints, hairs, lemonade, or cookie crumbs.
3. Heat ruins diskettes. Leaving a diskette in a hot car is a sure way to destroy it.
4. Pressure can damage a diskette. Never allow a disk to be caught by the ring of a binder. Never use a ballpoint pen to write on the disk label.

Read Only Memory (ROM)

There is another type of nonvolatile memory available for computers. This storage resembles main storage with one important difference—the contents of the memory cannot be changed by the computer user. This *ROM* (*Read Only Memory*) is filled with software by the manufacturer. Once inside the computer, the instructions may be executed, but not changed. ROM is actually hardware containing permanently stored software and is sometimes called *firmware.*

Floppies. Two sizes of diskettes used for microcomputers: *A.* 5¼-inch diskette. *B.* 3½-inch diskette.

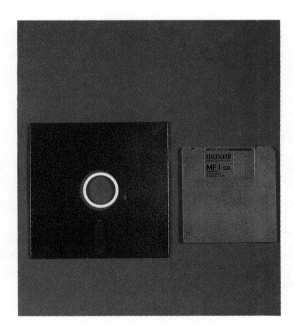

Mac with mouse. A mouse can be used for computer input. As the mouse is moved around the tabletop, the cursor moves on the screen.

Light pen. A light pen is a penlike wand attached to the computer by a wire. It can be used to select options from on-screen menus, to point at screen images, and even to draw graphic images.

Computer Input

As you have discovered, main storage must hold the program and some of the data to operate upon. How does this information get into storage? Since all data must be stored electronically, letters, numbers, words, or sounds must first be converted to a form that can be stored. Then these data can be moved into main storage. This conversion to electronic form, sometimes called digitizing, takes place in computer input devices.

The foremost input device is the keyboard. What happens when you press the *A* key on the keyboard? That keypress must be converted into digital electronic pulses that can be stored in computer memory.

Many other input devices are available for personal computers as well as their larger counterparts. Increasingly popular as input devices for personal computers are the joystick and the mouse, along with voice input. Optical scanners can digitize drawings, printed pages, or bar codes. Computer input may also come from the more traditional magnetic tape, magnetic disk, or more exotic sources such as thermocouples.

Computer Output

Since the entire reason for using computers is to produce some type of output, it makes sense to examine some of the choices available for that output.

The results of processing will be in main storage (temporarily). You must find a way either to present that information in a human-understandable form or to save the information for later reference.

The two most common forms of computer output are the screen display and the printout. However, many others are also available. In this text you will learn to store programs as well as data files on magnetic disk. Computers may also send their output to plotters, tape drives, card punches, voice speakers, and many types of switching devices.

Touchscreen. A touchscreen such as this one from Hewlett-Packard allows the user to input data by merely touching the screen next to a menu choice. Electrical sensors in the glass screen are grounded by this touch, indicating which portion of the screen was selected.

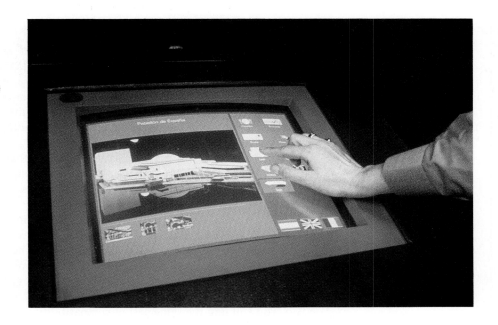

Touch pad. This pad can be used to input characters and graphics. The user draws on the pad, and the characters are interpreted and transferred to the computer.

Joystick. Input from joysticks is very popular for computer games.

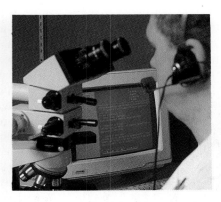

Voice input. This microphone is used to provide voice input to a computer.

Software

The instructions to take data from the input devices, manipulate that data, and send it to an output device are called software. Software can be broken down into two broad classifications: (1) *operating system software* (including utilities) and (2) *applications software.*

The necessary software to manage computer operation is called the operating system. This operating system, called **DOS (*D*isk *O*perating *S*ystem),** along with many utility programs, makes up operating system software. Nobody ever bought a computer so that they could use operating system software. People buy computers to produce some desired output. That output is produced by applications software.

Applications software includes accounting programs, games, word processing programs, business applications, scientific applications, medical applications, in fact anything you can name—anything, that is, except the programs to manage the computer itself.

The Operating System

There are many tasks to be done, if an application program is to be run. The disk must first be properly formatted so that programs and data may be stored. A directory must be maintained on the disk to indicate what is there, which parts of the disk are occupied, and which are still available. Programs must be read from the disk into main storage; sequences of characters must be sent from the input devices and to the output devices; and error messages must be sent. The **operating system** performs these, and many more, functions.

You probably will not be surprised to hear that not all operating systems are alike. Although each must solve the same set of problems, each does the job in a slightly different way—disk directories in different locations and in different formats, different codes to indicate similar conditions.

The situation could be compared to that of movie cameras and video recorders. There, the problem is to take pictures, to place them on film or tape, and to reproduce the pictures later. But how many different approaches are there? Different manufacturers use their own techniques and methods. The consumer must choose one, because they are not interchangeable. However, the differences may be mostly technical in nature and not affect the use of the equipment.

You will find the same sort of compatibility, or lack of it, in computer operating systems as in video systems. A video consumer may select from BETA, VHS, video disc, or several other options and have a measure of compatibility. If the user's goal is simply to record and to play back pictures, it makes no difference which is most popular, or how compatible the system will be with others. If the goal is to play tapes produced on other systems, it suddenly becomes important to know what and how much is available in each format.

A computer consumer may select any one of a number of operating systems. Some that have more users than others have become more "standard" simply because there are more programs available that are compatible with that system. Some computer manufacturers supply their own operating system with their computers, others purchase a "standard" operating system from a software company and supply that operating system with their computer. Popular operating systems that have been adopted by many manufacturers are MS-DOS (called PC-DOS by IBM), Unix, and Xenix. These operating systems can be said to be "standard," since they are in use on many different brands of computers.

Operating System Utilities

There are also many utility programs that are classified as operating system software. These utilities exist to make the development, use, and storage of applications software easier or more efficient. Some examples of utilities are: (1) program editors, which provide for entering and changing program lines; (2) copy programs, which will allow entire disks or parts of disks to be copied to another disk or device; (3) debugging aids, which are not for extermination but for finding program errors; (4) disk maintenance programs, which check the validity of data stored on diskette and perhaps make corrections to erroneous data; and (5) compilers and interpreters, which are for application program development and deserve much closer attention.

Compilers and Interpreters

The computer does not really speak or understand human language. Although the computer was designed to carry out instructions, those instructions must be in a strange language called *machine language*. The instructions written for the computer must be translated into machine language before the computer can understand or execute them.

For a moment, remember the robot analogy, and imagine that the robot helper speaks, reads, and writes only a strange robot dialect. Any request made of the robot must first be translated into "robotese."

Fortunately, there is one person who knows the robot dialect and can translate instructions. The translator understands only precise English and cannot translate any idioms or slang expressions. Instructions must be written carefully. Assume there is a long list of instructions for the robot. How are the instructions going to be translated? The translator will work in either of two methods.

In the first translation mode, the translator converts the first instruction, and the robot executes it. Then the translator translates the next instruction to robot language, and the robot executes it. The entire list is completed, one instruction at a time. If one instruction on the list can't be correctly translated, the robot will perform everything up to that point and stop. If any steps in the list must be repeated, those instructions must be retranslated.

The second method of translation calls for the entire list to be translated before the robot begins. The translator goes through the list, translating and checking. If there is anything in the list that won't properly translate, the translator discovers that before the robot begins. If some of the steps in the list must be repeated, they will need to be translated only once. When the translator is finished with the list, it is handed to the robot, who can now understand every word.

Which method is best? That depends on what the task is, how often it must be repeated, and whether it is more advantageous to get started quickly. Translating the whole list before starting will make the execution go much more quickly, but it will take time that perhaps could have been better spent executing instructions. What does all this have to do with computer languages anyway?

Since the computer instructions must be in machine language, a translator is required. That translator is computer software, which reads written instructions and converts them into machine language.

The translator program must be able to understand the written instructions. The instructions must be precise and correct. Many languages have been developed to aid in writing computer instructions. These languages are called computer *programming languages,* and each has strict rules for forming instructions to the computer.

What about the order of translation? Translator programs that convert one instruction at a time are called **interpreters.** Each instruction is executed immediately after it is interpreted. Translator programs that completely translate the entire program to machine code before any execution are called **compilers.** You will find that both methods have their advantages and disadvantages.

Programming Languages

There are literally hundreds of computer programming languages available for writing instructions to the computer. Each was developed to solve a particular type of problem. Some of the more common programming languages are:

1. BASIC (*B*eginner's *A*ll-purpose *S*ymbolic *I*nstruction *C*ode)—The most popular language in use for microcomputers. BASIC was developed as the first language to be interactive with a user.
2. FORTRAN (*FOR*mula *TRAN*slation)—The first of the high-level languages, designed for scientific and mathematically oriented programming.
3. COBOL (*CO*mmon *B*usiness *O*riented *L*anguage)—The most popular business language in use for larger computers.
4. Pascal—Popular with computer scientists, Pascal is known as a highly structured language. Pascal was named after Blaise Pascal, mathematician and inventor of the adding machine.
5. C—Developed by Bell Lab scientists. C is widely used for writing operating systems and utility software.
6. PL/I (*P*rogramming *L*anguage/I)—Developed as an all-purpose language, for both business and scientific applications, and used primarily on large mainframe computers. Subsets of the language are available for use on microcomputers.

7. RPG (*R*eport *P*rogram *G*enerator)—Used primarily for business applications on small business computers.
8. Ada—A relatively new language under development by the U.S. Department of Defense, along with several international organizations and governments. Ada's primary use is scientific, including missile guidance systems.
9. Assembly language—Included here as a class of languages, since each type of computer has its own assembly language. Assembly is extremely close to machine language and requires an intimate knowledge of the inner working of the computer and the machine's instruction set.

BASIC and Standardization

The language BASIC was developed at Dartmouth College in the 1960s as a simplified method for learning computer programming. The acronym BASIC stands for *Beginner's All-purpose Symbolic Instruction Code*. Early BASIC had only a fraction of the statements now included in most versions of the language.

As the BASIC language became more popular, new versions were implemented for many different computers. With new implementations came many new additions to the language in order to increase the usefulness of BASIC. Some of the capabilities added to BASIC after its introduction include statements for handling alphabetic data, statements allowing programs to read and write data in disk files, and statements providing a means to give programs better structure. These extensions to the language are both a blessing and a curse. The language is much more powerful and flexible than it once was, but these enhancements have not been uniformly implemented. Now the market abounds with many different versions of BASIC.

Which version of BASIC should you learn? Valid arguments can be made for many versions. This text will concentrate on QuickBASIC and QBASIC from Microsoft, Inc. This BASIC is one of a "new breed" of computer languages that has kept up with technology. New statements have been added to the language to implement current teachings in structured programming. The "smart editor" catches many programming syntax errors as each line is typed, making it easier to learn the correct form, and catch errors early. On-screen help and powerful new capabilities make it competitive with the best of modern programming languages, while retaining BASIC's ease of use.

BASIC consists of several parts. The first part is the language itself, which has vocabulary and rules for the construction of statements, just like any other language. Another important aspect of BASIC is called the *environment* or *user interface*. This refers to the way that we specify what we want to do. How do we specify that we want to run a program, save a program, type a new program, or quit? The BASIC environment has been designed to be as easy and understandable as possible for beginning programmers. Commands are selected from menus with either a keyboard or a mouse.

QuickBASIC and QBASIC

This text was written for QuickBASIC versions 4.0 and 4.5, as well as QBASIC version 1.0. For the sake of simplicity, all three versions will be referred to as QB (or just BASIC). There are very few differences in the BASIC language statements for the three versions. The main differences that you will notice are in the menu choices and Help feature. Also, QuickBASIC programs can be compiled into stand-alone executable programs; QBASIC and the educational version of QuickBASIC 4.0 are interpreters only and cannot be used to compile programs. All programs in this text are intended to be interpreted rather than compiled, so you will not be handicapped by the lack of the compile capability. (If you were to write commercial programs and put them into regular use, you would want to compile rather than interpret them.)

With the release of QuickBASIC 4.5, Microsoft added extensive Help screens. You can request Help at any point to give the syntax of BASIC statements and show examples; in fact, the entire reference manual is available on the Help screens. There are also two levels of menus in version 4.5, designed to make choices less confusing for the beginner. The programmer can choose between the simpler "Easy Menus" or select "Full Menus," which contain the more advanced options. With very few exceptions, everything that must be done in a beginning BASIC course is found on the simplified "Easy Menus."

QBASIC is the version of BASIC that is shipped with DOS version 5.0 and above. QBASIC has all the extended Help screens of QuickBASIC 4.5, but it interprets rather than compiles the programs. QBASIC has somewhat fewer choices on its menus, which only occasionally may be a handicap (such as in debugging programs and executing DOS commands).

All of the programs in this text can be written in any of the three versions of BASIC. On occasion, there are slight differences in the statements, which will be noted. As soon as we gain an understanding of an elementary BASIC program, the menu commands to execute a program will be presented.

A First BASIC Program

Following is an elementary computer program, written in the BASIC language.

Program Listing:

```
' *** Program to Calculate the Area of a Room ***
CLS
INPUT Length
INPUT Wdth
LET Area = Length * Wdth
PRINT "The area is"; Area
END
```

Program Execution:

```
? 25
? 35
The area is 875
```

The individual statements will be examined line by line.

The first line is called a remark statement. An apostrophe is used to denote the beginning of a remark. Remarks, sometimes called *comments,* are used for program documentation only, to make programs easier for humans to understand. Remarks are not translated to machine language or executed by the program. Any time the program is listed, the remarks appear along with the program lines. It is wise to make heavy use of remark statements in programs; establish the habit early.

When writing BASIC programs in other versions of BASIC, you may find that the apostrophe cannot be used to indicate a remark. In any version of BASIC (including QB), a remark statement may be indicated with REM. The first line of the program could be written

```
REM *** Program to Calculate the Area of a Room ***
```

The first statement that will actually be executed is CLS. This instructs QB to clear the screen before taking any other action. CLS will be the first statement in most programs.

The two following statements are called INPUT statements. Recall the diagram of computer processing.

The first step is input. The data must be put into the computer so that it can be operated upon.

Referring back to the example program for a moment, notice the program execution

```
?  25    ← typed by user
?  35    ← typed by user
The area is 875
```

This is the execution of the program. The computer is carrying out the instructions given in the program lines.

The first question mark is generated by the first INPUT statement. When an INPUT statement is encountered during program execution, a question mark is displayed on the screen. Execution is then suspended while the user types a number. In this case, the number 25 was assigned to Length.

The second question mark was placed there by the second INPUT statement. When the user keyed 35, that value was assigned to Wdth.

The LET statement corresponds to the middle box in the diagram of the input-process-output. The LET statement does the processing. In this case, it multiplies the value for Length by the value for Wdth and calls the answer Area. The names Length, Wdth, and Area are called **variables,** since the values assigned to those names may be changed.

> *Note:* When choosing variable names, the programmer must avoid a list of "reserved" words. Since the word Width is reserved, the variable was named Wdth. See appendix F for the complete list of reserved words.

The program output is performed by the PRINT statement. This will PRINT (display on the screen) both the literal words "The area is" and the value calculated for Area. The program output could be directed to the printer instead of the screen (assuming a printer is attached to the computer) by changing the PRINT statement to LPRINT.

```
LPRINT "The area is"; Area
```

This program could be executed many times, each with different room sizes.

Program Execution:

```
?  20
?  30
The area is 600
```

Program Execution:

```
?  10
?  30
The area is 300
```

The last line in the program, END, is the signal that processing is complete.

Program Planning

A series of program planning tasks must be performed before a computer program can be written. A construction crew would not begin building a house until all plans were drawn, and a programmer should not start a computer program until the plans are made. You may find programmers who begin writing the program as soon as they see the problem. You can also find carpenters who begin sawing and hammering without making plans. The analogy is a good one. Generally, the project results will look "slapped together." If the carpenter is experienced and has done this same sort of thing many, many times, chances are good that the project will come out well. A truly experienced programmer also may be able to begin without writing down the plans. In both cases, the reason for success is that the complete plan is really there in the person's head. So, until a programmer attains the level of experience to be able to picture *exactly* how the whole thing fits together, written plans must be made.

Steps in Program Development

1. *Clearly state the problem.* No one can solve a problem if it is not clear exactly what is to be done. The problem statement should have three parts.
   a. The output required.
      A computer program is designed always to produce some desired output. Find out exactly what output is required before proceeding.
   b. The inputs.
      What inputs are available, and what will you need in order to produce the desired output?
   c. The **algorithm** for solution.
      An algorithm is a list of steps necessary to accomplish the task. What processing must be done to get from input to output? This will include any formulas needed for calculations.

2. *Plan the logic of the program.* There are several popular methods for planning program logic. In this book **flowcharts, pseudocode,** and **hierarchy charts** are used. (These terms will be explained in depth in following sections.) In practice, you will probably find that one of these methods works best for you and adopt that method.

   The computer follows directions exactly and in the sequence given. You must be careful to plan each step, making sure the sequence is correct. *The logic should be thoroughly tested, with an operation sometimes called "playing computer," before continuing on to the next step.*

3. *Code the program.* Writing the program statements in a programming language such as BASIC is called coding. The program can be written on plain paper or on a specially designed form called a coding form.

4. *Key the program into the computer.* This generally means to type the program, one line at a time, on the computer keyboard. The QB editor gives a big assist, since it checks the syntax of the BASIC statements as they are typed, and displays an error message when it detects a violation of the rules of BASIC.

5. *Test and debug the program.* Once the program has been keyed into the computer, you are ready to see if it works. When the *Start* command is selected, the program begins executing. Did you get the exact output you expected? If the planning was done carefully and well, and no errors were made keying the program, then probably the answer is "yes." But you may want to change the appearance of the output; or maybe the output is *not* correct; or perhaps there was no output at all!

   Any programmer will tell you that programmers don't make mistakes, but that their programs sometimes get **bugs** in them. The process of finding and correcting any errors is called **debugging.**

   It cannot be emphasized too strongly that *all* computer output must be carefully checked. Too often there are reports of gigantic "computer errors" that resulted in overpayments being made or election results being miscalculated. In most cases, the actual errors were programmer errors. Programmers must thoroughly check every aspect of computer output before allowing a program to be used.

   One method of testing programs is to use *test data*. These data have been carefully selected and designed to test all options of a program where the expected results are already known.

6. *Complete the documentation.* **Documentation** is used as reference material for computer systems. The documentation includes the program plans (flowchart, hierarchy chart, pseudocode), descriptions of output and input, algorithms for problem solution, program listings, and instructions for the user. Looking back at steps 1 through 5, it is obvious that most of the documentation has already been prepared. The last step is to complete any loose ends and assemble the documentation into a finished product.

Program Planning with Flowcharts, Pseudocode, and Hierarchy Charts

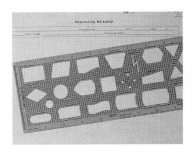

Template. Two basic program design tools: a flowchart template and a flowchart layout form.

Three methods of planning programs will be presented in this text. As an introduction to program planning, the sample program will be shown in pseudocode, hierarchy chart, and flowchart. (See figures 1.1, 1.2, and 1.3.)

Flowcharts

A flowchart is a graphic, or pictorial, view of the logic of a computer program. It has been said that "one picture is worth a thousand words." Many programmers have found that a flowchart helps to organize their thoughts and produce a well-organized program.

A flowchart is drawn before the program is coded as a planning aid. It also becomes part of the documentation for the completed program as an explanation of the logic. This documentation can be a great aid when modifications must be made to a completed program.

Figure 1.1
Pseudocode. Pseudocode shows the program logic in English-like statements.

Input room length

Input room width

Calculate area = length x width

Print area

Figure 1.2
Hierarchy chart. A hierarchy chart shows the program organization broken down into individual functions.

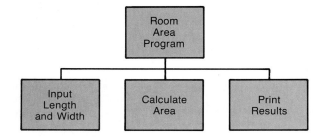

Figure 1.3
Flowchart. A flowchart shows the program logic in pictorial form using standardized symbols.

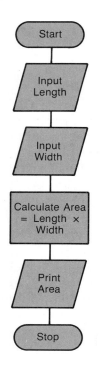

The American National Standards Institute (ANSI) and the International Organization for Standardization (ISO) have each adopted a set of standard flowcharting symbols to be used in computer programming (figure 1.4). This makes flowcharting an effective means of communication between programmers, since all use the same symbols to mean the same thing. (One note here: Just as you can always find people who misuse a spoken language, you may find people who misuse flowcharting symbols.)

Developing Flowcharts

For simple programs, a flowchart may seem superfluous. As programs become more complex, a picture can be an invaluable aid. As the diagram is drawn, often the details of the problem become more apparent. Many times it will become obvious that the boxes should be rearranged for more efficient processing.

When drawing a flowchart, test the logic by "playing computer." This means to step through the program, one line at a time, to determine what the computer output will be. Often there are special conditions that occur only at the beginning of the program or only at the end of the program. Make sure that those steps will always be handled correctly. And, of course, test for the steps that occur in the middle, or main processing, of the program.

There is no rule regarding the language used inside the flowchart symbols. English statements may be used, mathematical formulas, or BASIC statements. The idea is to convey the logic steps and be consistent in language type. (See figure 1.5 for three flowchart examples.)

Figure 1.4
ANSI standard symbols for program flowcharts.

Symbol	Name	Use
	Terminal	Indicates the beginning and end of a program.
	Process	A calculation or assigning a value to a variable. The process symbol generally corresponds to a LET statement in a BASIC program.
	Input/Output (I/O)	Any statement that causes data to be input to a program (INPUT, READ) or output from the program, such as printing on the display screen or line printer.
	Decision	Program decisions. Allows alternate courses of action based on a condition. A decision indicates a question that can be answered *yes* or *no* (or *true* or *false*).
	Predefined Process	A group of statements that together accomplish one task. Used extensively when programs are broken into modules.
	Connector	Can be used to eliminate lengthy flowlines. Its use indicates that one symbol is connected to another. Also used as the termination of IF-THEN-ELSE logic.
	Flowlines and Arrowheads	Used to connect symbols and indicate the sequence of operations. The flow is assumed to go from top to bottom and from left to right. Arrowheads are only required when the flow violates the standard direction.

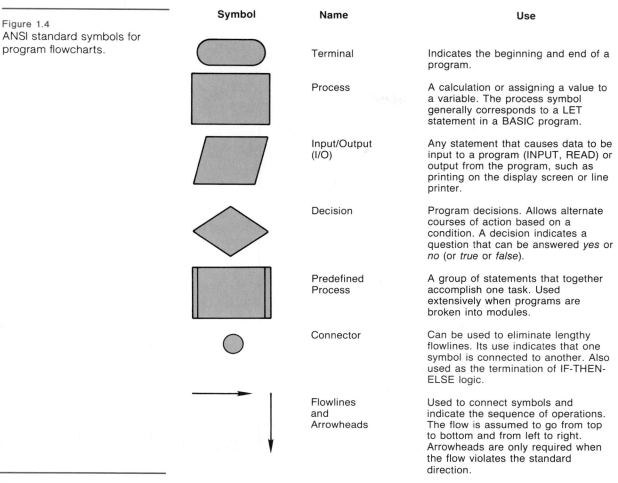

Figure 1.5
Three sample flowcharts. Can you determine what each will do?

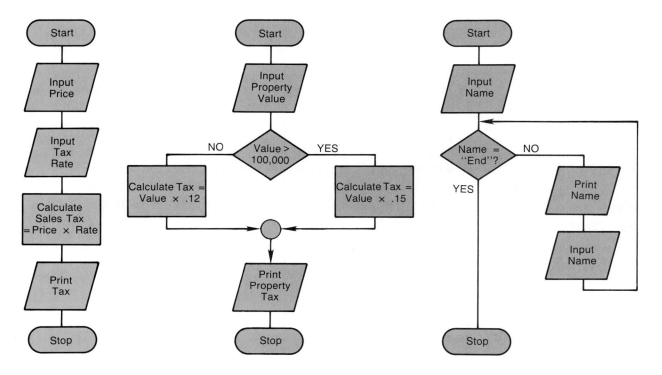

Pseudocode

In pseudocode, natural English statements are used for program planning. The main difference between pseudocode and flowcharts is the lack of pictorial symbols (figure 1.1). Some people find that to be an advantage, others find the written words less clear than the picture.

Pseudocode resembles a cross between a flowchart and the program code. The programmer is free to think about the logical solution to the problem, without being constrained either by selecting the correct symbol or by following the strict syntax rules of the programming language.

There are few rules or standards for the language used in pseudocode. This allows the program planner a great deal of freedom. However, certain conventions have been adopted as an aid to communication.

To be a useful tool, pseudocode should be written as short, imperative statements, with one statement per line. As program logic is developed in this book, the corresponding pseudocode will also be shown. You will find that indentation and alignment of pseudocode lines greatly increase readability and understanding.

These pseudocode examples illustrate the same three programs shown in figure 1.5 as flowcharts.

Sales Tax Computation
Input price
Input tax rate
Calculate tax = price × rate
Print tax
End

Print List of Names
Input name
Loop until name = "END"
    Print name
    Input name
End loop
End

Property Tax Computation
Input property value
If value > 100,000
  then
      calculate tax at 15%
  else
      calculate tax at 12%
Print tax amount
End

Hierarchy Charts

A hierarchy chart is also called a structure chart or a **VTOC (*Visual Table Of Contents*)**. The chart resembles an organization chart in both looks and function (see figure 1.2).

Hierarchy charts are useful when writing programs in a modular fashion. Since you won't learn about modular programming until chapter 2, the presentation of techniques for drawing hierarchy charts will be postponed until that time.

Developing an Example Program

Recall the room area problem presented earlier. This time, each step in program development will be shown.

1. *Clearly state the problem in terms of output, input, and processing.*

   OUTPUT: The area of the room, in square feet
   INPUT: The length and width of the room, in feet
   PROCESSING: Calculate area = length × width

2. *Plan the logic.* For this example, both a flowchart and pseudocode will be used (see figure 1.6). In actual practice, you will choose the one that works best for you.

Figure 1.6
Flowchart and pseudocode for
example program.

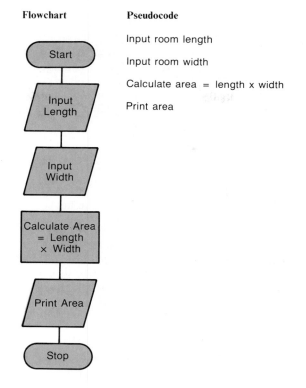

Flowchart

Pseudocode

Input room length

Input room width

Calculate area = length x width

Print area

Figure 1.7
Program coded on coding form.
Any eighty-column layout form
can be an aid in coding a
program.

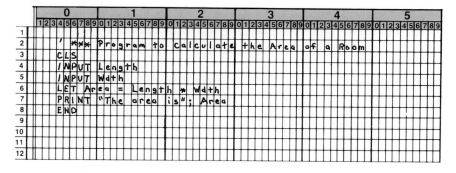

3. *Code the program.* Coding forms make the process easier. Figure 1.7 is a program coded on coding forms.

4. *Key the program into the computer.* Type each BASIC statement on a separate line. At the end of each line, press the ENTER/RETURN key. QB's smart editor converts any BASIC keywords to uppercase and displays an error message in a dialog box if it detects a syntax error. When a message appears, press ENTER or ESCAPE to clear the dialog box from the screen, and make the necessary corrections.

5. *Test and debug the program.* To test the program, select the *Start* command from the *Run* menu (or press Shift-F5). The statements in the program will be executed, one at a time.

6. *Complete the documentation.* Assemble the program planning documents from steps 1 and 2, a listing of the program, sample output, any test data used, and necessary instructions for running the program.

Using the BASIC Environment

Programs are entered using the **editor.** Functions such as running a program, saving a program, and starting a new program are all selected from **menus.** QB sends messages and asks for responses in **dialog boxes.** All together, these tools are called the QB **operating environment** or **user interface.** Fortunately, navigating the environment is quite easy and consistent. As soon as you have learned to select a menu choice and respond to a dialog box, you have mastered the entire QB environment.

The following sections give a quick introduction to the QB environment. For more complete reference, refer to appendix A or the QB reference manual.

Keyboard or Mouse?

Most QB environment commands may be entered with either the keyboard or a mouse. In this text, commands are given for the keyboard method of entry. Mouse users will find directions in appendix A.

Starting the BASIC Program

The specific manner of starting the QB program will vary depending on how and where the program has been installed on a floppy diskette or hard disk. Assuming the program has been installed on a diskette that also holds DOS, and that diskette is in the A: drive, the command for QuickBASIC is

```
A>QB
```
For QBASIC, the command is `A>QBASIC`

What appears next will depend on which version of QB you are using. Quick-BASIC 4.0 takes you directly to the editing screen; QuickBASIC 4.5 and QBASIC display a `Welcome` dialog box first, directing you to press Escape to clear the dialog box and proceed, or Enter to see some of QB's many Help screens. If you choose to view the "Survival Guide," notice the keystroke directions on the bottom of the screen, and remember that you can always clear any dialog box with the Escape key.

The Editing Screen and Menus

The main screen in QB is called the editing screen. Across the top of the editing screen you will find the names of the menus that are available. To open (or pull down) a menu, first press the Alt key to activate the menu bar. Then press the first letter of the menu name, and the menu choices will appear beneath the menu name. Example: *press the Alt key and then the F key to see the File menu.* Then, to select a command from the menu, use the DOWN arrow key to highlight the desired command. With the command highlighted, press Enter to execute the command. Each command also has a one-letter selector key, which appears highlighted in the name. You can type the one-letter selector to execute a command rather than the arrow keys and Enter if you prefer. Example: *to exit QB, press Alt and then F to open the File menu; then type X (for Exit) or use the DOWN arrow to highlight Exit and press Enter.*

A menu can be made to disappear without executing a command. Press the Escape key to close a menu. Or, if you have opened a menu and would like to see a different one instead, use the Right or Left arrow keys.

Dialog Boxes

Many times you will find what QB calls *dialog boxes* on the screen. Dialog boxes are used to enter needed information such as a file name, to display error messages, and to select options. The operation of these dialog boxes is consistent throughout.

When a dialog box appears, you will find one or more interior boxes for entering information or selecting options. The cursor will appear in the "current" box. Generally, you will be asked to type something in the box, such as the name of the file you wish to use. To move the cursor from one box to the next, use the Tab key (→), *not* the Enter key. If there are multiple options listed in one box, use the arrow keys to move among items.

Along the lower edge of the dialog box are what are called *buttons*. These buttons have words inside such as, *OK*, *Cancel*, or *Help*. When the dialog box appears, one of the buttons is highlighted (double-outlined in QB 4.0). Pressing Enter executes the command in the highlighted button. To change the highlight, use the Tab key and watch the highlight (and cursor) move from one to the next. Press Enter when the correct button is highlighted. Highlight *Cancel* and press Enter to get rid of the dialog box, or use the Escape key, which always cancels a dialog box or a menu.

Help

As noted earlier, Help has been improved from QB 4.0 to 4.5 and QBASIC. In 4.0, press the F1 key for Help, which gives information about keystrokes needed for the editor and environment. In QB 4.5 and QBASIC, Help will give explanations of the current operation. You can place the cursor on a BASIC keyword (such as PRINT) and press Shift-F1 for the syntax and examples of the statement. In either version, the Escape key cancels Help and returns to the operation in progress.

Using the QuickBASIC Editor to Enter a Program

The majority of your work will be done on the editing screen. That is where you will type the program.

Typing Program Lines

Whenever you are looking at the editing screen, you may type new text or make corrections to existing lines. Type your program one line at a time. Each line should be terminated by the Enter key. You can move the cursor to any location to make changes by pressing the arrow keys or by moving a mouse. (Note: If your computer's arrow keys are on the numeric keypad, NumLock must be OFF for the arrow keys to work.) There are also some shortcut keys for moving the cursor around rapidly; those are covered in appendix B.

Use a little care when pressing the Enter key, since this actually inserts a line-feed character at the current cursor location. If the cursor is in the middle of a line, the line-feed will split the line. Therefore, before pressing Enter, move the cursor to the beginning or end of a line.

If BASIC keywords are spelled correctly and followed by a space, the QB editor will convert the words to capital letters when you press the Enter key.

Insert Mode and Overtype Mode

Changes may be made in one of two ways: in Insert mode or Overtype mode. The default is Insert mode. This means that any characters you type at the cursor location will be inserted into the line, and any characters to the right will be moved further right to make room for them. In Overtype mode, any new characters you type will replace those already appearing on the line. If you wish to turn ON Overtype mode, press the Insert (Ins) key. The cursor changes shape and blinks to indicate Overtype mode. Press Insert again to turn Overtype mode OFF, and Insert mode back ON.

Deleting Characters

You can delete characters to the left of the cursor or under the cursor. The Backspace key deletes the character left of the cursor; the Delete key deletes the character under the cursor.

Inserting and Deleting Lines

Entire lines can be inserted or deleted. To delete a line, place the cursor anywhere on the line and press Ctrl-Y. The Enter key inserts lines, but be sure to place the cursor at the beginning or end of a line before pressing Enter. The Home key moves the cursor to the beginning of a line; the End key moves to the right end of the line. If you press Enter in the middle of a line, you can remove the resulting Line-feed with the Back-space key.

Executing a Program

Once the program has been typed and has passed the smart editor's syntax checking, you are ready to run the program. You can select *Start* from the *Run* menu (Alt key, *R* for *Run*, *S* for *Start*), or press the shortcut *Run* key, Shift-F5.

Program Errors

Did the program produce the expected output? Exactly? You may need to use a calculator to check the computer output. Is the spacing correct? Check each detail of the output. If the output is not correct, the program may have a *logic error.*

Perhaps the program did not produce what was expected at all. At times the program may halt with an error message in a dialog box. These **run-time errors** are caused by statements that cannot execute correctly. The statements are correctly formed BASIC statements that passed the syntax check by the editor. However, in execution, the statements fail. Run-time errors can be caused by such problems as the misuse of reserved words, and by attempts to do impossible arithmetic operations such as division by zero or the square root of a negative number.

When a run-time error occurs, the program halts and a dialog box appears with an error message. Either the Escape or Enter key will clear the dialog box and leave the offending statement highlighted. Locate and correct the error, then run the program again.

Run-Time Errors

This program produced a run-time error. Can you spot it? If this happened to your program, the offending line would be highlighted.

```
' *** Program to Calculate the Area of a Room ***
CLS
INPUT Length
INPUT Width
LET Area = Length * Width
PRINT "The area is"; Area
END
```

To locate this one, you must have been reading carefully when it was stated earlier that Width is a reserved word in BASIC. That was the reason to use Wdth for the variable name.

Logic Errors

Can you find the logic errors in these three programs?

Program Listing:

```
' *** Program to Calculate the Area of a Room ***
CLS
INPUT Length
INPUT Wdth
LET Area = Length * Wdth
PRINT "The area is"; A
END
```

Program Execution:

```
? 25
? 35
The area is 0
```

Program Listing:

```
' *** Program to Calculate the Area of a Room ***
CLS
INPUT Length
INPUT Wdth
LET Area = Length + Wdth
PRINT "The area is"; Area
END
```

Program Execution:

```
? 25
? 35
The area is 60
```

Program Listing:

```
' *** Program to Calculate the Area of a Room ***
CLS
INPUT Length
INPUT Wdth
PRINT "The area is"; Area
LET Area = Length * Wdth
END
```

Program Execution:

```
? 25
? 35
The area is 0
```

In these three examples, there were no syntax errors. QB was able to translate and execute each statement in the program, but the results were not correct. Before reading any further, see if you can find the logic error in each example.

In the first example, the result of the LET statement was called Area. Then the computer was told to print the value, not of Area, but A. Although it is perfectly legal to call a variable A, since no value was assigned to A, its value is zero.

In the second example, the arithmetic operation was incorrectly specified. Length should be multiplied by Wdth, not added.

The error in the third example may be a little more difficult to see. Recall the earlier discussion about the sequence of instruction execution. The statements are executed one at a time in the order given. When the PRINT statement was executed, the value of Area was still zero. Area was not actually calculated until *after* it was printed.

Correcting the Errors

Once the program error has been identified, it must be corrected. This is referred to as "debugging" the program. Use the mouse or the cursor movement keys to position the cursor on the offending line, and type the corrections. Re-run the program by selecting *Start* from the *Run* menu, or by pressing Shift-F5.

Saving and Reloading a Program

Once a program has been completed and is running correctly, what then? You may want to save the program on diskette so that it can be run sometime in the future.

If a program is to be saved, it needs a name. The name chosen will be used to store the program. It will also be used in the future when the program is to be run again.

The rules for naming programs (files) are specified by DOS (*D*isk *O*perating *S*ystem). A program name may be from one to eight characters long, followed by an optional period and up to three-character extension. When the extension is omitted (the recommended practice), BASIC will supply an extension of .BAS.

Sample Filenames for Programs

```
PROGRAM1.BAS      PROG1.BAS
A.PGM             PROG.1
```

The *File* menu is used to save programs as well as retrieve programs that were previously saved.

Save on Disk

To save a program, select *Save As* from the *File* menu. A dialog box opens; select a meaningful name that you will recognize in the future, and type it in the box. Press Enter (or click on *OK*) to execute the command. In the future, QB knows the name of the program, and the dialog box will appear with the name already filled in. If you want to keep the same name, press Enter; if you would like a new name, type the new name before pressing Enter.

A word about saving on diskette. Don't make the mistake of thinking that if you have saved the program once, that it will be updated. If you make changes to the program on the screen, those changes will not be saved on the disk unless you execute another *Save* command. Each time you save a program with the same name, the old version is replaced by the new version. If you would like to save both the old and new versions, give the new version a new name.

Reload a Program from Disk

To recall a program previously stored on disk, select *Open Program* (*Open* in QBASIC) from the *File* menu. The dialog box will ask for the name of the program. It also displays a list of all files with the extension .BAS. You may type the name of the program in the *File Name* box, or move the cursor and select the desired file name from the list. To select the name, use the Tab key to move the cursor into the box with the file names. Then use the arrow keys to highlight the selected file. With a file name highlighted, press Enter to execute the command.

Format of BASIC Statements

Throughout this text, new statements will be introduced. In order to maintain consistency and to conform to the manuals published by computer vendors, some conventions have been adopted.

1. Words in capital letters are *keywords* and must be typed as they appear. They may be entered in upper- or lowercase, but BASIC will convert them to uppercase.
2. Items appearing in square brackets ([ ]) are optional.
3. An ellipsis (...) indicates an item may be repeated as many times as desired.

Clearing the Screen

The first step in most programs is to clear the screen. The CLS statement will clear the screen and place the cursor in the upper left corner.

The CLS Statement

```
CLS
```

Formatting Program Output with the PRINT Statement

Many techniques for formatting computer output will be presented in later chapters. For now, there is one simple method of controlling output placement with PRINT and LPRINT statements.

The PRINT and LPRINT Statements—General Form

```
PRINT  items to print
LPRINT  items to print
```

The only difference between the PRINT and LPRINT statements is that PRINT displays its output on the display screen, while LPRINT places output on the printer (assuming one is connected to the computer). All comments about PRINT also apply to LPRINT. The "items to print" may be literals (the actual characters to print) or variables. They may be separated by semicolons or commas.

The PRINT and LPRINT Statements—Examples

```
                  literal              variable
PRINT "The length is"; Length
LPRINT "Length", "Width", "Area"
PRINT A;B;C
```

Vertical Spacing

To achieve vertical spacing in computer output, the PRINT statement may be used without any "items to print." This effectively prints blank lines and places the output in the desired location.

```
' *** Demonstrate Spacing Using PRINTS ***
CLS
PRINT "Top Line"
PRINT
PRINT
PRINT "Fourth Line"
END
```

Program Execution:

```
Top Line


Fourth Line
```

Horizontal Spacing— Semicolons and Commas

In the sample program shown earlier, both the literal "The area is" and the value of the variable Area were printed.

```
PRINT "The area is"; Area
```

Any mix of literals and variables can be included on a print statement, as long as each literal is enclosed in quotation marks.

```
PRINT "The area of a room"; Length; "feet by"; Wdth; "feet is"; Area; "square feet"
```

When run with this statement, the example program would produce this output:

```
? 20
? 30
The area of a room 20 feet by 30 feet is 600 square feet
```

Placing semicolons between elements to print causes no extra spaces to appear between the items.

```
PRINT "HELLO"; "MARTHA"
```

Program Execution:

```
HELLOMARTHA
```

If a space is desired between literals, a space may be included within the literal.

```
PRINT "HELLO "; "MARTHA"
```

Program Execution:

```
HELLO MARTHA
```

or

```
PRINT "HELLO  "; "  HARRY"
```

Program Execution:

```
HELLO    HARRY
```

There is one exception to this spacing rule. When the element to print is a number (variable), spaces are left between the items. When printing numeric values, BASIC leaves one space after each number and allows one print position for the sign of the number. If the number is negative, the position is taken by the minus sign. When the number is positive, the sign is suppressed, and a blank space precedes the numeric output.

```
LET Team = 6
PRINT "TEAM NUMBER"; TEAM
```

Program Execution:

```
TEAM NUMBER 6
             ↑
             ⋮
          Space for sign
```

Numeric values may also be printed directly, without the use of variables.

```
PRINT "TEAM NUMBER"; 6
```

Program Execution:

```
TEAM NUMBER 6
```

To print a series of numbers:

```
PRINT 2; 4; 6; 8; 10
```

Program Execution:

```
 2   4   6   8   10
```

These numbers are printed with two spaces between them—one for the sign and one for the trailing space supplied by BASIC. Now try two more examples:

```
PRINT 2; 4; 6; 8
PRINT 10; 12
```

Program Execution:

```
 2   4   6   8
 10   12
```

```
PRINT 2; 4; 6; 8;
PRINT 10; 12
```

Program Execution:

```
 2   4   6   8   10   12
```

Can you see the difference? Notice the trailing semicolon in the second group. After printing 2 4 6 8, the internal print pointer stays on the same line. So when the next PRINT is executed, the 10 appears right after the 8.

Using Print Zones for Spacing

Spacing on the line can also be controlled by taking advantage of the five *print zones,* each of which is fourteen columns wide. Using a comma between elements causes the internal print pointer to move to the start of the next zone before printing. When the item to print is a literal, it will be printed at the start of the zone. If the item to print is a numeric value, one space will precede the number (for the sign). Figure 1.8 is a print zone layout.

```
PRINT "ONE", "TWO", "THREE"
PRINT 1, 2, 3
```

Program Execution:

```
ONE             TWO             THREE
1               2               3
```

A comma may also be used at the end of a PRINT line. This causes the internal print pointer to move to the start of the next print zone. The next item to print will appear on that same line.

```
PRINT "HOW", "NOW",
PRINT "BROWN", "COW"
```

Program Execution:

```
HOW             NOW             BROWN           COW
```

Print zones function in a manner similar to the TAB key on a typewriter. It advances a variable number of spaces to the next preset position. This allows for aligning columns of data.

```
PRINT ,"SOCKS", "BRAVES"
PRINT
PRINT ,"ALEXANDER", "TOM"
PRINT ,"JOE", "KENNY"
PRINT ,"PASCUAL", "KIM"
```

Program Execution:

```
        SOCKS           BRAVES

        ALEXANDER       TOM
        JOE             KENNY
        PASCUAL         KIM
```

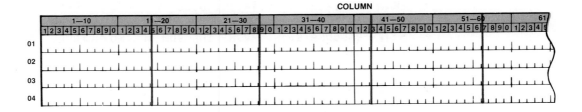

Figure 1.8
Print zones. Each zone is fourteen columns wide.

There are five print zones defined on the standard eighty-character line. If a command is given to advance to a zone beyond the end of a line, printing "wraps around"; that is, it advances to the next line and continues using the print zones.

```
PRINT "A", "B", "C", "D", "E", "F", "G"
```

Program Execution:

```
A               B               C               D               E
F               G
```

Feedback

What will print for each of these program segments? Try to determine the results by hand, then enter them into the computer to verify your results.

1.  ```
    PRINT "HALF A LOAF ";
    PRINT "IS BETTER THAN NONE"
    ```

2.  ```
    PRINT "HALF,", "MY EYE"
    ```

3.  ```
    PRINT "HAWKS";0, "DOVES";0
    ```

4.  ```
    PRINT 1,2,3,4,5,6,7,8,9,10
    ```

5.  ```
    PRINT 1,
    PRINT 2,
    PRINT 3,
    PRINT 4,
    PRINT 5,
    PRINT 6,
    PRINT 7,
    PRINT 8,
    PRINT 9,
    PRINT 10
    ```

Each of these program segments has at least one logic error, since the program will not do what the remarks claim. How can each error be corrected?

6.  ```
    ' *** INPUT AND PRINT A PERSON'S AGE
    INPUT A
    PRINT AGE
    END
    ```

7.  ```
    ' *** PRINT THE NUMBERS FROM ONE TO THREE
    PRINT ONE; TWO; THREE
    ```

8.  ```
    ' *** PRINT NUMBERS, ALL ON THE SAME LINE
    PRINT 2,4,6,8,10,12,14,16,18,20
    ```

9.  ```
    ' *** CALCULATE AND PRINT THE SUM OF TWO NUMBERS
    INPUT Num1
    INPUT Num2
    PRINT Sum
    ```

Summary

1. The computer is a tool for solving problems.
2. A computer needs instructions to be given in the correct sequence in order to do any task.
3. Software is the instructions the machine is given to follow.
4. Computer hardware is the physical components, such as the keyboard, screen, printer, disk drives, and internal circuitry.
    ```

5. The reason for employing a computer for a task is to produce some desired output. A computer program (software) consists of the instructions necessary to convert inputs into the desired outputs.

Input → Processing → Output

6. The hardware of the computer includes input devices, output devices, storage (or memory), the CPU (*C*entral *P*rocessing *U*nit), and assorted circuitry.

7. The CPU includes the ALU (*A*rithmetic and *L*ogic *U*nit) and the control unit. The ALU executes the instructions, doing the arithmetic and logical functions. The control unit coordinates and directs the execution of instructions.

8. Computer main storage is also called primary storage, internal storage, or RAM (*R*andom *A*ccess *M*emory).

9. Main storage must hold the program being executed and the data being operated upon.

10. A larger main storage size may be needed to store larger programs.

11. Main storage is measured in bytes, where one byte equates to one character. One K is 1024 bytes of storage. The amount of RAM is generally given in the number of K bytes, such as 640 K bytes.

12. Most main storage is volatile, which means that the contents are lost when the power source is removed.

13. Secondary storage is nonvolatile and can be used for long-term storage of data.

14. Secondary storage is also called auxiliary storage or external storage.

15. The most popular forms of secondary storage are magnetic disk and magnetic tape.

16. ROM (*R*ead *O*nly *M*emory) is hardware that has software permanently stored inside.

17. Input devices include the keyboard, optical readers, scanners, the joystick, mouse, magnetic disk, and magnetic tape.

18. Output devices are used to present computer results in a human readable form.

19. Output devices include the display screen, printers, plotters, speakers, magnetic disk, and magnetic tape.

20. Software can be broken into two types: (1) operating system software and (2) applications software.

21. Applications software includes all programs written to meet the needs of the end user, such as accounting programs, games, word processing, applications in business, science, medicine, law, and research.

22. Operating system software includes the *D*isk *O*perating *S*ystem (DOS) and utility programs designed to aid in the development and use of applications programs.

23. Operating system utility programs are available to aid in the development, storage, use, and maintenance of applications software.

24. Instructions to the computer must be translated to machine language (or machine code) before the instructions can be executed. The translation is done by a compiler or interpreter.

25. With an interpreter, program statements are translated and then executed, one at a time. However, with a compiler, the entire program is translated before any statements are executed.

26. There are many programming languages available. Some of the most popular are BASIC, FORTRAN, COBOL, Pascal, C, RPG, and Assembly language.

27. Many different versions of BASIC are in use, some offering more features than others. This book will concentrate on QuickBASIC.

28. The Remark statement in BASIC allows for comments within the program. The primary purpose of remarks is for program documentation and to make the program easier for humans to understand. Remarks are not translated to machine language.

29. The general pattern of computer programs is

$$Input \longrightarrow Processing \longrightarrow Output$$

        The BASIC statement presented for the input operation was INPUT. The statement to accomplish the processing was the LET statement. The program output was performed by the PRINT statement. The LPRINT may be used for output on the printer, rather than the display screen.

30. The steps in program development are:
    a. Clearly state the problem, in terms of its output, input, and processing.
    b. Plan the program logic with a flowchart, hierarchy chart, or pseudocode.
    c. Code the program.
    d. Key the program into the computer.
    e. Test and debug the program.
    f. Complete the documentation.

31. There is a set of standard flowcharting symbols used for drawing a pictorial representation of the program logic.

32. A flowchart is used for planning purposes and is drawn before the program is coded. Flowcharts are also used to document completed programs.

33. Pseudocode is English statements that are "like code." When writing pseudocode, the programmer need not be concerned with language syntax rules or flowchart symbols.

34. A hierarchy chart resembles an organization chart and shows the organization of program functions.

35. Once a BASIC program has been planned, coded, and entered into the computer, it can be executed.

36. The QuickBASIC environment includes the editor, menus, and dialog boxes.

37. QB's smart editor locates most syntax errors.

38. Syntax errors are caused by incorrectly using the elements of the language.

39. Two types of program errors that may occur during program execution are run-time errors and logic errors.

40. When there are no run-time errors but the program output is incorrect, the cause is a logic error.

41. Program errors are called bugs; locating and correcting the errors is called debugging the program.

42. Programs may be saved on diskette with the *Save As* command on the *File* menu.

43. A program saved on diskette may be reloaded into memory with the *Open Program* command on the *File* menu.

44. The CLS statement clears the screen, and will usually be the first statement in a program.

45. The PRINT and LPRINT statements can print combinations of literals and variables.

46. Vertical spacing can be achieved by printing blank lines, that is, including a PRINT statement with no items named for printing.

47. Horizontal spacing on a line can be controlled by the use of semicolons and commas between the items to print.

48. A semicolon between elements on a PRINT statement will cause the items to be printed next to each other. The internal print pointer remains in the position immediately following the last item printed.

49. A comma between elements to print causes the internal print pointer to move to the next print zone before the next item is printed.

50. Each print zone is fourteen positions wide.

Programming Exercises

For each of the programming assignments, plan the program with a flowchart or pseudocode. Include Remarks indicating your name, the exercise number, the date, and the purpose of the program.

1.1. Write a program to produce the following output. Use the print zones for the columns of data.

```
TEAM RECORD

NAME            AGE

PATRICIA         18
RONALD           20
MARIA            21
TIEN             19
KENNETH          22
```

1.2. Write a program that will output the following information: your name, address, major, and reason for studying BASIC programming. Include print statements for the screen and printer, and nicely format your output, using both semicolons and commas for spacing.

1.3. Write a program that will produce address labels for you and two other people. The labels will be printed "three up," which means that the three labels are next to each other, horizontally. All three are printed at the same time. Place your own name on the leftmost label, and use the name of two friends or acquaintances for each of the others.

Output must appear on the screen as well as the printer.

SAMPLE PROGRAM OUTPUT:

```
JERRY JAMISON          GEORGE GARNER          SILVIA SAUCEDO
127 CANYON DRIVE,      881 ELGIN COURT,       410 E. GLADSTONE,
CHINO, CA 91710        ONTARIO, CA 91764      WALNUT,CA 91789
```

1.4. Write a program that will input three numbers and print the sum and average of the numbers with appropriate labels. The program should work for *any* three numbers. Run the program several times with different numbers for each run.

Use LPRINT to show the output on the printer as well as the screen.

1.5. Write a program with a title and headings to print your three favorite TV programs, the day of the week they air, and the time they air. Use print zones for the columns of data.

1.6. Write a program to produce the following output using print zones.

```
   PERFECT PICTURE INC.
STORE #        SALES GOAL
_____        _____
LA-021           4525
LA-023           3121
LA-151           3769
LA-221           2987
```

1.7. Write a program to produce the following output using print zones.

```
THE PROGRAM THAT
          PRODUCED THIS OUTPUT
                        SHOWS THAT I KNOW HOW
          TO EFFECTIVELY USE
PRINT ZONES.
```

1.8. Write a program that will compute gallons per hour of gas used on a trip.

INPUT: The number of gallons used and the number of hours the trip took will be input from the keyboard.

OUTPUT: Print the number of gallons used per hour with an appropriate label.

PROCESSING: Calculate gallons per hour = gallons/hours.

1.9. Write a program to convert pints into quarts.

INPUT: The number of pints will be input from the keyboard.

OUTPUT: Print the calculated number of quarts.

PROCESSING: Calculate quarts = pints / 2.

1.10. Write a program to convert miles to kilometers.

INPUT: The number of miles will be input from the keyboard.

OUTPUT: Print the computed number of kilometers.

PROCESSING: Calculate kilometers = miles * 1.61

2 Modular Programs with Calculations and Strings

LET Statement
INPUT Statement
GOSUB Statement
RETURN Statement
INT Function

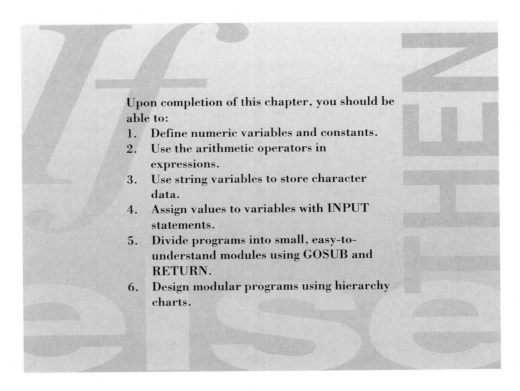

Upon completion of this chapter, you should be able to:

1. Define numeric variables and constants.
2. Use the arithmetic operators in expressions.
3. Use string variables to store character data.
4. Assign values to variables with INPUT statements.
5. Divide programs into small, easy-to-understand modules using GOSUB and RETURN.
6. Design modular programs using hierarchy charts.

Numeric Variables

As you saw in chapter 1, numeric values can be referred to by a name. These names are called *variable names,* since the actual number referred to is changeable. Picture each variable as a scratch pad with a name. Different values can be placed on the scratch pad. In this example, the variable (or scratch pad) is called Amt.

```
LET Amt = 100
```

Amt
100

After execution of this statement, Amt has a value of 100. You could print the value of Amt, use Amt in a calculation, or change Amt to any other chosen numeric value.

```
LET Amt = -1.25
```

Amt
−1.25

This LET statement will change the value of Amt to −1.25. The effect of the LET statement is to assign a value to a variable.

Variable Names

The BASIC language has a set of rules for naming variables. In addition, there are naming guidelines dictated by good programming practice. Many early versions of BASIC restrict variable names to a maximum of two **characters** in length, where the first character must be a letter of the alphabet. The second character, if present, must be a numeric digit (0–9). This allows for names like A, B, X1, X2, X3. This rule explains the look of many older BASIC programs with unintelligible variable names.

In QB, variable names may be as long as 40 characters, and must begin with a letter. The rest of the name can be made up of letters, numeric digits, and the period (.). No other special characters are allowed. (Later you will learn about the use of some characters—$ % ! # &—that have a special meaning in BASIC.) Note that QB is not case-sensitive, that is COUNT, Count, count, and COunt are equivalent. This text will adopt the practice of using a capital letter to begin a variable name, followed by lowercase letters.

A variable name cannot be a **reserved word** (see appendix F for a list of reserved words), but a reserved word may be embedded in a variable name. Thus Let is not a valid variable name, but Lettuce is acceptable. Some valid variable names are:

```
A                          Interest
Total                      Type1
NumberOfPiecesOfPie        R2D2
RateOfPay
```

Invalid variable names:

```
1Tot   (must begin with a letter)
A*     (special characters are not allowed)
End    (reserved word)
```

Good programming practice dictates that meaningful names should be used for variables. When reading a program, names such as Rate, Discount, Tax, and Bonus are descriptive and easy to understand. Names such as A, X, Y, D1, and T2 are much harder to decipher. Anyone who has attempted to read and to understand a program written by someone else (or even their own program after a lapse of a few months) will appreciate the value of descriptive variable names. Often, those who employ programmers prohibit the use of single character variable names.

Feedback

Which of the following is/are valid numeric variable names? For any that are invalid, give the reason.

```
PorcupinePie        Etc...          2A
Count#1             A2              Print
$Total              SooLong         PrintItOut
```

Numeric Constants

The actual numbers assigned to variables are called **constants.** In the example

```
LET Amt = 100
```

Amt is the variable, and 100 is the constant.

Constants are formed with combinations of the numeric digits (0–9) and an optional decimal point. An operational sign (+ or −) may precede the number, but it is optional for positive numbers. No other characters are allowed in constants, which rules out the use of commas, dollar signs, or percent signs. Examples of valid numeric constants are

25	+47	+47.0
−.00025	−47	+47.
2500.25	−47.5	

Examples of invalid numeric constants are

25%	(no special symbols are allowed)
1,250.50	(no commas are allowed)
$1.25	(no special symbols)
15−	(the sign must precede the number)

LET Statements

You have seen several examples of numbers being assigned to variables. In the example

```
LET Amt = 100
```

the constant 100 is assigned to the variable Amt. LET statements always operate from right to left; that is, the value appearing on the right side of the equal sign is assigned to the variable on the left of the equal sign. It is often helpful to read the equal sign as "be replaced by." The example above would read, "Let the value stored in Amt be replaced by 100."

The equal sign used in the LET statement does *not* imply equality. The operation indicated by the equal sign is actually *assignment*. A perfectly valid assignment statement is LET X = X + 1. If the equal sign here actually meant "is equal to," it would be difficult to find a value of X to satisfy the equation.

The LET Statement—General Form

```
LET  variable = variable
LET  variable = constant
LET  variable = arithmetic expression
```

LET statements must always have a variable name to the left of the equal sign. However, the value on the right side of the equal sign may be another variable, a constant, or an arithmetic expression.

The LET Statement—Examples

```
LET Profit = Sales
LET Balance = 10000
LET Sum = Num1 + Num2 + Num3
LET Total = Total + Amt
```

In each of these examples, the value on the right side of the equal sign is assigned to the variable on the left. In the first statement, the current value of the variable Sales is assigned to the variable Profit.

When the second statement is executed, the constant 10000 is assigned to the variable Balance. For calculations, the expression on the right of the equal sign is evaluated (that is, the *current* values of Num1, Num2, and Num3 are added together), and the result is assigned to the variable Sum. The last example statement will take the current value of Total, add Amt, and assign the results to Total. The effect is to add Amt to Total.

The word LET is optional. The example LET statements may be written:

```
Profit = Sales
Balance = 10000
Sum = Num1 + Num2 + Num3
Total = Total + Amt
```

Arithmetic Expressions

In the preceding example, Num1 + Num2 + Num3 is called an *expression*. Expressions are formed with combinations of variables and constants using **arithmetic operators.**

Table 2.1
Arithmetic operators.

Operator	Meaning	Example	Explanation
+	addition	A + B	add together the current value of A and the current value of B
−	subtraction	A − B	subtract the value of B from the value of A
*	multiplication	A * B	multiply the value of A times the value of B
/	division	A / B	divide the value of A by the value of B
∧	exponentiation	A ∧ B	raise the value of A to the power of B

Arithmetic Operators

It is important to determine the order in which operations will be performed. Consider the expression 3 + 4 * 2. What is the result? If the addition is done first, the result is 14. However, if the multiplication is done first, the result is 11.

The **hierarchy of operations** or *order of precedence* in arithmetic expressions (refer to table 2.1), from highest to lowest is

1. exponentiation
2. multiplication and division
3. addition and subtraction

In the previous example, the multiplication is done before the addition, and the result is 11. To change the order of evaluation, use parentheses: (3 + 4) * 2 will yield 14 as the result. One set of parentheses may be used inside another set. In that case, the parentheses are said to be **nested.** For example:

```
((Score1 + Score2 + Score3)/3) * 1.2
```

Extra parentheses can always be used for clarity. The expressions

```
2 * Cost * Rate and (2 * Cost) * Rate
```

are equivalent, but the second may be more easily understood.

When there are multiple operations at the same level (such as multiplication and division), the operations are performed from left to right. The example: 8 / 4 * 2 yields 4 as its result, not 1. The first operation is 8 / 4, then 2 * 2 is performed.

The process of evaluation of an expression is done in this order:

1. All operations within parentheses are evaluated first. If there are multiple operations within the parentheses, the operations are performed according to the rules of precedence.
2. All exponentiation is done. If there are multiple exponentiation operations, they are performed from left to right.
3. All multiplication and division is done. Multiple operations will be performed from left to right.
4. All addition and subtraction is done from left to right.

Although the precedence of operations in BASIC is the same as in algebra, take note of one important difference: there are no implied operations in BASIC. The following expressions would be valid in mathematics, but they are not valid in BASIC:

Mathematic Notation	*Equivalent BASIC Expression*
2A	2 * A
3 (X + Y)	3 * (X + Y)
(X + Y) (X - Y)	(X + Y) * (X - Y)

A word about spacing. The spaces between the operators and variables are optional. The expression 2*A is equivalent to 2 * A as well as   2   *   A.

Rounding and Functions

BASIC supplies many **functions** that may also be used in expressions. The INT function is used for a variety of purposes, including rounding numbers. (See chapter 10 for a list of more functions.) The purpose of the INT function is to find the largest integer (whole number). For a positive number, the effect is to truncate (chop off) all digits to the right of the decimal point, thus making a whole number (or integer). (For the effect on negative numbers, see the discussion in chapter 10.) This example is how a program for finding the largest integer would look:

```
' *** Make an Integer of a Decimal Fraction ***
CLS
LET Frac = 1.995
LET Whole = INT(Frac)
PRINT Whole
```

Program Execution:

```
1
```

The INT function can be used as a tool to round to as many decimal places as desired. When rounding a number, look to the next digit to the right of the desired place value. If the digit to the right is 5 or more, increase the digit immediately to s left by 1. If that right digit is not as large as 5, drop it and all digits to its right. N e these examples of rounding:

2.82549 rounded to the nearest whole number is 3
rounded to the nearest tenth is   2.8
rounded to the nearest hundredth is   2.83
rounded to the nearest thousandth is   2.825
rounded to the nearest ten-thousandth 2.8255

These are the steps necessary to round a number using the INT function:

1. Move the decimal point to the correct location (with multiplication).
2. Add .5 to the number.
3. Truncate all digits to the right of the decimal point, using the INT function.
4. Move the decimal point back to the starting location (with division).

This is how to round 2.82549 to the nearest hundredth using the four steps.

```
1.  2.82549 * 100 = 282.549
2.  282.549 + .5 = 283.049
3.  INT(283.049) = 283
4.  283/100 = 2.83
```

The program to round 2.82549 would be similar to this:

```
' *** Round a Number ***
CLS
LET Num = 2.82549
LET Num1 = INT(Num + .5)                         'Nearest whole
                                                 '  number
LET Num2 = INT(Num * 10 + .5) / 10               'Nearest tenth
LET Num3 = INT(Num * 100 + .5) / 100             'Nearest hundredth
LET Num4 = INT(Num * 1000 + .5) / 1000           'Nearest thousandth
LET Num5 = INT(Num * 10000 +.5) / 10000          'Nearest
                                                 '  ten-thousandth

PRINT Num1, Num2, Num3, Num4, Num5
```

Program Execution:

```
3        2.8       2.83      2.825      2.8255
```

Feedback

What will be the result of evaluation of these expressions?

X
2

Y
4

Z
3

```
1.  X + Y ^ 2
2.  8 / Y / X
3.  X * (X + 1)
4.  X * X + 1
5.  Y ^ X + Z * 2
6.  Y ^ (X + Z) * 2
7.  (Y ^ X) + Z * 2
8.  ((Y ^ X) + Z) * 2
```

Which of the following are valid statements? For those that are invalid, give the reason.

```
9.   LET Avg = (Num1 + Num2 + Num3) / 3
10.  LET 10 = Ten
11.  LET Mine = Yours
12.  LET Count = Count + 1
```

```
13.  LET Apples + Oranges = Salad
14.  LET Ans = Num(Num - 1)
15.  LET Result = (X+Y)/((X - Y)^2)
```

String Variables

In addition to storing numeric values in variables, strings of alphabetic characters, special characters, and digits can also be stored. Variables that store alphanumeric data such as this are called *string variables* and are named differently from numeric variables.

String variable names must have a dollar sign as the last (rightmost) character of the variable name. The remaining rules for string variable names are the same as those for numeric variables. Following is a summary of naming rules for string variables. Variable names:

1. must be terminated by a dollar sign ($).
2. may be any length up to forty characters.
3. may use combinations of letters, digits, and periods.
4. must begin with a letter.
5. must not be a reserved word such as LET or PRINT. Using LET$ as a variable name will cause a syntax error.

Values may be assigned to string variables with the LET statement.

```
LET Nam$ = "PORKY DUCK"
PRINT Nam$
```

Program Execution:

```
PORKY DUCK
```

One string variable may also be assigned to another string variable.

```
LET Last$ = First$
```

String Literals

In the above example, "PORKY DUCK" is called a *string literal*. String literals are also sometimes called *string constants* or *quoted strings*. When assigning a string literal to a string variable, quotation marks must enclose the literal. Valid string literals may be up to 32,767 characters and include combinations of alphabetic characters, special characters, blank spaces, and numeric digits.

```
LET Day$ = "Monday"
LET Code$ = "#402"
LET Curse$ = "%&#*/%!"
LET Heading$ = "  ACCOUNT NUMBER             NAME "
LET Title$ = "M O N T H L Y    R E P O R T "
LET AcctNum$ = "0550"
```

String literals are not stored in the same way that numeric constants are stored. Notice in the last line above that the string literal is all numeric. It is not possible to do any arithmetic operations with AcctNum$, and when printed, the left zero will not be suppressed. When a string literal is stored, the characters are stored one at a time, as individually coded characters. So "0550" is stored as a coded zero, five, five, zero. When the numeric constant 0550 is stored in a numeric variable, the value is actually numeric five hundred fifty.

```
' *** Demonstrate Difference Between String and Numeric ***
CLS
LET AcctNum$ = "0550"
LET AcctNum  = 0550
PRINT AcctNum$
PRINT AcctNum
```

Program Execution:

```
0550
 550
```

Feedback

Determine which are valid string variable names and which are invalid. For the invalid names, give the reason. Try them on the computer to see which ones will generate error messages.

1. `A$`
2. `PayClass$`
3. `$Person`
4. `Answer1$`
5. `Answer$1`
6. `Print$`

Which of these are valid statements? Give the reason for any which are invalid.

7. `LET PayClass = "M"`
8. `LET SSN$ = 550-51-5257`
9. `LET Sign$ = "$"`
10. `LET "SAMMY" = Person$`

INPUT Statements

Using LET statements to assign values to variables is a useful tool. However, if the data value must also be changed, the LET statement in the program must also be changed. In actual practice, changing the program for each set of values is cumbersome. BASIC provides a powerful statement that allows values to be entered during program execution and to be assigned to program variables.

The INPUT Statement—Elementary Form

```
INPUT  variable name
```

The INPUT Statement—Examples

```
INPUT Rate
INPUT Answer$
```

When an INPUT statement is encountered during the program run, execution pauses, and the program waits for the data to be typed at the keyboard. A question mark is displayed on the screen as a signal that an input is expected. Any valid constant can be typed in response to the input prompt. The value keyed in will be assigned to the variable named on the INPUT statement.

```
INPUT Rate
```

When this statement is executed, the program will print a question mark and pause, awaiting entry of a numeric constant.

Program Execution:

    ?   (execution paused)

When the **user** enters a constant and presses the ENTER key, that value is placed in the variable Rate.

```
INPUT Rate
```
Program Execution:

    ? .08   ←keyed by user

Rate
.08

The INPUT statement can also be used to input string data. The variable named must be a string variable. The data entered by the user may optionally be enclosed with quotation marks.

```
INPUT Month$
```
Program Execution:

? <u>JUNE</u>   ←keyed by user

Month$
JUNE

Prompting INPUT

Whenever data input is expected during the execution of the program, the user must be informed what to enter. Having only a question mark appear each time data are requested could be confusing and perhaps even infuriating. One way to **prompt** the user for the correct input is to place a PRINT statement immediately before the INPUT statement.

```
PRINT "Enter the rate of interest"
INPUT Rate
```

Program Execution:

```
Enter the rate of interest
? .08 ←keyed by user
```

If it is desirable to place the question mark generated by the INPUT statement on the same line as the prompt message, a semicolon can be placed after the PRINT statement.

```
PRINT "Enter the rate of interest";
INPUT Rate
```

Program Execution:

```
Enter the rate of interest? .08 ←keyed by user
                           ⌞__ placed by INPUT
```

It is important that the type (numeric or string) of the data entered be the same as the type of the variable named. More specifically, if inputting into a numeric variable, a valid numeric constant must be entered. If an invalid response is entered, the unfriendly message *Redo from start* will appear.

Since numeric digits are valid characters in a string literal, a number *can* be entered into a string variable.

Invalid INPUT into a Numeric Variable

```
INPUT Nuts
```
Program Execution:

? <u>CASHEW</u>

```
Redo from start
```

Valid INPUT into a Numeric or String Variable

```
INPUT DeptNum
PRINT DeptNum
```

Program Execution:

? <u>010</u>
10

```
INPUT DeptNum$
PRINT DeptNum$
```

Program Execution:

? <u>010</u>
010

Example Program

```
'***********Calculate Simple Interest on a Deposit ***********
'               Variables Used:
'
'       Rate            Rate of interest, decimal form
'       Deposit         Amount deposited
'       Years           Length of time deposit draws
'                       interest
'       Interest        Simple interest for period
'       Value           Ending value of deposit

'****************** Input Data ****************************

CLS
PRINT "ENTER THE INTEREST RATE, IN DECIMAL FORM";
INPUT Rate
PRINT "ENTER THE AMOUNT OF DEPOSIT";
INPUT Deposit
PRINT "ENTER THE NUMBER OF YEARS";
INPUT Years

'****************** Calculate Answer **********************

LET Interest = Deposit * Rate * Years
LET Value = Deposit + Interest

'****************** Program Output ************************

PRINT
PRINT
PRINT "THE INTEREST IS               ";Interest
PRINT "THE ENDING BALANCE IS         ";Value
END
'****************** End of Program ************************
```

Sample Program Execution

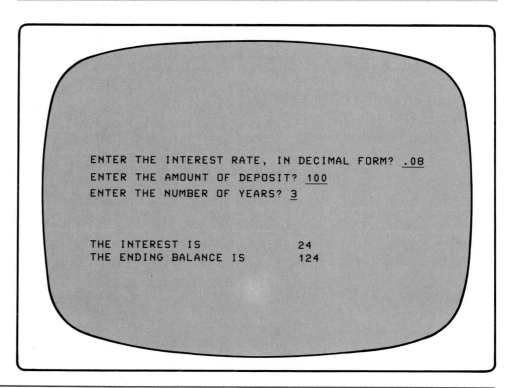

```
ENTER THE INTEREST RATE, IN DECIMAL FORM? .08
ENTER THE AMOUNT OF DEPOSIT? 100
ENTER THE NUMBER OF YEARS? 3


THE INTEREST IS            24
THE ENDING BALANCE IS      124
```

The example program can be reexecuted as often as needed with different values substituted for the deposit, rate, and number of years.

Combining Literals with INPUT Statements

INPUT statements in BASIC can also be used to print a literal message before the INPUT occurs. This would allow combining the PRINT and INPUT statements from the example program and simplify the programming of INPUT statements.

```
INPUT "ENTER INTEREST RATE"; Rate
::
::
```

Program Execution:

```
ENTER INTEREST RATE? ____ ←—value placed here will
                             be assigned to Rate
```

When this statement is executed, the message ENTER INTEREST RATE will first be printed, then the question mark. Execution will pause awaiting keyboard entry of the value to be assigned to the variable Rate.

As a further variation on this same statement, it is possible to suppress the question mark, which is printed to indicate that input is requested. By using a comma in the INPUT statement in place of the semicolon, the message will be printed and INPUT occur without the question mark.

```
INPUT "ENTER INTEREST RATE ", Rate
::
::                          |_____notice, extra space
```

Program Execution:

```
ENTER INTEREST RATE ____ ←—value placed here will
                           be placed in Rate
                    |_____notice, no question mark
```

The extra blank space included at the end of the literal prompt ("ENTER INTEREST RATE") is helpful but not required. When the prompt line is printed on the screen, the cursor remains at the space immediately following the last character printed. Then when the user begins to key in the response, it will appear run together with the prompt message. The blank space included in the literal prompt will separate the words and improve the appearance of the input dialogue.

The INPUT Statement—General Form

```
INPUT  [;] ["literal prompt";] variable name(s)
INPUT  [;] ["literal prompt",] variable name(s)
```

The INPUT Statement—Examples

```
INPUT "ENTER RATE, AMOUNT, AND TERM, SEPARATED BY COMMAS ", Rate, Amount, Term

INPUT "Who are you"; Nam$

INPUT "How many do you want"; Num

INPUT; "Enter rate ", Rate
```

The first example shows one INPUT to enter values for three variables. When the program is run, the user must take great care to enter three constants, to enter in the correct order, and to separate by commas. BASIC is not forgiving of an inexperienced user. The *Redo from start* message is printed in response to too few constants, too many constants, illegal characters embedded in the constants, or missing commas. Since one of the objectives in writing good programs is to make programs clear and easy to use (user friendly), it is obvious that multiple variables on the INPUT statement will only be used in exceptional circumstances.

When multiple variable names are placed on an INPUT statement, commas are required in two separate locations. The programmer must separate the variable names by commas. The user, when running the program, must separate the individual data items with commas.

```
INPUT "ENTER RATE, AMOUNT, AND TERM, SEPARATED BY COMMAS ", Rate, Amount, Term
::
::
```

Program Execution:

```
ENTER RATE, AMOUNT, AND TERM, SEPARATED BY COMMAS .08, 100, 3
```
← all three entered by user

Another technique is available for INPUT statements, as shown in this example:

```
INPUT; "ENTER RATE ", Rate
```
↑ extra semicolon

The extra semicolon immediately following the word INPUT serves the same function as a semicolon placed at the end of a PRINT statement; that is, after the input (or print) is completed, no carriage return or linefeed is sent. The next item to be printed will print on the same line, immediately following the last item printed.

Example Program

The use of INPUT statements can greatly increase the flexibility of programs. Each run of the program can have different values for the variables.

Program Listing

```
'** Program To Calculate the Average of Three Test Scores **
'          Variables Used
'
'          Student$              Name of student
'          Test1                 Score for test 1
'          Test2                 Score for test 2
'          Test3                 Score for test 3
'          Avg                   Test average

'*************** Input Data *****************************
CLS
INPUT "ENTER STUDENT NAME   ", Student$
INPUT "SCORE FOR TEST 1     ", Test1
INPUT "SCORE FOR TEST 2     ", Test2
INPUT "SCORE FOR TEST 3     ", Test3

'*************** Calculate Average *********************

LET Avg = (Test1 + Test2 + Test3) / 3

'*************** Print Output *************************

PRINT
PRINT "THE AVERAGE FOR "; Student$; " IS "; Avg
END

'*************** End of Program *********************
```

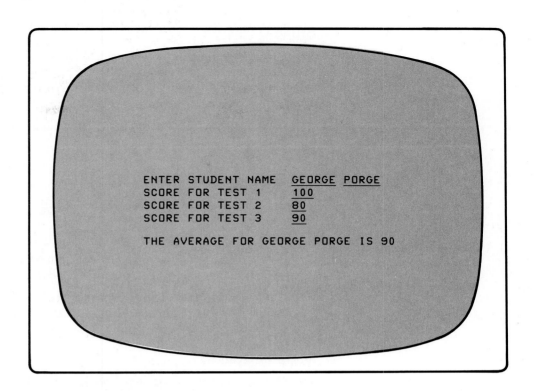

```
ENTER STUDENT NAME   GEORGE PORGE
SCORE FOR TEST 1     100
SCORE FOR TEST 2     80
SCORE FOR TEST 3     90

THE AVERAGE FOR GEORGE PORGE IS 90
```

Without changing the program, the user can rerun it.

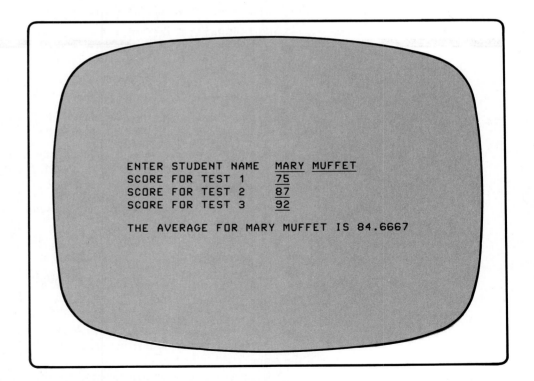

```
ENTER STUDENT NAME   MARY MUFFET
SCORE FOR TEST 1     75
SCORE FOR TEST 2     87
SCORE FOR TEST 3     92

THE AVERAGE FOR MARY MUFFET IS 84.6667
```

String Delimiters

A potential for error exists when string variables are input. When entering the data, the user may or may not use quotation marks around the literal. Commas are used as **delimiters** to separate literals. So, if a comma is needed within the string, quotation marks *must* be used.

```
INPUT "ENTER STUDENT NAME ", Student$
PRINT Student$
::
::
```

Program Execution:

```
ENTER STUDENT NAME CROCKETT, DAVEY

Redo from start
```

In this case, the comma was taken as a delimiter between two fields. The computer saw DAVEY as a second field of input when none was required and refused to cooperate.

```
INPUT "ENTER STUDENT NAME ", Student$
PRINT Student$
::
::
```

Program Execution:

```
ENTER STUDENT NAME "CROCKETT, DAVEY"
CROCKETT, DAVEY
```

The comma is the only special character that causes problems in string literals. Any other character may be included in the literal input without requiring quotation marks.

```
INPUT "WHAT IS THE PROBLEM"; Problem$
PRINT "THAT'S TOO BAD ABOUT "; Problem$
::
::
```

Program Execution:

```
WHAT IS THE PROBLEM? THE #$%&**! COMMAS
THAT'S TOO BAD ABOUT THE #$%&**! COMMAS
```

An important thing to remember is that the value entered for an INPUT must match the type of variable defined on the INPUT statement. The *Redo from start* message will be given if this rule is not followed.

```
INPUT "ENTER NAME AND AGE ", Names$, Age
::
::
```

Program Execution:

```
ENTER NAME AND AGE 25, SALLY MORRIS

Redo from start
```

The number 25 was first placed in Names$ without any problem. Remember, digits are legal characters in a string literal, but SALLY MORRIS cannot be placed in the numeric variable Age.

Another important point to notice about the previous example is that it is perfectly legal to have both string variable names and numeric variable names in one INPUT statement. As long as the user enters the values in the proper order, it will all work out correctly. Again, this is not considered good programming practice, since it requires a lot from the user and introduces an unnecessary potential for errors.

```
INPUT "ENTER PRODUCT NUMBER, DESCRIPTION, UNIT PRICE, AND QUANTITY, SEPARATED BY COMMAS ",
Number, Desc$, Price, Quantity
::
::
```

Program Execution:

```
ENTER PRODUCT NUMBER, DESCRIPTION, UNIT PRICE, AND QUANTITY, SEPARATED BY COMMAS
125, TORCH, 9.75, 12
```

Number	Desc$	Price	Quantity
125	TORCH	9.75	12

Feedback

1. Write the statements necessary to input a class name and class count.
2. Write the statements necessary to input and print out a name and address.
3. Write the INPUT statement necessary to input this value into Dat$.

Dat$
JAN. 15, 1940

Long Statements

Sometimes a program line is too long to fit on one screen line (80 characters). The solutions are a little less than ideal. QB's solution is to allow long statements to "hang off" the edge of the screen. A statement may be as long as 256 characters. When you type past column 80 on the screen, QB scrolls the entire document right, so that you are looking at the area to the right of column 80. When you press ENTER, the document will scroll back so that you will be viewing column 1. If you wish to see the right end of the line, place the cursor on the line and press the END key, use the mouse on the scroll bars, or use the editor's scroll keys:

Ctrl+PgUp Scrolls left one page
Ctrl+PgDn Scrolls right one page

The problem becomes a little more interesting when you print the program on the printer. How wide is the printer's carriage? And paper? Some printers can print long lines, others can't. On some printers, lines longer than 80 characters will "wrap." That is, any excess characters will print on the next line. On other printers, the entire statement will print on one line, whether the printer is loaded with narrow or wide paper. You can see that your choice may depend on the equipment you expect to use, now and in the future.

The preferred solution is to keep your statements to 80 characters. Sometimes it takes a little planning, but you can usually obtain the same results with more than one method. For example, these two methods achieve the same output:

Method 1—One long line.

```
PRINT "Report for the Year Ending December 31, 19"; Year$, "Page"; PageNo
```

Method 2—Joining the two lines when they are printed.

```
PRINT "Report for the Year Ending December 31, 19"; Year$,
PRINT "Page"; PageNo
```

Modular Programming

As programs become larger and more complex, it becomes more difficult to write clear, understandable solutions that work correctly. The goal of **modular programming** is to break up the program into small parts that are more easily understood. Then planning, coding, and testing can be done on these small, relatively simple units, rather than on one large, complex body of code. Remember the adage Divide and Conquer!

Programmers must develop the skill and the ability to look at a large problem and to decompose it into individual functions. The alternative is a phenomenon called "spaghetti code." Once a programmer has learned to modularize programs, programs will be coded more quickly, will be more likely to work correctly, and will certainly be easier to read and to be maintained by others.

Virtually all computer scientists recommend modular programming. The only disagreement seems to be at what point a programmer should begin writing what are called "subroutines." Many wait until programs become hopelessly complex. Then, introducing subroutines can save the day. The more practical approach is to begin using subroutines early. As programs become more complex, if correct habits are already in place, the programmer doesn't need to be "rescued." The solution to the problem is already in place.

Subroutines

A **subroutine** is a group of statements intended to accomplish an individual task. For example, all INPUT statements may be placed together in a subroutine. Another subroutine might contain all calculations for the program. Or, if the calculations become more complex, they may be divided into multiple subroutines, each one accomplishing a specific portion of the whole.

Subroutine Used for Report Headings

Main Program

```
GOSUB PrintHeadings              'Transfer control to subroutine
INPUT "Enter name ", Nam$
```

Subroutine

```
'  ************** Subroutine to Print Headings ***********
PrintHeadings:
    LPRINT ,, "CLUB ROSTER"
    LPRINT
    LPRINT
    LPRINT "NAME",, "ADDRESS",, "TELEPHONE"
    LPRINT
RETURN
```

When this program is run, execution proceeds one statement after another until the GOSUB statement is reached. At the GOSUB, control is transferred to the line containing PrintHeadings. The statements in the subroutine are executed one-at-a-time until the RETURN statement is reached. After the RETURN, control is transferred back to the statement immediately following the GOSUB. The INPUT statement is the next statement to be executed after the RETURN.

The GOSUB Statement—General Form

```
GOSUB subroutine name
```

The GOSUB Statement—Example

```
GOSUB  CalculateTotal
```

The RETURN Statement—General Form

```
RETURN
```

Each time a GOSUB is encountered during program execution, control passes to the subroutine named on the GOSUB. The statements in the subroutine are then executed. When a RETURN is encountered, control passes back to the statement immediately following the GOSUB.

Subroutines may be called from more than one location in a program and may be called any number of times. A subroutine may be called from within another subroutine, which is called *nesting* subroutines. In fact, you may nest as many levels of subroutines as you wish in QB.

Naming Subroutines

A subroutine is given a name with a **line label.** A line label must:

1. Be on a line by itself.
2. Be the first non-blank character on the line. It may begin in any column, however.
3. End with a colon.
4. Consist of one to forty letters and digits, with no blank spaces embedded. However, there may be a space between the line label and the colon.

Line labels are not case-sensitive. That is, PRINTSCORES: is equivalent to PrintScores: or printscores:.

Examples of valid line labels:
```
Totals:
123GO:
INITIALIZATION:
Sub1:
InputTheScores:
```

Examples of invalid line labels:

Mainline	(Does not end with a colon)
Heading Routine:	(No blank spaces allowed)
AdvanceToTheTopOfTheNextPageAndPrintATitle:	(Too many characters)

Writing "Good" Subroutine Names

Although you can name your subroutines anything you wish, some names are better than others. A line label should clearly indicate the function of the subroutine. Current good programming practice dictates that line labels should have a verb (an action being performed) and an object (on which the action takes place). Examples of good and bad line labels are:

Good	Bad
PrintTotals:	Totals:
InitializeVariables:	Initialization:
CalculateAverage:	Calculations:
InputTheName:	Name:

Feedback

1. Why would anyone want to use subroutines?
2. When a RETURN statement is executed, to what statement does execution "return"?
3. What do you think would happen if a RETURN statement were encountered in program execution, but there was no GOSUB? (Try it to see.)
4. What is the limit to the number of subroutines that may be in one program?

Forming Modular Programs—The Program Mainline

When a program is written with individual tasks in subroutines, a **mainline,** or *control program,* is needed. This control program is sometimes called the *program outline,* as it presents an overview of the program tasks. Another term sometimes used for the program mainline is the *driver.*

Example Program: The Interest Program Written with Subroutines

Program Listing

```
' *** Calculate Simple Interest On A Deposit ***

'           Variables Used

'           Rate          Rate of interest decimal form
'           Deposit       Amount deposited
'           Years         Length of time for interest
'           Interest      Simple interest for period
'           Value         Ending value of deposit
'***************** Program Mainline *********************

CLS
GOSUB InputData
GOSUB CalculateAnswer
GOSUB PrintOutput
END

'*************** Input Data **************************

InputData:
  INPUT "ENTER INTEREST RATE, IN DECIMAL FORM ", Rate
  INPUT "ENTER THE AMOUNT OF DEPOSIT          ", Deposit
  INPUT "ENTER THE NUMBER OF YEARS            ", Years
RETURN

'*************** Calculate Answer *********************

CalculateAnswer:
  LET Interest = Deposit * Rate * Years
  LET Value = Deposit + Interest
RETURN

'*************** Print Output *************************

PrintOutput:
  PRINT
  PRINT "THE INTEREST IS                      "; Interest
  PRINT "THE ENDING BALANCE IS                "; Value
RETURN

'*************** End of Program ***********************
```

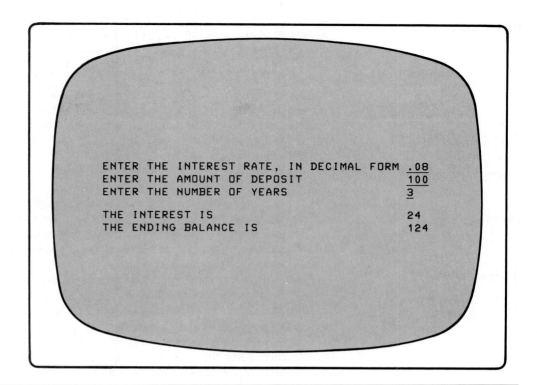

```
ENTER THE INTEREST RATE, IN DECIMAL FORM .08
ENTER THE AMOUNT OF DEPOSIT                100
ENTER THE NUMBER OF YEARS                  3

THE INTEREST IS                            24
THE ENDING BALANCE IS                      124
```

Notice how the program mainline is the outline of the tasks to be performed. The mainline controls execution of each task. Also note the addition of the END statement. This is the logical end, or the finish of execution of the program. This is necessary, so that execution does not "fall through" and accidentally enter a subroutine.

Modular Program Planning

There are several popular methods used for planning modular programs. Pseudocode or flowcharts may be used, with a slight modification for the subroutines; or, hierarchy charts may be used. The preceding example program will be shown using all three methods.

Pseudocode

When tasks are to be performed by a subroutine, show those statements indented below the main heading.

1. Input data
   1.1   Prompt and input rate, deposit amount, and number of years
2. Calculate results
   2.1   Calculate interest = deposit * rate * years
   2.2   Calculate ending balance = deposit + interest
3. Write Output
   3.1   Print interest and ending balance

Flowcharts

Modular flowcharts can be drawn using the *predefined process* symbol.

This symbol indicates that a particular function is to be performed, generally a series of statements that together accomplish a task. Use the predefined process symbol to indicate that a subroutine is to be executed. The subroutine itself will be flowcharted separately.

Use the terminal symbol to show the beginning and end of a subroutine. At the start of the subroutine, label the terminal symbol with the functional name of the subroutine (i.e., Print Headings, Compute Volume, Compute Mean). The ending terminal should contain the word Return (figure 2.1).

Hierarchy Charts

Many programmers who write modular programs prefer to plan their programs with hierarchy charts. An example of a hierarchy chart can be seen in figure 2.2. A hierarchy chart is used to plan and show program structure. It is constructed much like an organization chart. At the highest level (indicated by *A*), the entire program is shown. At the next level (*B*), the program is separated into its major functions. The mainline (main control module) will be coded directly from this *B* level on the chart. Any functions that are further broken down are shown at another (lower) level. The **modules** can be broken into smaller and smaller parts until the coding for each function becomes straightforward and often obvious.

Many programmers use a hierarchy chart to plan the overall structure of a program. Then, when the individual modules are identified, flowcharting or pseudocode will be used to plan the details of the logic.

Figure 2.1
A modular flowchart.

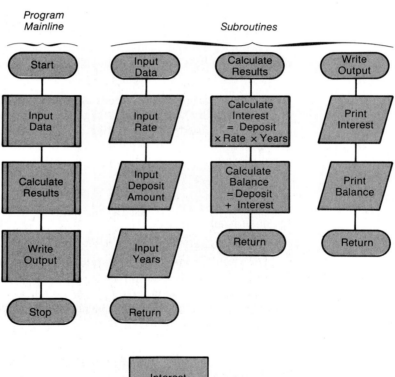

Figure 2.2
Hierarchy chart. Level *A* shows the entire program, which is broken down into major program functions on the *B* level. A more complicated program would be further broken down into lower levels.

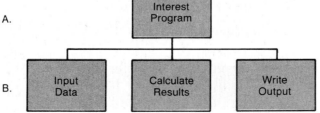

Example Program:
Test Score Program Written with Subroutines

Hierarchy Chart

Refer to figure 2.3.

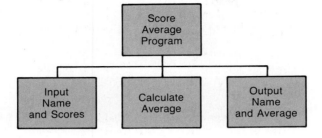

Figure 2.3
Program hierarchy chart for the test score program. The chart shows the three program modules.

Flowchart

Refer to figure 2.4.

Figure 2.4
Program flowchart for the test score program. This program inputs a person's name and three test scores. It then calculates and rounds the average score and prints it along with the name.

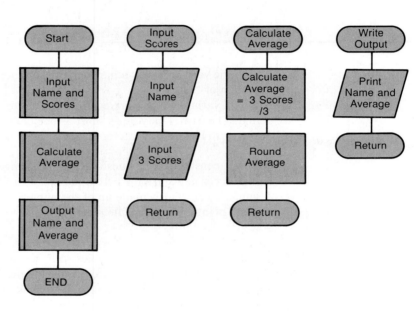

Program Listing

```
'*** Program To Calculate the Average of Three Test Scores ***
'
'              Variables Used:
'
'       Student$          Name of student
'       Test1             Score for test 1
'       Test2             Score for test 2
'       Test3             Score for test 3
'       Avg               Test average
'
'*************** Program Mainline ********************
CLS
GOSUB InputData
GOSUB CalculateAverage
GOSUB PrintOutput
END
```

```
'*************** Input Data ***************************

InputData:
   INPUT "Enter student name  ", Student$
   INPUT "Score for test 1    ", Test1
   INPUT "Score for test 2    ", Test2
   INPUT "Score for test 3    ", Test3
RETURN

'*************** Calculate Average ********************

CalculateAverage:
   LET Avg = (Test1 + Test2 + Test3) / 3
   LET Avg = INT(Avg + .5)
RETURN

'*************** Print Output ************************

PrintOutput:
   PRINT
   PRINT "The average for "; Student$; " is"; Avg
RETURN

'*************** End of Program *********************
```

Summary

1. A numeric variable holds a numeric value, which can be changed during execution of the program.
2. Numeric variable names are composed of letters, numeric digits, and the period. The names may be as short as one character or as long as forty characters. The first character of the variable name must be a letter of the alphabet.
3. Numeric constants are values that do not change.
4. Numeric constants are the actual numbers (digits) used in a program.
5. A numeric constant is made up of the numeric digits (0–9), and an optional decimal point. The sign of the number (+ or −) may also be included, if it precedes the digits.
6. No special characters ($, % #) may be included in a numeric constant.
7. Values can be assigned to variables with the LET statement.
8. The LET statement operates from right to left. The value on the right side of the equal sign is placed in the variable named on the left side of the equal sign.
9. A variable name must appear on the left side of the equal sign. On the right side of the equal sign, there may be another variable, a constant, or an arithmetic expression.
10. Since the equal sign means assignment, not equality, the statement LET Ans = Num1 + Num2 should read: LET Ans *be replaced* by Num1 + Num2.
11. Arithmetic expressions are used to perform calculations and are formed with combinations of variables, constants, and the arithmetic operators (+ − * / ∧).
12. Parentheses may be used to control the order of execution of operations. When one set of parentheses is enclosed inside another set, they are said to be nested.
13. The hierarchy of operations is:
    a. calculations within parentheses;
    b. all exponentiation, from left to right;
    c. all multiplication and division, from left to right;
    d. all addition and subtraction, from left to right.

14. The INT function truncates all digits to the right of the decimal point.
15. The INT function can be used to round numbers.
16. String variables are used to store alphabetic characters, special characters, and numeric digits.
17. String variable names must have a dollar sign as the rightmost character.
18. String literals are made up of alphabetic characters, blank spaces, special symbols, and numeric digits.
19. In most instances, string literals must be enclosed in quotation marks.
20. Although strings may hold numeric digits, no calculations may be done with strings.
21. A second way of assigning a value to a variable is with the INPUT statement.
22. When an INPUT statement is encountered during the run of a program, execution pauses and awaits keyboard entry. The value entered on the keyboard will be assigned to the variable named on the INPUT statement.
23. The INPUT statement may be used to input both numeric and string data.
24. When a numeric variable is named on an input statement, only valid numeric constants may be entered.
25. A literal prompt may be included on an INPUT statement. This is usually to inform the user what to enter.
26. Multiple variables may be requested with one INPUT statement, but this is usually considered poor programming.
27. When multiple variables are requested, the user must exactly match the number and type of data items.
28. Programs should be broken into small, easy-to-understand parts. These small parts are called modules.
29. Subroutines can be used to code program modules.
30. The GOSUB statement is used to call a subroutine.
31. The RETURN statement is placed at the end of a subroutine. When the RETURN statement is encountered in program execution, control is transferred back to the statement following the GOSUB that called the subroutine.
32. A subroutine may be called multiple times and may be called from more than one location in the program.
33. Subroutines may be nested; that is, one subroutine may call another subroutine, which may call another subroutine. Each RETURN transfers control back to the line following the most recent GOSUB.
34. Modular programs are generally written with a mainline and subroutines.
35. Modular programs can be planned with pseudocode, flowcharts, or hierarchy charts.
36. Subroutines are flowcharted with the predefined process symbol.
37. Hierarchy charts are similar to organization charts and show the structure of a program.
38. The top level of a hierarchy chart shows the entire program. The next-lower level shows the major program functions. Each major function is then broken down into smaller parts until each contains only one function and can be easily coded.
39. Many programmers draw hierarchy charts to identify the program modules and flowchart the individual modules.

Programming Exercises

Each of these exercises should be written as a modular program with a program mainline and subroutines. Plan the program with a modular flowchart, pseudocode, or a hierarchy chart. Run the program with the test data provided as well as additional data that you make up.

2.1. The stopping distance for a moving automobile can be calculated for any given rate of travel.

INPUT: The speed of the car, in miles per hour.
OUTPUT: The distance needed to stop the car, in feet.
PROCESSING: The formula for stopping distance is:

$$\text{Stopping distance in feet} = \text{Velocity} * 2.25 + \frac{\text{Velocity} \wedge 2}{21}$$

Where 2.25 is a factor for the time necessary to perceive and react to the situation, and 21 is a friction factor for stopping. Round the answer to the nearest foot.

SAMPLE PROGRAM OUTPUT:

```
VELOCITY? 25
THE DISTANCE REQUIRED TO STOP IS 86 FEET
```

TEST DATA: 25, 40, 55, 70

2.2. In retail sales, it is important for the manager to know the average inventory figure and the turnover of merchandise.

INPUT: Beginning inventory, ending inventory, cost of goods sold.
OUTPUT: The average inventory in dollars and the turnover in number of times the inventory was turned over.
PROCESSING: The values can be calculated from these formulas:

$$\text{Average inventory} = \frac{\text{Beginning inventory} + \text{Ending inventory}}{2}$$

$$\text{Turnover} = \frac{\text{Cost of goods sold}}{\text{Average inventory}}$$

Round the turnover to the nearest tenth.

SAMPLE PROGRAM OUTPUT:

```
Beginning Inventory = 58500
Ending Inventory =    47000
Cost of Goods Sold =  400000
Average Inventory =   52750
Turnover =            7.6
```

TEST DATA:

Beginning	Ending	Cost of Goods Sold
58,500	47,000	400,000
75,300	13,600	515,400
3,000	19,600	48,000

2.3. Calculate and print the area of a triangle.

INPUT: The base and height of the triangle.
OUTPUT: The area of the triangle.
PROCESSING: The formula for calculations:

$$\text{Area} = (1/2) * (\text{Base} * \text{Height})$$

SAMPLE PROGRAM OUTPUT:

```
Enter base of triangle   3
Enter height of triangle 4

The area is              6
```

TEST DATA:

Base	Height
4.5	6.2
10	15
1	1

2.4. A local recording studio rents its facilities for $200 per hour. The management charges only for the number of minutes used.

INPUT: Name of the group and number of minutes used.
OUTPUT: Print the name of the group and the total charges on both the screen and the printer.
PROCESSING: Calculate the per-minute cost as 1/60 of the hourly rate. Round the charges to the nearest cent.

SAMPLE PROGRAM OUTPUT:

```
Name of group? The Birddogs
Number of minutes? 45

Total charges = $ 150
```

SAMPLE PRINTER OUTPUT:

```
The charges for The Birddogs are $ 150
```

TEST DATA:

Group	Minutes
Pooches	95
Hounddogs	5
Mutts	480

2.5. Determine the future value of an investment at a given interest rate for a given number of years.

INPUT: Amount of investment, the interest rate (as a decimal fraction), and the number of years the investment will be held.
OUTPUT: The future value of the investment.
PROCESSING: The formula for calculations is:

$$\text{Future value} = \text{Investment amount} * (1 + \text{interest rate})^{\wedge}\ \text{years}$$

Where the interest rate is a decimal value (8 1/2% is entered as .085)
Convert the decimal rate to percent for output.
(Percentage = interest rate * 100)
Round the future value to the nearest cent.

SAMPLE PROGRAM OUTPUT:

```
Enter amount of investment         1000.00
Enter interest rate, decimal form  .125
Number of years                    5
The future value of $ 1000 invested at 12.5% for
 5 years is $ 1802.03
```

TEST DATA:

Amount	Rate	Years
2,000.00	.15	5
10,000.00	.185	5
1,234.56	.10	1

2.6. Calculate the shipping charge for a package, if the shipping rate is $0.12 per ounce.

INPUT: Package identification number (a six-digit code that contains letters and numbers) and the weight of the package in pounds and ounces.

OUTPUT: The shipping charge on both the screen and the printer.

PROCESSING: Find the total number of ounces (16 ounces in a pound) and multiply by .12 to find the charge.

SAMPLE PROGRAM OUTPUT:

```
Enter package ID   K2576C
Weight - Pounds 3
         Ounces 12

THE CHARGE FOR 60 OUNCES IS $ 7.2
```

SAMPLE PRINTER OUTPUT:

```
PACKAGE ID      WEIGHT          CHARGE
K2576C           3 LB. 12 OZ.   $ 7.2
|(zone 1)        |(zone 2)       |(zone 3)
```

TEST DATA:

ID	Weight
L5496P	0 lb. 5 oz.
J1955K	2 lb. 0 oz.
Z0000Z	1 lb. 1 oz.

2.7. Convert the temperature given in degrees Fahrenheit to the corresponding value in degrees Celsius.

INPUT: Temperature in degrees Fahrenheit.

OUTPUT: Temperature in degrees Celsius.

PROCESSING: The formula for conversion:

$$\text{Celsius} = (5/9) * (\text{Fahrenheit} - 32)$$

Round the temperature to the nearest whole number

SAMPLE PROGRAM OUTPUT:

```
Temperature in degrees Fahrenheit? 75
Temperature in degrees Celsius is 24
```

TEST DATA: 32, 90, 212

2.8. The charges for a rental car at the local agency are $15 per day, plus $0.12 per mile. Print an invoice for rental customers.

INPUT: Customer name, address, city, state, zip code, beginning odometer reading, ending odometer reading, and number of days the car was used.

OUTPUT: Print a customer bill, similar to the sample shown below.

PROCESSING: Subtract the beginning odometer reading from the ending odometer reading to find the miles driven. Multiply the miles driven by .12, and add the daily charge (15 * number of days). Round the charges to the nearest cent.

SAMPLE PROGRAM OUTPUT:

```
CUSTOMER NAME                          IVAN TERRIBLE
STREET ADDRESS                         2601 DISTANT STREET
CITY                                   NOWHERE
STATE                                  CA
ZIP CODE                               91711

BEGINNING ODOMETER READING             35202.5
ENDING ODOMETER READING                35700.9
NUMBER OF DAYS                         3

CHARGES                                $ 104.81
```

SAMPLE PRINTER OUTPUT:

```
                    AWESOME CAR RENTALS
                    CUSTOMER INVOICE

IVAN TERRIBLE
2601 DISTANT STREET
NOWHERE, CA 91711

NUMBER OF DAYS          MILES DRIVEN          TOTAL CHARGE
3                       498.4                 $ 104.81
```

TEST DATA:

	Beginning	Ending	Days
(You make up names	1,520.1	1,542.3	1
and addresses)	20,425.2	20,619.0	2
	50,402.5	53,212.2	5

2.9. Write a program to determine the discount and sale price of any item input.

INPUT: The description of the item, the base price, and the percentage of discount to be given will be entered from the keyboard.
OUTPUT: Print the description of the item, the base price, the sale price, and the discount.
PROCESSING:
　　1. Discount = base price * percent of discount / 100.
　　2. Sale price = base − discount.

2.10. Write a program to input five numbers and find the mean.

INPUT: Five numbers will be input from the keyboard.
OUTPUT: Print the calculated mean with the appropriate label.
PROCESSING: Calculate the mean = sum of numbers / 5.

2.11. Write a program to calculate the slope of a line.

INPUT: The X and Y coordinates of two points on a line will be input from the keyboard.
OUTPUT: The slope of the line.
PROCESSING: Calculate the slope $= \dfrac{Y_2 - Y_1}{X_2 - X_1}$

Note: Slope is the measure of the steepness of a line. X_1 and Y_1 are the coordinates for point 1, X_2 and Y_2 are the coordinates for point 2.

2.12. Write a program to input the titles of your three favorite books and their authors. Print a title, headings, the titles, and the authors. Output should be to both the screen and the printer.

2.13. Write a program to calculate net pay.

INPUT: Gross pay will be input from the keyboard.
OUTPUT: Calculated net pay, identified by an appropriate literal.
PROCESSING: Net pay = gross pay − deductions.
Deductions:
1. FICA = .0715 * gross pay
2. FED = .14 * gross pay
3. STATE = .09 * gross pay

2.14. Write a program to calculate an employee's net pay, and print a budget report based on the percentages given.

INPUT: The employee's name and dollar amount of sales earned this month will be input from the keyboard.
OUTPUT: Print an appropriate title and headings. Print the base pay, amount of sales, amount of commission, gross pay, deductions, net pay, and the dollar amount that can be spent on housing, food and clothing, entertainment, and miscellaneous items.
PROCESSING:
1. Gross pay = $900 a month + 6% commission on all sales over $200.
2. Commission = (total sales − $200) * 6%.
3. Net pay = gross pay − deductions.
4. Deductions = 18% of gross pay.
5. Housing = 30% of net pay.
6. Food and clothing = 15% of net pay.
7. Entertainment = 50% of net pay.
8. Miscellaneous items = 5% of net pay.

TEST DATA:
Base pay = $900
Sales = $1200

SAMPLE OUTPUT:

```
                          BUDGET REPORT FOR Joan Cooley
Base Pay      Sales       Commission      Gross      Deductions
 900           1200          60             960         172.8
Net
787.2

Housing          =  236.16
Food/Clothing    =  118.08
Entertainment    =  393.6
Miscellaneous    =  39.36
```

2.15. The Perfect Picture company has created a bonus program to give its employees some incentive. Each store has a sales goal to reach. For every dollar the store makes over the goal, the employees of that store receive 15% of sales. The amount each employee receives is based upon the percentage of hours they worked of the total hours the store was open. (There are two employees per store and no more than one employee working at any given time.) Write a program that will print a summary report for one store.

INPUT: Input from the keyboard the store number, name of employee 1, name of employee 2, total hours worked for employee 1, total hours worked for employee 2, store's sales goals, and actual sales.
OUTPUT: Print a title and column headings. Detail output will consist of store number, sales goal, actual sales, amount of sales over goal, each employee's name, number of hours each employee worked, and bonus amount each employee earned.

PROCESSING:
1. The store's bonus will be calculated as (actual sales — sales goal) *
   15%. Round the bonus to the nearest whole number.
2. Each employee's percent of the bonus is calculated as his or her hours
   divided by the total store hours.
3. For each employee, multiply the bonus earned for the store by the
   percent calculated in step 2 above. Round the amount to the nearest
   cent.

SAMPLE PROGRAM OUTPUT:

```
                Monthly Bonus Summary Report

Store #          LA-021
Store Goal       3800
Sales            4300
Store Bonus      75

Employee         Hours Worked      Bonus Earned

Anita Bonita         150              36.53
Mitzi Micro          158              38.47
```

3

Programs with Loops and Formatted Output

DO...LOOP Statements
UCASE$ Function
OR Operator
AND Operator
NOT Operator
TAB Function
SPC Function
PRINT USING Statement

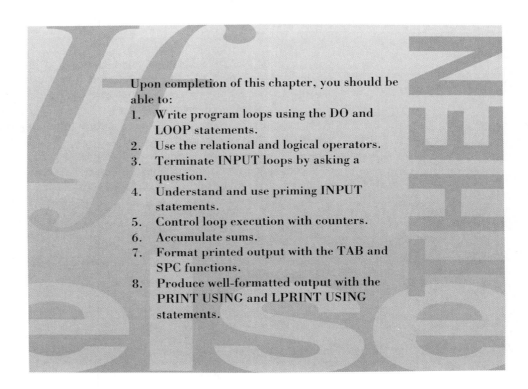

Upon completion of this chapter, you should be able to:

1. Write program loops using the DO and LOOP statements.
2. Use the relational and logical operators.
3. Terminate INPUT loops by asking a question.
4. Understand and use priming INPUT statements.
5. Control loop execution with counters.
6. Accumulate sums.
7. Format printed output with the TAB and SPC functions.
8. Produce well-formatted output with the PRINT USING and LPRINT USING statements.

Loops

Until now, each of the practice programs has only been able to process a single set of data. There has been no way to go back and repeat the same steps without rerunning the program. The computer is capable of repeating a group of instructions multiple times, without the necessity of rerunning the program for each set of new data. This process of repeating a series of instructions is called *looping*. The group of repeated instructions is called a **loop.**

```
'*** Calculate the Area of a Room ***
CLS
DO
   INPUT "Enter length"; Length
   INPUT "Enter width"; Wdth
   LET Area = Length * Wdth
   PRINT
   PRINT "The area is "; Area
   INPUT "Do you wish to continue"; Ans$
LOOP WHILE UCASE$(Ans$) = "YES"
PRINT
PRINT "Bye"
END
```

The new BASIC statements forming the loop are the DO and LOOP. Any time the program logic calls for repeating one instruction or a group of instructions, the DO and LOOP are the best way to accomplish the task.

The indented program lines between DO and LOOP form a loop and will be executed repeatedly until the user enters something other than YES to the question Do you wish to continue?

When you write a loop, you may choose how the loop is to terminate. You will need a condition (such as Ans$ = "YES"). Conditions are always written so that they evaluate as TRUE or FALSE (or YES or NO). Then, you may choose to execute the loop WHILE the condition is TRUE, or UNTIL the condition is true. Finally, you may place the condition at the top of the loop (on the DO), or at the bottom of the loop (on the LOOP statement).

The DO and LOOP Statements—General Form

```
DO {WHILE¦UNTIL} condition
        [statements in loop]
LOOP


or


DO
        [statements in loop]
LOOP {WHILE¦UNTIL} condition
```

The braces around WHILE¦UNTIL mean that one word or the other may be used.

The DO and LOOP Statements—Examples

```
DO
    [statements in loop]
LOOP UNTIL Count = 10


DO UNTIL Nam$ = "EOD"
    [statements in loop]
LOOP


DO
    [statements in loop]
LOOP WHILE Pieces > 0


DO WHILE Amount >= 10 AND Amount <= 20
    [statements in loop]
LOOP
```

The first form of the DO...LOOP tests for completion at the top of the loop. With this type of loop, also called a *pretest,* the statements inside the loop may never be executed if the terminating condition is true the first time it is tested. Example:

```
LET Total = 0
DO UNTIL Total = 0
        [statements in loop]
LOOP
```

Since Total = 0 the first time the condition is tested, the condition (Total = 0) is true, and the loop will not be executed. Control will pass to the statement following the LOOP statement.

The second form of the DO...LOOP tests for completion at the bottom of a loop (which means that the statements in the loop will *always* be executed at least once). This form of loop is sometimes called a *posttest.* Changing the example to a posttest, you can see the difference.

```
LET Total = 0
DO
        [statements in loop]
LOOP UNTIL Total = 0
```

In this case, the statements in the loop will be executed at least once. Assuming the value for Total does not change inside the loop, the condition (Total = 0) will be true the first time it is tested and control will pass to the first statement following the LOOP statement. Figure 3.1 shows both pre- and posttest loops, written with both WHILE and UNTIL.

Figure 3.1
Flowcharts of pre-test and post-test loops.

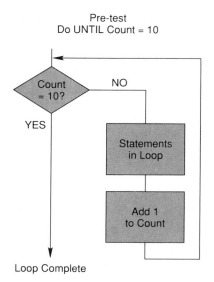

Pre-test
Do UNTIL Count = 10

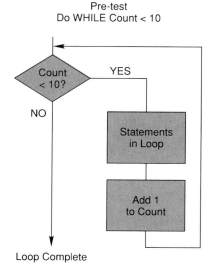

Pre-test
Do WHILE Count < 10

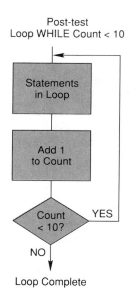

Post-test
Loop WHILE Count < 10

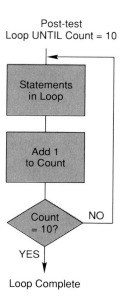

Post-test
Loop UNTIL Count = 10

Conditions

Control of the loop execution is based on a *condition*. To form the conditions, there are six **relational operators** (table 3.1) used to compare two values. The result of the comparison is either *true* or *false*.

The conditions to be tested can be formed with numeric variables and constants, string variables and constants, and arithmetic expressions. However, it is important to note that comparisons must be made on "like types"; that is, strings can be compared only to other strings, and numeric values can be compared only to other numeric values, whether a variable, constant, or arithmetic expression.

Comparing Numeric Variables and Constants

When numeric values are involved in a test, an algebraic comparison is made; that is, the sign of the number is taken into account. Therefore, -20 is less than 10, and -2 is less than -1.

	Symbol	Relation Tested	Examples		
Table 3.1 **The six relational operators.**	>	greater than	`Amt` `Item$`	`>` `>`	`Num` `"STAR"`
	<	less than	`Count` `Item$`	`<` `<`	`10` `Choice$`
	=	equal to	`Sum` `Nam$`	`=` `=`	`Total` `"BASIC"`
	<>	not equal to	`Choice` `Big$`	`<>` `<>`	`100` `Large$`
	>=	greater than or equal to	`Num` `Part$`	`>=` `>=`	`Guess` `Id$`
	<=	less than or equal to	`Amt` `String1$`	`<=` `<=`	`Limit` `String2$`

Even though an equal sign (=) means replacement in a LET statement, in a relation test the equal sign is used to test for equality. For example, the condition

```
DO WHILE Price = Max
```

is interpreted to mean "is the current value stored in Price equal to the current value stored in Max?"

Some Sample Comparisons

Alpha	Bravo	Charlie
5	4	−5

Condition	*Evaluates*
`Alpha = Bravo`	False
`Charlie < 0`	True
`Bravo > Alpha`	False
`Charlie <= Bravo`	True
`Alpha >= 5`	True
`Alpha <> Charlie`	True

Comparing Strings

String variables can be compared to other string variables or string literals enclosed in quotation marks. The comparison begins with the leftmost character and proceeds one character at a time from left to right. As soon as a character in one string is not equal to the corresponding character in the second string, the comparison is terminated, and the string with the lower ranking character is judged less than the other.

The determination of which character is less than another is made based on the code used to store characters internally in the computer. The code, called the **ASCII code** (pronounced ask-key), has an established order (called the collating sequence) for all letters, numbers, and special characters. Note in figure 3.2 that *A* is less than *B*, *L* is greater than *K,* and all numeric digits are less than all letters. Some special symbols are lower than the numbers and some are higher, and the blank space is lower than the rest of the characters shown.

Figure 3.2
ASCII Collating sequence
(American Standard Code for
Information Interchange). For a
more complete list of the ASCII
code, see appendix D.

ASCII CODE	CHARACTER	ASCII CODE	CHARACTER	ASCII CODE	CHARACTER
32	SPACE	64	@	96	'
33	!	65	A	97	a
34	"	66	B	98	b
35	#	67	C	99	c
36	$	68	D	100	d
37	%	69	E	101	e
38	&	70	F	102	f
39	'	71	G	103	g
40	(	72	H	104	h
41	)	73	I	105	i
42	*	74	J	106	j
43	+	75	K	107	k
44	,	76	L	108	l
45	-	77	M	109	m
46	.	78	N	110	n
47	/	79	O	111	o
48	0	80	P	112	p
49	1	81	Q	113	q
50	2	82	R	114	r
51	3	83	S	115	s
52	4	84	T	116	t
53	5	85	U	117	u
54	6	86	V	118	v
55	7	87	W	119	w
56	8	88	X	120	x
57	9	89	Y	121	y
58	:	90	Z	122	z
59	;	91	[	123	{
60	<	92	\	124		
61	=	93	]	125	}
62	>	94	^	126	~
63	?	95	_	127	DEL

Person1$	Person2$
JOHN	JOAN

The condition Person1$ < Person2$ evaluates *false*. The *A* in JOAN is lower ranking than the *H* in JOHN.

Word1$	Word2$
HOPE	HOPELESS

The condition Word1$ < Word2$ evaluates *true*. When one string is shorter than the other, it can be considered that the shorter string is padded with blanks to the right of the string, and the blank space will be compared to a character in the longer string.

C$	D$
300ZX	PORSCHE

The condition C$ < D$ evaluates *true*. When the number 3 is compared to the letter *P,* the 3 is lower, since all numbers are lower ranking than all letters.

Feedback

Determine which conditions will evaluate *true* and which ones *false*.

L		M		N		P$		R$
5		5		−5.5		CIS 10A		CIS 10B

1. L >= M
2. N < 0
3. N < M
4. L <> M
5. L + 2 > M * 2

6. P$ < R$
7. P$ <> R$
8. P$ > "D"
9. "2" <> "TWO"
10. "$" <= "?"

Comparing Uppercase and Lowercase Characters

When comparing strings, the case of the characters is important. An uppercase "Y" does not compare equal to a lowercase "y." Since the user may type either in response to the question "Do you wish to continue (Y/N)?", we must check for both. There are several ways to write such a test. The easiest and slickest way is to use the string function UCASE$, which returns the uppercase equivalent of any string. Example:

```
DO
    . . .
        INPUT "Do you wish to continue (Y/N)"; Ans$
    LOOP WHILE UCASE$(Ans$) = "Y"
```

The condition (UCASE$(Ans$) = "Y") will be TRUE if Ans$ contains either "Y" or "y," and the loop will be executed repeatedly as long as the user enters either.

The UCASE$ Function—General Form

```
UCASE$(string)
```

The UCASE$ function may be used anywhere that a string is legal.

The UCASE$ Function—Examples

```
PRINT UCASE$("Hello")
DO UNTIL UCASE$(Ans$) = "NO"
LET Response$ = UCASE$(Response$)
```

In each case, the function returns the uppercase equivalent of the string in parentheses.

If Test$ =	then UCASE$(Test$) returns
y	Y
Yes	YES
Yes I do	YES I DO
YES	YES
yes IT IS	YES IT IS

Note that the function does not change the value of the variable within parentheses.

```
LET Test$ = "Yes I can"
PRINT UCASE$(Test$)
PRINT Test$
```

Program Execution:

```
YES I CAN
Yes I can
```

Compound Conditions

Compound conditions, which allow more than one condition to be tested, can be formed using the **logical operators.**

Logical Operators	*Example*
OR—If one or the other condition is true, or both are true, the entire condition is true.	Num = 0 OR Num = 5
AND—Both conditions must be true for the entire condition to be true.	Num >= 1 AND Count <= 10
NOT—Reverses the condition, so that a true condition will evaluate false and vice versa.	NOT Count = 0

The OR Operator—Example

```
INPUT "Enter a number between 1 & 10 ", Num
DO WHILE Num < 1 OR Num > 10
    INPUT "Value not in range 1-10, Please re-enter ", Num
LOOP
```

If the value of *Num* is less than 1 or greater than 10, then the message will print. *Note that the Num must be repeated in the second condition.* If this were written IF Num < 1 OR > 10, BASIC would *not* assume that you meant Num > 10, but produce an error message.

When a compound condition contains an OR, the two conditions are tested independently. Then if one condition *or* the other is true, the entire condition evaluates true.

The AND Operator—Example

```
DO WHILE UCASE$(Ans$) <> "YES" AND UCASE$(Ans$) <> "NO"
    INPUT "Enter 'YES' OR 'NO'", Ans$
LOOP
```

In this example, if Ans$ contains *neither* YES nor NO, then the condition will be true. If Ans$ contains NO, then the first condition is true, the second condition is false, and the entire condition is false. The compound condition also evaluates false if Ans$ contains YES.

When two conditions are joined by AND, each condition is evaluated independently. Then, if both conditions are true, the entire compound condition is true. If one or the other is false, the entire condition tests false.

The NOT Operator—Example

```
DO WHILE NOT Response$ = "QUIT"
    GOSUB CalculateAnswer
    GOSUB PrintResult
    INPUT "Enter next one ('Quit' to end)", Response$
LOOP
```

In the example, if Response$ holds anything other than QUIT the condition evaluates true. The NOT operator reverses the truth of a condition and applies only to the condition it precedes.

The use of the NOT operator is generally confusing and difficult to evaluate and is therefore not recommended. Conditions usually can be constructed without the use of NOT (e.g., Response$ <> "QUIT" rather than NOT Response$ = "QUIT"). Refer to figure 3.3 for the outcomes of use of logical operators.

Figure 3.3
Effect of logical operators (truth tables).

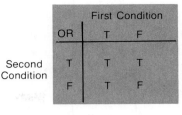

	First Condition	
OR	T	F

Second Condition

	T	T	T
	F	T	F

	First Condition	
AND	T	F

Second Condition

	T	T	F
	F	F	F

Condition	NOT Condition
T	F
F	T

Combining the Logical Operators

Combinations of AND and OR can be used in a single compound condition. When the operators are combined, the order of evaluation becomes important. The condition surrounding the AND is evaluated first, then the condition surrounding the OR is tested.

```
DO WHILE Score >= 0 AND Score <= 100 OR Score = 999
```

If the Score entered is in the range 0–100 or if 999 is entered, then the entire condition is true.

	Evaluated First			Evaluated Second			
Score	Score >= 0	AND	Score <= 100	AND Cond.	OR	Score = 999	Entire Cond.
0	TRUE	AND	TRUE	TRUE	OR	FALSE	TRUE
90	TRUE	AND	TRUE	TRUE	OR	FALSE	TRUE
100	TRUE	AND	TRUE	TRUE	OR	FALSE	TRUE
200	TRUE	AND	FALSE	FALSE	OR	FALSE	FALSE
−1	FALSE	AND	TRUE	FALSE	OR	FALSE	FALSE
999	TRUE	AND	FALSE	FALSE	OR	TRUE	TRUE
1000	TRUE	AND	FALSE	FALSE	OR	FALSE	FALSE

Compound conditions can be useful, but should only be used when thoroughly understood. Multiple ANDs, ORs, and NOTs may be used when necessary. The logic should be carefully worked out for all possible combinations before use. Parentheses may be used to alter the order of evaluation, with the conditions within the parentheses being evaluated first. Extra use of parentheses can also make the statement easier to understand.

Example: Parentheses used to clarify, but not alter, the sequence of operations:

```
DO WHILE (Score >= 0 AND Score <= 100) OR Score = 999
```

Example: Parentheses used to alter the sequence of operations:

```
DO WHILE (Num < 1 OR Num > 10) AND Num <> 999
```

Feedback

Determine which conditions will test *true* and which *false*.

A	B	C$
10	15	M

1. `A = B OR C$ = "M"`
2. `A = B AND C$ = "M"`
3. `A = 10 OR B = 15 AND C$ = "F"`
4. `(A = 10 OR B = A) AND C$ = "F"`
5. `(A = 10 OR B = 10) AND C$ = "M"`
6. For what value(s) of X would this condition be true?

   `X < 1 AND X > 10`

7. For what value(s) of Y would this condition be true?

   `Y >= 1 AND Y <= 10`

Example Program: Conversion of Miles to Kilometers

Program Listing

```
'*** Program to Convert Miles to Kilometers ***

'              Variables Used

'         Miles           Distance in miles
'         Km              Distance in kilometers
'         Ans$            Answer to question

'****************** Program Mainline ******************
CLS
DO
    GOSUB InputMiles
    GOSUB ConvertMiles
    GOSUB PrintResults
    INPUT "ANOTHER CONVERSION (Y/N)"; Ans$
LOOP WHILE UCASE$(Ans$) = "Y"
END

'****************** Input Miles ******************

InputMiles:
  PRINT
  INPUT "ENTER DISTANCE IN MILES ", Miles
  PRINT
RETURN

'****************** Convert Miles ******************

ConvertMiles:
  LET Km = Miles * 1.6
RETURN

'****************** Print Results ******************

PrintResults:
  PRINT Miles; "MILES IS EQUIVALENT TO"; Km; "KILOMETERS"
  PRINT
RETURN

'****************** End of Program ******************
```

Sample Program Output

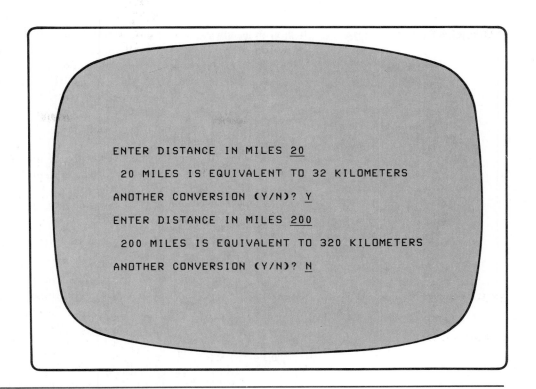

```
ENTER DISTANCE IN MILES 20

   20 MILES IS EQUIVALENT TO 32 KILOMETERS

ANOTHER CONVERSION (Y/N)? Y

ENTER DISTANCE IN MILES 200

   200 MILES IS EQUIVALENT TO 320 KILOMETERS

ANOTHER CONVERSION (Y/N)? N
```

Loop Indentation

Notice in the conversion program that the statements in the loop have been indented. This is done to improve the readability of programs. As the complexity of a program increases, good indentation practice becomes more and more important.

The DO and LOOP statements should be aligned with each other. This clearly indicates the beginning and end of the loop. Then all statements within the loop should be indented and aligned with each other. The precise number of spaces to indent is not important. Some programmers prefer two spaces, others pick a convenient TAB location. The important thing is to be consistent.

If you ever find yourself making changes in another person's program, or even returning to one of your own after a time delay, you will quickly appreciate the importance of good, consistent indentation practices for readability and understanding.

Endless Loops

Care must be taken when programming loops so that an *endless loop* does not occur.

```
'***An Endless Loop ***
CLS
DO WHILE Num <> 10
    PRINT "HELLO"
LOOP
```

In this example, there is no way for Num to become equal to 10, so the condition will always be *true*. This program will continue printing HELLO until one of two things occurs: (1) you turn off the power to the computer, or (2) you learn to interrupt a program on your computer. Simultaneously pressing the CTRL and BREAK (or CTRL-C) keys works for most computers; investigate yours. Try entering the endless loop program, run it, and make sure you can stop it. Then vow not to write that kind of program yourself.

Here is a cleaned-up version of the loop program.

```
'*** A Proper Loop ***
CLS
DO WHILE Num < 10
    PRINT "Hi there, Handsome"
    LET Num = Num + 1
LOOP
```

How many times will the PRINT statement be executed?

Terminating Loops

A loop must always have a way to terminate by using a variable that changes value within the loop. Then the loop condition will be tested again after each **iteration** (execution of the body of the loop). Three common ways of controlling loop exits are (1) questioning the user (e.g., Do you wish to continue?), (2) testing for a particular input value, and (3) using a counter.

Asking a Question to Terminate the Loop

When data is being input from the keyboard, the program can ask the question *Do you wish to continue?, Are there more data items?,* or some such question. Then the program can test the value of the data input. Since it is not practical to test for all possible answers (*yes, no, nope, y, n, no thanks, yes I do,* etc.), it is best to suggest the desired responses:

```
Do you wish to continue (Y/N)?
Are there more data (Yes/No)?
```

Check for the affirmative response to continue program execution. (Later you will learn to make sure that the response matches one response or the other. If not, you will re-request input.)

```
' *** Enter and Print Names and Distances ***
CLS
DO
      INPUT "Enter name       ", Nam$
      INPUT "Enter distance ", Dist
      PRINT Nam$, , Dist
      PRINT
      INPUT "Are there any more to enter (Yes/No)"; Ans$
LOOP WHILE UCASE$(Ans$) = "YES"
```

Terminating Loops with a Particular Data Value

Many times a certain value in a variable will be used to terminate an INPUT loop. Some common ways to end loops are:

```
INPUT "ENTER NAME (TYPE 'QUIT' TO END) ", Nam$
INPUT "ENTER SCORE (ZERO TO QUIT) ", Score
```

When using a predetermined value to end a loop, there are several things to remember. Be sure to choose an ending value that will make sense to the user. Some common ending values are QUIT, END, EOD (*End Of D*ata). Also, make certain that the terminating data requested is a valid constant for the field named on the INPUT statement. When inputting numeric data, you cannot request the word END, but you can select a value that is not a possible value for the field. Zero might or might not be a suitable value to use depending on the data to be entered—perhaps –1 or 999 would be suitable.

```
INPUT "ENTER GOLF SCORE (-1 TO QUIT) ", Score
INPUT "ENTER SALES AMOUNT (0 TO QUIT) ", Sale
```

Priming INPUT

Consider the timing of the condition test in a loop. The condition is tested only at the top or bottom of the loop—never in the middle. If the user is requested to "Enter Name (type 'END' to quit)," when should the program quit? You don't want to ask for additional information such as an address, or do any calculations, or print a line that says

"END" in place of the name. In order to keep from executing the body of the loop again after the user has entered the terminal value, the INPUT statement should immediately precede the condition test. Therefore, the INPUT should be the *last* statement in the loop, just before the LOOP.

```
DO UNTIL UCASE$(Nam$) = "END"
    GOSUB CalculateNumbers
    GOSUB PrintResults
    INPUT "Enter name (type 'End' to quit) ", Nam$
LOOP
```

This technique will work for all data items starting with the second INPUT. One more statement is needed to complete the logic. That statement is called the *priming INPUT*. It serves to get things going, to "prime the pump."

```
INPUT "Enter name (Type 'END' to Quit) ", Nam$
DO WHILE UCASE$(Nam$) <> "END"
    GOSUB CalculateAnswer
    GOSUB PrintResults
    INPUT "Enter name (Type 'END' to quit) ", Nam$
LOOP
```

Example Program:
A Variation on the Conversion Problem

Program Listing

```
'********** Program to Convert Miles to Kilometers ********

'                  Variables Used

'           Miles            Distance in miles
'           Km               Distance in kilometers

'****************** Program Mainline ********************

CLS
GOSUB InputMiles
DO WHILE Miles >= 0
        GOSUB ConvertMiles
        GOSUB PrintResults
        GOSUB InputMiles
LOOP
END

'****************** Input Miles ************************

InputMiles:
  PRINT
  INPUT "ENTER DISTANCE IN MILES (NEGATIVE NUMBER TO QUIT) ", Miles
  PRINT
RETURN

'****************** Convert Miles to Kilometers **********

ConvertMiles:
  LET Km = Miles * 1.6
RETURN

'****************** Print Results ********************

PrintResults:
  PRINT Miles; "MILES IS EQUIVALENT TO"; Km; "KILOMETERS"
RETURN

'**************** End of Program ********************
```

Sample Program Output

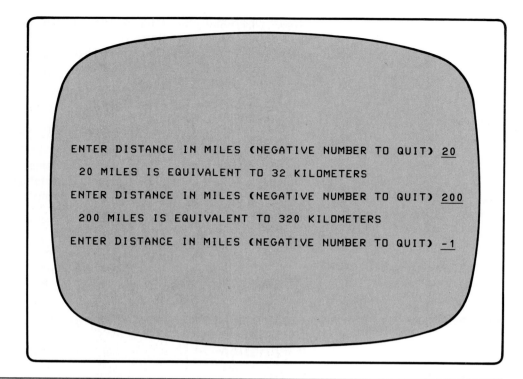

```
ENTER DISTANCE IN MILES (NEGATIVE NUMBER TO QUIT) 20

    20 MILES IS EQUIVALENT TO 32 KILOMETERS

ENTER DISTANCE IN MILES (NEGATIVE NUMBER TO QUIT) 200

    200 MILES IS EQUIVALENT TO 320 KILOMETERS

ENTER DISTANCE IN MILES (NEGATIVE NUMBER TO QUIT) -1
```

Counter-Controlled Loops

When a loop must be executed a given number of times, a variable can be used as a **counter.** For each execution of the loop, the counter is incremented by 1. The condition on the LOOP statement can then test for the terminal value needed.

```
'*** Print 10 Rows ***
LET Count = 0
DO
    LPRINT "----------------------------------"
    LET Count = Count + 1
LOOP UNTIL Count = 10
```

PROGRAM EXECUTION:

Value of
Count
```
 1   ----------------------------------
 2   ----------------------------------
 3   ----------------------------------
 4   ----------------------------------
 5   ----------------------------------
 6   ----------------------------------
 7   ----------------------------------
 8   ----------------------------------
 9   ----------------------------------
10   ----------------------------------
```

Or, an alternate solution:

```
'*** Print 10 Rows ***
LET Count = 10
DO
    LPRINT "----------------------------------"
    LET Count = Count - 1
LOOP UNTIL Count = 0
```

Either of these methods will work perfectly well. Which to use is strictly a matter of preference.

Sometimes the number of iterations of a loop must be variable. One possibility is to INPUT the value for the counter before beginning the loop.

```
'*** Print a Variable Number of Rows ***
INPUT "How many rows to print"; Count
DO
    LPRINT "-------------------------------------"
    LET Count = Count - 1
LOOP UNTIL Count = 0
```

Nested Loops

Often it will be necessary to place one loop inside another loop. These are called **nested loops.** A situation in which nested loops are needed is when input data must be checked for a valid response. If the user enters an invalid response, continuous requests must be made for a valid response. Whenever program statements must be repeated, a loop is needed.

```
'*** Enter and Print Names and Distances ***
CLS
DO
    INPUT "Enter name      ", Nam$
    INPUT "Enter distance ", Dist
    LPRINT Nam$,, Dist
    PRINT
    INPUT "Are there any more to enter? (Yes/No) ", Ans$
    '*** Check the Answer for a Valid Response ***
    DO WHILE UCASE$(Ans$) <> "YES" AND UCASE$(Ans$) <> "NO"
        INPUT "Please enter 'Yes' OR 'No' ", Ans$
    LOOP
LOOP WHILE UCASE$(Ans$) = "YES"
END
```

Or, as a further variation, the inner loop can be used to ask the question every time.

```
'*** Enter and Print Names and Distances ***
CLS
DO
    INPUT "Enter name      ", Nam$
    INPUT "Enter distance ", Dist
    LPRINT Nam$,, Dist
    PRINT
    LET Ans$ = " "
    '*** Keep Inputting Until "Yes" or "No" Entered ***
    DO
        INPUT "Are there any more to enter? (Yes/No) ", Ans$
    LOOP UNTIL UCASE$(Ans$) = "YES" OR UCASE$(Ans$) = "NO"
LOOP WHILE UCASE$(Ans$) = "YES"
```

QuickBASIC will allow nesting to as many levels as desired, as long as these rules are followed.

1. Each DO must have a LOOP.
2. Each LOOP will be matched with the last unmatched DO statement (regardless of any indentation). This means that an inner loop must be completely contained within an outer loop.

Good programming practice requires proper indentation of loops. This is especially important with nested loops.

```
DO WHILE <condition 1>
      statements for loop 1
      DO WHILE <condition 2>
            statements for loop 2
            DO WHILE <condition 3>
                  statements for loop 3
            LOOP
            more statements for loop 2
      LOOP
      more statements for loop 1
LOOP
```

Feedback

1. Code a BASIC loop that will print your name five times (one PRINT statement executed five times).
2. Write a BASIC loop that will print the numbers 1–10. This should be done with one PRINT statement executed multiple times. (PRINT X, where X changes in value for each iteration of the loop.)
3. Write a BASIC loop that will continuously input and print the names of contest participants, until QUIT is entered in place of the name.
4. How many times will the PRINT be executed?

```
DO WHILE Zed <> 0
    PRINT Zed
    LET Zed = Zed + 1
LOOP
```

5. What will print? Try this with several different values for Amt, such as 5, 10, 1, and 0.

```
INPUT Amt
DO WHILE Amt > 0
    PRINT "*";
    LET Amt = Amt - 1
LOOP
```

Accumulating Sums

A common task in programming is summing numbers. Earlier, three test scores were added with these statements:

```
INPUT Test1
INPUT Test2
INPUT Test3
LET Sum = Test1 + Test2 + Test3
```

What if there had been twenty scores or 500? Imagine the program necessary to input 500 scores and add them up! How would a program work if the exact number of scores were unknown?

Figure 3.4

Flowchart for summation in a
loop. The statements in the
loop will be repeated until -1 is
input for the score.

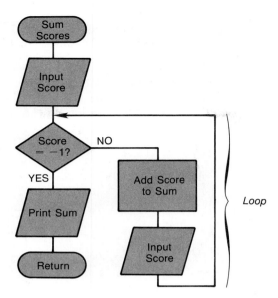

Fortunately, there is a simple solution to the problem—loops. The scores can be
input one at a time until all scores are entered. Of course, each time the INPUT statement in the loop is executed, a new score will replace the previous score. It is not necessary to save each individual score. What is needed is the total, so each score may be
added into the total as it is input. In this way, a running total is kept. Then, after all
scores have been entered, the total can be printed (see figure 3.4). The statements in
the loop will be repeated until -1 is input for the score.

It should be noted that at the start of program execution, BASIC sets all numeric
variables to zero. This eliminates the need for the initialization step required in many
programming languages.

```
'*** Sum Variable Number of Test Scores ***
CLS
PRINT "Enter test scores, (-1 to quit)"
INPUT Score
DO UNTIL Score = -1
      LET Sum = Sum + Score
      INPUT Score
LOOP
PRINT " The sum is "; Sum
```

To trace the execution of the program statements, enter scores of 100, 75, 90,
85, and −1 to end (see figure 3.5).

Figure 3.5
Hand tracing a summation loop.

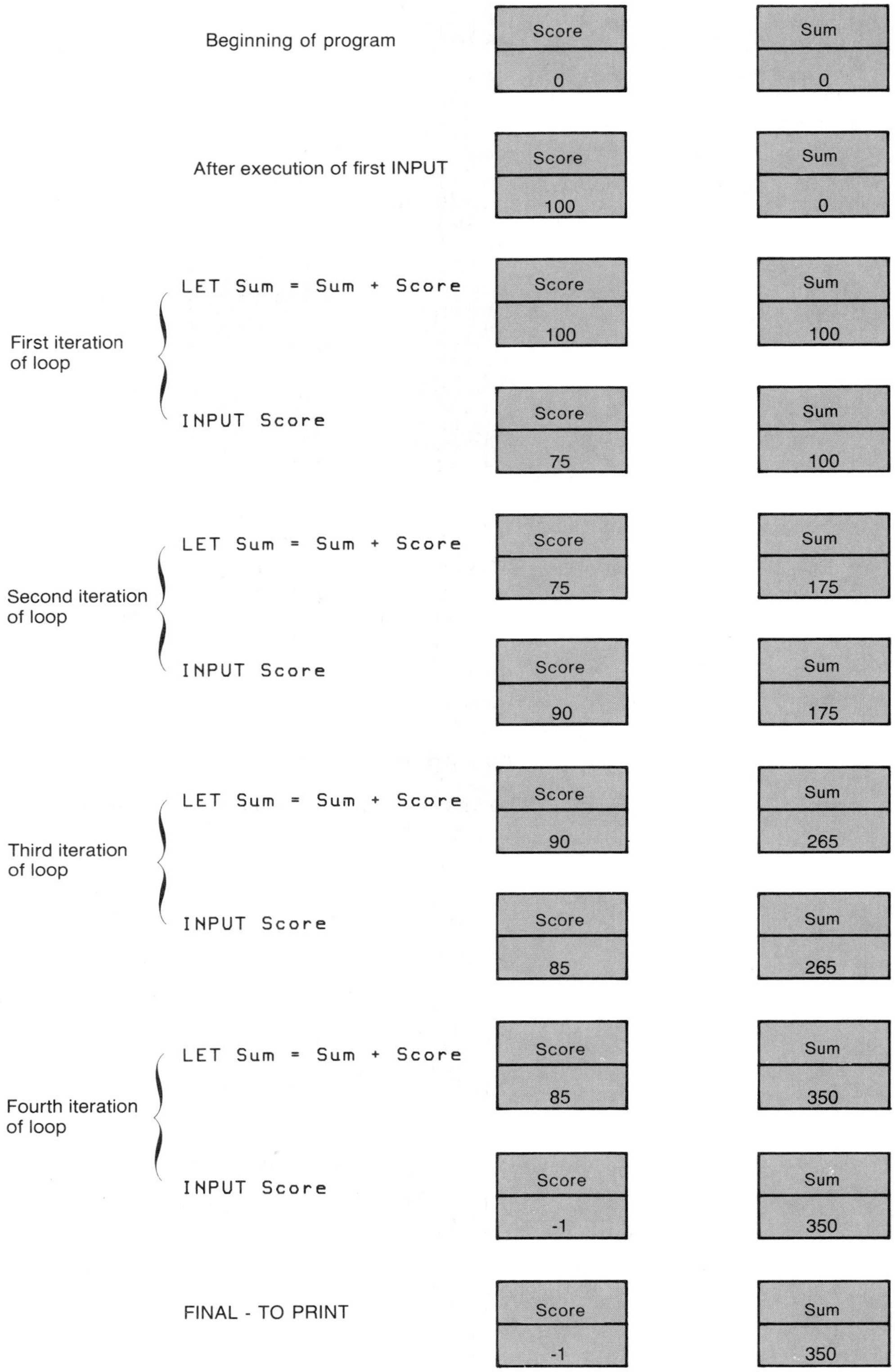

	Score	Sum
Beginning of program	0	0
After execution of first INPUT	100	0

First iteration of loop
LET Sum = Sum + Score — Score: 100, Sum: 100
INPUT Score — Score: 75, Sum: 100

Second iteration of loop
LET Sum = Sum + Score — Score: 75, Sum: 175
INPUT Score — Score: 90, Sum: 175

Third iteration of loop
LET Sum = Sum + Score — Score: 90, Sum: 265
INPUT Score — Score: 85, Sum: 265

Fourth iteration of loop
LET Sum = Sum + Score — Score: 85, Sum: 350
INPUT Score — Score: -1, Sum: 350

FINAL - TO PRINT — Score: -1, Sum: 350

Figure 3.6
Flowchart of subroutine to
average scores. The scores are
summed and counted in the
loop. Then after all scores are
entered, the average can be
calculated by dividing the sum
by the count of the scores.

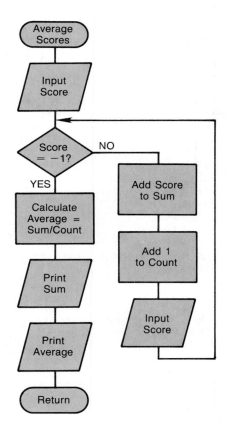

Averaging

To know the average of the scores, it is also necessary to know the number of scores entered. This can be accomplished with a counter in the loop. In figure 3.6, note how the scores are summed and counted in the loop. Then after all scores are entered, the average can be calculated by dividing the sum by the count of the scores. Note: this program has line numbers so that you can follow the program execution.

```
'*** Average Variable Number of Test Scores ***
CLS
PRINT "ENTER TEST SCORES, (-1 TO QUIT)"
INPUT Score
DO UNTIL Score = -1
   LET Sum = Sum + Score
   LET Count = Count + 1
   INPUT Score
LOOP
LET Avg = Sum / Count
PRINT " THE SUM IS "; Sum
PRINT " THE AVERAGE IS "; Avg
END
```

Statement	Value of Score	Value of Sum	Value of Count
CLS			
PRINT "ENTER TEST SCORES -1 TO QUIT"			
INPUT Score	100	0	0
DO UNTIL Score = -1 (Score is not −1 so it enters the loop)			
LET Sum = Sum + Score	100	100	0
LET Count = Count + 1	100	100	1
INPUT Score	75	100	1
LOOP			
DO UNTIL Score = -1 (Score is not − 1 so it enters the loop again)			
LET Sum = Sum + Score	75	175	1
LET Count = Count + 1	75	175	2
INPUT Score	90	175	2
LOOP			
DO UNTIL Score = -1 (Score is not −1 so it enters the loop again)			
LET Sum = Sum + Score	90	265	2
LET Count = Count + 1	90	265	3
INPUT Score	85	265	3
LOOP			
DO UNTIL Score = -1 (Score is not − 1 so it enters the loop again)			
LET Sum = Sum + Score	85	350	3
LET Count = Count + 1	85	350	4
INPUT Score	−1	350	4
LOOP			
DO UNTIL Score = -1 (sees the − 1 so it does not enter the loop again)			
LET Avg = Sum / Count	(350 / 4 = 87.5)		
PRINT "THE SUM IS"; Sum	(Prints 350)		
PRINT "THE AVERAGE IS"; Avg	(Prints 87.5)		

Table 3.2
Value of the variables, following the program execution.

Planning Programs with Loops

When planning the logic of a program, a good practice is to number each logic step. A relatively clear way to plan loop logic is to give the loop one number. Then for each step in the loop use the loop's number, a decimal point, and a sequential number within the loop. This is similar to an outline form.

1. Initialize variables
2. Print headings
3. Priming input
4. DO Loop until end of data
   4.1 Add to totals
   4.2 Print a line
   4.3 Input next data
5. Print totals
6. Stop

Flowcharting Loops

When flowcharting a loop, the decision belongs at the top or bottom (never in the middle). The decision determines whether or not the loop should be executed again. A decision is flowcharted with the diamond-shaped symbol (see figure 3.7). The question within the symbol is stated as a question that can be answered YES or NO, TRUE or FALSE. The statements in the body of the loop are repeated as long as the condition (MORE DATA?) is true.

Figure 3.7
Flowchart for a single loop. The
statements in the body of the
loop are repeated as long as
the condition (More Data?) is
true.

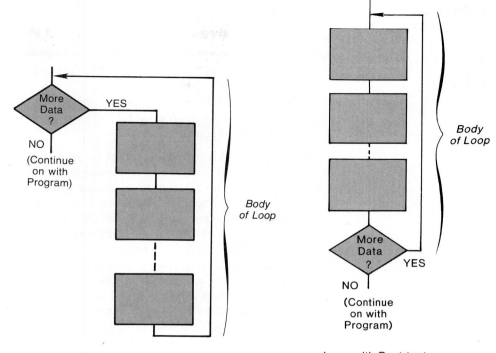

Loop with Post-test

Output Formatting

Creating program output that is pleasing, properly spaced, and aligned has sometimes
been a difficult task. BASIC has several statements and functions to assist in the formatting process. Those presented in the sections to follow are TAB, SPC, PRINT
USING, and LPRINT USING.

The PRINT Functions— TAB and SPC

TAB

The placement of variables and constants on the screen or printer can be controlled by
the use of the TAB function. It is similar to the tabs used on a typewriter.

The TAB Function—General Form

```
PRINT TAB(position) ; items to print
LPRINT TAB(position) ; items to print
```

The TAB Function—Examples

```
PRINT TAB(20); "UNDERWATER REPORT"
LPRINT TAB(5); "NAME = ";Names$;TAB(40); "CLASS = ";Class$

LET T1 = 5
LET T2 = 20
LET T3 = 45
LPRINT TAB(T1);Item;TAB(T2);Desc$;TAB(T3);Price

LET Spot = Spot + Column
PRINT TAB(10 + Spot); Figure
```

It is a good practice to use variables for the TAB position. Then, report layouts may be changed more easily.

If a TAB position is given that has already been passed on that line, BASIC will go to that TAB position on the next line to print.

```
PRINT TAB(10); "POSITION 10"; TAB(5); "POSITION 5"
```

Program Execution:

```
          POSITION 10
POSITION 5
```

The TAB function can only be used in PRINT and LPRINT statements. The keyword TAB is followed by an open parentheses (no intervening space allowed), then the desired position number, a closing parenthesis, and the data item to print. That data item may be a variable, a constant, or an expression. The items to print must be separated by semicolons. However, QB's smart editor adds them if you leave them out.

The position to occupy is an absolute position; that is, the first position on the line is TAB(1), and the twentieth position is TAB(20). The TAB location is limited by the line length of the video display or by the line length of the printer used. The position number may be a constant, variable, or arithmetic expression in the range 1–255. Any fractional values will be rounded up.

When the PRINT is executed, the internal print pointer moves to the position specified in the TAB, then the data value is printed in that exact position. A semicolon separates the TAB and data value, but watch out for the comma! A comma in a PRINT statement always means "go to the next zone," and the effects of the TAB will be lost. Do not use commas with TABs.

A layout form can be a helpful tool in planning program output (see figures 3.8 and 3.9).

```
' *** Illustrate Spacing With Tabs ***
CLS
PRINT TAB(25); "WEEKLY SALES"
PRINT
PRINT TAB(10); "NAME"; TAB(40); "AMOUNT"
PRINT
PRINT TAB(6); "Chuck Steak"; TAB(40); 25.25
```

Program Execution:

```
                        WEEKLY SALES

         NAME                           AMOUNT

     Chuck Steak                        25.25
```

SPC

Another function that can control horizontal spacing on the line is SPC. SPC differs from TAB in that TAB moves the print pointer to an absolute position on the line, but SPC moves the pointer a given number of spaces on the line (relative to the preceding item printed).

```
PRINT "ACCOUNT NUMBER"; SPC(5); "BALANCE"
```

Program Execution:

```
ACCOUNT NUMBER     BALANCE
```

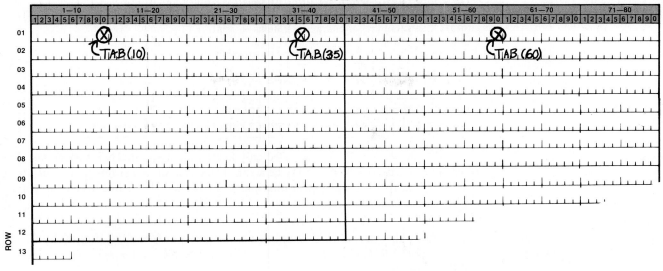

Figure 3.8
Layout showing TAB locations.

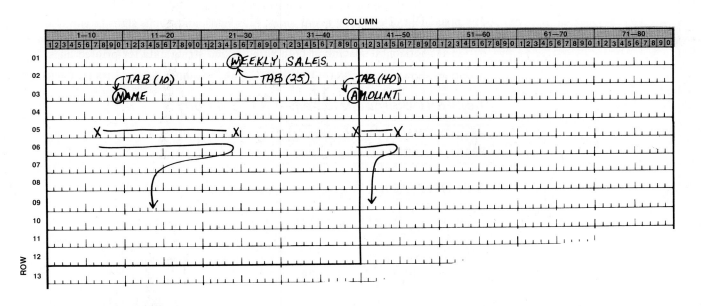

Figure 3.9
TAB example, using a layout
form.

The SPC Function—General Form

```
PRINT SPC(number of characters); items to print
LPRINT SPC(number of characters); items to print
```

The SPC Function—Examples

```
PRINT TAB(20); "COSTS = "; SPC(4); Cost
LPRINT Nam$;SPC(3);Addr$;SPC(3);City$;SPC(3);State$
```

Like the TAB, SPC can be used only in PRINT and LPRINT statements. The number of characters to space may be a variable, constant, or arithmetic expression in the range 1–255. SPC may appear multiple times on one PRINT line to control spacing all across the line.

Formatting Output with PRINT USING and LPRINT USING

A powerful aid to formatting screen and printer output is the USING option of the PRINT and LPRINT statements. The PRINT USING statement will provide for "editing" data such as

1. alignment of decimal points.
2. exact alignment of columns of data.
3. rounding to any desired number of decimal places.
4. forcing right zeros to print in decimal fractions.
5. placement of commas, dollar signs, plus signs, and minus signs in numeric values.
6. exact horizontal spacing of both numeric and string data for printed lines.

All options shown for the PRINT USING are also available for the LPRINT USING.

The PRINT USING Statement—General Form

```
PRINT USING "string literal"; items to print
PRINT USING (string variable); items to print
```

The PRINT USING Statement—Examples

```
PRINT USING " ###    ###.##    #,###.##"; Item, Pr, Tot

Execution:

   250    14.50    1,450.00

LET N$ = "###,###.##"
PRINT USING N$; 12.5
PRINT USING N$; 1.365
PRINT USING N$; .111
PRINT USING N$; 12345

Execution:

      12.50
       1.37
       0.11
  12,345.00
```

Editing Numeric Data

The formats for numeric values are defined by using the number sign (#), the decimal point, and the comma. The number of symbols used will determine the length and format of the results. Notice in the second example of the PRINT USING statement decimal points are aligned in the results, each output number has two digits to the right of the decimal point, short numbers have been padded with right zeros, and the long numbers (1.365 and .111) were rounded to print in the print image.

Editing Strings

Strings may also be printed with PRINT USING statements. The backslash character (\) is used to show the beginning and end of an edited string. The backslash characters are included in the length of the string. In the following example, there are six blank spaces between the backslashes, so the printed string length is eight characters. Any string longer than the edit image will be truncated when printed (see the results of the example following).

```
LET Dt$ = "\       \      ###.##"
PRINT USING Dt$; "SAM"; 4.5
PRINT USING Dt$; "JANET"; 25
PRINT USING Dt$; "HORNSWAGGLED"; 1
```

Program Execution:

```
SAM              4.50
JANET           25.00
HORNSWAG         1.00
```

The **print image,** or string used for formatting the data, can be a literal (as in the first two examples following) or a variable (third example following). The combination of special characters used in the print image will determine the format of the data printed. When there are multiple items to print, they are separated by semicolons.

```
PRINT USING "###   \      \   ##,###.##"; Num; Desc$; Amt

LET Prize = 1000
PRINT USING "##,###.##"; Prize

LET D$ = "  ###.#   ###.#   ###.#"
PRINT USING D$; R1; R2; R3
```

Rounding

One of the advantages of the PRINT USING is that numeric values will be rounded to the specified number of digits in the format.

```
LET Show = 1.625
PRINT USING " #    #.#    #.##    #.###    #.####"; Show; Show; Show; Show; Show
```

Program Execution:

```
2    1.6    1.63    1.625    1.6250
```

Defining Entire Print Lines Including Literals

Print images may contain formatting characters for multiple items along with literals to be printed on a line. The spacing in the print image will define the exact horizontal spacing on the printed line.

```
LET T$ = "TOTAL JOKES = ### -- TOTAL DUDS = ###"
PRINT USING T$; JokeTot; DudTot
```

Program Execution:

```
TOTAL JOKES = 125 -- TOTAL DUDS =    1
```

Formatting PRINT Images

Each print image should contain one specification for each variable to be printed. The variables will be placed into the specifications on the line on a one-for-one basis. The variable type (numeric or string) must correspond.

```
LET D$ = "  ##.#    ##.#   \      \   ##  "
PRINT USING D$; Num1; Num2; St$; Num3
```

In the above example, the first statement defines four specifications for data. Then in the PRINT USING, four variables are named in the correct order (numeric, numeric, string, numeric).

```
LET A$ = "  THE GROSS IS #,###.##    THE NET IS #,###.## "
PRINT USING A$; Gross; Net
```

The first statement specifies two literals to print, exactly as shown ("THE GROSS IS" and "THE NET IS"). Additionally, two numeric specifications are included for formatting the two variables Gross and Net. Assuming that Gross has a value of 1000 and Net has a value of 800, the output would be:

```
THE GROSS IS 1,000.00    THE NET IS   800.00
```

Short Numeric Formats

When the format given for a number is too short for the value, a percent sign is printed first, then the entire value. This will often cause columns of data to be misaligned. Whenever there is a percent sign at the beginning of the printed output, the first suspicion should be an inadequate numeric format.

```
LET G$ = "###.#"
PRINT USING G$; 1000
PRINT USING G$; 999.95
PRINT USING G$; 1000000
```

Program Execution:

```
%1000.0
%1000.0
%1000000.0
```

Placement of PRINT Images in the Program

Each program module should perform one, and only one, function. Setting up all print images for the program is a good example of a group of statements that together accomplish one task. Since a print image must be defined before the first time it is used, it makes sense to set up all print images at the start of the program in a step called initialization.

A further advantage to defining all print images in one subroutine is that it is easy to see that columns are aligned—headings will appear above the correct column of data, and totals will be exactly aligned below their columns.

Example Program: Using PRINT Images

Program Listing

```
'**** Example Using Print Image Lines ****
'************ Program Mainline **************

CLS
GOSUB InitializeImages
GOSUB PrintHeadings
GOSUB ProcessDetail
GOSUB PrintTotal
END

'************ Initialize Print Images ********

InitializeImages:
    LET H1$ = "     NAME           AMOUNT "
    LET D1$ = "     \           \    ###.## "
    LET T1$ = "            TOTAL = #,###.## "
RETURN

    '************ Print Headings ****************

PrintHeadings:
    LPRINT H1$
    LPRINT
    LPRINT
RETURN

    '************ Process Detail ****************

ProcessDetail:
    INPUT "Enter name ('Quit' to end) ", Nam$
    DO UNTIL UCASE$(Nam$) = "QUIT"
      INPUT "Enter amount given ", Amt
      LET Total = Total + Amt
      LPRINT USING D1$; Nam$; Amt
      INPUT "Enter name ('QUIT' to end) ", Nam$
    LOOP
RETURN

    '************ Print Total ****************

PrintTotal:
    LPRINT
    LPRINT USING T1$; Total
RETURN

    '************ End of Program **************
```

Sample Printer Output

```
      NAME               AMOUNT


   MAJOR GENERAL          2.75
   COLONEL CHICKEN       12.00
   PRIVATE PUNCH          4.01

          TOTAL =        18.76
```

What output will result for each of these examples? Check your answers with the computer.

```
1.  LET D$ = " ##   ##.#   ##.##   ##.### "
    LET Num = 25.3964
    PRINT USING D$; Num; Num; Num; Num

2.  LET P$ = "\       \  ##"
    PRINT USING P$; "FROGS"; 10
    PRINT USING P$; "TOADS"; 5
    PRINT USING P$; "POLLIWOGS"; 75

3.  LET T$ = " THE SCORE IS ## FOR THE \            \"
    PRINT USING T$; 12; "ROVERS"
    PRINT USING T$; 6; "BRAVES"
    PRINT USING T$; 125; "AMAZING AMAZONS"

4.  LET R$ = " \            \ SPENT ###.## ON \         \ "
    LET Money = 2
    LET Kid$ = "JOEY"
    LET Treat$ = "GUM"
    PRINT USING R$; Kid$; Money; Treat$

5.  LET A$ = " ### NEEDED BY \         \ "
    LET Dat$ = "12/25/95"
    LET Amt = 3.5
    PRINT USING A$; Dat$; Amt
```

Extended Numeric Editing

Numbers may also be edited with dollar signs, asterisks, and plus and minus signs. Dollar signs may be "fixed" at a particular location on the line or may be caused to "float."

Dollar Signs

Dollar signs may be placed in print images in one of two different ways.

1. The sign can be *fixed;* that is, it will always appear in the location defined.
2. A *floating dollar sign* will be printed to the left of the first significant digit of the number (first nonzero digit).

Fixed Dollar Sign   One dollar sign in the print image will fix the dollar sign.

```
PRINT USING "$##,###.##"; 25
```

Execution:

```
$    25.00
```

Floating Dollar Sign   Two dollar signs in the print image will cause the sign to be printed in the first position to the left of the formatted number.

```
PRINT USING "$$##,###.##"; 25
```

Execution:

```
$25.00
```

Since one dollar sign must always be printed by this print image, the largest number that can be printed in this image has five digits to the left of the decimal point (99,999).

Plus and Minus Signs

Without any help from a print image, positive numbers are printed without a sign, and negative numbers are printed with a leading minus sign. By using a print image, the sign may be printed at either end of the number, and plus signs may be forced to print.

The printing of the sign is controlled by the sign used in the print image. Using a plus sign will force a sign to print on all numbers—a plus sign for positive numbers and a minus sign for negative numbers. Using a minus sign in the image will cause a sign to be printed for negative numbers only.

Trailing Signs   The sign placed at the right end of the format specification will cause the sign to trail the formatted number.

```
LET P1$ = "###.#-    ###.#+"
PRINT USING P1$; 10; 10
PRINT USING P1$; -50.65; -50.65
PRINT USING P1$; .22; .22
```

Program Execution:

```
10.0       10.0+
50.7-      50.7-
 0.2        0.2+
```

Leading Signs   A plus sign placed at the left end of the format specification will cause the sign to be printed preceding (leading) the formatted number. However, a minus sign cannot be used on the left of a format specification.

```
LET S1$ = "+###.##    ###.##"
PRINT USING S1$; 10; 10
PRINT USING S1$; -1.555; -1.555
PRINT USING S1$; -100; -100
```

Program Execution:

```
 +10.00    10.00
  -1.55    -1.55
-100.00   %-100.00
```

Asterisk Check Protection

Two asterisks in a format specification specify *check protection*. All spaces to the left of the number will be filled with asterisks.

```
LET C$ = "**##,###.##"
PRINT USING C$; 1000
PRINT USING C$; 1.25
```

Execution:

```
***1,000.00
*******1.25
```

Combining a Floating Dollar Sign with Check Protection

To combine the floating dollar sign and asterisk check protection, use two asterisks and one dollar sign (**$).

```
LET D$ = "**$#,###.##"
PRINT USING D$; 50
PRINT USING D$; 2542.22
```

Execution:

```
*****$50.00
**$2,542.22
```

Number of Characters Printed

Each of the formatting characters (#, $. * + −) counts as one character. The floating dollar sign and asterisk check protection characters are each considered one digit position. If the number to be printed is too long, the editing characters will not print.

```
LET L$ = "**$,###.##"
PRINT USING L$; 10
PRINT USING L$; 1000
PRINT USING L$; 10000
PRINT USING L$; 100000
PRINT USING L$; 1000000
```

Execution:

```
****$10.00
*$1,000.00
$10,000.00
%$100,000.00
%$1,000,000.00
```

Editing String Data

Strings can be formatted to a specified length with the backslash character. The number of print positions used will be the number of spaces between the backslashes plus two, since the backslash characters are included in the length. Long strings will be truncated to fit the format, and short strings will be filled with blank spaces.

```
LET K$ = "\  \      \      \  \              \"
LET V$ = "ABCDEFGHIJ"
PRINT USING K$; V$; V$; V$
```

Execution:

```
ABCD      ABCDEF   ABCDEFGHIJ
```

Printing Variable Length Strings

When the entire string should be printed, regardless of the length, the ampersand (&) is used.

```
LET L$ = "& ## ####"
PRINT USING L$; "MAY"; 15; 1940
PRINT USING L$; "DECEMBER"; 1; 1995
```

Execution:

```
MAY 15 1940
DECEMBER  1 1995
```

Repeated PRINT Images

One print image can be used to format multiple numeric values. When the print image does not contain enough numeric specifications, the image is repeated. When this technique is used, it is advisable to include blank spaces within the image to control horizontal spacing between numeric values.

```
PRINT USING "##,### "; 25; 10000; 235
```

Execution:

```
   25   10,000    235
```

Feedback

What output will result for each of these examples?

```
1.  LET E$ = "**$#,###.##"
    PRINT USING E$; 1
    PRINT USING E$; 250000
    PRINT USING E$; .599
    PRINT USING E$; 999.999
    PRINT USING E$; 123456789
```

```
2.  LET Num1 = 4
    LET Num2 = -50.45
    LET Num3 = -100.63
    LET Num4 = 0
    PRINT USING " ###.#- "; Num1; Num2; Num3; Num4
    PRINT USING " ###.#+ "; Num1; Num2; Num3; Num4
    PRINT USING " +##.## "; Num1; Num2; Num3; Num4
    PRINT USING " $$##,###.## "; Num1; Num2; Num3; Num4
    PRINT USING "  $##,###.## "; Num1; Num2; Num3; Num4
```

Combining TABs and PRINT Images

It is permissible to combine TAB with PRINT USING, but only one TAB function may be used per line.

```
    PRINT TAB(20); USING "##.##    ##"; Total; Count
```

Notice the placement of the TAB between the PRINT and USING.

Feedback

Can you name any advantages of using a variable rather than a literal for the print image?

Programming Example: Jog-a-Thon Fund-Raising Drive

A jog-a-thon has been planned for a fund-raising drive. What is needed is a program to keep track of the runners and the donations they have earned. Each runner has received pledges of a certain amount of money for each lap run. After the event has been run, the amount each runner has earned for the cause must be calculated.

At the conclusion of the report, the program should show the totals of the amount pledged, the number of laps run, and the amount earned. Also, the organizers would like to know the average amount pledged per runner, the average number of laps run, and the average amount earned.

Input

1. Runner's name
2. Amount pledged per lap (for that runner)
3. Number of laps run

Output (printer)

1. All three input fields
2. Amount earned (one runner)
3. Totals for amount pledged, number of laps, and amount earned (all runners)
4. Averages for amount pledged, number of laps, and amount earned

Calculations

1. Amount earned = amount pledged * laps run
2. Total the amount pledged, laps run, and amount earned
3. Count the number of runners
4. Average the amount pledged, laps run, and amount earned

Pseudocode

1. Initialize print images
2. Print headings
3. Input runner name (priming input, name only)
4. DO Loop until END entered
    4.1   Input amount pledged and laps run
    4.2   Calculations
        4.2.1   Calculate amount earned
        4.2.2   Add to 3 totals
        4.2.3   Add 1 to count
    4.3   Output on printer
        4.3.1   Name, amount pledged, laps run, amount earned
    4.4   Input next runner name
5. Total calculations
    5.1   Average 3 fields
6. Print totals and averages
7. End

Hierarchy Chart Refer to figure 3.10.

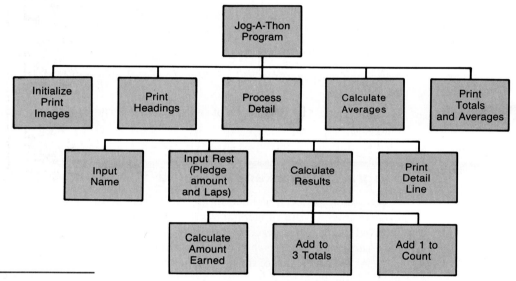

Figure 3.10
Jog-a-thon program hierarchy chart.

Flowchart

Refer to figure 3.11.

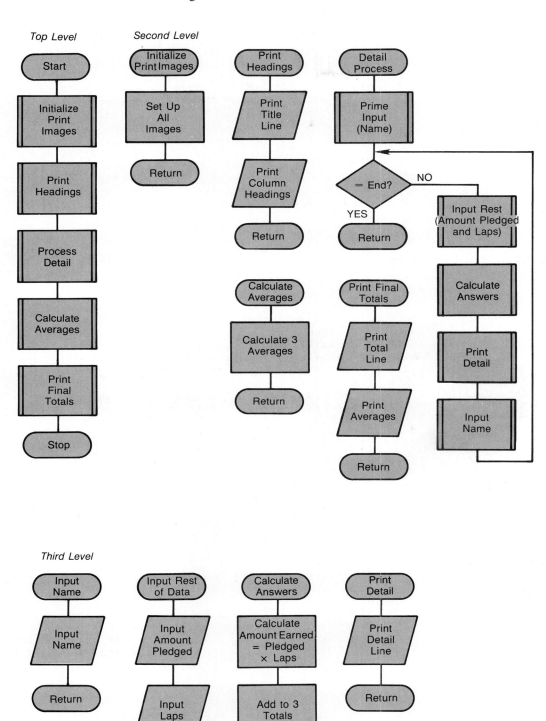

Figure 3.11
Jog-a-thon program flowchart.

Example Program

```
'*** Program to Keep Track of the Donations for the JOG-A-THON ***
'                  Variables Used

'                       Runner$         Name of runner
'                       Pledge          Amount pledged per lap
'                       Laps            Number of laps run
'                       Earned          Amount earned/one runner
'                       TotLaps         Total number of laps
'                       TotPledge       Total of pledge column
'                       TotEarned       Total of earned column
'                       Count           Count of number of runners
'                       AvgPledge       Average amount pledged per lap
'                       AvgEarned       Average amount earned per runner
'                       AvgLaps         Average number of laps per
'                                       runner
'                       T1$, H1$, H2$   Print Images
'                       D1$, TL$, S1$   Print Images
'                       S2$, S3$        Print Images


'******************** Program Mainline ********************

CLS
GOSUB InitializeImages
GOSUB PrintHeadings
GOSUB ProcessDetail
GOSUB CalculateAverages
GOSUB PrintTotals
END


'******************** Initialize Print Images ************

InitializeImages:
   LET T1$ = "          J O G - A - T H O N   D O N A T I O N S"
   LET H1$ = "     RUNNER           AMOUNT     LAPS       AMOUNT"
   LET H2$ = "                      PLEDGED     RUN       EARNED"
   LET D1$ = " \                  \    ###.##     ###     #,###.##"
   LET TL$ = "     TOTALS      #,###.##   ##,###   ###,###.##"
   LET S1$ = "     AVERAGE PLEDGED PER LAP    ###.##"
   LET S2$ = "     AVERAGE LAPS RUN            ##.#"
   LET S3$ = "     AVERAGE EARNINGS           ###.##"
RETURN


'******************** Print Headings ********************

PrintHeadings:
   LPRINT T1$                          'Title line
   LPRINT
   LPRINT H1$                          'First heading line
   LPRINT H2$                          'Second heading line
   LPRINT
   LPRINT
RETURN


'******************** Process Detail ********************

ProcessDetail:
   CLS
   GOSUB InputName
   DO UNTIL UCASE$(Runner$) = "END"
      GOSUB InputRest
      GOSUB CalculateAnswers
      GOSUB PrintDetail
      GOSUB InputName
   LOOP
RETURN
```

```
'******************** Input Runner Name ********************

InputName:
    INPUT "ENTER RUNNER NAME (TYPE 'END' TO QUIT)  ", Runner$
RETURN

'******************** Input Rest For One Runner ***********

InputRest:
    PRINT
    INPUT "AMOUNT PLEDGED PER LAP   ", Pledge
    PRINT
    INPUT "NUMBER OF LAPS RUN       ", Laps
    PRINT
RETURN

'******************** Calculate Answers ******************

CalculateAnswers:
    LET Earned = Pledge * Laps
    LET TotEarned = TotEarned + Earned
    LET TotPledge = TotPledge + Pledge
    LET TotLaps = TotLaps + Laps
    LET Count = Count + 1
RETURN

'******************** Print Detail ********************

PrintDetail:
    LPRINT USING D1$; Runner$, Pledge, Laps, Earned
RETURN

'******************** Calculate Averages ******************

CalculateAverages:
    LET AvgPledge = TotPledge / Count
    LET AvgLaps = TotLaps / Count
    LET AvgEarned = TotEarned / Count
RETURN

'******************** Print Totals ********************

PrintTotals:
    LPRINT
    LPRINT USING TL$; TotPledge, TotLaps, TotEarned
    LPRINT
    LPRINT
    LPRINT USING S1$; AvgPledge
    LPRINT USING S2$; AvgLaps
    LPRINT USING S3$; AvgEarned
RETURN
'******************** End of Program ********************
```

Sample Program Output

```
ENTER RUNNER NAME (TYPE 'END' TO QUIT)  RANDY

AMOUNT PLEDGED PER LAP  2.50

NUMBER OF LAPS RUN      30

ENTER RUNNER NAME (TYPE 'END' TO QUIT)  SUZANNE

AMOUNT PLEDGED PER LAP  1.50

NUMBER OF LAPS RUN      40

ENTER RUNNER NAME (TYPE 'END' TO QUIT)  JOEY

AMOUNT PLEDGED PER LAP  3.50

NUMBER OF LAPS RUN      20

ENTER RUNNER NAME (TYPE 'END' TO QUIT)  END
```

Sample Printer Output

```
          J O G - A - T H O N   D O N A T I O N S
         RUNNER              AMOUNT    LAPS      AMOUNT
                             PLEDGED   RUN       EARNED


         RANDY               2.50      30        75.00
         SUZANNE             1.50      40        60.00
         JOEY                3.50      20        70.00

         TOTALS              7.50      90        205.00


         AVERAGE PLEDGED PER LAP    2.50
         AVERAGE LAPS RUN           30.0
         AVERAGE EARNINGS           68.33
```

Summary

1. When one or more program statements are repeated, a loop is formed.
2. A loop is programmed with the DO and LOOP statements.
3. Each loop begins with the DO statement and ends with the LOOP statement.
4. The terminating condition for a loop may be written with WHILE or UNTIL.
5. The WHILE or UNTIL may be placed at the top of the loop on the DO statement (called a pretest), or at the bottom of the loop on the LOOP statement (called a posttest).
6. The condition for a WHILE or UNTIL is formed using one or more of the six relational operators: $>$ (greater than); $<$ (less than); $=$ (equal); $<>$ (not equal); $>=$ (greater than or equal); $<=$ (less than or equal). These operators may be combined with the logical operators AND, OR, and NOT to form compound conditions and may be grouped by using parentheses.

7. The UCASE$ function can be used to simplify comparing uppercase and lowercase characters.
8. Good, consistent indentation is important for program understandability and maintenance. Each DO and LOOP should be aligned, and the statements in the loop should be indented and aligned with each other.
9. A statement must be included in each loop that will cause the loop to terminate; otherwise, endless loops will result.
10. Loops containing INPUT statements may ask a question to determine whether the statements should be reexecuted.
11. INPUT loops often are terminated by the user entering a particular value to indicate the end of data. These values must match the type of variable being input (string or numeric).
12. When using a specific value to terminate the loop, the INPUT should be the last statement in the loop (before the LOOP). In order to start the execution, a priming INPUT is used.
13. Counters can be used to control the number of iterations of a loop.
14. Loops may be nested to any level.
15. Each LOOP will be matched with the last unmatched DO, regardless of indentation.
16. When totals are required for a listing, a running total is accumulated. During each iteration of the loop the current values are added into the totals.
17. List totals are generally printed after the main processing loop is completed.
18. When planning a loop with pseudocode, follow indentation and numbering guidelines.
19. A flowchart for a loop shows the decision at the top or bottom of the loop. The logic flow returns to the decision after each execution of the loop.
20. The PRINT USING and LPRINT USING statements are the most powerful of the formatting statements.
21. All options of the PRINT USING are also available with LPRINT USING.
22. The PRINT USING can be used to insert dollar signs, commas, asterisks, plus signs, and minus signs. It can align decimal points, round numbers, and force the printing of zeros to the right of the decimal point.
23. The string used to format the printing is called a print image, and it may be a literal or a variable.
24. A dollar sign used in a numeric format may be either fixed or floating. One dollar sign is a fixed sign, which will appear in the exact position placed. Two dollar signs in the format define a floating dollar sign, which will print immediately to the left of the number.
25. A plus sign placed in a numeric format will cause the sign of the number to print. The sign may be placed at the left or the right of the number.
26. A minus sign may be placed at the right of a numeric format. The printed output will have a minus sign for negative numbers, a blank for positive numbers.
27. Asterisk check protection is implemented with two asterisks in the numeric format.
28. When the print image is too short—that is, when there are not enough specifications for the variables named—the image will be repeated.
29. Any number to be printed that is too long for its format will print with a percent sign to the left of the number.
30. Strings can be printed with PRINT USING by using backslashes or an ampersand. The backslash method will print a specified number of characters for each string. An ampersand for formatting will print a variable length string.

Programming Exercises

Each of the following exercises should be written as a modular program with a program mainline and subroutines. Plan the program with a modular flowchart, pseudocode, or hierarchy chart. Run the program with the test data provided, as well as other data that you design. Any rounding of results should be accomplished with the (L)PRINT USING statement.

3.1. Modify the program in exercise 2.2 (merchandise turnover problem, p. 54) to have a program loop. The program should keep requesting new values for beginning inventory, ending inventory, and cost of goods sold, and keep printing the appropriate figures for average inventory and turnover. A negative number entered for beginning inventory will end the program. Accumulate and print totals for beginning inventory, ending inventory, and cost of goods sold.

Format the output with a title and column headings for beginning inventory, ending inventory, cost of goods sold, average inventory, and turnover. Align the total fields on the decimal point beneath the corresponding columns.

3.2. Modify the program in exercise 2.1 (automobile stopping distance problem, p. 54) to print a table of speeds and stopping distances. Print one line for each velocity, in 5-mph increments, from 30 mph to 80 mph. Round the stopping distances to the nearest tenth [use (L)PRINT USING]. Print an appropriate title on the report and the message END OF REPORT at the bottom of the list.

INPUT: None. Use a counter for the speeds.
SAMPLE PROGRAM OUTPUT:

```
                   AUTOMOBILE STOPPING DISTANCE TABLE

        SPEED (MPH)        DISTANCE REQUIRED TO STOP (FEET)

            30                      110.4
            35                      137.1
            40                      166.2
            45                      197.7
            50                      231.5
            55                      267.8
            60                      306.4
            65                      347.4
            70                      390.8
            75                      436.6
            80                      484.8
        END OF REPORT
```

3.3. Modify the program in exercise 2.4 (recording studio charges, p. 55) to calculate charges for all groups for an entire day. Keep requesting the name of a new group until END is entered for group name. Accumulate and print totals of the minutes used and the charges made. Format the report with a title and column headings. Each detail line should show Group Name, Number of Minutes, and Charges. The total line will show the total for Number of Minutes and Charges.

3.4. Compute the factorial for any integer.

INPUT: An integer (N) should be requested. After the output, continue requesting integers for calculation until zero is entered.
OUTPUT: Print the message

N! = xxxxxxx

PROCESSING: The factorial is calculated as

$$N \times (N\text{-}1) \dots \times 2 \times 1$$
$$\text{Example: } 5! = 5 \times 4 \times 3 \times 2 \times 1$$

TEST DATA: 10, 5, 25, 0

3.5. Modify the program in exercise 2.8 (car rental invoice, p. 56) to print multiple invoices. After each invoice is printed, ask the question: ANOTHER INVOICE TO PRINT?. As long as the user enters YES, print another invoice. Any answer other than YES will terminate the program. Format the output with (L)PRINT USING.

3.6. The Computer Club needs to keep a membership list with member names and telephone numbers.

INPUT: Names and telephone numbers will be input during program execution.

OUTPUT: Print a nicely formatted listing with appropriate title and column headings. Each detail line will consist of a member name and telephone number. At the end of the report, print the number of members with an identifying literal, such as

```
NUMBER OF MEMBERS = XX
```

PROCESSING: Accumulate a count of the number of members.

3.7. Modify the program in exercise 3.6 to include a data validity check. For each iteration of the loop, ask the question: ANOTHER MEMBER (Y/N)?. If any response other than Y or N is entered, print a message and allow the response to be re-entered. As a further variation, consider the possibility of lowercase letters as well as uppercase (Y or y, N or n).

3.8. Write a program to create a grocery list on the printer. Continue inputting items until QUIT is entered.

INPUT: Items for the grocery list will be input from the keyboard.
OUTPUT: The list of items should be printed on the printer.

3.9. Modify the program in exercise 2.15 (employee bonus program, p. 58) to handle multiple stores. Request input until QUIT is entered for the store number. Use print images to format your output.

3.10. Write a program that will input a number and print the number, the square of the number, and the cube of the number. Continue the operation until 999 is entered.

3.11. Write a program that will request the length and width of a rectangle until 0 is entered for either the length or the width. You will then print the area and the perimeter for each set of inputs.

INPUT: The length and width will be input from the keyboard.
OUTPUT: The area and perimeter will be printed with appropriate labels.
PROCESSING:
  1. Area = length * width.
  2. Perimeter = (length + width) * 2.

3.12. Write a program to create two lists for a potluck dinner party you are planning. The first list will be a guest list, and the second list will be an itemization of things to be brought.

INPUT: For the guest list, guest names should be input from the keyboard until QUIT is entered. For the second list, items to bring should be entered until QUIT is entered.
OUTPUT: Print an appropriate title for each list. Also, print the total number of people invited on the guest list.
PROCESSING: Keep a count of the total number of people invited.

3.13. Using nested loops, write a program to create a baseball statistics sheet for baseball teams until QUIT is entered for the team name and the player's name. Each team has twelve players.

INPUT: Input a team name. Then, for that team, input player's name, player's number, total home runs, total at bats, and total hits. At the conclusion of one team, input the next team name and players on that team.

OUTPUT: Team name, player's name, player's number, total home runs, total at bats, total hits, and the player's batting average will be output to the printer.

PROCESSING:

1. Calculate batting average $= \dfrac{\text{total hits}}{\text{total at bats}}$

3.14. Using nested loops, write a program to create a sheet of test results for multiple classes. Each student will have five test scores.

INPUT: Name of class, teacher, student's name, and test grades will be input from the keyboard. End a class group when QUIT is entered for student name. End processing when QUIT is entered for teacher name.

OUTPUT: Name of class, teacher, student's name, test grades, test average and the class score average will be output to the printer.

PROCESSING:

1. Calculate test average for each student $= \dfrac{\text{total for all tests}}{\text{number of tests}}$

2. Calculate class score average $= \dfrac{\text{total of all test scores for class}}{\text{number of students} * \text{number of tests (5)}}$

SAMPLE OUTPUT FOR ONE CLASS:

```
Class Name: Basket Weaving
Teacher: Mrs. Twine
```

Student Name	Test 1	2	3	4	5	Average
Steve Campbell	80	93	90	100	95	91.6
Chris Conley	79	80	100	100	80	87.8
Dean Cummings	63	50	55	60	80	61.6
Teresa Foss	75	78	80	90	100	84.6
Tricia Mills	85	90	95	100	83	90.6
Shawn Nelson	82	78	40	55	60	63.0
Albert Plucker	57	65	83	84	97	77.2
Jon Snow	98	100	85	80	84	89.4
Jim Spencer	76	81	91	88	59	79.0
Eric Stone	100	100	95	100	98	98.6

```
Class Score Average = 82.3
```

3.15. The Kiwi Karate Studio needs to purchase some GIs, belts, and weapons for its students. The GIs and belts are bought from one company and the weapons are bought from another. Write a program to create two purchase orders using the data given below.

INPUT: The date, name and address of vendor, karate studio name and address, and the sample data below will be input from the keyboard.

OUTPUT: Make up appropriate title and column headings. Include the date, name and address of vendor, karate studio name and address, item description, price, subtotal, tax, and total will be output to the printer.

PROCESSING:
1. Extended price = price * quantity.
2. Subtotal = sum of extended price column.
3. Tax = subtotal * .065.
4. Total = tax + subtotal.

TEST DATA:
PURCHASE ORDER 1:

Description	Price	Quantity
Size 1 GI	$65	5
Size 2 GI	$65	8
Size 3 GI	$65	10
Size 4 GI	$65	20
Size 5 GI	$65	7
Size 6 GI	$65	5
Brown belt	$20	10
Black belt	$18	15
Orange belt	$16	15
Blue belt	$14	20
Green belt	$12	30
White belt	$10	30

PURCHASE ORDER 2:

Description	Price	Quantity
Samurai sword	$50	25
Nunchucks	$15	30
Manrici	$20	30
Scye	$15	20
Joto	$5	40

4

Adding IF Statements and READ Statements to Programs

IF...THEN...ELSE Statement
Block IF Statement
  IF...THEN
  ELSEIF...THEN
  END IF
READ Statement
DATA Statement
RESTORE Statement

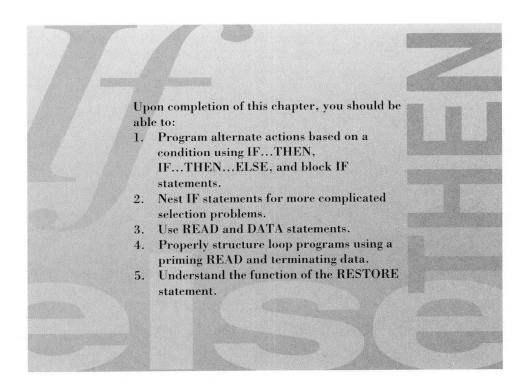

Upon completion of this chapter, you should be able to:

1. Program alternate actions based on a condition using IF...THEN, IF...THEN...ELSE, and block IF statements.
2. Nest IF statements for more complicated selection problems.
3. Use READ and DATA statements.
4. Properly structure loop programs using a priming READ and terminating data.
5. Understand the function of the RESTORE statement.

The Selection Process

The programs presented thus far have executed a single sequence of actions—not realistic for computer applications. One powerful asset of the computer is the ability to make decisions and to take alternate courses of action based on the outcome.

A decision made by the computer is formed as a question: Is a given condition true or false? If it is true, do one thing; if it is false, do something else.

like: IF   <u>the sun is shining</u>   (condition)
           THEN   <u>go to the beach</u>   (action to take if condition is true)
           ELSE   <u>go to class</u>   (action to take if condition is false)

or: IF   <u>you don't succeed</u>   (condition)
           THEN   <u>try, try again</u>   (action to take if condition is true)

Notice in the second example, no action is specified if the condition is not true.

Single-line IF...THEN...ELSE

Note the following example:

```
'****** An Agreeable Program ******
CLS
INPUT "Do you like this class?", Ans$
IF Ans$ = "YES" THEN PRINT "So do I" ELSE PRINT "Neither do I"
```

The condition Ans$ = "YES" will be tested. If the content of the variable Ans$ is equal to YES, then the condition evaluates *true,* and the first PRINT will be executed. If Ans$ has *any* value other than YES, then the condition is *false,* and the second PRINT will be executed. Too bad if Ans$ contains SURE DO.

Study this example:

```
'*** Give Discount Of 5% On A Sale Less Than $100, Or A
'          Discount Of 10% When Sale Is $100 Or More ******

GiveDiscount:
  INPUT "Enter amount of sale"; Amount
  IF Amount < 100 THEN LET Disc=Amount*.05 ELSE LET Disc=Amount*.10
  LET Total = Amount - Disc
  PRINT "The discount is "; Disc
  PRINT "The total is    "; Total
RETURN
```

Here the variable Amount will be tested to see if it is less than 100. Any amount less than 100 will cause the condition to be true, and a 5 percent discount calculated. If the condition is not true (an amount 100 or more), a 10 percent discount will be calculated. (What happens on exactly 100?) Figure 4.1 illustrates the discount selection.

The IF...THEN...ELSE Statement—General Form

```
IF <condition> THEN <statement> [ELSE <statement>]
```

The IF...THEN...ELSE Statement—Example

```
If X > Y THEN PRINT "X is greater" ELSE PRINT "X is not greater"
```

If the value of X is greater than the value of Y, then the condition X > Y is true, and the PRINT is executed. In any other case (including X = Y), the condition is false, and the second PRINT is executed.

Figure 4.1
The discount selection. When
the amount is less than 100, a
5% discount is given. For an
amount 100 or more, a 10%
discount is given.

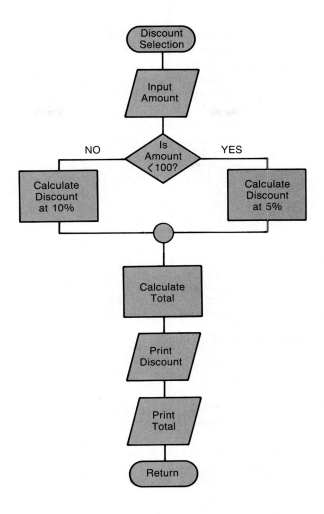

Effect of the IF...THEN...ELSE Statement

In an IF statement, when the condition is *true*, only the THEN clause is executed.
When the condition is *false*, only the ELSE clause, if present, is executed.

Conditions for IF Statements

There is no difference between the conditions used in DO...LOOP and the conditions
used in IF statements. In both instances, the conditions are formed with combinations
of the relational operators ($>$, $>=$, $<$, $<=$, $=$, $<>$), the logical operators (AND,
OR, NOT), and the parentheses (). Compound conditions may be used in IF statements:

```
IF Score >= 80 AND Score <= 90 THEN PRINT "Your grade is B"
```

Longer IF Statements

The disadvantage of these single-line IF statements is that the entire statement must
appear on one line. For one simple condition, single-line IF statements are satisfactory.
But when you want to code more complicated IF statements, with more than one action
to take for the THEN or ELSE condition, QB's block IF statement is the better solution.

Block IF...THEN...ELSE

One of the most important new features of QB is the block IF...THEN...ELSE statement. With block IFs you may write IF statements as large as you wish. Statements for the THEN and ELSE conditions appear on separate lines, terminated by an END IF statement. The block IF makes the BASIC language more like structured languages such as Pascal or Ada and can help make your programs more structured and understandable.

Single-line IF statements may be rewritten as block IFs. Generally, this adds clarity to the program. Here is the discount selection illustrated in figure 4.1, rewritten as a block IF.

```
IF Amount < 100 THEN
        LET Disc = Amount * .05
ELSE
        LET Disc = Amount * .10
END IF
```

A block IF...THEN...ELSE must always conclude with END IF. The word THEN must appear on the same line as the IF, with nothing following THEN (except a remark). Anything further on the line indicates to QB that it is an old-style, single-line IF statement. END IF and ELSE (if used) must appear alone on a line. The statements underneath the THEN and ELSE clauses are indented for readability and clarity.

The Block IF...THEN...ELSE Statement—General Form

```
IF <condition> THEN
    <statement(s)>
[ELSEIF <condition> THEN
    <statement(s)>]
[ELSE
    <statement(s)>]
END IF
```

Notice that the keyword ELSEIF is all one word, but that END IF is two words.

The Block IF...THEN...ELSE Statement—Examples

```
IF Price > Cost + Markup THEN
    PRINT "Error in pricing"
    INPUT "Enter cost:    ", Cost
    INPUT "Enter markup:  ", Markup
    INPUT "Enter price:   ", Price
END IF

IF X > Y THEN
    PRINT "X is greater"
ELSE
    PRINT "X is not greater"
END IF

IF Balance > Limit THEN
    GOSUB RejectTransaction
ELSEIF Balance = Limit THEN
    GOSUB PrintLimitMessage
    GOSUB AcceptTransaction
ELSE
    GOSUB AcceptTransaction
END IF
```

```
IF Sales > Quota THEN
   IF Quota > PriorQuota THEN
      LET Bonus = (Quota - Sales) * .15
   ELSE
      LET Bonus = (Quota - Sales) * .1
   END IF
ELSEIF Sales = Quota THEN
   LET Bonus = 100
ELSE
   LET Bonus = 0
END IF
```

Forms of the Block IF...THEN...ELSE

The block IF can be as simple or complex as you wish. The most simple has one condition and one action.

```
IF Count > 10 THEN
     PRINT Sum
END IF
```

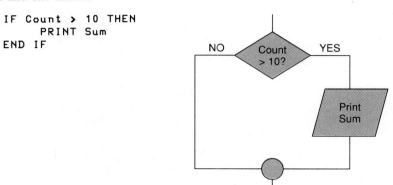

This is a block IF with both THEN and ELSE clauses.

```
IF Hours > 40 THEN
     GOSUB CalculateOvertimePay
ELSE
     GOSUB CalculateRegularPay
END IF
```

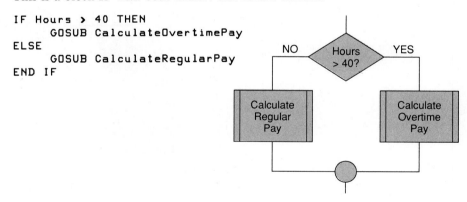

Multiple actions may be taken for either the THEN or ELSE.

```
IF Score >= 90 THEN
    LET Grade$ = "A"
    LET ACount = ACount + 1
END IF
```

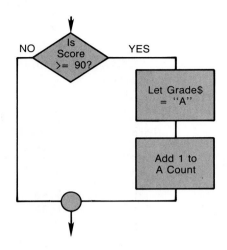

```
IF Score >= 60 THEN
    PRINT "You passed"
    LET Pass = Pass + 1
ELSE
    PRINT "You didn't pass"
    LET NoPass = NoPass + 1
END IF
```

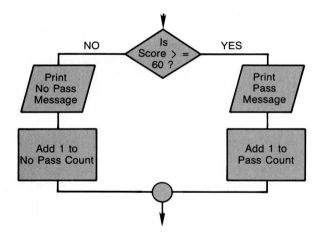

Nested IF Statements

Often it is desirable to have another IF statement as one of the statements to be executed when a condition tests *true* or *false*. IF statements containing additional IF statements are said to be **nested IF statements**. This is an example of a nested IF statement, with the second IF in the THEN portion.

```
IF Temp > 32 THEN
     IF Temp > 80 THEN
          PRINT "Hot"
     ELSE
          PRINT "Moderate"
     END IF
ELSE
     PRINT "Freezing"
END IF
```

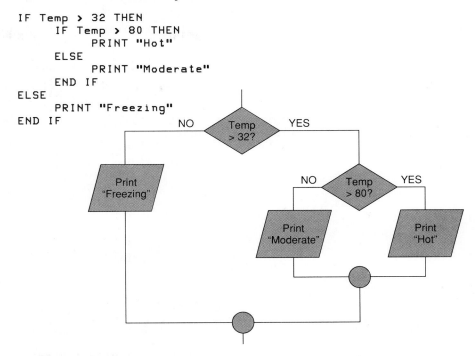

To nest IF statements in the ELSE portion, you may use either of the following approaches; however, your code is simpler if you use the ELSEIF...THEN statement. Both are flowcharted in the same way.

```
IF Temp <= 32 THEN
     PRINT "Freezing"          IF Temp <= 32 THEN
ELSE                               PRINT "Freezing"
     IF Temp > 80 THEN        ELSEIF Temp > 80 THEN
          PRINT "Hot"              PRINT "Hot"
     ELSE                     ELSE
          PRINT "Moderate"         PRINT "Moderate"
     END IF                   END IF
END IF
```

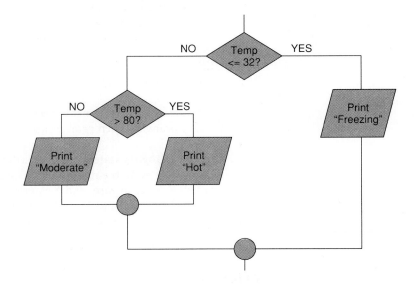

You may combine these, and nest IFs in both the THEN and ELSE. In fact, you may continue to nest IFs within IFs within IFs, as long as each IF has an END IF. However, programs become very difficult to follow (and may not perform as intended) when IFs become too deeply nested.

```
IF Code$ = "M" THEN
    IF Age < 21 THEN
        LET MinorMaleCt = MinorMaleCt + 1
    ELSE
        LET MaleCt = MaleCt + 1
    END IF
ELSE
    IF Age < 21 THEN
        LET MinorFemaleCt = MinorFemaleCt + 1
    ELSE
        LET FemaleCt = FemaleCt + 1
    END IF
END IF
```

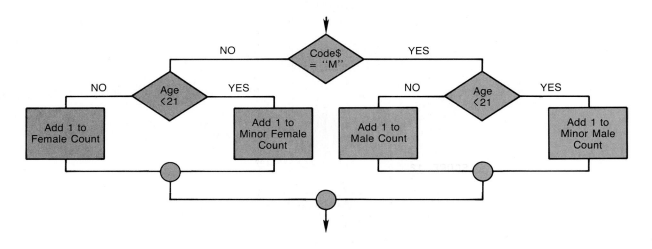

Feedback

Assume that Frogs = 10, Toads = 5, Polliwogs = 6. What will print for each of these statements?

1. IF Frogs > Polliwogs THEN PRINT "The frogs have it"
2. IF Frogs > Toads + Polliwogs THEN
       PRINT "It's the frogs"
   ELSE
       PRINT "It's the toads and polliwogs"
   END IF
3. IF Polliwogs > Toads AND Frogs <> 0 OR Toads = 0 THEN PRINT
       "It's true"
   ELSE
       PRINT "It's false"
   END IF
4. Write the BASIC statements necessary to input the price of apples and the price of oranges. Then print either "The apples cost more" or "The oranges cost more."
5. Write the BASIC statements that will test the current value of K. When K is greater than zero, the message THE ACCOUNT IS POSITIVE should be printed, K reset to zero, and Kcounter incremented by one. When K is zero or less, print the message THE ACCOUNT IS NOT POSITIVE (do not change the value of K or increment the counter).

Finding the Highest or Lowest Value in a List

When using IF statements, it becomes a simple task to find the highest or lowest value of a series. In this example, a series of names, along with the score for each, will be INPUT. At the end, the name of the person having the highest score, along with his score, will be printed out. Note that ties are not allowed in this solution.

The key to this technique is the two variables: HighScore and HighNam$. For each score input, the current score will be compared to the high score. When the current score is larger than the score stored in HighScore, the current score is placed in HighScore, and the name of the person who achieved that score is placed in HighNam$. In order to assure that the first score will be placed in high score to begin, HighScore should be initialized to a number lower than the lowest possible score.

```
'******** Find Highest Value from All Those Input ********
CLS
LET HighScore = -1                      'Initialize to low value
DO
    INPUT "NAME    ", Nam$
    INPUT "SCORE   ", Score
    IF Score > HighScore THEN
        LET HighScore = Score
        LET HighNam$ = Nam$
    END IF
    PRINT
    INPUT "ANOTHER SCORE (Y/N)"; Ans$
    PRINT
LOOP WHILE UCASE$(Ans$) = "Y"
PRINT "THE HIGHEST SCORE WAS"; HighScore; ", EARNED BY "; HighNam$
END
```

Program Execution:

```
NAME   LOU LOW
SCORE  12

ANOTHER SCORE (Y/N)? Y

NAME   HANK HIGH
SCORE  95

ANOTHER SCORE (Y/N)? Y

NAME   MARK MIDDLE
SCORE  50

ANOTHER SCORE (Y/N)? N

THE HIGHEST SCORE WAS 95 , EARNED BY HANK HIGH
```

The lowest score can be found in a similar manner. In this case, the comparison variable (LowScore) will be initialized to a value higher than the highest allowable score. This will assure that the first score input will be placed into the LowScore field.

```
'******** Find Lowest Value from All Those Input ********
CLS
LET LowScore = 101                      'Initialize to high value
DO
    INPUT "NAME    ", Nam$
    INPUT "SCORE   ", Score
    IF Score < LowScore THEN
        LET LowScore = Score
        LET LowNam$ = Nam$
    END IF
    PRINT
    INPUT "ANOTHER SCORE (Y/N)"; Ans$
    PRINT
LOOP WHILE UCASE$(Ans$) = "Y"
PRINT "THE LOWEST SCORE WAS"; LowScore; ", EARNED BY "; LowNam$
END
```

Program Execution:

```
NAME  LOU LOW
SCORE 12

ANOTHER SCORE (Y/N)? Y

NAME  HANK HIGH
SCORE 95

ANOTHER SCORE (Y/N)? Y

NAME  MARK MIDDLE
SCORE 50

ANOTHER SCORE (Y/N)? N

THE LOWEST SCORE WAS 12 , EARNED BY LOU LOW
```

Notes on Decision Making and Structured Programming

Guidelines for good structured programs require that programs and program segments have only one entry point and one exit point. To comply with this rule, program statements cannot be allowed to "branch around" indiscriminately. It is for this reason that neither the GO TO nor the "IF condition THEN branch" have been introduced. Although it is possible to write well-structured programs with these statements, the majority of beginning programmers start writing "spaghetti code" when introduced to these statements. The resulting programs are often difficult to debug and expensive to maintain. For these reasons, it is strongly recommended that all decision statements follow the form shown in this chapter.

Planning Program Decisions

Before beginning to code a program in BASIC, the logic should always be planned carefully. This planning can be in the form of a flowchart, pseudocode, hierarchy chart, or one of several other planning methods.

Flowcharts

When planning with flowcharts, always show the decision symbol and two possible courses of action (one for *true,* one for *false*). There will be statement(s) to execute when the condition is true, and there may be other statement(s) to execute when the condition is false. After these statements, the logic flow must return to a common point (the one exit point) before continuing with the program. It is suggested that the question in the decision symbol be stated so that it has a YES and a NO for the two possible courses of action.

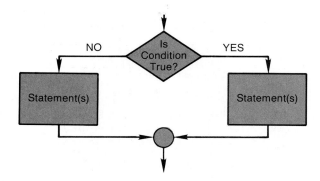

Pseudocode

When planning IF...THEN...ELSE logic with pseudocode, indentation should be in the same form as in BASIC code.

    IF condition THEN
        statement(s) to be executed when true
    ELSE
        statement(s) to be executed when false

When there are no statements to execute when the condition is false, use this form:

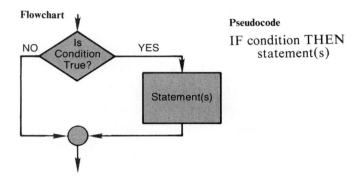

Pseudocode

IF condition THEN
     statement(s)

Hierarchy Charts

Hierarchy charts show neither the selection process nor the control structures needed to implement the logic. Only the modules are shown. When there are two modules and only one will be executed for each run of the program, show the two modules, but not the selection. Figure 4.2 shows the form for a hierarchy chart and a flowchart of an example with two modules.

The introduction of the IF statement adds new and powerful logic capabilities to programs. The next topic to be introduced will not add logical functions; instead, it will give a little more flexibility in offering another way to do a familiar task.

The READ and DATA Statements

Two methods have been shown for assigning a value to a variable—the LET and INPUT statements. There is a third method—READ and DATA statements.

Using READ and DATA allows for all data to be entered before program execution. This can save time and trouble for the user when running the program, especially when there is a large amount of data to enter. However, the results of the program will be exactly the same each time it is run.

The READ Statement—General Form

    READ list of variables, separated by commas

The READ Statement—Example

    READ A, B, C

The DATA Statement—General Form

    DATA list of constants, separated by commas

Figure 4.2
A. Hierarchy chart showing two
modules. B. Flowchart showing
two modules.

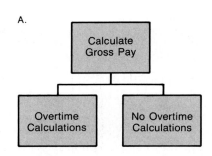

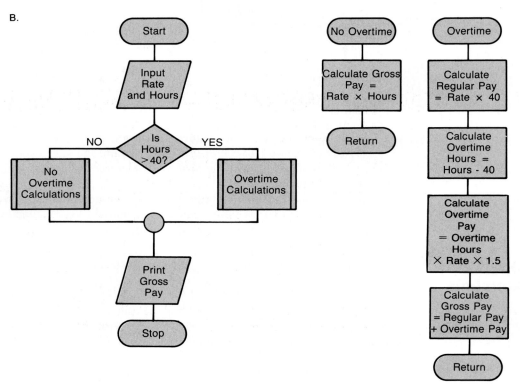

The DATA Statement—Example

```
DATA 1.25, 3.5, -20
```

Note that the data statement example could have been written as two or three
lines with the same results:

```
DATA 1.25            or        DATA 1.25, 3.5
DATA 3.5                        DATA -20
DATA -20
```

Here is an example calculating gas mileage.

```
'*** Calculate Gasoline Mileage ***
READ Miles, Gallons
LET Mileage = Miles / Gallons
PRINT "MILES ="; Miles; "GALLONS ="; Gallons; "MILEAGE ="; Mileage
DATA 265,10
END
```

Program Execution:

```
MILES = 265 GALLONS = 10 MILEAGE = 26.5
```

The READ statement causes the first DATA value (265) to be placed in the variable Miles and the second DATA value (10) to be placed in the second variable, Gallons.

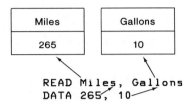

This next example involves string values.

```
'*** Read and Print Data Values ***
READ A$, B$, C$
PRINT C$; " "; B$; " "; A$
DATA THOUGHTS, YOUR, A PENNY FOR
END
```

Program Execution:

```
A PENNY FOR YOUR THOUGHTS
```

In the preceding example, THOUGHTS was assigned to the variable A\$, YOUR was placed into the variable B\$, and A PENNY FOR was placed in the variable C\$. Blank spaces included as part of a string constant will be included as long as the spaces are not leading or trailing. To include leading or trailing spaces, quotation marks must enclose the string constant.

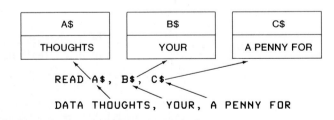

```
'*** Read and Print Data Values (With Quotes) ***
READ A$, B$, C$
PRINT C$; B$; A$
DATA " THOUGHTS ", " YOUR ", "A PENNY FOR"
END
```

Program Execution:

```
A PENNY FOR YOUR THOUGHTS
```

Note in the following example that if a comma is needed as part of a string constant, quotes are required. This is necessary because commas are delimiters (separaters) between the constants. To include colons in a constant also requires quotes.

```
'**** Read a Person's Name and Three Test Scores ****
'        and Print Out the Average Score
CLS
READ Nam$, Test1, Test2, Test3
LET Average = (Test1 + Test2 + Test3) / 3
PRINT "THE AVERAGE SCORE FOR "; Nam$; " IS"; Average
DATA "MARTIN, JOAN", 84, 67, 92
END
```

Program Execution:

```
THE AVERAGE SCORE FOR MARTIN, JOAN IS 81
```

Rules for READ and DATA Statements

1. The variables in READ statements must be matched by corresponding values in DATA statements.
2. READ statements contain one or more variable names separated by commas.
3. DATA statements contain one or more constants separated by commas.
4. The DATA values are assigned to variables with the READ statement on a one-to-one basis.
5. Items in the DATA list must be constants, either numeric values or character strings, and the type of value must agree with the variable type specified on the READ. If the types do not agree, a *Syntax error* will occur.
6. Character strings do not require quotation marks unless:
   a. they contain significant leading or trailing blanks. (Leading or trailing blanks will be ignored if the string is not quoted. Why do you suppose that is?)
   b. a comma or colon appears in the string.
7. DATA statements are nonexecutable and may be placed anywhere in the program.
8. A DATA statement may contain as many constants as will fit on one program line (255 characters), and any number of DATA statements may appear in a program.
9. The READ statement accesses the DATA values in order as they appear in the program. All DATA constants in the program may be thought of as one continuous list of items, regardless of how many items are on a line or where the lines are placed in the program.
10. As READ statements are executed, values are taken, one after another, from the data list. QB keeps track of the current element in the DATA list, even though the READ and DATA statements may be widely separated.
11. For every variable in a READ list, there must be a corresponding constant in DATA statement. If there are not enough data items to satisfy the READ, an *Out of data* error will occur. However, no error will occur if there are more elements in the DATA list than in the READ list.

Placement of READ and DATA Statements

Since DATA statements are nonexecutable, they may be placed anywhere in the program. Many programmers place all DATA statements at the beginning of the program or in a separate module placed at the physical end of the program just before the END statement. It generally works well to place the DATA statements in modular programs at the conclusion of the module that contains the READ. The goal is to make the DATA statements easy to find and easy to change when necessary, as well as to keep the logic of the program clean and easy to follow.

Comparison of READ/DATA, INPUT, and LET Statements

Using READ/DATA statements has an advantage over using LET statements and constants in calculations—there is more flexibility in the program. The data is easier to locate and change. However, the programs using READ/DATA statements cannot be considered **interactive** (or *conversational* between the user and the program). If nonprogrammers are going to run the program and make changes in the data values, the INPUT statement is preferable.

Many programs will have use for both READ/DATA and INPUT statements. When a large quantity of data is to be entered—perhaps a long list of words or a table of values that seldom change—READ and DATA statements will relieve the user of the task of entering all data for every program run. The data need be entered only once before program execution. Errors in the data can easily be corrected, and the data can be processed more than once without having to be retyped. READ/DATA can be useful for testing programs when multiple test runs must be made.

Using READ/DATA in a Loop

When data is read into a variable, it replaces whatever is already there. So when a READ is placed in a loop, a new value will be assigned to the variable for each execution (iteration) of the loop.

```
'*** Read and Data Statements in a Loop ****
CLS
DO UNTIL Nam$ = "END OF DATA"
     READ Nam$, Addr$
     PRINT Nam$, Addr$
LOOP
DATA ANN DOE, 1234 BAKER ST., BRUCE LEE, 457 HIGH ST.
DATA HOPE SEW, 222 BANK ST., END OF DATA, NO ADDRESS
END
```

Program Execution:

```
ANN DOE          1234 BAKER ST.
BRUCE LEE        457 HIGH ST.
HOPE SEW         222 BANK ST.
END OF DATA      NO ADDRESS
```

First execution of READ statement

Nam$	Addr$
ANN DOE	1234 BAKER ST.

Second execution of READ statement

Nam$	Addr$
BRUCE LEE	457 HIGH ST.

Third execution of READ statement

Nam$	Addr$
HOPE SEW	222 BANK ST.

Fourth execution of READ statement

Nam$	Addr$
END OF DATA	NO ADDRESS

Priming READ

Although the program works exactly as intended, the last line of output is not appealing. In order to have the program stop after the last READ without printing the contents of Nam$ and Addr$, the logic will have to be changed. What is wanted is to have the condition, Nam$ = "END OF DATA," tested *after* the READ but *before* the PRINT. The way to accomplish this is to place the READ *last* in the loop. Then, immediately after execution of the READ, the condition will be tested. Since Nam$ *will* be equal to END OF DATA, the condition will evaluate *true,* control will pass to the next statement following the LOOP, and the program will stop without printing END OF DATA on the list.

```
'**** Read and Data Statements in a Loop - A Better Way ***
CLS
READ Nam$, Addr$
DO UNTIL Nam$ = "END OF DATA"
    PRINT Nam$, Addr$
    READ Nam$, Addr$
LOOP
DATA ANN DOE, 1234 BAKER ST., BRUCE LEE, 457 HIGH ST.
DATA HOPE SEW, 222 BANK ST., END OF DATA, NO ADDRESS
END
```

Program Execution:

```
ANN DOE          1234 BAKER ST.
BRUCE LEE        457 HIGH ST.
HOPE SEW         222 BANK ST.
```

As you can see, this approach requires a *priming READ.* The initial READ will be executed only once at the beginning of the program. After that, the READ within the loop will take care of all reading. The purpose of the first READ is to start the process, or "prime the pump."

Data Terminators

Another principle can be observed from the preceding sample program. How many names and addresses is this program capable of reading and printing? You could insert as many pairs of names and addresses as desired, as long as END OF DATA, NO ADDRESS is last. Of course, the data can continue on many DATA statements, and the only limit will be the amount of main storage the computer has allocated for the program. The data item END OF DATA is generally called a **data terminator.** Sometimes data terminators are also called **trailers, trailer data, sentinels,** or **flags.**

The data terminator is generally selected by the programmer. There is no reason not to have selected a string of Xs, a certain name, or "*" as the terminator. As long as the condition in the UNTIL test checks for the same value as placed last in the data list, the program will find the value and stop on command.

Considering the way READ and DATA statements work, explain why NO ADDRESS appears after END OF DATA. How could the program be modified so that NO ADDRESS is not needed?

The RESTORE Statement

The data in the DATA list may be reread from the beginning by use of the RESTORE statement.

The RESTORE Statement—General Form

```
RESTORE
```

RESTORE returns the internal pointer back to the beginning of the program. Any subsequent READ will then reread the data from the beginning.

```
' *** Illustrate Restore Statement ***
CLS
READ A, B
RESTORE
READ C, D
PRINT A, B, C, D
DATA 25,50
END
```

Program Execution:

25   50   25   50

Feedback

1. Some of the following problems have syntax errors, others will not do what was intended. Identify each error, determine what type of error it is, and tell how to correct it.

   a. ```
   READ Nam1$, Score1, Nam2$, Score2
   PRINT Nam1$, Nam2$
   PRINT Score1, Score2
   DATA JOHN, MARTHA, 4, 5
   ```

   b. ```
   READ X, Y, Z
   PRINT X, Y, Z
   DATA 100, 200
   ```

   c. ```
   READ Nam$, Dat$
   PRINT Nam$, Dat$
   DATA HUMPTY DUMPTY, JAN. 15, 1994
   ```

   d. ```
   READ A, B
   PRINT B, A
   DATA 40, -21, 25, 16
   ```

   e. ```
   DO UNTIL F$ = "END"
       READ F$
       PRINT F$
   LOOP
   DATA APPLES, PEACHES, PLUMS, PEARS, BANANAS, END
   ```

2. Write the READ and DATA statements to assign these values to the variables.

| StTime$ | EndTime$ |
|---------|----------|
| 1:25    | 2:45     |

3. Write the statements necessary to read and print a series of words until END is read. At the end of the list, print a count of the number of words printed. Do *not* print or count the word END.
   ```

Programming Example

A Little League team wants to print a list of the players along with their batting averages. In addition, it would be helpful to know the overall team batting average, team totals for total number of official times at bat, and number of hits. As an added incentive, each week the program will print out the name and average of the player with the highest average and player with the lowest average.

Batting average is calculated as the number of hits divided by the number of official times at bats multiplied by 1000 (hits / at bats * 1000).

Input

Read each player's name, number of official times at bats, number of hits (use READ/DATA).

Output

1. Print the team name at the top of the page, and identify each column of output.
2. For each player, print the name, times at bats, number of hits, and batting average.
3. Print a total below the columns for times at bats and hits.
4. Print the player's name and batting average for the player who had the highest average and the one with the lowest average.

Calculations

1. Calculate the batting average for each player (hits / at bats * 1000).
2. Calculate a team batting average (total hits / total at bats * 1000).

Pseudocode

1. Initialize variables
   1.1   LET high average = −1
         LET low average = 1001
   1.2   Initialize print images
2. Print title and column headings
3. Detail processing loop
   3.1   Priming READ, name, at bats, and hits
   3.2   Loop until "END" entered
         3.2.1   Calculations
                 Batting average:
                 IF at bats > 0
                    THEN batting average = hits / at bats * 1000
                    ELSE batting average = 0
                 Add at bats and hits to totals
         3.2.2   Find lowest and highest average
                 IF average < lowest average so far
                    THEN save average and name as lowest
                 IF average > highest average so far
                    THEN save average and name as highest
         3.2.3   Print a line
         3.2.4   READ next name, at bats, and hits
4. Calculate team average
   total hits / total at bats * 1000
5. Write totals
   5.1   Print total line
   5.2   Print high average and name
   5.3   Print low average and name

Hierarchy Chart

Refer to figure 4.3 for the hierarchy chart.

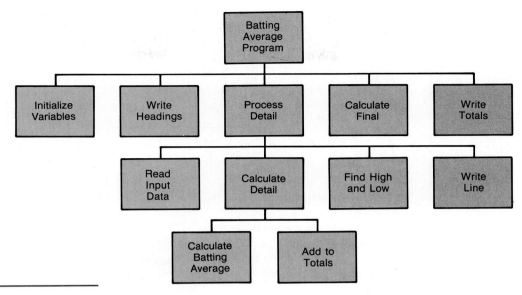

Figure 4.3
Hierarchy chart for batting
average program.

Flowchart

Refer to figure 4.4 for the flowchart.

Figure 4.4
Flowchart for batting average
program.

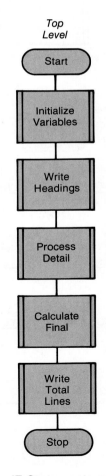

Figure 4.4—*Continued*

Second Level

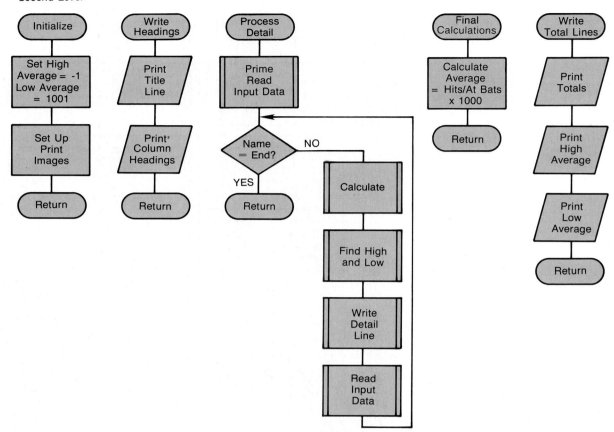

Third Level

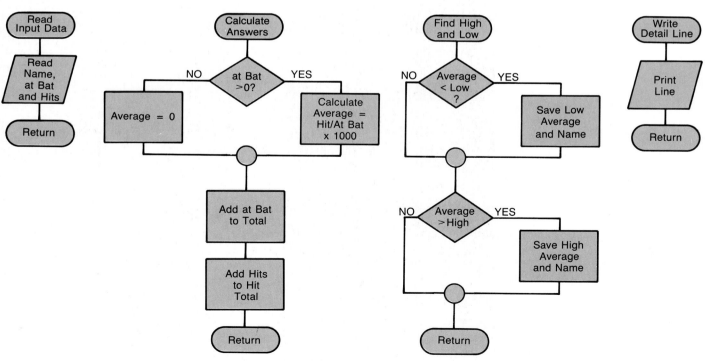

Chapter 4

Example Program

```
'      Program To Calculate Batting Average For Each Player On The
'          Team, Calculate The Team Batting Average, And Print Out The
'          Name Of The Player With The Highest Batting Average, And
'          The Lowest

'                        Variables Used

'                    Nam$                    Player's name
'                    AtBat                   Number of times at bat
'                    Hit                     Number of hits
'                    TotAtBat                Team total of number of
'                                                times at bat
'                    TotHit                  Team total of number of
'                                                hits
'                    Average                 Batting average

'                    HighAverage             Highest average on the team
'                    LowAverage              Lowest average on the team
'                    HighPlayer$             Name of player who achieved
'                                                high avg
'                    LowPlayer$              Name of player who achieved
'                                                low avg
'                    T1$, H1$, D1$,TL$       Print images
'                    S1$, S2$                Print images

'******************** Program Mainline ********************

CLS
GOSUB InitializeVariables
GOSUB PrintHeadings
GOSUB ProcessDetail
GOSUB CalculateFinalTotals
GOSUB PrintTotals
END

'******************** Initialize Variables ********************

InitializeVariables:
  LET HighAverage = -1
  LET LowAverage = 1001
  LET T1$ = "                    Y E L L O W   S O C K S"
  LET H1$ = "    PLAYER                    AT BATS      HITS      AVERAGE"
  LET D1$ = "\                \              ###          ##         ###"
  LET TL$ = "    TOTALS                     ####         ###        ###"
  LET S1$ = "    HIGH BATTING AVERAGE = ### by \                \"
  LET S2$ = "    LOW  BATTING AVERAGE = ### by \                \"
RETURN

'******************** Print Headings ********************

PrintHeadings:
  LPRINT
  LPRINT T1$                    'Print title line
  LPRINT
  LPRINT H1$                    'Heading line
  LPRINT
  LPRINT
RETURN
```

```
'******************** Process Detail ********************

ProcessDetail:
  GOSUB ReadData
  DO UNTIL UCASE$(Nam$) = "END"
        GOSUB CalculateAnswer
        GOSUB FindHighLow
        GOSUB PrintDetail
        GOSUB ReadData
  LOOP
RETURN

'******************** Read Input Data ********************

ReadData:
  READ Nam$, AtBat, Hit
  DATA KIRK BRAGGART, 20, 9
  DATA ROBERT ABLE, 15, 5
  DATA IAN BROTHER, 10, 3
  DATA SUZY SLEEPER, 12, 2
  DATA DON TREADER, 16, 4
  DATA RANDY RUNNER, 7, 1
  DATA MICHELLE ANGEL, 16, 7
  DATA TIM CODY, 8, 2
  DATA END, 0, 0
RETURN

'******************** Calculate Answer ********************

CalculateAnswer:
  IF AtBat > 0 THEN
        LET Average = INT(Hit / AtBat * 1000)
  ELSE
        LET Average = 0
  END IF
  LET TotAtBat = TotAtBat + AtBat
  LET TotHit = TotHit + Hit
RETURN

'******************** Find High and Low ********************

FindHighLow:
  IF Average < LowAverage THEN
        LET LowAverage = Average
        LET LowPlayer$ = Nam$
  END IF
  IF Average > HighAverage THEN
        LET HighAverage = Average
        LET HighPlayer$ = Nam$
  END IF
RETURN

'******************** Print Detail ********************

PrintDetail:
  LPRINT USING D1$; Nam$, AtBat, Hit, Average
RETURN

'******************** Calculate Final Totals ********************

CalculateFinalTotals:
  LET Average = INT(TotHit / TotAtBat * 1000)
RETURN
```

```
'********************* Print Total ************************

PrintTotals:
  LPRINT
  LPRINT USING TL$; TotAtBat, TotHit, Average
  LPRINT
  LPRINT
  LPRINT USING S1$; HighAverage, HighPlayer$
  LPRINT USING S2$; LowAverage, LowPlayer$
RETURN

'********************* End of Program ********************
```

Sample Program Output

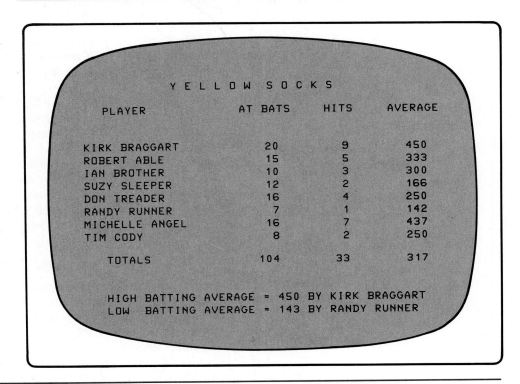

```
                    Y E L L O W   S O C K S

        PLAYER              AT BATS     HITS      AVERAGE


        KIRK BRAGGART          20          9         450
        ROBERT ABLE            15          5         333
        IAN BROTHER            10          3         300
        SUZY SLEEPER           12          2         166
        DON TREADER            16          4         250
        RANDY RUNNER            7          1         142
        MICHELLE ANGEL         16          7         437
        TIM CODY                8          2         250

        TOTALS                104         33         317


        HIGH BATTING AVERAGE = 450 BY KIRK BRAGGART
        LOW  BATTING AVERAGE = 143 BY RANDY RUNNER
```

Summary

1. The selection process is implemented with the IF...THEN...ELSE. A condition is evaluated. When the condition is true, one course of action is taken; when the condition is false, another course of action is taken.

2. The conditions for IF statements are formed with the six relational operators: > (greater than); < (less than); = (equal); <> (not equal); >= (greater than or equal); <= (less than or equal). These operators may be combined with the logical operators AND, OR, and NOT, and with parentheses to form compound conditions.

3. Single-line IF...THEN...ELSE statements must be written on one line.

4. Block IF statements are written on multiple lines and must be terminated with an END IF statement.

5. Block IF statements allow multiple actions for the THEN and the ELSE, as well as nested IFs.

6. Block IF statements are formed using the IF...THEN, ELSE, ELSEIF, and END IF statements.

7. Good indentation practices are important for producing programs that are clear and understandable. As the logic of programs becomes more complicated, proper indentation becomes more and more important.
8. Programs should be readable from "top to bottom" with no jumping around. In order to discourage unstructured code, no branch instructions will be used.
9. Programs must always be planned before the coding begins. Flowcharting, pseudocode, or hierarchy charts can be used for the planning step.
10. In hierarchy charts, only the individual modules are shown, not the control structure. IF statements are not indicated on the chart. The various actions to take *are* indicated.
11. READ and DATA statements can be used to assign values to variables.
12. An advantage that READ/DATA may have over INPUT statements is that all data can be entered before program execution.
13. A disadvantage of READ/DATA compared to INPUT is that the program will not be interactive. Nonprogrammers cannot be expected to change values in DATA statements.
14. READ/DATA can be more flexible than LET statements for assigning values to variables. DATA statements can be grouped together, making the values easier to locate and change than LET statements.
15. READ statements are executable, while DATA statements are not. The READ must be placed in the proper sequence for the logic of the program. The DATA statements may be placed anywhere.
16. It is recommended that the DATA statements be placed in a group, either at the beginning of the program or in the READ subroutine.
17. When a READ statement is executed, a value is placed into the variable or variables named, one at a time. Always the next unused value from the list of DATA values will be assigned to the next variable named on a READ statement.
18. The variable named on the READ and the corresponding value listed on the DATA statement must agree in type; that is, a numeric variable must receive a numeric value, and a string variable must receive a string value.
19. String values placed in DATA statements do not require quotation marks around them unless the value contains a comma or a colon, or there are leading or trailing blank spaces that must be included as part of the string.
20. A special item of data, called a data terminator, is usually placed at the end of a data list.
21. The data terminator is used to end the READ loop.
22. The data terminator may be any value and is chosen by the programmer.
23. A priming READ is generally required before a loop containing READ or INPUT statements. The loop condition is retested at the bottom of the loop, so the READ or INPUT statement should be last. Then the data terminator will be found by the condition test, and no further processing will be done on the termination data.
24. The RESTORE statement allows the DATA values in a program to be reread. Following execution of a RESTORE statement, the next READ executed will take its value from the first DATA statement in the program.

Programming Exercises

Each of these programs should be written as a modular program with a program mainline and subroutines. Plan the program with a modular flowchart, pseudocode, or hierarchy chart. Program remarks listing the program variables are required. Test your program with two or three different sets of data, making sure that it will perform correctly with any data. In most cases, data may be entered with either READ/DATA or with INPUT statements.

4.1. Piecework workers are paid by the piece. Often, workers who produce a greater quantity of output are paid at a higher rate.

1–199 pieces completed	$.50 each
200–399	.55 each (for all pieces)
400–599	.60 each
600 or more	.65 each

INPUT: For each worker, input the name and number of pieces completed. Data may be entered with READ or INPUT statements.

OUTPUT: Print an appropriate title and column headings. There should be one detail line for each worker, which shows the name, the number of pieces, and the amount earned. Compute and print totals of the number of pieces and the dollar amount earned.

PROCESSING: For each person, compute the pay earned by multiplying the number of pieces by the appropriate price. Accumulate the total number of pieces and the total dollar amount paid.

SAMPLE PROGRAM OUTPUT:

```
        PIECEWORK WEEKLY REPORT

    NAME              PIECES      PAY

    JOHNNY BEGOOD       265      145.75
    SALLY GREAT         650      422.50
    SAM KLUTZ           177       88.50
    PETE PRECISE        400      240.00
    FANNIE FANTASTIC    399      219.45
    MORRIE MELLOW       200      110.00

    TOTALS             2091     1226.20
```

TEST DATA: Test your program with the data shown in the sample output, as well as with another set of data that you make up.

4.2. Modify the program in exercise 4.1 to compute and print the following information. At the conclusion of the list, print additional lines naming the person with the greatest number of pieces and with the least number of pieces. Also, print the average number of pieces for all workers.

4.3. A battle is raging over the comparative taste of Prune Punch and Apple Ade. Each taste tester rates the two drinks on a scale of 1–10 (10 being best). The proof of the superiority of one over the other will be the average score for the two drinks.

INPUT: For each tester, input (or read) the score for each of the two drinks.

OUTPUT: Print a title and headings above the columns of scores. Then print one line on the report for each tester that shows his or her rating for each drink. At the bottom of the report, print the overall (average) score for each drink. Then print one line declaring the winner based on the comparative scores.

PROCESSING: Average the scores for each drink and round to the nearest tenth of a point. The winning drink will be the one with the highest average.

TEST DATA:

Prune Punch	Apple Ade
8	9.5
2	10
9	4
7.5	8.2
6	5

4.4. The local library has a summer reading program to encourage reading. A chart will be kept with the readers' names and bonus points earned.

INPUT: Each reader's name and number of books read. Use INPUT or READ.

OUTPUT: Print a title and headings over the columns of data. Each detail line will show the name, number of books read, and number of points earned. Print totals for the number of books and the number of points. Also, print the average number of points for all readers.

PROCESSING: Assign points according to this schedule. The first three books are worth 10 points each. The next three books are worth 15 points each. All books over six are worth 20 points each.

TEST DATA:

Name	Number of Books
SAM SONG	4
LINDA LOU	2
P. DEXTER	8
K. C. SMITH	6

4.5. Modify the program in exercise 4.4 to include the name of the winner (assume that no ties are allowed).

4.6. The Fox family is planning a large family reunion and wishes to accumulate some statistics on the size and distribution of the group.

INPUT: Input the name and age of each person attending. Use INPUT or READ statements.

OUTPUT: Print a title and headings over the columns of data. Print one line for each attendee showing the name and age. The average age should be printed along with the number of persons in each age group.

PROCESSING: Accumulate the number of family members in each of these groups:

<20
$20-39$
$40-59$
$60-79$
>79

TEST DATA: Make up a series of names and ages or use the list below. Be sure to include ages that fall on the boundaries, such as 39 and 40, 59 and 60.

Name	Age
GRANDPA	80
GRANDMA	79
AUNT VIXEN	60
MAMA	21
PAPA	20
CUBBY	1

4.7. Write a program to compute your checking account balance for one month's transactions.

> INPUT: The first input should be the bank balance from the previous month. Then deposits, checks, or service charges will be entered at the keyboard. The user should be prompted to enter D, C, S, or E (for *D*eposit, *C*heck, *S*ervice charge, or *E*nd), and the amount of the transaction.
>
> OUTPUT: Print a statement with a title and column headings, showing the beginning balance, each transaction as it is applied, and a current balance.
>
> PROCESSING: Add deposits to the balance, subtract checks and service charges.
>
> TEST DATA:

Beginning balance	$20.05
Check	15.00
Deposit	50.50
Check	45.57
Check	5.00
Deposit	60.00
Service charge	6.00
End	

4.8. Add error checking to the program in exercise 4.7. If any code other than D, C, S, or E is entered, print a message and reprompt for input. Continue checking the input until a correct code is entered.

4.9. Modify your program of exercise 4.7 or 4.8 to compute and print the following additional information: The total number of deposits and dollar total of deposits, the total number of checks, and dollar total of the checks.

4.10. Modify your program of exercise 4.7 (or 4.8 or 4.9) to not allow payment of any check not covered by sufficient funds. If there is not enough money to cover a check, it will be rejected with the message INSUFFICIENT FUNDS, and a service charge of $10 will be charged to the account. Make up additional data to test these routines.

4.11. A salesperson earns a weekly base salary plus a commission when sales are above quota. Write a program that will input the weekly sales and calculate the amount of pay.

> INPUT: Use READ statements to establish the base pay, the quota, and the commission rate (these will apply to all salespersons). Then, for each salesperson, INPUT the name, social security number, and amount of sales.
>
> OUTPUT: Print the salesperson's name, social security number, sales, commission, and total pay. When the salesperson has not earned a commission, omit the commission line. Do not print a line for commission = 0. After all sales have been entered, print report totals showing total sales, total commissions, and total pay.
>
> PROCESSING: Compare the sales to the quota. When the sales are equal to or greater than the quota, calculate the commission by multiplying the sales by the commission rate. Each salesperson will receive the base salary, plus the commission if one has been earned. Round the commission to the nearest cent.

SAMPLE PROGRAM OUTPUT:

```
NAME =                  SANDY SMUG
SOC. SEC. NUMB =        123-45-6789
SALES =                   1,000.00
COMMISSION =                150.00
PAY =                       400.00


NAME =                  SAM SADNESS
SOC. SEC. NUMB =        222-22-2222
SALES =                     999.99
PAY =                       250.00


NAME =                  JOE WHIZ
SOC. SEC. NUMB =        555-55-5555
SALES =                   2,000.00
COMMISSION =                300.00
PAY =                       550.00


TOTAL SALES =             3,999.99
TOTAL COMMISSIONS =         450.00
TOTAL PAY =               1,200.00
```

TEST DATA: Be sure to change the data to make certain your program will produce correct results with any values for quota, commission rate, base pay, and sales amounts. Use these values to test the program.

QUOTA = 1000
COMMISSION RATE = .15
BASE PAY = 250

4.12. Calculate and print a customer sales invoice. Separate totals will be accumulated for taxable and nontaxable items, the tax will be calculated, and an invoice total will be calculated.

INPUT: Input the item description, the quantity sold, the unit price, and whether or not the item is taxable. Alternately, READ and DATA statements may be used for the program input.

OUTPUT: Print an appropriate title and column headings at the top of the invoice. There should be one line in the body of the invoice for each item purchased. Each line should show (in this order) the quantity, item description, unit price, extended price, and the letters TX for any taxable item. At the bottom of the invoice, print the total of taxable items, the sales tax, the total of nontaxable items, and the invoice total.

PROCESSING: For each item of input, multiply the quantity times the unit price to obtain the extended price. Accumulate separate totals for taxable items and nontaxable items. After all data for one customer has been input and printed, calculate the sales tax at 6 percent (.06) times the taxable total. Do not calculate tax on each individual item. The total of taxable items, the sales tax, and the total of nontaxable items should be added together to produce the invoice total.

TEST DATA: Test your program with the following data. Also, create different data to thoroughly test your program. Test it with only taxable items and only nontaxable items. Turn in at least two invoices—one with the data exactly as shown, another with data that you create.

Quantity	Description	Unit Price	Taxable
2	NAPKINS	.59	YES
1	POTATO CHIPS	1.69	NO
2	SODA POP	.69	NO
3	BOWL	1.29	YES
1	PRETZELS	.89	NO

SAMPLE PROGRAM OUTPUT USING TEST DATA:

```
                    YOUR COMPANY NAME HERE

                       CUSTOMER INVOICE

    QUANTITY      DESCRIPTION      UNIT PRICE   PRICE

        2         NAPKINS               .59      1.18  TX
        1         POTATO CHIPS         1.69      1.69
        2         SODA POP              .69      1.38
        3         BOWL                 1.29      3.87  TX
        1         PRETZELS              .89       .89

                      TAXABLE ITEM TOTAL       5.05
                      SALES TAX                 .30
                      NONTAXABLE TOTAL         3.96
                                              -----
                      INVOICE TOTAL            9.31
```

4.13. Write a program that will calculate the current value of a portfolio of stocks. Given the stock name, number of shares, and the purchase price per share, input the current price per share. From that data, calculate and print the current value for each stock, the gain or loss, and the percentage gain or loss. Additionally, each of those figures is to be calculated for the portfolio as a whole.

INPUT: Stock name, number of shares, and original purchase price will be read from DATA statements. The current price per share of each stock will be INPUT from the keyboard.

OUTPUT: The output will be a printed report, with appropriate title and column headings centered over the columns of data. For each stock, print the name, number of shares, original price per share, current price per share, current value, the dollar amount of gain or loss, and the percent gain or loss. At the end of the report, print the total dollar valuation of the portfolio, the overall gain or loss, and the overall percentage gain or loss.

PROCESSING:

1. For each stock read, input the current price per share.
2. Calculate the original value of the stock as the original price per share times the number of shares.
3. Calculate the current value of the stock as the current price per share times the number of shares.
4. Calculate the gain or loss as the current value minus the original value.
5. Calculate the percent gain or loss as the gain or loss divided by the original value.
6. Accumulate totals of the current value of the stocks and the overall dollar gain or loss.
7. Calculate the overall (portfolio) gain or loss as the total current value minus the total original value.
8. Calculate the overall percentage gain or loss for the portfolio as the overall gain or loss divided by the total original value.

TEST DATA:

	From DATA Statements		*INPUT During Program Run*
STOCK	# SHARES	ORIG PRICE	CURRENT PRICE
AT&T	200	35	38
IBM	100	120	118
APPLE	50	20	22
WANG	20	30	21

For a second run of the program, consider finding *today's* price for each of the stocks.

4.14. Write a program that will produce a summary of the amounts due for Pat's Auto Repair Shop.

INPUT: Using DATA statements, enter job number, customer name, amount charged for parts, and hours of labor for each job. Use DATA statements for the tax rate and the hourly labor charge also, so that the program may be easily adapted if either changes. Current charges are $30 per hour for labor and 6 percent (.06) for the tax rate.

OUTPUT: Print a report with a title and column headings. Each detail line will consist of the job number, customer name, amount charged for parts, amount for labor, the sales tax, and the total charges for that customer. All dollar amounts will be rounded to the nearest cent and printed with decimal points aligned. Print a total line, indicating totals for parts, labor, tax, and customer total. The total fields must be decimal point aligned beneath the corresponding columns.

PROCESSING: Sales tax is charged on parts but not on labor. Multiply the amount for parts by the tax rate to determine the amount of sales tax. The labor charge is calculated as the hourly rate times the number of hours worked. The customer total is the sum of the amounts charged for parts, labor, and sales tax. Report totals must be accumulated for parts, labor, tax, and customer total.

TEST DATA:

tax rate = .06
labor charge = $30/hour

(job number, customer name, parts, hours of labor)
125, HARRY BUTLER, 27.50, 1.5
126, LEE HERNANDEZ, 45.37, 2.1
127, IAN ALTON, 1.75, 5.2
000, END, 0, 0

SAMPLE PROGRAM OUTPUT USING TEST DATA:

PAT'S AUTO REPAIR SHOP

JOB NUMBER	CUSTOMER NAME	PARTS	LABOR	TAX	TOTAL
125	HARRY BUTLER	27.50	45.00	1.65	74.15
126	LEE HERNANDEZ	45.37	63.00	2.72	111.09
127	IAN ALTON	1.75	156.00	.11	157.86
	TOTALS	74.62	264.00	4.48	343.10

4.15. Write a program using DATA statements to print a list of students, the college attended, and their ages.

INPUT: Use the test data below for your DATA statements.
OUTPUT: Print a title and headings over the columns of data. Each detail line will contain the student's name, the college attended, and age.

TEST DATA:

Name	College	Age
Dave Drive	Facetious University	25
Tricia Scudder	Swain College	20
Jane Adams	Rakish University	27
Lynn Steen	Ludicrous University	21
Anita Bonita	Charm College	37
Mary Berry	Outlandish College	18
Eric Pavy	Juvenile College	29
Brian Dudlin	Arachnid University	31
Mitzi Micro	Jaunty University	19
Judy Judlin	Convexity College	34

5

Structured Programming

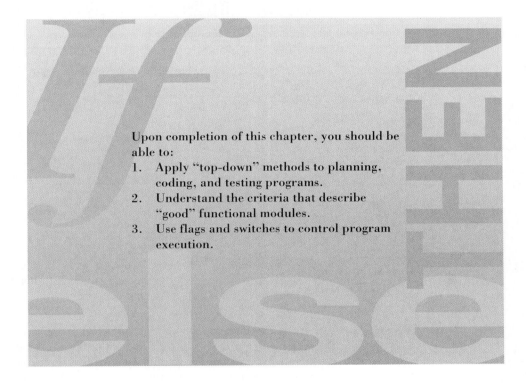

Upon completion of this chapter, you should be able to:
1. Apply "top-down" methods to planning, coding, and testing programs.
2. Understand the criteria that describe "good" functional modules.
3. Use flags and switches to control program execution.

Top-Down Programming

The term **top-down** is often used to describe well-structured, modular programs. Looking at the hierarchy chart in figure 5.1, you can visualize the top-down concept. First look at the entire program (or system of programs). Begin breaking the program into its functional parts. The process continues until, at the lowest level, relatively simple logic remains.

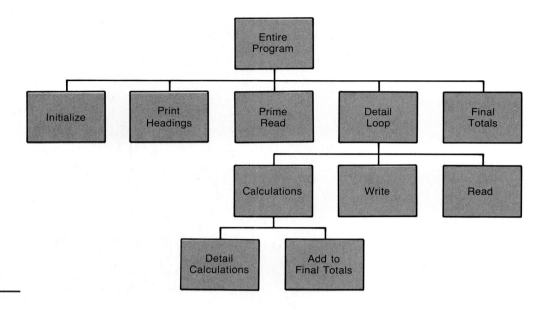

Figure 5.1
Hierarchy chart showing top-down organization.

Top-down programming has three parts: (1) plan the program with the top-down approach; (2) code the program—mainline first, then the subroutines; and (3) test the program in a top-down manner.

Top-Down Testing

In a large and complex program, *top-down testing* can save much time and effort. The program mainline is written first, and perhaps some of the subroutines. Other subroutines will be *stubbed in* (a dummy module written), so that the program can be tested. The overall program structure can be tested and debugged early in program development. Then, one at a time, individual subroutines may be added. If the program fails at any point, the most likely cause will be the last subroutine added.

Module Stubbing

As a simple example, the chapter 4 programming example (p. 120) will be shown with some modules stubbed in. Although the program is relatively small to actually be a candidate for stubbing, you will see that for complicated programs this could be helpful. Assume that the programmer was asked to begin coding the program, but the precise calculations to be done were uncertain. All the calculations could be left for later.

Example Program:
Module Stubbing for Top-Down Testing

Program Listing

```
'    Program To Calculate Batting Average For Each Player On The
'        Team, Calculate The Team Batting Average, And Print Out The
'        Name Of The Player With The Highest Batting Average, And The
'        Lowest

'               Program Variables

'               Nam$                    Player's name
'               AtBat                   Number of times at bat
'               Hit                     Number of hits
'               TotAtBat                Team total of number at bats
'               Average                 Batting average
'               HighAverage             Highest average on the team
'               LowAverage              Lowest average on the team
'               HighPlayer$             Name of player who achieved high
'                                           avg
'               LowPlayer$              Name of player who achieved low
'                                           avg
'               T1$, H1$, D1$           Print images
'               S1$, S2$, T1$           Print images

'****************** Program Mainline ***********************

GOSUB InitializeVariables
GOSUB PrintHeadings
GOSUB ProcessDetail
GOSUB CalculateFinalTotals
GOSUB PrintFinalTotals
END

'****************** Initialize Variables *******************

InitializeVariables:
  LET HighAverage = -1
  LET LowAverage = 1001
  LET T1$ = "               Y E L L O W   S O C K S"
  LET H1$ = "     PLAYER               AT BATS    HITS    AVERAGE"
  LET D1$ = "\                    \       ###        ##      ###"
  LET TL$ = "     TOTALS                 ####       ###      ###"
  LET S1$ = "   HIGH BATTING AVERAGE = ### BY \              \"
  LET S2$ = "   LOW BATTING AVERAGE  = ### BY \              \"
RETURN

'****************** Print Headings *************************

PrintHeadings:
  LPRINT
  LPRINT T1$                    'Print title line
  LPRINT
  LPRINT H1$                    'Heading line
  LPRINT
  LPRINT
RETURN
```

```
'****************** Process Detail ****************************

ProcessDetail:
  GOSUB ReadData
  DO UNTIL UCASE$(Nam$) = "END"
    GOSUB CalculateAnswer
    GOSUB FindHighLow
    GOSUB PrintDetailLine
    GOSUB ReadData
  LOOP
RETURN


'****************** Input Data ****************************

ReadData:
  READ Nam$, AtBat, Hit
  DATA KIRK BRAGGART, 20, 9
  DATA ROBERT ABLE, 15, 5
  DATA END, 0, 0
RETURN


'****************** Calculate Answer ********************
'               ********** Stub Module ************

CalculateAnswer:
  LET Average = 350
RETURN


'****************** Find High and Low ********************
'               ********* Stub Module ****************

FindHighLow:
  LET LowAverage = 300
  LET HighAverage = 400
  LET LowPlayer$ = "LOW GUY"
  LET HighPlayer$ = "HIGH GUY"
RETURN


'****************** Print Detail Line ********************

PrintDetailLine:
  LPRINT USING D1$; Nam$, AtBat, Hit, Average
RETURN


'****************** Calculate Final Totals ***************
'               *********Stub Module **********

CalculateFinalTotals:
  LET Average = 365
RETURN


'****************** Print Total Lines *******************

PrintFinalTotals:
  LPRINT
  LPRINT USING TL$; TotAtBat, TotHit, Average
  LPRINT
  LPRINT
  LPRINT USING S1$; HighAverage, HighPlayer$
  LPRINT USING S2$; LowAverage, LowPlayer$
RETURN

'****************** End of Program ********************
```

Structured Programming

Structured programming is one step beyond modular programming with guidelines for "good" modules and "poor" modules. The structured programming guidelines also define "proper" flow of control and coding standards (such as indentation). In many large programming projects for which statistics have been kept, it has been shown that structured programming has many demonstrable advantages over the old-style, unstructured programs.

1. Programs are more reliable. Fewer bugs appear in testing and later operation.
2. Programs are easier to read and understand.
3. Programs are easier to test and debug.
4. Programs are easier to maintain.

Most commercial programming shops report that at least 50 percent of programmer time is spent making changes and corrections in existing programs rather than developing new programs (some report more than 90 percent maintenance). Anything that will save time in correction and maintenance can save a company considerable money. It is easy to see why most commercial shops hiring programmers insist on structured programming techniques.

The current **definition of structured programming** includes standards for program design, coding, and testing that are designed to create proper, reliable, and maintainable software. These standards include coding guidelines and rules for flow of control and module formation.

Structured Coding Guidelines

The *structured coding guidelines* are designed to make programs more readable and easier to understand.

1. Use meaningful variable names.
2. Code only one statement per line.
3. Use remarks to explain program logic.
4. Indent and align all statements in a loop.
5. Indent the THEN and ELSE actions of an IF statement.

Flow of Control

In 1964, Italians Bohm and Jacopini proved mathematically that any program logic can be accomplished with just three control structures. Within a few years, studies were done declaring the GOTO statement to be harmful to good programming. In fact, in comparisons of selected large programming projects, there was a direct correlation between the number of GOTO statements and program bugs found.

BASIC was not designed as a structured language, but some of the current additions to the language now permit the programmer to adhere to the *three "proper" constructs*. All programming can be done with combinations of these three constructs.

Three "Proper" Constructs for Structured Programs

1. *SEQUENCE*—Statements are executed one after another in sequence.

```
INPUT Num
LET Total = Total + Num
PRINT Total
```

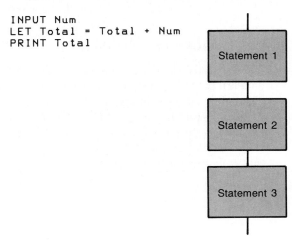

2. *SELECTION*—Choosing one course of action or another. In BASIC, the selection control is implemented with the IF...THEN...ELSE.

```
IF Num > 10 THEN
     PRINT "Limit Exceeded"
ELSE
     LET Count = Count - Num
END IF
```

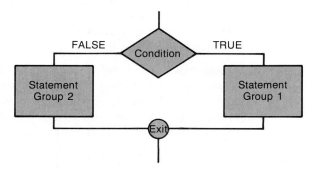

3. *ITERATION*—This is the loop structure. The BASIC statements learned for looping is the DO...LOOP. (In chapter 9 you will learn a second loop structure—the FOR/NEXT.)

```
DO WHILE Cat < 20
     .
     .
     .
     Let Cat = Cat + 1
LOOP
```

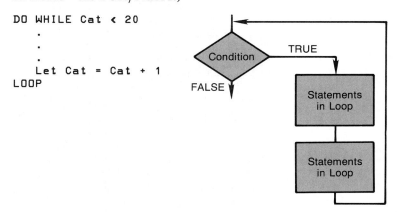

Structured Module Design Considerations

One Entry, One Exit

The primary rule for program modules is that each module must have only one entry point and one exit point. So, even though BASIC will allow a GOSUB to a line label within a subroutine and will allow multiple RETURN statements, such violations of the "one-entry, one-exit" rule should be avoided.

The "Black Box" Concept

A "black box" (program module) is designed to accomplish a task. Generally, some data is input to the module, a transformation occurs, and data is output from the module. The details of what happens within the "black box" are not important to the overall program. What *is* important is that for a given input, the module will reliably produce the correct output. That module could be replaced by another—perhaps in another language such as assembler—without changing the rest of the program. It is important that each module "stand alone."

Module Cohesion

Choosing the correct statements to combine into modules is an important skill for programmers to develop. "Good" or "bad" module design is often an elusive concept when beginning to modularize programs.

Cohesion refers to the internal strength of a module. It is an indication of how closely related each statement in a module is to the others. As cohesion is increased, module independence, clarity, maintainability, and portability are increased.

The "best" modules are those that accomplish one task; and all statements in the group relate to that one function. Some examples of good, functional modules would be:

> calculating detail data
> obtaining INPUT from the keyboard
> calculating subtotals
> validating input data
> printing headings

When other statements are "thrown in" because "they need to be done also" or "that's what comes next," the cohesion of a module is destroyed.

In order to improve the cohesion of modules, resist the urge to lump the PRINTs with the calculations or to group together all program preliminaries such as initializing variables, printing headings, and doing a priming READ.

It is not always possible to isolate each function into a module, especially in small programs. Such an attempt can cause many one-line modules. But one-line modules are not forbidden and are often preferable to an uncohesive, poor, utility module.

Module Coupling

Coupling refers to the connections, or interfaces, between modules. As a general rule, modules should be loosely coupled; that is, what goes on inside one module should not affect the operation in other modules.

The control for execution of program modules must "come from above." Looking at a hierarchy chart, a lower level module cannot determine what a higher level module should do—or even a module at the same level. For example, do not allow the detail read routine to determine that it is time to do final total calculations. That decision must be made by the mainline.

When a decision will determine which function to perform, place that decision at as high a level as possible.

Poor Construction

```
GOSUB Sub1
GOSUB Sub2
::
::

Sub1:
  IF Code$ = "A" THEN
::
::

Sub2:
  IF Code$ <> "A" THEN
::
::
```

Preferable Construction

```
IF Code$ = "A" THEN
     GOSUB Sub1
ELSE
     GOSUB Sub2
END IF
```

The decision to perform a function should not be made after calling the subroutine, but should be made at the higher level, if possible.

At times it is necessary to have lower ranking modules make a determination that will alter the program flow of control. Those lower modules may place values in variables that will be checked at a higher level. The variables used for this type of control are called switches or flags.

Using Switches and Flags

Sometimes you want to know "How did it go?" after an operation is complete. Was the data valid or invalid? Was this the end of data? Was a particular key pressed? A common practice is to use a variable to indicate the status of the operation. Some programmers refer to these variables as **switches,** others call them **flags.**

A switch (or flag) is nothing more than a variable that is allowed to have one of two values. Commonly, a numeric variable is used. Then a value of 1 means the switch is "on," and a value of 0 indicates the switch is "off." Many programmers prefer to use a string variable for the switch field. Then the two values would be Y and N for YES and NO, or T and F for TRUE and FALSE.

Use of a switch field generally requires three steps. The first step is to initialize the field—to know its initial state. Then, the switch will be set to indicate a condition. At a later point, the switch field can be tested to see how it was set.

Switches are commonly used in well-structured programs. However, care must be taken to observe proper flow of control. The preferred usage is to have the lower ranking module set the switch to indicate the condition. Then the higher ranking module will check the switch field to determine the correct subroutine to execute.

Example Program Segment: General Form for Using Switches

Program Listing

```
'****** General Form For Use of a Switch *************
LET Switch = 1                    'Set on (or off) to start
GOSUB TestACondition
IF Switch = 1 THEN
        ...                       'Still on - select course of action
: :
: :
```

Example Program Segment: Selection of Correct Subroutine with a Switch

Program Listing

```
'****** Selection of Correct Subroutine With Switch ****

    LET ReasonableFlag = 1              'Set switch on
    GOSUB CalculatePay

                                        'Select course of action
                                        'Based on ReasonableFlag


    IF ReasonableFlag = 1 THEN
            GOSUB PrintPaycheck
    ELSE
            GOSUB UnreasonablePay
    END IF
    ...
```

```
'***************** Calculate Pay *********************

CalculatePay:
  LET Pay = Hours * Rate
  IF Pay > MaxPay THEN
        LET ReasonableFlag = 0
  END IF
  IF Pay > (2 * PriorPay) THEN
        LET ReasonableFlag = 0
  END IF
  IF Pay < 0 THEN
        LET ReasonableFlag = 0
  END IF
RETURN

'***************** Print Paycheck *********************

PrintPaycheck:
  : :
  : :
RETURN

'***************** UnreasonablePay *********************

UnreasonablePay:
  PRINT "Error in pay calculations"
RETURN
```

Example Program Segment: Loop Control with a Switch

Program Listing

```
'****** Keep At It Until Good Field Entered ***********

LET Switch = 0                    'Set switch OFF to begin
DO WHILE Switch = 0
    GOSUB InputValidSelection
LOOP
  : :
  : :


'****************** Input Valid Selection ************

InputValidSelection:
  INPUT "Enter Selection Code (A, D, F) ", Code$
  '*** Switch set ON for valid data ***
  IF Code$ = "A" OR Code$ = "D" OR Code$ = "F" THEN
        LET Switch = 1
  END IF
RETURN
```

Feedback

1. What is the difference between the terms "top-down programming" and "structured programming"?
2. It would seem that coding a program as concisely as possible would be a desirable trait. Why not use one- or two-character variable names?
3. Consider a subroutine that adds to subtotals, prints a detail line, and reads the next data. Would this be a "good" subroutine? If not, is it an example of poor coupling or poor cohesion?

Summary

1. A hierarchy chart can be a useful tool for planning structured programs.
2. The entire program is shown at the highest level of a hierarchy chart. Then at each lower level, the program is further broken down into smaller and smaller parts.
3. Top-down programming applies to program design, coding, and testing.
4. In top-down design, the program is planned from the overall view first, then broken down into individual parts.
5. Top-down coding suggests that the main part (or top) of the program be written first. Details (or bottom level) can be added later.
6. In top-down testing, the program is tested and debugged in the midst of top-down coding. The overall structure of the program can be tested by "stubbing in" lower level modules.
7. Structured programming is a tool for creating proper, reliable, and maintainable software.
8. Structured programming includes rules for module formation, for flow of control, and for coding.
9. Coding guidelines include standards for naming variables, use of remarks, indentation, and alignment. The purpose of the rules is to make programs more readable and understandable.
10. Module formation rules include:
    a. One entry, one exit.
    b. Good cohesion—The statements of a module should be grouped together because they all contribute to one program function.
    c. Loose coupling—The statements in one module cannot be allowed to affect, alter, or interfere with those in any other module.
    d. Decisions for control must be made at the highest level possible.
11. There are three "proper" constructs for programming logic:
    a. sequence
    b. selection
    c. iteration
12. Sequence refers to executing one statement after another in sequence.
13. In selection, alternate courses of action are taken, depending on a condition. In BASIC, the selection construct is formed with IF...THEN...ELSE.
14. Iteration refers to program loops. Whenever a statement or group of statements is to be repeated, use the DO...LOOP.
15. A variable may be used as a switch (sometimes called a flag). A value of 1 in the field generally means the switch is ON, and 0 means the switch is OFF. This technique allows one module of the program to set the switch to indicate a condition. Then, in another module, the value of the switch variable can be checked to determine what that condition was. As a general rule, switches will be used to pass status information to a higher ranking module for determining flow of control.

5.1. Write a program to create an inventory list for your collection of model cars using the top-down approach in planning, coding, and testing the program. Code the main module and the detail module, and create stub submodules for the initialization, title, headings, read, calculations, output, and totals.

OUTPUT: Print a message such as HEADING ROUTINE for each GOSUB in the main module.

5.2. Code the initialization, title, and heading subroutines for the car inventory program in program 5.1. You will need a heading for manufacturer's number, year, make, model, description, and price.

5.3. Code and debug the read, calculation, output, and total subroutines for the car inventory program in exercise 5.1.

INPUT: Input can come from INPUT statements or READ/DATA statements. Use the test data below.
OUTPUT: Print a title, column headings, manufacturer's number, year, make, model, description, price, and total price on the printer and on the screen.
PROCESSING: Calculate the total price = sum of all purchase prices.
TEST DATA:

Manufacturer #	Yr	Make	Model	Description	Price
BMR-R79	49	FIAT	500B	GILLETTE RAZOR	7.99
HOTWELS-34	57	CHEVY	NOMAD	4/DR STATION WAGON	12.95
MATCHBX-878	73	FORD	BRONC	3/DR 4X4 RED SPARE WHL	25.99
MATCHBX-72	69	BUIK	CENTY	YELLOW TAXI	1.49
BRM-R88	34	BUGAT	TY575	RACER, BLACK	35.00
MATCHBX-25	80	LINCO	MRKIV	WHITE, LIMOUSINE	14.99
LESNEY-Y42	82	CHEVY	MALBU	4/DR GREEN PASSENGER	1.99
HASBRO-119	75	AMC	GRMLN	2/DR SEDAN, YELLOW	1.69
TABY-6332	71	TOYOT	CELIC	2/DR SEDAN, BLUE	2.99
BMR-SY238	36	ROLRY	SYLVC	4/DR SEDAN, SILVER-GRAY	60.00

6

Report Design and Subtotals

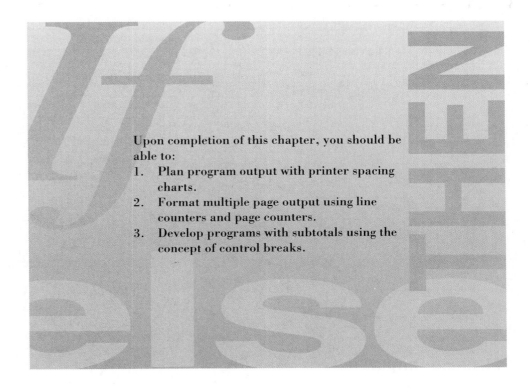

Upon completion of this chapter, you should be able to:
1. Plan program output with printer spacing charts.
2. Format multiple page output using line counters and page counters.
3. Develop programs with subtotals using the concept of control breaks.

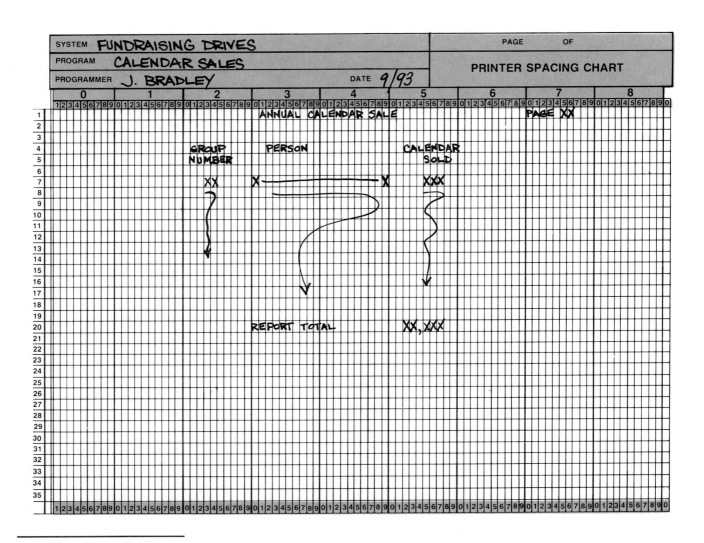

Figure 6.1
A completed printer spacing
chart.

Planning Output with Printer Spacing Charts

When designing the format of printed output, a *printer spacing chart* (or *print chart*) can be a valuable tool. The lines have been drawn to the standard scale, so it is easy to see how the completed output will look. Coding the print images in a program is far easier once a print chart has been drawn. See figure 6.1 for a typical printer spacing chart.

Printers vary a great deal in their specifications. Before designing output for any particular printer, a programmer should check the line length, horizontal spacing, and vertical spacing. It can be extremely discouraging to plan all program output for 132-character lines and then to find that the printer has only 80-character lines.

The horizontal spacing of a printer is generally stated in the number of *characters per inch* (*CPI*), with 10 CPI being the most common. The most common line lengths are 80 characters, 120 characters, and 132 characters.

Vertical spacing is measured in *lines per inch* (*LPI*), with 6 LPI being the most common. Many printers have a switch, which allows printing at 6 LPI or 8 LPI. Many of the popular printers for personal computers allow selection of line spacing in increments of 1/72 inch or even 1/216 inch.

If a programmer doesn't know what type of printer will be used for output, the safest practice is to plan for an 80-character line with 6 lines per inch. For standard 8 1/2-by-11-inch paper, this will allow for 66 lines of 80 characters (which would fill the entire sheet).

Some recommendations for planning output follow:

1. Allow 1 inch at the top of the paper above the title.
2. Allow at least 1 inch at the bottom of the sheet for a margin. (Subtracting 12 lines for top and bottom margin leaves 54 lines for printing.)
3. Center the title and triple space (2 blank lines). Consider adding the date and identification of the program that produced the output to the title line.
4. Generally 1 or 2 lines are needed for column headings, plus 1 blank line before the first detail line. (Subtract 6 lines for title, headings, and blank lines— leaving 48 lines for printing the detail lines.)
5. Decide where the data will appear for detail lines before placing the column headings. Plan the number of characters for each field, including edit characters (commas, decimal points, dollar signs). Then decide on the number of spaces to allow between columns of data, and *center the detail data on the 80-character line*. Columns of data too close together (2 or 3 spaces) are difficult to read. Columns too far apart (more than 10) cause difficulties for many people in visually aligning the data fields.
6. Once the detail line has been drawn on the chart, *then* center the headings above the columns of data. A slight abbreviation is acceptable if the meaning is clear. It is better to allow 2 (or even 3) lines of column headings than to code cryptic headings.
7. Draw wavy lines below the columns of data to show that more lines will be printed. Single spacing of detail lines is assumed unless a note appears to the contrary.
8. When totals are needed, indicate the spacing below the last line of detail data. Always make sure the total fields are decimal point aligned beneath their columns of data.
9. Will the report fit on one page? After subtracting the lines for the total line and spacing, there will be about 45 or 46 lines left for detail data. If the data is likely to require more than that, multiple pages are required. If it is possible to fit the report on one page with modest modification, it is probably a good idea.
10. If multiple pages are required, add the page number to the title line.

Multiple Page Output

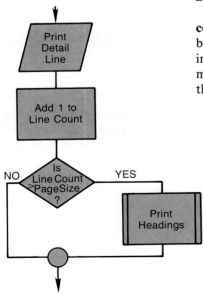

When a report must be printed on multiple pages, additional program logic is required. The detail lines must be counted as they are printed. When the page is filled, the paper must be advanced to the top of the next page, a page number and headings printed, and the lines on the new page counted.

Two counters must be added to a program that prints multiple pages. A **line counter** is needed to count the number of detail lines printed, and a **page counter** must be kept in order to print the page number on each page. The line counter must be re-initialized for each new page, while the page counter must begin at 1 and keep incrementing. As each detail line is printed, it must be counted. When the count goes over the specified number of lines, a page break occurs.

Figure 6.2
Flowchart of heading
subroutine.

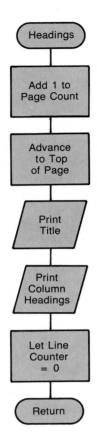

The heading subroutine must do several things (figure 6.2):

Increment the page counter
Advance to the top of the next page
Print the headings
Reset the line counter to zero (for the next page)

Question: How do you make the printer advance to the top of the page?
Answer: Two ways.

1. There are 66 lines on a page, and you know how many have been printed. So, print the correct number of blank lines to advance to the top of the page.
2. Trickier but better. Most printers respond to a special, nonprinting character, called the form-feed, by advancing to the top of the next page. The character is the twelfth code in the ASCII coding sequence and can be sent to the printer with this statement:

```
LPRINT CHR$(12);
```

The trailing semicolon keeps the internal print pointer on the first line, rather than allowing it to advance one more line.

There is one small catch to this—how does the printer know where the top of the next page is? When the printer is powered on (or reset), it establishes *that* line as top-of-form. It keeps its own internal counter as it prints lines. So, each time it receives the form-feed character [CHR$(12)], it advances to a point 66 lines from the last top-of-form. Obviously, if the paper is not set correctly in the beginning, the page breaks will be misplaced.

Note: For more information about controlling the printer with special characters, see appendix H. The CHR$ function is covered in more detail in chapter 7.

Coding the Heading Module

```
'****************** Print Headings *****************************
PrintHeadings:
  LET PageCt = PageCt + 1          'Add to page count
  LPRINT CHR$(12);                 'Advance to top of page
  LPRINT USING T$; PageCt          'Print title line
  LPRINT
  LPRINT
  LPRINT H1$                       'Print column headings
  LPRINT H2$
  LPRINT
  LET LineCt = 0                   'Reset line counter
  RETURN
```

The logic of the program will need to be altered to provide for the printing of headings when interspersed in the detail lines. In prior programs, the headings were always printed from the program mainline before the detail loop was begun. Now, the line counter must be tested in the detail loop. When the number of lines printed indicates the page is full, the heading module must be executed.

Programming Example

This program must print a summary of the calendars sold for the annual fund-raising drive. In order to demonstrate multiple page output without including great quantities of data, the number of lines per page has been set to 10.

Input

(from DATA statements)

1. Group number
2. Name of person
3. Number of calendars sold

Output

(on printer)

1. Report with title, column headings, and multiple page output.
2. For each person, print the group number, name, and number of calendars sold.
3. A report total is required for the total number of calendars sold.

Calculations

Add all calendar sales.

Pseudocode

Main Program

1. Initialize
       Print images and maximum page size
2. Print headings—for first page
3. Process detail
    3.1   Prime read
    3.2   DO Loop until end of data
           3.2.1   Calculations—add to total
           3.2.2   Print a line
                        Add to line counter
           3.2.3   If line counter > maximum allowed then
                        print headings
           3.2.4   Read next data
    3.3   End loop
4. Print final total

Heading Subroutine

1. Add to page counter
2. Advance to top of page
3. Print title and column heading lines
4. Reset line counter to zero

Flowchart

Figure 6.3 reflects the calendar sales flowchart form.

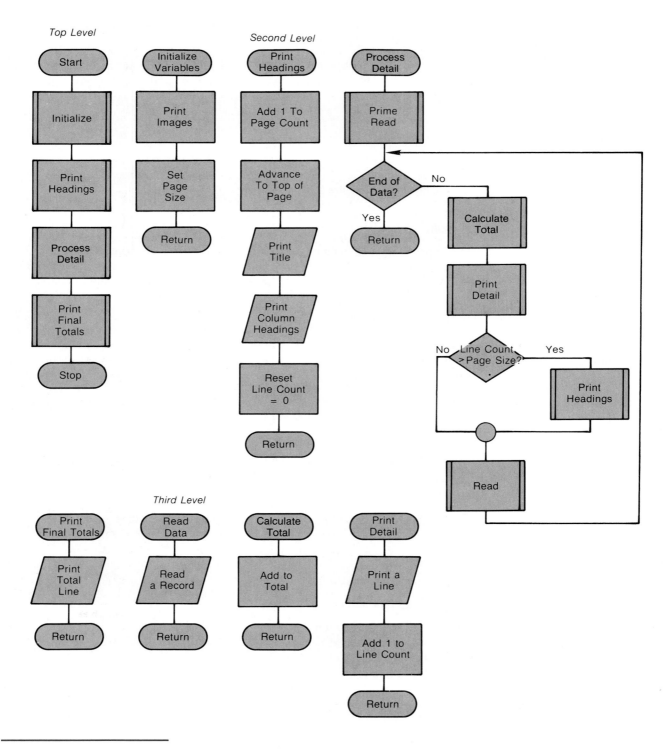

Figure 6.3
Calendar sales program
flowchart.

Program Listing

```
'Program To Report On The Annual Calendar Sale Drive.
' Includes Multiple Page Breaks, With The Number Of
' Lines Per Page Set To 10 To Demonstrate Page Counter.

'          Variables Used

'      Group$                 Group number
'      Per$                   Name of person
'      Cal                    Calendars sold
'      CalSubtot              Group subtotal
'      CalTot                 Report total
'      LineCt                 Line count
'      PageCt                 Page count
'      MaxLines               Maximum number of lines per page
'      T1$, H1$, H2$, D1$     Print images
'          Rt$                Print image

'***************** Program Mainline ********************

CLS
GOSUB InitializeVariables
GOSUB PrintHeadings
GOSUB ProcessDetail
GOSUB PrintTotals
END

'***************** Initialize Variables ******************

InitializeVariables:
  LET T1$ = "                    ANNUAL CALENDAR SALE   PAGE##"
  LET H1$ = "        GROUP           PERSON               CALENDARS"
  LET H2$ = "        NUMBER                                SOLD"
  LET D1$ = "          \\          \              \        ###"
  LET Rt$ = "                        REPORT TOTAL      ##,###"
  LET MaxLines = 10                   'Set page for short page to
                                      ' demonstrate
RETURN

'***************** Print Headings ********************

PrintHeadings:
  LET PageCt = PageCt + 1              'Add to page counter
  LPRINT CHR$(12);                     'Advance to top of page
  LPRINT USING T1$; PageCt             'Print title line
  LPRINT
  LPRINT
  LPRINT H1$                           'Print column headings
  LPRINT H2$
  LPRINT
  LPRINT
  LET LineCt = 0                       'Reset line counter
RETURN

'*************** Process Detail ********************

ProcessDetail:
  GOSUB ReadData
  DO UNTIL Group$ = "00"
    GOSUB CalculateTotal
    GOSUB PrintDetail
    IF LineCt >= MaxLines THEN
      GOSUB PrintHeadings
    END IF
    GOSUB ReadData
  LOOP
RETURN
```

```
'***************** Read Data ****************************

ReadData:
  READ Group$, Per$, Cal
  DATA 1A, CLEO THORPE, 4, 1A, BERTHA THOMAS, 6, 1A, KARL BETTS, 3
  DATA 1B, ANTHONY HOFFMAN, 12, 1B, DAVID YOUNT, 4, 2A
  DATA PHILLIP TIBBS, 6, 2B, VICTOR PROCTOR, 15, 2B, PAUL PARSONS
  DATA 25, 2B, BRENDA MILLER, 18, 3A, RALPH MAY, 6, 3A
  DATA DEANNA MC CLURE, 10, 3A, FLOYD SWANSON, 20, 3A, STEVE SUTTON
  DATA 3, 3A, BARBARA KIDWELL, 12, 3A, KENNETH KING, 22, 3B
  DATA PAUL DEMPSEY, 25, 3B, RUBY BAILEY, 12, 4A, BILL WILKINSON
  DATA 10, 4A, RUSSELL BUTLER, 21, 4A, CHARLES CAIN, 15, 4B
  DATA HARVEY CALDWELL 6, 5A, EILEEN FAY, 9, 5A, ALLEN FARMER, 14
  DATA 5B, ARTURO HERNANDEZ, 13, 5B, BERNICE HENDERSON, 7, 5B
  DATA LARRY HOLT, 30, 5B, WADE LEE, 25, 00, 00, 00
RETURN

'***************** Calculate Total ********************

CalculateTotal:
  LET CalTot = CalTot + Cal
RETURN

'***************** Print Detail ***********************

PrintDetail:
  LPRINT USING D1$; Group$, Per$, Cal
  LET LineCt = LineCt + 1
RETURN

'***************** Print Totals ***********************

PrintTotals:
  LPRINT
  LPRINT USING Rt$; CalTot
RETURN

'***************** End of Program *********************
```

Sample Program Output

```
         ANNUAL CALENDAR SALE                 PAGE 1

   GROUP        PERSON              CALENDARS
   NUMBER                           SOLD


    1A          CLEO THORPE             4
    1A          BERTHA THOMAS           6
    1A          KARL BETTS              3
    1B          ANTHONY HOFFMAN        12
    1B          DAVID YOUNT             4
    2A          PHILLIP TIBBS           6
    2B          VICTOR PROCTOR         15
    2B          PAUL PARSONS           25
    2B          BRENDA MILLER          18
    3A          RALPH MAY               6
```

```
•                         ANNUAL CALENDAR SALE                    PAGE 2
•
•       GROUP              PERSON                    CALENDARS
•       NUMBER                                       SOLD
•
•
•        3A            DEANNA MC CLURE                  10
•        3A            FLOYD SWANSON                    20
•        3A            STEVE SUTTON                      3
•        3A            BARBARA KIDWELL                  12
•        3A            KENNETH KING                     22
•        3B            PAUL DEMPSEY                     25
•        3B            RUBY BAILEY                      12
•        4A            BILL WILKINSON                   10
•        4A            RUSSELL BUTLER                   21
•        4A            CHARLES CAIN                     15
•
```

```
•                         ANNUAL CALENDAR SALE                    PAGE 3
•
•       GROUP              PERSON                    CALENDARS
•       NUMBER                                       SOLD
•
•
•        4B            HARVEY CALDWELL                   6
•        5A            EILEEN FAY                        9
•        5A            ALLEN FARMER                     14
•        5B            ARTURO HERNANDEZ                 13
•        5B            BERNICE HENDERSON                 7
•        5B            LARRY HOLT                       30
•        5B            WADE LEE                         25
•
•                      REPORT TOTAL                    353
•
```

Feedback

1. When multiple pages are needed, how will the printed output look if the line counter is not reset to zero in the heading routine?
2. Can you think of any reason why it might be better to advance to the next page by printing a form-feed character (ASCII code 12) rather than printing blank lines?
3. How many lines can be printed on a standard 8 1/2-by-11-inch paper?
4. What is the difference between detail lines and any other lines printed?

Subtotals with Control Breaks

Another technique often required for reports is printing subtotals. For the programming example for calendar sales, subtotals can be printed at the end of each group before beginning the next group. At the end of the entire list, the report totals can be printed.

```
                    ANNUAL CALENDAR SALE                    PAGE  1

        GROUP           PERSON              CALENDARS
        NUMBER                               SOLD


         1A         CLEO THORPE                 4
         1A         BERTHA THOMAS               6
         1A         KARL BETTS                  3

                    SUBTOTAL                   13

         1B         ANTHONY HOFFMAN            12
         1B         DAVID YOUNT                 4

                    SUBTOTAL                   16

         2A         PHILLIP TIBBS               6

                    SUBTOTAL                    6

         2B         VICTOR PROCTOR             15
         2B         PAUL PARSONS               25
         2B         BRENDA MILLER              18

                    SUBTOTAL                   58

                    REPORT TOTAL              93
```

There is a field controlling the totaling process to determine when subtotals are required. (In this case, group number controls the totals.) As long as the group number stays the same, detail lines are printed and totals are accumulated. As soon as the group number changes, subtotals are required. The field controlling the process is called the **control variable.** When the contents of the field change and subtotals are printed, this is called a **control break.**

When a control break occurs, several steps must take place:

1. The subtotals are printed (generally along with spacing before and after the subtotal line).
2. The subtotal fields are added into the report totals.
3. The subtotal fields are reset to zero (so that the next group subtotals will be correct).
4. The extra lines are added to the line counter.
5. The control variable is reset for the next group.

Figure 6.4 shows a flowchart of the subroutine needed when a control break occurs.

How do you know when it's time to print the subtotals? The only way to know that the last item in the group has been printed is to read the next record and to find that the group number is different. So, after each read, ask the question, "Is this group number different from the last one?" But if you use the statement

```
READ Group$, ...
```

the new group number replaces the old one, and a comparison cannot be made. For this reason, another variable is required to hold the previous group number.

```
READ Group$, ...
IF Group$ <> GroupSave$ THEN
    GOSUB PrintSubtotals
END IF
```

Figure 6.4
Flowchart of the subtotal
subroutine.

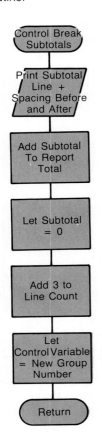

In the flowchart of the control break subroutine (figure 6.4), the contents of GroupSave\$ was altered so that the next group would use the new value as its control variable. Once this process gets going, it will work well. One problem remains—for the first group, GroupSave\$ will not have the correct value. Subtotals will print the first time the comparison is made. To solve this one last problem, the first group number is placed into the save field immediately after the priming READ.

```
'****************** Process Detail *************************

ProcessDetail:
  GOSUB ReadData
  LET GroupSave$ = Group$              'Save first group number
  DO UNTIL Group$ = "00"
        GOSUB CalculateAnswers
        IF LineCt > MaxLines THEN
                GOSUB PrintHeadings
        END IF
        GOSUB PrintDetail
        GOSUB ReadData
        IF GroupSave$ <> Group$ THEN
                GOSUB PrintSubtotal
        END IF
  LOOP
RETURN


'****************** Print Subtotal *********************

PrintSubtotal:
  LPRINT
  LPRINT USING St$; CalSubtot          'Print subtotal line
  LPRINT
  LET CalTot = CalTot + CalSubtot      'Add to report total
  LET CalSubtot = 0                    'Reset subtotal to zero
  LET LineCt = LineCt + 3              'Add to line counter
  LET GroupSave$ = Group$              'Save new group number
RETURN
```

One important point must be made. The input data *must* be in order by group number. Otherwise, subtotals would occur every time another group number was read.

The Page Headings

The alert reader may have noticed a change in the placement of the line counter test. This is largely a matter of aesthetics. If the last detail line of one group happens to be the last line on the page, the choice can be to have the subtotals appear in the bottom margin or as the first line on the new page. Generally, it is not considered good form to begin a page with subtotals. In order to keep from printing headings between the last detail line and the subtotal line, the decision has been placed *before* the PRINT.

Example Program: Calendar Sales

The program for calendar sales is ready to be shown in its entirety.

Pseudocode

Main Program
1. Initialize
    Print images and line count
2. Detail process
    2.1 Prime read
    2.2 Save group number
    2.3 DO Loop until group = 00
        2.3.1 Calculations—add to subtotal
        2.3.2 If line counter >= maximum allowed then
                print headings
        2.3.3 Print a line
                Add to line counter
        2.3.4 Read next data
        2.3.5 If new group then
                do subtotals
3. Print final totals

Subtotal Subroutine

1. Print subtotal line with space before and after
2. Add subtotal to report total
3. Reset subtotal to zero
4. Add 3 to line counter
5. Save group number

Hierarchy Chart   Refer to figure 6.5 for the chart.

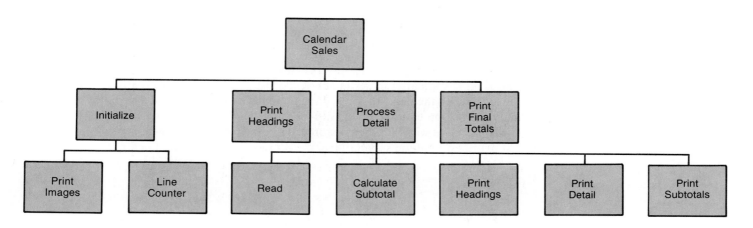

Figure 6.5
Calendar sales program
hierarchy chart.

Flowchart   Refer to figure 6.6 for the flowchart.

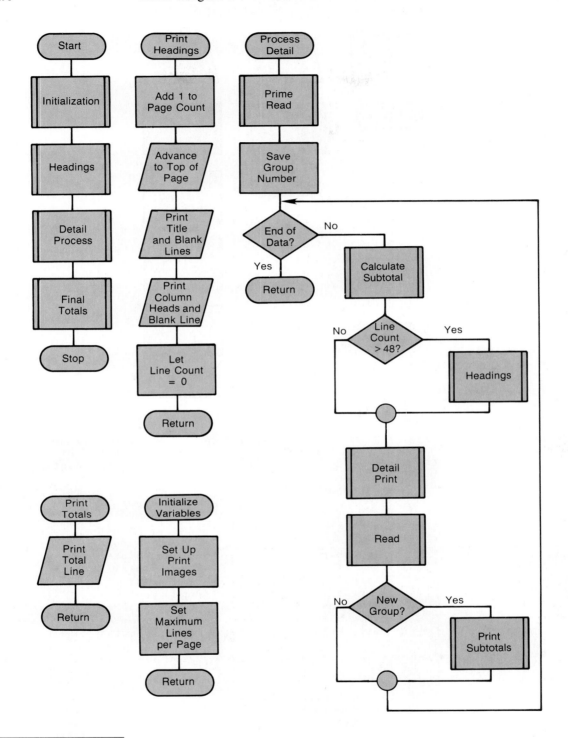

Figure 6.6
Calendar sales program
flowchart using control breaks.

Figure 6.6—*Continued*

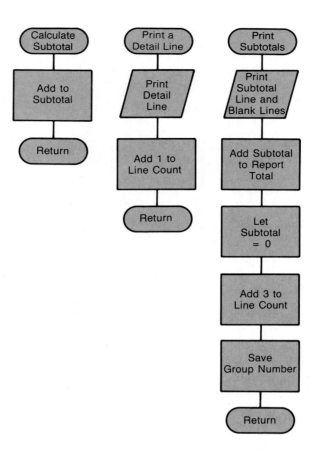

Program Listing

```
'*** Program To Report On The Annual Calendar Sale Drive.
' Includes Multiple Page Breaks, With The Number Of
' Lines Per Page Set To 30 To Demonstrate Page Counter.
'
'         Variables Used
'
'         Group$                      Group number
'         Per$                        Name of person
'         Cal                         Calendars sold
'         CalSubtot                   Group subtotal
'         CalTot                      Report total
'         LineCt                      Line count
'         PageCt                      Page count
'         MaxLines                    Maximum number of lines per page
'         T1$, H1$, H2$, D1$          Print images
'         St$, Rt$                    Print images
'
'****************** Program Mainline ********************
CLS
GOSUB InitializeVariables
GOSUB PrintHeadings
GOSUB ProcessDetail
GOSUB PrintTotals
END
```

```
'****************** Initialize Variables ******************

InitializeVariables:
  LET T1$ = "                    ANNUAL CALENDAR SALE  PAGE##"
  LET H1$ = "          GROUP         PERSON           CALENDARS"
  LET H2$ = "          NUMBER                             SOLD"
  LET D1$ = "            \\       \                 \    ###"
  LET St$ = "                    SUBTOTAL             #,###"
  LET Rt$ = "                    REPORT TOTAL        ##,###"
  LET MaxLines = 30
RETURN


'****************** Print Headings ******************

PrintHeadings:

  LET PageCt = PageCt + 1                'Add to page counter
  LPRINT CHR$(12);                       'Advance to top of page
  LPRINT USING T1$; PageCt               'Print title line
  LPRINT
  LPRINT
  LPRINT H1$                             'Print column headings
  LPRINT H2$
  LPRINT
  LPRINT
  LET LineCt = 0                         'Reset line counter
RETURN

'****************** Process Detail ******************

ProcessDetail:
  GOSUB ReadData
  LET GroupSave$ = Group$
  DO UNTIL Group$ = "00"                 'Save first group number
    GOSUB CalculateSubTotal
    IF LineCt >= MaxLines THEN
      GOSUB PrintHeadings
    END IF
    GOSUB PrintDetail
    GOSUB ReadData
    IF GroupSave$ <> Group$ THEN
      GOSUB PrintSubtotals
    END IF
  LOOP
RETURN

'****************** Read Data ******************

ReadData:
  READ Group$, Per$, Cal
  DATA 1A, CLEO THORPE, 4, 1A, BERTHA THOMAS, 6, 1A, KARL BETTS, 3
  DATA 1B, ANTHONY HOFFMAN, 12, 1B, DAVID YOUNT, 4, 2A
  DATA PHILLIP TIBBS, 6, 2B, VICTOR PROCTOR, 15, 2B, PAUL PARSONS
  DATA 25, 2B, BRENDA MILLER, 18, 3A, RALPH MAY, 6, 3A
  DATA DEANNA MC CLURE, 10, 3A, FLOYD SWANSON, 20, 3A, STEVE SUTTON
  DATA 3, 3A, BARBARA KIDWELL, 12, 3A, KENNETHY KING, 22, 3B
  DATA PAUL DEMPSEY, 25, 3B, RUBY BAILEY, 12, 4A, BILL WILKINSON
  DATA 10, 4A, RUSSELL BUTLER, 21, 4A, CHARLES CAIN, 15, 4B
  DATA HARVEY CALDWELL, 6, 5A, EILEEN FAY, 9, 5A, ALLEN FARMER, 14
  DATA 5B, ARTURO HERNANDEZ, 13, 5B, BERNICE HENDERSON, 7, 5B
  DATA LARRY HOLT, 30, 5B, WADE LEE, 25, 00, 00, 00
RETURN

'****************** Calculate SubTotal ******************

CalculateSubTotal:
  LET CalSubtot = CalSubtot + Cal
RETURN
```

```
'********************* Print Detail ************************
PrintDetail:
  LPRINT USING D1$; Group$, Per$, Cal
  LET LineCt = LineCt + 1
RETURN

'****************** Print SubTotals ***********************
PrintSubTotals:
  LPRINT
  LPRINT USING St$; CalSubtot          'Print subtotal line
  LPRINT
  LET CalTot = CalTot + CalSubtot      'Add to report total
  LET CalSubtot = 0                    'Reset subtotal to 0
  LET LineCt = LineCt + 3              'Add to line counter
  LET GroupSave$ = Group$              'Save new group
RETURN

'****************** Print Totals *************************
PrintTotals:
  LPRINT USING Rt$; CalTot
RETURN

'****************** End of Program ***********************
```

Sample Program Output

```
        •
        •          ANNUAL CALENDAR SALE   PAGE 1
        •
        •     GROUP        PERSON              CALENDARS
        •     NUMBER                            SOLD
        •
        •      1A     CLEO THORPE                 4
        •      1A     BERTHA THOMAS               6
        •      1A     KARL BETTS                  3
        •
        •             SUBTOTAL                   13
        •
        •      1B     ANTHONY HOFFMAN            12
        •      1B     DAVID YOUNT                 4
        •
        •             SUBTOTAL                   16
        •
        •      2A     PHILLIP TIBBS               6
        •
        •             SUBTOTAL                    6
        •
        •      2B     VICTOR PROCTOR             15
        •      2B     PAUL PARSONS               25
        •      2B     BRENDA MILLER              18
        •
        •             SUBTOTAL                   58
        •
        •      3A     RALPH MAY                   6
        •      3A     DEANNA MC CLURE            10
        •      3A     FLOYD SWANSON              20
        •      3A     STEVE SUTTON                3
        •      3A     BARBARA KIDWELL            12
        •      3A     KENNETH KING               22
        •
        •             SUBTOTAL                   73
        •
```

```
                    ANNUAL CALENDAR SALE    PAGE 2

        GROUP           PERSON                  CALENDARS
        NUMBER                                  SOLD

        3B              PAUL DEMPSEY            25
        3B              RUBY BAILEY             12

                        SUBTOTAL               37

        4A              BILL WILKINSON         10
        4A              RUSSELL BUTLER         21
        4A              CHARLES CAIN           15

                        SUBTOTAL               46

        4B              HARVEY CALDWELL         6

                        SUBTOTAL                6

        5A              EILEEN FAY              9
        5A              ALLEN FARMER           14

                        SUBTOTAL               23

        5B              ARTURO HERNANDEZ       13
        5B              BERNICE HENDERSON       7
        5B              LARRY HOLT             30
        5B              WADE LEE               25

                        SUBTOTAL               75


                        REPORT TOTAL          353
```

Feedback

1. When subtotals are printed, why is it called a *control break?*
2. What changes would need to be made in the program if there were two fields that needed subtotals and report totals?
3. Code the additional lines necessary to print the average number of calendars sold for each group (on the group subtotal line) and the average for the entire report (on the report total line).
4. Sometimes a third (or fourth) level of subtotals is needed. Consider the situation in which the groups are divided into divisions. What changes would be necessary in the program to print group subtotals, division subtotals, and report totals?

Summary

1. Printer spacing charts are used to plan program output.
2. The most common horizontal spacing for personal computer printers is 80-character lines (10 characters per inch).
3. The most common vertical spacing for printers is 6 lines per inch.
4. It is considered good practice to leave 1 inch at the top and bottom of the page for margins.
5. The detail line spacing should be determined before the column headings are placed on the print chart.
6. Column headings should not be abbreviated in a way that makes their meaning unclear.

7. If multiple pages will be needed, add page numbers to the report.
8. When multiple pages are needed, the program will need line counter and page counter fields.
9. The line counter field is used to count the detail lines printed. When the counter becomes greater than the specified number of lines, a new page is needed.
10. The tasks of the heading routine are to: (1) advance to the next page; (2) increment the page counter; (3) print the title and column headings; and, (4) reset the line counter to zero.
11. Advancing to the next page can be accomplished by printing blank lines or printing a form-feed character (ASCII code 12).
12. The printing of subtotals is also called control breaks.
13. The field controlling the subtotal process is called the control variable.
14. In order to compare the control variable for the current record to that of the previous record, a "save" field is required.
15. When the current control variable is different from the previous one, subtotals are printed.

Programming Exercises

Each of these programming assignments is to use line and page counters and to have multiple page output. A printer spacing chart must be prepared to document the report layout.

Note: The program output must *exactly* match the layout shown on the printer spacing chart.

6.1. Write a program to produce a report of the gross earnings of employees.

INPUT: The input data will be read from DATA statements. The data consists of the employee's name, the department number, hourly pay rate, and the number of hours worked.

OUTPUT:

1. Print an appropriate title and column headings at the top of each page of the report. The title should be centered on the title line. The title line must include the page number. The column headings must be meaningful and be aligned over the columns of data.
2. Each detail line is to include the employee's name, department number, hourly pay rate, number of hours worked, regular hours, overtime hours, regular pay, overtime pay, and gross pay.
3. Print a total of 20 detail lines per page.
4. At the end of the report, print a total line that includes totals of the number of hours worked, regular hours, regular pay, overtime hours, overtime pay, and total gross pay. The totals must be properly aligned below the detail line columns.
5. The data will fit (barely) on an 80-character line. If you are using a printer with a wider carriage and paper, you may take advantage of the width by placing these statements in your program.

```
WIDTH "LPT1:",132 'Set line length to 132 characters
WIDTH "LPT1:",80  'Set it back to 80 characters
```

Many dot matrix printers are capable of printing in smaller, condensed print. To print a longer line in condensed print, add these lines to your program. See appendix H, Using Special Functions of Printers for more explanation.

```
WIDTH "LPT1:", 132 'Set line length to 132 characters
LPRINT CHR$(15);    'Turn on condensed mode
```

And at the conclusion of the program, add these lines:

```
WIDTH "LPT1:", 80 'Set line length back to normal
LPRINT CHR$(18);    'Reset to normal characters
```

CALCULATIONS:

1. Calculate the regular pay for each employee. The first forty hours worked are the regular hours. The regular pay is to be calculated by multiplying regular hours times the hourly pay rate. Round the pay to the nearest cent.

2. Calculate the overtime pay for each employee. Any hours worked in excess of forty hours are the overtime hours. The overtime pay rate is to be equal to the hourly pay rate times 1.5. Overtime pay is to be calculated by multiplying overtime hours by the overtime pay rate. Round the pay to the nearest cent.

3. The gross pay is calculated as the sum of the regular pay and the overtime pay.

4. Accumulate report totals of the number of hours worked, regular hours, overtime hours, regular pay, overtime pay, and gross pay.

TEST DATA:

Name	Dept. No	Pay Rate	Hours Worked
FRANK BENSON	10	6.50	25.0
BETTY BERGMAN	10	6.80	40.0
ROGER BROWN	10	7.70	45.0
TONY CHAVEZ	12	6.70	32.20
ELLA COURTNEY	12	8.20	39.70
PAUL DERBY	10	5.50	41.0
EDWARD DUNLAP	20	10.70	15.0
LOUISE ERICKSON	20	7.90	40.0
HENRY GARCIA	20	8.10	40.0
MAX GOODRICH	20	9.00	1.0
CRAIG HILL	20	6.70	40.0
BEN ISAACSON	22	7.30	50.0
BRIAN KING	22	10.00	40.0
MARY LAMONT	22	8.60	40.0
NIEN LE	24	7.60	36.0
COLLEEN MARTIN	24	7.60	39.0
TIEN NGUYEN	24	8.20	20.20
HENRY OKADA	24	6.80	40.0
LEON PITTMAN	24	11.00	25.0
DON RIDGEWAY	24	8.20	23.0
LILLIAN SALINAS	28	12.00	40.0
THOMAS SHIPLEY	28	9.20	40.0
ANNA TAYLOR	28	7.80	40.0
PETER ULRICH	30	8.10	49.0
DAVID VERDUGO	31	7.60	42.0
END OF DATA	00	0.00	0.0 (not to be printed)

6.2. Modify the program in exercise 6.1 to include control breaks. For each department, print subtotals of the number of hours worked, regular hours, overtime hours, regular pay, overtime pay, and the gross pay. Double-space (1 blank line) before and after each subtotal line. The extra blank lines are to be counted as detail lines when determining page size.

6.3. Write a program using control breaks to produce a student grade report.

INPUT: The input will consist of the student number, the student name, the course code, the course title, number of units, and letter grade. The input data will be included on DATA statements within the program.

OUTPUT:

1. Print an appropriate title and column headings at the top of each page of the report. The title should be centered on the title line. The title line must include the page number. The column headings must be meaningful and be aligned over the columns of data.

2. A detail line is to be printed for each input record. The first line for each student will contain the student name and number, but the subsequent lines for that student will not. In addition to the name field, each detail line is to include the student ID, the course code, course title, number of units, and the letter grade.

3. A student total line (control break) is to be printed for each student. Leave 1 blank line before and after the total line.

4. Print a total of 10 detail lines per page. The blank lines before and after the student total lines are to be counted as detail lines for determining page size.

5. At the end of the report, double-space (1 blank line) and print a total line that includes the total number of units completed for all students. Double-space again and print a line showing the average number of units completed per student.

CALCULATIONS:

1. Accumulate the total number of units for each student.
2. Accumulate the total number of units for all students.
3. Calculate the average number of units for all students (total units / number of students).

TEST DATA:

Name	ID	Course Code	Title	Units	Grade
DAVID BASSETT	1462	0814	SYSTEMS ANALYSIS	3	B
DAVID BASSETT	1462	0813	DATA PROCESSING	3	A
DAVID BASSETT	1462	2625	DATA PROCESSING LAB	.5	A
DAVID BASSETT	1462	1823	ENGLISH	3	C
OSCAR FERNANDEZ	2145	2015	BASIC PROGRAMMING	3	B
OSCAR FERNANDEZ	2145	2016	BASIC PROGRAMMING LAB	1	A
MARIA GREEN	2452	1823	ENGLISH	3	B
MARCIA KNIGHT	3665	3333	ALGEBRA	4	B
MARCIA KNIGHT	3665	0814	SYSTEMS ANALYSIS	3	A
MARCIA KNIGHT	3665	4244	ACCOUNTING	4	B
LE NIEN	4891	0813	DATA PROCESSING	3	B
LE NIEN	4891	2625	DATA PROCESSING LAB	.5	B
LE NIEN	4891	3333	ALGEBRA	3	A
LE NIEN	4891	4244	ACCOUNTING	4	B
CHRIS REEVES	5678	3333	ALGEBRA	3	D

END OF DATA

SAMPLE PROGRAM OUTPUT USING TEST DATA:

```
                    REPORT TITLE                                PAGE  1

STUDENT                     COURSE
NAME              ID        CODE     TITLE                  UNITS    GRADE

DAVID BASSETT     1462      0814     SYSTEMS ANALYSIS        3.0      B
                  1462      0813     DATA PROCESSING         3.0      A
                  1462      2625     DATA PROCESSING LAB     0.5      A
                  1462      1823     ENGLISH                 3.0      C

                         TOTAL UNITS                         9.5
```

```
OSCAR FERNANDEZ  2145     2015   BASIC PROGRAMMING          3.0  B
                 2145     2016   BASIC PROGRAMMING LAB      1.0  A

                         TOTAL UNITS                        4.0

MARIA GREEN      2452     1823   ENGLISH                    3.0  B

                         TOTAL UNITS                        3.0
: :
: :
: :

              TOTAL UNITS FOR ALL STUDENTS            XXX.X

              AVERAGE NUMBER OF UNITS PER STUDENT      XX.X
```

6.4. Write a program using control breaks to produce a sales summary for charter hours booked for yachts.

INPUT: The program input may be read from DATA statements or INPUT statements. For each yacht, enter the length, the rate per hour, and the number of hours chartered.

OUTPUT: Print an appropriate title, column headings, and detail lines for each ship. Detail lines include the yacht type, length, hourly rate, hours chartered, and the total revenue for those hours chartered. Print subtotals for each yacht type and report totals at the end of the report. Subtotals and totals are to be printed for the charter hours column and charter revenue column.

PROCESSING: The charter revenue for each ship is calculated as the hourly rate times the number of hours chartered. Accumulate subtotals and totals for charter hours and charter revenue.

TEST DATA:

Type	Size	Rate	Charter Hours
Ranger	22	95.00	24
Ranger	22	69.00	12
Wavelength	24	69.00	6
Wavelength	24	89.00	12
Catalina	27	160.00	24
Catalina	27	99.00	6
Catalina	30	190.00	12
Catalina	30	225.00	24
Coronado	32	230.00	24
Hobie	33	192.00	33
Hobie	33	235.00	24
Hobie	33	137.00	6
Hobie	33	235.00	24
C & C	34	290.00	24
C & C	34	175.00	6
Catalina	36	185.00	6
Catalina	36	320.00	24
Hans Christian	38	400.00	24
Hans Christian	38	250.00	6
Excaliber	45	550.00	24
Excaliber	45	295.00	6

SAMPLE PROGRAM OUTPUT USING TEST DATA:

YACHT TYPE	SIZE	RATE	CHARTER	REVENUE
RANGER	22	95.00	24.0	$2,280.00
RANGER	22	69.00	12.0	828.00
RANGER SUBTOTAL			36.0	3,108.00
WAVELENGTH	24	69.00	6.0	414.00
: :	: :	: :	: :	: :
: :	: :		: :	: :
REPORT TOTAL			XXX.X	$XXX,XXX.XX

6.5. The local video arcade is sponsoring a summer team competition and is planning to give trophies to the members of the winning team. Also, the highest individual score on each team will earn a medal. There is one individual grand prize for the person with the highest score. Each team may have up to three players, and any number of teams may enter the contest.

INPUT: For each player, input the team number, the player's name, and the number of points scored. Data may be entered with INPUT statements or READ/DATA.

OUTPUT: Print a report with appropriate title and column headings. Each detail line will show the player name and points scored. The first detail line for each team must also indicate the team number. At the conclusion of each group, print the team total for points scored. Also, print the name of the player with the highest score for that team.
At the end of the report, print:
1. the team number of the winning team;
2. the number of points scored by the winning team; and,
3. the name of the individual with the highest score.

PROCESSING: Accumulate the total points scored for each team. Also, determine the highest-scoring contestant on each team and the highest-scoring individual for the entire contest.

SAMPLE PROGRAM OUTPUT:

```
                    THE SUMMER GAMES
                 VIDEO ARCADE SHOOTOFF

TEAM      NAME                            POINTS

  1       ACE BRADLEY                     10,000
          RICHARD OCHOA                    9,100
          JAY JOHNSTON                     5,050

          TOTAL POINTS                    24,150

          TEAM WINNER - ACE BRADLEY

  2       CHRIS JACKSON                   11,100
          KEN RYAN                         8,990
          : :
          : :

THE WINNING TEAM IS TEAM # XX WITH XXX,XXX POINTS

THE WINNING INDIVIDUAL IS XXXXXXXXXXXXX WITH XXX,XXX POINTS
```

6.6. Write a program to create a dues report for the Women's Club.

INPUT: Input will come from the test data below.

OUTPUT: Output should be to the printer. Print a title, column headings, member's name, number of years as a member, amount due, total number of members, and total amount due. Print a page number on each page, with only 10 detail lines per page.

PROCESSING:
1. If the person has been a member longer than six years, dues are $800.
2. If the person has been a member for six years or less, dues are $1200.
3. Count the total number of members.
4. Accumulate a sum of all dues owed.

TEST DATA:

Member Name	Years of Membership
Judy Niles	2
Elaine Norton	4
Mary Percel	7
Sarah Rivera	8
Beatrice Udell	10
Anita Ashley	1
Janice Wills	5
May Wong	3
Kim Smith	2
Louise Olsen	1
Jane Adams	11
Holly Johnstone	4
Sheree Drake	6
Lisa Kayhill	8
Susan Zank	9
Michelle Brown	12
Mandy Goodwill	2
Denise Jones	1
Carol Lang	1
Joanne Miller	4

6.7. Write a program to create a hospital billing report for Stateside Hospital.

INPUT: Use DATA statements for the patient's name, number of days in the hospital, and type of room. Use the test data below.

OUTPUT:
1. Output may be to the screen or the printer.
2. Print a title and page number on each page.
3. Print column headings for the patient's name, number of days, room type, and total bill.
    A. Room types are as follows:
        1. Intensive care
        2. Private
        3. Double
4. Print 10 detail lines per page.
5. Print a count of the total number of patients.
6. Print the total billing amount.

PROCESSING:
1. Intensive care = $355 a day.
2. Private = $275 a day.
3. Double = $150 a day.
4. Calculate the amount due for each patient.
5. Accumulate a report total of the amount due to the hospital.

TEST DATA:

Name	Days	Room Type
Greg Scott	3	I
John Nelson	12	I
Sally Goldsmith	14	P
Carol Dunckon	2	I
Kim Agnew	1	D
Tom Jones	7	D
Richard Hernandez	15	D
Deon Moore	18	I
Gail Kidd	17	I
Ray Redstone	12	P
Steve Sillo	6	P
Scott Brown	2	P
Peggy Smith	5	D
Sue Johnson	7	I
Martha Miller	21	P
Jaime Robinson	6	D
Pearl Russ	4	I
Diane Hanley	3	I
Mike Williams	19	D
Duane Nichols	14	D

6.8. Write a program using control breaks to produce a transaction list for the Yin-Yan Wholesale Company.

INPUT: Department number, transaction date, and amount of the order will come from DATA statements. Use the following sample data.

OUTPUT: Make up a title and column headings for the department number, transaction date, and amount of order. Print department subtotals and a report total for the amount field. Display the output on the screen.

PROCESSING:
1. Accumulate a subtotal of the amount field, by department.
2. Accumulate a report total of the amount field.

TEST DATA:

Dept. #	Trans. Date	Amount in Dollars
100	1–21–86	6.75
100	1–21–86	14.85
100	2–21–86	21.21
100	2–28–86	8.21
119	3–05–86	121.83
119	3–21–86	19.50
119	4–10–86	21.50
121	5–01–86	12.75
121	5–21–86	100.21
142	5–22–86	53.47

6.9. The Kafkaesque Bank wants to know which group of customers has the most money in the bank. Write a program using control break logic to print a customer listing.

INPUT: Customer code, customer name, and amount of money in the bank.

OUTPUT: Print a title and column headings for the customer code, customer name, and amount of money. Print subtotals and report totals for the amount column.

PROCESSING:
1. Accumulate a subtotal on the amount column, by customer code.
2. Accumulate a report total of the amount column.

TEST DATA:

Code	Name	Amount in Dollars
A	Andy Adams	500
A	Lisa Anderson	150
A	Loni Adler	50
B	Steve Brown	300
B	John Bone	173
B	Scott Burges	75
J	Sally Jensen	20
J	Tom Jones	275
M	Anita Millsap	10
M	Michelle Millspaugh	510
M	Jane Miller	100
S	Jim Setella	83
S	Mike Stone	321
S	Trish Sapp	25

6.10. You have a stamp collection, and you want to print a list broken down into groups. The three groups are plants, people, and miscellaneous.

INPUT: Type of stamp, name of stamp, first day of issue, and the face value will come from DATA statements. Use the sample data below.

OUTPUT: Make up an appropriate title and column headings for the type of stamp, name of stamp, first day of issue, and the face value. Print a subtotal for the face value field.

PROCESSING: Accumulate a subtotal and report total of the face value amount for each of the three types of stamps.

TEST DATA:

Type	Name	Issue Date	Face Value in Dollars
Plant	Agave	12–11–81	.20
Plant	Barrel Cactus	12–11–81	.20
Plant	Saguaro	12–11–81	.20
Misc	Ballooning	3–31–83	.20
Misc	In Flight	3–31–83	.20
Misc	Building A Snowman	8–28–82	.20
Misc	Lend A Hand	4–20–83	.20
People	Nathaniel Hawthorne	7–08–83	.20
People	Nikola Tesla	9–21–83	.20
People	Dr. Mary Walker	6–10–82	.20

6.11. Looney Toon Grocers needs to track its inventory on a monthly basis. Management needs a report on this inventory, by department. Print a report showing, by department, the inventory item, its unit cost, the quantity on hand, and the inventory cost, plus the total inventory cost.

INPUT: Input will come from DATA statements. Use the test data below.
OUTPUT:
1. The output of this program is a report printed on the screen.
2. Print a title, with a page number and column headings.
3. Print 15 detail lines per page. These 15 lines must include the subtotal lines.
4. Print the fields in the following order, from left to right:

Department Number
Inventory Item
Quantity On Hand
Unit Price
Inventory Cost

5. Double-space before and after printing the inventory cost for each department. Include the department number in the subtotal output line.

PROCESSING:
1. For each item, calculate the inventory cost by multiplying the quantity on hand by the unit cost.
2. Calculate a subtotal by department of inventory cost.
3. Accumulate the sum of the total inventory cost.

TEST DATA:

Inventory Item	Dept. #	Quantity	Unit Cost in Dollars
American cheese	14	50	1.92
Salted butter	14	41	2.53
Swiss cheese	14	32	3.55
Cider	17	20	1.98
Chowchow	17	40	3.02
Prunes	17	62	2.51
Sweet potatoes	17	72	3.38
Ketchup	21	80	1.75
Tapioca	21	94	3.50
Beans	21	81	3.20
Peas	21	42	2.53
Olives	21	32	3.15
Whipping cream	26	20	1.98
Brooms	26	72	4.95
Fly paper	26	61	2.56
Zinc bucket	26	52	3.65
Dog biscuits	28	50	1.05
Condensed milk	28	41	3.65
Apples	28	83	2.67
Apricots	28	22	5.06
Cocoa	35	90	1.61
Ceylon tea	39	30	1.10
Coffee	39	13	2.05
Dates	39	41	3.03
Figs	42	50	1.85
Raisins	42	72	2.45
Apple sauce	42	12	3.50
Crackers	53	60	1.95
Lemon extract	53	74	3.47
Noodles	53	31	4.05
Macaroni	53	12	2.60

6.12. The sales manager for the Far-Out Sales Company needs to track the sales amount and the commissions paid to the sales force for each sales office. Generate the following report showing, by sales office, the amount of commissions paid and the dollar amount of sales. Also, include report totals for amount of commissions and the dollar amount of sales.

INPUT: Input will come from DATA statements. Use the following test data.

OUTPUT:
1. Print the title SALES COMMISSION REPORT and a page number at the top of each page.
2. Use appropriate column headings above each column of output. Underline the headings with equal signs, then double-space.
3. Display 12 detail lines per page.
4. Leave a blank line before and after each subtotal line.

5. Display the detail data in the following sequence from left to right.
   a. Sales Region
   b. Sales Office Number
   c. Salesperson Name
   d. Sales Amount
   e. Commission Amount
6. Display the report totals under the appropriate columns of data, and align the decimal points with the detail data.

PROCESSING:
1. Compute a 10 percent commission for each salesperson.
2. Accumulate Sales Office totals for sales amount and commission amount.
3. Accumulate report totals for sale amounts and commission amounts.

TEST DATA:

Salesperson Name	Office #	Sales Amount in Dollars	Sales Region
Andy Atom	14	134.08	50
Brian Brown	14	145.16	41
Claudia Cool	14	170.56	32
Deon Done	19	189.54	20
Eric Espinosa	19	243.19	62
Frank Ferry	19	244.37	72
Greg Green	21	251.27	80
Hank Hanna	21	303.31	94
Isabel Isha	21	305.58	81
Jane Jones	21	340.61	42
Kevin Kline	21	341.47	32
Leon Lang	26	391.03	20
Molly Moore	26	432.21	50
Nina Nelson	26	443.21	72
Olivia Oston	42	456.98	12
Penny Pamper	42	490.07	71
Quinn Quiery	42	521.04	21
Randy Rich	42	525.14	83

6.13. Write a program with multilevel control breaks to produce a list of books on cassette available to the blind. The first-level control break will be for fiction or nonfiction. The second-level control break will be the subject category.

INPUT: The type of book (fiction or nonfiction), the subject category, the author, the title of the book, and the shelf number will be input using DATA statements. Use the following test data.

OUTPUT: Print a title and appropriate column headings, the type of book, subject category, author, title of book, shelf number, subtotal for each subject, a total of nonfiction and fiction books, and a report total of all books.

PROCESSING: Keep a subtotal for each subject category, a total of nonfiction books, a total of fiction books, and a report total of all books.

TEST DATA:

Type	Subject	Author	Title	Shelf #
F	Best-sellers	Anita Brokner	*Hotel Du Lac*	RC-21510
F	Best-sellers	John Fowles	*A Maggot*	RC-22954
F	Best-sellers	Robert Moss	*Moscow Rules*	RC-21509
F	Fantasy	Richard Adams	*Maia*	RC-21237
F	Fantasy	Michael Ende	*Momo*	RC-22829
F	Occult	Harriet Waugh	*Kate's House*	RC-22652
F	Occult	F. Paul Wilson	*The Tomb*	RC-22793
F	Religion	James Kavanaugh	*The Celibates*	RC-23389
F	Religion	Michael Delahaye	*On the Third Day*	RC-22277
F	Romance	Sandra Kitt	*Adam and Eve*	RC-23209
F	Romance	Edna Maye Manley	*Agatha*	RC-22636
F	Humor	Norma Levinson	*The Room Upstairs*	RC-22401
F	Humor	Maggie Brooks	*Loose Connections*	RC-22853
F	Humor	Jill McCorkle	*July 7th*	RC-22222
F	Science Fiction	Frederik Pohl	*Black Star Rising*	RC-23663
F	Science Fiction	William Sleator	*Interstellar Pig*	RC-22792
NF	Business	Michael Drosnin	*Citizen Hughes*	RC-21530
NF	Business	David Sinclair	*Dynasty*	RC-22259
NF	Business	Mark Singer	*Funny Money*	RC-23712
NF	Humor	Frank B. Gilbreth	*Cheaper by the Dozen*	RC-23282
NF	Humor	Bill Adler	*Kid's Letters to President Reagan*	RC-22848
NF	Women	Geraldine A. Ferraro	*Ferraro: My Story*	RC-23725
NF	Women	Karen Armstrong	*Beginning the World*	RC-22572
NF	Philosophy	Lewis Mumford	*The Conduct of Life*	RC-22264
NF	Philosophy	Mortimer Adler	*Ten Philosophical Mistakes*	RC-22827
NF	Education	Sara Gilbert	*How to Take Tests*	RC-23232
NF	Education	Eda LeShan	*When Your Child Drives You Crazy*	RC-23361

6.14. Write a program using multilevel control breaks to print a list of local gyms and their members. The first-level control break should be on the name of the gym. The second-level control break should be on sex (male or female). The third-level control break should be on age (under 25, 25 and over).

INPUT: Gym name, member name, sex, age, weight, and phone number will come from the following test data.

OUTPUT: Print a title and column headings, gym name, member name, sex, age, weight, phone number, and a subtotal of the number of members of each of the three levels of control breaks.

PROCESSING:

1. Accumulate a subtotal of the number of members at each of the three levels of control breaks.
2. On the first level control break (gym name) advance to a new page.

TEST DATA:

Gym	Member Name	Sex	Age (yr)	Weight (lb)	Phone #
Ersatz	Sue Stone	F	19	123	123–4287
Ersatz	Jenny Scott	F	21	105	467–8221
Ersatz	Rose Jones	F	23	110	867–4289
Ersatz	Molly Mist	F	18	125	966–4037
Ersatz	Holly Howe	F	24	130	862–3090
Ersatz	Lynn Long	F	25	121	334–0712
Ersatz	Kim Smith	F	30	150	332–0021
Ersatz	Debbie Doe	F	50	143	167–0072
Ersatz	John Jones	M	19	175	963–0421
Ersatz	Scott Miller	M	21	200	331–0021
Ersatz	Steven Brown	M	23	150	966–0404
Ersatz	Larry Show	M	43	189	967–0000
Ersatz	James Randal	M	67	178	339–0421
Licit	Vira Osmond	F	21	110	334–0202
Licit	Sandra Long	F	24	130	334–0212
Licit	Gaynel Sillo	F	19	110	332–0264
Licit	Joelle Derlap	F	27	100	960–0215
Licit	Jeannie Jones	F	30	137	960–1245
Licit	Mike Moore	M	23	170	962–0405
Licit	Jerry Sandoval	M	24	189	339–0211
Licit	Tom Tone	M	37	175	421–1234
Licit	Tim Short	M	40	183	330–1001
Fetid	Cathy Nelson	F	21	105	331–0219
Fetid	Sonia Song	F	19	142	967–0121
Fetid	Jackie Smith	F	24	189	337–7123
Fetid	Tricia Scudder	F	18	120	960–1234
Fetid	Nora Nomes	F	23	163	301–1243
Fetid	Randy Rich	M	24	152	961–1111
Fetid	Tony Hernandez	M	21	110	333–4444
Fetid	Tommy Foss	M	18	125	900–0000
Fetid	Doug Donley	M	85	129	312–3456

6.15. Write a program using control break logic to print a list of animals broken down into type and phylum.

INPUT: Type, name, phylum, class, order, and family will be input using DATA statements. Use the following test data.

OUTPUT: Print a title and column headings, type, name, phylum, class, order, family, a subtotal for each type, a subtotal for each phylum within each type, and a grand total of all animals.

PROCESSING:
1. Accumulate a subtotal count for each type of animal.
2. Accumulate a subtotal count for each phylum within each type.
3. Accumulate a grand total of all animals.

TEST DATA:

ARTHROPODS

Name	Phylum	Class	Order	Family
Bed Bug	Arthropoda	Insecta	Hemiptera	Cimicidae
Wart-Biter	Arthropoda	Insecta	Orthoptera	Tettigoniidae
Comet	Arthropoda	Insecta	Lepidoptera	Saturniidae
Goat Moth	Arthropoda	Insecta	Lepidoptera	Cossidae
Ant Lion	Arthropoda	Insecta	Neuroptera	Myrmeleonidae

WORMS

Name	Phylum	Class	Order	Family
Tapeworm	Platyhelminthes	Cestoda	Cyclophyllidae	Taeniidae
Flatworm	Platyhelminthes	Turbellaria	Tricladida	Bipalidae
Ribbon Worm	Nemertini	Anopla	Heteronemertini	Lineidae

MOLLUSCS

Name	Phylum	Class	Order	Family
Sea Ear	Mollusca	Gastropoda	Diotocardia	Haliotidae
Squid	Mollusca	Cephalopoda	Decapoda	Loliginidae
Paper Nautilus	Mollusca	Cephalopoda	Octopoda	Argonautidae
Periwinkle	Mollusca	Gastropoda	Monotocaroia	Littorinidae
Music Volute	Mollusca	Gastropoda	Monotocaroia	Volutidae

ECHINODERMS

Name	Phylum	Class	Order	Family
Basket Star	Echinodermata	Ophiuroidea	Euryalae	Euryalidae
Sea Cucumber	Echinodermata	Holothuroidea	Dendrochirotida	Cucumariidae

AMPHIBIANS

Name	Phylum	Class	Order	Family
Olm	Vertebrata	Amphibia	Urodela	Proteidae
Flying Frog	Vertebrata	Amphibia	Anura	Rhacophoridae

REPTILES

Name	Phylum	Class	Order	Family
Blind Snake	Vertebrata	Reptilia	Squamata	Typhlopidae
Flying Dragon	Vertebrata	Reptilia	Squamata	Agamidae

7

Data Validation and Interactive Programs

LOCATE Statement
SPACE$ Function
STRING$ Function
LEN Function
LEFT$ Function
RIGHT$ Function
MID$ Function and
  Statement
VAL Function
STR$ Function
INSTR Function
CHR$ Function
ASC Function
UCASE$ Function
LCASE$ Function
INKEY$ Function
INPUT$ Function
LINE INPUT Statement
DATE$ Function
TIME$ Function

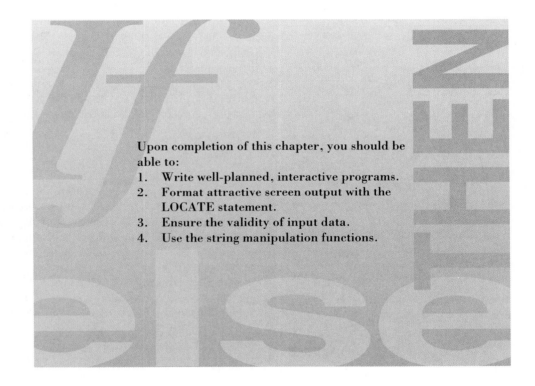

Upon completion of this chapter, you should be able to:
1. Write well-planned, interactive programs.
2. Format attractive screen output with the LOCATE statement.
3. Ensure the validity of input data.
4. Use the string manipulation functions.

User Friendly?

When writing computer programs, it should be assumed that the user (person who runs the program) will *not* be the programmer. Therefore, the programmer must strive to make the input dialogue clear and easy to understand. If the user makes mistakes or causes the program to malfunction, it must be assumed that the programmer is at fault. In this chapter, you will learn to "idiot proof" programs.

Guidelines for Interactive Programs

1. Make all program output clear, choosing terms the user will understand. *Never* use computerese. Use descriptive words rather than program variable names for INPUT prompts. If you had never run a program before, which would you rather see?

   ENTER BG __

   or

   ENTER BEGINNING BALANCE __

2. Design the layout of the screen so there will be no question about what is expected.
   a. Use menus, if possible, whenever there is a choice of options (see chapter 9 for menu programs).
   b. Whenever possible, place data in the same location every time. This requires that the screen *not* be allowed to scroll the print statements. This precise screen placement is accomplished with the LOCATE statement.
   c. Choose one area of the screen—perhaps the bottom line—to use for error messages. After the error has been corrected, clear the message. (Again, the LOCATE statement will help.)

3. Check the input data for validity. Many errors made by users can be caught at the point of entry. Finding and correcting the error early can often keep the program from producing erroneous results or "blowing up" during execution. Careful programmers include validity checking as a means of self-protection. It is better to reject bad data than to spend time attempting to debug the program only to discover (sometimes after hours or days) that the problem was caused by a "user error."

   In computer circles, you often hear the term, **GIGO** (*G*arbage *I*n, *G*arbage *O*ut). The accuracy of any program is only as good as the data it is given. The only way to hope to produce output that is not garbage is to make sure that garbage isn't allowed to enter.

   If the user was supposed to enter 3 and entered 4 instead, the program will not be able to detect the error as long as 4 is also a valid response. When there are only certain responses allowed, the program *can* check.

   In the following sections you will learn to check for these types of errors:
   a. reasonableness, or range checking
   b. matching a predetermined value, or code checking
   c. verifying that numeric fields are truly numeric
   d. consistency
   e. check digit calculations

4. Ask someone unfamiliar with computers to test your programs. Allow the tester to enter any values, to make sure your programs can function correctly, to identify the errors, and to not "blow up." Remember, a good programmer makes it easy to enter correct data and difficult to make mistakes.

Validity Checking

1. *Reasonableness, or range checking.* Numbers must be in a certain range, such as ID numbers less than 100 or hours in the range 0–100 (total hours a person could work in a week). Sometimes an upper (or lower) limit will be placed on amounts, such as checks written.

```
'************** Validate Range *********************
INPUT "Enter a number from 1-100 ", Num
DO WHILE Num < 1 OR Num > 100
    INPUT "Number must be between 1 and 100, reenter ", Num
LOOP
```

2. *Matching a predetermined value, or code checking.* Code only values of M (male) or F (female) allowed in a field, or perhaps a list of acceptable values in a field. This situation was handled earlier when checking for a YES or NO response.

```
'************** Validate Class Code ****************
INPUT "Enter class code", Code$
LET Code$ = UCASE$(Code$)
DO WHILE Code$ <> "FR" AND Code$ <> "SO" AND Code$ <> "JR"
    AND Code$ <> "SR"
        INPUT "Only values Fr, So, Jr, Sr allowed ", Code$
LOOP
```

3. *Verifying that numeric fields are truly numeric.* Many operations require valid numeric data. Of course, BASIC can do the checking. The statement

```
INPUT "ENTER A NUMBER", Num
```

requests input of a numeric constant. If the user presses the wrong key or enters a comma, a dollar sign, or a percent sign, what should happen? As it stands, the BASIC message *Redo from start* will be printed. This is apt to confuse the noncomputer person running the program, as well as mess up a carefully formatted screen. A much better solution is to input numbers as strings so that anything is allowed. Then, in the program, check for valid numeric values and print a friendly message for invalid data. The BASIC statements to accomplish the checking will be covered in the upcoming section on string manipulation functions along with a way to convert strings to numbers.

4. *Consistency.* Check the consistency of one data item against another. This could include checking that the ending date of a series is later than the starting date; that the return time for a flight is after the departure time; that the returns of an item don't exceed the sales of that item; that date fields are checked for the correct number of days in each month; or that a baseball player is not awarded more hits than the number of times at bat.

```
INPUT "Number of times at bat", Atbat
INPUT "Number of hits", Hits
IF Hits > Atbat THEN
    PRINT "Error: Number of hits cannot exceed the number ";
    PRINT "of times at bat"
END IF
```

5. *Check digit calculations.* When accounting is primarily based on ID numbers such as credit card processing, a great potential for error exists. A one-digit error or a simple transposition can result in the wrong party receiving charges or credits. Many different schemes have been developed to check the validity of ID numbers. Each usually involves an arithmetic operation on the digits of the number. Then the result of the operation will be added as an extra digit to the ID number. An example of a check digit calculation will be shown later in this chapter in figure 7.5.

Output Formatting

There are several functions available for formatting output. Some, like TAB and SPC, may be used for screen or printer output. The most powerful formatting statement, LOCATE, can only be used on the screen.

Precise Cursor Placement

The LOCATE statement is used to place the cursor at any spot on the video display screen. It is generally executed just prior to a PRINT or INPUT statement. The location is an absolute row and column position—not relative to the prior location of the cursor.

The LOCATE Statement—General Form

```
LOCATE [row],[col][,cursor]
```

Row and *col* are integer values that specify the exact location on the screen for the cursor. Since the standard screen has 24 rows and 80 columns, *row* can have any value 1–24 and *col* must be in the range 1–80. Any fractional values for *row* or *col* will be rounded up.

The third parameter on the LOCATE statement controls the visibility of the cursor. If the value of CURSOR is 0, then the cursor will not be visible. If CURSOR is 1, the cursor is on. If the parameter is omitted, the cursor remains unchanged.

The LOCATE Statement—Examples

```
LOCATE 1,1
PRINT "This is the upper left-hand corner"

LET Row = 4
LET Col = 20
LOCATE Row, Col
PRINT "THIS WILL APPEAR AT VERTICAL POSITION 4, HORIZONTAL POSITION 20"
```

Figure 7.1 shows the cursor position at LOCATE 4,20. Other variations are possible. Either the row or the column may be omitted. In that case, the current value is used.

```
LOCATE N
```

Move the cursor to row N, keeping the same column.

```
LOCATE ,C
```

Move the cursor to column C, without changing the current row.

```
LOCATE ,,0
```

This will make the cursor invisible, and leave its position unchanged.

Be aware that executing a LOCATE and PRINT will not clear the screen prior to execution. Any old data will remain where it was with the exception of the new characters printed. This can be disconcerting at times, if you are expecting to completely replace data on the screen. When a short string is printed in the same location as a longer one, for example, the excess characters from the first string will still appear. It may be necessary to erase areas of the screen by printing a string of blank spaces.

```
'*************** Blank Out Line on Screen ***************
LOCATE 5, 10
PRINT "                                               "
'************* Now Input At The Same Location *************
LOCATE 5, 10
INPUT "Name: ", Nam$
```

This will move the cursor to row 5, column 10 and blank out the space on the line. (Most likely there was another name in the spot from a prior iteration of the program.) Then, the cursor is placed back in the same spot. The input prompt "Name:" will begin on line 5, column 10.

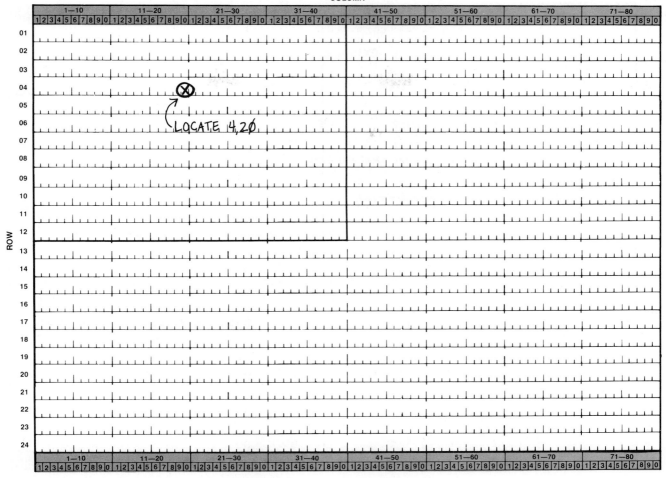

COLUMN

LOCATE 4,20

ROW

Figure 7.1
Screen layout showing cursor
location. The statement
LOCATE 4,20 will place the
cursor at row 4, column 20 on
the screen.

There can be many advantages to having the line not clear when new data is printed. A data entry form can be constructed on the screen with titles for all fields (see figure 7.2). Those titles can remain in place, with only the data fields changing. Try drawing a box on the screen and change the contents of that box. LOCATE will handle these situations beautifully.

Feedback

1. Using the LOCATE statement, write the statements necessary to print your name in the exact center of a clear screen.
2. Using the LOCATE statement, write the statements necessary to clear the screen and draw a box (using asterisks) in the center of the screen. Then place the cursor inside the box, and INPUT a number.

String Manipulation to Assist Screen Formatting

Joining Strings— Concatenation

Strings may be joined together by using the plus sign (+) to form longer strings. This joining is called **concatenation.**

```
LET A$ = "They shoot horses "
LET B$ = "don't they?"
LET C$ = A$ + ", " + B$
PRINT C$
```

Program Execution:

```
They shoot horses, don't they?
```

String Manipulation Functions

BASIC supplies many *functions* that provide a means for performing operations. The functions presented thus far include INT, TAB, SPC and UCASE$. A function can be thought of as a prewritten subroutine, which accomplishes one operation. Functions are used within other BASIC expressions, either string or numeric.

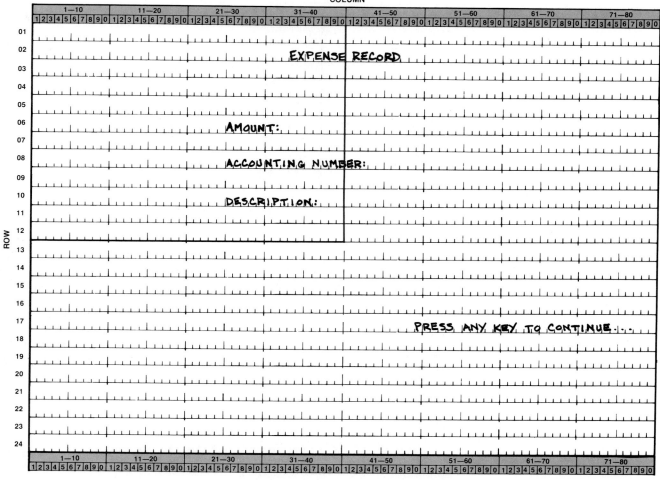

COLUMN

EXPENSE RECORD

AMOUNT:

ACCOUNTING NUMBER:

DESCRIPTION:

PRESS ANY KEY TO CONTINUE....

Figure 7.2
Data entry form drawn on the screen. Input will always appear in the same location.

SPACE$

The SPACE$ function is similar to the SPC function, since both produce a series of spaces. But SPACE$ does not have the limitation of always having to be included in a PRINT or LPRINT statement. SPACE$ may also be used to assign blank spaces to a string variable.

The SPACE$ Function—General Form

```
SPACE$(number of spaces)
```

The SPACE$ Function—Examples

```
PRINT SPACE$(15); "THIS IS IT"
LET Empty$ = SPACE$(40)
LET Draw$ = "XXX"+SPACE$(20)+"XXX"+SPACE$(20)+"XXX"
```

STRING$

Another function, which resembles SPACE$ and may prove useful in formatting output, is STRING$. This function produces a series of identical characters of the desired length.

The STRING$ Function—General Form

```
STRING$(length, character)
```

The STRING$ Function—Examples

```
PRINT STRING$(40,"*")

LET Star$ = STRING$(40,"*")

'**** Underline Columns of Data ****
LET ColWidth = 15
LET LineChar$ = "_"
LET Lin$ = STRING$(ColWidth, LineChar$)
PRINT TAB(10); Lin$; SPC(5); Lin$; SPC(5); Lin$
```

The first example will print forty asterisks on the screen. The second example assigns a string of forty asterisks to the variable Star$, presumably to print at a later point in the program. The technique shown in the third example can be used to underline columns of data.

The length specified in the STRING$ function may be a constant, a numeric variable, or an arithmetic expression. The character to duplicate may be given as a string literal, as a string variable, or as the number indicating the position in the ASCII coding sequence. For example, the ASCII code number for the asterisk is 42, so the first example given could have been written

```
PRINT STRING$(40,42)
```

Both statements have the same effect.

```
'*** A Pretty Screen, By Any Name ***
LET Lin$ = STRING$(80, "*")
LET Border$ = "**" + SPACE$(76) + "**"
CLS
PRINT Lin$;
PRINT Lin$;
LET Row = 3
DO WHILE Row < 22
    PRINT Border$;
    LET Row = Row + 1
LOOP
PRINT Lin$;
PRINT Lin$;
LOCATE 12, 36
PRINT "Hi, Mom"
```

What do you think the result would be if the semicolons were not placed at the end of each PRINT?

Formatting a Screen for Data Entry

When designing the layout for a screen, a layout form can be extremely helpful. See the example in figure 7.3. To use the form for data entry, these steps are necessary.

1. Draw the form on the screen.
2. Input the data.
3. Clear the data areas on the screen.

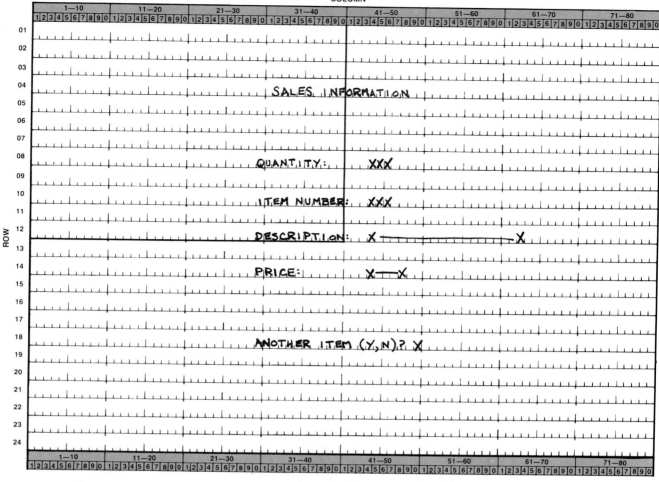

Figure 7.3
Using a screen layout to design
a data entry screen.

Example Program:
Inputting Data Using a Formatted Screen

Program Listing

```
' Program To Demonstrate Formatted Screen Data Entry
'  Inputs Data From Screen And Prints A Simple Report

'      Variables Used

'      Quan            Quantity
'      Item            Item number
'      Desc$           Item description
'      Price           Item price
'      Ans$            Answer - to continue

'*************** Program Mainline ************************

GOSUB PrintFormOnScreen
DO
   GOSUB InputData
   GOSUB CalculateTotal
   GOSUB PrintDetailLine
   GOSUB ClearDataFields
LOOP WHILE UCASE$(Ans$) = "Y"
END
```

184

```
'********************* Print Form on Screen *********************
PrintFormOnScreen:
  CLS
  LOCATE 4, 32
  PRINT "SALES INFORMATION"
  LOCATE 8, 30
  PRINT "QUANTITY:"
  LOCATE 10, 30
  PRINT "ITEM NUMBER:"
  LOCATE 12, 30
  PRINT "DESCRIPTION:"
  LOCATE 14, 30
  PRINT "PRICE:"
  LOCATE 18, 30
  PRINT "ANOTHER ITEM (Y/N)"
RETURN

'********************* Input Data *********************

InputData
  LOCATE 8, 44
  INPUT "", Quan
  LOCATE 10, 44
  INPUT "", Item
  LOCATE 12, 44
  INPUT "", Desc$
  LOCATE 14, 44
  INPUT "", Price
  LOCATE 18, 48
  INPUT Ans$
RETURN

'********************* Calculate Total *********************

CalculateTotal:
  LET Total = Quan * Price
RETURN

'********************* Print Detail Line *********************

PrintDetailLine:
  LPRINT Quan, Item, Desc$, Price, Total
RETURN

'********************* Clear Data Fields *********************

ClearDataFields:
  LOCATE 8, 44
  PRINT SPACE$(10)
  LOCATE 10, 44
  PRINT SPACE$(10)
  LOCATE 12, 44
  PRINT SPACE$(30)
  LOCATE 14, 44
  PRINT SPACE$(10)
  LOCATE 18, 48
  PRINT SPACE$(10)
RETURN

'********************* End of Program *********************
```

SALES INFORMATION

QUANTITY: 14

ITEM NUMBER: 234

DESCRIPTION: BED KNOBS

PRICE: 1.25

ANOTHER ITEM (Y/N) ? Y

SALES INFORMATION

QUANTITY: 21

ITEM NUMBER: 32

DESCRIPTION: TOE WARMERS

PRICE: .75

ANOTHER ITEM (Y/N) ? N

Figure 7.4
Screen output produced by
sample program.

Notice the INPUT statements in the InputData subroutine. The "empty prompt" was used to eliminate the question mark generated by an INPUT statement. See figure 7.4 for screen output.

More String Manipulation

When checking for valid input data, it is important to be able to check each individual character. Numeric data should be input as a string, checked for validity, and then converted to numeric form. The tools to implement this validity checking are presented in the sections following.

LEN

The number of characters in a string can be found with the LEN function.

The LEN Function—General Form

```
LEN(string)
```

The LEN Function—Examples

```
LET Count = LEN(A$)
PRINT TAB(20-LEN(C$)); C$
LET Vline$ = STRING$(LEN(K$), "-")
```

The second statement will right-justify C$ at print position 20. The last line assigns to Vline$ a series of dashes the same length as K$.

Any spaces embedded within a string are counted in the length of the string.

```
LET A$ = "PEACE OF MIND"
LET A = LEN(A$)
PRINT "THE LENGTH OF "; A$; " IS"; A
```

Program Execution:

```
THE LENGTH OF PEACE OF MIND IS 13
```

LEFT$

The function LEFT$ is used to extract characters from the left end of a string.

The LEFT$ Function—General Form

```
LEFT$(string, number of characters)
```

The LEFT$ Function—Examples

```
PRINT LEFT$("Hello", 4)
LET B$ = LEFT$(A$, N)
DO WHILE LEFT$(X$, 1) = "Y"
```

The LEFT$ function returns a string of the specified length.

```
Assume that P$ = "WASTE NOT WANT NOT"
Then LEFT$(P$, 1) is W
     LEFT$(P$, 5) is WASTE
     LEFT$(P$, 9) is WASTE NOT
```

A common use for LEFT$ is in checking a response when YES or NO is requested.

```
INPUT "DO YOU WISH TO CONTINUE"; Ans$
DO WHILE LEFT$(Ans$, 1) = "Y"
::
::
```

This will allow entry of Y or YES (or YEP or YESSIREE).

LEFT$ can be combined with UCASE$ to allow either upper- or lower-case entry.

```
DO
   ::
   ::
   INPUT "Any more"; Ans$
LOOP UNTIL LEFT$(UCASE$(Ans$), 1) = "Y"
```

RIGHT$

This function is used to extract characters from the right end of a string.

The RIGHT$ Function—General Form

```
RIGHT$(string, number of characters)
```

The RIGHT$ Function—Examples

```
LET B$ = RIGHT$(D$, 4)
IF RIGHT$(X$, 2) = "ED" THEN ...
```

Each of these "picks off" characters from the right end of the string.

```
If P$ = "WASTE NOT WANT NOT"
then RIGHT$(P$, 1) is T
     RIGHT$(P$, 3) is NOT
     RIGHT$(P$, 7) is ANT NOT
```

MID$

The MID$ function extracts characters from anywhere within a string. The starting location is given, and a count of the number of characters wanted.

The MID$ Function—General Form

```
MID$(string, starting location [,number of characters])
```

The MID$ Function—Examples

```
LET S$ = MID$(R$, 2, 4)
PRINT MID$(K$, B, N)
IF MID$(D$, 2, 1) = "," THEN ...
LPRINT MID$(N$, LEN(N$)/2)
```

When the third argument (number of characters) is missing, as in the last statement above, the MID$ function returns the rest of the string, beginning at the starting location.

```
If T$ = "A STITCH IN TIME SAVES NINE"
then MID$(T$, 3, 6) is STITCH
     MID$(T$, 8, 6) is H IN T
     MID$(T$, 18, 4) is SAVE
     MID$(T$, 18)    is SAVES NINE
     MID$(T$, 5, 4) is ITCH
```

Notes on string functions

1. If the starting location or number of characters is a fractional value, it will be rounded to the nearest whole number.
2. If the number of characters specified for LEFT$ or RIGHT$ is greater than the number of characters in the string, the entire string is returned.

MID$ Statement

MID$ may be used as a statement to replace characters in strings.

The MID$ Statement—General Form

```
MID$(string1, starting location [, number of characters]) = string2
```

The MID$ Statement—Examples

```
LET A$ = "XXXXX"
MID$(A$, 3) = "O"

LET D$ = "WATER"
MID$(D$, 2, 4) = "INE "
```

The first example changes A$ from XXXXX to XXOXX. The second example changes WATER into WINE.

VAL

The VAL function is used to convert a string value into a numeric value. The number 123 can be assigned to a numeric variable or a string variable.

```
LET V = 123
LET V$ = "123"
```

In order to do any arithmetic operations with the value, however, the numeric variable must be used.

The VAL Function—General Form

```
VAL(string)
```

The digits in the string will be converted to their numeric value. If there is a mixture of numeric digits and other characters in the string, VAL starts its conversion at the left and continues until the first nonnumeric character is found. In the event the first character of the string is not numeric, zero will be returned. The VAL function will accept a leading sign (if present), a decimal point, and the ten numeric digits (0–9).

The VAL Function—Examples

```
LET Amt = VAL(A$)
IF VAL(S$) = 0 THEN PRINT "NOT A VALID NUMBER"
PRINT TAB(40 - LEN(N$)); VAL(N$)
```

Statement: PRINT VAL(A$)

Value of A$	Printed
"1234"	1234
"+1.2B"	1.2
" -4C"	-4
"1 2 3"	123
"ABC"	0

An important use of the VAL function occurs during data validation. In order to properly check for *any* input values, numeric digits must be input into strings. After the validation, the data must be converted to a numeric value for computations.

```
INPUT "Enter number", Num$
GOSUB ValidateNumber
LET Num = VAL(Num$)
```

Numeric Validity Checking

Numeric data can now be INPUT as a string and checked for valid numeric characters, one digit at a time. To determine the number of digits to check, use the LEN function. For checking each character, the MID$ function allows selection of each digit individually. Once the data has been determined to be numeric, the VAL function will be used to place the digits into a numeric variable.

Example Subroutines: Numeric Validity Checking

Program Listing

```
'This program Asks The User To Input A Non-Negative Integer,
Then
'Checks Each Character To See That The Input Was Valid

'Variables Used

'NumAmt$    String value input by the user
'NumAmt     User input converted to its numeric equivalent
'P          Number of digits to check
'ValidSw    Switch for validity checking
```

```
'********************** Program Mainline **********************
CLS
DO
    INPUT "Type a non-negative integer: ", NumAmt$
    LET ValidSw = 1                    'Assume data good until proven bad
    GOSUB ValidateInput
    IF ValidSw = 0 THEN
            PRINT "Invalid entry...try again."
            PRINT
    ELSE
            LET NumAmt = VAL(NumAmt$)    'Convert to a numeric value
    END IF
LOOP UNTIL ValidSw = 1                  'Continue until data passes test
PRINT
PRINT "Congratulations...You Did It!"
END

'********************** Validate Input **********************

ValidateInput:

    LET P = LEN(NumAmt$)
    DO WHILE P > 0 AND ValidSw = 1
    IF MID$(NumAmt$, P, 1) < "0" OR MID$(NumAmt$, P, 1) > "9" THEN
            LET ValidSw = 0
    END IF
    LET P = P - 1                       'Prepare to check the next digit
    LOOP
RETURN
'********************** End of Program **********************
```

STR$

STR$ does the reverse operation of VAL. STR$ takes a numeric value and converts it into a string. The primary use for this function is to allow for the use of the string manipulation functions such as LEN or MID$.

The STR$ Function—General Form

```
STR$(numeric expression)
```

The STR$ Function—Examples

```
LET K$ = STR$(K)
LET L = LEN(STR$(Amt))
```

The last statement may return a slightly different value than expected. When Amt is converted to a string, the first character is reserved for the sign. If Amt is a negative number, the first character is a minus sign. When Amt is a positive number, the first character is a blank. In either case (blank or —), that first character is included in the length of the string.

More Handy String Functions

INSTR

The INSTR function searches a string for the occurrence of a second string. The value returned is the position within the first string where the second string begins.

The INSTR Function—General Form

```
INSTR([starting position,] string, string to search for)
```

The starting position may be omitted, in which case the entire string is searched. When the search is unsuccessful—that is, the second string is not found within the first string—the function returns zero.

The INSTR Function—Examples

```
LET Pointer = INSTR(Primary$, Search$)
LET C = INSTR(N, Nam$, ",")
```

INSTR may be used to count the occurrences of a substring (the second string) within the primary string.

Sample Program Output

```
Type a non-negative integer: Hello
Invalid entry...try again.

Type a non-negative integer: 12.5
Invalid entry...try again.

Type a non-negative integer: -16
Invalid entry...try again.

Type a non-negative integer: 123x45
Invalid entry...try again.

Type a non-negative integer: 1234

Congratulations...you did it!
```

Example Program:
Counting Occurrences of a Substring within a String

Program Listing

```
'**** Count Occurrences Of Substring Within String ****
INPUT "String"; A$
INPUT "Substring"; B$
LET P = 1                          'P is start position to check
DO
    LET N = INSTR(P, A$, B$)
    IF N <> 0 THEN
        LET Count = Count + 1
    END IF
    LET P = N + 1
LOOP UNTIL N = 0
PRINT B$; " occurred"; Count; "times in "; A$
END
```

Program Execution:

```
String? ABRACADABRA
Substring? A
A occurred 5 times in ABRACADABRA
```

Program Execution:

```
String? ABRACADABRA
Substring? BRA
BRA occurred 2 times in ABRACADABRA
```

At times, it is necessary to reverse the name within a string. If the name is stored as SMITH, JOHN, it may be preferable to print JOHN SMITH. Assume that names are stored LAST-NAME, FIRST-NAME. Use a combination of the string functions to place the names in the form FIRST-NAME LAST-NAME.

Example Program: Reversing Name Position

Program Listing

```
'**** Reverse Position Of Names ****
' P Used As A Pointer To The Position Of The Comma
READ Nam$
DO
   LET P = INSTR(Nam$, ",")
   LET Nam2$ = MID$(Nam$, P + 2) + " " + LEFT$(Nam$, P - 1)
   PRINT Nam$, Nam2$
   READ Nam$
LOOP UNTIL Nam$ = "end"
DATA "Last, First", "Jones, Pat", "Horton, Eric", "end"
END
```

Program Execution:

```
Last, First    First Last
Jones, Pat     Pat Jones
Horton, Eric   Eric Horton
```

CHR$

You have already seen the use of CHR$(12) to eject a page on the printer. In general, the CHR$ function returns one character specified by its number in the ASCII coding sequence. This can be useful when a character is required that is not on the keyboard of the computer you are using.

The CHR$ Function—General Form

```
CHR$(code number)
```

The CHR$ Function—Examples

```
PRINT CHR$(7)
PRINT CHR$(34); "HELLO,"; CHR$(34); " HE SAID"
```

These two examples show solutions to problems frequently encountered. The first example prints character 7, which is the bell (or speaker) on most computers. This will cause the bell to sound—perhaps for an error condition or a game. The second example solves a sticky problem. Since quotation marks are used to surround literals in a PRINT statement, how do you actually print quotation marks when needed? ASCII code 34, the quotation mark, does just what is wanted. The following two statements will give identical results, since ASCII code 65 is the letter A.

```
PRINT CHR$(65)
PRINT "A"
```

ASC

The ASC function does the opposite operation of CHR$. For any character, it will return the ASCII code number.

The ASC Function—General Form

```
ASC(character)
```

The ASC Function—Examples

```
IF ASC(C$) < 32 THEN
    PRINT "UNPRINTABLE CHARACTER"
END IF

IF ASC(D$) < 48 OR ASC(D$) > 57 THEN
    PRINT "NOT A VALID NUMERIC DIGIT"
END IF
```

The ASC function returns the decimal number corresponding to the character's position in the ASCII code. Referencing the chart in appendix D, all code numbers less than 32 are nonprinting control characters. There are times these codes need to be sent to a terminal or printer, however. Code 12 is a form-feed character. When the statement

```
LPRINT CHR$(12);
```

is executed, most printers will advance to the top of the next page (assuming the paper is correctly set).

LCASE$ and UCASE$

The twin functions LCASE$ and UCASE$ provide the capability to change the case of any string. LCASE$ returns the string converted to lower-case, while UCASE$ (which we have been using since chapter 3) returns the upper-case version of the string.

The LCASE$ and UCASE$ Functions—General Form

```
LCASE$(string)
UCASE$(string)
```

The LCASE$ and UCASE$ Functions—Examples

```
LET Upper$ = UCASE$("make my day")
DO WHILE LCASE$(Ans$) = "y"
PRINT UCASE$(Nam$)
LET Sentence$ = UCASE$(LEFT$(Text$,1))+LCASE$(MID$(Text$,2))
```

Free-Form Keyboard Entry

BASIC has two ways to allow characters to be input from the keyboard without the necessity of pressing RETURN/ENTER. These two statements, INKEY$ and INPUT$, have some things in common. Both return the key pressed as a string character, and neither **echoes** (displays) that character on the screen. This could be handy for passwords when screen display is not wanted. Both statements also cause the cursor to become invisible. To overcome that inconvenience, use the LOCATE statement. Recall from the discussion of LOCATE that LOCATE, , 1 makes the cursor visible.

There are some important differences between INKEY$ and INPUT$. INKEY$ does not halt program execution, but simply checks to see if there has been any key pressed lately. This could be useful for game playing, when the player presses keys during execution of the program. INPUT$ *does* halt program execution, similar to the INPUT statement. Another significant difference is that INPUT$ allows for input of multiple characters, while INKEY$ inputs a single keyboard character.

The INKEY$ Function—General Form

```
LET  string variable  =  INKEY$
```

When INKEY$ is used, the keyboard buffer is checked. If any key has been pressed, its value is placed into the variable named in the LET statement. The string returned will have a length of 0, 1, or 2 characters:

0—If no key has been pressed, the null string (of zero length) is returned.
1—The actual character pressed on the keyboard is placed in a one-character string.
2—Two-character strings are returned when the key pressed was one of the special control keys such as the cursor movement keys. See your system manual for this option.

The INKEY$ Function—Example

```
LET  X$  =  INKEY$
```

Since INKEY$ does not halt program execution, it is often used in a loop.

```
'**** Keep Printing Until A Key Is Pressed ****
PRINT "Press any key to stop program"
DO
    PRINT "This is a Test of the Emergency Broadcasting System"
    LET A$ = INKEY$
LOOP WHILE A$ = ""
```

The loop condition could also be written as:

```
DO WHILE LEN(A$) = 0
```

The INPUT$ Function—General Form

```
LET  string variable  =  INPUT$(number of characters)
```

INPUT$ will halt program execution and await the number of keystrokes specified. When the characters have been pressed, the string will then be assigned to the variable named. The RETURN/ENTER key is not required.

The INPUT$ Function—Examples

```
LET  V$  =  INPUT$(1)
LET  K$  =  INPUT$(N)
LET  R$  =  INPUT$(4)
```

When a screen full of data has been printed, the user needs a chance to read it before continuing. Print the message *Press any key to continue* to allow the user to control execution. The INPUT$ function accomplishes this task nicely.

```
PRINT "Press any key to continue"
LET X$ = INPUT$(1)
           .
           .
           .
```

(continue with program)

In this example, X$ is a **dummy variable,** since it doesn't matter what value it has, and it won't be used anywhere else.

Inputting Strings of Data with the INPUT$ Function

Since INPUT$ does not echo the characters on the screen, it may be necessary for the program to do so.

```
'**** Keyboard Entry Of A String Using INPUT$ ****
LOCATE ,, 1
LET Long$ = ""                      'Turn on the cursor
DO
    LET P$ = INPUT$(1)              'Get one character
    PRINT P$;                       'Echo on screen
    IF P$ <> CHR$(13) THEN
        LET Long$ = Long$ + P$      'Tack character onto string
    END IF                          'Keep going until Enter key pressed
LOOP UNTIL P$ = CHR$(13)
PRINT
PRINT Long$
```

More on Numeric Validity Checking

You now have more tools that will allow greater flexibility in numeric validity checking. Some programmers prefer to print an error message or sound the bell as an inappropriate key is pressed; others wait for the Enter key. Another approach is to "throw away" any bad characters and accept only the good ones.

Example Programs: Checking for "Good" and "Bad" Characters

Program Listing

```
'**** Check Each Good Character And Ignore Bad Ones ****

CheckGoodCharacter:
    LOCATE ,, 1                          'Set cursor to visible
    LET Invar$ = ""                      'Clear out string to begin
    LET C$ = INPUT$(1)                   'Get first character to get started
    DO
        IF ASC(C$) >= 48 AND ASC(C$) <= 57 THEN
            GOSUB SaveAndPrintGoodCharacter
        END IF
        LET C$ = INPUT$(1)
    LOOP UNTIL C$ = CHR$(13)             'Get next character from keyboard
    LET Invar = VAL(Invar$)              'Convert string to numeric value
    PRINT Invar                          'Let's see our good number
RETURN

'**** Save And Print Good Character ****

SaveAndPrintGoodCharacter:
    LET Invar$ = Invar$ + C$             'Tack character onto string
    PRINT C$;                            'Echo on screen
RETURN
```

```
'*** Check Each Character and Sound Bell for Bad Ones ***
CheckEachCharacter:
    LOCATE ,, 1                  'Set cursor to visible
    LET Invar$ = ""              'Clear out string to begin
    LET C$ = INPUT$(1)           'Get first character to get started
    DO
        IF ASC(C$) >= 48 AND ASC(C$) <= 57 THEN
            GOSUB SaveAndPrint
        ELSE
            GOSUB BadCharacter
        END IF
        LET C$ = INPUT$(1)       'Get next keyboard character
    LOOP UNTIL C$ =CHR$(13)
    LET Invar = VAL(Invar$)      'Convert string to numeric value
    PRINT Invar                  'Let's see our good number
RETURN

'*** Save and Print Good Characters ***

SaveAndPrint:
    LET Invar$ = Invar$ + C$     'Tack character onto string
    PRINT C$;                    'Echo on screen
RETURN

'*** Bad Character ***

BadCharacter:
    PRINT CHR$(7);               'Ring the bell
RETURN
```

If you prefer to wait until the entire input is entered before printing the error message, use the INPUT statement. Check the characters with MID$. See the example shown earlier in this chapter (p. 188).

Inputting Strings with the LINE INPUT Statement

An interesting situation can arise when a user types a response to an INPUT statement, such as

```
INPUT "Enter your answer", Answer$
```

With practically any response, the INPUT statement will execute correctly and the program proceed as expected. However, if the user enters a comma, BASIC interprets that as the separator between responses and stops the program with the error message *Redo from start*. You can eliminate this run-time error by using the LINE INPUT statement rather than the INPUT statement:

```
LINE INPUT "Enter your answer"; Answer$
```

With the LINE INPUT statement, an entire line of characters (including commas) is input into a string variable. All characters typed, up until the Enter key, are assigned to the string variable.

The LINE INPUT Statement—General Form

```
LINE INPUT [;] ["literal prompt";] stringvariable
```

The LINE INPUT Statement—Examples

```
LINE INPUT Address$
LINE INPUT "Enter address "; Address$
LINE INPUT; "Enter a sentence"; Sent$
```

Each of these examples will assign to the variable named all characters entered until the ENTER key is pressed. The extra semicolon in the last example suppresses the line feed and carriage return, which normally occur following keyboard entry. This might be helpful with formatted screens, to prevent scrolling.

Retrieving the Date and Time

The current system date and time can be retrieved by a BASIC program. Naturally, the computer operating system must have been set previously to the correct date and time.

The DATE$ Function—General Form

```
DATE$
```

DATE$ is a variable that returns the current date in a ten-character string in the form mm–dd–yyyy. The first two digits are the month, then a dash, then two digits for the day, another dash, and the year in the form 19xx.

For example, if the date is July 4, 1999, then DATE$ will return 07–04–1999.

The DATE$ Function—Examples

```
LET DA$ = DATE$
PRINT DATE$
```

Parts of the date may be used for other operations.

```
LET Month$ = LEFT$(DATE$, 2)
LET Year$ = RIGHT$(DATE$, 4)
LET Day$ = MID$(DATE$, 4, 2)
```

Or, if the values are needed in a numeric operation:

```
LET Month = VAL(LEFT$(DATE$, 2))
LET Year = VAL(RIGHT$(DATE$, 4))
LET Day = VAL(MID$(DATE$, 4, 2))
```

The TIME$ Function—General Form

The variable TIME$ will return an eight-character string in the form hh:mm:ss, in twenty-four-hour notation. The first two characters (hh) represent the hour (00–23); mm represents the minutes (00–59); ss represents the seconds (00–59).

When the TIME$ function is executed, the current value of the system clock will be placed in the variable. If it is 8:01 A.M., TIME$ will yield 08:01:00. For 8:01 P.M., you will see 20:01:00.

The TIME$ Function—Examples

```
LET T$ = TIME$
PRINT TIME$
LET Sec$ = RIGHT$(TIME$, 2)
```

Parts of the time may be accessed:

```
LET Hr = VAL(LEFT$(TIME$, 2))
LET Min = VAL(MID$(TIME$, 4, 2))
LET Sec = VAL(RIGHT$(TIME$, 2))
LET TotSec = Sec + Min * 60 + Hr * 3600
```

The keyword TIMER returns a time-related number; it is the number of seconds elapsed since last midnight. Or, if your computer has no clock capability, it is the number of seconds since it was turned on.

The TIMER Function—General Form

```
TIMER
```

The TIMER Function—Examples

```
LET Start = TIMER
  .  .  .  .  .
  .  .  .  .  .
  .  .  .  .  .
Let Finish = TIMER
Let ElapsedTime = Finish - Start
```

Table 7.1 summarizes the string manipulation functions.

Feedback

1. When might it be necessary to use this statement?

   ```
   LOCATE ,,1
   ```

2. How many ways can you think of to print a line of forty equal signs on the screen?
3. How can you find out the number of digits in a numeric variable?
4. What is the most likely situation to require the use of the VAL function?
5. Name one reason for using INKEY$ rather than INPUT.
6. Name one reason for using INKEY$ rather than INPUT$.
7. Name one reason for using INPUT$ rather than INKEY$.
8. Write the statements necessary to READ this series of words (until END is encountered) and print each word right-justified at column 30.

   ```
   DATA FIG, WATERMELON, PINEAPPLE, PLUM, MANGO, END
   ```

9. What will print when these statements are executed?

   ```
   LET A$ = "GOOD GRIEF"
   PRINT MID$(A$,4,1) + MID$(A$,2,1) + LEFT$(A$,1)
   ```

10. Write the statements necessary to print all characters following the period in P$. Assume that there will always be one and only one period in the string.
11. Write the statements necessary to print all characters following the period in P$. This time, do not assume that there will always be a period. If there is no period in the string, print nothing.
12. Write the statements necessary to advance the printer paper to the top-of-form.
13. Using INPUT$, keep inputting characters until an asterisk is entered. Echo all characters except the asterisk on the screen.

Check Digit Calculation

Many credit card companies and other institutions use a check digit to ensure validity of the account numbers. The check digit calculation is designed to catch errors in keying such as transpositions or misstrikes.

Table 7.1
Summary of string manipulation functions.

Function	Description
ASC(X$)	Returns the number corresponding to the ASCII code for the first character of X$. Reverse of CHR$ function.
CHR$(n)	Returns the string character that corresponds to the ASCII code n. Reverse of ASC function.
DATE$	Retrieves the system date, as a ten-character string in the form mm–dd–yyyy.
INKEY$	Allows keyboard entry of a single character without the RETURN key being pressed. Does not halt program execution.
INPUT$(n)	Allows keyboard entry of n characters without the RETURN key being pressed. Halts program execution to await entry.
INSTR([pos,]X$,X2$)	Searches for the occurrence of the substring X2$ in X$, starting at position *pos*. If *pos* is omitted, the start position is 1. Returns a numeric value that is the position where the substring begins; returns 0 if the substring is not found.
LCASE$(X$)	Returns the lower-case equivalent of X$.
LEFT$(X$,n)	Returns the leftmost n characters of X$.
LEN(X$)	Returns the length of X$ (a count of the number of characters in the string).
MID$(X$,pos[,n])	Extracts n characters from X$, starting at position *pos*. When n is omitted, the rest of the string, beginning at position *pos,* is returned.
RIGHT$(X$,n)	Returns the rightmost n characters of X$.
SPACE$(n)	Returns a string of blank spaces of n length.
STR$(n)	Returns the string value of the numeric expression. Used to convert numeric values to strings. Reverse of VAL function.
STRING$(n,C$)	Returns a string of length n, filled with the character named. The character may be a variable, a literal enclosed in quotes, or the ASCII code for the character.
TIME$	Retrieves the system time as an eight-character string in a twenty-four-hour format, in the form hh:mm:ss.
TIMER	Returns number of seconds since last midnight.
UCASE$	Returns the upper-case equivalent of X$.
VAL(X$)	Returns the numeric value of X$. Used to convert strings to numeric values. Reverse of STR$ function.

As a memory aid, it should be noted that all function names containing a dollar sign return a string value, and those function names not containing a dollar sign return a numeric value.

Many different algorithms have been devised for generating check digits. The general plan is to perform a calculation on the digits of the ID number. Then, the results of that calculation are appended to the ID number as an extra digit. Each time an ID number is used, the calculation can be performed to verify that the number is valid. (See figure 7.5.)

Figure 7.5
Check digit calculation.

SAMPLE CHECK DIGIT ALGORITHM

1. Double every other digit
2. Add the digits together
3. Use the right-most character of the sum as the check digit.

ID NUMBER	CHECK DIGIT CALCULATION	NEW ID NUMBER
45261	$4 + (5 \times 2) + 2 + (6 \times 2) + 1 = 29$	452619
54261	$5 + (4 \times 2) + 2 + (6 \times 2) + 1 = 28$	542618
45621	$4 + (5 \times 2) + 6 + (2 \times 2) + 1 = 25$	456215

Example Subroutines: Check Digit Calculation

Each time an ID number is entered, the program will calculate the check digit. If it matches, the ID number passes; if not, an error message is generated.

Program Listing

```
'****************** Check Digit Calculation *******************
CheckDigitCalculation:
   LET ValidSw = 0                              'switch OFF to start
   DO WHILE ValidSw = 0
      INPUT "Enter ID number ", IdNo
      GOSUB CheckValidity
      IF ValidSw = 0 THEN
         PRINT "Invalid ID number, reenter "
      END IF
   LOOP
RETURN

'**** Check Validity ****

CheckValidity:
   LET ID$ = STR$(IdNo)
   LET D1 = VAL(MID$(ID$, 2, 1))
   LET D2 = VAL(MID$(ID$, 3, 1))
   LET D3 = VAL(MID$(ID$, 4, 1))
   LET D4 = VAL(MID$(ID$, 5, 1))
   LET D5 = VAL(MID$(ID$, 6, 1))
   LET D6 = VAL(MID$(ID$, 7, 1))
   LET Check = D1 + (D2 * 2) + D3 + (D4 * 2) + D5
   LET Check = VAL(RIGHT$(STR$(Check), 1))
   IF Check = D6 THEN
      LET ValidSw = 1
   END IF
RETURN
```

Programming Example

As an example of an interactive program with screen formatting and validity checking, a math drill program will be developed. The user will be asked to enter the number to be practiced. Then the entire set (1–12) will be produced. A correct answer will produce the message RIGHT, while an incorrect (or invalid) response will cause TRY AGAIN to appear. The user will be allowed to quit (by entering Q) after each problem. When the set (1–12) is complete, the user may select a new set or quit.

This program is one that suggests many further enhancements, such as multiple messages and random selection of the problems. These will be left as an exercise for the programmer. (The random number function, RND, in chapter 10 could prove helpful.)

Input

1. Number to select problem set (validate for numeric and 1–12)
2. Answer to problem (validate for numeric)

Output

1. The problem
2. Messages for right or wrong answer

Processing

1. Check for correct answer
2. Validate all input
3. Hold messages on screen until a key is pressed
4. Blank out all messages

Pseudocode

Main Program

1. Print title
2. Select number
3. Math drill
4. Print ending message

Select Number Subroutine

2.1   Input a number
2.2   DO Loop until number found valid
    2.2.1   Validate number
    2.2.2   If not valid then
          print a message
          re-enter number
2.3   Return

Math Drill Subroutine

3.1 DO Loop until "Q" entered (once for each set)
    3.1.1   Begin problems in set with 1
    3.1.2   DO Loop until problem 12 or "Q" entered
        3.1.2.1 Print problem on screen
        3.1.2.2 Input the answer
        3.1.2.3 Validate answer
        3.1.2.4 If answer correct then
                print "RIGHT"
                else print "TRY AGAIN"
        3.1.2.5 Wait for keypress
        3.1.2.6 Clear out message areas
    3.1.3   End loop for set
    3.1.4   Choose a new set
3.2 Return

Hierarchy Chart   See figure 7.6.

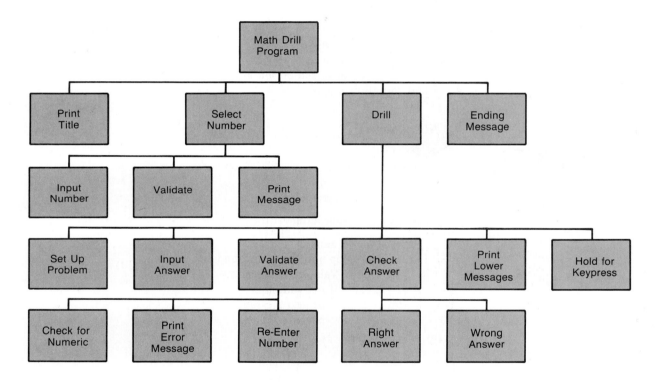

Figure 7.6
Hierarchy chart for math drill
program.

Flowchart   Refer to figure 7.7.

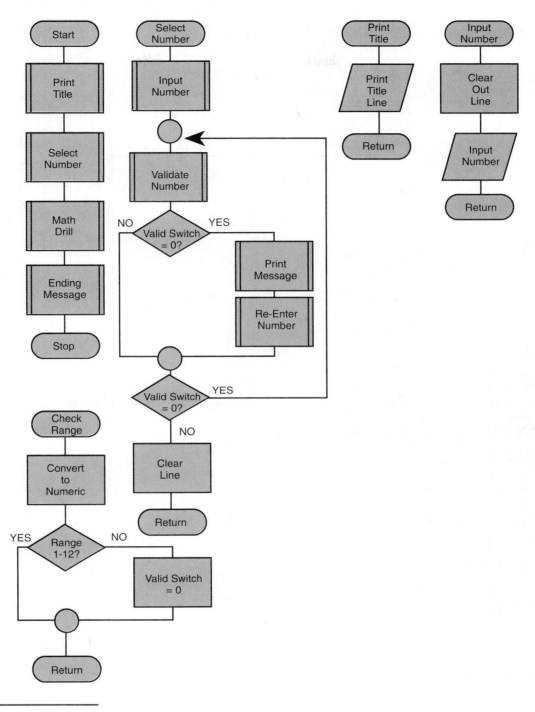

Figure 7.7
Flowchart for math drill
program.

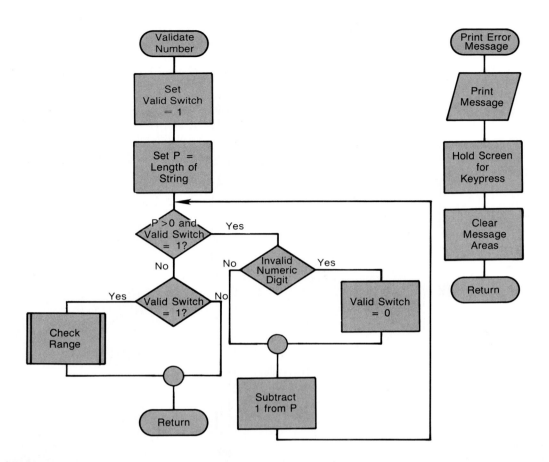

Figure 7.7—*Continued*

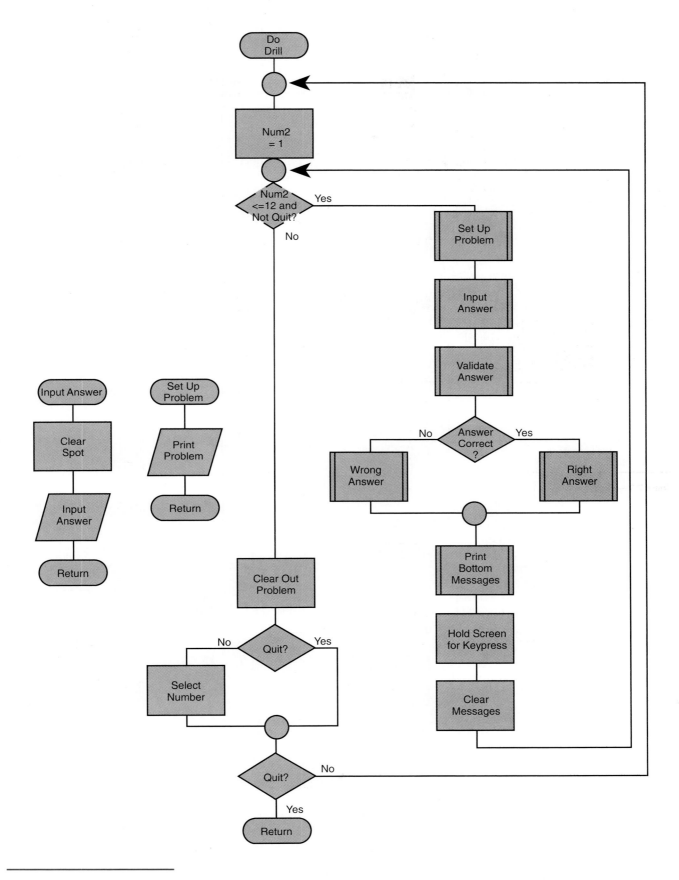

Figure 7.7—*Continued*

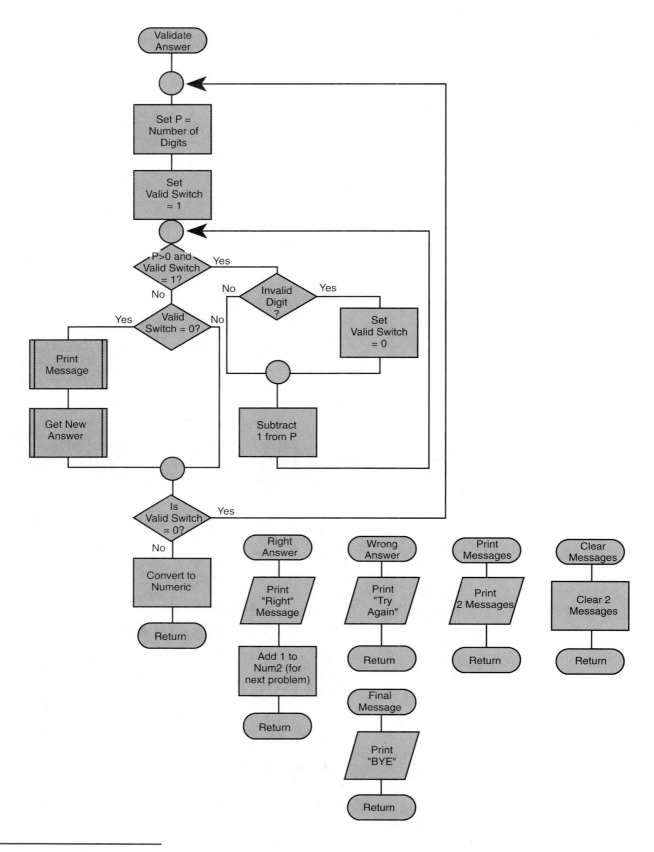

Figure 7.7—*Continued*

Program Listing

```
'Interactive Program To Practice Multiplication Tables
'  All Screens Formatted To Not Allow Scrolling

'        Variables Used

'        Num1$             Number to use for multiplier string form
'        Num1              Number to use for multiplier numeric form
'        Num2              Second number
'        P                 Digit position for checking number
'        Ans$              Answer to problem string form
'        Ans               Answer to problem numeric form
'        Res$              Response to message for quit
'        ValidSw           Switch for validity checking
'                                  1 = valid, 0 = invalid


'***************** Program Mainline *********************

GOSUB PrintTitles
GOSUB SelectNumber
GOSUB DoDrill
GOSUB SayGoodbye
END

'***************** Print Titles *************************

PrintTitles:
   CLS
   LOCATE 2, 20
   PRINT "M U L T I P L I C A T I O N    T A B L E S"
RETURN

'***************** Select Number ************************

SelectNumber:
   GOSUB InputNumber
   DO
      GOSUB ValidateNumber
      IF ValidSw = 0 THEN
         GOSUB PrintErrorMessage
         GOSUB InputNumber
      END IF
   LOOP UNTIL ValidSw = 1
   LOCATE 8, 22
   PRINT SPACE$(40)                   'Clear out the line
RETURN

'***************** Input the Chosen Number **************

InputNumber:
   LOCATE 8, 22
   PRINT SPACE$(40)                   'Clear out the line
   LOCATE 8, 22
   INPUT "WHAT NUMBER DO YOU WANT TO PRACTICE"; Num1$
RETURN

'***************** Validate Number **********************

ValidateNumber:
   LET ValidSw = 1       'Assume OK until proven bad
   LET P = LEN(Num1$)    'Find number of digits to check
   DO WHILE P > 0 AND ValidSw = 1
      IF MID$(Num1$, P, 1) < "0" OR MID$(Num1$, P, 1) > "9" THEN
         LET ValidSw = 0
      END IF
      LET P = P - 1                   'Check next digit
   LOOP
   IF ValidSw = 1 THEN
      GOSUB CheckRange
   END IF
RETURN
```

```
'****************** Check Range *****************************

CheckRange:
   LET Num1 = VAL(Num1$)                'Convert to numeric
   IF Num1 < 1 OR Num1 > 12 THEN
      LET ValidSw = 0
   END IF
RETURN

'***************** Print Error Message *********************

PrintErrorMessage:
   LOCATE 11, 29
   PRINT "I CAN'T DO THAT NUMBER"
   LOCATE 13, 32
   PRINT "I ONLY KNOW 1-12"
   GOSUB PrintBottomMsg
   LET Res$ = INPUT$(1)
   GOSUB ClearBottomMsg
   LOCATE 11, 29
   PRINT SPACE$(22)
   LOCATE 13, 32
   PRINT SPACE$(16)
RETURN

'******************** Do Drill ***************************

DoDrill:
   DO
      LET Num2 = 1                      'Start drill at 1
      DO WHILE Num2 <= 12 AND Res$ <> "Q"
         GOSUB SetupProblem
         GOSUB InputAnswer
         GOSUB ValidateAnswer
         IF Ans = Num1 * Num2 THEN
            GOSUB RightAnswer
         ELSE
            GOSUB WrongAnswer
         END IF
         GOSUB PrintBottomMsg
         LET Res$ = INPUT$(1)           'Get one char from keyboard
         LOCATE 12, 35
         PRINT SPACE$(9)                'Clear out messages
         GOSUB ClearBottomMsg           'Clear out bottom messages
      LOOP
      LOCATE 9, 35
      PRINT SPACE$(15)
      IF Res$ <> "Q" THEN
         GOSUB SelectNumber
      END IF
   LOOP UNTIL UCASE$(Res$) = "Q"
RETURN

'***************** Setup Problem ***********************

SetupProblem:
   LOCATE 9, 35
   PRINT Num1; "X"; Num2; "="
RETURN
```

```
'****************** Input Answer ****************************

InputAnswer:
    LOCATE 9, 44
    PRINT SPACE$(10)              'Clear out spot
    LOCATE 9, 44
    INPUT Ans$                    'Input the answer
RETURN

'****************** Validate Answer **********************

ValidateAnswer:
    DO                                  'To begin loop
        LET P = LEN(Ans$)               'To find number of digits
                                        '   to check
        LET ValidSw = 1                 'Set to good before check
        DO WHILE P > 0 AND ValidSw = 1
            IF MID$(Ans$, P, 1) < "0" OR MID$(Ans$, P, 1) > "9" THEN
                LET ValidSw = 0
            END IF
            LET P = P - 1
        LOOP
        IF ValidSw = 0 THEN
            GOSUB WrongAnswer
            GOSUB InputAnswer
        END IF
    LOOP WHILE ValidSw = 0
    LET Ans = VAL(Ans$)
RETURN

'****************** Right Answer **************************

RightAnswer:
    LOCATE 12, 35
    PRINT "RIGHT!"
    LET Num2 = Num2 + 1              'Go on to next number
RETURN

'****************** Wrong Answer **************************

WrongAnswer:
    LOCATE 12, 35
    PRINT "TRY AGAIN"
RETURN

'****************** Print Bottom Message ****************

PrintBottomMsg:
    LOCATE 21, 46
    PRINT "PRESS ANY KEY TO CONTINUE ..."
    LOCATE 23, 50
    PRINT "PRESS Q TO QUIT ..."
RETURN

'****************** Clear Bottom Message ****************

ClearBottomMsg:
    LOCATE 21, 46
    PRINT SPACE$(30)
    LOCATE 23, 50
    PRINT SPACE$(20)
RETURN
```

```
'******************* Say Goodbye ***************************

SayGoodbye:
    CLS
    LOCATE 10, 38
    PRINT "GOODBYE"
RETURN

'****************** End of Program **********************
```

Sample Program Output

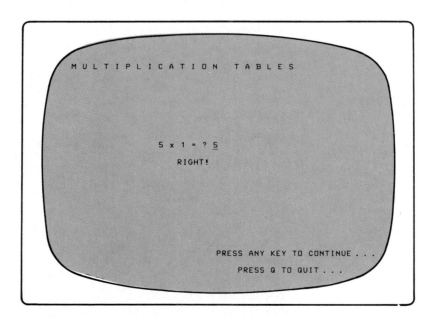

Summary

1. "Good" programs make it easy for users to enter correct data and difficult for them to make errors.
2. Program output should be in terms that a noncomputer person will understand. Never use computer jargon or program variable names in program output.
3. Format screen output pleasingly, with each item of data in the same location each time it appears.
4. Check input data for validity whenever possible.
5. GIGO means *Garbage In, Garbage Out.* Good validity checking can keep most garbage out of programs.
6. Range checking involves checking high and/or low limits for input values.
7. Many times data input must match preset values such as codes. Input data can be checked to verify that a match is found.
8. Try to shield the user from cryptic system errors such as *Redo from start* or *Type mismatch.* Whenever possible, allow the user to enter any value as a response. Then, have the program trap any errors and print friendly explanations.
9. Many times the value of one field can be compared to another for consistency.
10. A technique used for verifying the validity of ID numbers is called check digit calculation.
11. Ask an inexperienced computer user to test your programs.
12. The LOCATE statement is a powerful statement for formatting screen output. The internal print pointer is moved to an absolute row and column position on the screen.
13. LOCATE is generally used just prior to a PRINT statement.
14. Placing program output with the LOCATE statement does not erase the screen. This allows for placing new data intermixed with output previously written.
15. The visibility of the cursor can also be controlled with the LOCATE statement.
16. BASIC has many functions for manipulating string data.
17. Strings may be joined together, or added, in an operation called concatenation.
18. The SPACE$ function returns a string of blank spaces of the specified length.
19. A string of identical characters of any length (up to 255 characters) may be generated with the STRING$ function.
20. The LEN function can be used to determine the length of a string.
21. There are three functions that provide a means to extract a substring from a larger string. These are LEFT$, RIGHT$, and MID$.
22. LEFT$ returns a given number of characters from the left end of a string, while RIGHT$ takes characters from the right end of the string.
23. MID$ provides a way to extract any number of characters from anywhere in the string.
24. The VAL function is used to convert a string into its numeric equivalent. A popular use for VAL is in the editing of input data. Numeric input can be INPUT into strings, validated, and then converted to numeric variables.
25. STR$ converts a numeric expression into a string. STR$ is the opposite operation of VAL.
26. In order to search for the occurrence of one string (called the substring) within another string, the INSTR function is used. INSTR can search for one single character, for a whole word, or for a longer series of characters and spaces.
27. To use the CHR$ function, you must provide an ASCII code number. The function returns the corresponding character.
28. To use the ASC function, you specify a character. The ASC function returns the corresponding ASCII code number. ASC and CHR$ perform opposite operations.

29. The UCASE$ and LCASE$ functions can be used to change the case of strings. UCASE$ returns all uppercase; LCASE$ returns all lowercase.
30. There are two functions that provide a way to read the keyboard without requiring the RETURN/ENTER key. These two functions are INKEY$ and INPUT$. Neither function echoes the character on the screen.
31. INKEY$ takes a character from the keyboard buffer without halting program execution. If no key has been pressed, a null string (empty string) is returned. INKEY$ is generally used in a loop to keep checking for a keypress.
32. INPUT$ halts program execution and awaits keyboard entry, similar to the INPUT statement. For INPUT$, the number of characters to return is specified, while INKEY$ always returns one character.
33. The LINE INPUT statement can input any characters including commas and quotes into a string variable.
34. The system date and time can be retrieved with the DATE$ and TIME$ functions.

Programming Exercises

7.1. Modify the program in exercise 6.3 (student grade report, p. 166) to request input data from the keyboard, rather than use DATA statements. Verify that student ID, course ID, and number of units are valid numeric digits. The only acceptable values for the letter grade are A, B, C, D, F, I (incomplete), or W (withdrawal). The acceptable range for number of units is .5 to 5.0.

Design test data to verify that all data is correctly validated and that any error messages are cleared from the screen after the data is corrected.

7.2. Modify the program in exercise 6.1 (employee gross pay report, p. 164) to input the number of hours worked. Verify that the number of hours is a valid numeric value. Company policy does not allow working more than 50 hours per week. Verify that the hours do not exceed 50. DATA statements will still be used to enter the employee name, department number, and pay rate. Design test data to verify that all input data is correctly validated and that any error messages are cleared from the screen after the data is corrected.

7.3. Write an interactive program that will count the number of words in a sentence. The user will be prompted to type a sentence terminated by a period (*not* the ENTER key). Use the INPUT$ function to input characters, one at a time, until the period is entered. Each character must be echoed (printed) on the screen. Count the number of words (by checking for a blank character). When the entire sentence has been entered, print the sentence on the printer along with the word count. Continue inputting and printing sentences until the ENTER key is pressed.

SAMPLE PROGRAM OUTPUT:

```
TYPE A SENTENCE, TERMINATED BY A PERIOD.
    The quick brown fox jumped over the lazy dog's
back and ran after the three little pigs.
WORD COUNT = 17
```

7.4. Modify the program in exercise 7.3 to allow the user to erase a character by pressing the backspace key. (Hint: The backspace key sends CHR$(8) to the program.) To erase a character on the screen, a blank character must be printed.

7.5. Write a program that will find all words in a list beginning with a selected prefix (one or more characters).

INPUT: The user will be prompted to enter the prefix (letter or letters) for which to search. Read the list of words from DATA statements.

OUTPUT: Print the list of words that begin with the requested prefix. At the conclusion of the list, print the count of the words found.

PROCESSING: Count the number of words that begin with the selected prefix. After the count is printed, the user should be given the opportunity to enter a new prefix and to begin the search again.

TEST DATA: List of words for DATA statements.
ANIMALS, ANT, TAN, AUNT, ANTEATER, BANTER, LANTERN, PLEASANT

PROGRAM EXECUTION: Search for all words beginning with *A,* then search for the words beginning with *ANT.*

7.6. Write a program that will count all occurrences of the letter combination *ON* in a list of words.

INPUT: The list of words will be read from DATA statements.

OUTPUT: A count of the number of times the letters *ON* are found in the list.

PROCESSING: After reading each word, check for all occurrences of the *ON* combination. If the letter combination *ON* appears more than once in a word, it should be counted each time.

TEST DATA: List of words for DATA statements.
CONVERT, TON, BUN, NOPE, NONE, ONLY, ONE, ONION, AND, MARTIAN, MOON, MOUNTAIN

7.7. Write a program that will count the number of times one particular letter appears in a paragraph. The paragraph may be entered with a LINE INPUT statement. (Recall that the maximum length of a string variable is 32, 767 characters.)

INPUT: Request the paragraph and the search character.

OUTPUT: A count of the number of times the selected letter appears in the paragraph.

TEST DATA: Test your program by counting the number of times the letter *P* appears in this paragraph. Be sure to count both upper-case and lower-case characters.
Peter Piper picked a peck of pickled peppers. A peck of pickled peppers, Peter Piper picked. If Peter Piper picked a peck of pickled peppers, where's the peck of pickled peppers Peter Piper picked?

7.8. Write a program that will produce the following output by using the LEFT$ function.

```
O
ON
ONO
ONOM
ONOMA
ONOMAT
ONOMATO
ONOMATOP
ONOMATOPO
ONOMATOPOE
ONOMATOPOEI
ONOMATOPOEIA
```

7.9. Write a program using the MID$ and INSTR functions that will print only the last name when you input the first name, middle initial, and the last name.

7.10. Write a program using the STRING$ function to produce the following output. Erase the screen when a key is pressed.

```
* *
* * * *
* * * * * *
* * * * * * * *
* * * * * * * * *
* * * * * * * * * * *
* * * * * * * * * * * * *
* * * * * * * * * * * * * * *
```

7.11. Write a program using the MID$ function to produce the following output.

```
FUSSBUDGET
USSBUDGET
SSBUDGET
SBUDGET
BUDGET
UDGET
DGET
GET
ET
T
```

7.12. Write a program to print all of the characters from CHR$(128) to CHR$(255) on the screen.

7.13. Write a program to check input for a valid password. Use data validation to allow only alphabetic input.

INPUT: A password will be input from the keyboard.
OUTPUT: Print the message "VALID PASSWORD" or "INVALID PASSWORD" on the screen depending on the input.
PROCESSING: Use the INPUT$ function to validate input data. Make sure the input word is a valid password from the list.

VALID PASSWORDS

SPUD	KARATE	SHORT
BANANA	WORK	SWEET
HELP	FAST	WORD

7.14. Modify the program in exercise 2.15 (Perfect Picture bonus program, p. 58) to include data validation.

INPUT: The store number, name of employee number 1, name of employee number 2, total hours worked for employee number 1, total hours worked for employee number 2, store's sales goal, and actual sales will be input from the keyboard.
OUTPUT: See exercise 2.15.
PROCESSING:
1. Use the INPUT$ function and validate the input.
2. Total hours worked, store's sales goal, and actual sales goal should be validated as numeric fields.
3. Allow for the backspace or back arrow keys to be pressed in order to correct mistakes.

7.15. Write a program that produces a customer account number that consists of the first three digits of the last name, the first two digits of the first name, the zip code, and the last four digits of the address.

INPUT: Customer name, address, city, state, zip code, and phone number will be input from the keyboard.

OUTPUT: The customer name and account number should be printed on the screen with appropriate headings.

PROCESSING: All data should be validated.

8 Text Graphics, Color, and Sound

WIDTH Statement
KEY Statement
COLOR Statement
BEEP Statement
PLAY Statement
SOUND Statement

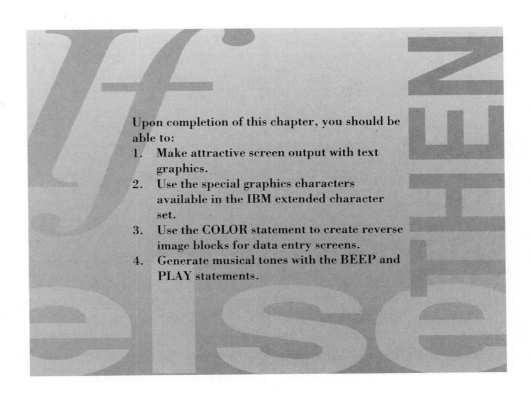

Upon completion of this chapter, you should be able to:

1. Make attractive screen output with text graphics.
2. Use the special graphics characters available in the IBM extended character set.
3. Use the COLOR statement to create reverse image blocks for data entry screens.
4. Generate musical tones with the BEEP and PLAY statements.

Text Graphics

There is more than one way to draw a picture. In this chapter, we will create graphics with text characters such as letters, digits, and special characters such as % # *] [. We will also use some additional characters called the IBM Extended Graphics Character Set.

Another way to draw pictures is to draw with individual dots (called **pixels**). Pixel graphics are covered in chapter 16.

The Text Screen

Until this point we have used a screen size of twenty-four lines of eighty characters each. But that is not the only choice. There is a twenty-fifth line on the screen that behaves differently than lines 1–24. Line twenty-five does not scroll like the other twenty-four lines. Whatever you print on the twenty-fifth line will "stay put," while lines 1–24 will scroll off the top of the screen when additional lines are printed.

The number of characters per line is selectable. We may choose to have either the normal eighty characters or forty larger ones. The WIDTH statement controls the number of characters on a line.

Characters may be placed anywhere on the screen with combinations of LOCATE and PRINT statements. You may refer to chapter 7 for a review of the LOCATE statement.

The WIDTH Statement—General Form

```
WIDTH 40
    or
WIDTH 80
```

The WIDTH Statement—Examples

```
WIDTH 40 'Change display screen to 40-column mode
WIDTH 80 'Change display screen to 80-column mode
```

Simple graphics may be created by printing letters on the screen.

Example Program:
Creating Graphics with Characters

Program Listing

```
'*************** Create Graphics With Characters ***************
CLS                         'Clean screen
WIDTH 40                    'Select wide characters
PRINT
PRINT " H     H  EEEEEE  L        L          OOO   "
PRINT " H     H  E       L        L         O   O  "
PRINT " HHHHHH   EEEE    L        L        O     O "
PRINT " H     H  E       L        L         O   O  "
PRINT " H     H  EEEEEE  LLLLLL   LLLLLL     OOO   "
END
```

Note: Wide characters appear on the screen, but not on the printer.

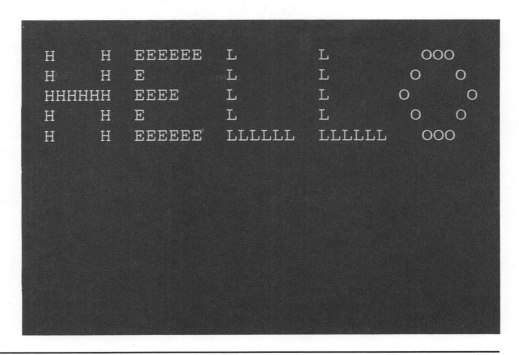

The Extended Graphics Character Set

The standard ASCII character set is made up of 128 characters. Some computer and printer manufacturers have developed their own, nonstandard additions to the ASCII code, to take advantage of special features of the hardware or to create special shapes to be used for foreign language symbols, mathematical symbols, and graphics. The IBM Extended Graphics Character Set, available with QuickBASIC, allows for many special shapes to be printed in text mode. See appendix C for a complete list of these special characters. Although the special characters are not on the keyboard, they may be printed by using the CHR$ function.

> *Note:* Not all printers are capable of printing the extended graphics characters. The printer must be dot matrix and support the IBM character set. Some printers have several modes and require a special control code to enable the IBM set. See your printer manual and appendix H for sending control codes.

Sample Graphics Characters

```
' Some of the graphics characters available in text mode
CLS
PRINT CHR$(191), CHR$(192), CHR$(193), CHR$(247), CHR$(219)
PRINT CHR$(194), CHR$(195), CHR$(168), CHR$(224), CHR$(225)
PRINT CHR$(3),   CHR$(4),   CHR$(5),   CHR$(6),   CHR$(251)
```

Program Execution:

Lines, boxes, and pictures can be drawn using combinations of the graphics characters.

Example Program:
Creating a Box with Graphics Characters

```
'Program To Display A Box On The Screen,
'    Using Special Graphics Characters

'        Variables Used

'        Uplft$              Upper left corner
'        Uprgt$              Upper right corner
'        Lolft$              Lower left corner
'        Lorgt$              Lower right corner
'        Vert$               Vertical line
'        Horiz$              Horizontal line
'        Margin              Distance to tab to center the box
'        Tall                Counter for height of box
'        Wide                Width of box
'****************** Initialize Print Strings ************

CLS
LET Uplft$ = CHR$(201)
LET Uprgt$ = CHR$(187)
LET Lorgt$ = CHR$(188)
LET Lolft$ = CHR$(200)
LET Vert$ = CHR$(186)
LET Horiz$ = CHR$(205)

'***************** Set Up Box Size *********************

INPUT "Enter width in characters (1-79)"; Wide
INPUT "Enter height in characters"; Tall
LET Margin = (80 - Wide) / 2
WIDTH 80

'***************** Print the Box *********************

CLS
PRINT TAB(Margin); Uplft$ + STRING$(Wide - 2, Horiz$) + Uprgt$
LET Tall = Tall - 2          'subtract for top and bottom lines
DO WHILE Tall > 0
    PRINT TAB(Margin); Vert$ + SPACE$(Wide - 2) + Vert$
    LET Tall = Tall - 1
LOOP
PRINT TAB(Margin); Lolft$ + STRING$(Wide - 2, Horiz$) + Lorgt$
END

'***************** End of Program *********************
```

Using Graphics Characters to Draw a Figure

This program uses a selectable graphics character to draw a figure. The shape of the figure is stored in DATA statements, in which each pair of numbers denotes a starting position and number of characters. Note that a screen layout form was used to plan the output.

Example Program:
A Company Logo Drawn with Graphics Characters

Program Listing

```
'*************** Draw A Picture With Characters ***************

LET Pic$ = CHR$(178)              'Select character to draw with
CLS                               'Clean screen
READ Start, Length
DO WHILE Start <> 0 AND Length <> 0
   PRINT TAB(Start);
   DO WHILE Length > 0
     PRINT PIC$;
     LET Length = Length - 1
   LOOP
   READ Start, Length
LOOP
'**** Data For Company Logo ****
DATA 18, 5, 17, 7, 16, 3, 21, 3, 14, 4, 21, 26, 14, 3, 21, 26, 14
DATA 4, 21, 3, 40, 5, 16, 7, 36, 11, 18, 4, 36, 5, 44, 4, 36, 2
DATA 39, 2, 43, 2, 46, 2, 0, 0
```

Program Output

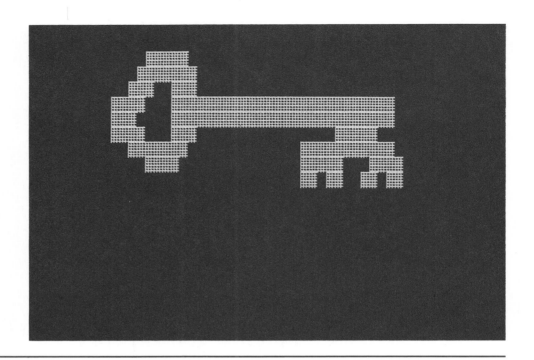

Producing the Extended Graphics Characters with the Keyboard

As we have seen, the extended graphics characters can be printed using the CHR$ function. It is also possible to produce the characters directly on the screen using the ALT key in combination with the numeric keypad. Holding down the ALT key, press the numbers corresponding to the ASCII code for the desired character. Example: To produce a solid block (ASCII code 219):

> Press and hold down the ALT key
> Press 2 (on the numeric keypad)
> Press 1 (on the numeric keypad)
> Press 9 (on the numeric keypad)
> Release the ALT key
> *(Note that the numeric keys on the top row of the keyboard will not produce the same results.)*

Using the ALT key method to produce the extended graphics characters allows their use in source listings. This can dress up our programs with fancy remarks, as well as show the actual characters to print for program output.

Program Listing

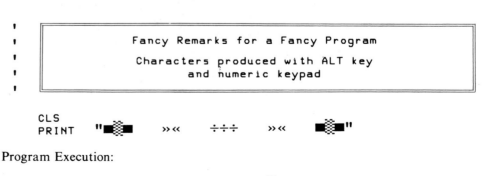

Program Execution:

A Bar Chart Program, Drawn with Graphic Characters

This simplified Bar Chart program demonstrates the use of graphic characters to make solid bars. A more comprehensive version, including scaling and colored bars, is found later in this chapter.

Example Program:
A Bar Chart Using Text Graphics

Program Listing

```
'   Program To Print A Bar Chart, Using Graphic Text Characters
'
'       Variables Used
'
'   Pic$                Character used to print bars for chart
'   Month$              Names of months, from DATA list
'   HowMany             Number of hamburgers sold for each month
'   Count               Counter for loops
'
'**************** Program Mainline **********************

LET Pic$ = CHR$(219)        'Select print character
GOSUB PrintHeading          'Print heading
GOSUB PrintDetail           'Print detail data
GOSUB PrintScale            'Print scale
END


'********************* Print Heading ********************

PrintHeading:
   CLS
   LOCATE 4, 25
   PRINT "HAMBURGER SALES"
   PRINT
   PRINT
   PRINT
RETURN


'********************* Print Detail *********************

PrintDetail:
   READ Month$, HowMany
   DO WHILE Month$ <> "END"
      PRINT Month$; TAB(10);              'Month name
      LET Count = 1
      DO WHILE Count <= HowMany
         PRINT Pic$;                      'Print the bar
         LET Count = Count + 1
      LOOP
      PRINT
      PRINT
      READ Month$, HowMany
   LOOP
RETURN
```

```
'********************* Print Scale *********************
PrintScale:
    PRINT TAB(9); CHR$(179);                'Start scale line
    LET Count = 1
    DO WHILE Count <= 14
        PRINT STRING$(4, 196); CHR$(179); 'Segments of line
        LET Count = Count + 1
    LOOP
    PRINT TAB(5);
    LET Count = 0
    DO WHILE Count <= 70
        PRINT USING "   ##"; Count;            'Print numbers
        LET Count = Count + 5
    LOOP
RETURN

'**************** Data For Hamburger Sales ****************
DataForHamburgerSales:
    '* Caution: numbers must be < 72 in this program.
    '* Scaling to graph variable size data appears in chapter 16
    DATA JUNE,40,JULY,70,AUGUST,55,SEPTEMBER,30,END,0
'********************* End of Program *********************
```

Program Output

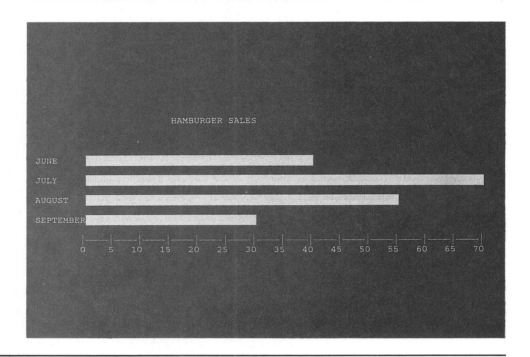

Color

You can control the color of text and graphic characters that you display on the screen. You can even use the COLOR statement on a black-and-white monitor to control such text attributes as high intensity, blinking, underlining, reverse image (black characters on a white background), and invisible (black characters on a black background).

With a color monitor and an appropriate adapter card, beautiful text is possible. The foreground (text) may be displayed in any of sixteen colors, the background in any of eight colors, and the border area around the edge of the screen in any of sixteen colors. Additionally, the foreground characters can be made to blink, for a total of thirty-two possible color choices. Table 8.1 shows these thirty-two color possibilities.

Table 8.1

Color available in low resolution text mode.

Color Number	Color	Color Number	Color
0	Black	16	Blinking black
1	Blue	17	Blinking blue
2	Green	18	Blinking green
3	Cyan	19	Blinking cyan
4	Red	20	Blinking red
5	Magenta	21	Blinking magenta
6	Brown	22	Blinking brown
7	White	23	Blinking white
8	Gray	24	Blinking gray
9	Light blue	25	Blinking light blue
10	Light green	26	Blinking light green
11	Light cyan	27	Blinking light cyan
12	Light red	28	Blinking light red
13	Light magenta	29	Blinking light magenta
14	Yellow	30	Blinking yellow
15	High-intensity white	31	Blinking high-intensity white

Some experimentation is necessary to select the best color combination for any monitor, as their adjustments may differ. You may want to try different combinations to find those most pleasing to you.

Use the COLOR statement to select the colors to display. You may select any of the thirty-two color choices shown in the table for the foreground. You can choose colors 0–7 for the background and colors 0–15 for the border. The border color does not display on monochrome or higher resolution color monitors.

BASIC can display colors in several different screen modes. In this chapter, only the text mode color is presented. Higher resolution graphics and their use of color are covered in chapter 16.

Each text character is drawn with dots in a block that is eight dots wide by eight dots tall. The dots that form the character itself are called the **foreground.** The dots surrounding the character are called the **background.**

The COLOR Statement in Low-Resolution, Text Mode—General Form

```
COLOR   [Foreground][,[Background][,Border]]
```

When any parameter is omitted that selection will remain unchanged. The *Border* parameter is valid for CGA hardware only. EGA, VGA, and MCGA do not support the border color.

```
COLOR 7,0      'White characters on black background
COLOR 15,1     'High-intensity white on blue background
COLOR 4        'Red characters, unchanged background
COLOR ,3       'Unchanged foreground, cyan background
COLOR ,,2      'Unchanged foreground and background,
               'green border
COLOR 0,7      'Reverse image, black characters on
               'white background
```

The sequence of your BASIC statements is important when you use COLOR statements. When you want to change the color of the entire screen, place a COLOR statement before a CLS statement:

```
COLOR 7, 1     'White foreground, blue background
CLS            'Changes screen color to blue
```

Any text that you print displays in the foreground color of the last COLOR statement executed:

```
COLOR 1, 0     'Blue foreground, black background
PRINT "This text is blue"
COLOR 2, 0     'Green foreground, black background
PRINT "This text is green"
```

The Bar Chart Program Revisited

With the addition of color, the bar chart program can be upgraded to be more visually pleasing. We have added scaling to the program, so that the chart will fill the screen even with very large or small numbers.

Example Program:
A Bar Graph Using Text Graphics and Color

Program Listing

```
'Program to Print a Bar Chart, Using Color Text Characters
'With Added Capabilities for Variable Scaling

'               Variables used

'      Pic$              Character used to print bars for chart
'      Month$            Names of months, from Data list
'      HowMany           Number of hamburgers sold for each month
'      Count             Counter for loops
'      MaxSales          Highest value to graph
'      ScaleFactor       Ratio to fit values on screen
'      Pretty            Color number for bars


'***************** Program Mainline ***************
GOSUB Initialize
GOSUB PrintHeadings
GOSUB PrintBarChart
GOSUB PrintScale
END
```

```
'****************** Initialize *********************
Initialize:
   LET Pic$ = CHR$(29)                'Character to use for bars
   LET MaxSales = -1
   READ Month$, HowMany               'Read data list
   DO UNTIL Month$ = "END"
      IF HowMany > MaxSales THEN
         LET MaxSales = HowMany
      END IF
      READ Month$, HowMany
   LOOP
   LET ScaleFactor = MaxSales / 70 'Scale to 70 characters on screen
   RESTORE                            'Reset data pointer
RETURN

'****************** Print Heading ******************
PrintHeadings:
   CLS
   LOCATE 4, 25
   PRINT "HAMBURGER SALES"
   PRINT
   PRINT
   PRINT
RETURN

'****************** Print A Bar Chart *************
PrintBarChart:
   READ Month$, HowMany
   DO UNTIL Month$ = "END"
      LET Pretty = Pretty + 1
      COLOR Pretty
      PRINT Month$; TAB(10);
      FOR Count = 1 TO INT(HowMany) / (ScaleFactor + .5)
         PRINT Pic$;                        'Print the bar
      NEXT Count
      PRINT
      PRINT
      READ Month$, HowMany
   LOOP
RETURN

'****************** Print Scale ******************
PrintScale:
   COLOR 7, 0                'Return to black & white
   PRINT TAB(9); CHR$(179);  'Start scale line
   FOR Count = 1 TO 10
       PRINT STRING$(6, 196); CHR$(179); 'Segments of line
   NEXT Count
   PRINT TAB(3);
   FOR Count = 0 TO MaxSales STEP MaxSales / 10
       PRINT USING " #####"; Count;        'Print numbers
   NEXT Count
RETURN

'**************** Data For Hamburger Sales ***********
DATA JUNE,250,JULY,500,AUGUST,450,SEPTEMBER,200,END,0
'*********************** End of Program ***************************
```

Text Graphics, Color, and Sound   227

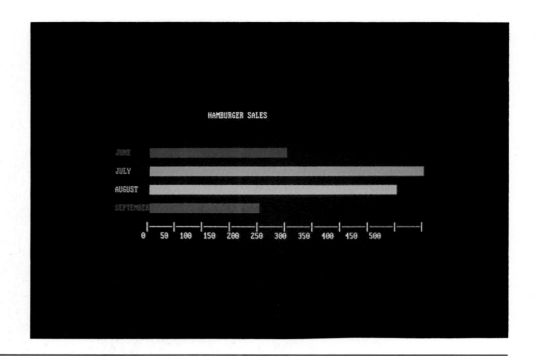

Color for Black-and-White Monitors

Although a black-and-white monitor cannot display in color, it can use the COLOR statement to control reverse image (black characters on a white background), high intensity, and invisible text (black on black).

Example Program: Color in Black and White

Program Listing

```
' Demonstrate Use of COLOR Statement for Black-and-White
Monitors
CLS
COLOR 0, 7              'Reverse image
PRINT "THIS IS REVERSE IMAGE"
COLOR 15, 0             'High intensity
PRINT "THIS IS HIGH INTENSITY"
COLOR 23, 0             'Blinking
PRINT "THIS IS A BLINKING LINE"
COLOR 31, 0             'Blinking high intensity
PRINT "THIS BLINKING LINE IS HIGH INTENSITY"
COLOR 7, 0             'Normal white on black
PRINT "ENTER YOUR PASSWORD ";
COLOR 0, 0             'Invisible
INPUT Password$
COLOR 7, 0             'Back to normal white on black
END
```

```
THIS IS REVERSE IMAGE
THIS IS HIGH INTENSITY
THIS IS A BLINKING LINE
THIS BLINKING LINE IS HIGH INTENSITY
ENTER YOUR PASSWORD ?
```

Reverse Image for Data Entry

When a user enters data into a screen, it is important to make the process as clear and easy as possible. One technique used for professional programs is to place a block on the screen where data is to be typed. This gives a clear indication of the location and length of required data. Printing spaces in reverse image gives a good-looking data entry block. In the example program segment that follows, note the technique used when the backspace key is pressed by the user.

Example Program: Using Reverse Image Blocks for Data Entry

Program Listing

```
' Use Reverse Image for Data Entry Areas
'       Uses COLOR statement on monochrome monitors
'
'*********** Print Data Entry Form **************************
CLS                                    'CLEAN SCREEN
LOCATE 10, 20
PRINT "Name:"
LOCATE 12, 20
PRINT "Telephone:"
COLOR 0, 7                             'Turn on reverse image
LOCATE 10, 40
PRINT SPACE$(20);                      'Print a bar for name
LOCATE 12, 40
PRINT SPACE$(15);                      'Print a bar for telephone
```

```
'************* Input Name ********************************
LOCATE 10, 40, 1                    'Place cursor for entry
LET Nam$ = ""
LET In$ = INPUT$(1)                 'Get one character
DO WHILE In$ <> CHR$(13)            'Check for return key
    IF In$ <> CHR$(8) THEN
        GOSUB GoodCharacter
    ELSE
        GOSUB EnterBackspaceCharacter       'Handle backspace character
    END IF
    LET In$ = INPUT$(1)             'Get one character
COLOR 7, 0                          'Return to normal print
END

'**************** Good Character ***************************

GoodCharacter:
    PRINT In$;                      'Echo character on screen
    LET Nam$ = Nam$ + In$           'Tack onto long string
RETURN

'**************** Backspace Character Entered ***************
EnterBackspaceCharacter:
    LET Nam$ = LEFT$(Nam$, LEN(Nam$) - 1)'Remove one character
    PRINT CHR$(29);                 'Move cursor back
    PRINT " ";                      'Print a space
    PRINT CHR$(29);                 'Replace cursor
RETURN
'********************** End of Program ***********************
```

Program Output

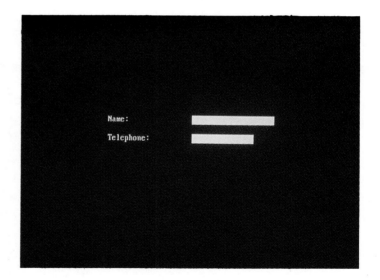

Sound

There are several statements available to make sounds. You can use the BEEP statement, which does just as the name implies. Or you can use more sophisticated statements like SOUND, PLAY, or ON PLAY to create more elaborate sounds. Music can be played in the background (at the same time other statements are executing) or in the foreground (completing execution before any other statements are executed). In this chapter we will cover only BEEP, SOUND, and some functions of PLAY. Consult the BASIC manual for more functions.

The BEEP Statement—General Form

```
BEEP
```

The BEEP Statement—Examples

```
BEEP                'Beep the speaker
PRINT CHR$(7);      'Exactly same effect as BEEP
IF ValidSw <> 1 THEN BEEP 'Beep on invalid data
```

The SOUND Statement—General Form

```
SOUND Frequency, Duration
```

The SOUND Statement—Examples

```
SOUND 262, 10       'Middle C

DO WHILE Frequency < 2500
    SOUND Frequency, .5
    Frequency = Frequency + 50
LOOP
```

The SOUND statement is used to accompany color and screen positioning to create lively and interesting programs, especially in input screens. For example, a correct input could be met with a happy sound, while an incorrect answer might result in a disappointing sound. The addition of SOUND can enhance utility as well as enjoyment for the user.

The values for both the frequency and sound must be unsigned numeric integers. The *frequency* is measured in hertz (cycles per second) and can range from 37 to 32,767. The *duration* is measured in clock ticks and can range from 0 to 65,535. There are 18.2 clock ticks per second, regardless of the CPU speed.

Frequencies for the SOUND statement, from a very low tone to a very high tone, are shown in table 8.2.

Table 8.2
Frequencies for the SOUND Statement.

A	55	110	220	440	880	1760	3520
A#	58	117	233	466	932	1857	3714
B	62	123	247	494	988	1976	3952
C	65	131	262	523	1046	2093	4186
C#	69	139	277	554	1109	2217	4434
D	74	149	294	587	1175	2349	4698
D#	78	156	311	622	1245	2489	4978
E	82	165	330	659	1319	2637	5274
F	87	175	349	698	1397	2794	5588
F#	93	185	370	740	1480	2960	5920
G	98	196	392	784	1568	3136	6272
G#	104	208	415	831	1661	3322	6644

Example Program: Segments Using SOUND

```
'*** Make a Happy Sound ***
LET Frequency = 50
LET Duration = .1

DO WHILE Frequency < = 5000
    SOUND Frequency, Duration
    LET Frequency = Frequency + 250
LOOP

'*** Make a Disappointing Sound ***
LET Frequency = 75
LET Duration = .1
LET Wavelength = 30
DO WHILE Frequency > 35
    SOUND Frequency, Duration
    LET Frequency = Frequency + Wavelength - 1
    LET Duration = Duration + .01
    LET Wavelength = Wavelength * - 1
LOOP

'*** Play the Scale ***
DO WHILE Count < 8
    READ Frequency
    SOUND Frequency, 5
    Count = Count + 1
LOOP

DATA 262, 294, 330, 349, 392, 440, 494, 523
```

PLAY

You can select actual notes to play with the PLAY statement. The music output sounds better on some computers than on others. However, without special equipment, none sounds like high-quality music.

The PLAY Statement—General Form

```
PLAY string
```

The PLAY statement takes its instructions from the characters included in the string, which may be a literal or variable. Some of the choices for this "tune definition language" are shown in figure 8.1. See the QB manual for more sophisticated commands, such as changing tempo.

The PLAY Statement—Examples

```
PLAY "O3 CDEFGAB O4 C"              'Scale in octave 3,
                                    'ending with C of octave 4
PLAY "MB O2 GFE-FGGG"               'Mary Had a Little Lamb
PLAY "C C+ D D+ E F F+ G G+ A A+ B" 'All notes in the
                                    'fourth octave
PLAY "L2 N40 L1 N42"                'Note 40 as a half-note,
                                    'note 42 as a whole-note
```

Figure 8.1
Tune definition for the PLAY
statement.

Tune Definition Language for the PLAY Statement

A to G, with optional ♯ , +, or −
Plays the indicated note. A sharp is indicated by ♯ or
+, a flat by −.

O n
Changes octave for the notes that follow. There are 7 octaves, numbered 0 to 6.
The default is Octave 4. Octave 3 begins with middle C.

L n
Sets the length for the notes that follow.
L1 Whole note
L2 Half note
L4 Quarter note (the default)
L8 Eighth note

P n
Pause (rest). The pause lengths are similar to the note lengths shown above.

T n
Sets the number of quarter notes in a minute, which may range from 32 to 255,
with default of 120.

MF
Plays music in the foreground (the default). This means that no other statements
will be executed until the music is finished.

MB
Music plays in the background, during execution of other statements. The notes
(up to 32) are placed in a buffer, and program execution continues.

N n
Plays a specific note, where n may range from 0 to 84. This is an alternate way of
selecting a note, rather than its octave (O n) and letter designation (A–G). Zero
represents a "rest," and the notes 1 to 84 select the possible notes in 7 octaves.

Feedback

1. How can you determine whether your printer is capable of printing the graphics characters?
2. How can the COLOR statement be used on a black-and-white monitor?
3. Why would it be unwise to draw a pie chart with text graphics?

Summary

1. Graphics may be created with text characters printed on the screen or printer.
2. The WIDTH statement can select either 40 or 80 characters per line on the screen.
3. There is a set of 128 graphics characters that may be displayed on the screen, as well as on some printers. Since these characters are not on the keyboard, they must be specified using the CHR$ function.
4. The COLOR statement can be used to display text in color, as well as to display special effects in black and white.
5. In low-resolution text operations, sixteen colors are available for the foreground (the text itself). Each of these colors can also be displayed as blinking, making a total of thirty-two colors.
6. The background (area around the text) can be displayed in any of eight colors.
7. On some monitors, a border can be specified in any of sixteen colors.
8. Black-and-white monitors are capable of displaying characters in reverse image, blinking, and high-intensity. These functions are controlled with the COLOR statement.
9. The SOUND statement generates tones, which can be used in programs to call attention to errors or reward correct responses.
10. The SOUND statement can be placed in loops, and the frequency and duration changed to create special effects.
11. BEEP sounds the computer's speaker.
12. Musical notes are played with the PLAY statement. A special "tune definition language" defines the notes to play.

Programming Exercises

8.1. Center your first name on the screen using the WIDTH and PRINT statements.

8.2. Using any graphic character you wish, draw a square on the screen.

8.3. Write a program to print ten graphic characters on the screen and beep after each one has been printed.

8.4. Use the PLAY statement to write a program to play all the notes in the third octave.

8.5. Write a program to create an input screen for the calculation of the markup on an item.

INPUT: Item description, retail selling price, and the cost of the item will be input from the keyboard. Use reverse image for the input fields.
OUTPUT: The item description, retail selling price, cost of the item, and the markup should be printed on the printer.
PROCESSING:
   1. Calculate markup = retail selling price − cost.

8.6. Write a program to create an input screen for the calculation of markup based on cost and the percentage of markup based on selling price.

INPUT: Item description, cost of item, and percentage of cost to be marked up will be input from the keyboard.
OUTPUT: Print the item description, cost of the item, percentage it was marked up, the amount of markup, and the selling price on the printer.
PROCESSING:
   1. Use reverse image for the input fields.
   2. Markup = percent * cost.
   3. Selling price = cost + markup.
   4. Markup as a percent of selling price = markup / selling price.

8.7. Write a program to create a bar chart that represents the demand of refrigeration units (in thousands) per quarter. The x-axis will indicate year-quarters for three years (e.g., Year 1, Quarter 1, Quarter 2, Quarter 3, Quarter 4; Year 2, Quarter 1, etc.). The y-axis will be the number of refrigeration units in demand in thousands. The y-axis will increase by 20,000 each step and go from 0 to 200.

Read the demand for each of four quarters for three years, and plot the values.

8.8. Draw a picture of the American flag, without stars, on the screen.

8.9. Write a program using the PLAY statement to play one of your favorite songs. While the song is playing, the title of the song, the composer, the year it was written, and the words to the song should be printed on the screen.

8.10. Modify the program in exercise 7.1 (student grade report, p. 212) to use reverse image for the data input fields on the screen. Allow entry of the backspace key to correct errors.

8.11. Modify the program in exercise 7.2 (employee gross pay report, p. 212) to use reverse image for the data input fields on the screen. Allow entry of the backspace key to correct errors.

8.12. Modify the program in exercise 7.13 (p. 214) to include appropriate sounds for good and bad passwords and color text for the messages.

8.13. Write a program that will display a box of any size in any location on the screen. Input from the user the starting row, starting column, ending row, and ending column. Also input the color number to use for the box. After drawing the box, ask the user whether to quit or draw another box of a new size.

9 Menus

SELECT CASE Statement
CASE Statement
END SELECT Statement

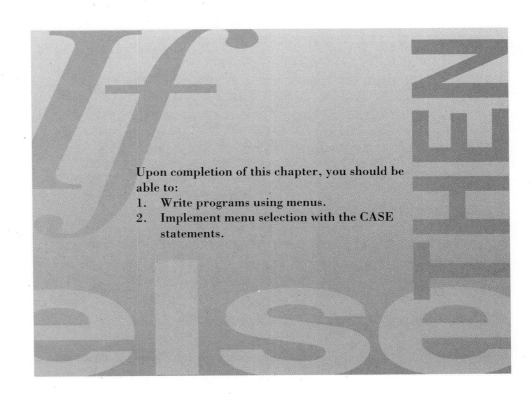

Upon completion of this chapter, you should be able to:
1. Write programs using menus.
2. Implement menu selection with the CASE statements.

Menu-Based Programs

An increasingly popular technique for interactive programs is the **menu.** Whenever the user has a choice to make, a menu is usually the best way to present the options available. Menus can be presented at any level of the program. In fact, many well-organized programs present successively lower levels of menus. Examples of menus abound in word processing programs, data base processing, and operating systems software, to name a few.

Top-Level Menu

```
        MENU

   1. APPETIZERS
   2. SALADS
   3. MAIN COURSES
   4. VEGETABLES
   5. DESSERTS

ENTER CHOICE 3
```

Second-Level Menu (After 3—MAIN COURSES chosen on above menu)

```
     MAIN COURSE MENU

   1. SEAFOOD
   2. CHICKEN DISHES
   3. MEATS
   4. VEGETARIAN DISHES

ENTER CHOICE 2
```

Third-Level Menu (After 2—CHICKEN DISHES chosen on second level)

```
     CHICKEN DISH MENU

   1. CHICKEN AND DUMPLINGS
   2. FRIED CHICKEN
   3. ROASTED CHICKEN
   4. CASHEW CHICKEN
   5. CHICKEN RIPPLE ICE CREAM

ENTER CHOICE _
```

Menus can provide the user with many choices. The options can become more narrow on each level, until an exact match is made. Printing a menu is a straightforward task. Any combination of the print formatting statements may be used, such as LOCATE, TAB, SPC.

Plan the menu to be user-friendly. Always arrange the menu screen to be pleasing to view, centered on the screen, with plenty of blank space. Too many choices can be confusing. When there are many options, it is far better to break the choices into groups and to present smaller menus.

Example Program: Printing a Menu Using TABs

Program Listing

```
'**** Print A Menu Using Tabs ****
CLS
PRINT TAB(35); "PRINT MENU"
PRINT
PRINT
PRINT
PRINT
PRINT TAB(27); "1. PRINT OUTPUT ON SCREEN"
PRINT
PRINT TAB(27); "2. PRINT OUTPUT ON PRINTER"
PRINT
PRINT TAB(27); "3. QUIT"
PRINT
PRINT
PRINT
PRINT TAB(22); "ENTER CHOICE (1-3)";
INPUT Choice
```

Example Program: Printing a Menu Using LOCATE

Program Listing

```
'**** Print A Menu Using Locate ****
CLS
LOCATE 5, 35
PRINT "PRINT MENU"
LOCATE 10, 27
PRINT "1. PRINT OUTPUT ON SCREEN"
LOCATE 12, 27
PRINT "2. PRINT OUTPUT ON PRINTER"
LOCATE 14, 27
PRINT "3. QUIT"
LOCATE 18, 22
PRINT "ENTER CHOICE (1-3)";
INPUT Choice
```

Sample Program Output

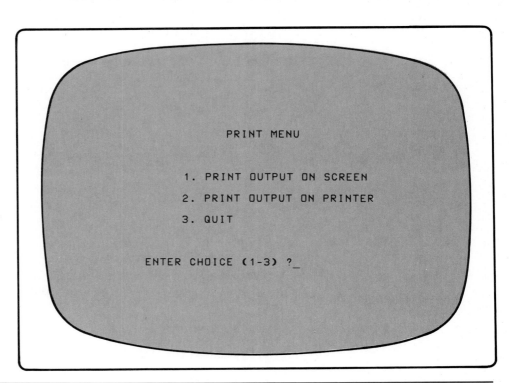

After displaying the menu and inputting the choice, the program must execute the correct subroutine. This could be accomplished with nested IF statements.

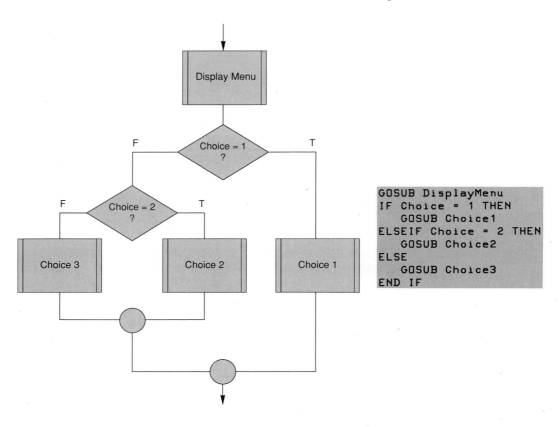

```
GOSUB DisplayMenu
IF Choice = 1 THEN
    GOSUB Choice1
ELSEIF Choice = 2 THEN
    GOSUB Choice2
ELSE
    GOSUB Choice3
END IF
```

The CASE Structure

Whenever you have multiple actions to take, depending on a condition, the CASE structure provides a flexible and powerful solution. You may have seen programs that use the ON...GOSUB or ON...GOTO statements for multiple actions. These statements have been made obsolete by QB's potent new CASE construct.

The SELECT CASE Statement—General Form

```
SELECT CASE expression
  CASE constant list
    [statement(s)]
  [CASE constant list
    [statement(s)]]
    .
    .
    .
  [CASE ELSE
      [statement(s)]]
END SELECT
```

The *expression* shown on the SELECT CASE statement will generally be a numeric or string variable that you wish to test. But it may be a more complex expression such as

```
Sum / Count
  or
VAL(RIGHT$(ID$,1))
  or
Last$ + First$
```

The *constant list* is the value that you want to match. It may be a single numeric or string constant, a range of values, a relational condition, or a combination of these. There is no limit to the number of *statements* that may be included.

The SELECT CASE Statement—Example 1

```
SELECT CASE Choice
   CASE 1
      GOSUB Choice1
   CASE 2
      GOSUB Choice2
   CASE 3
      GOSUB Choice3
END SELECT
```

In this example, the value of the variable Choice will be tested. If the value of Choice is 1, the Choice1 subroutine will be executed; if Choice has a value of 2, then Choice2 will be executed; a value of 3 will cause Choice3 to be executed. This process will be flowcharted as follows:

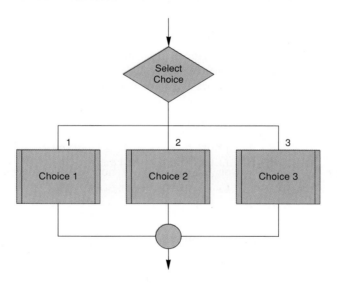

The SELECT CASE Statement—Example 2

```
SELECT CASE INT(Score)
   CASE   IS >= 100
      PRINT "Excellent score"
      PRINT "Give yourself a pat on the back"
   CASE   80 TO 99
      PRINT "Good score"
      PRINT "You should be proud"
   CASE   60 TO 79
      PRINT "Satisfactory score"
      PRINT "You should have a nice warm feeling"
   CASE ELSE
      PRINT "Your score shows room for improvement"
END SELECT
```

This example shows a combination of relational operators and constant ranges. Two points that were illustrated must be noted here:

1. When using a relational operator (i.e., IS >= 100) the word *IS* must be used.
2. To indicate a range of constants, use the word *TO* (i.e., 80 TO 89).

The elements used for *constant list* may have any of these forms:

Form	Example
constant[, constant ...]	CASE 2, 5, 8
constant TO constant	CASE 25 TO 50
IS relational-operator constant	CASE IS < 10

CASE ELSE

Generally, you will want to include a CASE ELSE clause in SELECT CASE statements. The statements associated with CASE ELSE will be executed only if none of the other CASE statements is matched. This will provide checking for any invalid or unforseen values of the expression being tested. If the CASE ELSE clause is omitted and none of the CASE conditions is true, the results will vary depending on the version of BASIC you are using. For QBASIC and QuickBASIC 4.5, no error message will occur and execution will continue with the END SELECT statement. With Quick-BASIC 4.0, the program will cancel with the run-time error message:

```
CASE ELSE expected
```

Writing a Menu Program

The top level of a menu program will display the menu and select the correct subroutine to execute. (See the hierarchy chart of a menu program in figure 9.1.) Each time one of the subroutines is completed, the menu should be redisplayed. The menu display and selection must therefore be placed in a loop.

```
'****** Mainline of a Menu Program ********
DO
    GOSUB PrintMenuAndInputChoice
    SELECT CASE Choice
        CASE 1
            GOSUB FirstItem
        CASE 2
            GOSUB SecondItem
        CASE 3
            GOSUB ThirdItem
        CASE 4
            GOSUB FourthItem
    END SELECT
LOOP UNTIL Choice = 5          '5 is ending value
PRINT "End of Program"
END
```

Figure 9.1
Hierarchy chart of a menu program.

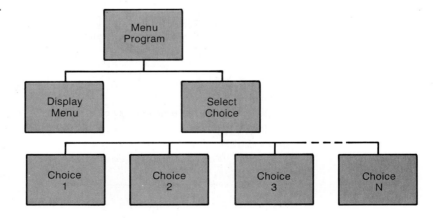

Another Approach to Menus— The Alphabetic Response

Sometimes menu selections are made with letters rather than numbers. In this menu, the user responds by entering the first character of the chosen item. Note that the only acceptable responses are N, P, S, or Q.

```
SELECTION MENU


N)AMES ONLY
P)HONE NUMBERS
S)ELECTIVE LIST
Q)UIT

SELECTION?_
```

Executing the correct subroutine may be done in one of two ways. Certainly nested IF statements will work.

```
IF UCASE$(Sel$) = "N" THEN
    GOSUB PrintNames
ELSEIF UCASE$(Sel$) = "P" THEN
    GOSUB PrintNumbers
ELSEIF UCASE$(Sel$) = "S" THEN
    GOSUB PrintSelectiveList
ELSEIF UCASE$(Sel$) = "Q" THEN
    CLS
ELSE
    GOSUB PrintErrorMessage
END IF
```

However, the SELECT CASE statement can handle this as easily as numeric choices.

Example Program: Menu Selection Using Alphabetic Characters

Program Listing

```
' Program Framework for Menu Selection Using Alphabetic
'    Characters for the Selection

'    Sel$      Menu selection (from keyboard)

'***************** MAIN PROGRAM **************************

DO
    GOSUB PrintMenu
    SELECT CASE Sel$
        CASE "N", "n"
            GOSUB PrintNames
        CASE "P", "p"
            GOSUB PrintNumbers
        CASE "S", "s"
            GOSUB PrintSelectiveList
        CASE "Q", "q"
            CLS
        CASE ELSE
            GOSUB PrintErrorMessage
    END SELECT
LOOP UNTIL UCASE$(Sel$) = "Q"
END
```

```
'******************** Print Menu **************************
PrintMenu:
   CLS
   LOCATE 5,30
   PRINT "Selection Menu"
   LOCATE 10,31
   PRINT "N)ames only"
   LOCATE 12,31
   PRINT "P)hone numbers"
   LOCATE 14,31
   PRINT "S)elective list"
   LOCATE 16,31
   PRINT "Q)uit"
   LOCATE 20,31
   INPUT "Selection"; Sel$
RETURN

'******************* Stub Module for Names Only *************
PrintNames:
   PRINT "Names only "
   LET X$ = INPUT$(1)              'Wait for keypress
RETURN

'****************** Stub Module for Phone Numbers **********
PrintNumbers:
   PRINT "Phone numbers "
   LET X$ = INPUT$(1)              'Wait for keypress
RETURN

'****************** Stub Module for Selective List *********
PrintSelectiveList:
   PRINT "Selective list"
   LET X$ = INPUT$(1)              'Wait for keypress
RETURN

'********************* Print Error Message ***************
PrintErrorMessage:
   PRINT "Please enter N, P, S, or Q"
   PRINT "Press any key to continue"
   LET X$ = INPUT$(1)              'Wait for keypress
RETURN
'********************* End of Program *********************
```

Programming Example:
Menu for a Personal Telephone Listing

A program is needed to keep personal telephone numbers. On demand, it must be able to print the list on the screen or the printer. A useful feature would allow the user to specify the area code, then print only those matching.

In the interest of brevity, the example program has been written with only those options named. Many other useful features quickly come to mind and are left for the programmer to add as further enhancements. Possible additions include selection by name—perhaps by the first letter of the name. As the size of the list grows, you will need to add multiple page breaks. A long list printed on the screen would scroll by too quickly to be read, so a good technique is to print one full screen of data and request the user to *Press any key to continue*. This allows time to read the first set before continuing.

Output

1. Complete list on the screen
2. Selective list (one area code) on the screen
3. Complete list on the printer
4. Selective list (one area code) on the printer

242

Input

1. List of names and phone numbers (in DATA statements)
2. Selection—screen or printer
3. Selection—"all" or area code

Pseudocode

1. Initialize variables
2. DO Loop until Choice = 3
   2.1 Display menu
   2.2 Input and validate choice
   2.3 Execute correct subroutine
      2.3.1 Print list on screen
      2.3.2 Print list on printer
3. Stop

   ** PrintListOnScreen Subroutine **

1. Allow choice of area code or all
   1.1 Input area code
   1.2 Validate
2. Print headings
3. Priming read—name
4. DO Loop until name = "END"
   4.1 Read phone number
   4.2 If match on area code or all chosen then print detail line
   4.3 Read next name
5. Hold screen output until a key is pressed
6. Return

Hierarchy Chart

Refer to figure 9.2 for the chart.

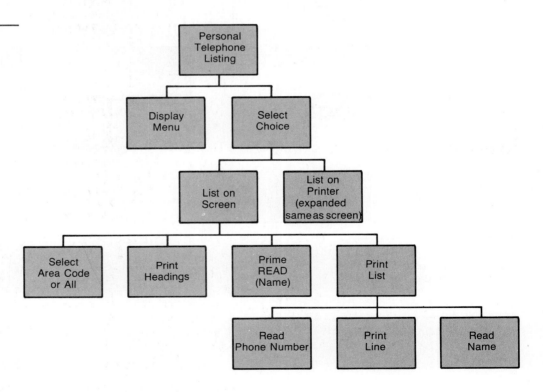

Figure 9.2
Hierarchy chart for personal telephone listing program.

Flowchart

Refer to figure 9.3 for the flowchart.

**Printer Spacing Chart
and Screen Layouts**

Refer to figure 9.4 .

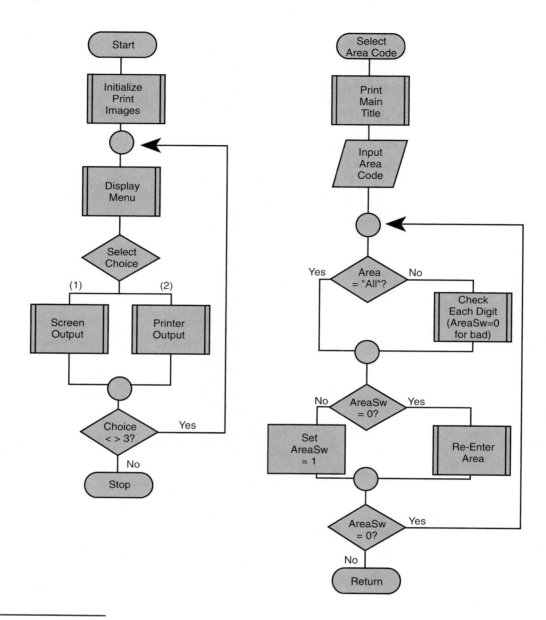

Figure 9.3
Flowchart for personal
telephone listing program.

Chapter 9

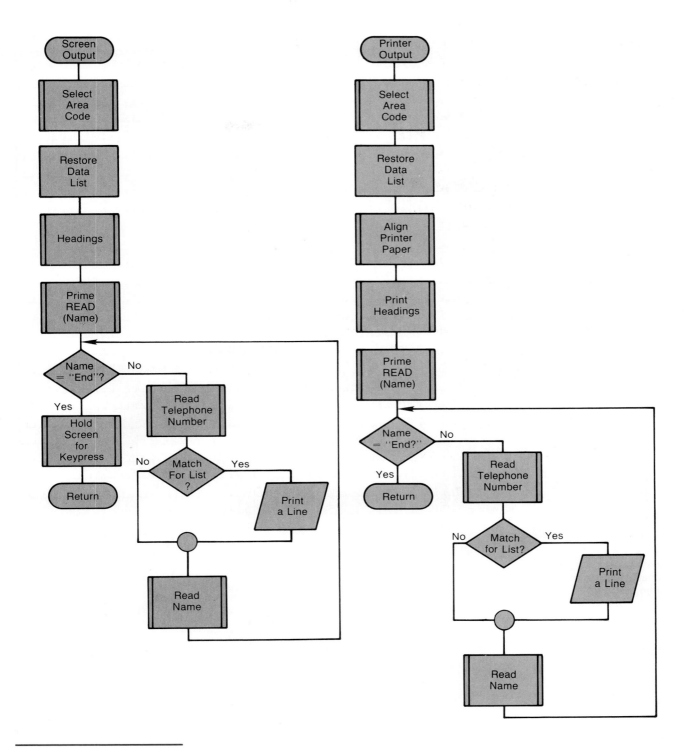

Figure 9.3—*Continued*

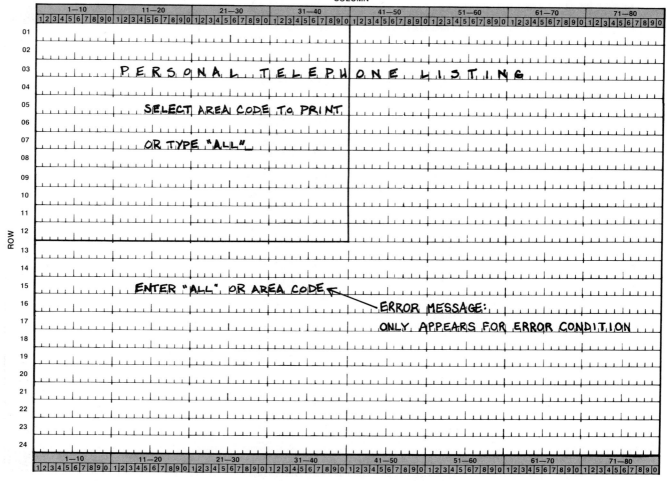

Figure 9.4
Screen and printer layouts for
personal telephone listing
program.

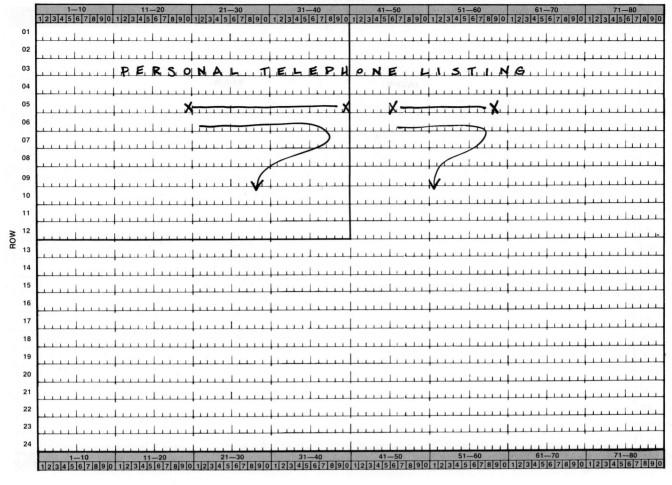

Figure 9.4—*Continued*

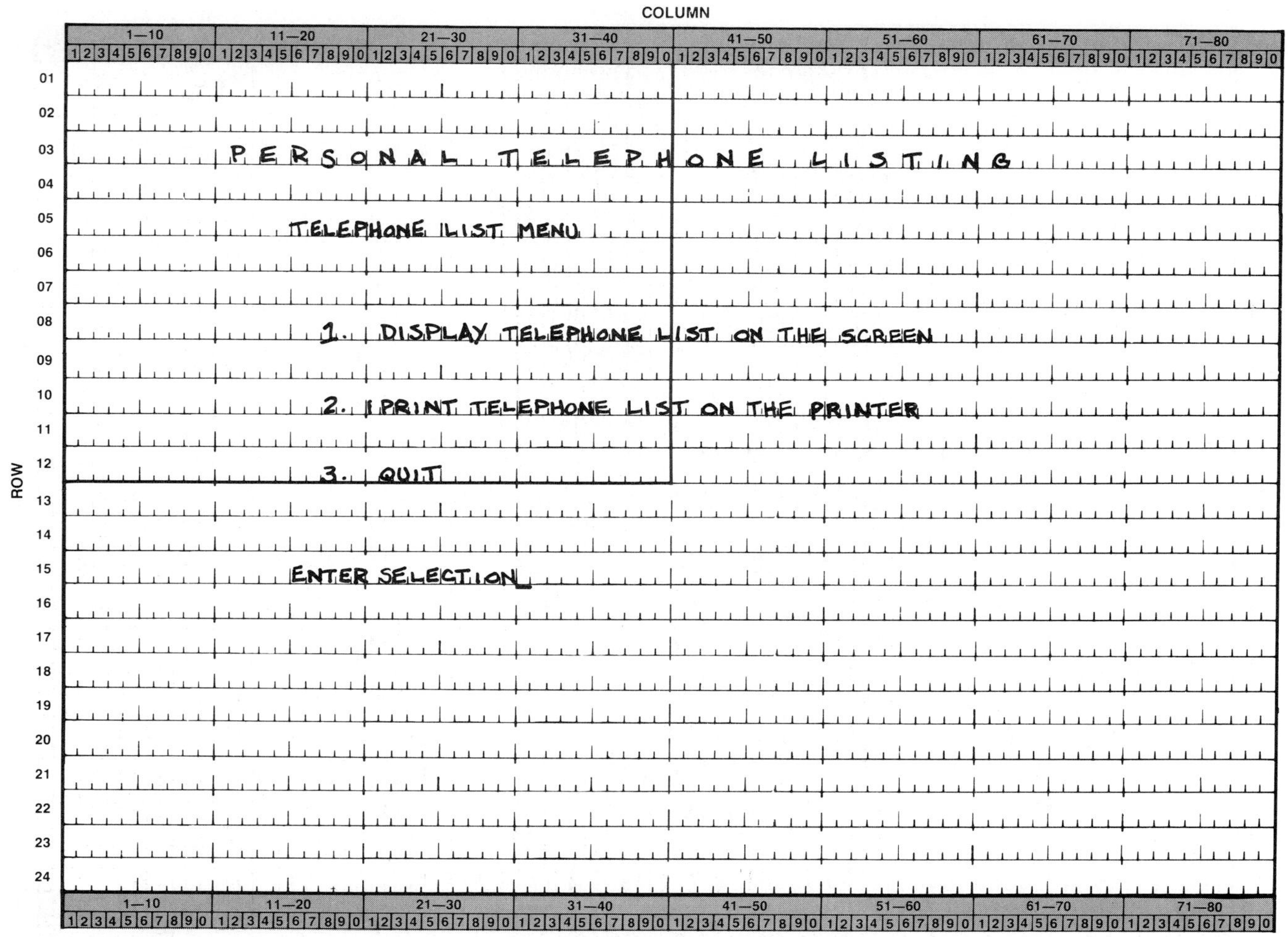

COLUMN
ROW
PERSONAL TELEPHONE LISTING
TELEPHONE LIST MENU
1. DISPLAY TELEPHONE LIST ON THE SCREEN
2. PRINT TELEPHONE LIST ON THE PRINTER
3. QUIT
ENTER SELECTION_

Figure 9.4—*Continued*

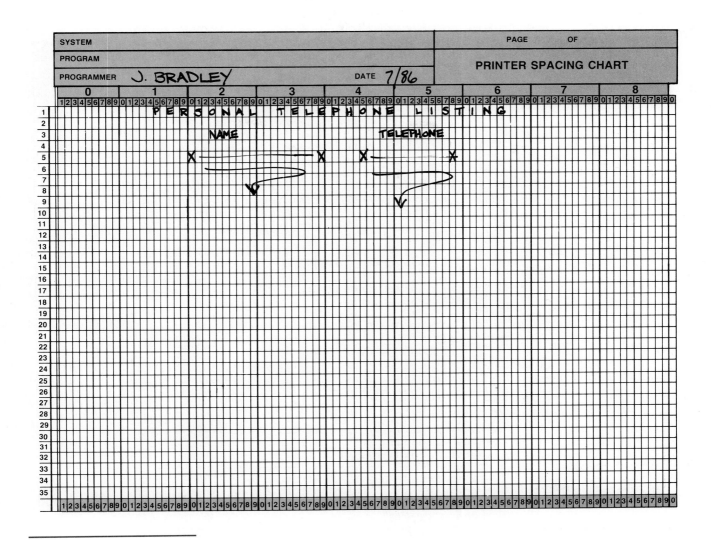

Figure 9.4—*Continued*

```
'          Program To Print Telephone Number Lists
'          Lists Will Be Printed In Their Entirety Or
'          Selected By Area Code

'       Variables Used

'       Nam$              Name
'       Tel$              Telephone number
'       Choice$           Menu choice for main menu
'       AreaSw            Switch to indicate good data for
'                           area code
'       Ck                Count of digits to check
'       Area$             Area code for selective list
'       Pt$               Print image for printer title
'       Pd$               Print image for detail line
'       D$                Dummy variable


'***************** Program Mainline ************************
GOSUB InitializePrintImages
DO
   GOSUB DisplayMainMenu
   SELECT CASE Choice$
      CASE "1"
         GOSUB ListOnScreen
      CASE "2"
         GOSUB ListOnPrinter
      CASE ELSE                    'No action, menu will repeat
   END SELECT
LOOP UNTIL Choice$ = "3"
END


'***************** Display Main Menu ***********************
DisplayMainMenu:
   GOSUB PrintMainTitle
   LOCATE 5, 26
   PRINT "TELEPHONE LIST MENU"
   LOCATE 8, 18
   PRINT "1. DISPLAY TELEPHONE LIST ON THE SCREEN"
   LOCATE 10, 18
   PRINT "2. PRINT TELEPHONE LIST ON THE PRINTER"
   LOCATE 12, 18
   PRINT "3. QUIT"
   LOCATE 15, 16
   PRINT "ENTER SELECTION ";
   LET Choice$ = INPUT$(1)
RETURN


'***************** Initialize Print Images ******************
InitializePrintImages:
   LET Pt$ = "   NAME                        TELEPHONE"
   LET Pd$ = "\                \    \                  \"
RETURN


'***************** Print Main Title For All Screens **********
PrintMainTitle:
   CLS
   LOCATE 3, 12
   PRINT "P E R S O N A L   T E L E P H O N E   L I S T I N G"
RETURN
```

```
'***************** Print Telephone List On Screen ************
ListOnScreen:
   GOSUB SelectAreaCode
   RESTORE                     'Start at top of data
   GOSUB PrintMainTitle
   LOCATE 7, 1                 'Set cursor for first detail line
   GOSUB ReadName
   DO UNTIL Nam$ = "END"
      GOSUB ReadPhoneNumber
      IF UCASE$(Area$) = "ALL" OR UCASE$(Area$) = MID$(Tel$, 2, 3) THEN
         PRINT TAB(20); USING Pd$; Nam$, Tel$
      END IF
      GOSUB ReadName
   LOOP
   GOSUB AllowTime
RETURN

'****************** Select One Area Code Or All To Print *****
SelectAreaCode:
   GOSUB PrintMainTitle
   LOCATE 5, 25
   PRINT "SELECT AREA CODE TO PRINT"
   LOCATE 7, 25
   PRINT "OR TYPE "; CHR$(34); "ALL"; CHR$(34); " ";
   INPUT Area$
   DO
      IF UCASE$(Area$) <> "ALL" THEN
         LET AreaSw = 1          'Set switch for good data before check
         GOSUB CheckDigits
         IF AreaSw = 0 THEN      'Bad data found
            GOSUB ReenterAreaCode
         END IF
      ELSE
         LET AreaSw = 1
      END IF
   LOOP WHILE AreaSw = 0
RETURN

'***************** Check Digits Of Area Code *****************
CheckDigits:
   LET Ck = 1
   DO WHILE Ck <= 3
      IF MID$(Area$, Ck, 1) > "9" or MID$(Area$, Ck, 1) < "0" THEN
         LET AreaSw = 0             'Set switch off (bad data)
      END IF
      LET Ck = Ck + 1
   LOOP
RETURN

'***************** Reenter Area Code ***********************
ReenterAreaCode:
   LOCATE 15, 24
   PRINT "ENTER "; CHR$(34); "ALL"; CHR$(34); " OR AREA CODE";
   LOCATE 7, 39
   PRINT "       "               'Clear out prior entry
   LOCATE 7, 39
   INPUT Area$                    'Input at same spot on screen
RETURN

'************** Allow Time to See Screen Before Clearing ******
AllowTime:
   LOCATE 24, 40
   PRINT "Press any key to continue";
   LET D$ = INPUT$(1)            'Wait for keypress
RETURN
```

```
'****************** Read A Name ********************************
ReadName:
    READ Nam$
RETURN


'****************** Read Telephone Number ********************
ReadPhoneNumber:
    READ Tel$
RETURN


'****************** Print List On Printer ********************
ListOnPrinter:
    GOSUB SelectAreaCode
    RESTORE                         'Start at top of data
    GOSUB AlignPaper
    GOSUB PrintTitlesPrinter
    GOSUB ReadName
    DO UNTIL Nam$ = "END"
        GOSUB ReadPhoneNumber
        IF UCASE$(Area$) = "ALL" OR Area$ = MID$(Tel$, 2, 3) THEN
            LPRINT TAB(20); USING Pd$; Nam$, Tel$
        END IF
        GOSUB ReadName
    LOOP
RETURN


'****************** Align Paper On Printer ********************
AlignPaper:
    LOCATE 20, 10
    PRINT "ALIGN PAPER TO TOP OF PAGE, AND PRESS RETURN WHEN READY"
    DO
        LET D$ = INPUT$(1)          'Get one character from keyboard
    LOOP UNTIL D$ = CHR$(13)
RETURN


'****************** Print Titles On Printer ********************
PrintTitlesPrinter:
    LPRINT TAB(15); "P E R S O N A L   T E L E P H O N E   L I S T I N G"
    LPRINT
    LPRINT TAB(20); Pt$
    LPRINT
RETURN


'****************** Data Begins Here ********************
DataBlock:
    DATA JOHNNY HARRINGTON, (714) 555-2145
    DATA SUZY WONG, (714) 555-4598
    DATA TIEN NGUYEN, (818) 555-4295
    DATA SCOTT HERRON, (213) 555-6214
    DATA RUBEN LOPEZ, (213) 555-2222
    DATA SANDRA WASHINGTON, (714) 555-2722
    DATA CURT KIRSCH, (714) 555-8118
    DATA MELINDA ROBB, (213) 555-4321
    DATA END
RETURN
'****************** End of Program ********************
```

Sample Program Output

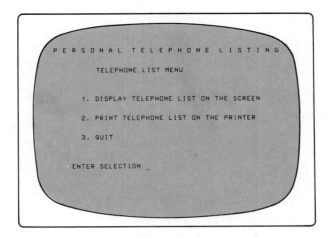

```
P E R S O N A L   T E L E P H O N E   L I S T I N G

          TELEPHONE LIST MENU


      1.  DISPLAY TELEPHONE LIST ON THE SCREEN

      2.  PRINT TELEPHONE LIST ON THE PRINTER

      3.  QUIT


    ENTER SELECTION _
```

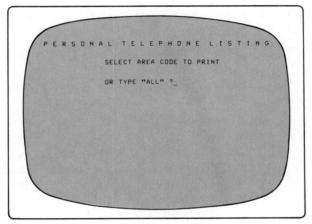

```
P E R S O N A L   T E L E P H O N E   L I S T I N G

       SELECT AREA CODE TO PRINT

       OR TYPE "ALL" ?_
```

Sample Printer Output

```
P E R S O N A L    T E L E P H O N E    L I S T I N G

      NAME                      TELEPHONE

   JOHNNY HARRINGTON          (414) 555-2145
   SUZIE WONG                 (714) 555-4598
   TIEN NGUYEN                (818) 555-4295
   SCOTT HERRON               (213) 555-6214
   RUBEN LOPEZ                (213) 555-2222
   SANDRA WASHINGTON          (714) 555-2722
   CURT KIRSCH                (714) 555-8118
   MELINDA ROBB               (213) 555-4321

P E R S O N A L    T E L E P H O N E    L I S T I N G

      NAME                      TELEPHONE

   SUZIE WONG                 (714) 555-4598
   SANDRA WASHINGTON          (714) 555-2722
   CURT KIRSCH                (714) 555-8118
```

Summary

1. Menus are a good way to present program choices to the user.
2. Often, several levels of menus will allow a user to quickly make precise choices.
3. The SELECT CASE statement provides a means to selectively execute one set of statements from many choices.
4. The CASE construct begins with SELECT CASE and ends with END SELECT.
5. The value to test in a SELECT CASE statement may be numeric or string and may be a constant, variable, or expression.
6. Each CASE statement handles one or more of the possible conditions named on the SELECT CASE statement.
7. A CASE ELSE statement is optional. If included, it will handle any situation not matched by a CASE statement.
8. Hierarchy charts are helpful in planning menu programs.

Programming Exercises

9.1. Write a menu program that will print various formulas and do calculation, if requested.

Menu Choices
1. Calculate the area of a triangle
2. Calculate the area of a rectangle
3. Calculate the area of a circle
4. Calculate the volume of a cube
5. End the program

For each menu choice, clear the screen and print the formula for the calculation. Then ask the user if a computation is desired. If the answer is affirmative, prompt for each necessary value. Then calculate and print the requested value. After each menu choice, the menu should be redisplayed.

Formulas
1. Area of a triangle $= 1/2 \times$ base $\times$ height
2. Area of a rectangle $=$ length $\times$ width
3. Area of a circle $= \pi \,(3.1416) \times$ radius^2
4. Volume of a cube $=$ length $\times$ width $\times$ depth

9.2. Write a menu program to convert currency. The menu must offer at least four choices in addition to the choice to end the program. You may use the menu choices suggested or select other currencies for the conversion.

Suggested Menu Choices
1. Convert U.S. dollars to British pounds
2. Convert British pounds to U.S. dollars
3. Convert U.S. dollars to Canadian dollars
4. Convert Canadian dollars to U.S. dollars
5. End the program

After the user selects a menu choice, clear the screen and prompt for the amount to be converted. Then print the converted amount with identifying literals. After each choice, the menu should be redisplayed. Find the current conversion rate or use the following (outdated) rates.

Conversion Rates
1 U.S. dollar $=$ 1.1330 British pounds
1 British pound $=$ .8826 U.S. dollars
1 U.S. dollar $=$ .7531 Canadian dollars
1 Canadian dollar $=$ 1.3277 U.S. dollars

9.3. Write a menu program to perform various conversions for cooking. For each choice, clear the screen and request the number to be converted. After printing the converted value, redisplay the menu.

Menu Choices
1. Tablespoons to teaspoons
2. Teaspoons to tablespoons
3. Cups to tablespoons
4. Tablespoons to cups
5. Cups to quarts
6. Quarts to cups
7. Quarts to gallons
8. Gallons to quarts
9. Quit

Formulas
1 tablespoon = 3 teaspoons
1 teaspoon = 1/3 tablespoon
1 cup = 16 tablespoons
1 tablespoon = 1/16 cup
1 cup = 1/4 quart
1 quart = 4 cups
1 quart = 1/4 gallon
1 gallon = 4 quarts

9.4. Write a menu program to list the "best" colleges to attend for a particular major.

Menu Choices
1. Computer Information Systems
2. Computer Programming
3. Business Economics
4. Photography
5. Quit

After the user selects a menu choice, clear the screen and print the list of colleges. After each choice, the menu should be redisplayed. Use DATA statements for the college names.

Colleges
1. Computer Information Systems
   a. University of Twilight Zone
   b. Bogus University
   c. State Polymetric University
   d. College of the Loafers
   e. University of the Atlantic
2. Computer Programming
   a. California Long-term College
   b. San Rose State University
   c. Romona State University
   d. Southern State University
   e. Bogus University
3. Business Economics
   a. Champain College
   b. Golden Bate University
   c. Holy Verbs College
   d. University of Sandy Beach
   e. Woodpecker University

4. Photography
   a. Art Center College
   b. Cooks Institute
   c. Coma Linda University
   d. Bills College
   e. University of Twilight Zone

9.5. Write a menu program to do various conversions.

Menu Options
1. Change a percentage to a decimal fraction
2. Change a percentage to a common fraction
3. Change a decimal to a percent
4. Change a common fraction to a percent
5. Quit

After the user has made a selection, clear the screen and display the conversion. Hold the screen for a keypress. After a key has been pressed, redisplay the menu.

Conversions
1. Percent to decimal fraction
   Divide number by 100
   Example: 25% = .25
2. Percent to a common fraction
   Make the number the numerator of a fraction that has 100 as its denominator
   Example: 50% = 50/100
3. Decimal to a percent
   Multiply number by 100
   Example: .375 = 37.5%
4. Common fraction to a percent
   Divide the numerator by the denominator and multiply by 100
   Example: 2/5 = 40%
   Note: Input the numerator and denominator separately.

10

Additional Control Structures and Numeric Functions

FOR / NEXT Statements
DEFTYPE Statements
Numeric Functions
MOD operator
RND Function
RANDOMIZE Statement
DEF FN Statement

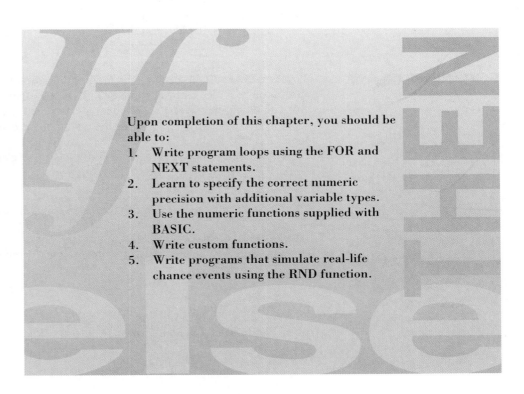

Upon completion of this chapter, you should be able to:

1. Write program loops using the FOR and NEXT statements.
2. Learn to specify the correct numeric precision with additional variable types.
3. Use the numeric functions supplied with BASIC.
4. Write custom functions.
5. Write programs that simulate real-life chance events using the RND function.

Figure 10.1
Flowchart of a counter-
controlled loop. The counter
variable must be initialized,
incremented, and tested for the
final value.

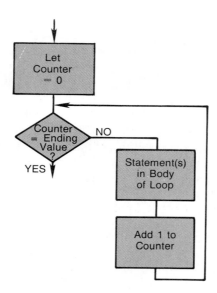

FOR/NEXT Loops

If you pause and look back at the programs written thus far, it becomes obvious that most require loops. Until now the DO...LOOP statements were used for all loops, and this could continue. But for the counter-controlled loop there is an easier way. Since looping is so common, BASIC provides a statement to automate the counter-controlled loop.

A counter-controlled loop generally has three elements (see figure 10.1).

1. Initialize the counter
2. Increment the counter—in the loop
3. Test the counter—to determine when it is time to quit

```
'***** Counter-Controlled DO...LOOP ****
LET Count = 0                  'Initialize
DO WHILE Count < 10            'Test
    PRINT Count
    LET Count = Count + 1      'Increment
LOOP
PRINT "End of list"
```

The following is an alternate way to accomplish the same result using a FOR/NEXT loop.

```
'**** Counter-Controlled FOR/NEXT Loop ****
FOR Count = 1 TO 10            'Initialize and test
    PRINT Count
NEXT Count                     'Increment
PRINT "End of list"
```

When the FOR statement is reached during program execution, several things occur. The variable, Count, is established as the loop counter and is initialized to 1. The final value for the Count (10) is also declared.

Execution is now "under control of" the FOR statement. After the value of Count is set, it is tested to see if Count is greater than 10 (the final value). If not, the statements in the body of the loop are executed—in this case, only the PRINT statement. The NEXT statement causes Count to be incremented by 1. Then control passes back to the FOR statement. Is the value of Count greater than 10? If not, the loop is again executed. When the test is made and Count *is* greater than 10, control passes to the statement immediately following the NEXT (PRINT "End of list" in the previous example).

```
        Initialize    TesT
                 ⏜         ⏜
FOR Count = 1 TO 10
NEXT Count
          ⏝
          Increment
```

The loop written with the FOR and NEXT statements has exactly the same effect as the DO...LOOP. In fact, all loops could be written with the DO and LOOP with no loss of programming capability. But FOR/NEXT offers a handy, concise way of doing the same thing and is the *only* loop control structure available in some dialects of BASIC. As you can see, two fewer statements are needed to code the loop with FOR/NEXT than with DO...LOOP. Moreover, counter-controlled loops, such as the previous example, execute much more quickly when written with FOR/NEXT.

The FOR and NEXT Statements—General Form

```
FOR  loop index = initial value TO  test value [STEP increment]
    ::
    ::  (Body of loop)
    ::
NEXT [loop index]
```

The *loop index* must be a numeric variable. *Initial value* and *test value* may be constants, variables, or numeric expressions. The optional word STEP may be included, along with the value to be added to the loop index for each iteration of the loop. When the STEP is omitted, the increment is assumed to be 1.

The FOR Statement—Examples

```
FOR Index = 2 TO 100 STEP 2
FOR Count = Start TO Ending STEP Incr
FOR Num = A - B TO A + B
FOR X = 1 TO LEN(A$) STEP 1
FOR Rate = .05 TO .25 STEP .05
FOR Countdown = 10 TO 0 STEP -1
```

Each of these FOR statements will also have a corresponding NEXT statement, which must follow the FOR. All statements between the FOR and the NEXT are considered to be the body of the loop and will be executed the specified number of times.

The first example FOR statement will count from 2 to 100 by 2. The statements in the body of the loop will be executed 50 times—once with Index = 2, once with Index = 4, once with Index = 6, and so forth.

When the comparison is done, the program checks for *greater than* the test value—not equal to. When Index = 100 in the preceding example, the body of the loop will be executed one more time. Then, at the NEXT statement, Index will be incremented to 102, the test made, and control will pass to the statement following the NEXT. If the value of Index were to print (or be used in any way) *after completion* of the loop, its value would be 102.

Using Variables to Control Loop Execution

It may be handy at times to input the beginning, ending, or increment values.

Example Program: Variables for Loop Control

Program Listing

```
******************* Temperature Conversion ********************
PRINT "CONVERSION FROM DEGREES FAHRENHEIT TO CELSIUS"
INPUT "ENTER LOWEST TEMPERATURE, IN FAHRENHEIT ", Low
INPUT "ENTER HIGHEST FAHRENHEIT TEMPERATURE    ", High
INPUT "ENTER VALUE FOR INCREMENT               ", Incr
FOR Fahren = Low TO High STEP Incr
   LET Celsius = 5 / 9 * (Fahren - 32)
   PRINT USING "##.#    ##.#"; Fahren, Celsius
NEXT Fahren
PRINT "END OF LIST"
END
'********************** End of Program ********************
```

Sample Program Output

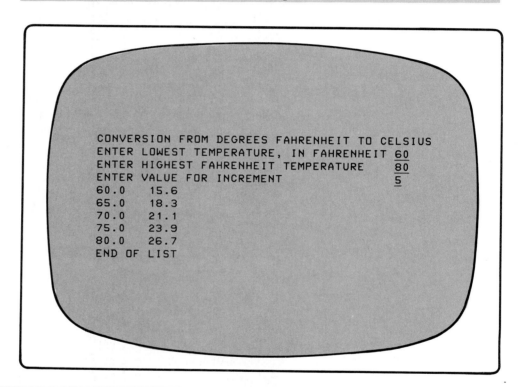

```
CONVERSION FROM DEGREES FAHRENHEIT TO CELSIUS
ENTER LOWEST TEMPERATURE, IN FAHRENHEIT  60
ENTER HIGHEST FAHRENHEIT TEMPERATURE     80
ENTER VALUE FOR INCREMENT                 5
60.0   15.6
65.0   18.3
70.0   21.1
75.0   23.9
80.0   26.7
END OF LIST
```

Negative Increment, or Counting Backward

The value for STEP may be a negative number. This has the effect of decreasing the loop index rather than increasing it. When the STEP is negative, BASIC will test for *less than* the test value instead of greater than.

```
'**** Count Backwards ****
FOR Count = 10 TO 0 STEP -1
   PRINT Count
NEXT Count
PRINT "BLAST OFF"
```

Condition Satisfied before Entry

At times, the terminal value will be reached before entry into the loop. In that case, the statements in the body of the loop will not be executed even once.

```
'**** An Unexecutable Loop ****
LET Term = 5
FOR Count = 6 TO Term
    PRINT "This will never print"
NEXT Count
```

Indentation

For ease of reading and debugging, the loop should be easily recognizable. Align the FOR and NEXT statements to show the beginning and end of the loop. The statements in the body of the loop should be indented and aligned with each other.

Flowcharting FOR/NEXT Loops

The logic of a FOR/NEXT loop is identical to a counter-controlled DO...LOOP and may be flowcharted in the same way. Figure 10.2 shows the ANSI standard symbols used to flowchart a FOR/NEXT loop.

Several nonstandard symbols have been developed to indicate a FOR/NEXT loop. Figure 10.3 illustrates one specialized FOR/NEXT symbol. Although the symbol is not included in the standards, it does have widespread use and will be used in this text.

Figure 10.2
ANSI standard flowcharting symbols used to plan a FOR/NEXT loop.

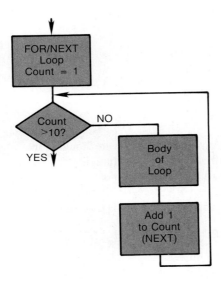

Figure 10.3
Nonstandard FOR/NEXT flowcharting symbol.

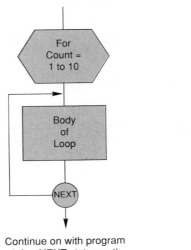

Continue on with program
(after NEXT statement)

Notes on Loops and Structured Programming

Consistent with the philosophy of this text, nothing has been said about branching into or out of FOR/NEXT loops. Good program modules have one entry point and one exit point. Therefore, a loop will always be entered at the top and exited at the bottom.

Many times it is desirable to end a counter-controlled loop before the test value is reached. BASIC does allow branching out, but structured programming guidelines do not. *If you need to terminate a loop early, always use a DO...LOOP rather than a FOR/NEXT loop.* According to the rules of BASIC, if execution branches out of a FOR/NEXT loop prior to normal termination, the variable used for the loop index will retain its current value. BASIC does *not* allow branching into the body of the loop. Execution must always begin with the FOR statement.

Altering the Values of the Control Variables

Once the FOR loop has been entered, the values for beginning, ending, and increment have already been set. Changing the value of the variables within the loop will have no effect on the number of iterations of the loop. Many texts admonish against changing the values within the loop. However, QB just ignores you if you try.

```
'*** Bad Example--Changing The Control Variables ***
LET Final = 5
LET Incr = 1
FOR Index = 1 TO Final STEP Incr
    PRINT Index
    LET Final = 10
    LET Incr = 2
NEXT Index
```

Program Execution:

```
1
2
3
4
5
```

Index will still go from 1 to 5, even though Final and Incr were changed within the loop. It should be obvious that changing the values is not possible and that the preceding coding is highly undesirable.

The value that BASIC *will* allow you to change within the loop is the index variable. Again an admonition: This is considered poor programming!

```
'*** Poor Programming ***
FOR Num = 1 TO 10 STEP 1
    PRINT Num
    LET Num = Num * 2
NEXT Num
PRINT "AFTER LOOP TERMINATION, Num ="; Num
```

Program Execution:

```
1
3
7
AFTER LOOP TERMINATION, Num = 15
```

The clue to the strange output here is to recall, step-by-step, what happens during execution. Each time the multiplication is executed (Num = Num * 2) the value of Num will double. Each time the NEXT statement is executed, 1 will be added to the current value for Num.

Feedback

1. Identify the statements that are correctly formed and those that have errors. For those with errors, state what is wrong and how to correct it.

   a. ```
   FOR N = 3.5 TO 6, STEP .5
   NEXT N
   ```

   b. ```
   FOR A = B TO C STEP D
   NEXT D
   ```

   c. ```
   FOR 4 = 1 TO 10 STEP 2
   NEXT For
   ```

   d. ```
   FOR K = 100 TO 0 STEP -25
   NEXT K
   ```

   e. ```
   FOR N = 0 TO -10 STEP -1
   NEXT N
   ```

   f. ```
   FOR X = 10 TO 1
   NEXT X
   ```

2. Write a FOR/NEXT loop to print the numbers counting by 3, from 3 to 100.

3. Using a FOR/NEXT loop, write the statements necessary to print "THIS IS A LARK" ten times.

4. What will be the output when each of these program segments is executed?

   a. ```
   FOR Rec = 1 TO 5
        READ Item$, Price
        LET Tot = Tot + Price
        PRINT Item$, Price
   NEXT Rec
   PRINT , Tot
   DATA BICYCLE,150,TRAIN,65,BALL,1.50,NERD,.27
   DATA GAME,6.95,BOX,4,END,0
   ```

   b. ```
   READ X,Y,Z
   FOR Index = X TO Y STEP Z
        PRINT Index
   NEXT Index
   DATA 10,15,2
   ```

   c. ```
   READ Term
   FOR Count = 1 TO Term
        PRINT "*";
   NEXT Count
   DATA 8.5
   ```

5. How many times will the body of the loop be executed for each of these examples? What will be the value of the loop index after normal completion of the loop?

   a. `FOR K = 2 TO 11 STEP 3`
   b. `FOR B = 10 TO 1 STEP -1`
   c. `FOR S = 3 TO 6 STEP .5`
   d. `FOR A = 5 TO 1`
   e. `FOR L = 1 TO 3`

## Nesting FOR/NEXT Loops

FOR/NEXT loops may be nested; that is, one loop may be placed inside another loop. The inner loop must be completely contained within the outer loop with no overlap. Each loop must use a unique variable name for the loop index. (The nonstandard symbol makes the logic flow easier to follow when nesting loops.)
   ```

Flowchart

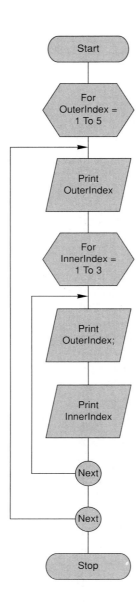

Example Program: Nested Loops

Program Listing

```
'*************** Nested Loops ******************
FOR OuterIndex = 1 TO 5
   PRINT "OUTER LOOP"; OuterIndex
   FOR InnerIndex = 1 TO 3
      PRINT TAB(6); "OUTER INDEX ="; OuterIndex;
      PRINT "INNER INDEX ="; InnerIndex
   NEXT InnerIndex
NEXT OuterIndex
```

```
 •
 •            OUTER LOOP 1
 •                 OUTER INDEX = 1 INNER INDEX = 1
 •                 OUTER INDEX = 1 INNER INDEX = 2
 •                 OUTER INDEX = 1 INNER INDEX = 3
 •            OUTER LOOP 2
 •                 OUTER INDEX = 2 INNER INDEX = 1
 •                 OUTER INDEX = 2 INNER INDEX = 2
 •                 OUTER INDEX = 2 INNER INDEX = 3
 •            OUTER LOOP 3
 •                 OUTER INDEX = 3 INNER INDEX = 1
 •                 OUTER INDEX = 3 INNER INDEX = 2
 •                 OUTER INDEX = 3 INNER INDEX = 3
 •            OUTER LOOP 4
 •                 OUTER INDEX = 4 INNER INDEX = 1
 •                 OUTER INDEX = 4 INNER INDEX = 2
 •                 OUTER INDEX = 4 INNER INDEX = 3
 •            OUTER LOOP 5
 •                 OUTER INDEX = 5 INNER INDEX = 1
 •                 OUTER INDEX = 5 INNER INDEX = 2
 •                 OUTER INDEX = 5 INNER INDEX = 3
 •
```

When the nested loop program is run, the inner loop will be executed three times for each iteration of the outer loop. In the first FOR statement, the outer loop is initialized and OuterIndex is set to 1. With OuterIndex still at 1, the inner loop is begun, and InnerIndex is set to 1. The body of the inner loop is executed and the inner NEXT InnerIndex is incremented and tested. Since it is not greater than 3, the inner loop is reexecuted. The outer NEXT will not be executed for the first time until the inner loop is completely satisfied. Then, when OuterIndex has a value of 2, the inner loop is reinitialized and must be completely satisfied before OuterIndex can go to 3.

In *nested FOR/NEXT loops,* the inner loop variable changes faster than the outer loop variable. This can be compared to the hands of a clock, on which the minute hand travels faster than the hour hand.

```
      '***** Properly Nested Loops ****
 ┌─FOR I = 1 TO 10
 │    ┌─FOR K = I TO 10
 │    └─NEXT K
 │    ┌─FOR L = 1 TO I
 │    │     FOR M = L TO 0 STEP -1
 │    │     NEXT M
 │    └─NEXT L
 └─NEXT I
```

Notice that each nested loop is completely contained within its outer loop. There is no crossing over. Also observe that I, the outermost loop index, is used as an initial value on one inner FOR and as a final value on the other. The loop index L is also used as an initial value on an inner loop. This technique is perfectly acceptable and is often a slick solution to programming problems. It is important, however, that each loop have its own, unique loop index.

```
'***** Improperly Nested Loops *****
┌FOR I = 1 TO 10
│   ┌FOR K = 1 TO 2
└NEXT I
    └NEXT K
    ┌FOR M = L TO 0 STEP -1
┌FOR L = 1 TO I
│   └NEXT M
└NEXT L
```

On execution, these loops would produce the error *NEXT without FOR*.

Example Program: Print Multiplication Tables

One application of nested loops is to print multiplication tables.

Program Listing

```
'***************** Print Multiplication Tables ****************
'                   Using Nested Loops
LET P$ = "### :"                    'Initialize print images
LET D$ = " ### "
CLS
PRINT "   :   0   1   2   3   4   5   6   7   8   9   10"
PRINT" -----------------------------------------------------"
FOR Row = 0 TO 10
   PRINT USING D$; Row;
   FOR Col = 0 TO 10
      LET Prod = Row * Col
      PRINT USING D$; Prod;
   NEXT Col
   PRINT
NEXT Row
END
'********************** End of Program **********************
```

Sample Program Output

```
     :   0   1   2   3   4   5   6   7   8   9  10
    ------------------------------------------------------
  0 :   0   0   0   0   0   0   0   0   0   0   0
  1 :   0   1   2   3   4   5   6   7   8   9  10
  2 :   0   2   4   6   8  10  12  14  16  18  20
  3 :   0   3   6   9  12  15  18  21  24  27  30
  4 :   0   4   8  12  16  20  24  28  32  36  40
  6 :   0   6  12  18  24  30  36  42  48  54  60
  7 :   0   7  14  21  28  35  42  49  56  63  70
  8 :   0   8  16  24  32  40  48  56  64  72  80
  9 :   0   9  18  27  36  45  54  63  72  81  90
 10 :   0  10  20  30  40  50  60  70  80  90 100
```

Feedback

1. What will print when the following program segment is run?

```
FOR Count = 2 TO 6 STEP 3
    FOR Index = 1 TO 3
        PRINT Count, Index
    NEXT Index
NEXT Count
```

2. a. What will print when the following program segment is run?
   b. What is the purpose of the PRINT before NEXT Row? What would the output look like if it were removed?

```
FOR Row = 1 TO 5
    READ Num
    FOR Star = 1 TO Num
        PRINT "*";
    NEXT Star
    PRINT
NEXT Row
DATA 5,2,10,6,1
```

Programming Example

The local children are on a fund-raising drive. Since none of the children excels in arithmetic, it was decided to print a chart to show the price for multiple items including tax. In order to keep the program flexible, the tax rate, description, and price of the items will be entered with DATA statements.

Input

1. Tax rate
2. Item description (for each of four items)
3. Item price (for each of four items)

Output

Refer to figure 10.4 for output layout.

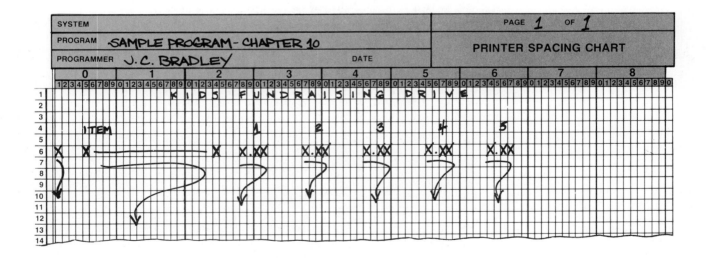

Figure 10.4
Output layout for fund-raising tax table program.

Processing

For each of four items:

Compute the price of 1, 2, 3, 4, and 5 items, including tax

$$(price * quantity) * (1 + rate)$$

Pseudocode

1. Initialize
    1.1   Print headings
    1.2   Initialize print images
2. Print table
    For each of 4 items
    2.1   Read description and price
    2.2   Print detail line
    2.3   For each of 5 quantities
          2.3.1   Calculate total including tax
          2.3.2   Print total
    2.4   Print blank line
3. End

Hierarchy Chart

Refer to figure 10.5 for the chart.

Flowchart

Refer to figure 10.6 for the flowchart.

Figure 10.5
Hierarchy chart for fund-raising
tax table program.

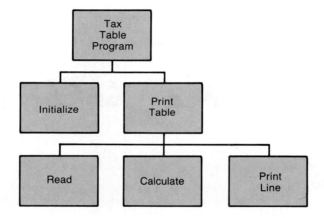

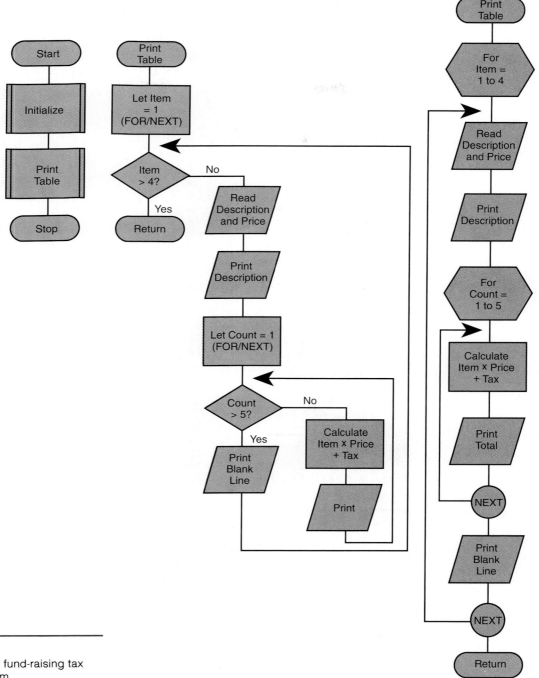

Figure 10.6
Flowchart of fund-raising tax
table program.

Program Listing

```
' Program For The Kids' Fundraising Drive
' Print A Chart That Shows Each Item Being Sold
' Along With The Price, For 1 - 5 Quantity, Including Tax

'      Variables Used

'      TaxRate          Tax rate (decimal fraction)
'      Desc$            Description of item
'      Price            Price of each item
'      Tot              Calculated total, including tax
'      Item             Item number, used to count
'      Count            Number of items sold
'      I1$, D1$         Print images
```

```
'***************** Program Mainline *********************

GOSUB InitializePrintImages
READ TaxRate
GOSUB PrintTable
END


*************** Initialize Print Images ********************

InitializePrintImages:
   CLS
   PRINT "          K I D S   F U N D R A I S I N G   D R I V E"
   PRINT
   PRINT
   PRINT "    ITEM              1         2         3         4         5"
   PRINT
   LET I1$ = "#  \                \ "
   LET D1$ = "   ##.##    "
RETURN


'****************** Print Table ************************

PrintTable:
   FOR Item = 1 TO 4
      READ Desc$, Price
      PRINT USING I1$; Item, Desc$;
      FOR Count = 1 TO 5
         LET Tot = (Count * Price) * (1 + TaxRate)
         PRINT USING D1$; Tot;
      NEXT Count
      PRINT
   NEXT Item


'****************** Data Begins Here ******************
DATA .06              'Tax rate
DATA CANDY BAR, .75, FUDGE COOKIES,1.25
DATA OATMEAL COOKIES, 1.00, MACAROONS, 1.45
'****************** End of Program ********************
```

Sample Program Output

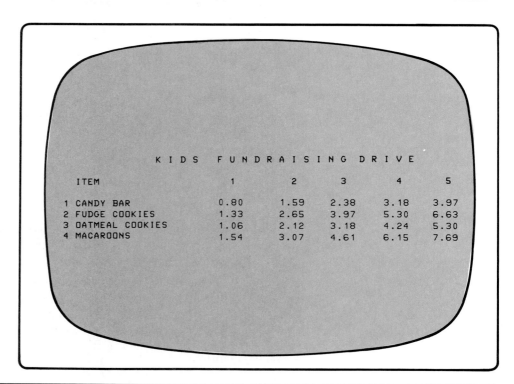

```
                K I D S   F U N D R A I S I N G   D R I V E

    ITEM               1         2         3         4         5

    1 CANDY BAR        0.80      1.59      2.38      3.18      3.97
    2 FUDGE COOKIES    1.33      2.65      3.97      5.30      6.63
    3 OATMEAL COOKIES  1.06      2.12      3.18      4.24      5.30
    4 MACAROONS        1.54      3.07      4.61      6.15      7.69
```

Numeric Precision

The **precision** of a number refers to the number of digits that can be stored accurately. The numeric variables used thus far are called *single-precision* variables. Due to the space allocated for variables, each variable can hold up to seven digits. Any numbers with more than seven significant digits may not be held accurately.

```
LET A = 112233445566
PRINT USING " ###,###,###,### ";A
```

Program Execution:

```
112,233,447,424
```

The first eight digits here are correct; the ninth digit is not even correctly rounded. The error here is 1,858. Is that close enough? For some applications, maybe yes. For others, it could be a disaster.

To increase the storage allocated for variables, and also the number of digits held, declare variables to be *double-precision*. A double-precision variable will hold fifteen digits accurately.

The storage in the computer is measured in bytes, where one byte will hold one alphanumeric (ASCII) character when strings are being stored. When numbers are being stored in computer memory, the numbers are converted to their binary value. If 123 is stored as a number, you won't find an ASCII coded 1, 2, 3. Instead, the numeric value for one hundred twenty-three is converted to binary and held in the standard size for a numeric variable. Recall from chapter 7 that the functions STR$ and VAL are used to convert from one form to the other.

The standard size for a single-precision numeric variable is four bytes. Whether zero is being stored or 1,000,000, it still takes four bytes. Double-precision variables always take eight bytes of storage.

Numbers may also be stored as **integers** (whole numbers). Integers may be either "short" or "long." Short integers take two bytes of storage and can hold any whole number in the range -32768 to $+32767$. Long integers take four bytes of storage and hold whole numbers in the range $-2,147,483,648$ to $+2,147,483,647$.

The way to specify the type of variable wanted is in the choice of variable names. You already found that a dollar sign as the rightmost character declared a string variable. Now learn to explicitly declare short integer variables with a percent sign (%), long integers with an ampersand (&), double-precision variables with a number sign (#), or single-precision with an exclamation point (!) as the rightmost character of the variable names. Table 10.1 summarizes the variable types and codes.

Table 10.1
Explicitly declaring variable types.

Variable Type	Character to Declare Type	Number of Bytes of Storage Allocated
String	$	1 for each character
Integer	%	2
Long Integer	&	4
Single-precision	!	4
Double-precision	#	8

When the type of numeric variable is not specified, BASIC sets up and uses single-precision variables. For most applications, this is fine, and there is little reason to change.

The occasions to consider changing variable types include:

1. When accuracy is needed for large numbers. Whenever more than seven digits must be held, double-precision is needed.
2. For large programs, when storage space is at a premium. Sometimes it may be necessary to use the smallest size consistent with usage.

3. When execution speed is an issue. The speed improvement can be substantial, and it *can* make a difference. Computations done with integers are faster than those done with either single- or double-precision. Single-precision computations are done more quickly than double-precision.
4. When decimal fractions are inaccurate due to the nature of binary fractions (see Binary Fractions and Accuracy, p. 273), it may be necessary to store fractional values such as dollars and cents as whole numbers of pennies.

Example Programs: Comparison of Execution Speeds for Four Variable Types

Counters on FOR/NEXT loops are good candidates for integers. The following loop programs were tested using a short integer, a long integer, a single-precision, and a double-precision loop counter. The short integer is obviously the preferred usage.

Short Integer

```
'*** Time A Loop With Integer Variable ***
LET Start = VAL(RIGHT$(TIME$, 2))
FOR Count% = 1 TO 25000
NEXT Count%
LET Finish = VAL(RIGHT$(TIME$, 2))
IF Start > Finish THEN LET Finish = Finish + 60
LET Et = Finish - Start
PRINT "Elapsed time = "; Et
END
```

Program Execution:

```
Elapsed time = 1
```

Long Integer

```
'*** Time A Loop With Long Integer Variable ***
LET Start = VAL(RIGHT$(TIME$, 2))
FOR Count& = 1 TO 25000
NEXT Count&
LET Finish = VAL(RIGHT$(TIME$, 2))
IF Start > Finish THEN LET Finish = Finish + 60
LET Et = Finish - Start
PRINT "Elapsed time = "; Et
END
```

Program Execution:

```
Elapsed time = 1
```

Single-Precision

```
'**** Time A Loop With Single-Precision Variable ***
LET Start = VAL(RIGHT$ (TIME$, 2))
FOR Count! = 1 TO 25000
NEXT Count!
LET Finish = VAL(RIGHT$(TIME$, 2))
IF Start > Finish THEN LET Finish = Finish + 60
LET Et = Finish - Start
PRINT "Elapsed time = "; Et
END
```

Program Execution:

```
Elapsed time = 8
```

```
'*** Time A Loop With Double-Precision Variable ***
LET Start = VAL(RIGHT$(TIME$, 2))
FOR Count# = 1 TO 25000
NEXT Count#
LET Finish = VAL(RIGHT$(TIME$, 2))
IF Start > Finish THEN LET Finish = Finish + 60
LET Et = Finish - Start
PRINT "Elapsed time = "; Et
END
```

Program Execution:

```
Elapsed time = 9
```

DEFTYPE Statements

Instead of affixing $, %, &, !, or # to the end of a variable, it is also possible to declare the variable type by using the DEFTYPE statement.

DEFTYPE Statement—General Form

```
DEFSTR Letter1 [- Letter2]    'String
DEFINT Letter1 [- Letter2]    'Integer
DEFLNG Letter1 [- Letter2]    'Long integer
DEFSNG Letter1 [- Letter2]     'Single-precision
DEFDBL Letter1 [- Letter2]     'Double-precision
```

Any variable names beginning with the letters specified by Letter1 through Letter2 will be the type determined by the last three letters of the statement.

DEFTYPE Statement–Examples

```
DEFSTR N        'Now N acts like N$
DEFDBL A-C      'A, B, and C act like A#, B#, C#
```

Feedback

1. When would it be a good idea to use integer variables?
2. Name one advantage of using double-precision numeric variables rather than single-precision numeric variables.
3. Name one advantage of using single-precision variables over double-precision variables.
4. What is the best type of variable to use as a counter for a loop?

Binary Fractions and Accuracy

The accuracy of fractional numbers is one of the stickiest issues in computer programming. It is expected that when the computer does computations, the answers must be accurate. Right? Wrong! Although a complete explanation of the binary number system, binary fractions, and computer storage is beyond the scope of this text, a little technical discussion is necessary to understand the occasional strange output.

In our decimal number system, some fractions cannot be held accurately and must be rounded. For example, consider

$$1/3 = .33333 \text{ (nearly)}$$
$$\text{and } 2/3 = .66667 \text{ (almost)}$$

The numbers stored in the computer memory are held, not in decimal, but in binary. In the binary number system, there are some fractions that cannot be held accurately. Unfortunately, those inaccurate fractions are some like 1/10 and 1/100. This means that decimal fractions holding dollars and cents will not be exact. Try taking $1.00, subtracting 100 pennies from it, and checking for zero. It won't be zero. Close, but not zero.

```
'************ Give Away 10 Pennies ***************
PRINT "I STARTED WITH .10"
FOR Wad = .09 TO 0 STEP -.01
    PRINT "I GAVE AWAY 1 PENNY, THEN I HAD"; Wad
NEXT Wad
```

Program Execution:

```
I STARTED WITH .10
I GAVE AWAY 1 PENNY, THEN I HAD .09
I GAVE AWAY 1 PENNY, THEN I HAD 8.000001E-02
I GAVE AWAY 1 PENNY, THEN I HAD 7.000001E-02
I GAVE AWAY 1 PENNY, THEN I HAD 6.000001E-02
I GAVE AWAY 1 PENNY, THEN I HAD 5.000001E-02
I GAVE AWAY 1 PENNY, THEN I HAD 4.000002E-02
I GAVE AWAY 1 PENNY, THEN I HAD 3.000002E-02
I GAVE AWAY 1 PENNY, THEN I HAD 2.000002E-02
I GAVE AWAY 1 PENNY, THEN I HAD 1.000001E-02
I GAVE AWAY 1 PENNY, THEN I HAD 1.490116E-08
```

The values for Wad are printed in **E (exponential) notation,** which is similar to scientific notation. The last printed value, 1.490116E–08, means "move the decimal point eight positions to the left." This gives .00000001490116, which is extremely close to zero (especially in dealing with pennies).

What to Do?

What action the programmer should take depends on the desired results. If the concern is the appearance of the output, PRINT USING is the solution. Since numbers are rounded to fit the print image, the program can be written to print the "right" numbers.

```
'************ Give Away 10 Pennies ***************
PRINT "I STARTED WITH .10"
FOR Wad = .09 TO 0 STEP -.01
    PRINT "I GAVE AWAY 1 PENNY, THEN I HAD";
    PRINT USING " .##"; Wad
NEXT Wad
```

Program Execution:

```
I STARTED WITH .10
I GAVE AWAY 1 PENNY, THEN I HAD .09
I GAVE AWAY 1 PENNY, THEN I HAD .08
I GAVE AWAY 1 PENNY, THEN I HAD .07
I GAVE AWAY 1 PENNY, THEN I HAD .06
I GAVE AWAY 1 PENNY, THEN I HAD .05
I GAVE AWAY 1 PENNY, THEN I HAD .04
I GAVE AWAY 1 PENNY, THEN I HAD .03
I GAVE AWAY 1 PENNY, THEN I HAD .02
I GAVE AWAY 1 PENNY, THEN I HAD .01
I GAVE AWAY 1 PENNY, THEN I HAD .00
```

Be aware of the accuracy problem in computations, also. If a DO...LOOP had been used and tested for zero, an endless loop would have been created.

```
'************ An Endless Loop *******************
LET Wad = .10
DO WHILE Wad <> 0
    LET Wad = Wad - .01
    PRINT Wad
LOOP
```

Sometimes you may need to check for a "close," rather than an exact, figure.

```
DO WHILE ABS(Wad) > .001
```

This loop will be terminated when the value of Wad gets close to zero.

Another possible solution is to always calculate with whole numbers. You can convert all decimal values to a whole number of pennies. Then, just before printing results, you will have to divide by 100. With this method you will never have to check for "close"; the results of all intermediate calculations will be accurate, and columns of dollars and cents will add up correctly. Since short integers can only hold a maximum of 32,767, long integers are recommended. Use double-precision for all fractional values if it is possible that more than seven digits must be held.

```
'******* Use Pennies Only For Calculations *******
INPUT "Enter dollar amount"; Dollars#
LET Cents& = Dollars# * 100

...

GOSUB CalculateWithPennies
...

'******* Print Out Results of Calculations *******
LET Dollars# = Cents& / 100#
PRINT USING " $###,###,###.##"; Dollars#
```

Numeric Functions

Many numeric functions are included in BASIC. Some have already been used, such as INT and ABS. Most of the common functions are listed in table 10.2.

Table 10.2
Numeric functions.

Function	Value Returned
ABS(X)	The absolute value of X. $\lvert X \rvert = X$ if $X >= 0$ $\lvert X \rvert = -X$ if $X < 0$
ATN(X)	The angle in radians whose tangent is X. The result will be in the range $-\pi/2$ to $+\pi/2$.
CINT(X)	The integer closest to X (rounded).
COS(X)	The cosine of X, where X is in radians.
EXP(X)	The value of e raised to the power X ($e = 2.718282...$).
FIX(X)	The integer portion of X (truncated).
INT(X)	The largest integer $<= X$.
LOG(X)	The natural logarithm of X, where $X > 0$.
MOD	The modulus operator. M MOD N calculates the remainder when integer M is divided by integer N.
RND	A random number in the range 0–1 (exclusive).
SGN(X)	The sign of X. -1 if $X < 0$ 0 if $X = 0$ 1 if $X > 0$
SIN(X)	The sine of X where X is in radians.
SQR(X)	The square root of X where X must be $>= 0$.
TAN(X)	The tangent of X where X is in radians.

Converting to Integers—INT, FIX, and CINT Functions

```
LET A = INT(X)
LET B = FIX(X)
LET C = CINT(X)
```

Each of these three functions will convert a **real number** (with digits to the right of the decimal point) to a whole number. Each does the conversion in a little different fashion.

Number Line

```
              −1.5                        +1.5
   |     |     |     |     |     |     |     |     |
  −3    −2    −1     0    +1    +2    +3
```

INT produces the largest integer not greater than X (the argument). Negative values of X return the next lowest integer. The largest integer will be to the left on the number line (more negative). INT(-1.5) returns -2.

FIX truncates (chops off) all digits to the right of the decimal point. For negative arguments, FIX returns the next larger (less negative) number, which is to the right on the number line. FIX(-1.5) returns -1.

CINT rounds up to the nearest integer and thus could go in either direction on the number line. CINT(-1.4) returns -1, CINT(-1.5) returns -2. Table 10.3 shows a summary of these functions.

Table 10.3
INT, FIX, and CINT functions.

Function	Return for Values of X			
	X = 1.5	X = −1.5	X = 1.4	X = −1.4
INT(X)	1	−2	1	−2
FIX(X)	1	−1	1	−1
CINT(X)	2	−2	1	−1

The MOD Operation

In mathematical applications it is frequently necessary to determine the quotient and remainder when one number, Num, is divided by another number, Denom. Here is a simple solution:

```
Let Quotient = INT(Num/Denom)
LET Remainder = Num MOD Denom
```

Another use of these two functions is to determine whether a number, Num, is even or odd.

Method 1
```
If Num/2 = Int(Num/2) THEN
   PRINT "EVEN"
ELSE
   PRINT "ODD"
END IF
```

Method 2
```
IF Num MOD 2 = 0 THEN
   PRINT "EVEN"
ELSE
   PRINT "ODD"
END IF
```

Arithmetic Functions— ABS, SGN, SQR

```
LET A = ABS(X)
LET B = SGN(X)
LET C = SQR(X)
```

Each of these functions returns a real number based on the value of X.

ABS is the absolute value function, written as |X| in mathematics. ABS has the effect of stripping the sign from a number. For a positive X, it will return X; for a negative X, it will return $-X$. ABS will always return the positive representation of the argument.

SGN is the sign function. It can be used to determine the sign (positive, negative, or zero) of any argument. SGN returns -1 for negative numbers, $+1$ for positive numbers, and 0 for zero.

SQR is the square root function. It will return the square root of any positive argument. A negative argument generates the error message: *Invalid function call.* Table 10.4 summarizes the ABS, SGN, and SQR functions.

Table 10.4
ABS, SGN, and SQR functions.

Function	Return for Values of X			
	X = 1.5	X = -1.5	X = 0	X = 4
ABS(X)	1.5	1.5	0	4
SGN(X)	1	-1	0	1
SQR(X)	1.224745	ERROR	0	2

```
'*** Convert Negative Numbers For SQR Function ***
INPUT X
IF SGN(X) = -1 THEN
      LET Y = SQR(ABS(X))
   ELSE
      LET Y = SQR(X)
END IF
```

Exponential and Trigonometric Functions

```
LET A = SIN(X)
LET B = COS(X)
LET C = TAN(X)
LET D = ATN(X)
LET E = LOG(X)
LET F = EXP(X)
```

These functions can be used to solve mathematic and trigonometric problems. The trigonometric functions operate with angles measured in radians, rather than degrees. To convert from degrees to radians, use this formula:

$$\text{Radians} = \text{Degrees} * (3.14159/180)$$

The EXP function returns the mathematical number e (2.718282) raised to the power of X.

```
LET Y = EXP(4)
```

yields Y = 54.59815

The LOG function returns the natural log and is the inverse of the EXP function.

```
LET Z = LOG(54.59815)
```

yields Z = 4

In the following example we use the SIN, COS, and TAN functions to generate a table of trigonometric values. The test statement is necessary because TAN is defined as SIN/COS. Hence, if COS = 0, we would get a Division by zero error. (In actual practice, COS is only *close* to zero, thereby producing a large, but meaningless value for TAN.)

Example Program: Use of SIN, COS, and TAN

Program Listing

```
'*********** Demonstrate The Use Of SIN, COS, TAN ***********
'    Variables Used
'    Deg            Loop counter to generate angle in degrees
'    Rad            Angle measured in radians
'    First          Starting angle in the table (user input)
'    Last           Ending angle in the table (user input)
'    Incr           Increment between successive angles (user
'                   input)
'    D1$, H$, U$    Print images


'******************** Program Mainline ********************

GOSUB InitializePrintImages
GOSUB GetUserInput
GOSUB OutputTheTable
END


'***************** Initialize Print Images *****************

InitializePrintImages:
    LET D$ = "   ###      ##.###   ##.####   ##.####  "
    LET H$ = "DEGREES RADIANS     SINE       COSINE        TANGENT"
    LET U$ = STRING$(40; "-")
RETURN


'********************* Get User Input *********************

GetUserInput:
    CLS
    INPUT "Starting value? ", First
    INPUT "Ending value? ", Last
    INPUT "Increment? ", Incr
RETURN


'******************** Output The Table ********************
OutputTheTable:
    CLS
    PRINT H$
    PRINT U$
    FOR Deg = First TO Last STEP Incr
        LET Rad = Deg * 3.14159 / 180
        PRINT USING D$; Deg: Rad; SIN(Rad); COS(Rad);
        IF ABS(COS(Rad)) < .0001 THEN
            PRINT " UNDEF "
        ELSE
            PRINT USING " ##.#### "; TAN(Rad)
        END IF
    NEXT Deg
RETURN
'******************** End of Program ********************
```

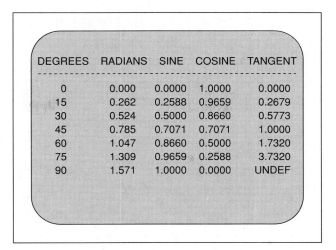

DEGREES	RADIANS	SINE	COSINE	TANGENT
0	0.000	0.0000	1.0000	0.0000
15	0.262	0.2588	0.9659	0.2679
30	0.524	0.5000	0.8660	0.5773
45	0.785	0.7071	0.7071	1.0000
60	1.047	0.8660	0.5000	1.7320
75	1.309	0.9659	0.2588	3.7320
90	1.571	1.0000	0.0000	UNDEF

Random Numbers—RND and RANDOMIZE

The function RND returns a number between 0 and 1. This means that any number from 0 to 1 (but not 0 or 1) is just as likely to come up as any other. RND is popular for use in games, as well as problems in probability and queuing theory.

The RND Function—General Form

```
RND
```

The RND Function—Examples

```
LET X = RND
LET Num = INT(RND*10)
PRINT RND
```

Here are ten random numbers generated by RND.

```
'*********** Generate Random Numbers **************
FOR Count = 1 TO 10
    PRINT RND
NEXT Count
END
```

Program Execution:

```
.7055475
.533424
.5795186
.2895625
.301948
.7747401
1.401764E-02
.7607236
.81449
.7090379
```

To generate numbers in a range 1–N:

```
LET Num = INT(RND * N + 1)
```

```
'****** Generate Numbers in a Given Range ********
INPUT "HIGHEST NUMBER"; Limit
FOR Index = 1 TO 10
   LET X = INT(RND * Limit + 1)
   PRINT X
NEXT Index
```

Program Execution:

```
HIGHEST NUMBER? 10
 1
 5
 9
 8
 4
 10
 9
 1
 10
 4
```

Unfortunately, the numbers are not really random. Every time the program is executed, the same sequence of "random" numbers is generated. To generate a different series of random numbers for each program run, the RANDOMIZE statement is used (once) at the beginning of the program. This is called *seeding* the random number generator.

The RANDOMIZE Statement—General Form

```
RANDOMIZE [numeric expression for seed]
```

The RANDOMIZE Statement—Examples

```
RANDOMIZE

INPUT "ENTER A NUMBER BETWEEN 1 AND 100", Seed
RANDOMIZE Seed

RANDOMIZE TIMER
```

RANDOMIZE can be used with or without the optional numeric expression. When the expression is omitted, BASIC suspends program execution and requests the seed from the keyboard.

```
Random number seed (-32768 to 32767)?__
```

The second example is a nicer way to request the seed from the user. The numbers 1–100 are not really required, but may seem less confusing to some users than −32768 to 32767.

The last example uses the internal clock for the seed as a way of selecting a different seed for each program run. (Recall that TIMER returns the number of seconds elapsed since last midnight.)

Example Program:
Using Random Numbers in a Guessing Game

Program Listing

```
'************************* Guessing Game ************************
CLS
RAMDOMIZE TIMER                        'Seed random number generator
LET Num = INT(RND * 100 + 1)          'Generate random number
INPUT "I'M THINKING OF A NUMBER BETWEEN 1 AND 100--YOUR GUESS";Guess
DO UNTIL Guess = Num
    IF Guess > Num THEN
        PRINT "TOO HIGH, GUESS AGAIN";
    ELSE
        PRINT "TOO LOW, GUESS AGAIN";
    END IF
    INPUT Guess
LOOP
PRINT "RIGHT ON!"
END
'************************* End of Program ***********************
```

Sample Program Output

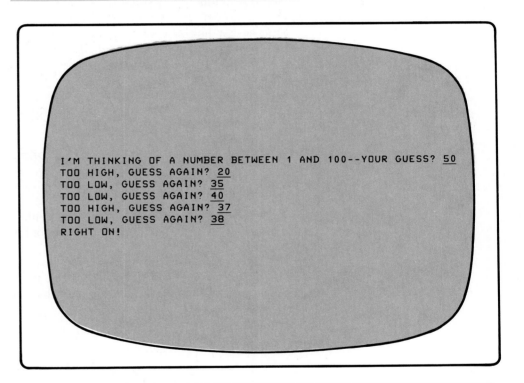

```
I'M THINKING OF A NUMBER BETWEEN 1 AND 100--YOUR GUESS? 50
TOO HIGH, GUESS AGAIN? 20
TOO LOW, GUESS AGAIN? 35
TOO LOW, GUESS AGAIN? 40
TOO HIGH, GUESS AGAIN? 37
TOO LOW, GUESS AGAIN? 38
RIGHT ON!
```

User-Defined Functions

In addition to the built-in functions, you can define your own functions. Any calculations done with **user-defined functions** can also be done without them. However, defining a relationship in a function can simplify programming. This is especially true when a complicated operation must be done in more than one location in the program.

QB offers two ways to write functions—single-line functions and multiple-line functions. The multiple-line functions are more powerful and are treated as separate program modules. Multiple-line functions will not be covered in this text.

```
'*********** Function to Round to 2 Decimal Places *****
DEF FNRound(X) = FIX(X * 100 + .5 * SGN(X)) / 100
:::
'***** Use the Function in Various Locations **********
LET Amt = FNRound(Amt)
:::
PRINT FNRound(A), FNRound(B), FNRound(C)
:::
LET Tax = FNRound(Sale * .065)
```

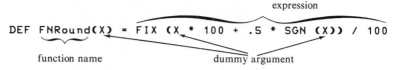

The DEF FN statement defines a function called FNRound. X is called a *dummy argument,* since it is holding the place for the actual argument. When the function is called later in the program, the actual argument named is substituted for X in the function definition. The expression on the right side of the equal sign is the operation to be carried out each time the function is referenced.

The first time the function is referenced, the current value for Amt will be rounded. Amt takes the place of X in the function expression.

In the second example, the function FNRound is referenced three times, each time with a different argument. A, B, and C will each be rounded according to the rule named in the DEF FN statement.

When the last statement is executed, first Sale will be multiplied by .065, then the result rounded by the function FNRound.

The DEF FN Statement—General Form

> DEF FNname(argument(s)) = expression

The naming of the function follows the rules for naming variables. The function name will be FN + the name given. The type of function (numeric or string) is defined by the name given.

There may be multiple arguments named (or none). The arguments that appear in the function definition serve only to define the function. They don't bear any relationship to any program variables that may have the same name.

```
'***** String Function to Print a Pattern *********
DEF FNPt$(A$) = STRING$(5, A$) + SPACE$(5) + STRING$(5, A$)
LET A$ = "B"
PRINT FNPt$("=")
```

This will print:

```
=====     =====
```

The LET A$ = "B" statement has no effect on the function. The argument of the function is the equal sign ("="), which was passed when the function was called.

An **argument** is data that is passed to the function. The variables named in the expression may or may not appear as arguments. However, the function may reference (use in calculations) variables that are not named as arguments. When a variable is an argument, the value of the argument is supplied when the function is called. When the variable is not an argument, the current value of the variable will be used.

Example Program: Variable Used in Function Expression

Program Listing

```
'*********** Variable Used In Function Expression ************
DEF FNPn$ (X$) = STRING$(Size, X$) + SPACE$(Size * 2) + STRING$(Size, X$)

CLS
LET P$ = "#"
FOR Size = 1 TO 10
    PRINT FNPn$(P$)
NEXT Size
END
'******************** End of Program ********************
```

Sample Program Output

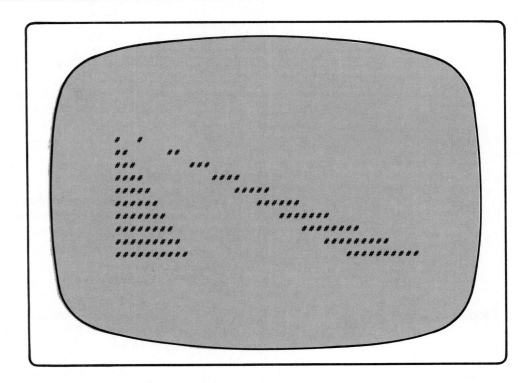

Functions with No Arguments

Although most versions of BASIC require at least one argument for functions, QB does not. There may be occasions when no arguments are required.

```
' *** A Function With No Arguments ***
CLS
DEF FNMonth = VAL(LEFT$(DATE$, 2))

'*** Function may be used anywhere a numeric expression is legal
IF FNMonth > 6 THEN
    GOSUB PrintSecondHalf
END IF

PRINT USING " The number of this month is ## "; FNMonth
```

Functions with Multiple Arguments

One function may be defined with multiple arguments, as long as the function is called with the same number of arguments. The arguments may be any precision numeric variables or string variables. No matter what the precision of the arguments, a numeric function will always return a single-precision number.

```
' *** Function to Center String on any Length Line ***
DEF FNCent$ (X$, L) = SPACE$((L - LEN(X$)) / 2) + X$
   .
   .
   .
INPUT "Type a heading: ", Hd$
PRINT FNCent$(Hd$, 80)
LPRINT FNCent$(Hd$, 120)
```

This function will center a string on whatever length line is specified. The function (FNCent$) is a string function. The function name is defined with a dollar sign, so the value returned will be a string. It is perfectly acceptable to have both string and numeric arguments, as long as the number, type, and order of arguments on the function reference exactly match those on the DEF FN statement. The actual arguments are substituted for the dummy arguments on a one-for-one basis depending on their position.

Referencing User-Defined Functions

In a program, user-defined functions are referenced (called) in the same way as built-in functions. The function must always be referenced by its full name (including FN) and may appear in any expression.

```
LET Y = INT(FNX(A) / FNY(A))
PRINT TAB(FNA(K)); K
LET Strange = SQR(ABS(FNR(Z)))
```

Order of Execution
The DEF FN statement must be executed before any reference to the function is made. The general practice is either to place all function definitions at the beginning of the program or to place them in an initializing subroutine.

Hierarchy of Operations

Functions rank above parentheses and exponentiation in the hierarchy of operations. If functions are used within other functions, the innermost operations are performed first.

```
'***** Example To Show Order of Operations *********
LET What = SQR(INT(ABS(A / B)) * 2) + A ^ 2
            ↑    ↑   ↑    ↑      ↑     ↑   ↑
            5    3   2    1      4     7   6
```

Feedback

1. Evaluate the following functions:

   a. INT(2.1)   e. SQR(-9)

   b. FIX(2.1)   f. ABS(4)

   c. CINT(2.1)   g. ABS(-4)

   d. SQR(9)   h. SGN(-4)

2. What will print?

   a.
   ```
   DEF FNK (A) = SQR(ABS(A))
   LET A = 9
   LET B = -25
   PRINT FNK(B)
   ```

   b.
   ```
   DEF FNA (X,Y,Z) = (X+Y+Z)/3
   PRINT FNA(10, 20, 30)
   ```

   c.
   ```
   DEF FNLn$ (C$) = C$+" "+C$+" "+C$+" "+C$
   PRINT FNLn$("*")
   ```

   d.
   ```
   DEF FNUc$(A$) = CHR$(ASC(A$) -32)
   READ Res$
   DATA Yes Please
   FOR Ct = 1 TO LEN(Res$)
       LET R$ = MID$(Res$,CT,1)
       IF ASC(R$) >= 97 AND ASC(R$) <= 122 THEN
           MID$(Res$,Ct,1) = FNUc(R$)
       END IF
   NEXT Ct
   PRINT Res$
   ```

3. What is a dummy argument?
4. How many operations may be done in the expression of a DEF FN statement?
5. Can you think of a good application for user-defined functions that was not mentioned in the chapter?

Summary

1. Loops that are controlled by a counter have three distinct steps. The counter must be initialized, incremented, and tested for completion.
2. The FOR and NEXT statements can be used to control the execution of a loop.
3. In the FOR statement, the counter variable is established and initialized. Also, the increment amount is defined.
4. The initial value, test value, and increment may be numeric constants, variables, or arithmetic expressions.
5. If the test condition is true before entry into the loop, the body of the loop will not be executed at all.
6. The NEXT statement marks the bottom of the loop. When NEXT is reached during execution, the counter is incremented, and control is passed back to the FOR statement to test the condition again.
7. The condition is tested for "greater than" the final value. In the case of a negative increment, the test is for "less than."
8. FOR/NEXT loops may be nested to any level. When nesting FOR/NEXT loops, the inner loop must be completely contained within the outer loop.
9. The loop index for the inner loop is incremented faster than the outer loop index.

10. Single-precision numeric variables hold up to seven digits accurately.
11. Double-precision numeric variables can hold up to fifteen digits accurately.
12. Integer variables hold whole numbers in the range -32768 to $+32767$.
13. Long integers can hold whole numbers in the range $-2,147,483,648$ to $+2,147,483,647$.
14. Numeric variables that are not explicitly defined default to single-precision.
15. To explicitly define the type of variables, the rightmost character must be % for integers, & for long integers, ! for single-precision, # for double-precision, and $ for string variables.
16. The unit of measurement for computer storage is the byte. Integer variables take two bytes, long integers take four bytes, single-precision variables take four bytes, double-precision variables take eight bytes, and string variables take one byte for each character stored.
17. The correct selection of variable type can affect the accuracy of the program, the speed of execution, and the program size.
18. Fractional numbers may not be stored accurately due to the nature of binary fractions.
19. When using fractional values, it may be necessary to check for "close" rather than exact numbers.
20. Many numeric functions are available in BASIC. A function performs the prescribed operation using the value passed as the argument.
21. The RND function returns a "random" number between 0 and 1 (exclusive).
22. To generate random numbers in the range 1–N, use the formula INT(RND * N + 1).
23. Every run of the program generates the same series of "random" numbers, unless the RANDOMIZE statement is used.
24. The functions INT, FIX, and CINT convert fractions to whole numbers, each in a little different manner.
25. INT returns the largest integer not greater than the argument. Negative numbers return the next lower integer.
26. FIX returns the integer portion of the argument by truncating all digits to the right of the decimal point. Negative numbers return the next higher integer.
27. CINT returns the nearest integer determined by rounding. Negative numbers may return a higher or lower number, whichever is closer.
28. ABS returns the absolute value of the argument.
29. SGN is used to determine the sign of a number. SGN returns -1 for a negative argument, $+1$ for a positive argument, and 0 for a zero argument.
30. SQR returns the square root of a positive argument.
31. The trigonometric functions, SIN, COS, TAN, and ATN operate on angles measured in radians.
32. The exponential functions EXP and LOG perform opposite operations using natural logarithms.
33. Additional functions can be defined by the programmer.
34. User (programmer)-defined functions are established with the DEF FN statement.
35. The DEF FN statement consists of the function name, the argument(s), and an expression that establishes the operation to be performed.
36. The variable(s) named as arguments in the DEF FN statement are called dummy arguments, since they are not actual program variables. The dummy arguments are used to indicate the operation to perform on the actual arguments.
37. Functions have higher priority than exponentiation in the hierarchy of operations for evaluating expressions.

Programming Exercises

10.1. Write a program that will print a table for conversion between pounds and kilograms.

INPUT: None
OUTPUT:
1. Print an appropriate title and column headings centered over the columns of data.
2. Print one detail line for each weight in pounds, beginning with .5, in increments of .5, ending with 20 pounds.

CALCULATIONS:
1. Use a FOR/NEXT loop to control the processing. The index of the loop must be the number of pounds. (Hint: Use .5 as the STEP.)
2. The formula for conversion:
   1 pound is approximately equal to .45 kilograms

10.2. Write a math drill program for elementary school students, allowing a choice of addition, subtraction, multiplication, or division. The selection of problem type is to be presented to the user as a menu. After the completion of one group of problems, the menu must be redisplayed.

MENU: Clear the screen and present a centered menu. The choices should be (1) Addition, (2) Subtraction, (3) Multiplication, (4) Division, and (5) Quit.
INPUT: Input the name of the student and the menu selection. After each problem is presented, the student's answer must be input.
OUTPUT: Present each problem on the screen. After the user's response, print a message that indicates whether the answer was correct or incorrect. Clear the problem and any messages before presenting the next problem.
PROCESSING:
1. The numbers for the problems are to be generated with the RND function. Use digits 0–9 for operands.
2. Each group should present ten problems.
3. If the user gives an incorrect answer three times for one problem, print the correct answer and proceed to the next problem. (Give encouraging messages.)
4. Subtraction problems must not require a negative answer.
5. Division problems will have integer answers (in the range 0–9).
6. No problem will require division by zero.
7. At the end of a group of problems, indicate how many were answered correctly on the first attempt. Then redisplay the menu (after a reasonable pause).
8. Validate the number input for menu item choice. The only valid response is a number in the range 1–5.

10.3. Print a table showing X, X^2, X^3, and $\sqrt{X}$, for X = 1 to 10. A FOR/NEXT loop must be used to increment X.

INPUT: None
OUTPUT: Complete this table.

X	X^2	X^3	$\sqrt{X}$
1	1	1	1.000
2	4	8	1.414
3	9	27	1.732
.	.	.	.
.	.	.	.

10.4. If one cent were placed in an investment that doubles in value each day, what would be the value of the investment at the end of thirty days? Write a program (using a FOR/NEXT loop) that calculates and prints the value of the investment for each of thirty days.

INPUT: None
OUTPUT: Complete the output shown.

```
DOUBLE OR NOTHING INVESTMENT COMPANY

DAY                 VALUE OF INVESTMENT

1                        .01
2                        .02
3                        .04
.                        .
.                        .
.                        .
```

10.5. On a clear day, you can see forever (almost). The distance you can see depends on your altitude while viewing and can be determined by this formula:

$$\text{distance in miles} = \text{SQR(altitude)} * 1.22$$

Write a program that will print a table of distances from an altitude of 1,000 feet to 10,000 feet in increments of 1,000 feet. Use a FOR/NEXT loop for the altitude with a step of 1000.

```
        VIEWING DISTANCES

    ALTITUDE            DISTANCE

     1,000               38.6
     2,000               54.6
     3,000               66.8
      .                    .
      .                    .
      .                    .
```

10.6. Simulate a coin toss twenty times, and count the number of heads and the number of tails thrown. Use the RND function. Assume that any value $> .5$ is heads, the rest tails. Be sure to use the RANDOMIZE statement, so that each program run will produce different results.

INPUT: A random number seed.
OUTPUT: For each run, print the number of heads and the number of tails produced.

10.7. Some line printers can only print uppercase characters. Write a program that will print address labels, converting all lowercase letters to uppercase.

INPUT: During program execution, request input of a name, address, city, state, and zip code. Continue inputting and printing until END is entered for the name.

OUTPUT: Print one address label for each person. The labels will be printed "one-up," which means that each label is directly below the preceding one. The most commonly used labels have room for five printed lines, with one more line lost between labels. Therefore a new label should begin every six lines (one inch). All alphabetic output must be uppercase.

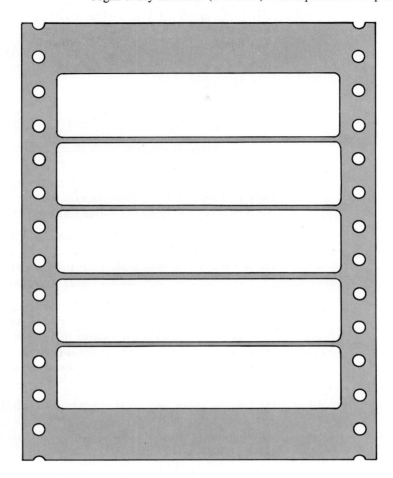

PROCESSING: Any lowercase letters must be converted to uppercase.

10.8. Write a program that will randomly place dots on the screen until a key is pressed.

10.9. Write a program to randomly place squares made with graphics symbols on the screen until a key is pressed.

10.10. Write a program to print a list of ten random numbers between 1 and 100. Print the numbers on the screen.

10.11. Write a program to print the absolute value, square root, and square of any number input from the keyboard.

10.12. Use a FOR/NEXT loop to total the numbers from 1 through 100. Print the numbers on the screen.

10.13. Modify program 3.15 (karate studio purchase orders, p. 100) to use FOR/NEXT loops instead of DO...LOOP.

10.14. Write a program using FOR/NEXT loops to find the standard deviation and midrange of a set of fifty numbers.

INPUT: The fifty numbers will come from DATA statements.
OUTPUT: Print the standard deviation, the midrange, and the 50 numbers on the printer.
PROCESSING:

1. Standard deviation = square root of $\dfrac{n(\text{sum of } x^2) - (\text{sum of } x)^2}{n(n-1)}$

2. Midrange = $\dfrac{\text{highest score} + \text{lowest score}}{2}$

10.15. Write a program to print addition, subtraction, multiplication, and division tests. Use FOR/NEXT loops to print fifty problems per page and use the RANDOMIZE statement so each test is different.

INPUT: Choose an option from a menu: addition, subtraction, multiplication, division, or quit.
OUTPUT: Print a title, a place for the student's name and score, and fifty problems on the printer. Format the output using print images.

10.16. To test the RND function and verify that the numbers are random, generate 10,000 numbers between 0 and 99. For each number, determine which decile (0–9, 10–19, 20–29, etc.) it belongs to and add 1 to a counter for that decile. When finished, print the counts for the ten deciles. If the random number routine is working properly, it will generate a number falling in any one decile about one-tenth of the time.

10.17. Do problem 10.16 with short integers and with single-precision numbers. Time each of them, compare the times, and have the computer report which was faster and what percentage improvement in speed can be gained from using a proper numeric type.

10.18. Write a program using a time value of money function to show the present value of a lump sum of money to be received in the future. Input the interest rate to be used and the amount to be received. Print a report showing the present value of the money decreasing as the time for it to be received fades into the future.

Hint: the present value formula is:

$$\text{Present Value} = \text{Amount} \left[\frac{1}{[1 + \text{interest rate}]^N} \right]$$

where N is the number of time periods in the future when the Amount is to be received.

10.19. As a variation on the situation in problem 10.18, assume that you have won the lottery, and have a choice of accepting an immediate payment of $1,000,000 (after taxes!) or contracting to receive $100,000 per year (also after taxes) for the next twenty years. Include color and sound in your input and output screens. Have the computer give a definitive answer regarding which alternative to choose, assuming interest rates of 5%, 8%, and 11%. Calculate the present value using a function.

Hint: the present value of a future stream of income is:

$$\text{Present Value} = \text{Amount} \left[\frac{[1 - [1 + i]^{-N}]}{i} \right]$$

where N is the number of time periods in the future during which the Amount is to be received, and i is the interest rate.

11

Single-Dimension Arrays

DIM Statement

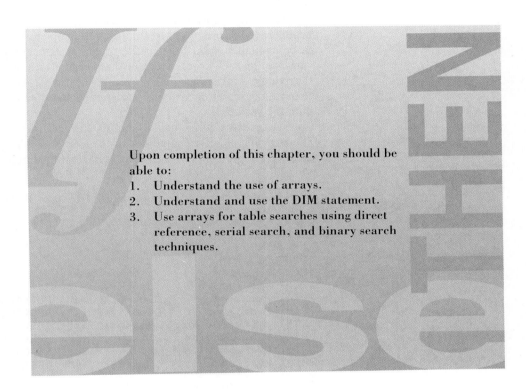

Upon completion of this chapter, you should be able to:

1. Understand the use of arrays.
2. Understand and use the DIM statement.
3. Use arrays for table searches using direct reference, serial search, and binary search techniques.

Introduction

In this chapter a method will be presented to overcome a problem that has arisen in some earlier programs. Whenever data is input in a loop, the new value for a variable replaces the prior value.

```
'***************** Average Scores ********************
INPUT Score
DO UNTIL Score = -1
    LET Count = Count + 1
    LET Tot = Tot + Score
    INPUT Score
LOOP
LET Avg = Tot / Count
PRINT "Average score = "; Avg
END
```

Although each score is accumulated in the loop, the individual scores are no longer available to the program after the loop is complete. Sometimes these scores may need to be available again later in the program. A common operation is to compute the variance for each score, which is the measure of how far an individual score is from the average [variance = ABS(average − score)]. For that operation, we would need to input the scores once to find the average and then input them a second time to compute the variance.

A second solution could be to give every score a unique variable name, so that all are available after completion of the loop. For this approach, the number of scores must be known ahead of time. In the interest of simplicity, six scores are used for the example.

```
'********* Calculate Variance For Six Scores *********
INPUT Score1
INPUT Score2
INPUT Score3
INPUT Score4
INPUT Score5
INPUT Score6
PRINT Avg = (Score1 + Score2 + Score3 + Score4 + Score5 + Score6) / 6
PRINT "Variance for"; Score1;" is"; ABS(Avg - Score1)
PRINT "Variance for"; Score2;" is"; ABS(Avg - Score2)
PRINT "Variance for"; Score3;" is"; ABS(Avg - Score3)
PRINT "Variance for"; Score4;" is"; ABS(Avg - Score4)
PRINT "Variance for"; Score5;" is"; ABS(Avg - Score5)
PRINT "Variance for"; Score6;" is"; ABS(Avg - Score6)
```

This program does solve the problem. The individual scores were retained in memory by giving each a unique variable name. With a little work, a search could find the highest score, print that one first, then the next highest, and so forth, to produce a sorted list. Stop and picture the program required to handle 30 scores or 100 scores.

Fortunately, there is a much better way. To hold related multiple variables, use an **array**. An array is a series of individual variables, all referenced by the same name.

Programming with Arrays

> An ARRAY can be defined as a series (or a group) of variables that are all referred to by one name.

In mathematics, multiple scores could be noted:

$$S_1, \quad S_2, \quad S_3, \quad S_4, \quad \ldots, \quad S_N$$

In BASIC, an array may be referenced in much the same way:

```
S(1), S(2), S(3), S(4), S(5), S(6)
```

These are read S sub one, S sub two, S sub three, and so forth.

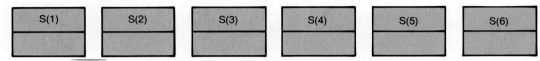

Each individual variable is called an *element* of the S array. The individual elements, also called **subscripted variables,** are treated the same as any other variable used and may be used in any statement such as LET, PRINT, INPUT, and READ.

```
LET S(1) = 5

LET Tot = Tot + S(4)

READ S(2)

INPUT S(5)

PRINT S(1), S(2), S(3), S(4)
```

Subscripts

The real advantage of arrays is not realized until variables are used for **subscripts** in place of the constants.

```
LET S(N) = 5

LET Tot = Tot + S(Index)

READ S(Index)

INPUT S(ScSub)

PRINT S(K), S(K+1), S(K+2), S(K+3)
```

Subscripts may be constants, variables, or numeric expressions. Although the subscripts must be integers, BASIC will round any noninteger subscript.

The problem to compute the variance for six scores becomes much easier.

```
'********** Input Scores and Compute Average *********
FOR Count = 1 TO 6
    INPUT S(Count)
    LET Tot = Tot + S(Count)
NEXT Count
LET Avg = Tot / 6                'Calc average

'*********** Compute and Print Variance ************
FOR Count = 1 TO 6
    LET Variance = ABS(Avg - S(Count))
    PRINT "The variance for"; S(Count); " is"; Variance
NEXT Count
```

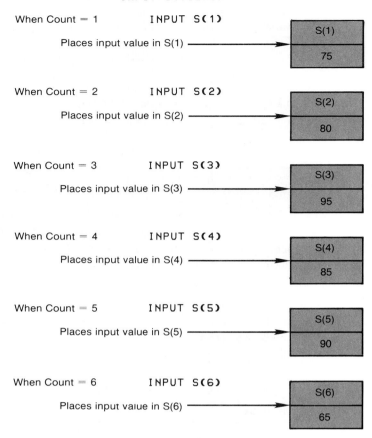

INPUT S(Count)

When Count = 1   INPUT S(1)

Places input value in S(1) ———————→

S(1)
75

When Count = 2   INPUT S(2)

Places input value in S(2) ———————→

S(2)
80

When Count = 3   INPUT S(3)

Places input value in S(3) ———————→

S(3)
95

When Count = 4   INPUT S(4)

Places input value in S(4) ———————→

S(4)
85

When Count = 5   INPUT S(5)

Places input value in S(5) ———————→

S(5)
90

When Count = 6   INPUT S(6)

Places input value in S(6) ———————→

S(6)
65

If the scores had not been added in the input loop, the elements of the array could be totaled quickly after the values were entered.

```
'******** Total the Elements in the S Array ***************
TotalElements:
   FOR Count = 1 TO 6
      LET Total = Total + S(Count)
   NEXT Count
RETURN
```

To print all scores, a routine similar to the following might be used.

```
'******** Print All Elements of the S Array **************
PrintElements:
   FOR Count = 1 TO 6
      PRINT S(Count)
   NEXT Count
RETURN
```

To print the scores in the reverse order from which they were input, use a routine similar to the following.

```
'*********** Print Scores in Reverse Order *****************
PrintScoresReversed:
   FOR Count = 6 TO 1 STEP -1
      PRINT S(Count)
   NEXT Count
RETURN
```

What changes would need to be made in the programs to handle more than six scores? Like 30 or 100?

A question has probably occurred to you by now—how many elements *are* there in the S array? The answer is that the programmer defines the number of elements in the array before its first use with the DIM (DIMension) statement.

It was possible to omit the DIM statements in the examples thus far because, in the absence of a DIM statement, BASIC allocates ten elements. Even though elements 1–6 were used, #7, 8, 9, and 10 were still available. In fact, there is one more—element 0—but more about that later.

Dimensioning an Array

The DIM Statement—General Form

```
DIM ArrayName(number of elements) ...
or
DIM ArrayName (lower subscript TO upper subscript) ...
```

The DIM Statement—Examples

```
DIM Score(100)
DIM Nam$(50)
DIM A(20),B(20),C(40),N$(50),P(10)
DIM Item$(101 TO 500)
DIM ID$(1000 TO 9999)
DIM Result(-100 TO 100)


INPUT Count
DIM S(Count)
```

The DIM statement allocates storage space for the specified number of elements and initializes each to zero. In the case of string arrays, each element is set to a null string (no characters).

Placement of the DIM statement is critical. DIM must be executed before any statement that references the array. Most programmers place all DIM statements at the start of the program, after the initial remarks and before the program mainline. The only exception to that practice would be the case shown in the last example above, where the size of the array is determined during program execution. Arrays dimensioned with a variable as a subscript, as in the last example, are referred to as *dynamic;* otherwise they are *static* arrays.

One program may have multiple DIM statements, and one DIM statement may dimension multiple arrays. Either of these approaches is valid:

```
DIM Apples(20), Bananas(20), Fruit$(40)
```

or

```
DIM Apples(20)
DIM Bananas(20)
DIM Fruit$(40)
```

Each static array may be dimensioned only once in a program. Any attempt to change the size of an array after its first use causes the error message: *Array already dimensioned.* Dynamic arrays, however, may be redimensioned using the REDIM statement. In this text all arrays are treated as static.

The maximum number of elements in one array is 32767 (that familiar number again!). A more practical limit for programming with arrays is the memory size of the computer. Each array element (and each regular variable) causes memory to be set aside. Many large arrays can quickly take the entire memory of small computers.

Without a DIM statement, BASIC arrays default to ten elements. However, *it is strongly recommended that all arrays be dimensioned, even those with ten elements or less.* Having the DIM statements appear together in the program is an aid to documentation and program debugging.

As mentioned earlier, BASIC also allocates an element zero for each array. The statement

```
DIM S(6)
```

actually defines seven elements: S(0), S(1), S(2), S(3), S(4), S(5), and S(6). In actual practice, the 0th (say zeroeth) element is commonly ignored. If there is no need for an element zero, one of three approaches may be taken: (1) ignore element zero; (2) use the OPTION BASE statement, which defines the lower limit for array elements; or (3) define the lower and upper limits in the DIM statement.

```
OPTION BASE 1
```

or

```
OPTION BASE 0  (the system default)
```

OPTION BASE 1 declares that all program arrays will begin with element 1 (instead of zero). This could save space if the program uses many arrays. If the OPTION BASE statement is used, it must appear before any array is dimensioned or used.

Declaring lower and upper bounds for arrays is a new addition to the BASIC language that is a big improvement.

```
DIM S(1 to 6)
```

More on Subscripts

A subscript (which may also be called an index) must reference a valid element of the array. If a list contained ten names, it wouldn't make sense to ask, "What is the fifteenth name on the list?" Try asking for the −1st name or the 2½th name on the list. BASIC rounds fractional subscripts and gives the error message: *Subscript out of range* for invalid subscripts.

Feedback

```
DIM A(20)
LET I = 10
```

After execution of the preceding statements, which of the following are valid subscripts?

1.	A(20)	5.	A(0)
2.	A(I)	6.	A(I-20)
3.	A(I*2)	7.	A(I/3)
4.	A(I*3)	8.	A(I/5-2)

Filling an Array with READ and DATA Statements

Using the READ to fill an array is similar to using the INPUT statement.

```
'******** Fill Ten-Element Array With READ/DATA ******
DIM Cost(1 TO 10)
FOR Index% = 1 TO 10
   READ Cost(Index%)
NEXT Index%
DATA 2.00,2.10,2.50,2.75,3.00,3.15,3.45,4.10,4.85,5.25
```

Here is an alternate method:

```
'**** Fill Array With READ/DATA Until Terminal Value ****
DIM Cost(1 TO 20)
LET Index% = 1
READ Cost(Index%)
DO WHILE Cost(Index%) >= 0 AND Index% < 20
    LET Index% = Index% + 1
    READ Cost(Index%)
LOOP
DATA 2.00,2.10,2.50,2.75,3.00,3.15,3.45,4.10
DATA 4.85,5.25,5.85,6.45,-1
```

Feedback

Use this statement for both problems:

```
DIM Nam$(1 TO 50)
```

1. Using INPUT, write the statements that will request names from the keyboard, and fill the Nam$ array with those names until EOD is entered.
2. Write the READ/DATA statements necessary to READ names into the Nam$ array until EOD is read.

Parallel Arrays

Consider the test score example again. If keeping names along with the scores is desired, a second array is required, one for the set of scores and another for the set of names.

```
'*********** Read Data Into Parallel Arrays **********
DIM Nam$(1 TO 6), Score(1 TO 6)
FOR Index% = 1 TO 6
    READ Nam$(Index%), Score(Index%)
NEXT Index%
DATA J. SPRAT,75,M. MUFFETT, 80,L. BOPEEP,95,B. SHAFTOE,85
DATA L. BOYBLUE,90,O. L. SHOE, 65
```

	Nam$ array		Score array
(1)	J. SPRAT	(1)	75
(2)	M. MUFFETT	(2)	80
(3)	L. BOPEEP	(3)	95
(4)	B. SHAFTOE	(4)	85
(5)	L. BOYBLUE	(5)	90
(6)	O. L. SHOE	(6)	65

The elements in the two **parallel arrays** correspond; that is, the first name goes with the first score, second with second, and so forth. The complete list could be printed out, or any single element.

```
'****** Print List Of All Names And Scores **********
PrintList:
    FOR Index% = 1 TO 6
     PRINT Nam$(Index%), Score(Index%)
    NEXT Index%
RETURN
```

In this example, the highest score is found, and the score and corresponding name are printed.

```
'*********** Find High Score ************************
FindHighScore:
    LET HighIndex% = 1
    FOR Index% = 2 TO 6
        IF Score(Index%) > Score(HighIndex%) THEN
        LET HighIndex% = Index%
        END IF
    NEXT Index%
    '* Now HighIndex% holds the subscript of the high score
    PRINT "Highest person was "; Nam$(HighIndex%);
    PRINT " with a score of"; Score(HighIndex%)
RETURN
```

Arrays Used for Accumulators

Array elements are regular variables, just like all variables used thus far. These subscripted variables may be used in any way chosen, such as for counters or total accumulators.

To demonstrate the use of array elements as total accumulators, eight totals will be accumulated. For the example, eight scout groups are selling raffle tickets. A separate total must be accumulated for each of the eight groups. Each time a sale is made, the number of tickets must be added to the correct total. The statement

```
DIM Total(1 TO 8)
```

will establish the eight accumulators.

Initializing the Array

Although all program variables are initially set to zero, it is often necessary to re-initialize variables. Such is the case when printing subtotals. After the subtotals are printed, the fields must be reset to zero. To zero out an array, each element must be individually set to zero.

```
'*************** Zero Out Total Array **************
FOR Index% = 1 TO 8
    LET Total(Index%) = 0
NEXT Index%
```

Total array

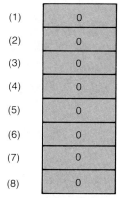

```
(1)    0
(2)    0
(3)    0
(4)    0
(5)    0
(6)    0
(7)    0
(8)    0
```

Adding to the Correct Total

Assuming that a program inputs a group number and number of tickets, the problem is to add that ticket count to the correct total. The sales will be input in any order, with multiple sales for each group.

```
'******** Input Group Number and Ticket Sale ********
INPUT "Enter group number ", Group
INPUT "Number of tickets sold ", Sale
```

After execution of the input statements, Group holds the group number, and Sale holds the amount of this sale. Assume for the first sale that 4 was entered for the group number and 10 tickets were sold.

In order to add 10 to the group 4 total, use Group as a subscript to add to the correct Total element.

```
LET Total(Group) = Total(Group) + Sale
```

After execution of this statement, Total(4) contains the value 10.

Of course, there is always the danger that the user will incorrectly enter the group number. Since it is undesirable for the user to get the error message *Subscript out of range,* the group number must be validated.

```
'**** Add Sale to Correct Total or Print Error Msg ***
IF Group >= 1 AND Group <= 8 THEN
        LET Total(Group) = Total(Group) + Sale
ELSE
        PRINT "Invalid group number, re-enter this sale"
END IF
```

Using the group number as an index to the array is a technique called direct reference.

Direct Table Reference

There are many occasions when it is useful to use an input variable as a subscript to point to an array element. Another example of direct reference is the use of a table to look up the month names. If a month number is input (perhaps part of the date), the corresponding month name can be printed out.

When using tables for reference, it is necessary to *load* the table as an initialization step in the program. The entire table must be in memory and available during all processing.

```
'*************** Load Month Table ******************
DIM Month$(1 TO 12)
FOR MonthSub% = 1 TO 12
    READ Month$(MonthSub%)
NEXT MonthSub%
DATA JANUARY, FEBRUARY, MARCH, APRIL, MAY, JUNE, JULY
DATA AUGUST, SEPTEMBER, OCTOBER, NOVEMBER, DECEMBER
```

Month$ array

(1)	JANUARY
(2)	FEBRUARY
(3)	MARCH
(4)	APRIL
(5)	MAY
(6)	JUNE
(7)	JULY
(8)	AUGUST
(9)	SEPTEMBER
(10)	OCTOBER
(11)	NOVEMBER
(12)	DECEMBER

PRINT Month$(MonthNum)

MonthNum
10

Output: OCTOBER

Lookup by Direct Reference

The month number can be used to directly access (or look up) the correct array element. If the month number is input, it is a simple task to print out the corresponding month name.

```
'****** Input Month Number And Print Month Name ******
INPUT "Enter month number ", MonthNum
IF MonthNum >= 1 AND MonthNum <= 12 THEN
      PRINT Month$(MonthNum)
END IF
```

If the user entered 10 for MonthNum, then the tenth element of the Month$ array would be printed—which is OCTOBER.

Table Lookup— Serial Search

Things don't always work out so neatly as month numbers or group numbers that can be used to directly access the table. Sometimes a little work must be done to **look up** the correct value. Go back to the eight scout groups and their ticket sales. Now the groups are not numbered 1–8, but 101, 103, 110, 115, 121, 123, 130, and 145. The group number and the number of tickets sold will still be input, and the number of tickets will be added to the correct total. But, another step is needed—determine to which element of the Sales array to add.

The first step in the program will be to establish a parallel array with the group numbers. Then, before any processing is done, the group numbers must be loaded into the table.

```
DIM Total(1 TO 8), GrNum(1 TO 8)

'************** Load Group Number Array ************
LoadArray:
    FOR Gr% = 1 TO 8
        READ GrNum(Gr%)
    NEXT Gr%
    DATA 101, 103, 110, 115, 121, 123, 130, 145
RETURN
```

	GrNum array			Total array
(1)	101		(1)	0
(2)	103		(2)	0
(3)	110		(3)	0
(4)	115		(4)	0
(5)	121		(5)	0
(6)	123		(6)	0
(7)	130		(7)	0
(8)	145		(8)	0

Again, the subroutine to input group number and sales will be executed.

```
'******* Input Group Number and Ticket Sale***********
InputData:
    INPUT "Enter group number ", Group
    INPUT "Number of tickets sold ", Sale
RETURN
```

The technique used is called **serial table lookup,** or **table search.** In the table lookup, the object is to find the element number (1–8) of the group number and use that element number as a subscript to the total table. So, if the third group number (110) is entered, the sale will be added to the third total. If the seventh group number (130) is entered, the sale will be added to the seventh total, and so on. Hence, we need a way, given the group number (Group), to find the corresponding subscript (GroupSub) of the Total array.

When BASIC executes the statement

```
LET Total(GroupSub) = Total(GroupSub) + Sale
```

the value of GroupSub must be a number in the range 1–8. The task for the lookup operation is to find the number to place in GroupSub, based on the value of Group. Figure 11.1 shows the variables used for the lookup. Figure 11.2 shows the flowchart of the lookup logic.

Figure 11.1
Diagram of arrays and variables
for lookup.

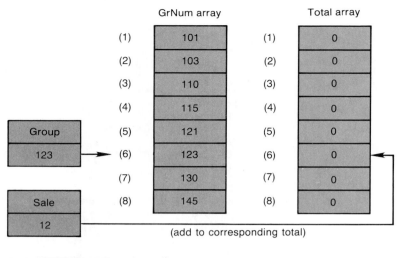

Figure 11.2
Flowchart of lookup logic.

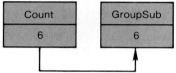

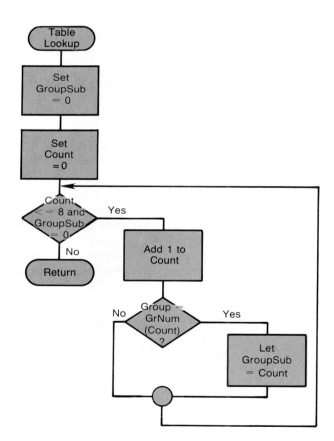

Coding a Table Lookup

```
'*********** Table Lookup For Group Number ***********
LookUpGroupNumber:
    LET GroupSub = 0               'Initialize to enter loop
    LET Count = 0                  'Begin counter at zero
    DO WHILE Count < 8 AND GroupSub = 0
        LET Count = Count + 1
        IF Group = GrNum(Count) THEN
            LET GroupSub = Count
        END IF
    LOOP                 '** GroupSub now contains correct element
                         '   number, or zero, if no match was found
RETURN
```

After execution of the LookUpGroupNumber subroutine, GroupSub will hold the subscript corresponding to the Group that was entered. If the count went all the way to 8 and a match was not found, then GroupSub will still hold 0. So, after the lookup, the program can test for 0 in GroupSub. This only slightly changes the AddToTotal subroutine.

```
'** Add Sale To Correct Total or Print Error Message**
AddToTotal:
    IF GroupSub <> 0 THEN
        LET Total(GroupSub) = Total(GroupSub) + Sale
    ELSE
        PRINT "Invalid group number, re-enter this sale"
    END IF
RETURN
```

Example Program: Serial Table Lookup

Now the entire program can be put together.

Hierarchy Chart and Flowchart

Figure 11.3 shows a hierarchy chart and a flowchart of the table lookup program.

Figure 11.3
Hierarchy chart and flowchart of table lookup program.

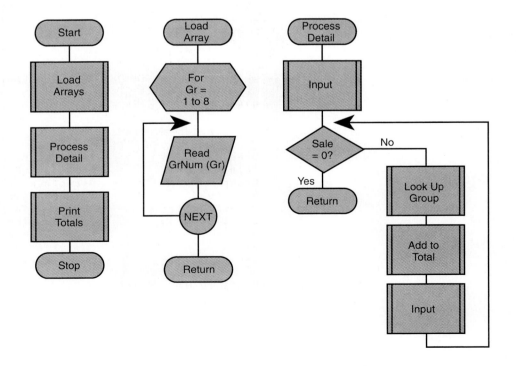

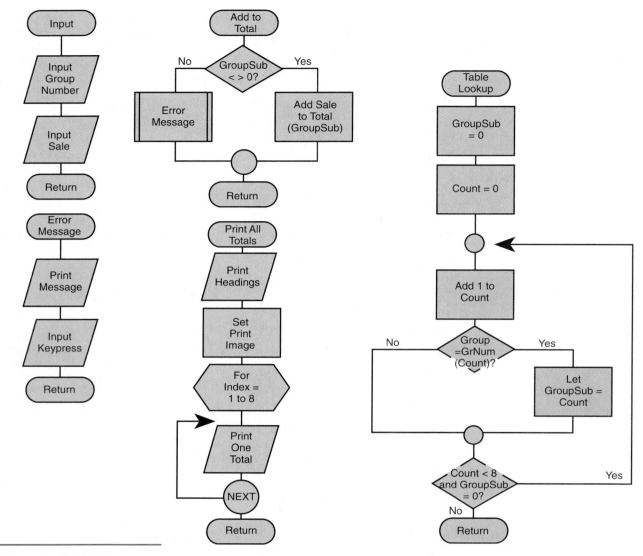

Figure 11.3—*Continued*

Program Listing

```
'Program To Demonstrate Serial Table Lookup Operation

'    Tabulates Total Sales For Eight Scout Groups

'          Variables Used

'     GrNum(1 TO 8)          Table to hold group numbers
'     Total(1 TO 8)          Array to hold totals for each group
'     Group                  Group number
'     GroupSub               Subscript to add to total table
'     Index%                 Loop counter to output total sales
'     Count                  Loop counter used in table lookup
'     Gr%                    Loop counter to load GrNum array
'     Sale                   Number of tickets sold
'     D$                     Dummy variable for pause

DIM GrNum(1 TO 8), Total(1 TO 8)
```

```
'***************** Program Mainline ******************
GOSUB LoadArray
GOSUB ProcessDetail
GOSUB PrintGroupTotals
END


'*************** Load Group Number Array *************
LoadArray:
   FOR Gr% = 1 TO 8
       READ GrNum(Gr%)
   NEXT Gr%
   DATA 101, 103, 110, 115, 121, 123, 130, 145
RETURN


'****************** Detail Processing ****************
ProcessDetail:
   GOSUB InputData                    'Priming input for ticket sales
   DO UNTIL Sale = 0
       GOSUB LookUpGroupNumber
       GOSUB AddToTotal
       GOSUB InputData
   LOOP
RETURN


'********* Input Group Number And Ticket Sale *********
InputData:
   CLS
   LOCATE 4, 15
   INPUT "Enter group number ", Group
   LOCATE 6, 15
   INPUT "Number of tickets sold (or zero to end) ", Sale
RETURN


'************* Table Lookup For Group Number *********
LookUpGroupNumber:
   LET GroupSub = 0              'Initialize to enter loop
   LET Count = 0                 'Begin counter at zero
   DO WHILE Count < 8 AND GroupSub = 0
      LET Count = Count + 1
      IF Group = GrNum(Count) THEN
         LET GroupSub = Count
      END IF
   LOOP            '** GroupSub now contains correct element
                   '**  number, or zero, if no match was found
RETURN


'**** Add Sale To Correct Total Or Print Error Msg ***
AddToTotal:
   IF GroupSub <> 0 THEN
      LET Total(GroupSub) = Total(GroupSub) + Sale
   ELSE
      GOSUB PrintErrorMsg
   END IF
RETURN


'***************** Print Error Message ************
PrintErrorMsg:
   LOCATE 20, 10
   PRINT "Error in group number, re-enter this sale"
   LOCATE 22, 20
   PRINT "Press any key to continue"
   LET D$ = INPUT$(1)              'Hold for Keypress
RETURN
```

```
'*************** Print All Group Totals *************
PrintGroupTotals:
   CLS
   PRINT "      GROUP          SALES"
   FOR Index% = 1 TO 8
     PRINT USING "        ###          #,### "; GrNum(Index%), TOTAL(Index%)
   NEXT Index%
RETURN

'******************** End of Program ***************
```

Table Lookup with String Data

The table lookup process works exactly the same way for string data as for numeric. However, sometimes a little caution is needed when looking up a name. The search is only successful on an exact match, character by character. For example, Joan T. Smith.

does not match	JOAN T. SMITH
or	Joan T Smith
or	Joan Smith

Programming Example

This program will keep a personal telephone number directory. A person's name will be entered, and their telephone number will be displayed on the screen.

Input

1. Names and telephone numbers to establish the table (directory).
2. During execution—one name for lookup.

Output

1. Telephone number—corresponding to name.
2. Error message, if name not in directory.

Pseudocode

1. Load the tables
2. Inquiry loop
   2.1 Input a name
   2.2 Loop until name = "END"
        2.2.1 Look up name
        2.2.2 If name found then
                  display phone number
               else
                  display error message
        2.2.3 Pause before clearing screen
        2.2.4 Input next name
3. End program

Hierarchy Chart and Flowchart

Figure 11.4 shows both a hierarchy chart and a flowchart for the program.

Figure 11.4
Planning for personal telephone
directory program.

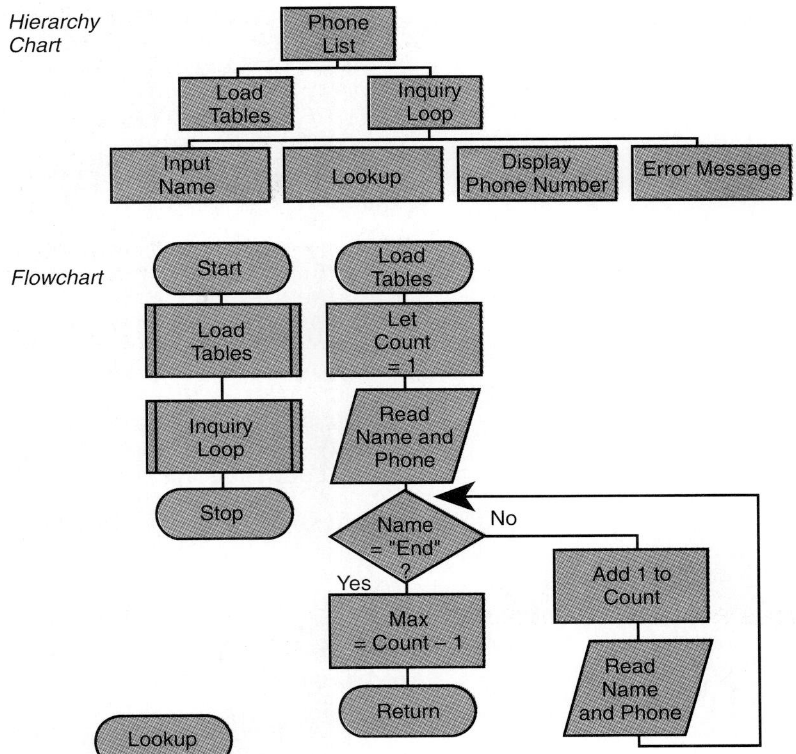

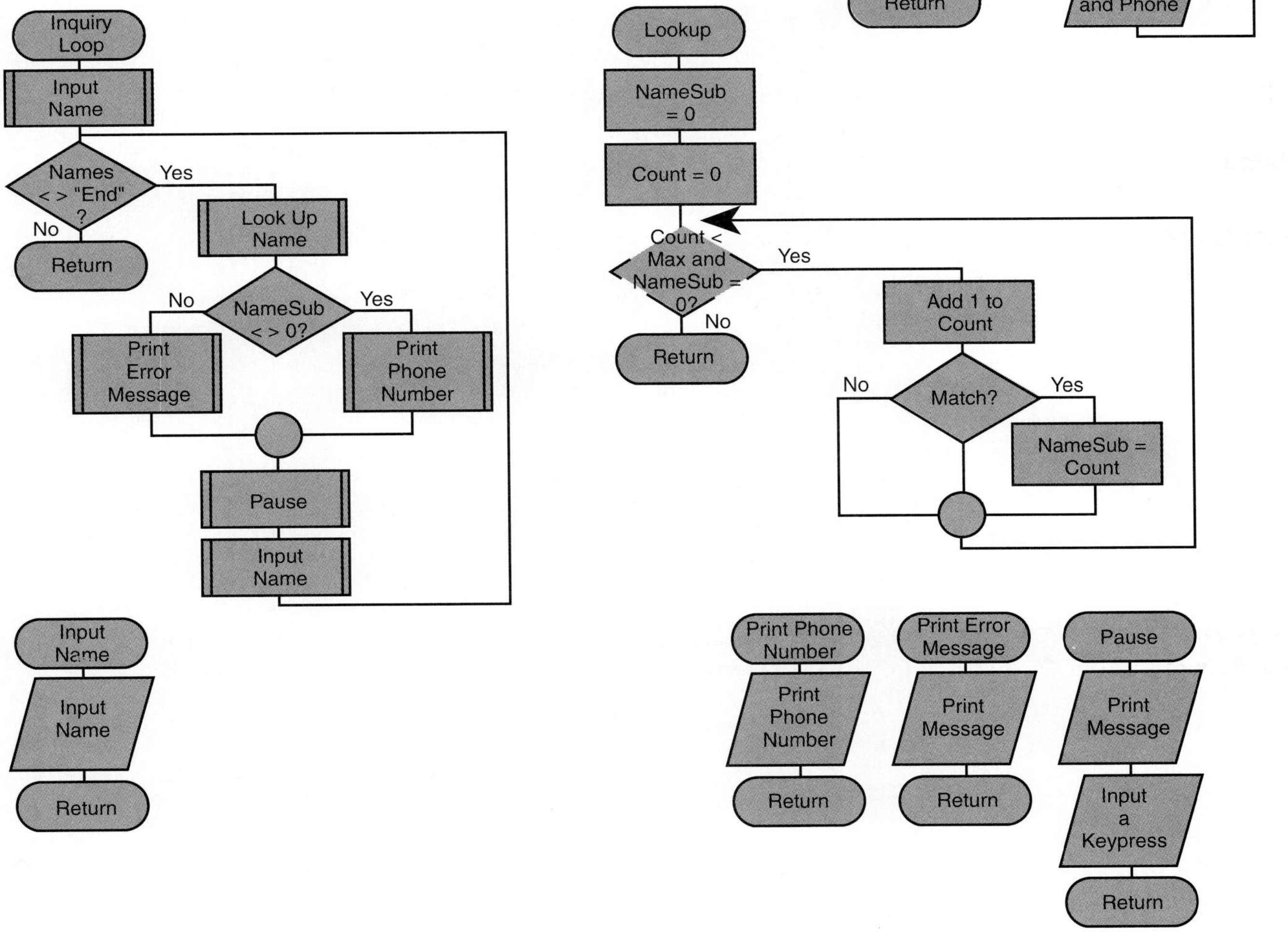

Hierarchy Chart

Flowchart

Single-Dimension Arrays   309

Program Listing

```
'              Personal Telephone Directory

'   Look Up Name and Print Person's Telephone Number

'          Variables used

'     Nam$(50)           Table to hold names
'     Phone$(50)         Table to hold phone numbers
'     Nm$                Name for inquiry input
'     NamSub             Subscript for correct number
'     Count              Loop counter used in table lookup
'     Max                Maximum number of names
'     D$                 Dummy variable for pause

DIM Nam$(1 TO 50), Phone$(1 TO 50)

'***************** Program Mainline ****************
GOSUB LoadTables
GOSUB LoopInquiry
CLS
END


'****************** Load Tables ********************
LoadTables:
   LET Count = 1
   READ Nam$(Count), Phone$(Count)         'Priming READ
   DO UNTIL UCASE$(Nam$(Count)) = "END"
      LET Count = Count + 1
      READ Nam$(Count), Phone$(Count)
   LOOP
   LET Max = Count - 1
   DATA Leanne Lott, 555-1243, Jill James, 555-3225
   DATA George Hill, 555-9119, John Short, 555-5926
   DATA Bill Rogers, 555-2290, Anita Paz, 555-5611
   DATA Alice Allison, 555-2345, Harry Hold, 555-4921
   DATA Bob Step, 555-3333, Carl Brown, 555-6543
   DATA END, END
RETURN


'*************** Inquiry Loop **********************
LoopInquiry:
   GOSUB InputName
   DO UNTIL UCASE$(Nm$) = "END"
      GOSUB LookUpName
      IF NamSub <> 0 THEN
         GOSUB PrintPhoneNumber
      ELSE
         GOSUB PrintErrorMsg
      END IF
      GOSUB Pause
      GOSUB InputName
   LOOP
RETURN


'****************** Input Name *****************
InputName:
   CLS
   LOCATE 10, 10
   INPUT "Enter name, 'End' to quit ", Nm$
RETURN
```

```
'************************ Look Up Name **************
LookUpName:
   LET NamSub = 0
   LET Count = 0
   DO WHILE Count < Max AND NamSub = 0
      LET Count = Count + 1
      IF Nm$ = Nam$(Count) THEN
         LET NamSub = Count
      END IF
   LOOP
RETURN

'******************** Print Phone Number ************
PrintPhoneNumber:
   LOCATE 12, 37
   PRINT Phone$(NamSub)
RETURN

'***************** Print Error Message ************
PrintErrorMsg:
   LOCATE 16, 40
   PRINT "Name not on file"
RETURN

'********************** Pause *********************
Pause:
   LOCATE 22, 40
   PRINT "Press any key to continue . . . ";
   LET D$ = INPUT$(1)          'Hold for Keypress
RETURN

'****************** End of Program ***************
```

The serial search technique will work for any table, numeric or string. It is not necessary for the fields being searched to be arranged in any sequence. The comparison is done to one item in the list, then the next, and the next, until a match is found. In fact, it's possible to save processing time by arranging the table with the most-often-used entries at the top, so fewer comparisons must be made. When a table gets really large, say more than 100 items, the serial search can become extremely slow. For these large tables, a **binary search** may be the best solution.

Binary Search

In a binary search, it is not necessary to search the entire table for a match. The table entries are arranged in sequence—whether numeric or string. The search can be quickly narrowed to a particular section of the table.

The first step in the search process is to compare the **search argument** (field to be matched) to the middle table element. If the search argument is higher than the middle element, the first half of the table can be discarded. Then that second half is again divided in half, and the comparison is made to the middle element. Again, half of the remaining group is discarded. This process continues until the table is narrowed down to one element, or a *hit* is made sooner.

Searching in this manner may seem cumbersome, but it is actually quite efficient. To serially search a 1,000-element table, an average of 500 comparisons would be required. For a binary search of a 1,000-element table, a *maximum* of ten comparisons is required. If a high percentage of the items to be matched is not in the table, the advantage of a binary search increases dramatically.

In the following example, a twelve-element table (Part$) of part numbers is searched. The search argument (part number to look up) is called Search$. Suppose the Part$ array contains the following part numbers:

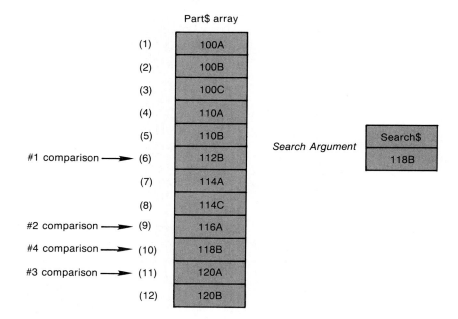

Moreover, suppose Search$ has been input as 118B. To begin, Search$ is compared with the part number stored in the middle of the list, that is, Part$(6). Since 118B is bigger than this number (112B), we can ignore that half of the array preceding Part$(6). We then compare Search$ with the part number stored in the middle of the remaining list; that is, Part$(9). Again, 118B is bigger than this part number (116A), so we ignore everything preceding Part$(9). Hence, our third comparison is with Part$(11). Since Search$ is smaller than this part number (120A), we ignore everything following Part$(11) and make our fourth comparison with Part$(10), which is halfway between Part$(9) and Part$(11), and finally find a match.

We now know that the matching part number is located in that element of the Part$ array whose subscript is 10. This subscript will be placed in the variable PartSub for later reference. If no match had been found, zero would be placed in PartSub to indicate that the required part number is not in the table.

Figure 11.5 shows the logic for a binary search.

Flowchart of Binary Search

Set upper limit for search
to number of elements in
array + 1

Set lower limit for search
to zero

Set middle point to halfway
between upper and
lower limits (low + upper)/2

Is there a match at the
middle element or a
determination that there
is no match?

While not finished:

    If the search argument
    < middle element
        then set new upper
        limit at middle
        else set new lower
        limit at middle
    Set new middle, halfway
        between lower and
        upper limits

While end

Finished. Now check
to see why. (Was there
a match or not?)

    If no match found
    (middle will be equal
    to lower limit)
        then let Subscript = 0
        else let Subscript = middle

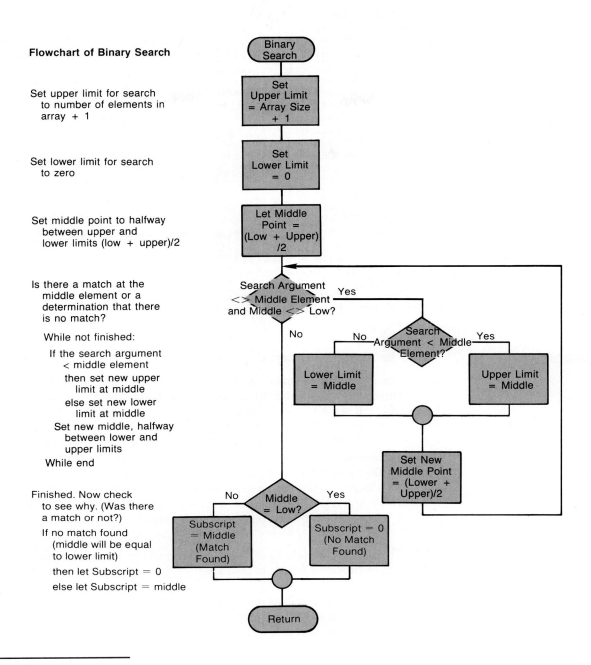

Figure 11.5
Flowchart of binary search.

Coding of a Binary Search

The coding in the following subroutine could be used to replace the serial lookup subroutine in the program on page 310. You will recall that the search argument was Group, and the table being searched was GrNum.

```
'***************** Binary Search *********************
BinarySearch:
    LET UpperLimit = 9          'Array size +1
    LET LowLimit = 0
    LET Middle = INT((LowLimit + UpperLimit) / 2)
    DO WHILE GrNum(Middle) <> Group AND Middle <> LowLimit
      IF Group < GrNum(Middle) THEN
          LET UpperLimit = Middle
      ELSE
          LET LowLimit = Middle
      END IF
      LET Middle = INT((LowLimit + UpperLimit) / 2)
    LOOP
    IF Middle = LowLimit THEN
        LET GroupSub = 0        'No match found
    ELSE
        LET GroupSub = Middle
    END IF
RETURN
```

Feedback

Write the BASIC statements to:

1. Set up a twenty-element array called K, and initialize each element to 100.
2. Divide all even-numbered elements in the K array by 2.
   [K(2), K(4), K(6), ... K(20)]
3. Subtract 1 from every element of the K array.
4. Print all elements of the K array, ten per line.
5. Dimension and load a table with the following data:
   DATA candy, ice cream, popcorn, gum, cookies, gum drops
6. How does a binary search differ from a serial lookup operation?
7. When would it be better to use a binary search?
8. When would it be better to use a serial search?

Summary

1. An array is a group of variables all referenced by the same name.
2. Arrays provide a means to hold multiple field values in memory at the same time.
3. The individual variables in an array are called elements.
4. To refer to an individual element in an array, a subscript is added to the array name. For this reason the elements are also referred to as subscripted variables.
5. Subscripted variables may be used exactly the same way as regular (unsubscripted) variables.
6. A subscript may be a constant, variable, or numeric expression. Any fractional subscript is rounded to the nearest integer.
7. A subscript cannot be a negative number or greater than the number of elements in the array.
8. The number of elements in an array is established by the DIM (DIMension) statement.
9. An array may be dimensioned for up to 32767 elements.
10. One program may have multiple DIM statements; one DIM statement may dimension multiple arrays.

11. The DIM statement for any array must be executed before any statement referencing that array.
12. If an array is not dimensioned before its first use, eleven elements are automatically defined—elements 0–10.
13. BASIC established arrays with an element 0. However, if the statement OPTION BASE 1 is used before the first DIM or array reference, all arrays will begin with element 1.
14. A variable may be used in the DIM statement as in DIM Arr(N). However, the size of a static array cannot be changed once it has been established.
15. The DIM statement may assign a lower-limit and an upper-limit for the subscripts.
16. When the DIM statement is executed, BASIC allocates the storage for the variables and initializes them to zero. In the case of string arrays, the elements are initialized to null strings (no characters).
17. Array elements may be filled with READ/DATA statements, INPUT, or assignment statements.
18. In parallel arrays, the elements of one array correspond to those in another array.
19. Array elements may be used as accumulators.
20. When using an input data item for a subscript, the value should always be validated. Otherwise the user is apt to receive the system error message, *Subscript out of range.*
21. Table elements may be accessed by direct reference, serial search (or lookup), and binary search.
22. For direct reference of a table, the actual subscripts (1–N) must be available.
23. In table lookup (serial search), multiple comparisons are made until the correct element is found.
24. The item to seek is called the search argument.
25. Table lookup requires an error handling routine in case a match is not found.
26. A search may be performed for numeric or string search arguments.
27. For a serial search, the table elements may be arranged in any order. However, for a binary search, the elements must be sorted in order.
28. A binary search should be considered for a large table (more than 100 elements) that can be arranged in sequence.

Programming Exercises

11.1. Write a program using single-dimension arrays to analyze an income survey. The statistics for each home include an identification code, the number of members in the household, and the yearly income.

INPUT: Use READ/DATA to enter the identification, annual income, and number of persons for each household. Use the test data provided.

OUTPUT: Produce a three-part report that shows:
1. A three-column table displaying the input data. The data will fit on one page.
2. A listing of the identification number and income for each household exceeding the average income.
3. The percentage of households having incomes below the poverty level.

The output must be nicely formatted with titles and column headings.

PROCESSING: Read the data into three arrays. *After* the arrays are filled, print out the data in three columns, showing the ID number, annual income, and number of persons. (Do *not* print the data as it is being read.)

Calculate the average income, and print one line for each household with income greater than average.

Calculate the poverty level for each household, and compute the percentage of households whose income falls below poverty level. The poverty level can be calculated as $8,000 for a family of one or two, plus $2,000 for each member more than two.

TEST DATA:

ID Number	Annual Income	Number of Persons
2497	$12,500	2
3323	13,000	5
4521	18,210	4
6789	8,000	2
5476	6,000	1
4423	16,400	3
6587	25,000	4
3221	10,500	4
5555	15,000	2
0085	19,700	3
3097	20,000	8
4480	23,400	5
0265	19,700	2
8901	13,000	3

11.2. Write a menu program to keep track of concert ticket sales by your club. Ticket prices are based on the section of the auditorium in which the seats are located. Your program should calculate the price for each sale, accumulate the total number of tickets sold in each section, display the ticket price schedule, and print a summary of all sales.

MENU: Clear the screen, and print the menu with an appropriate title and these choices:
1. Calculate ticket sales
2. Display ticket prices
3. Print sales summary
4. Quit

The user should be prompted to enter a choice between 1 and 4. (Validate their response.) The menu will be redisplayed after execution of choices 1, 2, or 3.

Menu Item #1—Calculate ticket sales

This is an interactive display (no printer involved), designed to calculate and to display the total price for each sale. Request the section and number of tickets, look up the unit price, calculate the total price (number of tickets times the unit price), and print the sales total on the screen. The sales should be accumulated in a table for later printing.

Give the user the option of entering more sales or returning to the menu after each sale.

Menu Item #2—Display ticket prices

Display the table of ticket prices on the screen:

Section	Ticket Price
A	20.00
W	17.50
B	15.00
M	11.00

Menu Item #3—Print sales summary

Print out (on the printer) the summary of all ticket sales made. For each section, print the number of tickets sold and the dollar amount. Also, print report totals of number of tickets sold and total amount of money collected. The report must include appropriate title, column headings, and numeric alignment of columns of detail data and totals.

Menu Item #4—Quit

Print an appropriate message, and end the program.

Special Considerations:

All screens should be well designed and printed with LOCATE. Do not allow the output to scroll on the screen.

"Idiot proof" all input, so that invalid values will be found and "friendly" messages printed. Do not allow the user to receive BASIC error messages for numeric values out of range or a section not in the table.

11.3. Write a menu program that will keep track of a list of items. The item names will be entered from the keyboard. As each item name is entered, the list should be checked to see if that item has already been entered. If the item is not already on the list, add it to the list. If it already appears on the list, count it.

Use a string array to hold the item names and a parallel numeric array to hold the counts. Allow array space to hold 100 items.

MENU CHOICES:
1. Enter items
2. Print the item list and counts
3. Quit

Choice 1: Clear the screen and request input of an item. Allow entry of items until a terminal value is entered (perhaps END or QUIT). Redisplay the menu when the entry is complete. Assume that the user may again choose #1 and wish to add more items to the list.

Choice 2: Print a list of the items entered so far and the count of the number of times each has been entered. Be aware of the number of lines on the screen (24), and do not print the list so fast that it scrolls off the top of the screen too quickly to read. If the list is long, print one screenful and a message to press a key to continue.

Choice 3: Clear the screen, and print an end-of-job message.

11.4. Write a program to look up state names and their two-letter abbreviations. Given a name, look up the abbreviation; given the abbreviation, look up the name. In the event that a match cannot be found for the state input, print an appropriate error message.

MENU CHOICES:
1. Find a state name from the abbreviation
2. Find the abbreviation from a state name
3. End the program

Choice 1: Clear the screen and request the two-character abbreviation. Print out the corresponding state name, and hold the screen by requesting a keypress. After a key is pressed, return to the menu.

Choice 2: Similar to choice 1, except request the state name and print out the abbreviation.

Choice 3: Clear the screen, and print an end-of-job message.

TABLE DATA:

AL	Alabama	MT	Montana
AK	Alaska	NE	Nebraska
AS	American Samoa	NV	Nevada
AZ	Arizona	NH	New Hampshire
AR	Arkansas	NJ	New Jersey
CA	California	NM	New Mexico
CZ	Canal Zone	NY	New York
CO	Colorado	NC	North Carolina
CT	Connecticut	ND	North Dakota
DE	Delaware	CM	Northern Mariana Island
DC	District of Columbia	OH	Ohio
FL	Florida	OK	Oklahoma
GA	Georgia	OR	Oregon
GU	Guam	PA	Pennsylvania
HI	Hawaii	PR	Puerto Rico
ID	Idaho	RI	Rhode Island
IL	Illinois	SC	South Carolina
IN	Indiana	SD	South Dakota
IA	Iowa	TN	Tennessee
KS	Kansas	TX	Texas
KY	Kentucky	TT	Trust Territories
LA	Louisiana	UT	Utah
ME	Maine	VT	Vermont
MD	Maryland	VA	Virginia
MA	Massachusetts	VI	Virgin Islands
MI	Michigan	WA	Washington
MN	Minnesota	WV	West Virginia
MS	Mississippi	WI	Wisconsin
MO	Missouri	WY	Wyoming

11.5. In many applications, such as interest calculations, it is necessary to compute the exact number of days between two dates. Write a program that will compute the number of days between two dates in the same year, as well as print the number of days in any month.

Use an array to store the number of days in each month. Be aware that in leap year, February has twenty-nine days.

MENU CHOICES:
1. Find the number of days in a month
2. Find the number of days between two dates
3. Quit

After each menu choice is complete, the menu should be redisplayed.

Choice 1: Clear the screen and request input of a month name. Look up and print the number of days in the month. Hold the output on the screen until a key is pressed.

Choice 2: Clear the screen and request input of two dates in the same year. Request the month name, spelled out, and the day. Using the month array, compute and print the number of days between the two dates. The ending date should be counted, but not the beginning date. Thus the number of days between January 1 and January 2 is 1. The number of days between January 15 and February 10 is 26 [(31 − 15) + 10].

Choice 3: Clear the screen and print a signoff message.

11.6. Write a program using single-dimension arrays to request a month of the year and print the holidays in that month. Allow for a maximum of three holidays in one month.

11.7. Write a program using single-dimension arrays to request the name of a city and print the corresponding zip code. If the city is not in the table, print a message telling the user that no zip code was found.

11.8. Write a program using single-dimension arrays to request the name of a state in the United States and print the corresponding capital. If the user types in a nonexistent state, print a message that there is no such state.

11.9. Write a program using single-dimension arrays to create a word-guessing game.

INPUT: The user will input, from the keyboard, the word he/she thinks the computer "guessed."
OUTPUT: If the user guesses the word, print an appropriate message. If the user doesn't guess the word after three tries, print the word the computer picked and print a message asking the user if he/she wants to play again.
PROCESSING:
1. Create a table with thirty words in it.
2. Use the randomize statement and the RND function for the computer's choice.

11.10. Write a program using single-dimension arrays to keep track of scores for the karate tournament for the Kiwi Karate Studio.

INPUT: Students' names will come from DATA statements. The scores will be input from the keyboard.
OUTPUT: Print a title, headings, student name, points for each event, total points, and which student was the grand champion.
PROCESSING:
1. The grand champion is the student with the most points.
2. Events:
   1. Sparring
   2. Open-hand Kata
   3. Weapons Kata
   4. Soft Kata
   5. Breaking
3. Not every student will participate in every event; some students may participate in only one or two.

TEST DATA:
Brian Boon
Chris Cook
Eric Mills
Mandy Moon
Nancy Noon
Scott Peck
Peter Smith
Sam Snoop
Trish Little

11.11. Write a program using single-dimension arrays to keep track of merchandise, prices, and the items that can be sold at the promotional price of three-for-the-price-of-two. Employees should be able to type in the merchandise code and receive the corresponding price and promotion.

INPUT: Merchandise code, price, and promo code will come from DATA statements.

OUTPUT: Print the price and promo for the item requested on the screen.

PROCESSING: If the item is a promo item, print the savings for the customer if the item is purchased.

TEST DATA:

Item	Price	Promo	Item	Price	Promo
P–1600–24	4.39	3/2	KX–135–24	3.89	None
PO–135–24	2.99	3/2	KX–135–36	4.89	None
PO–135–36	3.18	3/2	PS–135–36	3.29	3/2
P2–110–12	1.99	3/2	PD–135–24	3.49	3/2
P2–110–24	2.99	3/2	PD–135–36	4.49	3/2
P2–126–24	2.99	3/2	PL–135–24	4.59	3/2
P2–135–24	3.89	3/2	PL–135–36	5.59	3/2
P2–135–36	4.38	3/2	PLA–594	7.99	None
P4–135–24	4.38	3/2	PMA–464	8.99	None
P4–135–36	5.38	3/2	PN–135–24	3.49	None
KA–135–24	3.09	None	PN–135–36	4.49	None
KA–135–36	4.09	None	PR–135–24	3.89	None
KB–110–24	3.20	None	PR–135–36	4.89	None
KB–135–24	4.09	None	P–DISK–15	2.49	3/2
KB–135–36	5.09	None	P–DISK–15–2	4.18	3/2
KF–135–24	5.99	None	P600	9.37	None
KM–135–24	6.09	None	PSX70	9.37	None
			PSPEC	9.37	None

11.12. Write a program using single-dimension arrays to find the mean, midrange, range, variance, and standard deviation of a set of 100 I.Q. scores.

INPUT: The I.Q. scores will come from DATA statements.

OUTPUT: The mean, median, midrange, range, variance, and standard deviation will be printed on the screen.

PROCESSING:
1. Mean = total of all scores/number of scores.
2. Midrange = (highest score + lowest score)/2.
3. Range = highest value − lowest value.
4. Variance = [number of scores $*$ (sum of X^2) − (sum of X)^2]/ [number of scores $*$ (number of scores − 1)]. (Note: X represents each of the 100 scores.)
5. Standard deviation = square root of the variance.

11.13. Write a program using single-dimension arrays to find the critical value of the linear correlation coefficient and the linear correlation coefficient (r) for nine pairs of data and a significance level of .05.

INPUT: The table values and the nine pairs of data will come from DATA statements.

OUTPUT: The critical value, the linear correlation coefficient, and the type of correlation between the pairs of data should be output to the screen.

PROCESSING:

1. r = number of pairs * sum of $x*y$ — (sum of x) * (sum of y) / the square root of [the number of pairs * (sum of x^2) — (sum of x)²— the square root of [the number of pairs * (sum of y^2) — (sum of y)²].

2. The critical value should be looked up in the following table.

3. If the magnitude of r exceeds the critical value found in the table, there is a significant linear relationship between x and y.
   A. If the relationship is significant and r is positive, there is a positive linear correlation.
   B. If the relationship is significant and r is negative, there is a negative linear correlation.

4. If r is less than the critical value, there is no correlation.

TABLE OF CRITICAL VALUES			PAIRS OF DATA	
N	.05	.01	X	Y
4	.950	.999	10	12
5	.878	.959	15	11
6	.811	.917	20	10
7	.754	.875	25	13
8	.707	.834	30	9
9	.666	.798	35	8
10	.632	.765	40	6
			45	4
			50	1

11.14. Write a program using single-dimension arrays to find the sum of x, the sum of y, the sum of $x*y$, the sum of x^2, the sum of y^2, and the sum of x^2*y^2.

INPUT: The numbers for x and y will come from DATA statements.
OUTPUT: Print the output on the printer as follows:

x	y	$x*y$	x^2	y^2	x^2y^2

Totals

TEST DATA:

x	y
10	12
9	14
7	17
4	19
2	15
1	10
11	21
3	2
8	8
5	7

11.15. Write a program using single-dimension arrays to do a binary search for a requested name and date of birth.

INPUT:

1. The list of names and birth dates will come from DATA statements. The names are given, and you will need to make up corresponding birth dates.

2. The requested name will be input from the keyboard.

OUTPUT: Once you have found the name, print it and the corresponding birth date on the screen.

PROCESSING: Perform a binary search.

TEST DATA:

Alan
Bob
Brian
Chris
Connie
Dave
Henry
John
Kevin
Luis
Mindy
Nancy
Peter
Rose
Rudy
Scott
Steve
Tom
Tony
Wendy
Zena

11.16. Write a program using single-dimension arrays to keep track of belt color, weapon specialty, and name of the students at the Kiwi Karate Studio.

INPUT:

1. Student name, belt color, and weapon will be read from DATA statements.
2. A request for a choice of a complete list of students or a single student will come from the keyboard.

OUTPUT:

1. If a complete list is requested, it should be printed on the printer.
2. If a single student is requested, it should be printed on the screen.

TEST DATA:

Name	Belt Color	Weapon
Aline Ash	Orange	Joto
Anu Brown	Black	Scye
Kim Cook	Blue	Manrici
Sandy Campbell	White	Samurai Sword
Alice Drake	Brown	Joto
Tag Garison	Brown	Samurai Sword
Kristen Bosco	Black	Nunchucks
Jim Snow	White	Manrici
Larry Robles	Blue	Joto

12 Advanced Array Handling

SWAP Statement

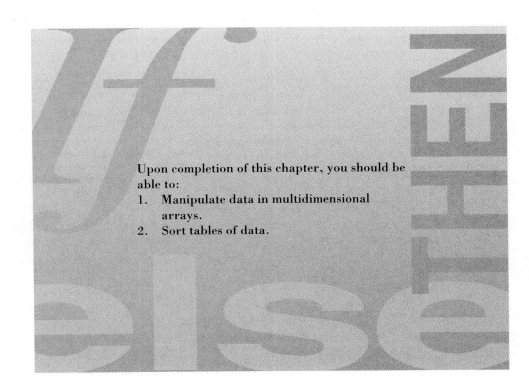

Upon completion of this chapter, you should be able to:
1. Manipulate data in multidimensional arrays.
2. Sort tables of data.

Two-Dimensional Arrays

The arrays discussed in chapter 11 were one-dimensional arrays. Each element in the array is identified by one subscript, which indicates its position in the list. Often there is a need to identify data by two subscripts. Such is the case in tabular data, where data is arranged into rows and columns.

Many applications of two-dimensional tables quickly come to mind—insurance rate tables, tax tables, addition and multiplication tables, postage rates, foods and their nutritive value, population by region, rainfall by state.

To define a *two-dimensional array* or **table,** the DIM statement specifies the number of rows and columns in the array.

```
DIM Table(4,6)
         ↑ ↑
         | | Columns
         Rows
```

or

```
DIM Table (1 TO 4, 1 TO 6)
```

Either of these two statements establishes an array of twenty-four elements, with four rows and six columns (assuming OPTION BASE 1). When referring to individual elements of the Table array, two subscripts must always be used. The first subscript should always be the row, the second the column. Figure 12.1 shows a diagram of this two-dimensional array.

Figure 12.1
Two-dimensional array showing subscripts.

(1,1)	(1,2)	(1,3)	(1,4)	(1,5)	(1,6)
(2,1)	(2,2)	(2,3)	(2,4)	(2,5)	(2,6)
(3,1)	(3,2)	(3,3)	(3,4)	(3,5)	(3,6)
(4,1)	(4,2)	(4,3)	(4,4)	(4,5)	(4,6)

The elements of the array may be used as any other variable—as accumulators, counts, reference fields for lookup, in statements like LET, PRINT, INPUT, READ and forming conditions. Some valid references to Table include:

```
LET Table(1,2) = 0
LET Table(N+1,N-1) = N
LET N = Table(J,K/2)
IF Table(4,6) > 0 THEN...
READ Table(Row,Col)
PRINT Table(Row,Col)
```

Invalid references for the four-by-six table in figure 12.1 would include any value for the first subscript greater than 4 or the second subscript greater than 6.

Initializing Two-Dimensional Arrays

Although the array elements are initially set to zero, many situations require that an array be re-initialized—to zero or some other value. Nested loops are an ideal way to set each array element to an initial value.

```
'********** Initialize Two-Dimensional Array ********
InitializeArray:
   DIM Table(1 TO 4, 1 TO 6)
   FOR Row% = 1 TO 4
      FOR Col% = 1 TO 6
         LET Table(Row%, Col%) = 0
      NEXT Col%
   NEXT Row%
RETURN
```

The LET statement in the inner loop will be executed twenty-four times, once for each element of Table. How can you confirm that?

A two-dimensional table can be filled with READ/DATA statements and nested loops. The programmer may choose to fill the table one row at a time or one column at a time, as long as the DATA statements are in the corresponding order. Figure 12.2 shows the array filled with values.

```
'*** Fill A Two-Dimensional Table, One Row At A Time **
FillTable:
    FOR Row% = 1 TO 4
        FOR Col% = 1 TO 6
            READ Table(Row%, Col%)
        NEXT Col%
    NEXT Row%
    DATA 20, 45, 1.2, 7, 6, 1.6, 12, -1, 14, -17, 19, -16
    DATA 17.5, 21, -2.5, 21.3, 5, 3, 19, -2.2, 2.1, -3, 8.6, 9.8
RETURN
```

Figure 12.2
Array filled with values from data statements.

(1,1) 20	(1,2) 45	(1,3) 1.2	(1,4) 7	(1,5) 6	(1,6) 1.6
(2,1) 12	(2,2) -1	(2,3) 14	(2,4) -17	(2,5) 19	(2,6) -16
(3,1) 17.5	(3,2) 21	(3,3) -2.5	(3,4) 21.3	(3,5) 5	(3,6) 3
(4,1) 19	(4,2) -2.2	(4,3) 2.1	(4,4) -3	(4,5) 8.6	(4,6) 9.8

Printing a Two-Dimensional Table

To print a two-dimensional table, again employ nested loops. Each execution of the PRINT statement in the inner loop will print one element of the Table array.

```
'********** Print A Two-Dimensional Table ***********
PrintTable:
    FOR Row% = 1 TO 4
        FOR Col% = 1 TO 6
            PRINT USING " ###.# "; Table(Row%, Col%);
        NEXT Col%
    NEXT Row%
RETURN
```

Summing a Two-Dimensional Table

Tables may be summed in various ways. Either the columns or the rows of the array may be summed. Or, as in a crossfoot, the figures may be summed in both directions and the totals double-checked.

```
                                                            ROW
                                                            TOTALS
             20.0    45.0     1.2     7.0     6.0     1.6    80.8
             12.0    -1.0    14.0   -17.0    19.0   -16.0    12.0
             17.5    21.0    -2.5    21.3     5.0     3.0    65.3
             19.0    -2.2     2.1    -3.0     8.6     9.8    34.3
             ----    ----    ----    ----    ----   -----   -----
  COLUMN
  TOTALS    68.5    62.8    14.8     8.3    38.6    -1.6   191.4
                                                            ↑
                                                    crossfoot total
```

To sum the array in both directions, each column needs one total field and each row needs one total field. Two, one-dimensional arrays will work well for the totals. Figure 12.3 shows a diagram of the necessary arrays. The following DIM statement establishes the necessary total fields.

Table	Columns							RowTot
	(1)	(2)	(3)	(4)	(5)	(6)		
Rows (1)	20	45	1.2	7	6	1.6	(1)	80.8
(2)	12	-1	14	-17	19	-16	(2)	11
(3)	17.5	21	-2.5	21.3	5	3	(3)	65.3
(4)	19	-2.2	2.1	-3	8.6	9.8	(4)	34.3
ColTot	68.5	62.8	14.8	8.3	38.6	-1.6		191.4
	(1)	(2)	(3)	(4)	(5)	(6)		GrandTot

Figure 12.3
Summing an array into two, one-dimensional arrays. Each row is summed into the corresponding element of the RowTot array. Each column is summed into the corresponding element of the ColTot array.

```
DIM RowTot(1 TO 4), ColTot(1 TO 6)

'********** Sum Two-Dimensional Array ******************
SumArray:
    FOR Row% = 1 TO 4
        FOR Col% = 1 TO 6
            LET RowTot(Row%) = RowTot(Row%) + Table(Row%,Col%)
            LET ColTot(Col%) = ColTot(Col%) + Table(Row%,Col%)
        NEXT Col%
    NEXT Row%
RETURN
'************** Sum the Row Totals *************************
ChecktheTotals:
    FOR Row% = 1 TO 4
        LET GrandTot = GrandTot + RowTot(Row%)
    NEXT Row%

    '********** Sum the Column Totals **********
    FOR Col% = 1 TO 6
        LET CheckTot = CheckTot + ColTot(Col%)
    NEXT Col%
    IF GrandTot <> CheckTot THEN
        PRINT "The programmer blew it"
    END IF
RETURN
```

Feedback

Write the BASIC statements to:

1. Dimension the following table (call it Grid).

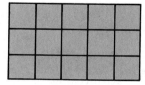

2. Set each element in the first row of Grid to 1.
3. Set each element in the second row of Grid to 2.
4. For each column of Grid, add together the elements in rows 1 and 2, placing the sum in row 3. (Even though the sum for every column will be 3, perform the addition operation for every column.)
5. Print the entire table.

Lookup Operation for Two-Dimensional Tables

To look up items in a two-dimensional table, you can use any of the three techniques learned in chapter 11—direct reference, serial search and binary search. The limitations are the same as in a one-dimensional table.

1. Direct reference: Must have row and column subscripts readily available. For an example, the hours used for each of five machines (identified by machine numbers 1–5) and each of four departments (identified by department numbers 1–4) may be tallied. In the example, the number of hours (5) is added to the total for machine #4 in department #2.

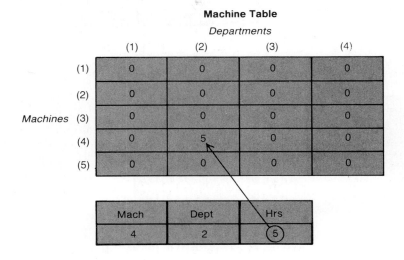

Machine Table

```
DIM Machine(1 TO 5, 1 TO 4)

'******* Input Data **********
INPUT "Department Number"; Dept
INPUT "Machine Number"; Mach
INPUT "Hours Used"; Hrs

'**** Add to Correct Total ****
LET Machine(Mach, Dept) = Machine(Mach, Dept) + Hrs
```

2. Binary search: The elements to be searched must be in sequence in the table. When the table is large *and* in sequence, a binary search is the preferred technique.
3. Serial table lookup: This is the most common technique used for lookup.

Many two-dimensional tables used for lookup require additional one-dimensional tables to aid in the lookup process. For an example, use a shipping rate table (figure 12.4) to look up the rate to ship a package. In this example, a one-dimensional table holds the weight limits, and another holds the zones. The five-by-four rate table is two-dimensional.

As an initialization step, the three tables shown in figure 12.5 must be set up. The first step in the program would be to establish and fill the three arrays. The Wt array perhaps needs a bit of explanation, since only four elements were dimensioned, and there are five rows in the rate table. However, the last row is open-ended; that is, any package heavier than 10 pounds will use the last row. No upper bound is required.

Figure 12.4
Shipping rate table.

		Zone A	B	C	D
Weight not to Exceed	1 lb.	1.00	1.50	1.65	1.85
	3 lb.	1.58	2.00	2.40	3.05
	5 lb.	1.71	2.52	3.10	4.00
	10 lb.	2.04	3.12	4.00	5.01
	any > 10 lb.	2.52	3.75	5.10	7.25

Rate array

	(1)	(2)	(3)	(4)
(1)	1.00	1.50	1.65	1.85
(2)	1.58	2.00	2.40	3.05
(3)	1.71	2.52	3.10	4.00
(4)	2.04	3.12	4.00	5.01
(5)	2.52	3.75	5.10	7.25

Wt array

(1)	1
(2)	3
(3)	5
(4)	10

Zn$ array

(1)	A
(2)	B
(3)	C
(4)	D

Figure 12.5
Shipping rate table arrays. The two-dimensional Rate array is used to hold the rates. The two, one-dimensional arrays are used to hold the weight limits and the zones to be used for lookup.

```
DIM Rate(1 to 5, 1 to 4), Wt(1 TO 4), Zn$(1 TO 4)

'***************** Load Tables *****************
'***************** Wt Table *****************
FOR Index% = 1 TO 4
    READ Wt(Index%)
NEXT Index%
DATA 1,3,5,10

'***************** Zone Table *****************
FOR Index% = 1 TO 4
    READ Zn$(Index%)
NEXT Index%
DATA A,B,C,D

'***************** Rate Table *****************
FOR Row% = 1 TO 5
    FOR Col% = 1 TO 4
        READ Rate(Row%, Col%)
    NEXT Col%
NEXT Row%
DATA 1,1.5,1.65,1.85,1.58,2,2.4,3.05,1.71,2.52,3.1,4
DATA 2.04,3.12,4,5.01,2.52,3.75,5.1,7.25
```

In order to print the rate to ship a package that weighs 4 pounds to zone B, the correct row and column must first be found.

```
'*************** Input Request ********************
InputRequest:
    INPUT "Enter weight of package ", Weight
    INPUT "Enter zone              ", Zone$
    PRINT
RETURN
```

To print the correct rate, these statements *could* be used:

```
LET Row = 3
LET Col = 2
PRINT Rate(Row%,CoL%)
```

This will print the correct rate (2.52), but it is not a practical solution. In order to find the correct values for Row% and Col%, a lookup operation must be done for each.

```
'************ Find Rate In Table ***************
FindRate:
    GOSUB LookUpRow
    GOSUB LookUpColumn
    IF Col% <> 0 THEN
        PRINT USING " ##.## "; Rate(Row%, Col%)
    ELSE
        PRINT "Incorrect zone "
    END IF
RETURN
```

The following subroutines show the coding to look up the row and column before the rate is printed. For the row, an exact match is unnecessary, only a weight not greater than the limit for that row. Any package too heavy for row 4 is assigned to row 5.

```
'********************** Lookup Row **********************
'** Note That Any Wt > 4th Element uses Sub Of 5 **
LookUpRow:
    LET Row% = 1
    DO WHILE Weight > Wt(Row%) AND Row% < 5
        LET Row% = Row% + 1
    LOOP
RETURN

'********************* Lookup Column *********************
LookUpColumn:
    LET Col% = 0
    LET Count% = 0
    DO WHILE Count% <= 4 AND Col% = 0
        LET Count% = Count% + 1
        IF Zone$ = Zn$(Count%) THEN
            LET Col% = Count%
        END IF
    LOOP
RETURN
```

Multidimensional Arrays

Arrays may be defined for more than two dimensions. The need for *three-dimensional arrays* is fairly common. Although QB allows dimensions as high as 60, rarely will there be more than three. Many versions of BASIC allow for only two dimensions.

Assume that for the shipping rate table, there were three different classes of shipping rates—Class I, II, and III. To manually look up the correct rate, first find the correct chart (Class I, II, or III), then find the correct weight and zone. Figure 12.6 illustrates the three-dimensional table.

The dimension statement for this three-dimensional array looks like this:

```
DIM Table(3,5,4)
              └Columns
            └Rows
          └Classes (or planes)
```

or

```
DIM Table(1 TO 3, 1 TO 5, 1 TO 4)
```

In the computer program, the lookup procedure would be done the same way as manually. Three lookup operations are needed in order to find the correct class, weight, and zone. The statement to print the rate is:

```
PRINT Table(Class%, Row%, Col%)
```

Figure 12.6
Three-dimensional table. Each
element can be identified by a
class number as well as a row
and column.

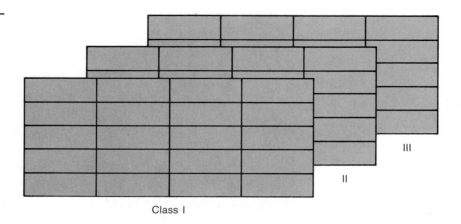

Class I

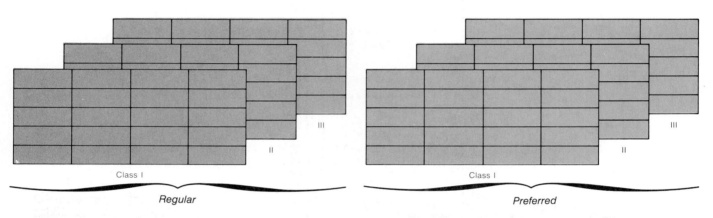

Regular

Preferred

Figure 12.7
Four-dimensional table.

Now, assume a further revision to the shipping tables. The company has two classes of customers—regular and preferred. To reflect this, there are two complete sets of these tables. Figure 12.7 illustrates the four-dimensional rate table.

The dimension statement for the four-dimensional table is:

```
DIM Table(2,3,5,4)
```

or

```
DIM Table(1 TO 2, 1 TO 3, 1 TO 5, 1 TO 4)
```

The subscripted variable to reference one element of the table is this:

```
Table(Cust%, Class%, Row%, Col%)
```

To carry this example to an extreme, set up three different rate schedules, one for each of three different regions of the country. The five-dimensional table is illustrated in figure 12.8.

The dimension statement is:

```
DIM Table(3,2,3,5,4)
```

or

```
DIM Table(1 TO 3, 1 TO 2, 1 TO 3, 1 TO 5, 1 TO 4)
```

A subscripted reference is:

```
Table(Region%, Cust%, Class%, Row%, Col%)
```

The statement *PRINT Table(1,2,1,2,3)* would print the value for region 1, preferred customer, Class I, weight greater than 10 pounds, to zone C.

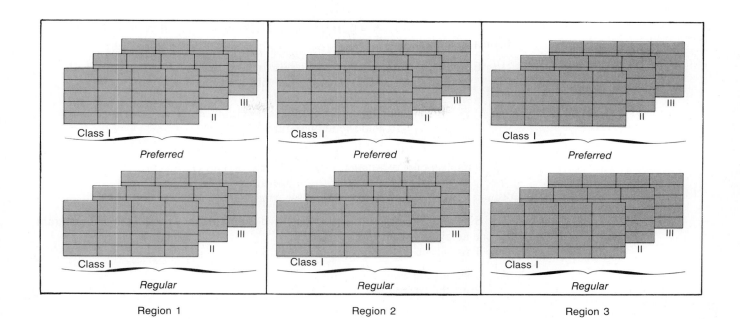

Figure 12.8
Five-dimensional table.

		Actual Temperature in Degrees Fahrenheit							
		30	20	10	0	-10	-20	-30	-40
	10	16	3	-9	-22	-34	-46	-58	-71
Wind	20	4	-10	-24	-39	-53	-67	-81	-95
Speed	30	-2	-18	-33	-49	-64	-79	-93	-109
(MPH)	40	-5	-21	-37	-53	-69	-84	-100	-115

Figure 12.9
Windchill table.

Programming Example:
Two-Dimensional Tables

Both temperature and wind cause heat loss from body surfaces. When the effects of temperature and wind are combined, the body feels colder than the actual temperature. Looking at the chart in figure 12.9, you can see that if the temperature is 10 degrees Fahrenheit and the wind 20 mph, the temperature felt by the body is −24 degrees.

For the computer program, input the temperature and wind speed, and display the windchill factor.

When establishing two-dimensional tables for lookup, there is a choice of two distinct methods:

1. Establish one, two-dimensional table, four-by-eight
   one, one-dimensional table with four elements
   to hold the wind speeds
   one, one-dimensional table with eight elements
   to hold the temperatures
   or

2. Establish one, two-dimensional table, five-by-nine
   Use the top row for temperatures
   Use the first column for wind speeds

Since the three-array method was used in the earlier example, in this program the one-array approach will be selected.

This will be a menu program with choices:

1. Look up the windchill factor
2. Print the entire table
3. Quit

Hierarchy Chart

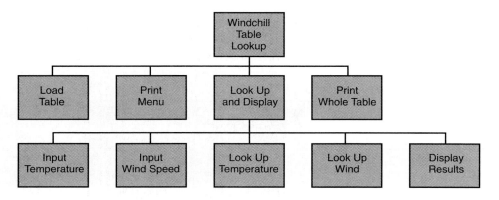

Figure 12.10
Hierarchy chart for windchill program.

Program Listing

```
' Program To Look Up Windchill Factor, Given Temperature, Wind Speed

'                 Variables Used

'      Chill(5,9)              Windchill Table
'      Wind                    Wind speed
'      Temp                    Temperature
'      Count%                  Loop counter for lookup
'      Choice                  Menu Choice
'      Row%                    Row subscript
'      Col%                    Column subscript
'      F1$, P1$                Print images
'      D$                      Dummy variable for pause

DIM Chill(1 TO 5, 1 TO 9)

'***************** Program Mainline ******************
GOSUB LoadTable
GOSUB PrintMenu
DO
    SELECT CASE Choice
        CASE 1
            GOSUB DisplayWindchillFactor
        CASE 2
            GOSUB DisplayEntireTable
        CASE 3
            CLS
    END SELECT
    GOSUB PrintMenu
LOOP UNTIL Choice = 3
END
```

```
'**************** Load Table ************************
LoadTable:
   FOR Row% = 1 TO 5
      FOR Col% = 1 TO 9
         READ Chill(Row%, Col%)
      NEXT Col%
   NEXT Row%
   DATA 0,30,20,10,0,-10,-20,-30,-40
   DATA 10,16,3,-9,-22,-34,-46,-58,-71
   DATA 20,4,-10,-24,-39,-53,-67,-81,-95
   DATA 30,-2,-18,-33,-49,-64,-79,-93,-109
   DATA 40,-5,-21,-37,-53,-69,-84,-100,-115
RETURN

'**************** Print Menu ************************
PrintMenu:
   CLS
   LOCATE 4, 32
   PRINT "WINDCHILL FACTOR"
   LOCATE 10, 25
   PRINT "1. DISPLAY A WINDCHILL FACTOR"
   LOCATE 12, 25
   PRINT "2. DISPLAY ENTIRE TABLE"
   LOCATE 14, 25
   PRINT "3. QUIT"
   LOCATE 24, 29
   PRINT "ENTER SELECTION "
   LET Choice = 0
   DO WHILE Choice < 1 OR Choice > 3
      LOCATE 24, 45
      LET Choice = VAL(INPUT$(1))
   LOOP
RETURN

'************ Display A Windchill Factor **************
DisplayWindchillFactor:
   GOSUB InputTemp
   GOSUB InputWindSpeed
   GOSUB LookUpTemp
   GOSUB LookUpWindSpeed
   GOSUB DisplayWindchill
RETURN

'************ Input and Round Temperature **************
InputTemp:
   CLS
   DO
      LOCATE 8, 26
      INPUT "ENTER TEMPERATURE (+30 TO -40) "; Temp
   LOOP WHILE Temp < -40 OR Temp > 30
   LET Temp = FIX(Temp / 10 + .5 * SGN(Temp)) * 10
RETURN

'************ Input and Round Wind Speed **************
InputWindSpeed:
   DO
      LOCATE 11, 26
      INPUT "ENTER WIND SPEED (10 TO 40 MPH) "; Wind
   LOOP WHILE Wind < 10 OR Wind > 40
   LET Wind = FIX(Wind / 10 + .5 * SGN(Wind)) * 10
RETURN
```

```
'***************** Look Up Temperature *****************
LookUpTemp:
   LET Col% = 0
   LET Count% = 1
   DO WHILE Count% < 9 AND Col% = 0
      LET Count% = Count% + 1
      IF Temp = Chill(1, Count%) THEN
         LET Col% = Count%
      END IF
   LOOP
RETURN

'***************** Look Up Wind Speed *****************
LookUpWindSpeed:
   LET Row% = 0
   LET Count% = 1
   DO WHILE Count% <= 4 AND Row% = 0
      LET Count% = Count% + 1
      IF Wind = Chill(Count%, 1) THEN
         LET Row% = Count%
      END IF
   LOOP
RETURN

'***************** Display Windchill *****************
DisplayWindchill:
   CLS
   LOCATE 8, 15
   PRINT "FOR A TEMPERATURE OF "; Temp
   LOCATE 10, 15
   PRINT "AND A WIND OF "; Wind; "MPH"
   LOCATE 12, 15
   PRINT "THE WINDCHILL FACTOR IS "; Chill(Row%, Col%)
   LOCATE 22, 40
   PRINT "PRESS ANY KEY TO CONTINUE . . ."
   LET D$ = INPUT$(1)        'Hold for Keypress
RETURN

'***************** Display Entire Table *****************
DisplayEntireTable:
   CLS
   LOCATE 2, 30
   PRINT "WINDCHILL TABLE"
   PRINT
   PRINT
   PRINT
   LET P1$ = "  ####"
   LET F1$ = "            ### :"
   FOR Row% = 1 TO 5
      FOR Col% = 1 TO 9
         IF Col% = 1 THEN
            PRINT USING F1$; Chill(Row%, Col%);
         ELSE
            PRINT USING P1$; Chill(Row%, Col%);
         END IF
      NEXT Col%
      PRINT
      IF Row% = 1 THEN
         PRINT TAB(13); STRING$(45, "-")
      END IF
   NEXT Row%
   LOCATE 22, 40
   PRINT "PRESS ANY KEY TO CONTINUE . . .";
   LET D$ = INPUT$(1)        'Hold for Keypress
RETURN

'***************** End of Program *****************
```

Sample Program Output

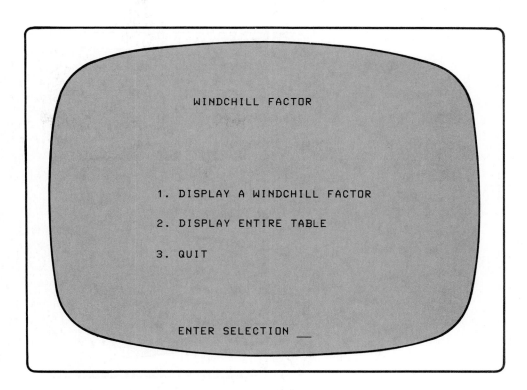

```
              WINDCHILL FACTOR




        1. DISPLAY A WINDCHILL FACTOR

        2. DISPLAY ENTIRE TABLE

        3. QUIT




           ENTER SELECTION __
```

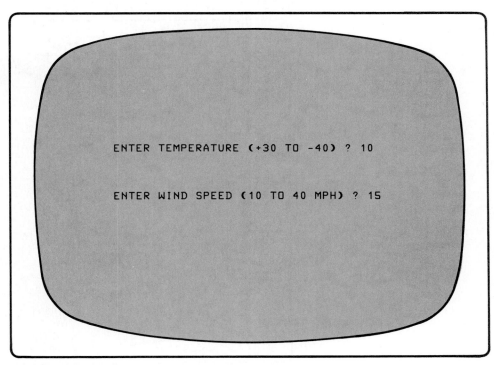

```
     ENTER TEMPERATURE (+30 TO -40) ? 10


     ENTER WIND SPEED (10 TO 40 MPH) ? 15
```

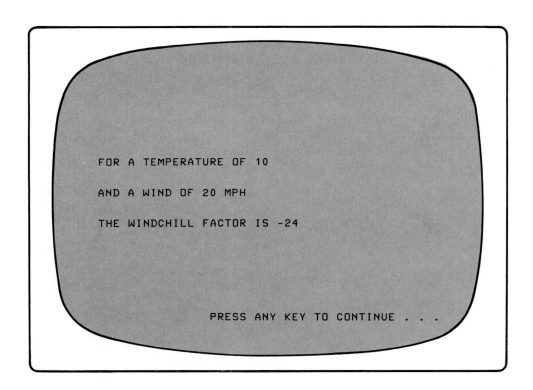

```
FOR A TEMPERATURE OF 10

AND A WIND OF 20 MPH

THE WINDCHILL FACTOR IS -24




                    PRESS ANY KEY TO CONTINUE . . .
```

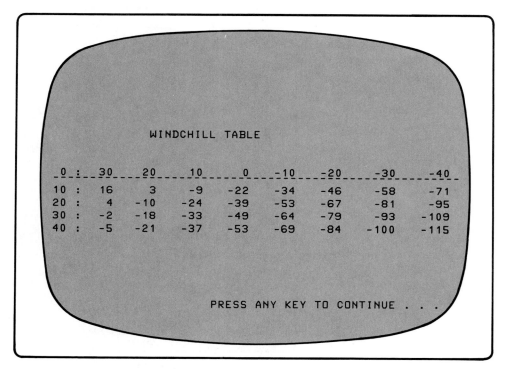

```
                    WINDCHILL TABLE

     0 :   30     20     10      0    -10    -20     -30     -40
    10 :   16      3     -9    -22    -34    -46     -58     -71
    20 :    4    -10    -24    -39    -53    -67     -81     -95
    30 :   -2    -18    -33    -49    -64    -79     -93    -109
    40 :   -5    -21    -37    -53    -69    -84    -100    -115




                    PRESS ANY KEY TO CONTINUE . . .
```

Sorting

A common and useful technique in computing is **sorting**—rearranging table entries in alphabetic order, numeric order, by date, or by time. Data can be arranged in *ascending* (low to high) or *descending* (high to low) order. Dates may be sorted by year, by month, by quarter, or any other convenient arrangement.

If a list is to be printed in a different order than it was input, it only makes sense that all data items must be in memory. The lowest entry can't be found unless all are checked. Is it any wonder then that sorting is covered in the unit on arrays? The data items to be sorted can be stored in an array and then rearranged or printed in any chosen order.

There are many methods used for sorting—some faster than others. Some are faster for short lists, others for long. Some can take advantage of lists already partially in order, others can't. Much research has been done and whole books written on sort algorithms and their relative merits.

In this text, two sort algorithms will be presented—the **bubble sort** and the **Shell sort.** The bubble sort is presented since it is relatively easy to understand. However, in real life it seldom will be used except to sort short lists of data. The more efficient Shell sort gains more advantage the more items there are to sort.

The Bubble Sort

In a bubble sort, adjacent entries are compared. If the first entry is larger than the second, the two entries are exchanged. This process is repeated many times, as the highest entries are moved to the highest position in the array. This process of "rising to the top" is the basis for the name "bubble" sort.

Sort Example

Original List   *Sorted List*

Collins   Allen
Bradley   Bradley
Turner   Collins
Allen   Norton
Norton   Turner

The Bubble Sort Process

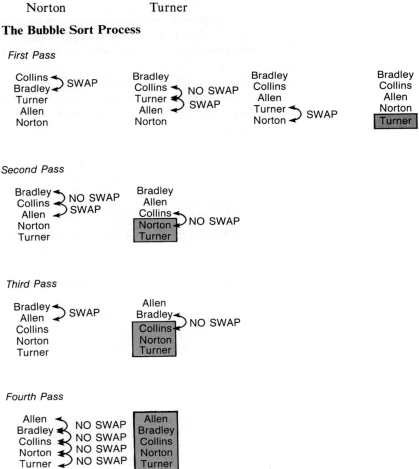

First Pass

Second Pass

Third Pass

Fourth Pass

Notice that on the last pass, no exchanges were made. This is the signal that the sort is complete.

Coding for Bubble Sort

```
'********************* Bubble Sort **********************
Bubblesort:
    LET Max% = Elements - 1       'Elements = # of Elem. To Sort
    LET SwapFlag% = 0
    DO WHILE SwapFlag% = 0
        LET SwapFlag% = 1
        FOR TableSub% = 1 TO Max%
            IF Table$(TableSub%) > Table$(TableSub% + 1) THEN
                SWAP Table$(TableSub%), Table$(TableSub% + 1)
                LET SwapFlag% = 0
            END IF
        NEXT TableSub%
    LOOP
RETURN
```

What Happens in the Bubble Sort?

It can be seen from the diagram (p. 337) that the program goes through the entire list once for each element (less one). On the first pass, the highest element is placed in the highest position in the list. On the second pass, the second highest element is placed in the second highest position. This process continues until one complete pass is made with no elements changing place. In the program coding, two items may need explanation: The use of the field called SwapFlag, and the new BASIC statement introduced, the SWAP statement.

In the Bubblesort subroutine, SwapFlag is used as a switch field (or flag). You recall that a switch is a variable that takes one of two possible values to indicate a condition. Here, when SwapFlag = 0, it means that at least one more pass is needed. SwapFlag is initially set to zero, so that the loop will be entered. Then, for each pass, the flag is set to 1. If any exchange is made during the pass, the flag is set back to zero, saying, "A swap was made during this pass, so you must make at least one more pass to make sure the list is in order." As soon as one complete iteration of the DO...LOOP is made (one pass) with no swap, the sort is complete. Figure 12.11 illustrates the logic of the bubble sort.

The SWAP Statement—General Form

```
SWAP variable1, variable2
```

The SWAP statement seems to be designed especially for the sort. It will exchange the values of two variables. The variables may be of any type (single-precision, double-precision, integer, long integer, or string) as long as the two variables are the same type. The two variable names must be separated by a comma.

The SWAP Statement—Examples

```
SWAP Table$(Index%), Table$(Index%+1)
SWAP X,Y
SWAP Arr(R,C), Arr(R+1,C)
SWAP A$, B$
SWAP I%, J%
```

Figure 12.11
Flowchart of a bubble sort.

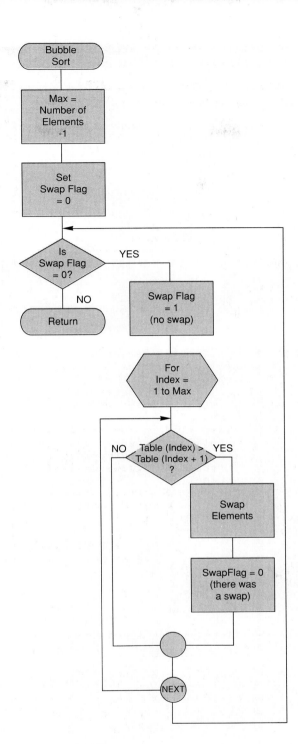

Example Program: The Bubble Sort

A program will be created to input a series of names until END is entered and to print out the list in alphabetic order.

Processing

1. Input names in a loop, counting the entries
2. Sort the list of names
3. Print out the sorted list

Hierarchy Chart

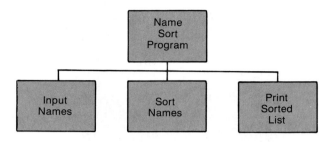

Program Listing

```
' Program To Input A Series Of Names, Sort Them Into
'    Alphabetical Order Using A Bubble Sort, And Print
'    The Sorted List

'          Variables Used

'         Count%        Count of names input
'         Lst$()        Array to hold names
'         NamSub%       Subscript  to reference names
'         Max%          Maximum # of entries to sort
'         SwapFlag%     Switch field
'                       1 = no switch made
'                       0 = switch made this pass

DIM Lst$(1 TO 50)

'**************** Program Mainline ******************
GOSUB InputNames
GOSUB SortNames
GOSUB PrintList
END

'******************* Input Names *******************
InputNames:
   CLS
   PRINT "ENTER NAMES, TYPE 'END' TO QUIT "
   LET Count% = 1
   INPUT Lst$(Count%)                  'Priming INPUT
   DO WHILE UCASE$(Lst$(Count%)) <> "END" AND Count% < 50
      LET Count% = Count% + 1
      INPUT Lst$(Count%)
      IF Count% = 50 AND UCASE$(Lst$(Count%)) <> "END" THEN
         PRINT "SORRY, I CAN ONLY HANDLE 50 NAMES"
      END IF
   LOOP
   IF Count% <> 50 THEN
      LET Count% = Count% - 1
   END IF
RETURN
```

```
'****************** Sort the Names ******************
SortNames:
   LET Max% = Count% - 1
   LET SwapFlag% = 0
   DO WHILE SwapFlag% = 0
      LET SwapFlag% = 1
      FOR NamSub% = 1 TO Max%
         IF Lst$(NamSub%) > Lst$(NamSub% + 1) THEN
            SWAP Lst$(NamSub%), Lst$(NamSub% + 1)
            LET SwapFlag% = 0              'There was a swap
         END IF
      NEXT NamSub%
   LOOP
RETURN

'****************** Print the Sorted List *************
PrintList:
   CLS
   PRINT TAB(5); "SORTED LIST"
   PRINT
   FOR NamSub% = 1 TO Count%
      PRINT Lst$(NamSub%)
   NEXT NamSub%
RETURN

'****************** End of Program ******************
```

Sample Program Output

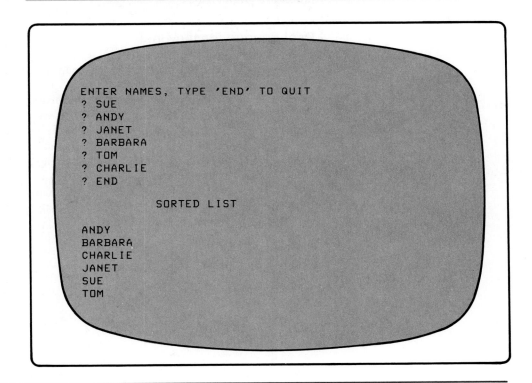

```
ENTER NAMES, TYPE 'END' TO QUIT
? SUE
? ANDY
? JANET
? BARBARA
? TOM
? CHARLIE
? END

               SORTED LIST

ANDY
BARBARA
CHARLIE
JANET
SUE
TOM
```

The Shell Sort

The bubble sort can work well for sorting short lists of data. However, for long data lists, the processing can be excessively slow. The Shell sort (named for its author, Donald Shell) has proven to be a much more efficient sort. The longer the list to be sorted, the greater the advantage. Table 12.1 shows a comparison of times.

Table 12.1	Number of Items	Bubble Sort	Shell Sort
Times using a bubble sort and a Shell sort, using QuickBASIC 4.5 on a 386 based PC (sorting single-precision data items).	20	.1 sec.	.1 sec.
	100	2.4 sec.	.8 sec.
	500	64.4 sec.	5.6 sec.
	1000	4.1 min.	15.1 sec.
	2000	17.5 min.	39.8 sec.

The Shell sort is similar to the bubble sort, except the comparisons and exchanges are made over a greater distance. Rather than compare and swap adjacent elements, a larger gap (distance between the elements) is used. To begin, the gap is equal to half the length of the list [Gap = INT(Count/2) where Count is the number of elements to be sorted].

Each time a pass is completed with no exchange, the Gap is divided in half, and the comparison and exchange process continues. The Gap is continually halved, until it reaches 1. When the Gap is at 1, adjacent elements are compared, and the sort proceeds in the same fashion as the bubble sort. Figure 12.12 details the Shell sort procedure graphically.

Pseudocode for the Shell Sort

1. Initialize Gap = Count/2 (where Count is the number of elements to sort)
2. Loop while Gap > 0
    2.1   Set SwapFlag to 0 (to begin the loop process)
    2.2   Loop while SwapFlag = 0 (repeat as long as any swaps are made)
        2.2.1   Set SwapFlag = 1 (to indicate NO swap made)
        2.2.2   For Index = 1 TO (Count-Gap)
            2.2.2.1   If Element(Index) > Element (Index + GAP) then
                    SWAP elements
                    Set SwapFlag = 0
    2.3   Calculate Gap = Gap/2
3. END

Figure 12.12
The Shell sort.

Count = 12   (items to sort)
Gap = 6

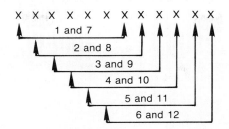

With Gap = 6, comparisons and exchanges
are made until a pass occurs where no
exchanges are made.

Then:
    Gap = INT(Gap/2)
    Gap = 3

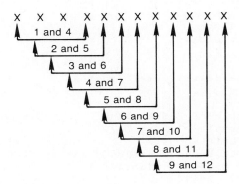

With Gap = 3, comparisons and exchanges
are made until a pass occurs where no
exchanges are made.

Then:
    Gap = INT(Gap/2)
    Gap = 1

and adjacent entries are compared and
exchanged, just as in the bubble sort.

Example Program: The Shell Sort

The previous sort example will be modified to replace the bubble sort with a Shell sort. Only the one subroutine (and a few remarks) need be changed.

Program Listing

```
' Program To Input A Series Of Names, Sort Them Into
'    Alphabetical Order Using A Shell Sort, And Print
'    The Sorted List

'          Variables Used

'          Count%        Count of names input
'          Lst$          Array to hold names
'          NamSub%       Subscript to reference names
'          Max%          Maximum # of entries to sort
'          SwapFlag%     Switch field
'                        1 = no switch made
'                        0 = switch made this pass
'          Gap%          Spread used for comparisons

DIM Lst$(1 TO 50)

'******************** Program Mainline ****************
GOSUB InputNames
GOSUB SortNames
GOSUB PrintList
END

'******************** Input Names ********************
InputNames:
   CLS
   PRINT "ENTER NAMES, TYPE 'END' TO QUIT "
   LET Count% = 1
   INPUT Lst$(Count%)                  'Priming INPUT
   DO WHILE UCASE$(Lst$(Count%)) <> "END" AND Count% < 50
      LET Count% = Count% + 1
      INPUT Lst$(Count%)
      IF Count% = 50 AND UCASE$(Lst$(Count%)) <> "END" THEN
         PRINT "SORRY, I CAN ONLY HANDLE 50 NAMES"
      END IF
   LOOP
   IF Count% <> 50 THEN
      LET Count% = Count% - 1
   END IF
RETURN

'******************** Sort the Names ****************
SortNames:
   LET Gap% = INT(Count% / 2)
   DO WHILE Gap% > 0
      LET SwapFlag% = 0
      DO WHILE SwapFlag% = 0
         LET SwapFlag% = 1
         FOR NamSub% = 1 TO Count% - Gap%
            IF Lst$(NamSub%) > Lst$(NamSub% + Gap%) THEN
               SWAP Lst$(NamSub%), Lst$(NamSub% + Gap%)
               LET SwapFlag% = 0    'There was a swap
            END IF
         NEXT NamSub%
      LOOP
      LET Gap% = INT(Gap% / 2)          'There was a swap
   LOOP
RETURN
```

```
'****************** Print the Sorted List **************
PrintList:
    CLS
    PRINT TAB(5); "SORTED LIST"
    PRINT
    FOR NamSub% = 1 TO Count%
        PRINT Lst$(NamSub%)
    NEXT NamSub%
RETURN


'******************* End Of Program ******************
```

Sample Program Output

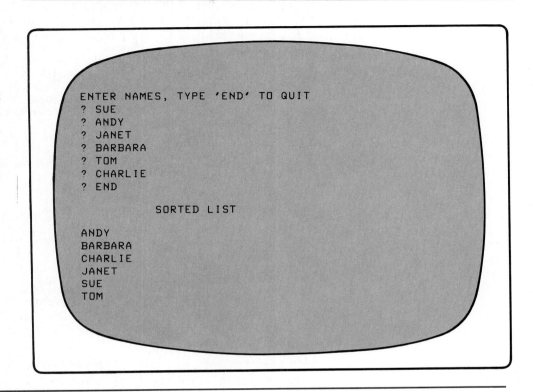

```
ENTER NAMES, TYPE 'END' TO QUIT
? SUE
? ANDY
? JANET
? BARBARA
? TOM
? CHARLIE
? END

            SORTED LIST

ANDY
BARBARA
CHARLIE
JANET
SUE
TOM
```

Multiple Fields to Be Sorted

A more realistic sort example would have additional fields to accompany each name. In the following example, each record consists of a name, date of last payment, and payment amount.

In a case such as this, the data will be read into three parallel arrays (one for the names, one for the dates, and one for the payments). If the records are sorted by the name field, the corresponding arrays must be kept in the same order as the names. Few modifications are required in our sort example program to accommodate the additional data.

Example Program:
Sorting a List with Additional Data Items

```
' Program To Input A Series Of Names, Dates, And Payment
'    Amounts, Sort Them Into Alphabetical Order Using A Shell
'    Sort, And Print The Sorted List

'            Variables Used

'         Count%        Count of names input
'         Lst$          Array to hold names
'         Dat$          Array to hold dates
'         Pmt           Array to hold payment amounts
'         NamSub%       Subscript to reference names
'         Max%          Maximum # of entries to sort
'         SwapFlag%     Switch field
'                       1 = no switch made
'                       0 = switch made this pass
'         Gap%          Spread used for comparisons

DIM Lst$(1 TO 50), Dat$(1 TO 50), Pmt(1 TO 50)

'********************* Program Mainline *********************
GOSUB InputNames
GOSUB SortNames
GOSUB PrintList
END

'********************** Input Names **************************
InputNames:
    CLS
    LET Count% = 1
    INPUT "NAME ('END' TO QUIT) ", Lst$(Count%)
    DO WHILE UCASE$(Lst$(Count%)) <> "END" AND Count% < 50
        INPUT "DATE OF LAST PAYMENT ", Dat$(Count%)
        INPUT "PAYMENT AMOUNT       ", Pmt(Count%)
        LET Count% = Count% + 1
        INPUT "NAME ('END' TO QUIT) ", Lst$(Count%)
        IF Count% = 50 AND UCASE$(Lst$(Count%)) <> "END" THEN
            PRINT "SORRY, I CAN ONLY HANDLE 50 NAMES"
        END IF
    LOOP
    IF Count% <> 50 THEN
        LET Count% = Count% - 1
    END IF
RETURN

'********************** Sort the Names **********************
SortNames:
    LET Gap% = INT(Count% / 2)
    DO WHILE Gap% > 0
        LET SwapFlag% = 0
        DO WHILE SwapFlag% = 0
            LET SwapFlag% = 1
            FOR NamSub% = 1 TO Count% - Gap%
                IF Lst$(NamSub%) > Lst$(NamSub% + Gap%) THEN
                    SWAP Lst$(NamSub%), Lst$(NamSub% + Gap%)
                    SWAP Dat$(NamSub%), Dat$(NamSub% + Gap%)
                    SWAP Pmt(NamSub%), Pmt(NamSub% + Gap%)
                    LET SwapFlag% = 0      'There was a swap
                END IF
            NEXT NamSub%
        LOOP
        LET Gap% = INT(Gap% / 2)
    LOOP
RETURN
```

```
'******************* Print the Sorted List ********************
PrintList:
    CLS
    PRINT TAB(15); "SORTED LIST"
    PRINT
    FOR NamSub% = 1 TO Count%
        PRINT Lst$(NamSub%), Dat$(NamSub%), Pmt(NamSub%)
    NEXT NamSub%
RETURN

'********************* End of Program *********************
```

Sample Program Output

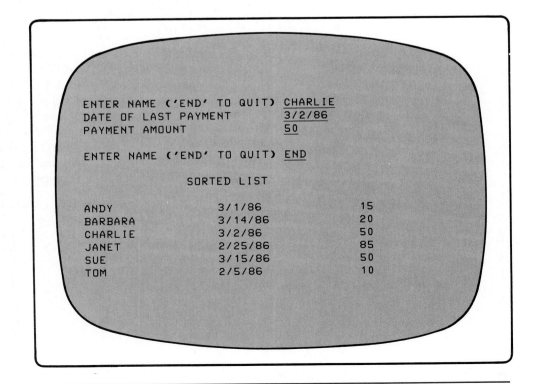

Summary

1. In a one-dimensional array, each element is identified by one subscript. In a two-dimensional array, each element is identified by two subscripts.
2. A two-dimensional array can be pictured as a table with rows and columns.
3. In dimensioning and subscripting a two-dimensional array, the first subscript identifies the row, the second the column.
4. Nested loops are an ideal tool for processing two dimensional tables.
5. Two-dimensional tables may be used in table lookups and binary searches.
6. Arrays may be dimensioned for three or more dimensions (up to 60). A three-dimensional array requires three subscripts for reference to an array element.
7. Numeric or string data stored in an array may be sorted into ascending (low to high) or descending (high to low) sequence.
8. The bubble sort rearranges data elements by continually exchanging data elements until the highest elements are at the high end of the array.
9. The Shell sort is more efficient than the bubble sort, especially for long lists of data.
10. The SWAP statement is used to exchange the contents of two variables. The two variables must be the same type (string, single-precision, double-precision, short integer, or long integer).

Programming Exercises

12.1. A club is raising funds through the sale of candies. They will be selling three different types—mints, peanut clusters, and English toffee. Write a program that will produce two reports, a detail of each sale and a summary report.

INPUT: Candy sales will be entered with READ/DATA statements. For each sale reported, an entry will be made containing the member name, type of candy sold, the quantity sold, and the date of sale.

PROCESSING: Use one-dimensional arrays to store the member names, candy types, and months of the year. Use a two-dimensional array to store the counts and the total sold per member.

Club Members		Types of Candies
DOUG	1	MINTS
MIMI	2	PEANUT CLUSTERS
KARL	3	ENGLISH TOFFEE
SCOTT		
JANNETTE		

OUTPUT: The detail report must contain the member name, the type of candy sold, and the quantity sold. Each line must also contain the date the sale was recorded with the month spelled out.

The summary report must contain the names of the members, the total count of each type sold per member, the total quantity sold per member, and the total of each type for the entire club.

TEST DATA: This data is supplied for test purposes. Remember, your program must be able to work for *any* data supplied, any month name, any quantity of these three candy types, and in any sequence entered.

Member (*Names* must be entered)	Type	Quantity	Date
KARL	1	3	3/21
KARL	3	5	3/21
MIMI	1	5	3/21
SCOTT	2	4	4/4
DOUG	3	3	4/4
DOUG	1	8	4/4
MIMI	1	8	4/11
KARL	2	4	9/11

SAMPLE PROGRAM OUTPUT USING TEST DATA:

SALES REPORT

NAME	TYPE	QUANTITY	DATE
KARL	MINTS	3	MARCH 21
KARL	TOFFEE	5	MARCH 21
MIMI	MINTS	5	MARCH 21
SCOTT	CLUSTERS	4	APRIL 4
DOUG	TOFFEE	3	APRIL 4
DOUG	MINTS	8	APRIL 4
MIMI	MINTS	8	APRIL 11
KARL	CLUSTERS	4	SEPTEMBER 11

SUMMARY REPORT

NAME	MINTS	CLUSTERS	TOFFEE	TOTAL
DOUG	8	0	3	11
MIMI	13	0	0	13
KARL	3	4	5	12
SCOTT	0	4	0	4
JANNETTE	0	0	0	0
TOTAL	24	8	8	40

12.2. A questionnaire has been sent to 100 households concerning the insulation of their homes. The form has fifteen questions, each with five possible answers. The possible responses are:

1. Always
2. Usually
3. Sometimes
4. Seldom
5. Never

What is needed is an item analysis that lists each question and the number of persons responding with choice 1, choice 2, choice 3, and so forth.

INPUT: The input data may come from DATA statements or INPUT statements. For each questionnaire received, enter a response (1–5) for each of the fifteen questions. Although 100 questionnaires were distributed, not all were returned. Test your program with different numbers of questionnaires returned.

Sample Data (Make up your own data to resemble the sample):
For each questionnaire

Question	Response
1	2
2	5
3	1
4	5
5	5
6	5
7	2
.	.
.	.
.	.
15	2

PROCESSING: Accumulate the number of each possible response for each question. Use a two-dimensional array for the accumulators.

Questions	(1)	(2)	(3)	(4)	(5)
(1)					
(2)					
(3)					
(4)					
(5)					
(6)					
(7)					
(8)					
(9)					
(10)					
(11)					
(12)					
(13)					
(14)					
(15)					

OUTPUT: Print an item analysis that shows the question number and the count of each possible response.

QUESTION	CHOICE 1	CHOICE 2	CHOICE 3	CHOICE 4	CHOICE 5
1	5	2	0	4	6
2	2	2	10	2	1
3	17	0	0	0	0
.	.	.	.	.	.
.	.	.	.	.	.
.	.	.	.	.	.

12.3. Students in a programming course have each taken three exams. Write an interactive program that will input each student's name and the three exam scores and will produce a listing showing each student's average and the class averages.

INPUT: Make up your own test data, similar to the data shown.

Name	Exam 1	Exam 2	Exam 3
Jan Shanks	80	75	92
Andy Mills	83	92	88
Ken Bird	72	65	80
.	.	.	.
.	.	.	.
.	.	.	.

Although the exact number of students is not known prior to entry, there will be no more than fifty students in the class. Be sure to INPUT all data into arrays before any calculations are done. Use a one-dimensional array for the student names and a two-dimensional array to hold the exam scores.

CALCULATIONS: After inputting all data into the arrays, calculate the average for each student and the class average for each exam. Use two, one-dimensional arrays to store the averages.

OUTPUT: Print appropriate title and column headings and one detail line for each student. Each line must show the student name, three exam scores, and average score. At the bottom of the list, print a summary line that shows the average for each exam. Align the averages beneath their corresponding columns of data.

12.4. Modify the program in exercise 12.3 to print the list sorted into rank order. This places the student having the highest average at the top of the list, and the student with the lowest average at the bottom of the list.

12.5. Modify the program in exercise 12.4 to include a menu with these choices:

1. Enter student names and scores
2. Display data for one student on the screen
3. Print class list in rank order
4. Print class list in alphabetic order
5. Quit

12.6. Write a program that will generate a series of random integers in the range 1–50 and will count the number of times each of those integers occurs. Present a menu with these choices:

1. Generate random numbers
2. Print the set of random numbers
3. Print the counts in numerical order
4. Print the counts in rank order by occurrence
5. Quit

Choice 1: Generate random numbers.
Request input of how many numbers to generate. Then, using the RND function, generate the specified number of integers in the range 1–50, counting the number of occurrences of each integer. Hint: Set up a one-dimensional array of fifty elements, using element 1 to count the occurrences of the integer 1, element 2 to count the 2's, and so forth. Each time the program is run, it must generate a different set of random numbers (use RANDOMIZE).

Choice 2: Display the list of random numbers. If possible, print all the numbers on one screen rather than allow them to scroll.

Choice 3: Print the list of numbers and their occurrences.

NUMBER	OCCURRENCES
1	4
2	3
3	4
4	6
.	.
.	.
.	.

Choice 4: Print the list sorted by the number of occurrences with the numbers occurring most frequently at the *top* of the list.

Choice 5: Print an appropriate sign-off message.

12.7. Modify the program in exercise 12.6 to graph the output with a series of asterisks. For each integer (1–50), print asterisks corresponding to the number of times the integer occurred.

Sample Output

```
1  * * * *
2  * * *
3  * * * *
4  * * * * * *
   .  .
   .  .
   .  .
```

12.8. Modify the program in exercise 12.7 to print the graph turned sideways. Hint: Create a two-dimensional string array, fifty-by-fifty. First fill each array position with a blank space. Then store the appropriate number of asterisks in the correct positions.

Sample Output

```
            *
            *
   *    *   *
   *  *  *  *
   *  *  *  *
   *  *  *  *

   1  2  3  4  . . .
```

12.9. A program is needed to keep track of sales of computer software for five salespersons. The group is selling ten different products by item number. Accumulate sales statistics and print a summary report.

TABLES: Use DATA statements to set up the tables for lookup.

Product Table

Item #	Product Name	Unit Price
A101	Accounting Made Easy	125.00
A102	Credits and Debits and Stuff	75.00
A103	Accounting for Turtle Factories	200.00
A104	Accounting for Preschoolers	10.00
B101	Wordy Processing	150.00
B102	The Big Word	115.00
B104	Only Words	210.00
C201	Spelling Games	85.00
C203	Games of Chance	30.00
C205	Games of Skill	40.00

Salesperson Table

Salesperson Number	Salesperson Name
101	Dot Mannix
105	Daisy Wharton
114	Ian Jet
118	Kathy Baud
120	Al Grithom

INTERACTIVE PROGRAM OPERATION: During interactive program execution, request the salesperson number, the item number, and the quantity sold. For that sale, display the salesperson's name, item description, unit price, quantity sold, and extended price (quantity $\times$ unit price). Accumulate the quantity sold by item number and salesperson.

If an item number or salesperson number is not in the table, print an error message and allow reentry of the data.

PRINTER OUTPUT: After all sales have been entered, print a summary report of the data. For each item number, print the item number, item name, number sold by each salesperson, the total units sold (for all salespersons), the unit price, and the total sales price of those items.

Report totals are required for the sales for each salesperson, as well as for the total units and total price. Design the output similar to this.

ITEM NO.	ITEM DESCRIPTION	PERSON 1	PERSON 2	PERSON 3	PERSON 4	PERSON 5	TOTAL UNITS	UNIT PRICE	SALES PRICE
XXXX	XXXXXXXXXXXXX	XXX	XXX	XXX	XXX	XXX	X,XXX	XXX.XX	X,XXX.XX
	TOTALS	XXXX	XXXX	XXXX	XXXX	XXXX	X,XXX		XX,XXX.XX

12.10. Write a program that will look up the distance between two cities by highway.

TABLE: Create the table with DATA statements.

Ref.	City
1	BOSTON
2	CHICAGO
3	DALLAS
4	LAS VEGAS
5	LOS ANGELES
6	MIAMI
7	NEW ORLEANS
8	TORONTO
9	VANCOUVER
10	WASHINGTON DC

	1	2	3	4	5	6	7	8	9	10
1	0	1004	1753	2752	3017	1520	1507	609	3155	448
2	1004	0	921	1780	2048	1397	919	515	2176	709
3	1753	921	0	1230	1399	1343	517	1435	2234	1307
4	2752	1780	1230	0	272	2570	1732	2251	1322	2420
5	3017	2048	1399	272	0	2716	1858	2523	1278	2646
6	1520	1397	1343	2570	2716	0	860	1494	3447	1057
7	1507	919	517	1732	1858	860	0	1307	2734	1099
8	609	515	1435	2251	2523	1494	1307	0	2820	571
9	3155	2176	2234	1322	1278	3447	2734	2820	0	2887
10	448	709	1307	2420	2646	1057	1099	571	2887	0

INTERACTIVE PROCESSING: Request input of the cities of departure and destination, and display the corresponding mileage. Format the screen so that the city names always appear in the same location, and data is not allowed to scroll.

If either the departure or destination city is not in the table, print an error message. Be sure to clear the message for any further processing.

12.11. The Plain Wrap Auto Supply Store sells its own brand of spark plugs. In order to cross-reference to major brands, they keep a table of equivalent part numbers. They would like to computerize the process of looking up part numbers in order to improve their customer service.

TABLE:

Plain Wrap	Brand A	Brand C	Brand X
PR214	MR43T	RBL8	14K22
PR223	R43	RJ6	14K24
PR224	R43N	RN4	14K30
PR246	R46N	RN8	14K32
PR247	R46TS	RBL17Y	14K33
PR248	R46TX	RBL12-6	14K35
PR324	S46	J11	14K38
PR326	SR46E	XEJ8	14K40
PR444	47L	H12	14K44

INTERACTIVE PROGRAM EXECUTION: Request input of a manufacturer's code (A, C, or X) and the part number. Then display the corresponding Plain Wrap part number.

12.12. Write a program that will allow for the input of names and print the list of names in alphabetical order. Use LINE INPUT so that names can be sorted by last name.

12.13. Write a program that will generate thirty random numbers and perform a bubble sort of the numbers. Print the numbers on the screen before and after the sort.

12.14. Write a subroutine to perform a binary search on the data sorted in exercise 12.12.

12.15. Write a subroutine that will fill a 5 × 5 array with random numbers and print row and column totals.

12.16. Write a program to print the sum and the average of each column in a 4 × 4 array. Use DATA statements to fill the array.

12.17. Modify the example program in this chapter for a binary search so that it will generate its own set of random numbers rather than reading them from DATA lines. Allow the number of random numbers to be generated to be input from the keyboard. The numbers are to be sorted in ascending order, using a Shell sort, so that a binary search for any chosen number can be performed.

12.18. The following table shows the effect of temperature and humidity on apparent temperature and explains why we feel much hotter in humid areas. Write a program to input a temperature and a humidity and to search the table for the correct apparent temperature. The areas off the chart in the upper right can result in a "Too hot to estimate" message.

Temperature
(Degrees Fahrenheit)

	10	20	30	40	50	60	70	80	90	100
125	123	141								
120	116	130	148							
115	111	120	135	151						
110	105	112	123	137	150					
105	100	105	113	123	135	149				
100	95	99	104	110	120	132	144			
95	90	93	96	101	107	114	124	136		
90	85	87	90	93	96	100	106	113	122	
85	80	82	84	86	88	90	93	97	102	108
80	75	77	78	79	81	82	85	86	88	91
75	70	72	73	74	75	76	77	78	79	80
70	65	66	67	68	69	70	70	71	71	72

Humidity %   10   20   30   40   50   60   70   80   90   100

13

Sequential Data Files

OPEN Statement
CLOSE Statement
WRITE# Statement
INPUT# Statement
EOF(n) Function
PRINT# Statement
PRINT# USING Statement

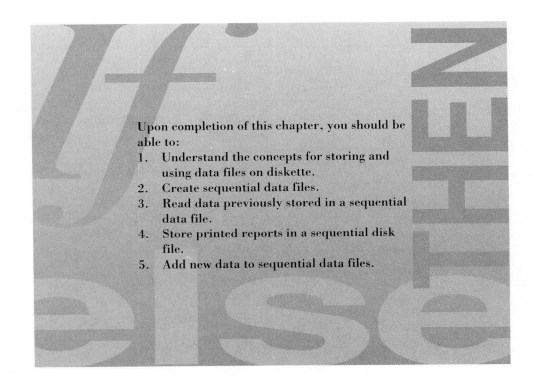

Upon completion of this chapter, you should be able to:
1. Understand the concepts for storing and using data files on diskette.
2. Create sequential data files.
3. Read data previously stored in a sequential data file.
4. Store printed reports in a sequential disk file.
5. Add new data to sequential data files.

Introduction

All of the example programs written until now have had their data entered with INPUT, DATA, or LET statements. While this is satisfactory for many applications, there are many situations requiring large quantities of data.

Many computer applications require data to be saved from one program run to the next. Some examples are personal tasks such as budgeting, mailing lists, and sports team records and business applications such as inventory records, customer files, and master files. This chapter and the next deal with methods to store and access **data files** on diskette.

Diskette Storage

There are several popular sizes of diskettes, or floppy disks. The most common sizes are, 5¼ inch and 3½ inch.

The actual diskette is encased in an outer protective case. Figure 13.1 illustrates a floppy diskette and its covering.

Data are stored along **tracks,** which are concentric circles on the surface of the disk. Each track is further broken down into **sectors.**

The capacity of diskettes varies greatly, even within the same size. The computer, disk drives, controller, and operating system all play a part in determining the storage capacity of a diskette. Some popular sizes are 360 K bytes (360 × 1024 characters), 720 K bytes, 1.2 megabytes (1.2 × 1,024,000 characters), and 1.44 megabytes. The difference depends on the number of characters per sector (512 for a PC), the number of sectors per track, and the number of tracks per diskette. When a file is stored, the required number of sectors are allocated. Whenever data is written to the disk or read from the disk, an entire sector (512 bytes) is written or read.

Data Files and Program Files

In computer terminology, anything stored on the diskette or hard disk is given its own unique name and called a *file*. Each program written and saved is called a *file*. However, these *program* files differ from the *data* files to be created now. One application will probably have one program file containing the program instructions, in addition to another file (or more) containing the actual data (names and addresses, inventory amounts, account balances, etc.).

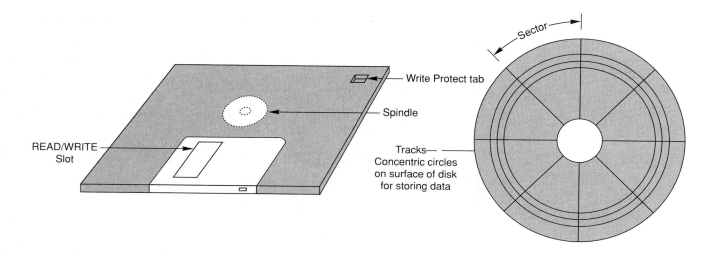

Figure 13.1
A floppy disk (diskette) in its outer protective case. At the right is a diskette showing tracks and sectors.

QB displays a list of program files from the *File Open* dialog box. Normally, program files have the extension .BAS. To see *all* files on the diskette (not just those having an extension of .BAS), change the *File Name* from `*.BAS` to `*.*`.

```
command.com
qb.exe
program9.bas
prog1.bas
test.dat
mydata
listing.txt
```

Recall from chapter 1 the naming rules for disk files: a one-to-eight-character name, optionally followed by a period and up to three-character extension. The three-character extension is generally used to identify and group the files into types. Most BASIC program files end with .BAS. Some other common extensions are

`.COM`—Command files (programs that are ready to execute)
`.EXE`—Executable program files
`.ASM`—Assembler program files
`.OBJ`—Compiled programs (object files)
`.TXT`—Text files (ASCII form, to be printed out)
`.DAT`—Data files
`.DOC`—Documentation files

Hard Disks

Many desktop computers are equipped with a hard disk. It is called 'hard' because each surface has a rigid metal base, rather than the flexible mylar base of the floppy diskette. A hard disk usually has two or more platters operating on a spindle so that there are several surfaces or sides for data to be stored upon. A hard disk revolves much faster than a floppy diskette, making access times much quicker.

With a very accurate mechanism for finding the track to read or write upon, combined with a sealed clean air environment, hard disk data can be placed very close together to increase storage capacity. Forty and one hundred megabyte hard disks are common, with some much larger. Table 13.1 shows the comparative capacities of floppy and hard disks.

The diskette drives are usually referred to as A: and B:, while the hard drive is commonly called C: or D:.

Table 13.1
Disk drive specifications.

	5¼" Diskettes		8½" Diskettes		Hard Disk (typical)
	360K	1.2Meg	720K	1.44Meg	30Meg
Surfaces	2	2	2	2	4
Tracks per Surface	40	80	80	80	613
Sectors per Track	9	15	9	18	25
Bytes per Sector	512	512	512	512	512
Total Bytes	368,640	1,228,800	737,280	1,474,560	31,385,600

Note that file names may be preceded by a drive specification. If the file resides on a drive other than the currently logged disk drive, include the drive and a colon.

```
A:MYFILE.DAT
B:DATAFILE.DAT
```

Files may also be stored in a subdirectory on a disk. The complete specification then includes the subdirectory name.

```
C:\PROGRAMS\PROG1.BAS
A:\DATA\MYFILE.DAT
B:\BASICDAT\DATAFILE.DAT
```

In order to discuss data files, some terminology must be agreed upon. The entire collection of data is called a **file.** The file is made up of **records**—one record for each entity in the file.

Examples: In a customer file, the data for one customer would be one record. In a name and address file, the data for one person is one record. Each record can be further broken down into individual **fields** (also called **data elements**).

Example: In the customer file, one customer record would have an account number field, a name field, an address field, perhaps a field to indicate credit rating, another to store the current balance, and another to store the date the account was opened. Each of these fields relates to the same customer.

The data stored in files is nearly always entered in an organized manner. Records may be stored in account number order, alphabetically by name, by date, or by the sequence in which they are received. One field in the record is the organizing factor for the file (such as account number, name, or date). This field, which is used to determine the order of the file, is called the **record key,** or *key field.*

A key field may be either a string or numeric field. In the customer file, if the records are in order by customer number, then customer number is the key field. If the order is based on customer name, then the name is the key field.

File Organizations

The manner in which data are organized, stored, and retrieved is called the *file organization.* BASIC supports two file organizations: **sequential** and **random.** A third file organization, called **indexed files,** is also popular in data processing applications. Indexed organization is supported by some other programming languages, such as COBOL, PL/I, and RPG. In BASIC, a combination of a sequential file, a table, and a random file can be used to create indexed files. The remainder of this chapter is devoted to sequential files; chapter 14 deals with random files, and chapter 15 covers special file handling techniques including indexed files.

Feedback

1. What is a disk track?
2. What is a sector?
3. How many characters can be stored in one disk sector?
4. What is the difference between a program file and a data file?
5. For the file specification

```
B:REPORT.PRT
```

   a. What does B: signify?
   b. What is .PRT?

6. Consider the situation in which an instructor stored data about the students in a class. For each student, the required data was name, identification number, five quiz scores, and three exam scores. The student data is in alphabetic order by student name.

   a. The student identification number is a _____ .
      (field, record, file)

   b. All of the data for one student is a _____ .
      (field, record, file)

   c. The key field is _____ .

   d. All of the data for all students is called a _____ .
      (field, record, file)

Sequential File Organization

Sequential files are the easiest to create and read in BASIC. Data elements (fields) are stored one after another in sequence. When the data is read *from* the disk, it must be read in the same sequence. Conceptually, a data file on the disk is similar to DATA statements in a program. In order to read any particular element of data, all fields preceding that one must be read first. As data elements are written on diskette, the fields are separated by commas. Records are generally terminated by a carriage return character. Figure 13.2 illustrates data fields stored on diskette.

Figure 13.2
One record stored on a diskette.

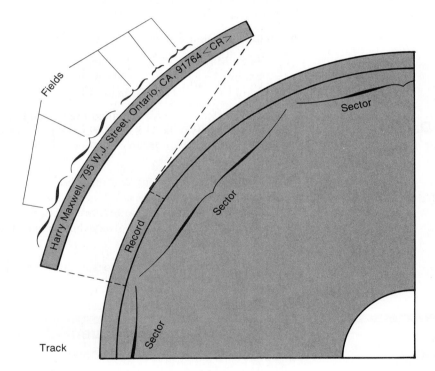

As an example program, a name and address file will be created (for a person with few friends).

Sample Data

First Record

Name field:	Harry Maxwell
Address field:	795 W. J Street
City field:	Ontario
State field:	CA
Zip code field:	91764

Second Record

Name field:	Jennifer Helm
Address field:	201 Cortez Way
City field:	Pomona
State field:	CA
Zip code field:	91766

Third Record

Name field:	Craig Colton
Address field:	1632 Granada Place
City field:	Pomona
State field:	CA
Zip code field:	91766

This data stored in a disk data file would look like this:

"Harry Maxwell","795 W. J Street","Ontario","CA", "91764"<CR>
"Jennifer Helm","201 Cortez Way","Pomona","CA","91766"<CR>
"Craig Colton","1632 Granada Place","Pomona","CA","91766"<CR>

Writing Data to a Disk File

Writing data to a disk file is similar to PRINTing data on the screen or printer. The data is *output* from the program. There are three steps necessary to place data on the disk.

1. *Open* the file. Before any data may be placed on the disk, the file must be opened as an *output file.*
2. *Write* the data elements to be stored.
3. *Close* the file. This should always be the last step in a program that handles disk data files.

Examine the following example program and the explanation of the individual program statements.

Example Program: A Sequential Disk File

Program Listing

```
' Program To Create A Sequential Disk File
'   Inputs Names & Addresses
'   And Writes Each Record On The Disk File

'   Variables Used

'   Nam$      Name        (user input)
'   Addr$     Address     (user input)
'   City$     City        (user input)
'   St$       State       (user input)
'   Zip$      Zip code    (user input)
```

```
'***************** Program Mainline *********************
CLS
GOSUB CreateFile
GOSUB LoadFile
GOSUB CloseFile
END

'********************** Create The File *********************
CreateFile:
   OPEN "NAMES.DAT" FOR OUTPUT AS #1
RETURN

'*********************** Load The File ***********************
LoadFile:
   INPUT "ENTER NAME, 'END' TO QUIT ", Nam$
   DO UNTIL UCASE$(Nam$) = "END"
      INPUT "STREET ADDRESS ", Addr$
      INPUT "CITY           ", City$
      INPUT "STATE          ", St$
      INPUT "ZIP            ", Zip$
      PRINT
      WRITE #1, Nam$, Addr$, City$, St$, Zip$
      INPUT "ENTER NAME, 'END' TO QUIT ", Nam$
   LOOP
RETURN

'***************** Close The File *********************
CloseFile:
   CLOSE #1
RETURN

'***************** End of Program *********************
```

Sample Program Output

```
ENTER NAME, 'END' TO QUIT Harry Maxwell
STREET ADDRESS 795 W. J Street
CITY           Ontario
STATE          CA
ZIP            91764

ENTER NAME, 'END' TO QUIT Jennifer Helm
STREET ADDRESS 201 Cortez Way
CITY           Pomona
STATE          CA
ZIP            91766

ENTER NAME, 'END' TO QUIT Craig Colton
STREET ADDRESS 1632 Granada Place
CITY           Pomona
STATE          CA
ZIP            91766

ENTER NAME, 'END' TO QUIT END
```

Before any data file may be accessed (created or read), the file must be opened.

The OPEN Statement—General Form

```
Format 1:
                          ⎧ INPUT  ⎫
    OPEN "filename" FOR   ⎨ OUTPUT ⎬  AS #filenumber
                          ⎩ APPEND ⎭

Format 2:
             ⎧ "I" ⎫
    OPEN,    ⎨ "O" ⎬,  #filenumber, "file name"
             ⎩     ⎭
```

Either version of the OPEN statement may be used. The elements shown in braces are the *file mode*. The braces indicate that a choice may be made, but that the entry is required.

The OPEN Statement—Examples

```
OPEN "DATAFILE.DAT" FOR OUTPUT AS #1
or
OPEN "O", #1, "DATAFILE.DAT"

OPEN "B:NAMES.DAT" FOR INPUT AS #2
or
OPEN "I", #2, "B:NAMES.DAT"
```

The first example opens a file called DATAFILE.DAT as an output file, calling it file #1. The second example opens a file on the B: drive called NAMES.DAT as an input file, calling it file #2.

File Mode	Explanation
OUTPUT-"O"	Data will be output from the program and written on the disk. This is used to create a data file.
INPUT-"I"	Data will be input into the program from the disk. This will read data previously stored on the disk.
APPEND-"A"	Data will be output from the program and written on the disk. The new data will be added to the *end* of a previously created data file.

Remember that a data file must *always* be opened prior to being used for output or input. When a data file is opened for output, the following actions are taken.

1. The directory is checked for the named file. If the file does not exist, an entry is created for this file. Note that if a file already exists, the old file contents will be lost. The new data will *replace* the previous contents of the file.
2. A **buffer** is established in memory. This is simply setting aside enough main storage to hold 512 bytes of data. As the program instructs BASIC to WRITE data on the disk, the data is actually placed in the buffer. Not until the buffer is filled is the data physically written on the disk.
3. A *file pointer* is set to the beginning of the file. The concept of a file pointer is similar to that in a DATA list in the program. The pointer is always updated to indicate the current location in the file.
4. The file is given a *file number* for future reference. In the example program, it was called file #1. Each file used in one program must be assigned a unique number; however, the numbers need not begin with #1. If you wish, you may call the first file #3. The allowable range is from 1 to 255.

At the conclusion of processing, the file should be closed.

The CLOSE Statement—General Form

```
CLOSE [#filenumber, ...]
```

The CLOSE Statement—Examples

```
CLOSE #1
CLOSE #1, #2, #3
CLOSE
```

The CLOSE statement is used to terminate processing of a disk file. When used without a file number (third example), all open files are closed. The CLOSE statement performs many "housekeeping" tasks:

1. Physically writes the last partially filled buffer on the disk. Data are placed in the buffer by the WRITE statement and are not written to the disk until the buffer is filled. Generally, there will be data in the buffer at the end of the program. That data must be written to the disk.
2. Writes an *End Of File mark (EOF)* at the end of the file.
3. Releases the buffer.
4. Releases the file number. The file number may be reused in another OPEN for a different (or the same) file.

Note that executing an END statement will automatically close all open files. However, it is *not* recommended procedure to rely upon this. If a program terminates in any manner other than an END statement, the files will remain open and probably be "garbaged." A good rule is always to explicitly CLOSE every file that has been opened in the program.

The WRITE# Statement—General Form

```
WRITE #filenumber, fields to write
```

Use the WRITE# statement to place data into a sequential data file. Before the WRITE# statement can be executed, the file must be opened in either the output mode or the append mode. The list of fields to write may be string and/or numeric expressions and may be separated by commas or semicolons.

The WRITE# Statement—Examples

```
WRITE #1, Acct, Desc$, Unit, Price
WRITE #3, A, B, C, D
WRITE #2, Nam$, Addr$, City$, St$, Zip$
```

The WRITE# statement outputs data fields to the disk. As you recall, those fields must have commas written between them as they appear on the disk. The WRITE# statement places commas between each element of data, encloses string data in quotation marks, and inserts a carriage return and a linefeed character after the last item in the list.

Sample name and address data written to the disk file by the WRITE# statement.

```
"Harry Maxwell","795 W. J Street","Ontario","CA","91764"<CR><LF>
"Jennifer Helm","201 Cortez Way","Pomona","CA","91766"<CR><LF>
"Craig Colton","1632 Granada Place","Pomona","CA","91766"<CR><LF>
```

Looking at the Data File on Diskette

Generally, the reason for writing data on diskette is the need to be able to read it in the future. The best way to check the data written on the disk is to write another program that reads the file and prints the contents. Such a program will soon be written.

A second way to "see" the data written on the disk is to open the file with the BASIC editor, and view it on the screen. To do this, make sure to first save your program. Then choose *Open Program* from the File menu. (The command is *Open* in QBASIC.) The files you see in the *Files List* are those that have an extension of .BAS. You can display any filenames you wish by changing the entry in the *File Name* box. Change the entry to *.DAT* to see all files with the extension .DAT, or change it to * . * to see all filenames, all extensions. When you see your data file name in the *Files List*, choose to open it. The data file will appear on the editing screen; if you want to continue working on your program, you must *Open* it again.

Feedback

1. Why must the data elements in a sequential disk file be separated by commas?
2. What is the purpose of the OPEN statement?
3. What would happen if the CLOSE statement were left out of a program?
4. You might choose a name for your data file without realizing that there was already a file on the disk with the same name. Your program would have an open statement, and a file by that name would already exist. What would happen?
5. What happens when a file is opened for output and the file is not already in the directory?

Writing a Program to List the Data File

To read the data from the disk, an input operation is needed. The concept is similar to the READ statement, where each field read brings in the next element in the list. The steps to read data from the disk are

1. Open the file for input
2. Read the data from the disk (and print it on the screen or printer)
3. Close the file

Example Program: Reading the Name and Address File and Printing Address Labels

Program Listing

```
' Read The Sequential Name And Address File
'   And Print Address Labels

'   Variables Used
'   Names$      Name        (from disk file)
'   Address$    Address     (from disk file)
'   City$       City        (from disk file)
'   State$      State       (from disk file)
'   Zip$        Zip code    (from disk file)

'******************** Program Mainline ********************
CLS
GOSUB OpenFile
GOSUB PrintLabels
GOSUB CloseFile
END

'***************** Open File For Input ******************
OpenFile:
    OPEN "NAMES.DAT" FOR INPUT AS #1
RETURN
```

```
'***************** Read Data File And Print Labels ******
PrintLabels:
    DO UNTIL EOF(1)
        INPUT #1, Names$, Address$, City$, State$, Zip$
        LPRINT Names$
        LPRINT Address$
        LPRINT City$; ", "; State$; " "; Zip$
        LPRINT
        LPRINT
    LOOP
RETURN

'***************** Close The File **********************
CloseFile:
    CLOSE #1
RETURN

'***************** End of Program *********************
```

Sample Printer Output

```
Harry Maxwell
795 W. J Street
Ontario, CA 91764

Jennifer Helm
201 Cortez Way
Pomona, CA 91766

Craig Colton
1632 Granada Place
Pomona, CA 91766
```

A new BASIC statement (INPUT#), a new function [EOF(n)], and a file opened for input were illustrated in the sample program.

Opening a File for Input

When a data file is opened for input, there is a slight change in the functions performed by the OPEN. When a file was opened for output, a new directory entry was created if the file did not exist. If a file is opened for input, and the file does not exist, an error message is printed and the program terminated. The OPEN, then, performs these functions:

1. The directory is checked for the named file.
2. The buffer is established.
3. The file pointer is set to the beginning of the file.
4. The file is given a number for future reference.

The INPUT# Statement—General Form

```
INPUT #filenumber, fields to read
```

The filenumber named on the INPUT# statement must be the number of a previously opened data file. The fields named should be separated by commas.

The INPUT# Statement—Examples

```
INPUT #1, Act, Des$, Unit, Pr
INPUT #3, Alfa, Bravo, Charlie, Delta
INPUT #2, Names$, Address$, City$, State$, Zip$
```

The data on the disk are stored in a manner similar to the items on a DATA statement; that is, no variable names are associated with the data elements. It doesn't matter what variable names were used when the data was written to the disk. When the data elements are read from the disk, they may be called by the same variable names or completely different ones. In the example programs, the variable names were purposely changed to illustrate that point.

Finding the End of the Data File

There is more than one way to find the end of the data file. One way would be to keep reading until the data are exhausted. However, this will cause an error message and program cancellation. The second way to find the end of the data file was illustrated in the example program. The BASIC function EOF(n) was used to indicate the *end of file* condition.

The EOF(n) Function—General Form

```
EOF(filenumber)
```

This function returns *false* (0) as long as the end of file has not been found. As soon as the end of file mark has been found, the function returns *true* (-1).

The filenumber included in parentheses must be the file number of a currently open disk file. Notice that *no* number sign (#) is used in this function for file number.

The EOF(n) Function—Examples

```
DO UNTIL EOF(1)
IF EOF(1) THEN . . .
IF EOF(2) <> 0 THEN . . .
```

Recall in the discussion of the CLOSE statement that one of the functions of the CLOSE is to write an End of File mark. That mark is actually an ASCII code 26, written after the last field of data.

Notice the placement of the test for end of file. There is *no* priming INPUT of the data. When data are being read with the INPUT# statement, the last read of *good* data also includes the EOF mark.

```
DO UNTIL EOF(1)
      INPUT #1, Nam$
      PRINT Nam$
LOOP
```

A program in this form will read and print all good data and will *not* print anything for the EOF mark.

A third way to find the end of the data file is to place a terminal value there yourself. A common approach is to write some value such as EOF, END, or zero amounts at the end of the file when it is created. This technique would be quite similar to placing terminating data in a DATA list. The following program writes terminating data at the end of a file after all good data has been written.

Example Program: Creating a File with Terminating Data

Program Listing

```
' Program To Create A Sequential Disk File
'     Inputs Names And Addresses And Writes
'     Each Record On the Disk Data File
'     Adds Terminating Data To End Of File

'     Variables Used

'     Nam$       Name         (user input)
'     Addr$      Address      (user input)
'     City$      City         (user input)
'     St$        State        (user input)
'     Zip$       Zip code     (user input)

'********** Program Mainline **********
CLS
GOSUB CreateFile
GOSUB LoadFile
GOSUB CloseFile
END

'********** Create the File *******
CreateFile:
   OPEN "NAMES2.DAT" FOR OUTPUT AS #1
RETURN

'********** Load the File **********
LoadFile:
   INPUT "Ente name, 'END' to quit ", Nam$
   DO UNTIL UCASE$(Nam$) = "END"
      INPUT "Street address", Addr$
      INPUT "City           ", City$
      INPUT "State          ", St$
      INPUT "Zip            ", Zip$
      WRITE #1, Nam$, Addr$, City$, St$, Zip$
      INPUT "Enter name, 'END' to quit ", Nam$
   LOOP
   WRITE #1, "END", "END", "END", "END", "END"
RETURN

'********** Close The File **********
CloseFile:
   CLOSE #1
RETURN
'***************** End of Program ********************
```

The program that reads the data file will test for the terminating data.

Example Program: Reading a File with Terminating Data

Program Listing

```
'Read The Sequential Name and Address File
'   And Print Address Labels
'   Test For Dummy Terminating Data

'   Variables Used

'   Names$       Name        (from disk file)
'   Address$     Address     (from disk file)
'   City$        City        (from disk file)
'   State$       State       (from disk file)
'   Zip$         Zip code    (from disk file)


'************** Program Mainline **************
CLS
GOSUB OpenFile
GOSUB PrintLabels
GOSUB CloseFile
END

'***************** Open File for Input *****************
OpenFile:
    OPEN "NAMES2.DAT" FOR INPUT AS #1
RETURN

'************** Read Data File And Print Labels ************
PrintLabels:
    INPUT #1, Names$, Address$, City$, State$, Zip$
    DO UNTIL UCASE$(Names$) = "END"
        LPRINT Names$
        LPRINT Address$
        LPRINT City$; ", "; State$; " "; Zip$
        LPRINT
        LPRINT
        INPUT #1, Names$, Address$, City$, State$, Zip$
    LOOP
RETURN

'***************** Close The File *******************
CloseFile:
    CLOSE #1
RETURN
'**************** End of Program ******************
```

Storing Printed Reports

A common application for sequential data files is temporarily to store a printed report. The report may be completely formatted with titles, column headings, and page breaks and written to a disk file rather than a print file. Then, at a more convenient time, the disk file can be printed out.

There are several situations that might require that printed reports be stored on the disk and printed later. One reason might be that several computers share one printer. Or, sometimes one program may print multiple reports—perhaps a detail report and a summary report. One report could be printed as the program runs and the other stored on the disk.

Example Program: Store a Report on Disk

Program Listing

```
'Program To Read Data And Create A Formatted Report
'     That Is Stored On A Disk Data File

'          Variables Used

'     Tree$      Species of trees
'     Count      Number of trees of that species
'     Total      Report total of all trees
'     T$, H$     Print images
'     D$, F$     Print images


'********************* Program Mainline *********************
OPEN "TREEREPT.TXT" FOR OUTPUT AS #1
CLS
GOSUB InitializePrintImages
GOSUB PrintHeadings
GOSUB PrintReport
GOSUB Terminate
CLOSE #1
END

'****************** Initialize Print Images ******************
InitializePrintImages:
    LET T$ = "          CITY TREE INVENTORY"
    LET H$ = "          SPECIES        COUNT"
    LET D$ = "          \          \     #,###"
    LET F$ = "              TOTAL = ###,###"
RETURN

'********************* Print Headings *********************
PrintHeadings:
    PRINT #1, CHR$(12);        'Advance to top of page
    PRINT #1, T$               'Print title
    PRINT #1, " "              'Print blank line
    PRINT #1, H$               'Print column headings
    PRINT #1, " "              'Print blank line
RETURN

'********************* Print Report *********************
PrintReport:
    GOSUB ReadData
    DO UNTIL UCASE$(Tree$) = "END"
        LET Total = Total + Count
        PRINT #1, USING D$; Tree$; Count
        GOSUB ReadData
    LOOP
RETURN

'********************* Read Tree Data *********************
ReadData:
    READ Tree$, Count
    DATA ALDER,100,ASH,225,BIRCH,75,ELM,305,EUCALYPTUS,145
    DATA LAUREL,90,MAPLE,250,OAK,125,SYCAMORE,275,WILLOW,110,END,0
RETURN

'************************* Terminate *************************
Terminate:
    PRINT #1, " "
    PRINT #1, USING F$; Total
RETURN
'********************* End of Program *********************
```

Running this program produces no visible output, except for the "disk busy" light on the disk drive. After the report has been saved in the disk file, the report may be printed with the DOS command TYPE or PRINT. To execute a DOS command in QB, select *DOS Shell* from the *File* menu. (In QB 4.5, first select *Full Menus.*) If you are using QBASIC, you must choose *File Exit* to go to DOS before executing a DOS command.

```
A>TYPE TREEREPT.TXT          to view the report on the screen
```

Or

```
A>TYPE TREEREPT.TXT>PRN      to send the report to the printer
```

```
          CITY  TREE  INVENTORY

          SPECIES          COUNT

          ALDER             100
          ASH               225
          BIRCH              75
          ELM               305
          EUCALYPTUS        145
          LAUREL             90
          MAPLE             250
          OAK               125
          SYCAMORE          275
          WILLOW            110

            TOTAL =       1,700
```

Two new statements were introduced in this program, the PRINT# and PRINT# USING.

The PRINT# Statement—General Form

```
PRINT#  filenumber, list of expressions
```

PRINT# actually functions much like the PRINT statement. Each of the items to print are formatted the same as in a PRINT. There will be one space for the sign preceding positive numbers and one space following the numbers. It responds to semicolons and commas in the print list just as if the data were going to the screen. So, any commas in the print list will be treated as tabs to print zones and cause extra spaces to be inserted between the data elements.

The PRINT# Statement—Examples

```
PRINT #1, "The result is :"; Result
PRINT #2, TAB(10); Nam$; TAB(40); Amount
```

The PRINT# USING Statement—General Form

```
PRINT #filenumber, USING "image string"; variables to print
```

The PRINT# USING Statement—Examples

```
PRINT #1, USING P$; Desc$; Amt
PRINT #3, USING "###.##"; X; Y; Z
```

The PRINT# USING is similar to the PRINT USING statement. All characters used to format the image string for PRINT USING are also valid for PRINT# USING. Notice the punctuation in the statement. A comma must follow the file number, and a semicolon follows the print image. The expressions to print must also be separated by semicolons.

Making Changes to the Data in Sequential Files

It is not a simple task to make changes in the data stored in a sequential file. Recall that opening the file for output places the file pointer at the start of the file, destroying any data in the file. There isn't any way to input data, make changes (like perhaps to change an address), and write the data back to the file. The only way to make changes in a sequential file is to create an entirely new file. Updating sequential files will be covered in chapter 15.

Adding Data to Sequential Files

At some time new names and addresses may need to be added to the end of a name and address file. APPEND mode provides an easy method to accomplish the task.

APPEND Mode

Referring back to the format for the OPEN statement (p. 364), one of the options was to open the file in APPEND mode. When a file is opened for APPEND, the file pointer is placed at the *end* of the file in output mode. Then the WRITE# statement is used to add data to the file.

Example Program:
Adding Data to a Sequential File with APPEND

Program Listing

```
' Program To Append Data To A Sequential Disk File
'    Inputs Names And Addresses And Writes
'    Each Record At The End Of The Disk Data File

'    Variables Used

'    Nam$        Name        (user input)
'    Addr$       Address     (user input)
'    City$       City        (user input)
'    St$         State       (user input)
'    Zip$        Zip code    (user input)

'****************** Program Mainline ************
CLS
GOSUB OpenFile
GOSUB AddToFile
GOSUB CloseFile
END

'***************** Open File for Append *********
OpenFile:
    OPEN "NAMES.DAT" FOR APPEND AS #1
RETURN
```

```
'***************** Create The File ***************
AddToFile:
    INPUT "Enter name, 'END' to quit ", Nam$
    DO UNTIL UCASE$(Nam$) = "END"
        INPUT " Street Address ", Addr$
        INPUT " City          ", City$
        INPUT " State         ", St$
        INPUT " Zip           ", Zip$
        WRITE #1, Nam$, Addr$, City$, St$, Zip$
        PRINT
        INPUT "Enter name, 'END' to quit ", Nam$
    LOOP
RETURN

'***************** Close The File ***************
CloseFile:
    CLOSE #1
RETURN

'***************** End of Program ***************
```

Feedback

1. What happens if a file is opened for input, and the file does not exist?
2. What is the purpose of the file buffer?
3. Does the file number used for the INPUT# statement have to be the same as the file number used when the file was written? Why or why not?
4. How would you know what variable names to use when reading data from the disk?
5. Why is it not necessary to use a priming INPUT# when using the EOF(n) to test for end of file?
6. Why is it necessary to create a new file to make changes in a data file?

Summary

1. Data may be saved from one program run to the next by using data files on a hard disk or diskette.
2. The most common sizes of diskettes, or floppy disks, are 5 1/4 inch and 3 1/2 inch.
3. Data are stored along concentric circles, called tracks, on the surface of the disk.
4. Each track on the disk is divided into sectors of 512 bytes.
5. Both program files and data files can be stored on a disk.
6. Filenames may be one to eight characters in length optionally followed by a period and up to a three-character extension.
7. A file is a collection of records.
8. A record is a collection of fields (or data elements).
9. One field in each record is generally called the key field. This record key is the field used to determine the order for the file.
10. BASIC supports two file organizations: sequential and random.
11. Sequential files are always created and read in sequence. In order to read any data element in the file, all preceding elements must first be read.
12. In sequential files on disk, commas must separate all fields, and a carriage return character separates records.
13. In order to read or write data in a disk file, the file must first be opened.
14. At the conclusion of processing, the data file must be closed.
15. When a data file is opened for output, certain actions occur:
    a. Check for existence of the file. Create an entry if it doesn't exist.
    b. Establish a file buffer.
    c. Set the file pointer to the start of the file.
    d. Establish a correspondence between the filename and the filenumber.

16. The close statement will accomplish these tasks:
    a. Write the last partial buffer to the disk.
    b. Write an End of File mark at the end of the file.
    c. Release the file buffer.
    d. Release the filenumber.
17. Data is written in the disk file with the WRITE#, PRINT#, or PRINT# USING statements.
18. The WRITE# statement is the most efficient of the data file output statements. The data written on the disk with the WRITE# statement will have the necessary commas separating the fields and quotation marks surrounding string elements.
19. In order to check the data written in a disk file, the *Open* option may be used.
20. A program may be written to print the contents of a data file. To accomplish this, the file must first be opened, then the data fields read and printed. At the conclusion of processing, the file must be closed.
21. When a data file is opened for input, the file must exist or an error message is printed and the program terminated.
22. The BASIC statement to read data from a disk file is the INPUT# statement.
23. The end of a data file is indicated with the EOF(n) function. The function returns a value of *false* as long as data remains in the file. When the End of File mark is read, the EOF(n) function returns a value of *true*.
24. Often sequential files are used to temporarily store printed reports.
25. The PRINT# and PRINT# USING statement can be used to store formatted data in a data file.
26. The only way to make changes in a sequential file with a BASIC program is to create a new file.
27. Data may be appended to the end of a sequential file with APPEND mode. After opening a file in APPEND mode, the file pointer is placed at the end of the file in output mode.

Programming Exercises

13.1. Write two programs: one to create a sequential data file, and the second to read the file and calculate commission amounts.

Program 1
INPUT: Input from the keyboard the salesperson's number, name, commission rate, and amount of sales.
OUTPUT: Create a sequential file that contains all input data.

Program 2
INPUT: The input data will be the sequential file created in the first program. Input fields are the salesperson's number, name, commission rate, and amount of sales.
OUTPUT: Print a report with a title and column headings. One detail line will be printed for each salesperson (each input record). The fields on the detail line are to be the salesperson's number, name, sales amount, commission rate, and commission amount.
CALCULATIONS: Compute the commission amount as the sales amount multiplied by the commission rate.
TEST DATA:

Salesman Number	Salesman Name	Sale Amount	Commission Rate
1245	HERMAN HOLLERITH	1157.85	6.5%
1386	BLAISE PASCAL	2540.00	5%
1457	CHARLES BABBAGE	1853.70	4%
1819	JOHN ATANASOFF	650.00	4%
1722	JOHN VON NEUMANN	1000.00	5%

13.2. This assignment entails writing five programs. The first will create a data file to be used by the other four programs. Each of programs 2 through 5 relies on the data file created by program 1. However, the latter four programs do not depend on each other in any way and need not *all* be written.

Program 1

Write a program to create a data file of the book inventory at an elementary school. For each book, store the title, author, grade level, and room location.

Data should be requested from the keyboard and written to the data file. You may make up your own data, find some "real-life" data, or use the test data provided.

TEST DATA:

Title	Author	Grade Level	Room Location
BIG TREES	COGSWELL	4	2
FANTASTIC FRIDAY	CASEY	5	4
FRIENDS	HANOVER	3	2
FUN WITH PHYSICS	HAU	6	1
JANE AND DICK	ADAMS	1	3
MAGICAL MICE	MANNY	5	4
SMALL WORLD	ZANE	5	5
TRY AGAIN	KANT	6	1

Program 2

A program is needed that prints out the entire file on the printer. Format the report with appropriate title and column headings. Add a line at the bottom of the report with a count of the number of books.

Program 3

The teachers need to find the titles at a particular grade level. Write a program that will INPUT a grade level number from the keyboard. Then read through the file, printing only the records matching the selected grade level. If there are no books on that level, print a message to that effect.

Program 4

Write a menu program that will print the entire file sorted into one of four different orders. For this program, the entire file must first be read into arrays. It can then be sorted into any sequence desired.

Menu:
1. Print book list by title
2. Print book list by author
3. Print book list by location
4. Print book list by grade level
5. Quit

Program 5

Write a menu program to access the book file.

Menu:
1. Display the book file on the screen
2. Print the book file on the printer
3. Add new books to the file
4. Quit

For choice 3 (add books), input new records from the keyboard, and add them to the end of the book file. The program should be able to move back and forth between the menu options; that is, add some records, display the file, add some more records, and display the file again.

13.3. When tables must be used in a program, a common approach is to store the tables in data files rather than in the program. This makes the table data independent from the program, which is preferable in two specific situations: (1) The table data must be used by more than one program; or (2) the table data must be changed periodically.

Modify the program in exercise 12.9 (p. 352) to store the two tables in data files. This will entail two small programs to INPUT the table data from the keyboard and write it to disk files. Create one file for the product table and another file for the salesperson table.

In the main (third) program, follow the specifications for the program in exercise 12.9. However, do *not* use DATA statements. Instead, read the data files to fill the tables.

13.4. Write a program to create a sequential data file for the video selection at Jose's Video Store as well as a listing of the data.

INPUT: Input from the keyboard the name of the video, the number of VHS copies available, and the number of BETA copies available.
OUTPUT:
  1. Create a sequential file on disk.
  2. Print a report with a title, column headings, the name of the video, number of VHS copies available, and number of BETA copies available. The report should be printed on the printer.

13.5. Write a program to create a sequential data file for a list of names.

INPUT: The names should come from INPUT statements.
OUTPUT: Create a sequential file on disk, and print the names on the screen.
PROCESSING: Give the user the option of printing the names sequentially or in alphabetical order.

13.6. Write a program to create a sequential employee file for Dan's Dance Studio.

INPUT: Employee name, address, phone number, account number, number of dependents, and pay rate should be input from the keyboard.
OUTPUT: Create a sequential file and print all the input information on the screen or printer depending on what the user wants.
PROCESSING:
  1. Design a nice-looking screen for data entry.

  Menu Options
  1. Enter employee information
  2. Print file on screen
  3. Print file on printer
  4. Quit

13.7. Write a program to create an employee file for the employees at Gonzo's Gunite Company.

INPUT: Employee name, address, phone number, employee number, number of dependents, marital status, and pay rate will be input from the keyboard.
OUTPUT: Create a sequential file on disk and print the entire employee file on the printer or one record on the screen, whichever the user wishes to do.

  Menu Option
  1. Add a record
  2. Print file on printer
  3. Display one record on the screen
  4. Quit

13.8. Write a program to create a sequential file for the company information for Gonzo's Gunite Company's subcontracters.

INPUT: The company name, address, phone number, and representative should be input from the keyboard.

OUTPUT: A list of the companies and all the company information should be printed on the printer, and a sequential file should be created on disk.

Menu Options
1. Add a record
2. Print file sequentially on printer
3. Print file in alphabetical order on printer
4. Quit

13.9. Write a program to create a sequential file to keep track of your stamp collection.

INPUT: The Scott's number, description, and value will be input from the keyboard.

OUTPUT: Output should be to the screen. The user should be able to display the entire file or just one record. Also, a sequential file should be output to disk.

Menu Options
1. Add a record
2. Display entire file
3. Display one record
4. Quit

TEST DATA:

Scott's No.	Description	Value
C13	65 c Green Graf Zeppelin	2700.00
C14	1.30 Brown Graf Zeppelin	5150.00
C15	2.60 Blue Graf Zeppelin	9000.00
15–16	3c, 5c Refugees	26.75
17–18	3c, 5c U.P.U.	30.00
19–20	3c, 5c Technical Assist	15.00
21–22	3c, 5c Human Rights	40.00
1455	8c Family Planning	8.75
1456	8c Glassmaker	.22
1460	6c Olympics-Bicycling	7.25
1461	8c Olympics-Bobsledding	8.75
1462	15c Olympics-Running	16.00
1470	8c Tom Sawyer	8.75
1471	8c Christmas Angel	8.75

13.10. Write a program to keep track of your software collection in a sequential file.

INPUT: Item number, description, publisher, and price will be input from the keyboard.

OUTPUT: Output should be to the screen. The user should be able to display the entire file or just one record. Also, a sequential file should be created on disk.

Menu Options
1. Add a record
2. Display entire file
3. Display one record
4. Quit

TEST DATA

Item No.	Description	Publisher	Price
208	Grand Bridge	Electric Inc.	59.95
209	Chess 1000	Electric Inc.	39.95
214	Resume Maker	InfoTron	49.95
203	Form and Tool	Black Corp.	95.00
218	Will Maker	No Press	49.95
238	Insect	IOU Software	99.00
202	Pro Grames	Delayed Microsys.	59.95
200	World of Golf	Electric Inc.	49.95
227	NewsLetter	Benson	99.95
240	Fast Mail	Sys. & Soft.	79.95
226	Squeeze	Turnover Pub.	79.95
100	Glu Master	Benson	59.95
213	The Tutor	No Soft.	94.95
216	Power Balance	Minds	49.95
223	Orbit Rider	Byte	49.95
217	Graph	New Soft.	97.60
211	Quacky DOS	Gaze Systems	69.95
224	Jet in the Air	Subline Inc.	49.95
221	Disk Destroyer	No Soft.	59.95
121	Gee Wiz	Byte	39.95

13.11. Write a program to create a sequential checkbook file.

INPUT: Check number, transaction date, description of transaction, and payment amount will be input from the keyboard. Only the transaction date and amount will be input for deposits.

OUTPUT: Format the output and send it to the printer.

PROCESS:
1. When a check is written, subtract the amount from the current balance.
2. For a deposit, add the amount to the current balance.

Menu Options
1. Enter a check
2. Enter deposit
3. Enter beginning balance
4. Print checkbook balance
5. Quit

13.12. Create a sequential file to keep track of your magazine collection.

INPUT: Magazine title, cover story, year, month, and comments you want to make about the issue should be input from the keyboard.

OUTPUT: Create a sequential file on disk. If the whole file is to be printed, it should be sent to the printer. If just one record is to be displayed, it should be displayed on the screen.

Menu Options
1. Add a record
2. Print entire file
3. Display one record
4. Quit

14 Random Data Files

OPEN Statement
CLOSE Statement
TYPE Statement
END TYPE Statement
GET Statement
PUT Statement
LOF Function

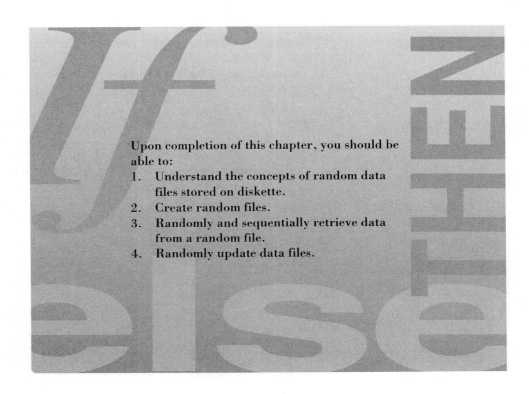

Upon completion of this chapter, you should be able to:

1. Understand the concepts of random data files stored on diskette.
2. Create random files.
3. Randomly and sequentially retrieve data from a random file.
4. Randomly update data files.

Introduction

The two types of files supported by BASIC are sequential files and random files. Chapter 13 dealt with sequential files. In this chapter, the concept of random files will be developed.

The primary difference between sequential files and random files is that data may be written and read in any order in a random file. In sequential files, it was always necessary to start at the beginning of the file and proceed in order through the file.

Programs to handle sequential files are a little easier to code than those for random files, but generally the extra statements required for random files are well worth the effort. Random files offer greater speed as well as the capability for random access. Also, when storing numeric data a random file will generally use less disk storage space than the same data stored in a sequential file. This decrease occurs for two reasons— numeric data is stored in a compressed binary form, and there is no need to store commas between the fields of data.

Random Files

Random files can be visualized like a table, where each entry may be referenced by its relative position. Each entry in a file is one record, which is referred to by its record number. Figure 14.1 illustrates the table concept of random files. Any record in the file may be read or written without the necessity of reading the preceding records.

File Design

We have seen that it is helpful to plan the spacing of a printed report, and that putting the layout of a screen design on paper makes programming easier. It is also helpful to plan a disk file on paper before entering the program for it.

In particular, a random access file needs careful planning. You need to determine the file name, record structure, number of fields, number of characters in each field, and approximate file size. You will find that committing these to paper before beginning to program is a significant aid in clarifying the material and results in shorter programming times.

Figure 14.1
Layout of a random file. Each record consists of a name field, a phone number field, and an amount field. The record is identified by its position in the file (record 1, record 2, etc.).

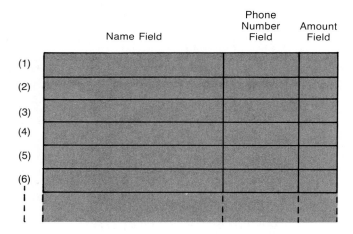

When the initial programming effort is over and the software system is in use, the file design chart, along with the screen layouts and printer spacing charts, becomes part of the permanent program documentation. This is a great help to the maintenance of the program, and an aid to understanding the system when changes are required.

A form for planning a disk file is shown in figure 14.2. A blank form for this purpose is found along with the other planning forms in appendix G.

Creating a Random File

As an example, a program to keep track of concert ticket sales by the Contemporary Music Club will be developed. One record will be stored for each member, consisting of three fields—the member name, telephone number, and the number of tickets sold to date. The member number will be used as the record number in the file.

Random files may be *created* either sequentially or randomly. When creating the file for the Contemporary Music Club, the member names may be entered in sequential order (1, 2, 3, . . .) or in any random order. By specifying the record number (which is assigned as the member number), you may first write record #5, then #1, then #20, or any other order. When record #5 is written in the file, BASIC skips enough space

Figure 14.2
A disk file planning form.

FILE DESIGN CHART

FILENAME _MEMBER. DAT_

FILE TYPE _RANDOM_

RECORD STRUCTURE:

FIELD NAME	FIELD WIDTH	TYPE
MEMBER NAME	30	STRING
PHONE NUMBER	14	STRING
TICKETS SOLD	2	INTEGER

RECORD LENGTH _46_

APPROXIMATE NUMBER OF RECORDS _100_

Figure 14.3
Writing record 5. The record is
written into the fifth location in
the file.

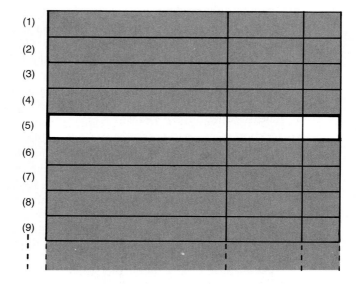

for four records and writes in the fifth physical location. Record positions 1–4 remain empty until such time as records are written in those locations. See the diagram in figure 14.3.

Here are the steps necessary to write data in a random file. Each of the new statements will be explained in the sections that follow.

1. Define the structure of the record (with TYPE and END TYPE)
2. Establish the name of the record (with DIM)
3. Open the file in random mode
4. Loop until finished
   - 4.1   Input the record data from the keyboard
   - 4.2   Output the data in the record to the disk (using the PUT statement)
   - 4.3   Ask the user if finished
5. Close the file
6. End

Defining the Record Structure

Each record in a random file is exactly the same size. The fields within the record are fixed in length and position. That is, if the name takes the first 30 bytes (characters) in one record, every record will have the first 30 bytes allocated for the name. This is a departure from sequential files, with their variable length fields and records. Before reading or writing a random file, the record structure, or layout, must be defined. The TYPE and END TYPE statements are used to set up record structures in Quick-BASIC.

The TYPE and END TYPE Statements—General Form

```
TYPE StructureName
    Element AS VariableType
    Element AS VariableType
    . . .
END TYPE
```

The *StructureName* is considered by QB to be a new variable type, and the naming rules are the same as those for forming variable names (1–40 characters, beginning with a letter).

Figure 14.4
Club member file buffer. Forty-
six characters are allocated for
the file buffer.

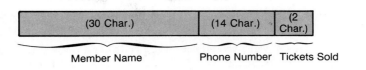

Member Name   Phone Number   Tickets Sold

The *Element* entries are programmer-defined names for each field in the record. The names for *elements* also follow the naming rules for variables. The *VariableType* entries define the type of variable (string, integer, long-integer, single-precision, or double-precision), as well as the length of the field, in bytes. The new concept of *fixed-length strings* must be introduced for record structures.

The TYPE and END TYPE Statements—Examples

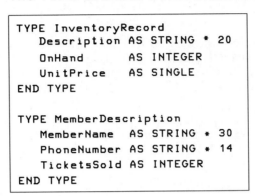

```
TYPE InventoryRecord
    Description AS STRING * 20
    OnHand      AS INTEGER
    UnitPrice   AS SINGLE
END TYPE


TYPE MemberDescription
    MemberName  AS STRING * 30
    PhoneNumber AS STRING * 14
    TicketsSold AS INTEGER
END TYPE
```

The record length for InventoryRecord will be 26 bytes. For MemberRecord, the length is 46 bytes. The binary format used for numeric values corresponds to the manner variables are held in main storage, where integers require 2 bytes, long-integers and single-precision take 4 bytes, and double-precision variables use 8 bytes.

Selecting and Defining Field Size and Record Length

Before a file is created, some planning is required to choose the optimum field size. In the club member example file, thirty characters were allocated for the member name field. You may choose to use fewer characters in order to save space; or, more characters may be necessary if some members have long names. Since the field size must be the same length, whether storing the name for J. Doe (six characters) or for Ebeneezer Abernathy Hornblower, Jr. (thirty-five characters), the length chosen will generally be a compromise. The phone number field was defined as fourteen characters in the form (XXX) XXX-XXXX, to allow space for an area code and number including the parentheses and hyphen. The club member record is illustrated in figure 14.4.

The numeric field to store the number of tickets sold was defined as an integer. Due to the compressed form used for numeric values, integer variables require two bytes of storage in a random data file.

Establishing the Record Name

The TYPE statement establishes a record structure that can now be used. Think of the *StructureName* as an overlay that can be placed over a variable. In the club member example, any variable we define as having a type of *MemberDescription* will be 46 bytes long—the first 30 bytes for *MemberName*, the next 14 bytes for *PhoneNumber*, and the last 2 bytes for *TicketsSold*. To declare a new variable with a type of MemberDescription, we use the DIM statement in a little different manner than seen with arrays.

The DIM Statement Used for Record Descriptions—General Form

```
DIM VariableName AS StructureName
```

The DIM Statement Used for Record Descriptions—Example
To continue with the club member example:

```
DIM MemberRecord AS MemberDescription
```

After the DIM has been executed, the program has a new variable called MemberRecord, of the type MemberDescription. Remember that MemberDescription defines the structure, but it is not a program variable.

Opening a Random File

The OPEN statement for a random file is only slightly different from the OPEN for a sequential file. Rather than being opened for INPUT or OUTPUT, the file is opened in *RANDOM mode*. This will allow both input and output while the file is open. Additionally, the *record length* should be specified each time a file is opened. If the length is not specified the length defaults to 128 bytes, which can cause problems.

The OPEN Statement for Random Files—General Form

```
Format 1:
OPEN "filename" FOR RANDOM AS #filenumber LEN = reclength
Format 2:
OPEN "R", #filenumber, "filename", reclength
```

The file mode shown, "RANDOM" in Format 1 or "R" in Format 2, indicates that both input and output may be performed on the file and that the records may be read or written in any sequence. In Format 2 of the OPEN statement, "R" is a required entry. However, in the first format, if the mode does not appear, the QB editor inserts FOR RANDOM when you press the Enter Key on the line.

The OPEN Statement for Random Files—Examples

```
OPEN "MEMBER.DAT" FOR RANDOM AS #1 LEN = 46
OPEN "MEMBER.DAT" FOR RANDOM AS #1 LEN = LEN(MemberRecord)
OPEN "R", #1, "MEMBER.DAT", 46

OPEN DataFile$ FOR RANDOM AS #2 LEN = RecLength
OPEN "R", #2, DataFile$, RecLength
```

Each of these groups of OPEN statements has the same effect. Before the OPEN in the second group can be executed, the two fields DataFile$ and RecLength must be given a value. This may be done with an INPUT statement to allow flexibility.

Using the Defined Record for Input and Output

The input/output statements for random file processing differ from those used for sequential files in several important respects. Data is read from the file with the GET statement and written with the PUT statement. The GET and PUT include the record position number and the name of the variable defined as the record description.

```
GET #1, recno, RecordName
PUT #1, recno, RecordName
```

The *recno* field on these statements indicates the record number in the file to read or write.

When the statement

```
GET #1, 5, MemberRecord
```

is executed, the entire record at location five is placed into the record variable. Then the field names from the record structure can be used to reference the data.

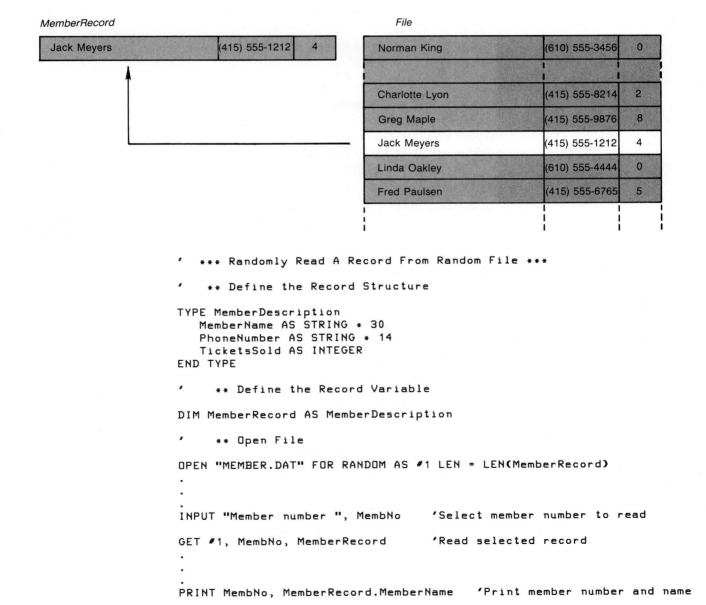

```
'  *** Randomly Read A Record From Random File ***

'   ** Define the Record Structure

TYPE MemberDescription
    MemberName AS STRING * 30
    PhoneNumber AS STRING * 14
    TicketsSold AS INTEGER
END TYPE

'   ** Define the Record Variable

DIM MemberRecord AS MemberDescription

'   ** Open File

OPEN "MEMBER.DAT" FOR RANDOM AS #1 LEN = LEN(MemberRecord)
.
.
.
INPUT "Member number ", MembNo      'Select member number to read

GET #1, MembNo, MemberRecord        'Read selected record
.
.
.
PRINT MembNo, MemberRecord.MemberName    'Print member number and name
```

Similarly, when a record is written to the disk file with the PUT statement, the contents of the record variable are placed on the disk.

```
PUT #1, 2, MemberRecord
```

MemberRecord

Dorothy Lombardi	(415) 555-2222	6

File

Norman King	(610) 555-3456	0
Dorothy Lombardi	(415) 555-2222	6
Charlotte Lyon	(415) 555-8214	2
Greg Maple	(415) 555-9876	8
Jack Meyers	(415) 555-1212	4
Linda Oakley	(610) 555-4444	0
Fred Paulsen	(415) 555-6765	5

The GET and PUT always transfer an entire record, by record number. In order to access the individual fields within the record, the elements must be referenced by the record name, a period, and the element name. Recall that the element names are defined within the TYPE statement. Any BASIC statement that normally uses a variable name may also reference a record element.

Examples:

```
PRINT MemberRecord.MemberName
INPUT "Enter telephone number ", MemberRecord.PhoneNumber
LET MemberRecord.TicketsSold = MemberRecord.TicketsSold + 1
```

Caution: Be sure to use the record name (from the DIM statement) rather than the structure name (from the TYPE statement).

Reading and Writing the Random Data File

You can now set up one record and PUT (write) it into the random file.

```
'    *** Randomly Write A Record Into A Random File ***

'    ** Define the Record Structure

TYPE MemberDescription
   MemberName AS STRING * 30
   PhoneNumber AS STRING * 14
   TicketsSold AS INTEGER
END TYPE

'    ** Define the Record Variable

DIM MemberRecord AS MemberDescription

'    ** Open File

OPEN "MEMBER.DAT" FOR RANDOM AS #1 LEN = LEN(MemberRecord)
   .
   .
```

```
'     ************ Input Data From Keyboard ************
INPUT "Member number ", MembNo
INPUT "Member name   ", MemberRecord.MemberName
INPUT "Phone number  ", MemberRecord.PhoneNumber
INPUT "Tickets sold  ", MemberRecord.TicketsSold
   .
   .
   .
'     ************* Write Record in File **************
PUT #1, MembNo, MemberRecord
   .
   .
   .
```

To read one record and print the contents of that record on the screen, add a little more coding.

```
'***************** Accept Inquiry **********************
INPUT "Enter Member number ", MembNo
   .
   .
   .
'**************** Read Selected Record ****************
GET #1, MembNo, MemberRecord
   .
   .
   .
'********** Display The Record On The Screen ***********
PRINT "Member name   "; MemberRecord.MemberName
PRINT "Phone number  "; MemberRecord.PhoneNumber
PRINT "Tickets sold  "; MemberRecord.TicketsSold
   .
   .
   .
```

The GET Statement—General Form

```
GET #filenumber, [RecordNumber], RecordName
```

The GET statement reads data from a random disk file and places the data into the record named. When the record number is omitted from the statement, the *next* record is read from the file.

The GET Statement—Examples

```
GET #1, 4, ItemRecord
GET #2, Custno, CustomerRecord
GET #1, , MemberRecord
```

Either a variable or a constant may be used for the record number. Generally you will want to use a variable to allow selection of any record in the file.

```
INPUT "Enter customer number ", Custno
GET #1, Custno, CustomerRecord
```

The PUT Statement—General Form

```
PUT  #filenum, [RecordNumber], RecordName
```

The PUT statement takes the contents of the record named and writes it on the disk. The *record number* determines the relative location within the file for the record. If the record number is omitted, the record will be placed in the next location after the last record PUT into the file. (This is not necessarily following the final record in the file, only the prior record PUT in this program run.)

The PUT Statement—Examples

```
PUT #1, AcctNum, AccountNumber
PUT #2, 1, PartNumber
PUT #3, , InventoryRecord
```

As with the GET, the record number may be a variable or a constant. Using a variable gives the most flexibility.

Printing Selected Records from a File

A program that *selectively* reads a particular disk record will follow this pattern:

1. Define the record structure (with TYPE)
2. Name the record (with DIM)
3. OPEN the file
4. Loop until finished
   4.1 INPUT (from keyboard) the desired record number
   4.2 GET the record
   4.3 Print the record (on screen or printer)
   4.4 Ask user if finished
5. CLOSE the file
6. END

Example Program:
Selectively Print One Record from a Random File

Program Listing

```
'     Program To Demonstrate The Selective Printing Of
'        One Record In A Random File
'
'          Variables used
'
'       Ans$                 Answer to question
'       MemberRecord         Record variable
'       MembNo               Member number
'                              (Used for record number)
TYPE MemberDescription
   MemberName    AS STRING * 30
   PhoneNumber   AS STRING * 14
   TicketsSold   AS INTEGER
END TYPE

DIM MemberRecord AS MemberDescription
```

```
'***************** Program Mainline *********************
OPEN "MEMBER.DAT" FOR RANDOM AS #1 LEN = LEN(MemberRecord)
CLS
DO
   PRINT
   INPUT "MEMBER NUMBER      ", MembNo
   IF MembNo > 0 AND MembNo < 100 THEN
      GET #1, MembNo, MemberRecord
      GOSUB PrintRecord
   END IF
   INPUT "DISPLAY ANOTHER RECORD? (Y/N) ", Ans$
LOOP WHILE UCASE$(Ans$) = "Y"
CLOSE #1
END

'***************** Print The Record *********************
PrintRecord:
   PRINT
   PRINT "MEMBER NAME     "; MemberRecord.MemberName
   PRINT "PHONE NUMBER    "; MemberRecord.PhoneNumber
   PRINT "TICKETS SOLD    "; MemberRecord.TicketsSold
   PRINT
RETURN

'***************** End of Program *********************
```

Sample Program Output

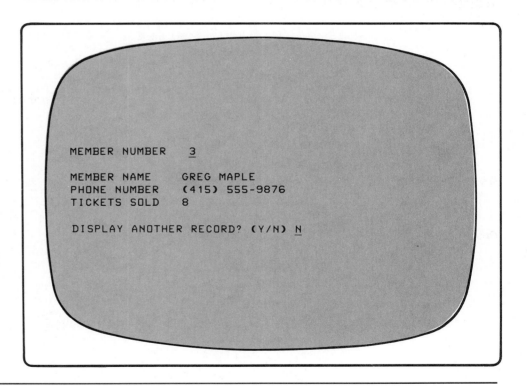

```
MEMBER NUMBER    3

MEMBER NAME      GREG MAPLE
PHONE NUMBER     (415) 555-9876
TICKETS SOLD     8

DISPLAY ANOTHER RECORD? (Y/N) N
```

Printing Out an Entire File

A program that reads and prints all of the records in a random file in order would follow this pattern:

1. Define the record structure (with TYPE)
2. Name the record (with DIM)
3. OPEN the file
4. Loop until end of file
    - 4.1 GET a record
    - 4.2 PRINT the fields from the file buffer
5. CLOSE the file
6. END

Finding the End of a Random Data File with the EOF Function

The EOF function may be used to signal the end of a random file as well as a sequential file. However, with random files, EOF is *true* when a GET is unable to read an entire record. Therefore EOF is not *true* until *after* the last good record is read. This will require a priming GET in order to prevent printing past End Of File.

Example Program: Printing an Entire Random File

Program Listing

```
'     Program To Demonstrate Printing an Entire Random File
'        using the EOF function for detecting End Of File
'        Note:  Any unused record positions will print garbage

TYPE MemberDescription
    MemberName    AS STRING *30
    PhoneNumber   AS STRING *14
    TicketsSold   AS INTEGER
END TYPE

DIM MemberRecord AS MemberDescription

'********************* Program Mainline *********************
OPEN "MEMBER.DAT" FOR RANDOM AS #1 LEN = LEN(MemberRecord)
CLS
GET #1, , MemberRecord
DO UNTIL EOF(1)
PRINT MemberRecord.MemberName, MemberRecord.PhoneNumber, MemberRecord.TicketsSold
    GET #1, , MemberRecord
LOOP
CLOSE #1
END
'********************* End of Program *********************
```

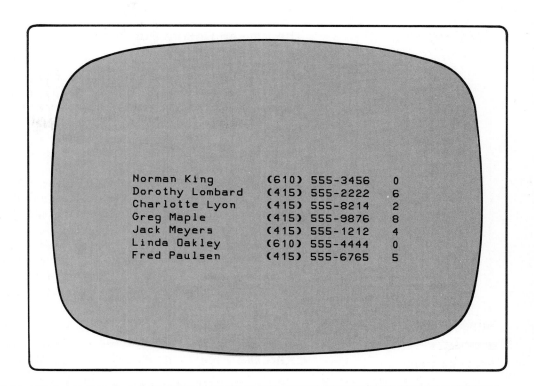

```
                   Norman King         (610) 555-3456   0
                   Dorothy Lombard     (415) 555-2222   6
                   Charlotte Lyon      (415) 555-8214   2
                   Greg Maple          (415) 555-9876   8
                   Jack Meyers         (415) 555-1212   4
                   Linda Oakley        (610) 555-4444   0
                   Fred Paulsen        (415) 555-6765   5
```

Finding the End of a Random Data File with the LOF Function

With random files, a second method exists for finding the End Of File that is superior to the EOF function. The LOF function returns the size of the file in bytes. By dividing this number by the record size, the last record number can be determined. Knowing the highest record number in a file makes it possible to add a new record to the end of the file, or print the entire file with a FOR/NEXT loop.

```
LET RecNum = LOF(1) / LEN(MemberRecord) + 1
PUT #1, RecNum, MemberRecord

LET LastRec = LOF(1) / LEN(MemberRecord)
FOR RecNum = 1 to LastRec
    GET #1, RecNum, MemberRecord
    GOSUB PrintTheRecord
NEXT RecNum
```

The LOF Function—General Form

```
LOF(FileNumber)
```

The LOF Function—Examples

```
LET LastRecord = LOF(1) / LEN(DataRecord)
PRINT "This file holds "; LOF(2); " bytes"
```

The Unused Record Positions

The EOF sample program will work well for a data file with *no* empty record positions. However, another approach must be used when some record positions will be unused (empty cells). As mentioned earlier, writing a record in record position 5 (for example) does not disturb any other records. If *you* haven't written anything in positions 1–4, that doesn't mean that those positions are blank.

To understand why "garbage" may be found in the midst of a file, you must understand a little bit about how the operating system (DOS) saves and deletes files. When any files (programs or data files) are saved on a diskette, those sectors are reserved as "in use." When a file is deleted from the diskette, DOS frees those sectors to be reused, but the file is *not erased*. Therefore, all available diskette space that has been previously used will hold the remains of old files. When the record in position 5 is written, positions 1–4 may hold *anything*.

There are two possible solutions to this dilemma: (1) assign record numbers in sequence with no unused record positions, or (2) initialize all record positions before writing any good records in the file. The second solution is the one chosen for the sample program for the Contemporary Music Club's ticket sales.

Example Program: Random File Maintenance

Now the complete program can be written to handle the data for the Contemporary Music Club. Notice that the menu allows choices to add members, update ticket sales, selectively print the record of one member, print a list of all members, or initialize the file. A maximum file size of 100 records was chosen for the initialization process.

Hierarchy Chart   Refer to figure 14.5.

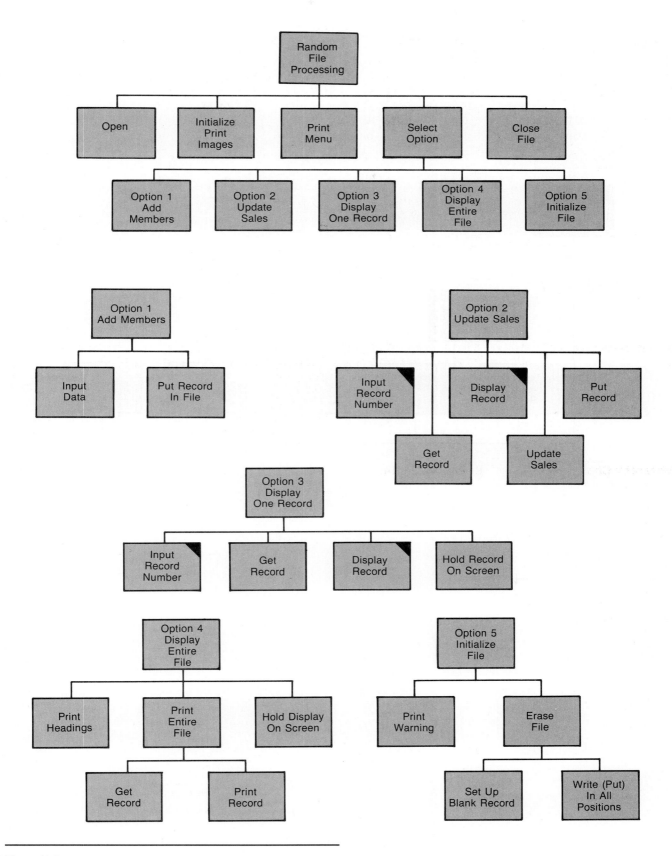

Figure 14.5
Hierarchy chart for random file processing program. Any
subroutines that are executed from more than one location are
shown with shaded corners. This indicates a shared module.

Flowchart   Refer to figure 14.6.

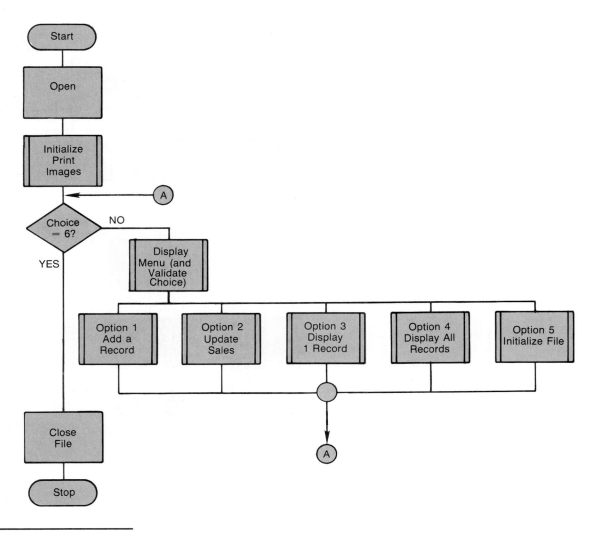

Figure 14.6
Flowchart for random file
processing program.

Figure 14.6—*Continued*

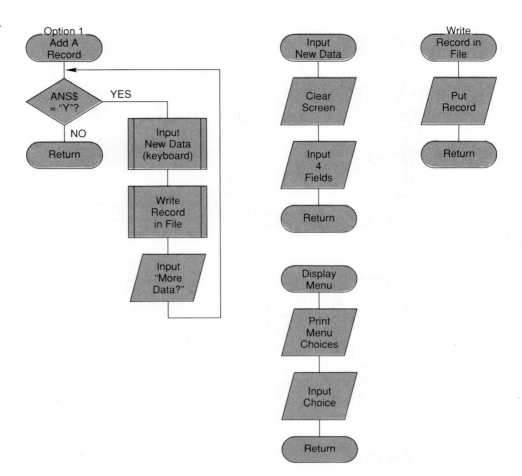

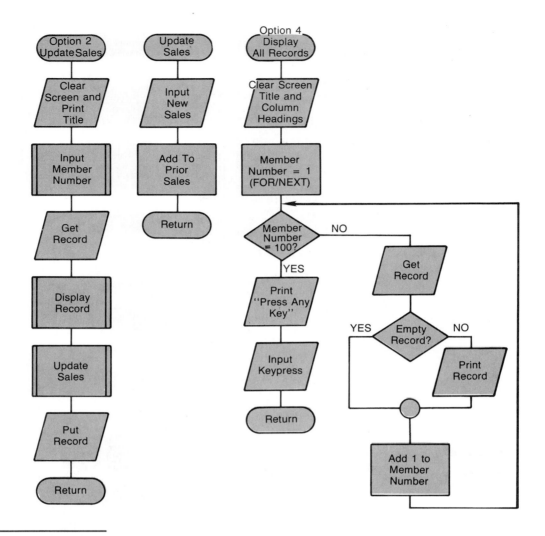

Figure 14.6—*Continued*

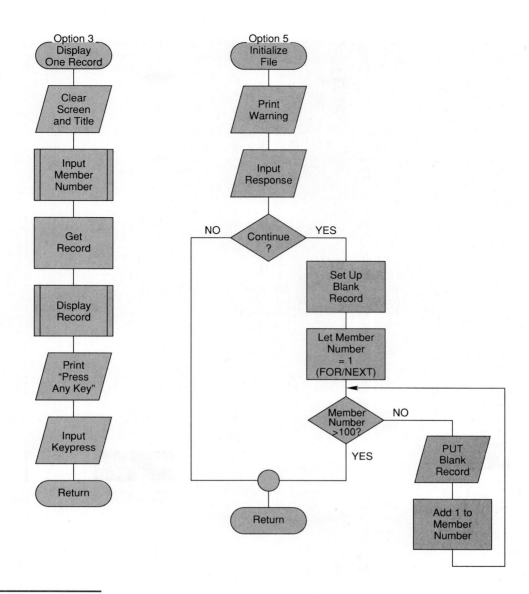

Figure 14.6—*Continued*

```
'      Program To Create And Maintain A Random Data File
'         To Be Used By The Contemporary Music Club
'            For Recording Member Information And Concert
'         Ticket Sales

'               Variables used

'      MembNo              Member number (record number)
'      Memb$               Member name
'      Phone$              Member phone number
'      Tick                Number of tickets sold
'      Ans$                Answer to question
'      Title$              Screen title
'      H1$, T2$, D1$       Print images
'      Sales               New sales for update
'      Choice and Choice$    Menu choice
'      MemberRecord        Record variable

TYPE MemberDescription
   MemberName   AS STRING * 30
   PhoneNumber  AS STRING * 14
   TicketsSold  AS INTEGER
END TYPE


DIM MemberRecord AS MemberDescription

'****************** Program Mainline ******************
OPEN "MEMBER.DAT" FOR RANDOM AS #1 LEN = LEN(MemberRecord)
GOSUB InitializePrintImages
DO
   GOSUB DisplayMenu
   SELECT CASE Choice
      CASE 1
         GOSUB AddRecord
      CASE 2
         GOSUB UpdateTickets
      CASE 3
         GOSUB DisplayOneRecord
      CASE 4
         GOSUB DisplayAllRecords
      CASE 5
         GOSUB InitializeFile
      CASE 6
         CLS
      CASE ELSE
         LOCATE 19, 44
         PRINT "         "
   END SELECT
LOOP UNTIL Choice = 6
CLOSE #1
END


'****************** Initialize Print Images ******************
InitializePrintImages:
   LET Title$ = "CONTEMPORARY MUSIC CLUB"
   LET T2$ = "CONCERT TICKET SALES "
   LET H1$ = "MEMBER          NAME          TELEPHONE TICKETS SOLD"
   LET D1$ = "  ###   /              /   /   /     ####"
RETURN
```

```
'***************** Display Menu **************************
DisplayMenu:
   CLS
   PRINT
   PRINT TAB(20); Title$
   PRINT
   PRINT TAB(31); T2$
   PRINT
   PRINT
   PRINT TAB(21); "1. ADD MEMBERS TO FILE"
   PRINT
   PRINT TAB(21); "2. UPDATE TICKET SALES"
   PRINT
   PRINT TAB(21); "3. DISPLAY INFORMATION FOR ONE MEMBER"
   PRINT
   PRINT TAB(21); "4. DISPLAY INFORMATION FOR ALL MEMBERS"
   PRINT
   PRINT TAB(21); "5. INITIALIZE THE FILE"
   PRINT
   PRINT TAB(21); "6. QUIT"
   PRINT
   PRINT TAB(24); "ENTER CHOICE (1 - 6) ";
   LOCATE 19, 44
   INPUT Choice$
   LET Choice = VAL(Choice$)
RETURN


'***************** Add a Record To File ******************
AddRecord:
   DO
      GOSUB InputDataKeyboard
      GOSUB WriteRecord
      INPUT "ADD ANOTHER MEMBER"; Ans$
   LOOP WHILE UCASE$(LEFT$(Ans$, 1)) = "Y"
RETURN


'***************** Input Data From Keyboard ***************
InputDataKeyboard:
   CLS
   INPUT "MEMBER NUMBER ", MembNo
   PRINT
   INPUT "MEMBER NAME    ", MemberRecord.MemberName
   PRINT
   INPUT "PHONE NUMBER   ", MemberRecord.PhoneNumber
   PRINT
   INPUT "TICKETS SOLD   ", MemberRecord.TicketsSold
   PRINT
   PRINT
RETURN


'***************** Write Record In The File ***************
WriteRecord:
   PUT #1, MembNo, MemberRecord
RETURN


'***************** Update Ticket Sales *******************
UpdateTickets:
   CLS
   PRINT TAB(20); Title$
   GOSUB InputValidRecordNo
   GET #1, MembNo, MemberRecord
   GOSUB PrintRecord
   GOSUB UpdateSales
   PUT #1, MembNo, MemberRecord
RETURN
```

```
'***************** Input Valid Record Number **************
InputValidRecordNo:
   PRINT
   INPUT "ENTER MEMBER NUMBER ", MembNo$
   DO WHILE VAL(MembNo$) < 1 OR VAL(MembNo$) > 100
      LOCATE 5, 10
      PRINT "MEMBER NUMBER MUST BE IN RANGE 1-100"
      LOCATE 3, 21
      INPUT "", MembNo$
      LOCATE 5, 10
      PRINT "
   LOOP
   LET MembNo = VAL(MembNo$)
RETURN

'******************** Print The Record ********************
PrintRecord:
   PRINT
   PRINT
   PRINT "MEMBER NAME        "; MemberRecord.MemberName
   PRINT "PHONE NUMBER       "; MemberRecord.PhoneNumber
   PRINT "TICKETS SOLD       "; MemberRecord.TicketsSold
   PRINT
RETURN

'******************* Update Sales **********************
UpdateSales:
   PRINT
   PRINT
   INPUT "ENTER NEW SALES ", Sales
   LET MemberRecord.TicketsSold = MemberRecord.TicketsSold + Sales
RETURN

'****************** Display One Record From The File ******
DisplayOneRecord:
   CLS
   PRINT TAB(20); Title$
   GOSUB InputValidRecordNo
   GET #1, MembNo, MemberRecord
   GOSUB PrintRecord
   PRINT "PRESS ANY KEY TO CONTINUE";
   LET X$ = INPUT$(1)
RETURN

'***************** Display All Records In File ************
DisplayAllRecords:
   CLS
   PRINT TAB(20); Title$
   PRINT
   PRINT TAB(12); H1$
   PRINT
   FOR MembNo = 1 TO 100
     GET #1, MembNo, MemberRecord
     IF LEFT$(MemberRecord.MemberName, 1) <> " " THEN
      PRINT USING  D1$; MembNo;   MemberRecord.MemberName;
      MemberRecord.PhoneNumber; MemberRecord.TicketsSold
     END IF
   NEXT MembNo
   PRINT
   PRINT
   PRINT "PRESS ANY KEY TO CONTINUE";
   LET X$ = INPUT$(1)
RETURN
```

```
'***************** Initialize The File *********************
InitializeFile:
   CLS
   LOCATE 8, 30
   PRINT "CAUTION, THIS WILL ERASE ALL MEMBER DATA IN THE FILE"
   PRINT
   PRINT
   PRINT
   INPUT "          DO YOU WISH TO PROCEED"; Ans$
   IF UCASE$(LEFT$(Ans$, 1)) = "Y" THEN
      LET MemberRecord.MemberName = "  "
      LET MemberRecord.PhoneNumber = "  "
      LET MemberRecord.TicketsSold = 0
      FOR MembNo = 1 TO 100
         PUT #1, MembNo, MemberRecord
      NEXT MembNo
   END IF
RETURN

'***************** End of Program ***************************
```

Sample Program Output

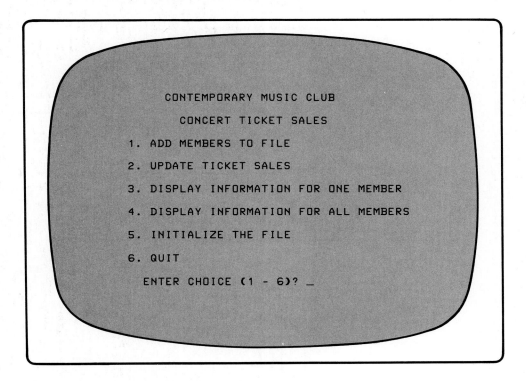

Choice 1—Add Members to File

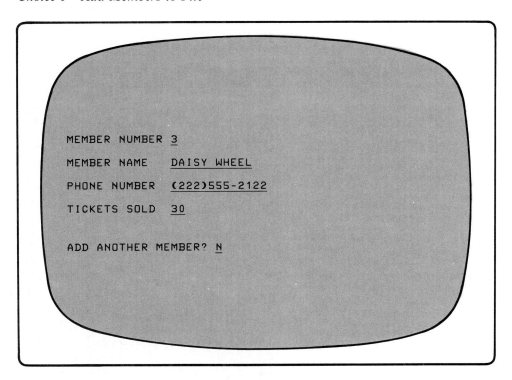

```
MEMBER NUMBER 3

MEMBER NAME    DAISY WHEEL

PHONE NUMBER   (222)555-2122

TICKETS SOLD   30

ADD ANOTHER MEMBER? N
```

Choice 2—Update Ticket Sales

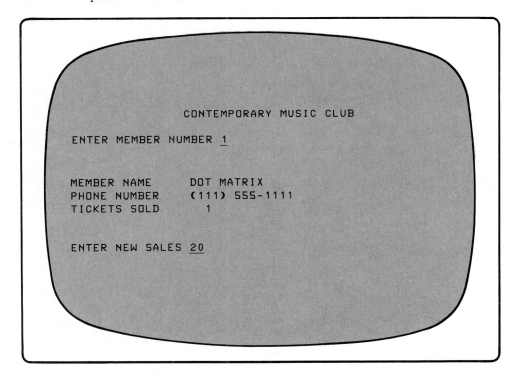

```
                    CONTEMPORARY MUSIC CLUB

ENTER MEMBER NUMBER 1

MEMBER NAME       DOT MATRIX
PHONE NUMBER      (111) 555-1111
TICKETS SOLD         1

ENTER NEW SALES 20
```

Choice 3—Display Information for One Member

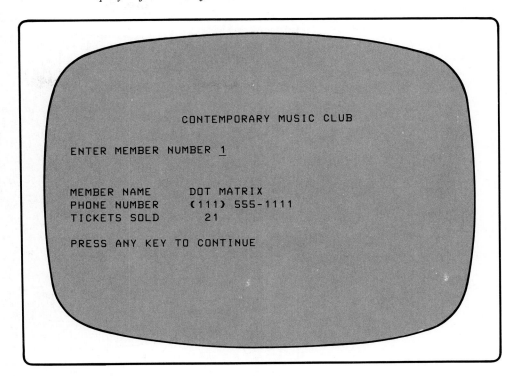

```
                    CONTEMPORARY MUSIC CLUB

ENTER MEMBER NUMBER 1


MEMBER NAME       DOT MATRIX
PHONE NUMBER      (111) 555-1111
TICKETS SOLD        21

PRESS ANY KEY TO CONTINUE
```

Choice 4—Display Information for All Members

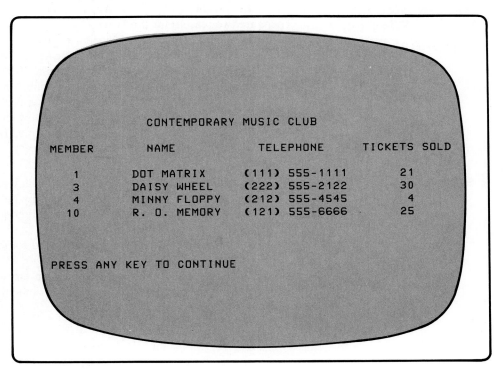

```
                 CONTEMPORARY MUSIC CLUB

MEMBER        NAME           TELEPHONE      TICKETS SOLD

   1       DOT MATRIX      (111) 555-1111       21
   3       DAISY WHEEL     (222) 555-2122       30
   4       MINNY FLOPPY    (212) 555-4545        4
  10       R. O. MEMORY    (121) 555-6666       25




PRESS ANY KEY TO CONTINUE
```

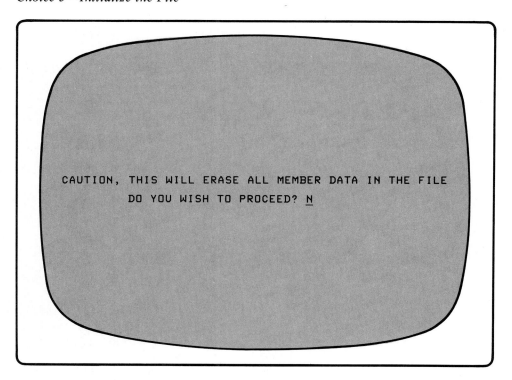

```
CAUTION, THIS WILL ERASE ALL MEMBER DATA IN THE FILE
        DO YOU WISH TO PROCEED? N
```

Relative Size of Random Files vs. Sequential Files

As a general rule, random disk files take less space than sequential files on a diskette. There are two reasons for this size difference: (1) numeric data is stored in compressed binary form, and (2) it is not necessary to write commas between the fields of data and place the linefeed and carriage return characters between records.

However, for some files sequential organization will use less space than random. In a sequential file, string data fields are variable in length. Only as many characters as are necessary are written, followed by a comma. In a random file, the string data fields must be fixed in length, probably resulting in wasted space. If the majority of the fields in the record are variable length strings rather than numeric fields, it may be that the sequential file will occupy less space.

Feedback

1. Would BASIC be able to randomly read any record in the file if the records were not all the same length? Why or why not?
2. How is the record length specified for a random file?
3. How are the field lengths specified?
4. Explain how field lengths are determined for string variables. For numeric variables.
5. Explain the use of the record description for writing data on the disk.
6. How is the record description used for randomly reading a record from the file?

7. Use these statements for reference.

```
TYPE InventoryStructure
    Description AS STRING * 10
    Quantity    AS INTEGER
END TYPE
DIM InventoryRecord AS InventoryStructure
OPEN "INVEN.DAT" FOR RANDOM AS #1 LEN = LEN(InventoryRecord)
```

Write the BASIC statements to accomplish the following:
a. Read the fourth record in the file INVEN.DAT, and print the description and quantity on the screen.
b. Input (from the keyboard) an item number, description, and quantity. Place the data into the file buffer, and write the record (using the item number for the record number).
c. List the entire INVEN.DAT file. Use the EOF function to find the end of file.

Summary

1. The records in a random file may be written and read in any order.
2. The advantages of using random files over sequential files include:
   a. capability for random access (rather than being limited to sequential access);
   b. random files are faster; and
   c. the random file will generally occupy less space on diskette.
3. Each record in a random file is referenced by its record number, which is its relative position in the file.
4. A random file may be created sequentially or randomly.
5. The file is opened in random mode, which allows for both input and output in any sequence.
6. All records in the file must be the same length. This record length is specified on the OPEN statement.
7. Each field within the record must be a fixed size. The size of the field is declared within the type specification.
8. The structure of a record is defined with the TYPE and END TYPE statements.
9. String elements within a record structure must be defined as fixed length.
10. Numeric elements within a record structure are defined as INTEGER, LONG, SINGLE, or DOUBLE, and require 2, 4, or 8 bytes of storage.
11. The DIM statement is used to assign a variable name to the record structure.
12. The I/O statements for a random file are GET and PUT.
13. Both the GET and PUT statements include a record number. This is the indication of which record position should be read or written. When the record number is omitted, it will read or write the *next* record.
14. When there are unused record positions in a file, the empty cells may contain garbage. Initializing the file to blank spaces will solve this problem.
15. The EOF function may be used to indicate an End Of File condition.
16. The LOF function returns the size of the file in bytes and may be used to calculate the last record number.

Programming Exercises

14.1. Establish a random file for reserving airplane seats. The plane has forty rows, numbered 1–40. Each row has six seats (three on each side of the aisle), referred to as A, B, C, D, E, and F.

Set up a random file of forty records. Each record will have six fields for the six seats. Make each field long enough to hold a passenger's name. Initially, each seat must be set to the value AVAILABLE. Then, as seats are assigned, place the name of the passenger in that field position.

Use a menu, with these choices:

1. Assign a seat
2. Display list of available seats
3. Print list of passengers with seat assignments
4. Initialize all seats as available
5. End

Choice 1: Prompt the user for a requested seat location. If that seat is available, assign the passenger to that seat. (Place the passenger's name in the corresponding field and rewrite the record.) If the seat is not available, the program might offer another choice or perhaps display the list of remaining available seats (menu choice 2).

Choice 2: Print out all seat locations that are still available. If no seats are available, print a message that the plane is full.

Choice 3: Print out the list of passengers along with their seat locations. This will be in seat-number order.

Choice 4: Print an appropriate sign-off message.

14.2. Modify the program in exercise 14.1 to print the passenger list in alphabetic order. This will require reading the entire file into arrays and sorting the data. The order of the file will remain unchanged (in seat-number order).

14.3. Modify the program in exercise 14.1 (or 14.2) to indicate which seats are next to windows or which are aisle seats. The aisle is in the middle of the plane, so seats A and F are window seats, and C and D are aisle seats. Allow the user to request any available window or aisle seat.

14.4. The company needs to store personnel records in a data file. Each employee will be assigned an employee number, beginning with number 1. Write a program that will create and update a random access file for storing personnel records.

PERSONNEL FILE: The fields in each personnel record should be name, address, social security number, marital status, exemptions, and department number.

MENU PROGRAM: The solution should be written as a menu program with options to create the file, to update individual records, to list the file on the printer, to display the file on the screen, or to quit.

a. *Create the File*—Request input of each of the fields for each employee. The records should be assigned employee numbers, beginning with #1. Use the employee number as record number, and write each record in the random file.

b. *Update Option*—Request the employee number to update. Then display the data for that employee, and give the user the option of changing *no* fields if this is not the correct employee. Allow the user to change as many fields as desired for that employee. When all updates for that employee are complete, return to the menu.

      c. *List the File on the Printer*—Design a report layout with an appropriate title. Create a company name.

      d. *Display the File on the Screen*—Design a pleasing screen layout, and display all records.

      e. *Quit*—Print a sign-off message.

    INPUT DATA: Make up data for at least five employees. For each, enter the name, address, city, state, zip code, social security number, marital status, exemptions, and department number.

    CHANGES: Make up changes to the file, testing all change options. List the file between changes to determine that the changes have been correctly made.

14.5. Modify the program in exercise 14.4 to include data validation and formatted screens for data entry.

    a. Data validation—both for the create and update.

      (1) Social security number—check for correct number of digits.

      (2) Marital status—check for M or S.

      (3) Exemptions—valid numeric characters, between 0 and 15.

      (4) Department number—the only valid department numbers are 40, 41, 45, 50, and 55.

    b. Formatted screens—make data entry easy and clear. Do not allow screens to scroll. Any error messages must be cleared after corrections are made.

14.6. Establish a random file to maintain inventory information for parts. The part numbers are in the range 1–100 and can be used as record numbers in the file.

Record Layout

Part number	integer
Description	25 characters
Unit price	single-precision
Quantity on hand	integer

Write the program as a menu, with these choices:

1. Increase part inventory
2. Decrease part inventory
3. Display parts inventory file on the screen
4. List parts inventory file on the printer
5. Initialize the parts inventory file
6. Sign off

Choice 1: Increase part inventory—Prompt the user for the part number. Then retrieve and display the part description, unit price, and quantity on hand. Then request input of the number of units to *add* to the inventory.

Choice 2: Decrease part inventory—Similar to choice 1, only enter number of units to *subtract* from inventory.

Choice 3: Display file on screen—Display a list of the entire file. However, do not list any part numbers that do not have data in the file (empty record positions). When a screenful of data has been printed, hold the display with the message: PRESS ANY KEY TO CONTINUE.

Choice 4: List file on printer—List the entire file on the printer, leaving out any part numbers for which there is no data (empty record positions). Format the report with an appropriate title and column headings. Multiple page output must have headings on each page with the page number on all pages.

Choice 5: After printing a warning message, initialize the entire file (record numbers 1–100). Numeric fields (part number, unit price, and quantity on hand) should be set to zero, the descriptions should be set to blanks. Then allow the user to enter data for part numbers, along with corresponding description, unit price, and quantity on hand. Part numbers may be entered in any order. Use the part number for record number.

Choice 6: Clear the screen and print an appropriate sign-off message.

PROGRAM TESTING: Run your program, selecting choice 5 to establish the file. Make up your own data, using noncontiguous part numbers such as 1, 5, 20, 25, 50, 100. Be sure to use record positions 1 and 100. Place sufficient parts in the file to test the multiple screen and multiple page options of menu choices 3 and 4.

Once the file has been established, select options to add parts, list the file, subtract parts, and list again, making sure that all requested changes are made.

ERROR CHECKING: Verify that requested part numbers are in the range 1–100 before attempting to read or write in the file. This must be done for menu choices 1, 2, and 5.

14.7. Modify the program in exercise 14.6 to include a formatted screen to make data entry easier and more clear. Do not allow screens to scroll. Any error messages must be cleared after corrections are made.

14.8. Modify the program in exercise 14.6 (or 14.7) to include a field for a reorder point in the file. Any inventory reduction that causes the quantity of a part to drop to or below the reorder point should cause a printed notice. Also, add a menu option to print a list of all items at or below the reorder point.

14.9. Modify the program in exercise 14.6 (or 14.7 or 14.8) to include an option to change the description or unit price (or reorder point from 14.8). Prompt the user for the part number, and display the corresponding data from the file. Then allow the user to change the required field(s).

14.10. Write a random file program to create a plane rental file for West End Airport Flight School. The program should have a menu with these options:

1. Add a record
2. Change a record
3. Delete a record
4. Print available planes on screen
5. Search for one plane
6. Quit

TEST DATA:

Plane Number	Plane	Rental Rate (dollars/hr)	Number Available
1	Cessna 152	26.90	8
2	Cessna 182	45.70	2
3	Piper Warrior	37.00	1
4	Cessna T120	91.00	1
5	Cessna 172	35.80	3
6	Cessna 150	24.00	2

14.11. Write a random file program to create and list a file for the students attending Dan's Dance Studio.

INPUT: Student name and telephone number should be input from the keyboard.

OUTPUT: Create a random file on disk. Then print a list of the file on the screen.

> *Menu Options*
> 1. Add a record
> 2. Change a record
> 3. Delete a record
> 4. View the file
> 5. Quit

14.12. Write a random file program to create a customer file for Jose's Video Store.

INPUT: Customer name, address, phone number, and status should be input from the keyboard.

OUTPUT: Create a random file on disk. Print the file on the printer if requested.

PROCESSING:
1. Status is either "NO DEBTS" or "OWES MONEY."

> *Menu Options*
> 1. Add a record
> 2. Change a record
> 3. Delete a record
> 4. Print the file on the printer
> 5. Quit

14.13. Write a program to create a random file to keep track of Girl Scout Troop #21.

Input the scout's number, name, age, and number of badges from the keyboard, and create a random file on diskette.

Allow the user to enter the scout's number, and display that person's information on the screen or print the entire file on the screen.

> *Menu Options*
> 1. Add a scout to the file
> 2. List all scouts
> 3. Display information for one scout
> 4. Quit

14.14. Write a program to create a random file for MacPac's division managers.

Input the division number, the division, and the manager's name and home phone number from the keyboard to create the file.

Allow the user to enter a division number and display the information for the corresponding manager.

> *Menu Options*
> 1. Add records
> 2. View one record
> 3. Quit

TEST DATA:

Division #	Division	Manager's Name	Phone No.
1	Accounting	John Price	432–6542
2	Sales	Steve Johnstone	946–3749
3	Receiving	Marla Keating	720–4800
4	Shipping	Kim Smith	439–0000
5	Stock	Dave Sillo	987–9111

15

Additional File Handling Concepts

The KILL Statement
The NAME Statement

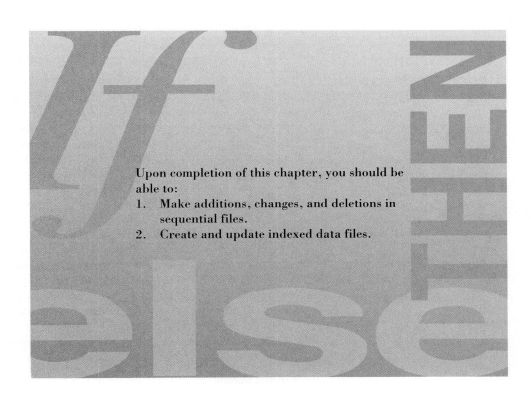

Upon completion of this chapter, you should be able to:
1. Make additions, changes, and deletions in sequential files.
2. Create and update indexed data files.

Updating Sequential Files

Sequential files are not easily updated. A program may read a file (input) or write data in a file (output), but it cannot do both to one file. Therefore, if data in a file must be changed, it must be read from one file and written in another file. That new file must contain all data from the old file as well as any changes that were made.

Traditionally, sequential updates have been a *batch operation* (as opposed to an on-line, interactive process). A group of updates is accumulated and sorted into key sequence. Then the update program reads both the master file and the transaction file (which holds the updates). The program produces a new master file as well as an error report to indicate any updates that cannot be processed. Possible errors include changes or deletions for records that do not exist or records for addition that duplicate a record already in the file. This style of batch processing is not well suited for the interactive processing generally done on a microcomputer or for timesharing on a larger computer system.

One of the advantages of microcomputer processing (and timesharing) is the interactive nature of operations. The user will enter the update transactions from the keyboard. Since it is not reasonable to require the user to enter the transactions in key sequence, another method must be used.

When a sequential file must be updated, there are several different approaches available.

1. Allow the user to enter multiple transactions (adds, changes, deletes), and store these transactions in a separate file. The transaction file would need to be sorted into key sequence before the update program could be run. As mentioned earlier, this technique is used extensively for batch processing (as opposed to on-line, interactive processing). This is the method of choice when a majority of the records in the file must be updated.
2. For each transaction entered from the keyboard (add, change, or delete), process the entire file, creating a new file. This method *does* allow multiple changes to be made in an interactive mode. However, this technique is reasonable only for a relatively small file. To read and write every record in a large file for each transaction would be extremely slow.
3. Read the entire file into arrays in memory. Then data may be added, deleted, or changed in the arrays. At the conclusion of processing, the entire file must be rewritten. This method will work only for a small file. Since the arrays must all be held in the main storage of the computer, the limiting factor is main storage size.
4. Use a random file. For a file that must be updated often, random organization is generally the best choice.

Each of the update choices has major drawbacks; but there are occasions when a file simply must be sequential and must be updated.

Although BASIC *can* be used for batch processing, in reality it seldom is. Either choice #2 or #3 above could be used for interactive updating. The array method (#3) *cannot* be used on a large file, and the single transaction method (#2) *should* only be used for a relatively small file requiring few updates.

In this text, the single transaction method (#2) will be demonstrated. Remember that an entirely new file will be created for *every transaction* entered.

In the example, the key field will be an item number. Therefore the master file must be in sequence by item number.

Old Master File

Item	Item	Item
Number	Description	Price

```
101,"CARDS - ALL OCCASION",1.75
102,"CARDS - ALL OCCASION",2.45
105,"CARDS - BIRTHDAY",1.5
110,"FOLDING NOTES",2.05
114,"POSTCARDS",3.5
122,"STATIONERY",2
125,"STATIONERY",3.25
136,"ENVELOPES",1.85
```

Adding a Record

Record Added from Keyboard

```
Item number? 108
Item description? CARDS - HUMUROUS

Item price? 4.50
```

New Master File

Item	Item	Item
Number	Description	Price

```
101,"CARDS - ALL OCCASION",1.75
102,"CARDS - ALL OCCASION",2.45
105,"CARDS - BIRTHDAY",1.5
108,"CARDS - HUMOROUS",4.5
110,"FOLDING NOTES",2.05
114,"POSTCARDS",3.5
122,"STATIONERY",2
125,"STATIONERY",3.25
136,"ENVELOPES",1.85
```

The steps necessary to add a record are:

1. Open the old master file for input
2. Open the new master file for output
3. Input the new record from the keyboard (record to be added)
4. Loop until end of old master file
    4.1   Read a record from the old master file
    4.2   Compare the item number from the new record with the item
          number from the master file. The new record should be inserted
          when the master item number is higher than the new item number.
          IF master item number > new item number THEN
             write new record in new master file
             set switch field to indicate that the add has been made
    4.3   Write the record from the old master file into the new master file
5. Close both files
6. Kill the old master file
7. Rename the new master file to be the current master file
8. End

Two new statements are needed to accomplish the file transfer, KILL and NAME. KILL is a vicious way to delete a disk file and will be used to remove the old master file after the update. NAME is used to rename a file; its function will be to make the temporary output file into the master file after the update.

The KILL Statement—General Form

```
KILL "filename"
```

The KILL Statement—Examples

```
KILL "MASTER.DAT"
KILL "B:PROG5.BAS"
KILL "DATAFILE.DAT"
```

KILL will delete a file from disk. The file must be present and *not open* for the operation to be successful.

The NAME Statement—General Form

```
NAME "old filename" AS "new filename"
```

The NAME Statement—Examples

```
NAME "TEMP.DAT" AS "MASTER.DAT"
NAME "B:PROG1.BAS" AS "PROG2.BAS"
```

The NAME statement simply changes the name of a disk file without moving the file or altering its contents in any way. The file named as "old filename" must exist, and the "new filename" mut *not* exist for the NAME statement to be successful.

The following subroutines will add a record in its proper position in a sequential file.

Example Subroutines: Adding a Record to the File

Program Listing

```
'*********** Add A Record To The Fle ******************
AddRecordToFile:
    OPEN "ITEMS.DAT" FOR INPUT AS #1
    OPEN "ITEMS.TMP" FOR OUTPUT AS #2
    LET AddedSw = 0                 'Set switch for no add yet
    GOSUB InputNewRecord
    DO UNTIL EOF(1)
        INPUT #1, Item1, Desc1$, Price1
        IF Item1 >= Item2 AND AddedSw <> 1 THEN
            GOSUB WriteRecord       'Write new record in file
        END IF
        WRITE #2, Item1, Desc1$, Price1
    LOOP
    IF AddedSw <> 1 THEN
        GOSUB WriteRecord                  'Write record at end of file
    END IF
    CLOSE #1, #2
    KILL "ITEMS.DAT"                'Remove old master file
    NAME "ITEMS.TMP" AS "ITEMS.DAT" 'New file is now master
RETURN
```

```
'**************** Input The New Record *****************
InputNewRecord:
    CLS
    PRINT
    PRINT
    PRINT
    PRINT TAB(10); "ADD AN ITEM TO THE FILE"
    PRINT
    PRINT
    INPUT "ITEM NUMBER        ", Item2
    PRINT
    INPUT "ITEM DESCRIPTION   ", Desc2$
    PRINT
    INPUT "ITEM PRICE         ", Price2
RETURN

'**************** Write The New Record *****************
WriteRecord:
    IF Item1 <> Item2 THEN
        WRITE #2, Item2, Desc2$, Price2
    ELSE
        PRINT
        PRINT TAB(15); "ERROR--This item number is already in the file"
        LET Wait$ = INPUT$(1)    'Wait for keypress
    END IF
    LET AddedSw = 1                  'Set switch to indicate record added
RETURN
```

Deleting a Record

When deleting a record from the file, it is also necessary to rewrite the entire file. However, the deleted record will be left out of the new file. In all other respects, the new file will be an exact copy of the old file. The master file must be read until a match is found—that is, the item number of the master record matches the item number to be deleted.

Example Subroutines: Deleting a Record from the File

Program Listing

```
'*********** Delete A Record From The File ************
DeleteRecord:
    OPEN "ITEMS.DAT" FOR INPUT AS #1
    OPEN "ITEMS.TMP" FOR OUTPUT AS #2
    LET DelSw = 0                  'Set switch off for no delete yet
    GOSUB ItemNumberToDelete
    DO UNTIL EOF(1)
        INPUT #1, Item1, Desc1$, Price1
        IF Item1 <> Item2 THEN
            WRITE #2, Item1, Desc1$, Price1
        ELSE
            LET DelSw = 1          'Set switch on - record deleted
        END IF
    LOOP
    IF DelSw <> 1 THEN
        PRINT "ERROR - Item not in file"
        LET Wait$ = INPUT$(1)    'Wait for keypress
    END IF
    CLOSE #1, #2
    KILL "ITEMS.DAT"                'Remove old master file
    NAME "ITEMS.TMP" AS "ITEMS.DAT"  'New file is now master
RETURN
```

```
'*********** Input Item Number To Delete *************
ItemNumberToDelete:
    CLS
    PRINT
    PRINT
    PRINT
    PRINT TAB(10); "DELETE A RECORD FROM THE FILE"
    PRINT
    PRINT
    INPUT "ITEM NUMBER TO DELETE"; Item2
    PRINT
    PRINT
RETURN
```

Changing a Record

To change the data in a record in the master file, the item number of the changed data must match an item number in the file. The file must be read until a match is found, and the new (changed) data will replace the old data. The new master file will contain all of the data from the old file with the exception of the changed data.

Example Subroutines: Changing Data in a File

Program Listing

```
'*************** Change A Record In The File ************
ChangeRecord:
    OPEN "ITEMS.DAT" FOR INPUT AS #1
    OPEN "ITEMS.TMP" FOR OUTPUT AS #2
    LET ChangeSw = 0            'Set switch for no change yet
    GOSUB ChangedData
    DO UNTIL EOF(1)
        INPUT #1, Item1, Desc1$, Price1
        IF Item1 <> Item2 THEN
            WRITE #2, Item1, Desc1$, Price1
        ELSE
            WRITE #2, Item2, Desc2$, Price2
            LET ChangeSw = 1        'Set switch on - record changed
        END IF
    LOOP
    IF ChangeSw <> 1 THEN
        PRINT "ERROR - item not in file"
        LET Wait$ = INPUT$(1)   'Wait for keypress
    END IF
    CLOSE #1, #2
    KILL "ITEMS.DAT"                'Remove old master
    NAME "ITEMS.TMP" AS "ITEMS.DAT"  'New file is now master
RETURN

'*************** Input Changed Data *******************
ChangedData:
    CLS
    PRINT
    PRINT
    PRINT
    PRINT TAB(30); "CHANGE DATA IN THE FILE"
    PRINT
    PRINT
    INPUT "ITEM NUMBER        ", Item2
    PRINT
    INPUT "ITEM DESCRIPTION   ", Desc2$
    PRINT
    INPUT "ITEM PRICE         ", Price2
    PRINT
    PRINT
RETURN
```

Example Program: Adding, Changing, and Deleting Records in a Sequential File

The program to utilize these subroutines can best be done with a menu. The user will be given a choice of the desired function, and the correct subroutine will be performed.

Program Menu

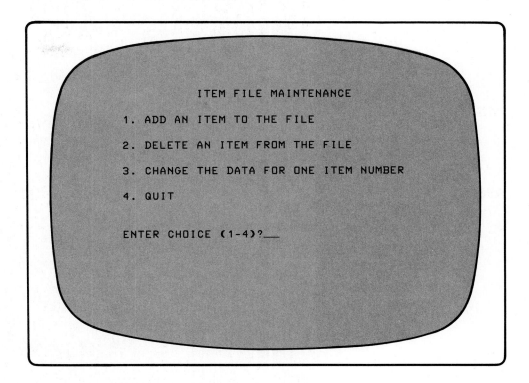

```
                ITEM FILE MAINTENANCE

    1. ADD AN ITEM TO THE FILE

    2. DELETE AN ITEM FROM THE FILE

    3. CHANGE THE DATA FOR ONE ITEM NUMBER

    4. QUIT


    ENTER CHOICE (1-4)?__
```

Program Listing

```
'Program To Update A Sequential Data File
'    Updates Are Entered In An Interactive Mode,
'    With Menu Selection of Update Function
'    Master File is ITEMS.DAT
'    Temporary File For Update is ITEMS.TMP

'          Variables Used

'    Item1      Item number from (old) master file
'    Desc1$     Item description from (old) master file
'    Price1     Item price from (old) master file
'    Item2      Item number for record update
'    Desc2$     Item description for new or changed record
'    Price2     Item price for new or changed record
'    AddedSw    Switch field to indicate that add was made
'    ChangeSw   Switch field to indicate that change was made
'    DelSw      Switch field to indicate that delete was made
'               Switches -- 0 = no action(add, change, or delete)
'                           1 = action taken
'    Wait$      Dummy variable to hold for keypress
```

```
'*** Sequential File Maintenance -- Program Mainline ***
DO
   CLS
   GOSUB PrintMenu
   SELECT CASE Choice
      CASE 1
         GOSUB AddRecord
      CASE 2
         GOSUB DeleteRecord
      CASE 3
         GOSUB ChangeRecord
      CASE 4
         CLS
   END SELECT
LOOP UNTIL Choice = 4
END


'************ Print the Menu and Get Choice ***********
PrintMenu:
   PRINT
   PRINT
   PRINT TAB(20); "ITEM FILE MAINTENANCE"
   PRINT
   PRINT
   PRINT
   PRINT TAB(15); "1. ADD AN ITEM TO THE FILE"
   PRINT
   PRINT TAB(15); "2. DELETE AN ITEM FROM THE FILE"
   PRINT
   PRINT TAB(15); "3. CHANGE THE DATA FOR ONE ITEM NUMBER"
   PRINT
   PRINT TAB(15); "4. QUIT"
   PRINT
   PRINT
   PRINT TAB(15); "ENTER CHOICE (1 - 4)";
   INPUT Choice
RETURN


'************* Add A Record To The File ***************
AddRecord:
   OPEN "ITEMS.DAT" FOR INPUT AS #1
   OPEN "ITEMS.TMP" FOR OUTPUT AS #2
   LET AddedSw = 0            'Set switch for no add yet
   GOSUB InputNewRecord
   DO UNTIL EOF(1)
      INPUT #1, Item1, Desc1$, Price1
      IF Item1 >= Item2 AND AddedSw <> 1 THEN
         GOSUB WriteRecord
      END IF
      WRITE #2, Item1, Desc1$, Price1
   LOOP
   IF AddedSw <> 1 THEN
      GOSUB WriteRecord
   END IF
   CLOSE #1, #2
   KILL "ITEMS.DAT"                      'Remove old master file
   NAME "ITEMS.TMP" AS "ITEMS.DAT"   'New file is now master
RETURN
```

```
'*************** Input The New Record ********************
InputNewRecord:
   CLS
   PRINT
   PRINT
   PRINT
   PRINT TAB(10); "ADD AN ITEM TO THE FILE"
   PRINT
   PRINT
   INPUT "ITEM NUMBER        ", Item2
   PRINT
   INPUT "ITEM DESCRIPTION   ", Desc2$
   PRINT
   INPUT "ITEM PRICE         ", Price2
RETURN


'**************** Write The New Record *****************
WriteRecord:
   IF Item1 <> Item2 THEN
      WRITE #2, Item2, Desc2$, Price2
   ELSE
      PRINT
      PRINT TAB(15); "ERROR-This item number already in the file"
      LET Wait$ = INPUT$(1)   'Hold for keypress
   END IF
   LET AddedSw = 1              'Set switch to indicate record added
RETURN


'************* Delete A Record From the File ***********
DeleteRecord:
   OPEN "ITEMS.DAT" FOR INPUT AS #1
   OPEN "ITEMS.TMP" FOR OUTPUT AS #2
   LET DelSw = 0          'Set switch off for no delete yet
   GOSUB ItemNumberToDelete
   DO UNTIL EOF(1)
      INPUT #1, Item1, Desc1$, Price1
      IF Item1 <> Item2 THEN
         WRITE #2, Item1, Desc1$, Price1
      ELSE
         LET DelSw = 1
      END IF
   LOOP
   IF DelSw <> 1 THEN
      PRINT "ERROR - Item not in file"
      LET Wait$ = INPUT$(1)           'Hold for keypress
   END IF
   CLOSE #1, #2
   KILL "ITEMS.DAT"                 'Remove old master file
   NAME "ITEMS.TMP" AS "ITEMS.DAT"  'New file is now master
RETURN


'************* Input Item Number To Delete ************
ItemNumberToDelete:
   CLS
   PRINT
   PRINT
   PRINT
   PRINT TAB(10); "DELETE A RECORD FROM THE FILE"
   PRINT
   PRINT
   INPUT "ITEM NUMBER TO DELETE"; Item2
   PRINT
   PRINT
RETURN
```

```
'**************** Change A Record In The File **********
ChangeRecord:
   OPEN "Items.Dat" FOR INPUT AS #1
   OPEN "Items.Tmp" FOR OUTPUT AS #2
   LET ChangeSw = 0                'Set switch for no change yet
   GOSUB ChangedData
   DO UNTIL EOF(1)
      INPUT #1, Item1, Desc1$, Price1
      IF Item1 <> Item2 THEN
         WRITE #2, Item1, Desc1$, Price1
      ELSE
         WRITE #2, Item2, Desc2$, Price2
         LET ChangeSw = 1      'Set switch on - record changed
      END IF
   LOOP
   IF ChangeSw <> 1 THEN
      PRINT "ERROR - Item not in file"
      LET Wait$ = INPUT$(1)    'Hold for keypress
   END IF
   CLOSE #1, #2
   KILL "ITEMS.DAT"                      'Remove old master
   NAME "ITEMS.TMP" AS "ITEMS.DAT"  'New file is now master
RETURN

'**************** Input Changed Data *******************
ChangedData:
   CLS
   PRINT
   PRINT
   PRINT
   PRINT TAB(10); "CHANGE DATA IN THE FILE"
   PRINT
   PRINT
   INPUT "ITEM NUMBER            ", Item2
   PRINT
   INPUT "ITEM DESCRIPTION    ", Desc2$
   PRINT
   INPUT "ITEM PRICE            ", Price2
   PRINT
   PRINT
RETURN
'********************** End of Program ***************************
```

Sample Program Output

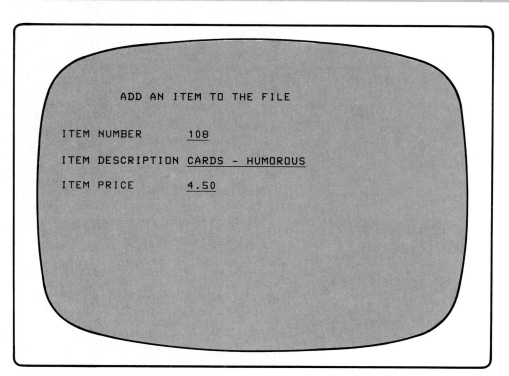

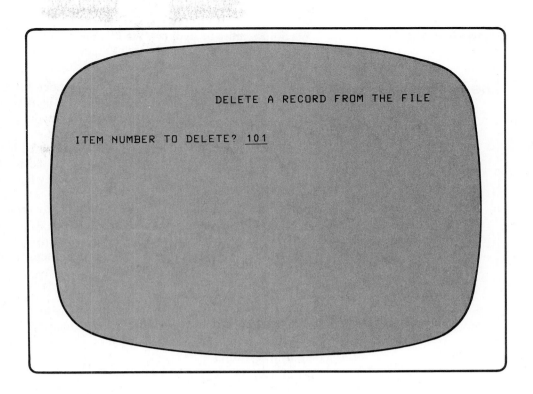

```
                        DELETE A RECORD FROM THE FILE


ITEM NUMBER TO DELETE? 101
```

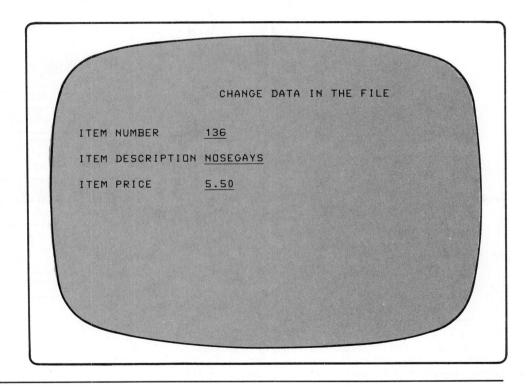

```
                        CHANGE DATA IN THE FILE


ITEM NUMBER        136

ITEM DESCRIPTION  NOSEGAYS

ITEM PRICE         5.50
```

Indexing Files

When files must be updated, random file organization is generally the preferred approach. However, the limitations of random files sometimes make their use difficult.

The Random File

Random files must be accessed by record number. Ideally, those record numbers begin with #1 and proceed consecutively through the number of records in the file. A file may certainly have unused record positions. However, each unused record location requires disk space just as if a record were stored there.

More often than not, the key fields associated with files do not lend themselves to conversion to record numbers. Numeric key fields such as account numbers, item numbers, or customer numbers or alphabetic key fields such as names are common in data files.

One common solution is to use an *index* for the data file. The index is an array that holds the key fields. For any access to the data file, the array is used to look up the record number. Then a random read may be initiated to retrieve the correct record. This concept is illustrated in figure 15.1. The steps to retrieve one record from the file would be:

1. The user enters item #114.
2. A table lookup produces a match on the fifth element.
3. Record position 5 is randomly read from the file.

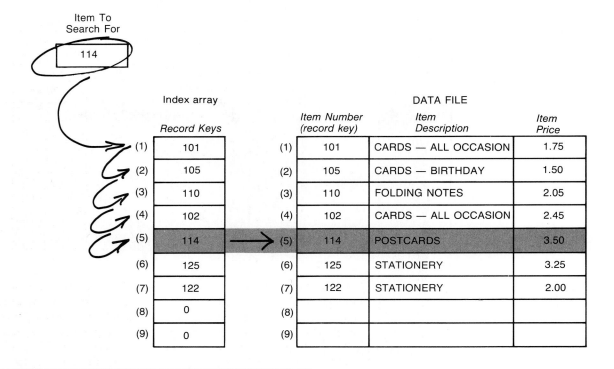

Figure 15.1
Using an index to find the record. Each position of the index array is checked for a match. When a hit is made, the corresponding record is read from the random file.

The technique of using tables to look up the record number is called indexing files and is commonly used to allow random access by any record key. Although the record number (for a random file) must always be numeric, the key field may be either numeric or string. A table lookup works equally well for numeric or string data.

The Index File

A second file must be used to store the index table. In previous programs, when a table was used for lookup, the table data was read from DATA statements in the program. Since the index table will be changed as records are added and deleted, the data to fill the table must be stored in a data file between program runs. For each run of the program, there must be an initialization step to read the index file into the array. At the termination of a program run, the index array must be rewritten in the index file.

Two Files

An indexed file will always have two parts: (1) the *primary data file,* which will be a random file, and (2) the *index file,* which will be a sequential file. Figure 15.2 illustrates the two files to be used. Note that the record keys in the index file are in the same sequence as those in the primary data file.

Figure 15.2
The index file and the data file. The record keys in the index file are in the same sequence as those in the primary data file.

INDEX FILE		DATA FILE		
Record Keys		Item Number (record key)	Item Description	Item Price
101	(1)	101	CARDS — ALL OCCASION	1.75
105	(2)	105	CARDS — BIRTHDAY	1.50
110	(3)	110	FOLDING NOTES	2.05
102	(4)	102	CARDS — ALL OCCASION	2.45
114	(5)	114	POSTCARDS	3.50
125	(6)	125	STATIONERY	3.25
122	(7)	122	STATIONERY	2.00
0	(8)			
0	(9)			

Using the Index to Access the File

Initially, all elements of the index array are set to zero. When a record is added to the file, an empty record position must be found to hold the new record. The index array is searched for the first zero entry (which indicates an available slot). Then the record is written in the data file at that record position, and the corresponding array element is set to the record key. See the illustration of record addition in figure 15.3.

Records to be deleted are not actually erased from the file. Instead, the index entry for the deleted record is set to zero. The zero index entry flags that location as available. (In some applications, a delete *does* actually cause blank spaces to be written in the record position.) A delete operation is shown in figure 15.4.

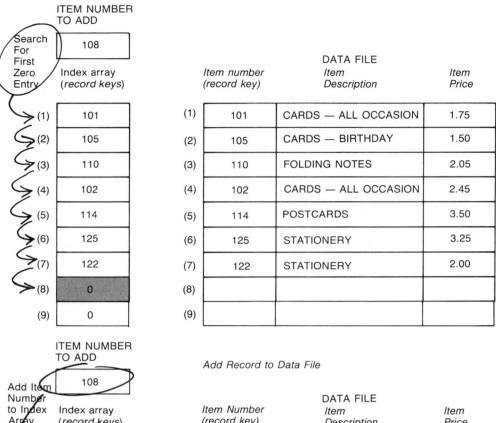

ITEM NUMBER TO ADD

108

Search For First Zero Entry

Index array (record keys)

(1)	101
(2)	105
(3)	110
(4)	102
(5)	114
(6)	125
(7)	122
(8)	0
(9)	0

DATA FILE

	Item number (record key)	Item Description	Item Price
(1)	101	CARDS — ALL OCCASION	1.75
(2)	105	CARDS — BIRTHDAY	1.50
(3)	110	FOLDING NOTES	2.05
(4)	102	CARDS — ALL OCCASION	2.45
(5)	114	POSTCARDS	3.50
(6)	125	STATIONERY	3.25
(7)	122	STATIONERY	2.00
(8)			
(9)			

ITEM NUMBER TO ADD

108

Add Item Number to Index Array

Index array (record keys)

(1)	101
(2)	105
(3)	110
(4)	102
(5)	114
(6)	125
(7)	122
(8)	108
(9)	0

Add Record to Data File

DATA FILE

	Item Number (record key)	Item Description	Item Price
(1)	101	CARDS — ALL OCCASION	1.75
(2)	105	CARDS — BIRTHDAY	1.50
(3)	110	FOLDING NOTES	2.05
(4)	102	CARDS — ALL OCCASION	2.45
(5)	114	POSTCARDS	3.50
(6)	125	STATIONERY	3.25
(7)	122	STATIONERY	2.00
(8)	108	CARDS — HUMOROUS	4.50
(9)			

Figure 15.3
Adding a record to the file.

Look Up Item Number in the Index Array

ITEM NUMBER
TO DELETE

125

	Index array (record keys)
(1)	101
(2)	105
(3)	110
(4)	102
(5)	114
(6)	125
(7)	122
(8)	108
(9)	0

DATA FILE

	Item Number (record key)	Item Description	Item Price
(1)	101	CARDS — ALL OCCASION	1.75
(2)	105	CARDS — BIRTHDAY	1.50
(3)	110	FOLDING NOTES	2.05
(4)	102	CARDS — ALL OCCASION	2.45
(5)	114	POSTCARDS	3.50
(6)	125	STATIONERY	3.25
(7)	122	STATIONERY	2.00
(8)	108	CARDS — HUMOROUS	4.50
(9)			

Change the Item Number to Zero

ITEM NUMBER
TO DELETE

125

	Index array (record keys)
(1)	101
(2)	105
(3)	110
(4)	102
(5)	114
(6)	0
(7)	122
(8)	108
(9)	

DATA FILE

	Item Number (record key)	Item Description	Item Price
(1)	101	CARDS — ALL OCCASION	1.75
(2)	105	CARDS — BIRTHDAY	1.50
(3)	110	FOLDING NOTES	2.05
(4)	102	CARDS — ALL OCCASION	2.45
(5)	114	POSTCARDS	3.50
(6)	125	STATIONERY	3.25
(7)	122	STATIONERY	2.00
(8)	108	CARDS — HUMOROUS	4.50
(9)	0		

Figure 15.4
Deleting a record from the file.

Establishing the Index File

A one-time initialization program must establish the index file before the first run of the program that accesses the primary data file. Alternately, the index file (which is only a series of zero fields) may be created with an editor.

One important step is to establish the maximum file size. The number of elements chosen for the index array will determine the maximum number of records the file may hold. For the example program, the number 100 has been chosen.

```
'*** Initialize Index File ***
'     A One-Time Operation
OPEN "ITEM.NDX" FOR OUTPUT AS #2
FOR Ndx% = 1 TO 100
    WRITE #2, 0
NEXT Ndx%
CLOSE #2
END
```

Programming Example

The item file from the sequential update program has been changed to an indexed file. By entering an item number (the record key), any record may be retrieved from the file. A record may be displayed, added, deleted, or changed.

Pseudocode

1. Open the random file
2. Initialize the index array
   - 2.1 Open the index file for input
   - 2.2 Read the entire file into the index array
   - 2.3 Close the index file
3. LOOP until menu option #5 (QUIT) chosen
   - 3.1 Display the menu and input choice
   - 3.2 Execute the correct subroutine:
     - 3.2.1 Display a record
     - 3.2.2 Add a record
     - 3.2.3 Delete a record
     - 3.2.4 Change a record
4. Rewrite the index file
   - 4.1 Open the index file for output
   - 4.2 Write the entire index array into the index file
   - 4.3 Close the index file
5. Close the random file
6. Stop

Display a Record Subroutine

1. Input the item number to display
2. Look up the item in the index array
   Use a table lookup, setting FoundSw = 1 when a match is found, FoundSw = 0 when no match found. When a match is found, Posn will hold the record position to be used for the random read.
3. IF the item number was found (FoundSw = 1) THEN
   - read the record and display it

   ELSE
   - display an error message
4. Hold the record (or the error message) on the screen until a key is pressed
5. Return

Add a Record Subroutine

1. Input the data for the new record
2. Look up the item number (checking for a duplicate). FoundSw = 1 means that a match was found (duplicate record), FoundSw = 0 means that the record can be added.
3. IF a match was found (FoundSw = 1) THEN
        print an error message
     ELSE
        add the record
          3.1 Search the index array for the first zero entry (set Posn to the first available record position)
          3.2 Save the item number in the index array
          3.3 PUT the record
4. Return

Delete a Record Subroutine

1. Input the item number to delete
2. Look up the item number in the index array. FoundSw = 1 means a match was found, FoundSw = 0 means that no match was found. Posn will hold the record position where the match was found.
3. IF the record was found THEN
        delete the record
          3.1 Read the record and display it on the screen
          3.2 Request verification of delete
          3.3 IF verified THEN
              set index array element to zero
          ELSE
              print an error message
4. Return

Change a Record Subroutine

1. Input the item number to change
2. Look up the item number in the index array. FoundSw = 1 means a match was found, FoundSw = 0 means that no match was found. Posn will hold the record position where the match was found.
3. IF the record was found THEN
        change the record
          3.1 Read the record and display it on the screen
          3.2 Input new description
          3.3 Input new price
          3.4 Rewrite the record (PUT)
     ELSE
        print an error message
4. Return

```
'          Indexed File Maintenance Program
'            Menu Selection to Choose Action:

'          1) Display data for one item
'          2) Add an item to the file
'          3) Delete an item from the file
'          4) Change the data for an item
'          5) Quit

'          Variables used

'     Item              Item number
'     Desc$             Item Description
'     Price             Item price
'     Max               Maximum number of records in file
'     Index(Max)        Index array
'     FoundSw           Switch used to indicate a match found in index
'                       1 = Match found, 0 = No match found
'     Posn              Position for record key in index and file
'     Ans$              Response to confirm delete
'     X$                Dummy variable for keypress
'     Ndx%              Index variable for index array

   TYPE RecordStructure
      ItemNumber AS INTEGER
      ItemDescription AS STRING * 20
      ItemPrice AS SINGLE
   END TYPE

   DIM RecordItem AS RecordStructure

'****** Indexed File Maintenance -- Program Mainline ***
LET Max = 100
GOSUB SetUpRandomFile
GOSUB InitializeIndex
DO
   CLS
   GOSUB PrintMenu
   SELECT CASE Choice
      CASE 1
         GOSUB DisplayItem
      CASE 2
         GOSUB AddRecord
      CASE 3
         GOSUB DeleteRecord
      CASE 4
         GOSUB ChangeRecord
      CASE 5
         GOSUB RewriteIndexArray
         CLOSE #1
         CLS
      CASE ELSE
   END SELECT
LOOP UNTIL Choice = 5
END


'*************** Initialize Random File *****************
SetUpRandomFile:
   OPEN "ITEM.DAT" FOR RANDOM AS #1 LEN = LEN(RecordItem)
RETURN
```

```
'**************** Initialize Index ********************
InitializeIndex:
   DIM Index(Max)                  'Establish index array
   OPEN "ITEM.NDX" FOR INPUT AS #2
   FOR Ndx% = 1 TO Max             'Fill the index array with item
      INPUT #2, Index(Ndx%)        'Numbers from the index file
   NEXT Ndx%
   CLOSE #2
RETURN

'***************** Print Menu and Get Choice ***********
PrintMenu:
   PRINT
   PRINT
   PRINT TAB(20); "ITEM FILE MAINTENANCE"
   PRINT
   PRINT
   PRINT
   PRINT TAB(15); "1. DISPLAY THE DATA FOR ONE ITEM"
   PRINT
   PRINT TAB(15); "2. ADD AN ITEM TO THE FILE"
   PRINT
   PRINT TAB(15); "3. DELETE AN ITEM FROM THE FILE"
   PRINT
   PRINT TAB(15); "4. CHANGE THE DATA FOR ONE ITEM NUMBER"
   PRINT
   PRINT TAB(15); "5. QUIT"
   PRINT
   PRINT
   PRINT TAB(15); "ENTER CHOICE (1 - 5)";
   INPUT Choice
RETURN

'************* Display Item Number From File ************
DisplayItem:
   GOSUB InputNumber
   GOSUB LookUpItemNumber
   IF FoundSw = 1 THEN
      GOSUB GetRecord
      LET X$ = INPUT$(1)                      'Hold for keypress
   ELSE
      GOSUB PrintErrorMessage
   END IF
RETURN

'*************** Input Item Number To Display ************
InputNumber:
   CLS
   PRINT
   PRINT
   PRINT
   PRINT TAB(10); "DISPLAY AN ITEM FROM THE FILE"
   PRINT
   PRINT
   INPUT "ITEM NUMBER TO DISPLAY"; Item
RETURN
```

```
'************ Get Record And Display On Screen *********
GetRecord:
   GET #1, Posn, RecordItem
   PRINT
   PRINT
   PRINT TAB(15); "ITEM NUMBER          "; RecordItem.ItemNumber
   PRINT
   PRINT TAB(15); "ITEM DESCRIPTION     "; RecordItem.ItemDescription
   PRINT
   PRINT TAB(15); "ITEM PRICE           "; RecordItem.ItemPrice
   PRINT
   PRINT
RETURN

'*************** Look Up Item Number In Index **********
LookUpItemNumber:
   LET FoundSw = 0            'Set switch for no match found
   LET Posn = 0              'Set to begin at start of index
   DO WHILE Posn < Max AND FoundSw = 0
      LET Posn = Posn + 1
      IF Index(Posn) = Item THEN
         LET FoundSw = 1        'A match is found
      END IF
   LOOP
RETURN

'****************** Print Error Message *****************
PrintErrorMessage:
   PRINT
   PRINT
   PRINT "ERROR: THIS ITEM IS NOT IN THE FILE"
   LET X$ = INPUT$(1)         'Hold for keypress
RETURN

'***************** Add A Record To The File ************
AddRecord:
   GOSUB InputNewRecord
   GOSUB LookUpItemNumber
   IF FoundSw = 1 THEN
     GOSUB ErrorField
   ELSE
     GOSUB FindFirstEmptyEntry
   END IF
RETURN

'***************** Input the New Record *****************
InputNewRecord:
   CLS
   PRINT
   PRINT
   PRINT
   PRINT TAB(10); "ADD AN ITEM TO THE FILE"
   PRINT
   PRINT
   INPUT "ITEM NUMBER       ", Item
   PRINT
   INPUT "ITEM DESCRIPTION  ", RecordItem.ItemDescription
   PRINT
   INPUT "ITEM PRICE        ", RecordItem.ItemPrice
RETURN
```

```
'*********** Find The First Empty Entry In The Index *****
FindFirstEmptyEntry:
   LET Posn = 1                              'Begin with position 1
   DO WHILE Index(Posn) <> 0 AND Posn < Max
      LET Posn = Posn + 1
   LOOP
   'Posn Points To Empty Record Position Unless File is Full
   IF Posn = Max AND Index(Posn) <> 0 THEN
      GOSUB FileFull
   ELSE
      GOSUB WriteNewRecord
   END IF
RETURN


'**************** Set Up and Write New Record *************
WriteNewRecord:
   LET Index(Posn) = Item              'Save item number in index
   LET RecordItem.ItemNumber = Item
   PUT #1, Posn, RecordItem
RETURN


'**************** Error - Duplicate Key Field *************
ErrorField:
   PRINT
   PRINT
   PRINT
   PRINT TAB(15); "ERROR - THIS ITEM NUMBER ALREADY IN THE FILE"
   LET X$ = INPUT$(1)                      'Hold for keypress
RETURN


'******************* The File Is Full ********************
FileFull:
   PRINT "ERROR - RECORD CANNOT BE ADDED"
   PRINT
   PRINT
   PRINT "THE FILE IS FULL"
   LET X$ = INPUT$(1)                      'Hold for keypress
RETURN


'************** Delete A Record From The File ************
DeleteRecord:
   GOSUB DeleteItem
   GOSUB LookUpItemNumber
   IF FoundSw = 1 THEN
      GOSUB DeleteTheRecord
   ELSE
      GOSUB PrintErrorMessage
   END IF
RETURN


'*************** Input Item Number To Delete ************
DeleteItem:
   CLS
   PRINT
   PRINT
   PRINT
   PRINT TAB(20); "DELETE AN ITEM FROM THE FILE"
   PRINT
   PRINT
   INPUT "ITEM NUMBER TO DELETE"; Item
RETURN
```

```
'******************* Delete The Record *********************
DeleteTheRecord:
   GOSUB GetRecord
   PRINT TAB(20); "DELETE THIS RECORD (YES TO CONFIRM)";
   INPUT Ans$
   IF UCASE$(Ans$) = "YES" THEN
      LET Index(Posn) = 0
   END IF
RETURN

'******************* Change a Record In the File ***********
ChangeRecord:
   GOSUB InputChangedData
   GOSUB LookUpItemNumber
   IF FoundSw = 1 THEN
      GOSUB ChangeData
   ELSE
      GOSUB PrintErrorMessage
   END IF
RETURN

'******************* Input Changed Data *****************
InputChangedData:
   CLS
   PRINT
   PRINT
   PRINT
   PRINT TAB(10); "CHANGE DATA IN FILE"
   PRINT
   PRINT
   INPUT "ITEM NUMBER TO CHANGE ", Item
RETURN

'***************** Change The Data ***********************
ChangeData:
   GOSUB GetRecord
   INPUT "NEW DESCRIPTION (PRESS ENTER FOR NO CHANGE)", Desc$
   PRINT
   PRINT
   INPUT "NEW PRICE (PRESS ENTER FOR NO CHANGE)", Price$
   IF Desc$ <> "" THEN
      LET RecordItem.ItemDescription = Desc$
   END IF
   IF Price$ <> "" THEN
      LET RecordItem.ItemPrice = VAL(Price$)
   END IF
   PUT #1, Posn, RecordItem
RETURN

'*************** Rewrite Index Array In Index File *********
RewriteIndexArray:
   OPEN "ITEM.NDX" FOR OUTPUT AS #2
   FOR Ndx% = 1 TO Max
      WRITE #2, Index(Ndx%)
   NEXT Ndx%
   CLOSE #2
RETURN
'******************* End of Program ************************
```

Sample Program Output

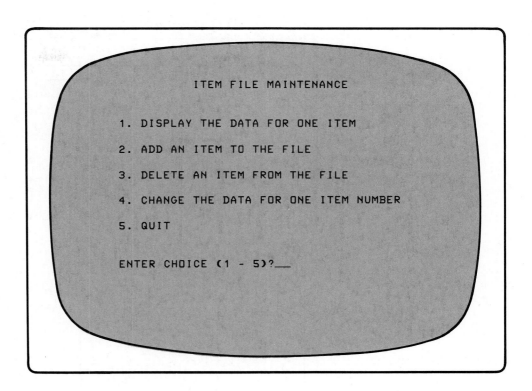

Choice 1

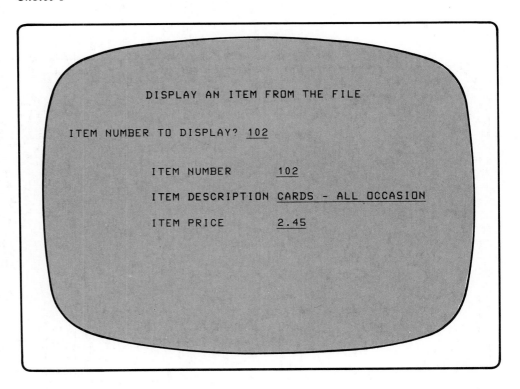

Choice 2

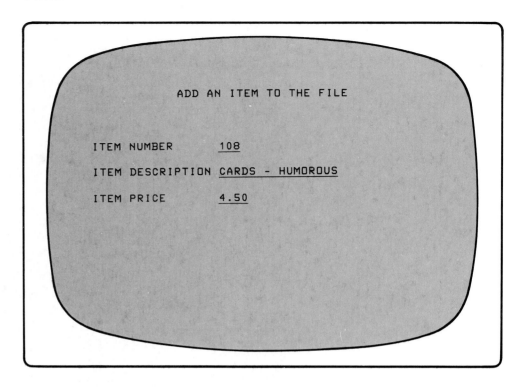

```
                ADD AN ITEM TO THE FILE


     ITEM NUMBER        108

     ITEM DESCRIPTION   CARDS - HUMOROUS

     ITEM PRICE         4.50
```

Choice 3

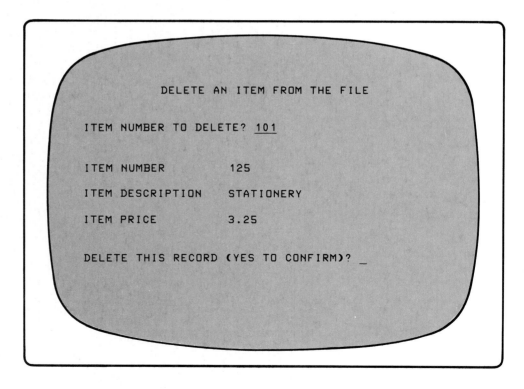

```
              DELETE AN ITEM FROM THE FILE

     ITEM NUMBER TO DELETE? 101

     ITEM NUMBER          125

     ITEM DESCRIPTION     STATIONERY

     ITEM PRICE           3.25

     DELETE THIS RECORD (YES TO CONFIRM)? _
```

Choice 4

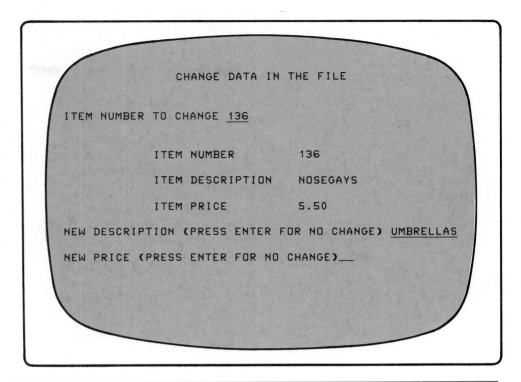

```
                    CHANGE DATA IN THE FILE


ITEM NUMBER TO CHANGE 136


              ITEM NUMBER         136

              ITEM DESCRIPTION    NOSEGAYS

              ITEM PRICE          5.50

NEW DESCRIPTION (PRESS ENTER FOR NO CHANGE) UMBRELLAS

NEW PRICE (PRESS ENTER FOR NO CHANGE)___
```

Summary

1. To update a sequential file, an entirely new file must be created.
2. In batch processing, updated transactions are accumulated. Then, the transactions are sorted and all updates are applied in a group.
3. The interactive style of program execution generally used with BASIC programming is not conducive to batch updates.
4. There are two methods of sequential updates that *do* allow for interactive program execution. However, neither should be used on a large file or one needing frequent updates. The two methods are:
    a. Create an entirely new file for each transaction (add, change, or delete).
    b. Read the file into arrays in memory, do all updating in the arrays, and rewrite the file when finished.
5. Files that need frequent updating should be organized as a random file, if possible.
6. When a record key field of a file cannot be used as a relative record number, indexed files may be used.
7. An indexed file actually consists of two files:
    a. A random file for the data records.
    b. An index file, which holds the record keys and their corresponding record number. The index file is generally stored in a sequential file and read into an array at the beginning of any program that accesses the primary file.
8. The KILL statement deletes a file from disk.
9. The NAME statement renames a disk file.

Programming Exercises

15.1. *Sequential Update*—Write a program to update the sequential file created by the program in exercise 13.1 (p. 375) (salesperson file). The program must be able to add new salespersons, delete salespersons, or change the data for any salesperson. Fields that may be changed are the name, sales amount, and the commission rate (*not* the salesperson number). Any new salespersons are to be added in order by the salesperson number (the key field). Use the listing program written for exercise 13.1 to verify that all changes are correctly made.

15.2. Combine the two programs written for exercise 13.1 with exercise 15.1 in a menu program, which will create the file, add records, delete records, change records, and list the file.

15.3. Modify the program in exercise 15.1 (or 15.2) to make the change routine easier to operate. After the user has entered the salesperson number of the record to change or delete, display the old data for that person on the screen. For a change, allow the user to accept or change each field (except the key field). For the delete, display a message, and allow the user to verify that the correct record is being deleted.

15.4. Modify the program in exercise 15.1 (or 15.2 or 15.3) to include screen formatting. Do not allow any screens to scroll.

15.5. *Sequential Update*—Write a program that will allow changes to be made in the book file created by the program in exercise 13.2 (p. 376). Since the file is in alphabetic order by book title, the title is the key field. The program must allow new books to be added to the file (in sequence), books to be deleted from the file, or the room location of any book to be changed.

15.6. *Sequential Update*—Write a program that will allow changes to be made in the two table files created by the program in exercise 13.3 (p. 377).

PRODUCT TABLE: Products may be added or deleted, or the price of any item may be changed. The table file is in order by item number (and must remain that way).

SALESPERSON TABLE: Salespersons may be added to the table file, deleted from the file, or the name may be changed.

15.7. *Indexed File*—Change the organization of the salesperson file created by the program in exercise 13.1 and updated by the program in exercise 15.1. Use the salesperson number as the key field, and establish an index file for random access.

Use a menu with these choices:
1. Display data for a salesperson
2. Add a salesperson to the file
3. Delete a salesperson from the file
4. Change a salesperson's name
5. Change a sales amount
6. Change a commission rate
7. Quit

15.8. *Indexed File*—Change the organization of the book file from the programs in exercises 13.2 and 15.5 to an indexed file. The key field is the book title. See the program in exercise 15.5 for the update program requirements.

15.9. *Indexed File*—Modify the program in exercise 14.4 (personnel file, p. 408) to create an indexed file. Rather than assign sequential employee numbers as in the program in exercise 14.4, use the employee name as the key field. Follow the specifications shown to include file creation, updating, and listing. Additionally, include an option to add an employee to the file.

15.10. The Perfect Picture Company has had some problems with customers who write bad checks. The area office has sent out a list of customers who have written bad checks, so that the sales clerks will not accept any more checks from those people. Write a program to create an indexed file to aid the credit checking. Use the customer last name as the record key.

MENU CHOICES

1. *Check credit for a customer*—Input the customer last name. Display a list of all customers in the file with that last name. If that name is not on file, print a message to that effect.
2. *Display the file*—Display the entire file on the screen. Be sure to hold the screen for a keypress, so that names do not scroll by too quickly to be read.
3. *Add a customer to the file*—Input last and first name, placement date, check date, and check number from the keyboard. Add the customer to the file.
4. *Delete a customer from the file*—Input the last and first name from the keyboard. Display the entire record on the screen, and ask the clerk to verify the delete.
5. *Change customer information*—Input the customer last name. Display the data on the screen, and allow the user to change fields.
6. *Quit.*

TEST DATA:

Last Name	First Name	Placement Date	Check Date	Check No.
Jones	Ray	2–14–88	2–5–88	121
Smith	Andy	3–21–88	3–2–88	83
Brown	Barbara	5–8–88	5–1–88	301

16 Pixel Graphics

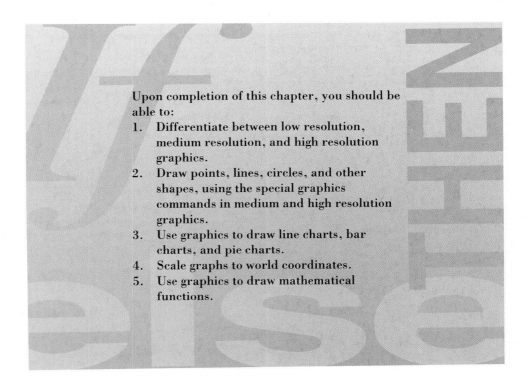

Upon completion of this chapter, you should be able to:

1. Differentiate between low resolution, medium resolution, and high resolution graphics.
2. Draw points, lines, circles, and other shapes, using the special graphics commands in medium and high resolution graphics.
3. Use graphics to draw line charts, bar charts, and pie charts.
4. Scale graphs to world coordinates.
5. Use graphics to draw mathematical functions.

Introduction to Graphics

Computer graphics may be undertaken strictly for fun or to make program output more understandable. Businesses use graphics to convert columns of numbers into meaningful visual displays as line graphs, bar charts, and pie charts.

QB offers several modes for displaying graphics. Each mode has its own distinct rules, statements, advantages, and disadvantages. The choices are also expanded by the possible hardware configurations. The graphics capabilities of computers vary greatly, depending on the display adapter installed and the monitor type in use. The graphics statements selected must be consistent with the hardware of the computer running the program. Table 16.1 shows the ten available graphics modes.

Table 16.1
Graphics modes.

Modes available for CGA hardware.

	Low Resolution (Text)	Medium Resolution	High Resolution
Screen mode	0	1	2
Resolution	80 Horizontal 25 Vertical or 40 Horizontal 25 Vertical	320 Horizontal 200 Vertical	640 Horizontal 200 Vertical
Color	16 Foreground 8 Background 16 Border	4 at a time from 1 of 2 sets called palettes	None

Four additional modes for EGA hardware.

	Medium Resolution	High Resolution	Enhanced Resolution	Monochrome Enhanced Resolution
Screen mode	7	8	9	10
Resolution	320 Horizontal 200 Vertical	640 Horizontal 200 Vertical	640 Horizontal 350 Vertical	640 Horizontal 350 Vertical
Color	16	16	16 (at a time from a choice of 64)	None (8 blinking and intensity levels)

Additional modes available for VGA or MCGA hardware.

	Very High Resolution	Very High Resolution	Medium Resolution
Screen mode	11	12	13
Resolution	640 Horizontal 480 Vertical	640 Horizontal 480 Vertical	320 Horizontal 200 Vertical
Color	2 at a time from 256K	16 at a time from 256K	256 at a time from 256K

Note that modes 3, 4, 5, and 6 are not listed. Mode 3 is for a Hercules adapter. Modes 4, 5, and 6 are for hardware not supported by QB.

Terms used to describe display adapters are MDA (Monochrome Display Adapter), CGA (Color Graphics Adapter), EGA (Enhanced Graphics Adapter), MCGA (MultiColor Graphics Array), and VGA (Video Graphics Array). The adapters are listed in order of increasing capabilities. MCGA and VGA adapters are always paired with monitors that match their functions. However, CGA and EGA adapters can be used with monochrome monitors. If you find this confusing, imagine writing graphics programs that can be run on many different machines.

Graphics Modes

You can create graphics with text characters, as presented in chapter 8; or, you can draw graphics on the screen with much smaller blocks called **pixels** (for picture elements). The number and size of the pixels determines the clarity of the graphics, the amount of detail that you can display, and the smoothness of the lines. Figure 16.1 shows the various screen resolutions for graphics along with the screen mode for each. Table 16.2 summarizes the hardware requirements for each screen mode.

After you learn to select the screen mode, you will learn to create pixel graphics. QB provides statements to draw points, lines, circles, arcs, and boxes. You can choose to draw in black and white or in color (with the proper hardware). The number of colors that you can display on the screen at any one time varies with the screen mode and the hardware in use.

Low Resolution or Text Mode Graphics

The normal operating mode of the video display terminal (VDT) is text (screen mode 0). Each position on the screen (width 40 or 80 by 25 lines) can display any one of the printable ASCII characters. As you learned in chapter 8, you can draw pictures and graphs with text characters—in color with color hardware.

Medium Resolution Graphics

In medium resolution graphics (screen modes 1, 7, and 13), there are 320 horizontal pixels and 200 vertical pixels. Although the number of pixels on the screen is relatively low, you can use all of the graphics commands to draw circles, arcs, lines, and boxes. The quality of the graphics will not be as good as those that you create in the higher resolution modes.

High Resolution Graphics

High resolution graphics (screen modes 2 and 8) provide twice as many pixels on the screen (640 horizontal by 200 vertical). Of course, when you have more pixels, each pixel is smaller, and your pictures can have smoother curves and rounder circles.

Enhanced Resolution Graphics

With an EGA or VGA display adapter and monitor, an enhanced resolution mode (screen modes 9 and 10) is possible. Figure 16.1 shows that enhanced mode provides 640 horizontal pixels by 350 vertical pixels.

Very High Resolution Graphics

Very high resolution graphics, available with VGA and MCGA hardware, gives the highest resolution—640 horizontal pixels by 480 vertical pixels (screen modes 11 and 12). You also have more choices of color with very high resolution graphics.

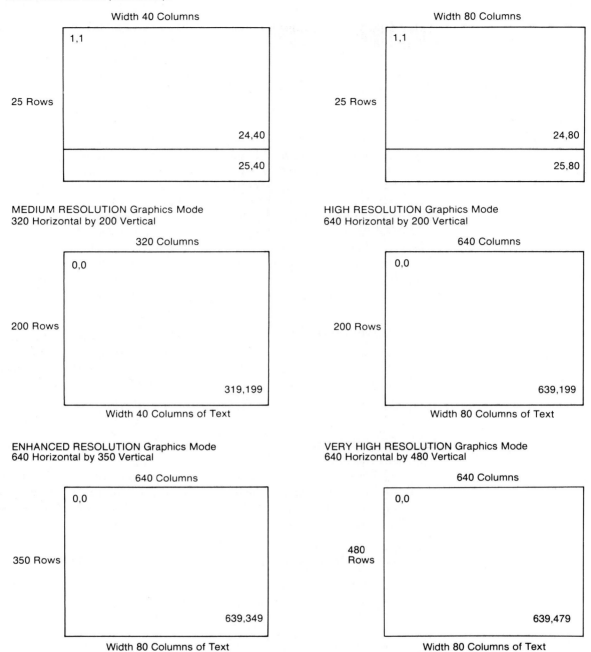

Figure 16.1
The various screen resolutions
available for graphics.

Table 16.2
Hardware requirements for graphics.

Display Adapter	Monitor	Graphics Possible	Screen Mode
Monochrome (MDA)	Monochrome	Low res text only	0
Color graphics adapter (CGA)	Composite black-and-white	Low res, medium res, high res (no color)	0,1,2
Color graphics adapter (CGA)	Standard color	Low res or medium res (with color), or high res	0,1,2
Enhanced graphics adapter (EGA)	Standard color	Low res, medium res, or high res	0,1,2, 7,8
Enhanced graphics adapter (EGA)	Enhanced color	Low res, medium res, high res, or enhanced res	0,1,2 7,8,9
Enhanced graphics adapter (EGA)	Monochrome	Low res, medium res, or high res (no color)	0,10
Video graphics array (VGA)	VGA	Low res, medium res, high res, enhanced res, very high res	0,1,2,7 8,9,10 11,12,13
Multicolor graphics array (MCGA)	MCGA	Low res, medium res, high res, very high res	0,1,2 11,13

Switching the Mode

The SCREEN statement is used to switch between low resolution, medium resolution, and high resolution modes. Until this point, the SCREEN statement was unnecessary, since low resolution text mode is the default. From this point on, we will always include a SCREEN statement in each graphics program.

SCREEN

The SCREEN statement does several things: It sets the mode, clears any prior COLOR statements, and clears the screen.

The SCREEN Statement—General Form

> SCREEN   Mode [,Colorburst]

The values for mode are:

    0 = Low Resolution Text Mode
        (width 40 or 80)
        up to 16 colors
    1 = Medium Resolution Mode
        (320 × 200)
        4 colors at a time, from 1 of 2 sets, called palettes
    2 = High Resolution Mode
        (640 × 200)
        2 colors, normally black and white

Note: The following modes require an EGA or VGA display adapter:

7= Medium Resolution Mode
(320 × 200)
with up to 16 colors
8 = High Resolution Mode
(640 × 200)
with up to 16 colors
9 = Enhanced Resolution Mode
(640 × 350)
with up to 16 colors, chosen from 64
10 = Monochrome Enhanced Resolution graphics
(640 × 350)
on a monochrome monitor with an EGA adapter

Note: The following modes require VGA or MCGA hardware:

11= Very High Resolution Mode
(640 × 480)
up to 256K colors, 2 available at a time
VGA or MCGA
12= Very High Resolution Mode
(640 × 480)
up to 256K colors, 16 available at a time
VGA only
13= Medium Resolution Mode
(320 × 200)
up to 256K colors, 256 available at a time
VGA or MCGA

The SCREEN Statement—Examples

```
SCREEN   0        'Switch to Text Mode
SCREEN   1        'Switch to Medium Resolution Mode
SCREEN   12       'Switch to Very High Resolution Mode
                     (VGA hardware only)
SCREEN   2        'Switch to High Resolution Mode
SCREEN   7        'Switch to Medium Resolution Mode
                     (VGA or EGA hardware only)
SCREEN   8        'Switch to High Resolution Mode
                     (VGA or EGA hardware only)
```

Medium and High Resolution Graphics

As you can see, the variety of graphics hardware is amazing. You may be using a monochrome or color monitor, with many possible combinations of display adapters. The order of topics and graphics programs in this chapter are designed to work on *any* graphics hardware. In order to do this, the programs use only screen modes 1 and 2. Later in the chapter, the higher resolution modes will be addressed.

Mixing Graphics and Text

You will be drawing pixel graphics in various screen modes. When you want to add text to your graphics, it is very easy to use LOCATE and PRINT statements. In some screen modes, the screen is automatically in WIDTH 40, so the text prints double wide; in others, the screen is in WIDTH 80, and text is normal size. You can use a WIDTH statement before the LOCATE and PRINT statements if you want to change the text size.

Specifying Color

With most of the graphics modes you can draw graphics in color. In screen mode 1 you can use four colors at a time; in screen mode 2 you can only use two colors (which are normally black and white). In this section, color will be included for screen mode 1; all of the screen mode 2 programs will be in black and white. Later in the chapter you will learn to assign two colors of your choice for screen mode 2.

COLOR

The four colors that you can specify for screen mode 1 are chosen from one of two sets, called palettes (like an artist's palette). For each palette, you select the background color, and the other three colors are fixed. After you have chosen the palette (with the COLOR statement), subsequent plotting instructions select the color from the palette. Table 16.3 shows the colors available for the background (called attribute zero), and table 16.4 shows the two palettes with their color choices.

The format and use of the COLOR statement is different in medium resolution than in text mode. COLOR selects the background color and the palette (0 or 1).

Table 16.3
Color numbers available for the background.

Color Number	Color
0	Black
1	Blue
2	Green
3	Cyan
4	Red
5	Magenta
6	Brown
7	White
8	Gray
9	Light blue
10	Light green
11	Light cyan
12	Light red
13	Light magenta
14	Yellow
15	High-intensity white

Table 16.4
Two palette choices in medium resolution mode.

Attribute	Palette 0	Attribute	Palette 1
0	Background (any color 0–15)	0	Background (any color 0–15)
1	Green	1	Cyan
2	Red	2	Magenta
3	Brown	3	White

The COLOR Statement in Medium Resolution Mode—General Form

```
COLOR   [Background][,[Palette]]
```

The choices for Background are any color 0–15. Palette should have a value of 0 or 1, however any even number will select palette zero, and any odd number will select palette one.

When any parameter is omitted, that selection will remain unchanged.

The COLOR Statement in Medium Resolution Mode—General Form

```
COLOR 0,0      'Select background black, palette zero
               ' (green, red, and brown)
COLOR 9,0      'Select background light blue, palette
               ' zero (green, red, and brown)
COLOR ,1       'Leave the background unchanged select
               ' palette one (cyan, magenta, white)
COLOR 0        'Change background to black, leaving
               ' palette unchanged
COLOR 14,1     'Select background yellow, palette one
               ' (cyan, magenta, white)
```

When you specify a color to be used for drawing, the only choices are 0, 1, 2, or 3. These numbers are not actually the color numbers, but rather the color's position in the current palette. Microsoft refers to these palette colors as *color attributes*. In any of the graphics statements that allow you to choose a color, use these four color attributes.

If color plotting is desired, the COLOR statement must be executed prior to any of the plotting instructions such as PSET, LINE, and CIRCLE. When CLS is executed after a COLOR statement, the entire screen changes to the background color. An interesting phenomenon occurs when a COLOR statement changes the palette after colors have already been plotted on the screen: The entire screen changes to the new palette. Green becomes cyan, red becomes magenta, brown becomes white, and the new background color replaces the old.

The Plotting Instructions

After specifying a color palette, you are ready to draw pixel graphics on the screen. You will use the PSET (for Point Set), LINE, and CIRCLE statements to draw. Each of these statements specifies a screen location with two numbers, called coordinates. The first coordinate is the horizontal position across the screen, generally referred to as X; the second coordinate is the vertical position down the screen, called Y. For screen mode 1, X may be any number from 0 to 319, and Y ranges from 0 to 199. (In screen mode 2, which will be covered later, X ranges from 0 to 639.) Therefore, the upper-left corner of the screen is position 0, 0, and the lower-right corner is position 319, 199.

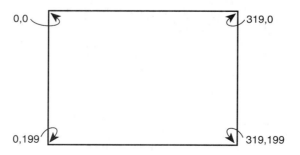

Plotting Points

You can turn on or off individual pixels on the screen with the PSET (Point Set) and PRESET (Point Reset) instructions. In addition, you can set each point to any of the four color attributes on the current palette. PSET statements can be used to draw any shapes you wish and to graph mathematical functions. Later in this chapter you will find examples of graphing functions.

PSET and PRESET

The instruction:

```
PSET (50,100)
```

turns on the point at horizontal (X) position 50 and vertical (Y) position 100.

To plot points in color, be sure to place a COLOR statement before the first PSET statement. The statements

```
SCREEN 1
COLOR 0,0
PSET (120,10),2
```

turn on medium resolution graphics, set the background color to 0 (black), select palette 0 (green, red, brown), and then plot a point in red (attribute 2) at horizontal (X) position 120 and vertical (Y) position 10.

The PSET and PRESET Statements—General Form

```
PSET (X, Y) [, ColorAttribute]
PRESET (X, Y) [, ColorAttribute]
```

The value for X is the horizontal position across the line (0–319 for medium resolution, 0–639 for high and enhanced resolution). The value for Y is the vertical position down the screen (0 to 199 for medium and high resolution). The Color-Attribute option refers to the four possible choices on the previously selected palette, and must have a value 0–3. Omitting the ColorAttribute parameter has different effects depending on whether a COLOR statement was previously executed. If no COLOR statement precedes the PSET statement, the point will be plotted in white on black. If a palette has been selected with a COLOR statement, and the Color-Attribute parameter is omitted, the point will be plotted in ColorAttribute 3.

You can erase a point with either the PSET or the PRESET statement. If ColorAttribute is selected on a PSET statement, the point will be plotted in the background color, effectively erasing the point. PRESET automatically resets the point to the background color.

The PSET and PRESET Statements—Examples

```
PSET (0, 0) 'Plot a point in the upper left corner
PSET (Across, Down) ,2          'Plot a point in
                                'ColorAttribute 2
PRESET (Across, Down)           'Erase the point
                                'plotted above
PSET (Left+Offset, Top+Offset)  'Plot a point at the
                                ' location calculated
```

Example Program: Plotting Points

Can you tell what this program will do? Try it to see.

```
' Program to Plot Points

SCREEN 1                    'Medium Resolution
COLOR 0, 1                  'Background black, palette 1
CLS                         'Clear screen
LOCATE 1, 1
INPUT "Horizontal position (0 - 319): ", Horiz
INPUT "Vertical position (0-199): ", Vert
PSET (Horiz, Vert), 1    'Plot point in ColorAttribute 1 (Cyan)
END
```

Using Relative Coordinates

Each of the preceding examples plots points using their absolute screen coordinates, without regard for the last point plotted. Rather than specify the location for each point with its X and Y screen coordinates, you can instead specify a relative position—how far from the last point plotted. Adding STEP to the PSET command changes the coordinates to relative.

STEP

The statement

```
PSET STEP(5, 2), 1
```

plots a point five pixels to the right and two pixels down from the last point plotted, in ColorAttribute 1.

The following program draws a diagonal line across the screen by plotting each point two pixels to the right and one pixel up from the last point.

Example Program: Plotting Points with Relative Coordinates

```
'** Program To Plot Points Using Step For Relative Position **

SCREEN 1                    'Medium Resolution
CLS
PSET (0, 200)
FOR Count = 1 TO 200
    PSET STEP(2, -1)
NEXT Count
END
```

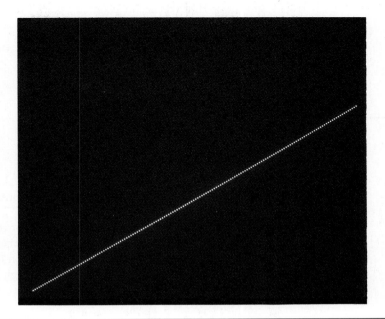

Drawing Lines

You can draw lines on the screen by plotting individual points. But a much easier method exists. The LINE statement draws a line from one screen point to another—in color or black and white. The statement

```
LINE (0,0) - (100,100)
```

draws a line from point 0,0 (upper-left corner) to point 100,100 (100 pixels right, 100 pixels down). Adding color to the statements

```
SCREEN 1
COLOR 9,0
LINE (0,0) - (100,100), 1
```

draws the line in green (ColorAttribute 1) on a light blue background.

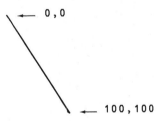

0,0

100,100

LINE

You can use the LINE statement to draw lines or boxes, solid or open. When "B" is specified, BASIC uses the two coordinates as corners for a box. And including "BF" makes the Box Filled with the same color used for plotting.

```
SCREEN 1                        'Medium Resolution
CLS                             'Clear screen
COLOR 0,1                       'Select palette
LINE (20,10) - (30,25), 1, BF   'Draw a filled box
```

The following statement will draw a solid filled box with upper-left corner at position 10,10 and lower-right corner at position 20,50. Can you tell what color the box will be? Note that when you omit the ColorAttribute parameter, two commas are required:

```
LINE (10,10) - (20,50),,BF 'DRAW A FILLED BOX
```

The LINE Statement—General Form

```
LINE   [(X.Start, Y.Start)] — (X.End, Y.End) [,[ColorAttribute] [,B [F] ] ]
```

X.Start and Y.Start specify the coordinates for the beginning of the line; X.End and Y.End specify the coordinates for the point at the end of the line. The X coordinates may range from 0 to 319 in medium resolution (0–639 in high resolution). The Y coordinates range from 0 to 199 in medium or high resolution. "B" specifies a box; "BF" produces a filled box.

The LINE Statement—Examples

```
LINE (0,0) - (100,100)          'Draw a diagonal line
LINE (X,Y) - (X+10, Y+15) , 3, B 'Draw an open box
LINE (X.Pt, Y.Pt) - (X.Pt - 20, Y.Pt - 12)
LINE - (New.X, New.Y), 1        'Draw from the last
                                'point referenced to
                                'a new point
LINE (10,10) - (200,100),,BF 'Draw a solid box in the
                                'default color
```

Connecting Lines

You can draw a line from the last point plotted to a new location without specifying the starting location.

```
LINE - (60,80)
```

draws a line from the last point plotted to a new point at position 60,80.

Drawing Circles and Ellipses

You can use the circle statement to draw circles, ellipses, or arcs. To draw a circle, you must specify the center point and the radius in pixels. Optionally, you may also specify a color for the circle.

CIRCLE

The statement

```
CIRCLE (160, 100), 50, 2
```

draws a circle with its center point at 160,100 (center of the screen in medium resolution), radius of 50 pixels across, in ColorAttribute 2. Note that QB will adjust for the shape of the pixels and make the circle round. So a radius of 50 will produce a circle 100 pixels wide and fewer pixels vertically, depending on the resolution chosen.

CIRCLE may also be specified with relative coordinates by adding the STEP option, as described in the PSET statement. The statement:

```
CIRCLE STEP(5,10), 50
```

draws a circle with its center five pixels to the right and ten pixels down from the last point referenced. When a circle is drawn, QB treats the center of the circle as the last point referenced.

Example Program: The Step Option

```
'** Draw Two Circles, Illustrating the STEP Option**
SCREEN 1
CLS
CIRCLE (160, 100), 50
CIRCLE STEP(5, 10), 50
END
```

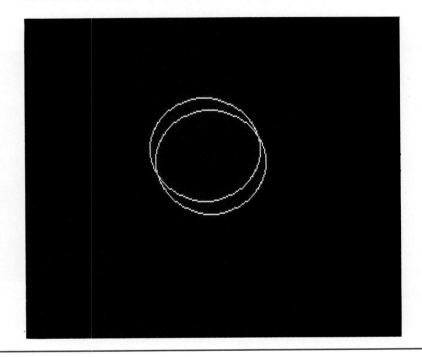

Arcs of a Circle

You can also use the CIRCLE statement to draw parts of a circle, by specifying the beginning and ending points of the arc. The endpoints for the arc are determined by a measurement in radians, counterclockwise from the 0 or 2 PI point. The angle reference is illustrated in the following figure.

The statements

```
SCREEN 1
LET PI = 3.14159
CIRCLE (160, 100), 50, 2, 0, PI
```

draw the top half of a circle, beginning at the right side (angle 0) and proceeding over the top to the left side (angle PI). The arc will be drawn in ColorAttribute 2, with a radius of 50 pixels.

453

Another parameter of the CIRCLE statement changes the aspect ratio and can be used to draw ellipses and elliptical arcs. The aspect ratio refers to the comparative length of a radius drawn on the horizontal to a radius drawn vertically. When this parameter is omitted, the aspect ratio is assumed to be 1, and the figure drawn is a circle. When the aspect ratio is less than 1, the elliptical figure will be wider than it is tall on the screen. When the aspect ratio is greater than 1, the ellipse will display on the screen taller than it is wide.

Example Program: Three Figures

Program Listing

```
' Draw Three Figures With Different Aspect Ratios

SCREEN 1
CLS
CIRCLE (100, 50), 20                    'Circle
CIRCLE (150, 50), 20, , , , .5          'Wide Ellipse
CIRCLE (200, 50), 20, , , , 1.5         'Tall Ellipse
```

Program Output

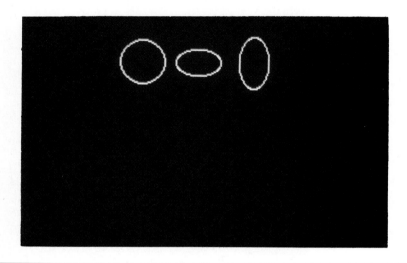

Example Program: Shapes Drawn with CIRCLE

Program Listing

```
'**Program to Display a Happy Face, Using the CIRCLE Statement**

SCREEN 1                                      'Set up screen in medium res
CLS                                           'Clear screen
LET PI = 3.14159                              'Define constant
CIRCLE (160, 100), 60                         'Draw outer circle
CIRCLE (160, 100), 40, , PI * 1.2, PI * 1.8   'Draw mouth
CIRCLE (140, 90), 5                           'Draw left eye
CIRCLE (180, 90), 5                           'Draw right eye
END
```

Program Output

Segments of a Pie

You can draw an arc with its end points connected to the center of the circle, creating a slice of pie. If you give end point as a negative number, a radius will be drawn from the end point to the center point.

Note: The minus sign preceding the end point is strictly to specify the radius, *not* to indicate a negative angle.

Example Program: Pie Segment

Program Listing

```
SCREEN 1
CLS
LET PI = 3.14159
CIRCLE (50, 100), 30, , -PI / 2, -PI
END
```

Program Output

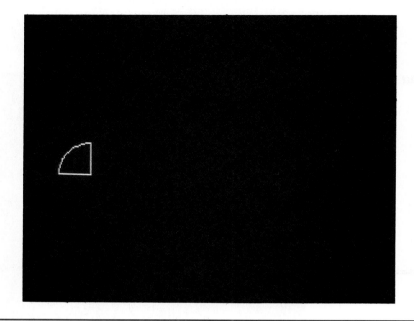

These pie segments can be used to create pie charts.

Example Program: Pie Chart

Program Listing

```
'** A Piece of Pie **
SCREEN 1
CLS
LET PI = 3.14159
CIRCLE (160, 100), 20, , -PI / 2, -2 * PI
CIRCLE STEP(5, -4), 20, , -2 * PI, -PI / 2
END
```

Program Output

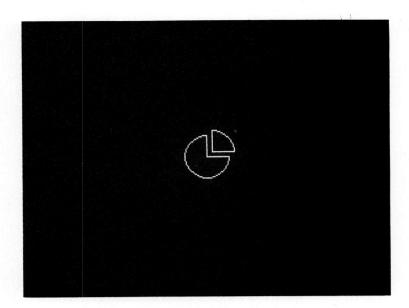

You can combine plotting instructions with LOCATE and PRINT to produce a chart with labels and legends. Remember that in medium resolution mode, text will be in WIDTH 40 (double-wide characters).

Example Program: Labeled Pie Chart

Program Listing

```
'** An Exploded Pie **

SCREEN 1
CLS
LET PI = 3.14159
CIRCLE (160, 100), 20, , -PI / 2, -2 * PI
CIRCLE STEP(5, -4), 20, , -2 * PI, -PI / 2
LOCATE 14, 10
PRINT "HOUSING";
LOCATE 11, 25
PRINT "FOOD";
LOCATE 24
END
```

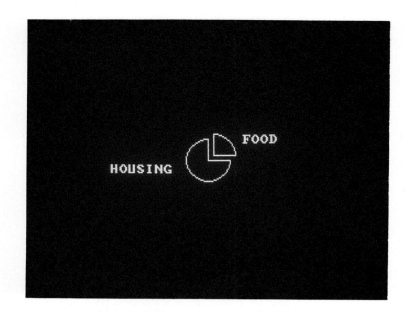

The CIRCLE Statement—General Form

```
CIRCLE (X, Y),   Radius [, ColorAttribute [, StartAngle, EndAngle [,AspectRatio]]]
```

X and Y specify the coordinates of the center of the circle, and Radius defines the radius in pixels on the horizontal axis. The ColorAttribute chooses a color from a previously selected palette and may be 0–3. If ColorAttribute is omitted, the circle will be drawn in ColorAttribute 3 when a COLOR statement has been executed, or in white if not.

If StartAngle and EndAngle are included, an arc will be drawn. Negative numbers for the angles will link the ends of the arc to the center of the circle.

The AspectRatio determines the shape of the figure drawn.

The CIRCLE Statement—Examples

```
CIRCLE (10, 20), 5 'Circle with center on 10,20 with
                 '    a radius of 5 pixels
CIRCLE (X, Y), Radius, Attrib, P.Start, P.End, Shape
CIRCLE (X, Y), 100, 2, 0, PI/2 'Plot an arc with a
                               ' radius of 100
```

Painting the Figures

After you have drawn figures on the screen, you can fill them with the PAINT statement. PAINT specifies a point within the figure to fill, the color to use, and the color that forms the boundary for filling. Carefully choose the correct boundary, and do not have any breaks in the boundary —otherwise, the color will "bleed" into other figures, and may fill the entire screen.

PAINT

The PAINT Statement—General Form

```
PAINT (X, Y)   [[, FillColor][,BoundaryColor]]
```

Both FillColor and BoundaryColor must be chosen from the current palette. The coordinates *X* and *Y* specify a point *within* the figure to fill. (Do not specify a point that is *on* the boundary.) If the FillColor is omitted, it will default to the foreground color. PAINT may also be used to draw solid shapes in black and white.

The PAINT Statement—Examples

```
PAINT (10, 20)        'Paint with the default foreground color
PAINT (X, Y), 1, 2 'Paint with ColorAttribute 1, the
                      ' figure formed with ColorAttribute 2
```

Example Program: Using PAINT to Fill Shapes

Program Listing

```
'Program To Demonstrate The Use of PAINT
'  It draws circles and boxes, then fills them in with color

SCREEN 1
COLOR 9, 0
CLS

'**************** Draw The Figures ******************
LET XCorner = 10
LET YCorner = 10
FOR Figure = 1 TO 3                   'Draw three figures
                                      'Draw a brown circle
    CIRCLE (XCorner + 30, YCorner + 25), 25, 3
                                      'Draw a green box around the circle
    LINE (XCorner, YCorner)-(XCorner + 60, YCorner + 50), 1, B
    LET XCorner = XCorner + 100
NEXT Figure
LINE (1, 1) - (278, 68), 2, B         'Draw a red box around all three figures
LOCATE 23                             'Move the cursor out of the way
LET Pause$ = INPUT$(1)                'Pause to see open figures on screen

'**************** Paint The Figures ****************
' Use a point within the first circle, using a boundary of brown
PAINT (40, 35), 2, 3                        'Paint the circle red
'Use a point within the second circle, but a boundary of green
PAINT (140, 35), 2, 1                       'Paint the circle red
'Use a point within the third circle, but a boundary of red
PAINT (240, 35), 1, 2                       'Paint the entire outer box with
'                                            green, up to all red boundaries
'                                            around the filled circle and square
END
```

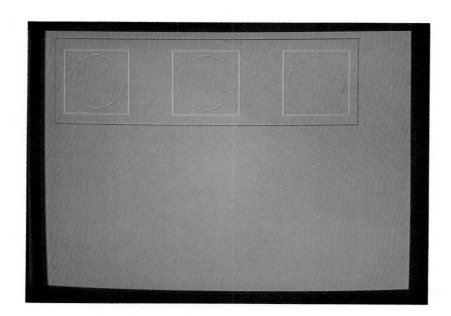

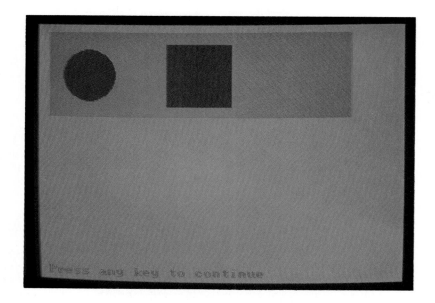

Clipping

What would happen if you drew a circle so close to the edge of the screen that the entire circle would not fit? In many programming languages and other versions of BASIC, the picture will "wrap around" to the opposite edge of the screen, producing some strange-looking results. In QB, the graphics image is "clipped" so that any points beyond the limits of the screen will not appear. **Clipping** is done automatically by QB for any graphics image (not just circles).

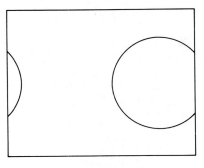

Circle "Wrapped"

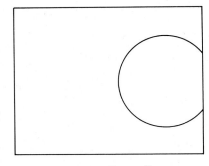

Circle "Clipped"

World Coordinates

Scaling the Screen to Fit the Numbers at Hand

When you want to plot graphs on the screen, seldom do your values fit neatly in the ranges allotted (0–320 horizontal by 0–199 vertical). Converting from the numbers you have to the screen coordinates requires some mathematics. Fortunately, QB has given us a tool that performs the necessary calculations with ease. We refer to the values to plot as the **world coordinates,** or their location in the "real" world. The world coordinates are mapped to screen coordinates by the WINDOW statement.

WINDOW

The WINDOW Statement—General Form

```
WINDOW   (W.Left, W.Top) - (W.Right, W.Bottom)
```

The first set of numbers gives the world coordinates to assign to the top-left corner of the screen. The second set of numbers defines the coordinates of the lower-right corner.

The WINDOW Statement—Examples

```
WINDOW (0, 0) - (100, 100) 'Redefines screen to 100 x 100
WINDOW (-20, 15) - (20, -15) 'Places 0,0 at the center
             ' of the screen with positive values up
             ' and to the right, negative values down
             ' and to the left
```

After execution of the WINDOW statement, you can display any values in the range defined, without the need for conversion to screen coordinates. The second example statement will be of particular interest to mathematicians, because now a function may easily be graphed using the familiar mathematical notation that has zero at the center. Note that any values outside the range defined will be clipped.

Example Program: To Plot a Sine Wave

Program Listing

```
'Plot a function using standard mathematical notation for coordinates.
'   In order to make 0,0 at the center of the screen, negative values
'   for X go to the left and positive values are right. For Y, positive
'   values are plotted in the top half of the screen, negative values in
'   the bottom half.

SCREEN 1
CLS
LET WLeft = -10                    'Minimum X value (left)
LET WRight = 10                    'Maximum X value (right)
LET WTop = 5                       'Maximum Y value (top)
LET WBot = -5                      'Minimum Y value (down)
WINDOW (WLeft, WTop)-(WRight, WBot)    'Map new coordinates to screen
FOR XCord = WLeft TO WRight STEP .1
   LET YCord = SIN(XCord)          'Find the sine of a new X coordinate
   PSET (XCord, YCord)             'Plot one point of the sine wave
NEXT XCord
END
```

Program Output

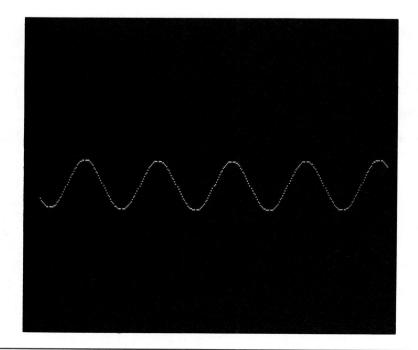

Graphing Functions

The following program will graph a mathematical function. You can change the function that appears in the mainline to graph any function that you choose. The user is asked to enter the highest and lowest values for X and Y. Then the WINDOW statement maps those coordinates to the screen. Notice that the Y coordinates have been increased by 20% so that the highest value for Y will not appear at the very top of the screen.

Example Program: Graphing a Mathematical Function

Program Listing

```
'This Program Graphs a Function That Is Defined By the User
'in the Program Mainline. The User Specifies the Highest and
'Lowest Value for X, and the Highest and Lowest Values for Y.

'          Variables Used

'    HighX          Highest value of X
'    LowX           Lowest value of X
'    HighY          Highest value of Y
'    LowY           Lowest value of Y
'    X              The x-coordinate of the function
'    Y              The y-coordinate of the function
'    Incr           The value by which X is incremented


'******************** Program Mainline *********************
DEF FNF (X) = SIN(X) / X              'Function goes here
GOSUB InputRanges
GOSUB SetUpGraph
GOSUB GraphTheFunction
GOSUB DrawTheAxes
END


'********************* Input Ranges ************************
InputRanges:
    INPUT "Lowest value of X"; LowX
    INPUT "Highest value of X"; HighX
    INPUT "Lowest value of Y"; LowY
    INPUT "Highest value of Y"; HighY
    INPUT "Increments on the X-axis (.1 is a good starting value)"; Incr
RETURN


'********************* Set Up Graph ************************
SetUpGraph:
    SCREEN 2                                      'High resolution graphics
    WINDOW (LowX, LowY * 1.2) - (HighX, HighY * 1.2)   'Map coordinates to screen
RETURN


'********************* Graph the Function*********************
GraphTheFunction:
    FOR X = LowX TO HighX STEP Incr
        LET Y = FNF(X)
        PSET (X, Y)
    NEXT X
RETURN


'********************* Draw the Axes ***********************
DrawTheAxes:
    LINE (0, HighY * 1.2) - (0, LowY * 1.2)         'y-axes
    LINE (LowX, 0) - (HighX, 0)                     'x-axes
RETURN
'******************** End of Program ***********************
```

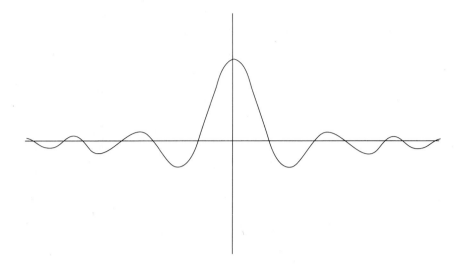

Viewports

Using Only a Part of the Screen

At times you may want to use an area smaller than the entire screen for your graph. You may want to draw multiple graphs on the screen at once. The VIEW statement provides a method to define a rectangular area for graphing, called a **viewport.** This viewport may be any size, up to the dimensions of the full screen. Combining VIEW with WINDOW allows you to define the location on the screen, and then adjust the coordinates of the area to the problem at hand.

The viewport established by the VIEW statement may also be colorful. When a palette is active (COLOR has been executed), you can set the background color of the viewport, as well as an optional border around the viewport.

VIEW

The VIEW Statement—General Form

```
VIEW   (V.left, V.top) - (V.right, V.bottom) [,[ColorAttribute] [, Boundary]]
```

The View coordinates given are the actual screen coordinates of the area you wish to use for graphing. The first set of numbers gives the screen coordinates to use for the top-left corner of the viewport. The second set of numbers defines the lower-right corner of the viewport.

The VIEW Statement—Examples

```
VIEW (0, 0) - (160, 99) 'Makes viewport in upper left
                         ' quarter of the screen
VIEW (60, 20) - (260, 179) 'Creates large viewport in
                ' the center of the screen
VIEW (10, 10) - (20, 20), 1, 2 'Viewport of color 1
                ' from the current palette, outlined
                ' in color 2
VIEW (200, 100) - (319, 199),,3 'Creates a viewport
                ' and draws a box around it in color 3
                ' from the current palette
```

After a VIEW statement has been executed, a CLS statement clears only the viewport, not the entire screen. To clear the screen manually, press Ctrl-Home. You can clear the viewport by executing another VIEW statement. VIEW by itself (no parameters) resets the screen to its normal mode.

```
VIEW          'Reset the viewport to use the entire screen
```

Combining the SCREEN, VIEW, and WINDOW statements gives great flexibility in drawing graphs. Be sure to specify the statements in the correct order:

```
SCREEN 1                       'Select medium resolution
                               ' graphics
VIEW (20,10) - (60,100),,3     'Set aside a screen area
                               ' and draw a box around it
WINDOW (1,100) - (500,0)       'Establish world coordinates
                               ' within the viewport
```

Note: If color is desired, the COLOR statement should appear between the SCREEN statement and the VIEW statement.

Example Program: A Bar Chart Program with Viewport and World Coordinates

Program Listing

```
'Program to plot any five values in a viewport in the center of
'  the screen. The viewport is always scaled to the current data
'  with the WINDOW statement.

'****************** Program Mainline **************************
GOSUB InputValues
GOSUB SetupScreen
GOSUB PlotValues
GOSUB DrawScale
GOSUB CleanupScreen
END


'****************** Input Values To Plot *********************
InputValues:
   CLS
   FOR Count = 1 TO 5
      PRINT "Value # "; Count;
      INPUT "", Value(Count)
      IF Value(Count) > Highest THEN
         LET Highest = Value(Count)
      END IF
      IF Value(Count) < Lowest THEN
         LET Lowest = Value(Count)              'Zero if no negative values
      END IF
   NEXT Count
RETURN


'****************** Set Up The Screen ***********************
SetupScreen:
   SCREEN 1
   COLOR 0, 1
   ' ***** Set Viewport to use a box in the center of the screen
   VIEW (80, 50)-(240, 150), 2, 3
   ' ** Scale the viewport Y axis to the current data
   ' ** X Axis scaling allows for 5 bars, + 0.5 for spacing
   WINDOW (.5, Highest)-(6, Lowest)
RETURN
```

```
'********************* Plot the Values ***************************
PlotValues:
    FOR Count = 1 TO 5
        LET Height = Value(Count)
        LINE (Count, Height)-(Count + .5, 0), , BF 'Bar is filled box
    NEXT Count
RETURN

'****************** Label The Y Axis To Show The Scaling ******************
DrawScale:
    ' **Find the range between ticks
    LET TickRange = (Highest - Lowest) / 4
    LET TickRow = 150 / 8          'Lower edge of viewport, 8 pixels per row
    LET TickValue = Lowest         'Print the lowest value first
    FOR Count = 1 TO 5             'Divide the viewport into five sections
        LOCATE TickRow, 2          'Place the label on the screen row
        PRINT USING "####.# -"; TickValue;
        LET TickRow = TickRow - 3    'Find the next higher row for label
        LET TickValue = TickValue + TickRange  'What value to print
    NEXT Count
RETURN

'******************** Clean Up The Screen ************************
CleanupScreen:
    LET Dummy$ = INPUT$(1)
    SCREEN 0
    WIDTH 80
    CLS
RETURN

'********************* End of Program ****************************
```

Sample Program Output

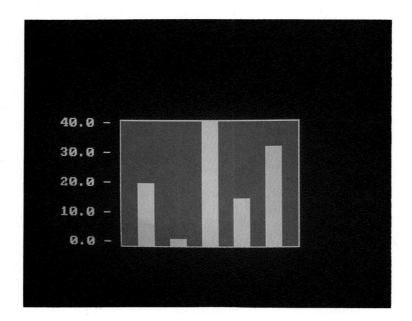

Creating Pie Charts

To produce pie charts, a little math is required. The angles are measured in radians rather than in degrees. Finding the location to place the legends can cause some headaches.

Using Radians

When using degree measurement, a circle has 360 degrees. A half-circle, then, is 180 degrees.

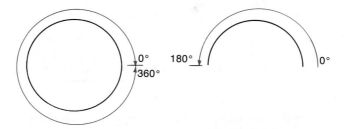

In radian measurement, the term π is the fraction 3.14159. A complete circle is 2π radians, so a half-circle is π radians.

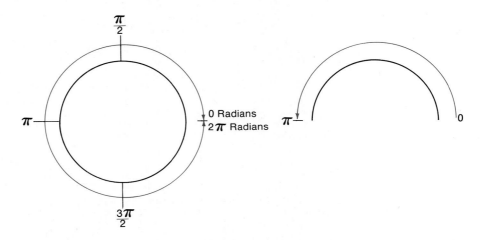

Therefore, if the number of degrees is known, you can convert to radian measurement with this calculation:

$$\text{Radians} = \text{Degrees} / 180$$

Finding Points around a Circle

If you want to place labels on a pie chart, you must find a point midway in the pie section but located on a larger (imaginary) circle outside the chart. A little trigonometry can be used to find the points, but another wrinkle makes it even more interesting. Since pixels are taller than they are wide, an adjustment must be made. For high resolution, a ratio of .42 works well.

The *X* coordinate can be found by multiplying the radius by the cosine of the angle that is the midpoint of the section:

```
LET X.Coord = Radius * COS ((StartAngle + EndAngle) / 2)
```

If pixels were square, the *Y* coordinate would be found by multiplying the radius by the sine of the angle. However, we must adjust for the shape. In high resolution, use this statement

```
LET Y.Coord = Radius * SIN((StartAngle + EndAngle) / 2) * 0.42
```

Adding Labels

You can combine text with pictures. Use LOCATE and PRINT to place text on the screen. Remember that in medium resolution the text is in WIDTH 40, and in high resolution the text will appear in WIDTH 80. At times you may need to convert from *XY* screen coordinates to a row or column number for printing. In high resolution each character is eight pixels wide by eight pixels tall. So the formulas for converting from *XY* pixel locations to rows and columns are

```
Row    = 1 + Y.Coordinate/8
Column = 1 + X.Coordinate/8
```

1. The Color Attribute range is limited to 0–3 in screen mode 1 or in screen mode 9 if the EGA has no more than 64K of memory; for screen mode 2 and 11 the ColorAttribute range limit is 0–1; for screen mode 13 the range is 0–255.

Example Program:
A Pie Chart Program in High Resolution Graphics

Program Listing

```
'Program to Plot a Pie Chart, Using High Resolution Graphics

'               Variables used

'      Class               Counter for 4 classification
'      Howmuch             Value to plot for each segment
'      Label$              Label for pie segment
'      StartPoint          Beginning angle for pie segment, in radians
'      EndPoint            Ending point for pie segment, in radians
'      Share               Size of pie segment, in radians
'      XCord               X coordinate for placing segment label
'      YCord               Y coordinate for placing segment label
'      Row                 Row for printing segment label
'      Col                 Column for printing segment label
'      PI                  Constant, 3.14159

'****************** Program Mainline *********************
GOSUB Initialize
GOSUB PrintHeadings
GOSUB PlotSegments
LOCATE 23, 1                           'Place cursor out of the way
END

'********************** Initialize *********************
Initialize:
   SCREEN 2
   CLS
   WINDOW (-320, 100)-(319, -100)       'Make 0,0 in the center
   LET PI = 3.14159
   FOR Class = 1 TO 4                   'Add up all values to plot
       READ Howmuch, Label$
       LET Total = Total + Howmuch
   NEXT Class
   RESTORE
RETURN

'********************** Print Headings *******************
PrintHeadings:
   LOCATE 2, 23
   PRINT "OFFICE EXPENSES"
RETURN
```

```
'******************* Plot Pie Segments *******************
PlotSegments:
   LET EndPoint = 0
   FOR Class = 1 TO 4
      READ Howmuch, Label$
      GOSUB CalculateShare
      CIRCLE (0, 0), 100, , -StartPoint, -EndPoint
      GOSUB PrintLabel
   NEXT Class
RETURN

'*************** Calculate Share Of Pie *******************
CalculateShare:
   LET StartPoint = EndPoint
   LET Share = Howmuch / Total * 2 * PI
   LET EndPoint = StartPoint + Share
   IF Class = 4 THEN
      LET EndPoint = 2 * PI              'Take care of rounding errors
   END IF
RETURN

'*************** Print Label For Segment *******************
PrintLabel:
   'Find the location on a circle of radius for the end
   '  point for the label for each segment.
   'For the Y coordinate, use a correction of 0.42 for pixel
   '  shape.
   LET XCord = 120 * COS((StartPoint + EndPoint) / 2)
   LET YCord = 120 * SIN((StartPoint + EndPoint) / 2) * .46
   LET Row = 13 - YCord / 8            'Each row made up of 8 pixels
   LET Col = 41 + XCord / 8            'Each column is 8 pixels wide
   IF Col <= 40 THEN
      LET Col = Col - LEN(Label$)   'Print label to left of spot
   END IF
   LOCATE Row, Col
   PRINT Label$
RETURN

'*************** Data To Graph ***************************
DATA 25,Utilities,60,Rent,15,Office Expense,5,Telephone

'*************** End of Program ***************************
```

Program Output

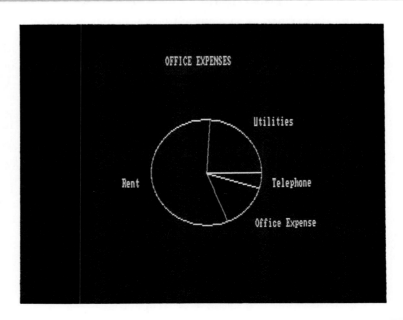

The Higher Resolution Graphics Modes—Screen Modes 7–13

The higher resolution graphics modes provide the greatest number of colors on the screen with the best resolution. However, to run the programs you must have an EGA, VGA, or MCGA display adapter. Screen modes 0, 1, and 2 will run on *any* color hardware, and may be the safest choice if you want your program to run on different computers. Table 16.5 shows the capabilities and requirements for the higher resolution modes.

Specifying Color

With the higher resolution graphics and the right hardware, you can specify many more colors. Each screen mode specifies the number of available ColorAttributes. For example, in screen mode 8, you can specify up to sixteen ColorAttributes. For each color that you want to use, you assign a color number (from the chart in table 16.3) to a ColorAttribute number. Then when you use the graphics statements, you specify the ColorAttribute (not the color number). To plot a red circle in screen mode 8, you could use these statements:

```
SCREEN 8                  'Set the mode
PALETTE 1, 4              'Assign color 4 (red) to ColorAttribute 1
CIRCLE (320, 100), 50, 1  'Draw in ColorAttribute 1
```

Table 16.5
Higher resolution graphics modes.

Screen Mode	Hardware	Number of ColorAttributes
7 Medium resolution (320 × 200)	EGA adapter, standard or enhanced monitor; or VGA	16
8 High resolution (640 × 200)	EGA adapter, standard or enhanced monitor; or VGA	16
9 Enhanced resolution (640 × 350)	EGA adapter, standard or enhanced monitor	16
10 Monochrome enhanced resolution (640 × 350)	EGA adapter, monochrome monitor	N/A
11 Very high resolution (640 × 480)	VGA or MCGA	2
12 Very high resolution (640 × 480)	VGA	16
13 Medium resolution (320 × 200)	VGA or MCGA	256

PALETTE

The PALETTE Statement—General Form

```
PALETTE   [ColorAttribute, ColorNumber]
```

The ColorAttribute must be an integer in the range 0–15 generally.[1] The value for ColorNumber must be an integer (long integer for VGA and MCGA). Its legal values are also dependent on the screen mode. For screen modes 1, 2, 7, and 8 the range is 0–15. For screen modes 0 and 9 the allowable range for ColorNumber is 0–63.

The PALETTE statement can only be used when an EGA, VGA, or MCGA display adapter is present in the computer. Error messages will result if the program is run on a computer without the required adapter.

The PALETTE Statement—Examples

```
SCREEN 8              'Select high resolution enhanced color
PALETTE 0, 1          'Assign color 1 (blue) to ColorAttribute 0
PSET (X,Y), 0         'Plot a blue point


SCREEN 7              'Select medium resolution enhanced color
PALETTE 5, 14         'Assign color 14 (yellow) to ColorAttribute 5
CIRCLE (X,Y), 20, 5   'Plot a yellow circle of radius 20


PALETTE               'Reset all attributes to their default
```

The PALETTE statement can be used to change the color of something previously displayed on the screen.

```
SCREEN 8                          'Select highresolution enhanced color
LINE (250, 50) - (390, 150), 2, BF 'Draw a box in ColorAttribute 2
PRINT "Press any key to continue"
LET DUMMY$ = INPUT$(1)            'Wait for a keypress
PALETTE 2, 4                      'Change ColorAttribute 2 to 4 (red)
```

Printing Graphics Images

Pixel graphics are intended for display on the screen. In graphics modes the Shift-PrtSc key combination will not transfer a graphics image to the printer unless a special DOS utility program has been executed *before* loading BASIC. With the DOS master diskette in the A: drive, type

```
A>GRAPHICS
```

then QuickBASIC can be loaded.

```
A>QB
```

or

```
A>QBASIC
```

When the GRAPHICS program has been executed before BASIC, the Shift-PrtSc key combination will send the graphics images to the printer correctly.

Note: These commands are for the IBM-PC and compatible dot matrix printers. Many other computers and printers have similar utilities.

Summary

1. There are several graphics modes: low resolution, medium resolution, high resolution, enhanced resolution, and very high resolution. The BASIC statements operate differently in each mode.
2. The possible screen resolution and color capabilities depend on the monitor and display adapter installed on the computer.
3. The number of pixels (picture elements) depends on the screen mode in use.
4. The SCREEN statement sets the graphics mode.
5. Screen modes 1 and 2 will work on any graphics hardware. The other screen modes each require specific hardware.
6. The LOCATE and PRINT statements can be used to combine text with graphics. Some screen modes put the text into WIDTH 40, others use WIDTH 80.
7. In screen mode 1, colors are chosen from one of two palettes. The COLOR statement is used to select the palette.
8. The plotting instructions use two coordinates (X and Y) to determine the placement of the graphics. X is the horizontal position across the screen; Y is the vertical position down the screen.
9. The PSET statement plots points. PRESET can be used to reset points.
10. Using STEP in a graphics statement makes the coordinates relative to the last point plotted, rather than absolute screen coordinates.
11. The LINE statement can be used to draw lines, open boxes, or fill boxes.
12. The CIRCLE statement is used to draw circles, ellipses, and arcs. A radius can be drawn from the endpoint of an arc by specifying the angle as a negative number.
13. The PAINT statement fills graphics with colors selected from the current palette.
14. When graphics are specified for a location off the screen, the shape is clipped so that only the visible portion is displayed.
15. The coordinates of the screen may be adjusted to conform to the problem at hand (called world coordinates) by using the WINDOW statement.
16. Mathematical functions can easily be graphed after selecting the screen coordinates with a WINDOW statement.
17. The VIEW statement provides a way to select an area of the screen to use for graphics.
18. To create pie charts, use the trigonometric functions SIN and COS to determine the placement of the segments and the labels.
19. The PALETTE statement is used to assign color numbers to ColorAttributes for the higher resolution graphics modes.
20. Graphics images will not print using the Print Screen key unless a special utility program is loaded before running QB.

Programming Exercises

16.1. Draw three solid squares on the screen using the LINE command.

16.2. Using only the circle command, draw a border around the screen.

16.3. Draw a line from the top left corner to the bottom right corner and another line from the top right corner to the bottom left corner of the screen.

16.4. Create a pie chart to represent the calculated data from program 2.14 (Budget Report).

16.5. Write a program using any of the graphics commands to draw a house and background scenery on the screen.

16.6. The Perfect Picture Company wishes to put a glamorous advertisement in every popular magazine to promote its film. Create a design for the ad using any graphics commands you wish.

16.7. Write a program using the PAINT statement to paint the entire screen eight different colors. Hold the screen for a keypress between colors.

16.8. Write a program using the PSET and PRESET statements to print a blinking dot on the screen.

16.9. Using any of the graphics statements discussed thus far, write a program that will create a weekly material log screen for data entry. Design the form to fit on the screen and include the following input areas:

1. Title
2. Week ending date
3. Signature
4. Employee number
5. Cost code
6. Description
7. Order number
8. Quantity
9. Job number
10. Department

16.10. Write a program that will draw five circles, with a radius of 21, on the screen. Then use the PAINT statement to fill each circle.

16.11. Write a program to create a bar chart to depict the percentage of karate matches won by each karate student at the Kiwi Karate Studio.

INPUT: Data will come from DATA statements.
OUTPUT:
1. Output should be to the screen.
2. Print a title on the chart.
3. Label both the x- and y-axes.
PROCESSING:
1. The x-axis will be the student's last name.
2. The y-axis will be the percentage of matches won.
3. Percentage won = matches won/total matches.
4. Use the LINE statement to create the bars.
TEST DATA:

Name	Number of Matches	Matches Won
Brian Boon	5	0
Chris Cook	6	5
Eric Mills	4	4
Mandy Moon	7	6
Nancy Noon	10	7
Scott Peck	8	7
Peter Smith	9	9
Sam Snoop	12	6
Trish Little	20	20

16.12. Using the PSET statement, graph the following ellipse:

$$\frac{X^2}{4} + \frac{Y^2}{9} = 1$$

INPUT: After the above ellipse is plotted, the user should have the option of graphing an ellipse with different intercepts.

OUTPUT: Display the ellipse on the screen.

PROCESSING:

1. Equation of an ellipse $= \dfrac{X^2}{a^2} + \dfrac{Y^2}{b^2} = 1$

2. To graph an ellipse, plot the four intercepts a, $-$a, b, and $-$b, and sketch an ellipse through the intercepts.

3. Since a and b are squared in the equation and not in the problem given, you must take the square root of the numbers to obtain a and b. e.g., a = the square root of 4.

16.13. Write a program using VIEW, WINDOW, and CIRCLE to print a happy face on the screen, in the middle of the window.

16.14. Write a program to randomly place circles on the screen with lines connecting the center of the circles.

16.15. Write a program using PSET and PRESET to create the effect of a moving dot. The dot should keep moving until a key is pressed.

Appendixes

Appendix A
The BASIC Environment

BASIC Versions

This text was written for QuickBASIC release 4.0 and 4.5 and QBASIC 1.0. The version currently for sale by dealers is QuickBASIC release 4.5. The version that accompanies DOS 5 is QBASIC 1.0; DOS 6 comes with QBASIC 1.1. The BASIC statements are the same for all versions; the changes are found in the environment. QuickBASIC 4.5 and QBASIC were updated to make the environment more friendly and easy to comprehend for a beginning programmer. The Help system was greatly expanded and improved, and the menus were simplified.

QuickBASIC release 4.5 can be run in either *Full Menu* or *Easy Menu* mode. Since everything in this text can be accomplished with *Easy Menus,* there is very little reason to turn on *Full Menus. Full Menus* in release 4.5 is nearly identical to the menus in 4.0, with the exception of the *Options* menu. The menus in QBASIC offer fewer choices than QuickBASIC.

The Opening Screen

When QB 4.5 or QBASIC is started, a *Welcome* dialog box is displayed. Press Escape to clear the dialog box, and proceed to the editing screen. When starting QB 4.0, the editing screen appears automatically.

The Editing Screen

Programs are entered and changed on the editing screen. Across the top of the screen the Menu Bar is displayed. Below the Menu Bar is a line called the Title Bar. If a program has been loaded or saved by name, that name appears in the center of the Title Bar; otherwise, the title reads "Untitled." Across the bottom and down the right side of the screen you will see scroll bars. Mouse users will find the scroll bars handy; keyboard users may want to remove them.

You can alter the appearance of the editing screen to suit your preferences. See the discussion of the Options Display.

Navigation of the QuickBASIC Environment

Menu selections and options may be selected with the keyboard or a mouse. The descriptions that follow assume keyboard use only. Instructions for using a mouse are found at the end of this appendix.

The Menu Bar

There are slight differences in the menu bars for the three BASIC versions.

QuickBASIC 4.5:

```
    File   Edit   View   Search   Run   Debug   Calls   Options
```

QuickBASIC 4.0:

```
    File   Edit   View   Search   Run   Debug   Calls
```

QBASIC 1.0:

```
    File   Edit   View   Search   Run   Debug   Options
```

Opening a Menu

Each of the words on the Menu Bar indicate the name of a menu that can be displayed, or "opened." To open a menu, press the Alt key to activate the Menu Bar; then press the first letter of the menu name. Example: to open the *File* menu, press the Alt key, then the *F* key. You can use the right and left arrow keys to switch menus after one has been selected.

Closing a Menu

If you change your mind and want to close the menu without executing any option, press the Escape key. Executing any option from the menu will automatically close the menu.

Format of Menu Choices

Each menu consists of a series of options. An option that ends with an ellipsis (. . .) means that additional information will be requested in a dialog box. For example, here is the *File* menu in QB 4.5:

```
New Program
Open Program...
Save As...
Print...
Exit
```

The commands *New Program* and *Exit* will be executed immediately when chosen; the commands *Open Program, Save As,* and *Print* will prompt for additional information in a dialog box.

Selecting a Command from a Menu

There are several ways to choose a command to execute.

1. Use the Down and Up arrow keys to highlight the command. When the correct command is highlighted, press Enter.
2. A little shortcut: After the menu has been opened, press the highlighted letter of the desired command. The command will be executed without the necessity of the Enter key.
3. Some popular options have "Quick Keys" that will execute the option without opening the menu. For example, on the *Run* menu is the *Start* option. You can always use method 1 or 2 to execute the *Start* command, or you can use its Quick Key and type Shift-F5 from the editing screen, without opening the menu.

You can tell which menu options have Quick Key equivalents—the keystrokes are shown to the right of the commands. For example, this is the *Run* menu for QBASIC:

```
Run

Start       Shift+F5
Restart
Continue        F5
```

The *Start* and *Continue* commands have Quick Keys; the *Restart* command does not. Once you learn the Quick Key commands, you will find them much quicker than using the menu commands.

Dialog Boxes

QB displays a dialog box on the screen when it needs a response from you. The cursor will appear in the location that you are expected to type an answer, such as a file name. When there are multiple boxes on the screen, move the highlight from one box to the next with the Tab key. When you have highlighted the correct choice, press the Enter key to execute the command. See the discussion of the *Open Program* command for a complete example. Table A.1 (p. 478) summarizes dialog box operation.

Table A.1
Dialog Box Summary

Cancel a dialog box	Press Escape. *or* Use Tab to highlight the *Cancel* button, and press Enter.
Move the Input Focus (highlight) to another box	Press Tab. *or* Hold down Alt and press the key for the highlighted letter in the desired item.
Select an item from a List Box (example: a file name)	Use the direction arrow keys to highlight the desired item, and press Enter.
Select an item in a Choice Box [X]	Press the Spacebar to toggle the option on or off. An empty box [ ] indicates the option is off; an X in the box indicates the option is on.
Select one of a group of options (•)	Use the direction arrow keys to move among the choices. Only one of the group may be chosen at any time.
Activate a command	Press Enter. The double-outlined or highlighted button will be executed. *or* Use Tab to move the Input Focus to the desired button and press Enter or the Spacebar.
Change the drive or directory (QB 4.0)	In the *File Name* box, type the new drive or directory name (followed by *.BAS to see a list of all BASIC files). Examples: B:*.BAS C:\PROGRAMS*.BAS
Change the drive or directory (QB 4.5 or QBASIC)	Use Tab to move to the **Dirs/Drives** box, use the direction arrow keys to highlight your choice, and press Enter.

Help

QB's *Help* differs greatly in the three versions. In any version you can press F1 to request *Help;* press Escape to cancel *Help* mode.

QB 4.0 Help

In QB 4.0 there are four *Help* screens. When you press F1, a handy summary of keystrokes appears. You may want to press the Print Screen key to print a hard copy of this summary. A second and third screen show the ASCII code, and a fourth screen shows the BASIC keywords.

QB 4.5 and QBASIC Help

In QB 4.5 and QBASIC there are several types of *Help* available. For general *Help*, press Shift-F1. When several items appear on the screen, you may use the Tab key to move the cursor among items, and press the Enter key to select a topic for further explanation. Or, as you are editing, you may request *Help* on a specific topic by placing the cursor on the BASIC keyword (such as PRINT or INPUT) and pressing F1. The *Help* screens are scrollable; that is, you can use the cursor control keys (Down or PgDn) to see any information that does not fit on one screen.

Another new feature has been added to Help that should make learning to program easier. You can display the *Help* screen that shows the format for any BASIC statement, cut and paste the statement into the editing screen, and make any changes necessary to customize the statement for your program. To move the cursor into the Help window, press F6 (Window key) two times. (One press of F6 moves the cursor to the Immediate window, the next F6 press moves the cursor to the Help window, when it is open, the next press of F6 moves the cursor back to the Edit window.) Cutting and pasting is covered in appendix B.

The Immediate Window

The area along the lower edge of the screen is called the Immediate window. At any time you can move the cursor into the Immediate window and execute a BASIC statement. This gives an opportunity to test a statement before adding it to your program. It also comes in handy for debugging, since you can use the Immediate window to PRINT any variable or even assign a new value to a variable.

To use the Immediate window, press F6 (Window key). The cursor will move into the window. Each press of the F6 key moves the cursor to the next window, and can be used to jump back and forth. Type a BASIC statement into the Immediate window and press the Enter key. The statement will be executed. If the statement is a PRINT or INPUT, the output screen will display. The statement remains in the window, and may be re-executed by placing the cursor on the line and pressing Enter.

The File Menu

Open the *File* menu by pressing the Alt key, then the *F*.

The *File* menu varies somewhat with the three BASIC versions:

QuickBASIC 4.5 Easy Menus	QuickBASIC 4.5 Full Menus	QuickBASIC 4.0	QBASIC 1.0
File	File	File	File
New Program	New Program	New Program	New
Open Program...	Open Program...	Open Program...	Open...
Save As...	Merge...	Merge...	Save
Print...	Save	Save	Save As...
Exit	Save As...	Save As...	Print...
	Save All	Save All	Exit
	Create File...	Create File...	
	Load File...	Load File...	
	Unload File...	Unload File...	
	Print...	Print...	
	DOS Shell	DOS Shell	
	Exit	Exit	

Exit—Exiting QuickBASIC

Selecting *Exit* from the *File* menu takes you out of QB, back to the operating system.

Open Program— Retrieving a Program from Disk into Memory

Selecting *Open* or *Open Program* from the *File* menu produces a dialog box with several internal boxes. When the *Open Program* dialog box appears, the entry in the *File Name* box is displayed in reverse image. Press the Tab key a few times and watch the highlight, or "input focus," change from one box to the next.

With the input focus on the *File Name* box, you can type a new entry. If you begin typing, the new characters will replace the ones already appearing there. The default entry (*.BAS) requests QB to display a list of all files with an extension of .BAS, which should be all BASIC files on the currently logged disk. If you wish to see a list of all BASIC files on a different disk, type the drive letter and a colon (i.e., B:). (In QB 4.5 or QBASIC, you can tab to the *Dirs/Drives* box, and use the Down arrow to select the correct drive.)

Rather than type a file name, you can select a file from the list displayed in the center *Files* box. Move the input focus to the list of files by pressing the Tab key. Then use the arrow keys to highlight the selected file name, and notice that the highlighted name also appears above in the *File Name* box.

Once the correct name appears in the *File Name* box, it is time to execute the command. This can be done in two different ways (three, if you count the mouse). First, pressing the Enter key executes the default "button" (that's the OK button at the bottom of the dialog box). Or, you can shift the input focus to the desired button with the Tab key. With OK highlighted, press the Enter key to execute the command.

Save As—Saving the Current Program to Disk

The program that appears on the screen is in the computer's temporary memory only. Execute the *Save As* command to copy the program to disk.

The operation of the *Save As* option varies depending on whether or not QB knows the name of the current program. If you loaded the file by name or have previously saved it, that name will appear in the *File Name* text box; otherwise the text box will appear empty. You can type a new name for the file, even if a name appears in the text box, thus making a new file without disturbing the old one.

The rules for naming BASIC program files are the same as the DOS file-naming rules: one to eight characters, followed by an optional period and one to three character extension. Do not include blank spaces in the file name. If you omit the extension, QB will supply the extension .BAS. This is the recommended practice as it will save you keystrokes, will cause all program files (and only program files) to be displayed by QB, and will help to organize your diskettes by making BASIC program files easily identifiable.

The *Format* box in the *Save As* dialog box (QB 4.0 and 4.5 only) can normally be ignored. The option marked by a dot is the one that will be executed. The default, (QuickBASIC Fast Load and Save), is the best choice for most programs. However, if you need to edit the program with another editor, or import the program into a word processor, or produce an ASCII file for some reason, you will need to save the program with the *Text* option selected. Use the Tab key to move the input focus to the *Format* box, and use the arrow keys to select *Text*. Programs saved as *Text* take a little longer to save and load and usually take more disk space than QuickBASIC's format.

The three BASIC versions have different formats for saving programs on disk. In QBASIC, you have no choice—programs are saved in ASCII text. In QB 4.0 and QB 4.5, your choices are:

```
QuickBASIC-Fast Load and Save
Text-Readable by Other Programs
```

If you are using more than one version of QB, you should be aware of the differences in file formats. All three versions can load and save Text files. QB 4.5 can load and save its own QuickBASIC format as well as QB 4.0's QuickBASIC format. However,

QB 4.0 cannot read QB 4.5 QuickBASIC format, and QBASIC cannot read either 4.0 or 4.5 QuickBASIC format. Therefore, if you plan to move your programs from one version to another, the best advice is to always save your programs as Text.

Print—Printing a Program or Part of a Program

The *Print* option makes a listing of the current program on the printer. Note that a printer *must* be attached to the computer. QB will only print a listing of the program currently in memory, not a program file from disk. If you wish to make a list of a program on disk, you must *Open* the program first.

The *Print* dialog box appears with the default option selected to print the *Current Module,* which refers to the entire program currently open. (QBASIC says *Entire Program.*) Press Enter to execute the command.

If you wish to print part of the program, you must first select the text to print. Select text using the editor:

1. Place the cursor at the start of the text you wish to select.
2. Use a combination of the Shift key and the cursor-movement keys (Up, Down, Left, Right, PgUp, PgDn, Home, End) to highlight a block of text.
3. Choose the menu option *File Print.* When the dialog box appears, the option *Selected Text* will be marked for execution.
4. Press Enter to execute the command.

New Program— Clearing the Screen

The *New Program* (or *New*) option will clear the screen (and memory) of the current program, so that you can begin a new program. If you have not saved the current program, QB will print a warning and allow you to save the program. However, you will not be given an opportunity to change the name of the program (unless you haven't named it yet). If you wish to save the program with a new name, first select *Save As,* then *New Program.*

DOS Shell—Briefly Visiting DOS

At times it is necessary to see a DOS directory or view a data file from the DOS prompt. If your intention is to immediately return to QuickBASIC, it is not necessary to exit QuickBASIC and then restart it from the beginning. With *DOS Shell,* you have complete access to DOS for these brief visits. To return to your same position in QuickBASIC, just type EXIT at the DOS prompt. (Note that *DOS Shell* is not available in QBASIC.)

The Run Menu

Press the Alt key, then the *R* to open the *Run* menu. The most popular option on the *Run* menu is *Start,* which executes a program.

The options on the *Run* menu vary, depending on the version of BASIC you are using:

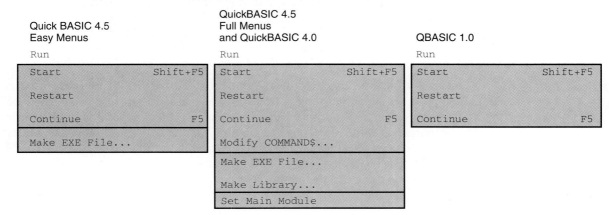

Start—Running a Program

Start is the option you will want to use to execute your programs most of the time. The *Start* command has a shortcut key that allows you to execute it from the editor, without opening the *Run* menu. Hold down Shift, and press F5.

Restart— Reinitializing a Program

Restart is an option that you will use only when using the debugger to single-step program execution. It will be covered in appendix C, which describes debugging.

Continue— Continuing Program Execution

If your program has halted during execution, perhaps due to a runtime error or to debugging, you may continue execution from the current location, rather than start again from the beginning. Select *Continue* from the *Run* menu, or press the shortcut F5 key.

Make EXE file— Making a Stand-Alone Program

Note: This option is only available in QuickBASIC 4.5.

The *Make EXE* option will compile the program and place the compiled version on disk. The compiled version will have a file extension of .EXE, rather than .BAS. The .EXE version of the program may be executed from the operating system prompt, rather than from within QuickBASIC. However, if you wish to make changes to the program, you must go back to the .BAS version, make the changes, and make a new .EXE version. This option is the one used to make "production" programs that will be executed on a regular basis.

The View Menu

The *View* menu changes significantly in the three BASIC versions. The *Options* choice in release 4.0 has been moved and expanded to an entire *Options* menu in release 4.5 and QBASIC. However, the most useful choice, *Output Screen*, appears in both versions.

QuickBASIC 4.5 Easy Menus	QuickBASIC 4.5 Full Menus	QuickBASIC 4.0	QBASIC 1.0
View	View	View	View

```
QuickBASIC 4.5        QuickBASIC 4.5        QuickBASIC 4.0        QBASIC 1.0
Easy Menus            Full Menus

View                  View                  View                  View

SUBs...        F2     SUBs...        F2     SUBs...        F2     SUBs...        F2

Output Screen  F4     Next SUB  Shift+F2    Next SUB  Shift+F2    Split

Included Lines        Split                 Split                 Output Screen F4

                      Next Statement        Next Statement

                      Output Screen    F4   Output Screen    F4

                      Included File         Include File

                      Included Lines        Included Lines

                                            Options...
```

Output Screen— Viewing the Program Output

When a program executes, any output produced by PRINT or INPUT statements appears on the output screen. Once you respond to "Press any key to continue," the editing screen and your source program reappear. Sometimes it is helpful to view the output again while correcting the program. You may view the output screen as often as you wish by selecting *Output Screen* from the *View* menu, or pressing the shortcut key, F4. The F4 key is a toggle, so pressing it repeatedly will switch the display between the output screen and the editing screen.

Options—Changing the Appearance of the Screen (Release 4.0)

Although screen changes are made from the *Options* choice on the *View* menu in QB 4.0, the same operations are done from the *Options* menu in QB 4.5 and QBASIC. Therefore, the directions for screen changes will appear in the section *Options* Menu.

The Options Menu

The *Options* menu is available in QB 4.5 and QBASIC. It centralizes the options that can be set by the user.

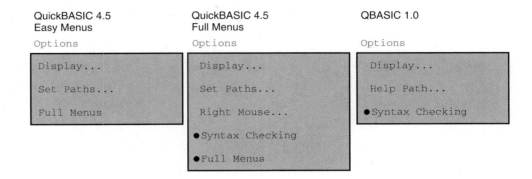

Full Menus—Viewing All Menu Choices

Release 4.5 of QuickBASIC has been simplified for the beginning programmer. However, all its power is still available, only slightly hidden. To see complete menus, including advanced options, choose *Full Menus*. Choosing Full Menus again returns QB 4.5 to *Easy Menu* mode. When the menu appears, you will see a dot in front of *Full Menus* when the option is currently ON.

Display—Changing the Appearance of the Screen

QB allows you to remove the scroll bars, set the number of spaces to tab, and control the colors to display on the screen. In QB 4.5 or QBASIC choose *Display* from the *Options* menu; in QB 4.0, select *Options* from the *View* menu.

Color options allow you to change the foreground (characters themselves) or background (area around the characters) on color monitors. To change colors, move the cursor with the Tab key. When the cursor is in the desired box, move up and down with the arrow keys to select your choice. With a monochrome monitor, you can switch to reverse image by selecting any color other than black for the background color.

Scroll bars are the vertical bar at the right edge of the screen and the horizontal bar at the bottom of the editing window. The bars are handy for mouse users, and take up space for nonmouse users. The *Scroll Bars* entry in the *Display* dialog box will be marked with an *X* when *Scroll Bars* are turned ON. Turn it off by using the Tab key to move the cursor to the entry, and pressing the Spacebar to remove the *X*.

The *Tab Stops* option is a handy one; it allows you to change the number of spaces the editor will insert each time you press the Tab key. To change the default of 8 spaces, use the Tab key to move the cursor to the *Tab Stop* box, and type the number you would like to use for indentation. Four is a nice number.

The Edit and Search Menus

The *Edit* and *Search* menus are useful when editing a program, and are covered in appendix B.

The Debug Menu

You will use the *Debug* menu when debugging a program. See appendix C for debugging.

Navigating with a Mouse

If you have a mouse attached to your computer, you will find menu navigation and scrolling a breeze, since QB was designed to be used with a mouse. You can mix keyboard and mouse commands, giving additional flexibility. All mouse control is done with one mouse button. If your mouse has more than one button, use the leftmost button.

Terminology

These are the terms used for describing mouse action:

pointer	The rectangular box on the screen that indicates the mouse position.
cursor	The flashing underline character that indicates where characters are to be entered from the keyboard.
mouse button	The leftmost button on a multi-buttoned mouse.
point	Move the mouse until the pointer is on the selected item.
press	Hold down the mouse button.
click	Quickly press and release the mouse button.
drag	Move the mouse while holding down the mouse button.
double click	Quickly press and release the mouse button, twice in succession.

Menu Selection

You can open a menu and select a menu option with the mouse:

Point to the desired menu name on the menu bar and click.
The menu will open, displaying the options.
Point to the selected option and click.
The command will be executed.

If you decide that you don't want to execute one of the menu commands after opening the menu, move the pointer off the menu and click.

Dialog Boxes

It is easy to make selections from dialog boxes with a mouse. Point to the desired selection and click. The pointer can be anywhere on the word, or in the box when one appears. When choices appear in command buttons, such as

move the pointer to the desired button and click. The double-lined box or highlighted entry indicates the default option.

Example—Loading a File Using a Mouse

Point to *File* on the menu bar and click the mouse button.
Point to *Open Program,* and click.
    The *Open Program* dialog box will appear.
Point to the file name desired, from the list of files.
Double-click the mouse button. This retrieves the selected file.

You can change the file list if the file you need is in a different disk or directory. When the dialog box appears, the cursor is in the *File Name* text box. Type a new drive or directory designation, and press Enter (QB 4.0), or double-click on the desired drive in the *Dir/Drives* box (QB 4.5 and QBASIC).

Using the Mouse for Scrolling and Editing

Appendix B covers editing commands. The mouse controls for scrolling and editing are covered there.

Appendix B
The BASIC Editor

When the QB program begins, the edit screen appears. On the edit screen you will type and change programs. QB's editor is a full-screen editor, which means that you may type and make changes anywhere on the screen.

Moving the Cursor

You can move the cursor one character at a time with the direction keys, or move greater distances with other special keys and key combinations. See table B.1 for the complete list of cursor movement keys.

Changing Text

When you wish to make changes to existing text, there are two choices—inserting or overtyping. QB is, by default, in insert mode. That means that when you type new characters, the old characters will be moved to the right to make room for the new.

Overtype Mode

In overtype mode, any new characters you type will replace the characters previously typed. Overtype mode is toggled ON and OFF with the Insert key (Ins). When overtype mode is in effect, the cursor changes to a blinking box and remains ON until the Insert key is pressed a second time.

Deleting Characters

Delete the character to the left of the cursor with the Backspace key (←). The character under the cursor is deleted with the Delete (Del) key.

Adding New Lines

The Enter key is used to insert new lines. However, a little care must be used when pressing Enter. The Enter key actually inserts a line-feed character at the current cursor location. If the cursor is in the middle of a line, the line feed will split the line. (Use the Backspace key to remove an accidentally placed line feed.) Before pressing Enter, press either Home or End, to move the cursor to the beginning or end of the line.

Selecting Text

When you want to delete, move, or copy text, the first step is to *select* the text. Selecting is sometimes called *marking a block*. Text is selected by combining the Shift key with the cursor movement keys. For example, press and hold down Shift-Right Arrow to select a series of characters. See table B.1 for the complete list of key combinations.

Indenting Text

QB's smart editor knows that program lines should be indented and tries hard to help. When you indent a line with the Tab key and press Enter, QB places the cursor on the next line, indented to the same location. Chances are, that's what you wanted. If not, it can easily be changed.

To indent one tab stop, press Tab.
To unindent (move left one indent-level), press Backspace.
To indent an entire block of code (like a loop or a subroutine), select the text and press Tab. The entire block of text will be indented.

Table B.1

Notes: Combination keystrokes are shown with the hyphen. The key combination Ctrl-Right means "Hold down the Ctrl key, press the Right arrow key, and release both keys." The words Up, Down, Left, Right refer to the arrow direction keys. A comma between keystrokes means to press and release the first key, then press and release the second.

Moving the Cursor

Up, down, left, right	Up, Down, Left, Right arrow keys
Right one word	Ctrl-Right
Left one word	Ctrl-Left
Beginning of line	Home
End of line	End
Top of screen	Ctrl-Q, E
Bottom of screen	Ctrl-Q, X
Beginning of file	Ctrl-Home
End of file	Ctrl-End

Scrolling

Up one line	Ctrl-Up
Down one line	Ctrl-Down
Up one screen	PgUp
Down one screen	PgDn
Left one window	Ctrl-PgUp
Right one window	Ctrl-PgDn

Deleting

Character left of cursor	Backspace
Character under cursor	Delete
Current line, Saving in clipboard	Ctrl-Y
To end of line, Saving in clipboard	Ctrl-Q,Y
Word	Ctrl-T
Selected text, Not saving in clipboard	Delete
Selected text, Saving in clipboard	Shift-Delete

Inserting a New Line   End, Enter

Selecting Text

Characters	Shift-Right or Shift-Left
Lines	Shift-Up or Shift-Down
A word	Shift-Ctrl-Right or Shift-Ctrl-Left

Starting a New Line

At the current cursor position   Enter

Combining Programs

At times you may need to combine two programs. QuickBASIC provides a way to merge files. QBASIC does not. The *Merge* option is on the *File* menu in QB 4.0, but not in QB 4.5. However, *Merge does* appear on the full *File* menu in QB 4.5. Therefore, in QB 4.5, first select *Full Menus* from the *Options* menu. Then, in either version, select *Merge* from the *File* menu. *Merge* retrieves a second program from the disk, inserting it at the current cursor location.

The Edit Menu

The *Edit* menu provides the commands to move a block of text from one location to another, or to make a copy of text in another location. Experienced users will prefer to use the shortcut keys, bypassing the *Edit* menu entirely.

Cut, Copy, and Paste—Moving and Copying Text

QB uses the concept of a "clipboard" to move text from one location to another, or to make a copy of text in a new location. In order to move or copy a block of text, the text must first be *selected* (see *Selecting Text,* p. 491). After selecting the text, use *Cut* or *Copy* to place the selected text in the clipboard. Use *Cut* when you want to move the text; it will delete the selected text and place it in the clipboard. Then move the cursor to the new location and *Paste.*

Use *Copy* when you want to reproduce text in a new location. *Copy* places a duplicate of the selected text in the clipboard without disturbing the original. To copy, first select the text, then *Copy.* Move the cursor to the new location and *Paste.*

If text has not been selected previously, *Cut* and *Copy* have no effect. Notice that you can use the keyboard shortcuts: Shift-Delete to cut, Ctrl-Insert to copy, and the Shift-Insert to paste, without opening the *Edit* menu.

Each time you place text in the clipboard, the new text replaces the old—it does not accumulate.

A Cut-and-Paste Example

1. Move the cursor to the beginning of the text you wish to move.
2. Select the text by holding down the Shift key along with cursor movement keys (Right, Left, Up, Down).
3. Press Alt and then *E* to open the *Edit* menu.
4. Highlight *Cut* and press Enter. This will remove the text from the screen, placing it in the clipboard.
5. Move the cursor to the new location, where you want the text to appear.
6. Press Alt and then *E* to open the *Edit* menu.
7. Highlight *Paste,* and press Enter. The text from the clipboard will be inserted at the new location.

Note that pasting does not empty the clipboard. You may move the cursor to a new location and *Paste* again, producing another copy of the selected text.

Shortcut method:

1. Place the cursor.
2. Highlight the text.
3. Press Shift-Delete (the shortcut key for *Cut*).
4. Move the cursor to the new location.
5. Press Shift-Insert (the shortcut key for *Paste*).

A Copy Example, Using the Shortcut Method

1. Move the cursor to the beginning of the text to copy.
2. Highlight the text using the Shift key along with cursor movement keys (Up, Down, Left, Right).
3. Press Ctrl-Insert (the shortcut key for *Copy*). Although the appearance of the screen hasn't changed, the selected text has been placed in the clipboard.
4. Move the cursor to the new location.
5. Press Shift-Insert (the shortcut key for *Paste*).

If you want additional copies of the text, repeat steps 4 and 5.

The Search Menu

The *Search* menu is used to quickly move the cursor to a new location, and optionally make changes in text at the new location (with the *Change* option).

Find—Searching for Text

Find searches for a particular string of text. You can specify a single character or entire words and phrases. This facility is handy for quickly moving the cursor to a particular block of code, or searching for all occurrences of a specific word.

1. Press Alt then S to open the *Search* menu.
2. Highlight *Find,* and press Enter.
3. The cursor appears in the *Find What* text box. Type the word or phrase for which you wish to search. You may type more text than fits in the box—it will scroll.
4. You can also select further options. These options are both toggles.
   a. *Whole Word.* Select this option if you want to match on whole words only. For example, *and* would find *sand* and *candy,* unless *Whole Word* were selected. To match on whole words only, press the Tab key to highlight *Whole Word,* then press the Spacebar to turn on the option.
   b. *Match Upper/Lowercase.* With this option turned ON, *Find* will only match if the case matches exactly. If you leave it turned OFF, *total* will match *total, Total* or *TOTAL.*
5. Press Enter to execute the *Find* command. The cursor will appear at the first occurrence of the text.

You can continue and *Find* the next occurrence of the text by pressing the F3 key, the shortcut key for *Repeat Last Find.*

Change—Searching for Text and Replacing with New Text

With the *Change* option you can find a particular word or phrase, and replace it with a different phrase or word. You can choose to change all occurrences of a search string, with or without verification.

1. Press Alt then *S* to open the *Search* menu.
2. With *Change* highlighted, press Enter.
3. In the *Find What* box, type the search string (text for which you wish to search).
4. Press the Tab key to move the cursor to the *Change To* box.
5. Type the new text that you want to replace the old text.
6. If you wish to change the *Whole Word* or *Match Upper/Lowercase* options, see the *Find* command.
7. Now you must choose between replace methods. Do you want QB to stop after each occurrence of the search string and ask for permission to change it, or go through the whole file and change them all without asking? Be extremely careful here, especially if you have not specified *Whole Words,* you may find things changed that were not your intention. The safest method is to verify each change.
8. For the verification method, press Enter. That will execute the highlighted command *Find and Verify.*
9. For the self-confident (or foolhardy) you can replace without asking. Press the Tab key to highlight *Change All,* and press Enter to execute the command.

Using a Mouse

A mouse is very useful in QB, even when editing text. With the mouse you can quickly scroll text, move the cursor to any spot, select text, execute menu commands, and make selections from dialog boxes. Executing menu commands and dialog boxes were covered in appendix A, along with the basic terminology of mouse operation.

Scrolling Text

The scroll bars down the right side and across the bottom of the screen are used to scroll text. You can move the text one character at a time, or quickly move to a general vicinity in the program (beginning, middle, or end of the file).

Scrolling One Character at a Time

You can scroll text one character at a time, using the arrow symbols at each end of the scroll bars. Each click on an arrow moves the text one character right or left or one line up or down. Holding the button while pointing to an arrow will make the text move continuously.

Quickly Scrolling to a Position in the File

You can quickly move to a general area of the file (i.e., top, middle, bottom) with the mouse. On each scroll bar you will see a dark spot called the *scroll box*. Point to the scroll box and drag it to the desired location. For example, if you want to look at some program lines that are near the end of the file, drag the scroll box to a position near the bottom of the vertical scroll bar.

Scrolling One Screenful at a Time

To scroll one screenful at a time, click on the gray area of the scroll bar. Click above the scroll box to scroll up, below the scroll box to scroll down.

Moving the Cursor

With the mouse you can quickly move the cursor to a new location on the editing screen. Move the pointer to the desired location and click.

Selecting Text

Several operations, such as *Cut* and *Paste, Copy,* and *Print Selected Text,* require that text first be selected. With the mouse this is particularly easy. Point to the beginning of the text to select, press the mouse button and drag the highlight to cover the desired area, and release the mouse button. Then execute the appropriate menu command.

Quickly Selecting Text with a Mouse

To select:

Characters	Point to the character following the desired character, press the button and drag left. Dragging left selects characters to the left of the pointer. Dragging right selects text beginning with the character under the pointer.
A word	Point anywhere on the word and double-click.
A line	Point to the beginning of the line, press the mouse button, and drag down one line. Dragging up selects the line above the pointer.
Several lines	Point to the first line to select, press the mouse button, and drag up or down through the desired lines.
To unmark selected text:	Point to a location outside the selected text and click.

Mouse Example—Copying Text

1. Move the mouse pointer to the beginning of the text to be copied.
2. Press and hold the mouse button.
3. Move the mouse pointer to the end of the text to be copied. The text will be highlighted.
4. Release the mouse button.
5. Move the mouse pointer to *Edit* on the menu bar and click.
6. Point to *Copy* and click. This will copy the selected text into the clipboard.
7. Move the pointer to the location where you would like the copied text to appear.
8. Click the mouse button. The cursor will jump to the new location.
9. Press the Shift-Insert key (the shortcut key for *Paste*). The text will appear in the new location (as well as the old one).

Appendix C
The BASIC Debugger

A computer is supposed to produce correct results. However, too often the output is not correct. Many beginning programmers believe that if the program runs, it must be finished. But all aspects of the output must be carefully checked before a program can be turned over to a user. All available methods should be used to verify the correctness of the program output.

Use Test Data

One method of verifying the correctness of program output is to run the program with test data. This is data that will produce known results. If test data is carefully designed, the chances are good that any program errors will be found.

Many times a program will work correctly for all "normal" inputs; but when given extreme values, errors pop up (sometimes not until a program has been in use for weeks or months). In selecting test data, be sure to exercise all options of a program. If a discount is given for sales of 100 or more units, be sure to test 99, 100, and 101 as well as 0—perhaps even a negative number.

A pattern that will fit many programs is one in which there are three distinct cases to validate. These three cases correspond to the beginning, middle, and end. In testing, make sure that the normal cases will be correctly handled (the middle). Then determine "Will the first input and/or calculation be handled correctly?" Then, "What will happen when the last record is read?"

Any situation that is a potential for error should be carefully checked. In a program with subtotals, be sure to check the first record, the last, the last record of one group, and the first record of the next group.

Use a Calculator

The calculator method of checking output may seem tedious, but it is definitely worth the trouble. It may be necessary to verify an entire report with the calculator; or it may be enough to validate only certain test cases. In a report that calculates gross pay for employees, use the calculator to verify at least one of each possibility—one person with 0 hours, one with less than 40 hours (if that is the cutoff point for overtime); one with exactly 40 hours; one with a fraction of an hour overtime (worked 40.5 hours); and one with a large amount of overtime (worked 55 hours).

Develop a Proofreader's Eye

A calculator won't help much for alphanumeric data. The way to catch errors is to carefully proofread all output, comparing the output to the input or to the desired output, if available. Proofreading is a skill that improves with practice.

Bugs in the Program

Only when all output has been carefully checked and proven correct is the program ready to go. If any errors are found, these are called program **bugs.** The process of locating and correcting the errors is called **debugging.**

The Immediate Window

The **immediate window,** along the lower edge of the screen, can be a big help for debugging, as well as for testing program lines. At any time you can switch to the immediate window, and enter a BASIC statement for immediate execution. You can display the contents of a variable, change the value of a variable, or try any statement you wish. Pressing F6 jumps the cursor to the immediate window, pressing F6 again jumps it back into the edit window (main portion of the screen).

Pressing the Enter key on any line in the immediate window executes the statement. Lines previously typed scroll up, but remain in the window. To re-execute any statement, move the cursor to the line and press Enter.

It is likely that most statements you will execute in the immediate window will be PRINT statements, so a little shortcut will come in handy. The question mark can be used as a shorthand symbol in place of the word PRINT.

Example:

? SubTotal
is equivalent to
PRINT SubTotal

The QB Debugger

The QB debugger is a useful tool to help you debug your programs. With the debugger you can watch the source code as the program executes, execute one line at a time, stop the execution, determine which branch of an IF...THEN...ELSE was taken, watch changing values in program variables, and set breakpoints so that the program will stop when it reaches a specific location. Several new terms are unique to the QB debugger:

Trace	Watch the execution of a program, line by line. As each source statement is executed, it is highlighted.
Watch Variable	Any program variable (or expression) that you would like to observe during program execution.
Breakpoint	Location in the program where you would like to pause the execution. You can use breakpoints to determine which parts of the program are being executed, and to stop to examine the value of a variable at a strategic location.
Watch Window	Area at the top of the screen that opens when you have defined watch variables. The current values of the expressions are shown during program execution.

The keystrokes used for the debugger are summarized in table C.1.

Table C.1
Summary of Debug Keyboard Commands

Command	Key(s)
Help	F1
Switch to or from the output screen	F4
Continue Execution from the current statement	F5
Begin execution	Shift-F5
Switch to or from the immediate window	F6
Single Step execution	F8
Set or clear a breakpoint	F9
Instant Watch	Shift-F9
Step through subprograms	F10

Summary of Debug Menu Commands
```
Add Watch . . .
Delete Watch . . .
Toggle Breakpoint (same as F9)
Clear All Breakpoints
```

Single-Stepping Program Execution

The easiest and most rewarding way to start using the debugger is to press F8 to execute one program statement. Repeatedly pressing F8 will single-step through program execution. When a PRINT or INPUT statement is executed, QB will show the output screen momentarily, and return to the source code. You can switch back and forth between the output screen and the source code with F4 (or *Output Screen* on the *View* menu). If the debugger had only one feature, single-stepping would be the number-one choice.

For programs containing subprograms, you can press F10 to step through the entire program, including subprograms.

GO—Executing without Tracing

If you wish to resume normal execution of the program, after tracing a portion of the program, press F5 (GO). The program will continue to execute until it reaches a STOP or END statement or until it reaches a runtime error or a breakpoint.

Using Breakpoints

A breakpoint is a location in the program where you would like execution to pause. Using breakpoints, you can rapidly execute a program up to a chosen location, and then pause. You then can begin a single-step trace or perhaps examine the contents of a variable using the immediate window or *Instant Watch*.

Select locations for breakpoints where you are suspicious of a problem. A good location is often right after the calculations. You may wish to examine the variables used for the calculation as well as the result. Another popular location is immediately after reading input data. This can be particularly helpful when the output does not match what you *thought* was the input.

Setting Breakpoints

Breakpoints are easily marked and unmarked. Move the cursor to the desired line and press F9 (or *Toggle Breakpoint* on the *Debug* menu). F9 is a toggle; that is, pressing it once sets the breakpoint, pressing it again turns it off. The line you have marked will appear in reverse image or red.

Clearing Breakpoints

A single breakpoint may be cleared by pressing the F9 key, or you can choose to clear *all* breakpoints. Select *Clear All Breakpoints* from the *Debug* menu to remove all breakpoints you have set.

Using Watch Variables

A watch variable is a program variable whose value you would like to display continuously during program execution. When you select variables to watch, the Watch window opens at the top of the editing screen, and the variable names and their current values are placed in the window. As you single-step through the program execution (F8), the values of the watch variables in the window are updated when any change in their values occur. Note that watch variables are available in QuickBASIC but not in QBASIC.

Setting Watch Variables

To set a new watch variable, select the *Add Watch* command from the *Debug* menu. Be sure to spell the variable name exactly as it appears in the program.

Deleting Watch Variables

Any watch variable can be deleted (cleared) from the watch window. Select *Delete Watch* from the *Debug* menu.

Instant Watch

A new feature in QB 4.5 provides a shortcut method to display or watch a program variable. With *Instant Watch,* you can look at the contents of any variable and optionally add the variable to the watch window as a new watch variable. To select a variable for Instant Watching, move the cursor to any variable name. The variable may be on the current line when single-stepping or on any other line. With the cursor on a variable name, press Shift-F9. A dialog box will appear with the name of the variable and its current value. You can select to add the variable to the watch window, or cancel the dialog box, which makes it disappear. *Instant Watch* provides an even more convenient method of displaying a variable's contents than printing in the immediate window.

Advanced Features

There are some additional, more advanced debugging features available in QB 4.0 and in QB 4.5 when *Full Menus* are selected (from the *Options* menu). An *Animated Trace* may be selected, in which the program executes rapidly, highlighting the current line as it is executed. Begin the trace by selecting *Trace On* from the *Debug* menu. The *History* feature allows replay of the last 20 instructions executed. In addition to watch variables, you can set a *Watchpoint,* in the form of a condition. When the condition becomes *TRUE,* program execution will halt (similar to a breakpoint). For more information on these advanced features, consult the QB manual or the Help screens.

Appendix D
The ASCII Code

ASCII CODE	CHARACTER	CONTROL CHARACTER	ASCII CODE	CHARACTER	ASCII CODE	CHARACTER
0	(null)	NUL	43	+	86	V
1	○	SOH	44	,	87	W
2	●	STX	45	-	88	X
3	♥	ETX	46	.	89	Y
4	♦	EOT	47	/	90	Z
5	♣	ENQ	48	0	91	[
6	♠	ACK	49	1	92	\
7	(beep)	BEL	50	2	93	]
8	■	BS	51	3	94	$\wedge$
9	(tab)	HT	52	4	95	_
10	(line feed)	LF	53	5	96	'
11	(home)	VT	54	6	97	a
12	(form feed)	FF	55	7	98	b
13	(carriage return)	CR	56	8	99	c
14	♫	SO	57	9	100	d
15	☼	SI	58	:	101	e
16	▶	DLE	59	;	102	f
17	◀	DC1	60	<	103	g
18	↕	DC2	61	=	104	h
19	‼	DC3	62	>	105	i
20	¶	DC4	63	?	106	j
21	§	NAK	64	@	107	k
22	▬	SYN	65	A	108	l
23	↨	ETB	66	B	109	m
24	↑	CAN	67	C	110	n
25	↓	EM	68	D	111	o
26	→	SUB	69	E	112	p
27	←	ESC	70	F	113	q
28	(cursor right)	FS	71	G	114	r
29	(cursor left)	GS	72	H	115	s
30	(cursor up)	RS	73	I	116	t
31	(cursor down)	US	74	J	117	u
32	SPACE		75	K	118	v
33	!		76	L	119	w
34	"		77	M	120	x
35	#		78	N	121	y
36	$		79	O	122	z
37	%		80	P	123	{
38	&		81	Q	124	:
39	'		82	R	125	}
40	(		83	S	126	~
41	)		84	T	127	⌂
42	*		85	U		

ASCII CODE	CHARACTER	ASCII CODE	CHARACTER	ASCII CODE	CHARACTER
128	Ç	171	½	214	╓
129	ü	172	¼	215	╫
130	é	173	¡	216	╪
131	â	174	≪	217	┘
132	ä	175	≫	218	┌
133	à	176	░	219	■
134	a	177	▒	220	▬
135	ç	178	▓	221	▪
136	e	179	│	222	▫
137	ë	180	┤	223	▬
138	è	181	╡	224	α
139	ï	182	╢	225	β
140	í	183	╖	226	Γ
141	ì	184	╕	227	π
142	Ä	185	╣	228	Σ
143	Å	186	║	229	σ
144	É	187	╗	230	μ
145	æ	188	╝	231	τ
146	Æ	189	╜	232	◊
147	o	190	╛	233	⊖
148	ö	191	┐	234	Ω
149	ò	192	└	235	δ
150	u	193	┴	236	∞
151	ù	194	┬	237	$\emptyset$
152	ÿ	195	├	238	$\in$
153	Ö	196	─	239	$\cap$
154	Ü	197	┼	240	$\equiv$
155	¢	198	╞	241	$\pm$
156	£	199	╟	242	$\geq$
157	¥	200	╚	243	$\leq$
158	Pt	201	╔	244	$\lceil$
159	f	202	╩	245	$\rfloor$
160	á	203	╦	246	$\div$
161	í	204	╠	247	$\approx$
162	ó	205	═	248	°
163	ú	206	╬	249	•
164	ñ	207	╧	250	·
165	Ñ	208	╨	251	$\sqrt{}$
166	ª	209	╤	252	n
167	º	210	╥	253	^{2}
168	¿	211	╙	254	■
169	⌐	212	╘	255	(blank 'FF')
170	¬	213	╒		

Appendix E
Answers to Chapter Feedback

Chapter 1, Feedback, p. 26

1. `HALF A LOAF IS BETTER THAN NONE`
2. `HALF,        MY EYE`
3. `HAWKS 0        DOVES 0`
4.

1	2	3	4	5
6	7	8	9	10

5. Same as #4.
6. The use of a variable name must be consistent. Change the INPUT to:

   `INPUT Age`

   (The problem could also be corrected by changing the PRINT to PRINT A.)
7. What will print is not the numbers 1, 2, 3, but the contents of the variables ONE, TWO, and THREE. Unless a value has been assigned to the variables, each has the value zero.
8. The numbers will not all print on the same line. Since the numbers are separated by commas, they will print in the print zones. Only five numbers will be printed on one line.
9. The sum was not calculated. Add a line before the PRINT:

   `LET Sum = Num1 + Num2`

Chapter 2, Feedback, p. 33

`PorcupinePie`	valid
`Count#1`	invalid—illegal # imbedded in name
`$Total`	invalid—no dollar sign in numeric variables
`Etc...`	valid
`A2`	valid
`SooLong`	valid
`2A`	invalid—must begin with a letter
`Print`	invalid—reserved word
`PrintItOut`	valid

Chapter 2, Feedback, p. 36

1. 18
2. 1
3. 6
4. 5
5. 22
6. 2048
7. 22
8. 38
9. Valid
10. Invalid. The variable must appear to the left of the equal sign.

11. Valid
12. Valid
13. Invalid. Any calculations must appear on the right side of the equal sign. The results of the calculation are then assigned to the variable named on the left of the equal sign.
14. Invalid. No operations are assumed in BASIC. If multiplication is needed, it must be stated. Without an operational sign, this will generate a syntax error.

    ```
    LET Ans = Num * (Num - 1)
    ```
15. Valid

Chapter 2, Feedback, p. 38

1. Valid
2. Valid
3. Invalid—$ must be rightmost character.
4. Valid
5. Invalid—$ must be rightmost character.
6. Invalid—PRINT is a reserved word.
7. Invalid—PayClass is numeric. The value "M" cannot be assigned to a numeric variable.
8. Invalid—The value must be enclosed in quotation marks.

    ```
    LET Ssno$ = "550-51-5257"
    ```
9. Valid
10. Invalid—The string literal ("SAMMY") must appear to the right of the equal sign, the variable to the left.

    ```
    LET Person$ = "SAMMY"
    ```

Chapter 2, Feedback, p. 45

1.
   ```
   INPUT "ENTER CLASS NAME ", Class$
   INPUT "ENTER THE CLASS COUNT ", Count
   ```

2.
   ```
   'Input Name and Address
   INPUT "ENTER NAME ", Nam$
   INPUT "ADDRESS    ", Addr$
   'Print Name and Address on Printer
   LPRINT Nam$
   LPRINT Addr$
   ```

3. Note: quotation marks will be needed around the data when it is input in order to accept the comma.

   ```
   INPUT "ENTER THE DATE, SURROUNDED BY QUOTATION MARKS ", Dat$
   ```

Chapter 2, Feedback, p. 48

1. Subroutines are a good way to group statements that together perform one function. Subroutines are also useful when a task must be performed from more than one location in a program.
2. Execution returns to the statement immediately following the GOSUB.
3. Try this on the computer.
4. No limit.

Chapter 3, Feedback, p. 67

1. True
2. True
3. True
4. False
5. False
6. True
7. True
8. True
9. True
10. True

Chapter 3, Feedback, p. 70

1. True
2. False
3. True
4. False
5. True
6. No possible value of X satisfies the condition.
7. Any value for Y in the range 1–10 would make the condition true.

Chapter 3, Feedback, p. 76

1.
```
'Program to Print Name 5 Times
DO UNTIL Count = 5
    PRINT "LOUIE LOOP"
    LET Count = Count + 1
LOOP
END
```

2.
```
' Print the Numbers 1 - 10
DO WHILE Numb < 10
    LET Numb = Numb + 1
    PRINT Numb
LOOP
END
```

3.
```
' Input and Print Participant Names
INPUT "ENTER NAME (TYPE 'QUIT' TO END) ", Nam$
DO UNTIL UCASE$(Nam$)="QUIT"
  LPRINT Nam$
  INPUT "ENTER NAME (TYPE 'QUIT' TO END) ", Nam$
LOOP
END
```

4. None—since ZED = 0 (by default), the loop would never be entered.

5.
```
X = 5     *****
X = 10    **********
X = 1     *
X = 0     No output
```

Chapter 3, Feedback, p. 88

1. `25 25.4  25.40  25.396`

2. ```
   FROGS      10
   TOADS       5
   POLLIWOGS  75
   ```

3. ```
   THE SCORE IS 12 FOR THE ROVERS
   THE SCORE IS  6 FOR THE BRAVES
   THE SCORE IS %125 FOR THE AMAZING AMAZ
   ```

4. ```
   JOEY        SPENT    2.00 ON GUM
   ```

5. *Illegal function call*—error message. The two variables must be reversed on the PRINT USING to match the print image.

Chapter 3, Feedback, p. 91

1. ```
   ******$1.00
   $250,000.00
   ******$0.60
   **$1,000.00
   %$123,456,789.00
   ```
2. ```
       4.0     50.5-  100.6-     0.0
       4.0+    50.5-  100.6-     0.0+
      +4.00   -50.45  %+100.63   +0.00
          $4.00       $-50.45     $-100.63      $0.00
      $    4.00    $   -50.45  $ -100.63 $     0.00
   ```

Chapter 3, Feedback, p. 91

1. Placing all print images at the beginning of the program will make them easier to find and to alter.
2. The actual print statements will be shorter, cleaner, and easier to read.
3. If a line is to be printed on both the screen and the printer, the print image can be shared.
4. It would be possible to change a print image during program execution, based on a condition in the program.

Chapter 4, Feedback, p. 110

1. `The frogs have it`
2. `It's the toads and polliwogs`
3. `IT'S TRUE`
4. ```
   'Compare the relative prices of apples & oranges
   INPUT "How much are the apples"; Apple
   INPUT "How much are the oranges"; Orange
   IF Apple > Orange THEN
      PRINT "The apples cost more"
   ELSE
      PRINT "The oranges cost more"
   END IF
   ```
5. ```
   IF K > 0 THEN
      PRINT "THE ACCOUNT IS POSITIVE"
      LET K = 0
      LET Kcounter = Kcounter + 1
   ELSE
      PRINT "THE ACCOUNT IS NOT POSITIVE"
   END IF
   ```
   ```

Chapter 4, Feedback, p. 119

1. a. The variable types do not match in the READ and DATA statements. One way to correct:

    ```
    DATA JOHN, 4, MARTHA, 5
    ```

    b. Out of data error. Another value is needed in the DATA list.
    c. In order to read a date (with an imbedded comma), quotation marks are needed.

    ```
    DATA HUMPTY DUMPTY, "JAN. 15, 1990"
    ```

    d. No error will be generated, but only the first two values in the data list will be read.
    e. This will print the word "END" at the bottom of the list. One way to correct is to use a priming READ and reverse the READ and PRINT statements inside the loop.

    ```
    READ F$
    DO UNTIL F$ = "END"
        PRINT F$
        READ F$
    LOOP
    ```

2.
    ```
    READ StTime$, EndTime$
    DATA "1:25", "2:45"
    ```

    Note: Quotation marks are needed because of the colons in the string values.

3.
    ```
    READ Word$
    DO UNTIL Word$ = "END"
        PRINT Word$
        LET WordCount = WordCount + 1
        READ Word$
    LOOP
    PRINT "THE NUMBER OF WORDS IS"; WordCount
    DATA list of words, separated by commas
    DATA END
    ```

Chapter 5, Feedback, p. 143

1. The term *top-down* means to break the program into its individual functions. The top-down idea can best be illustrated with a hierarchy chart, where each level shows breaking the program into successively smaller parts. Structured programming includes the top-down concept, as well as several other ideas and guidelines intended to produce "good" programs. The standards include rules for flow of control, module formation, and coding guidelines such as indentation, variable names, and remarks.
2. Short variable names do indeed make programs more concise. However, the programs will be more cryptic and difficult to read, debug, and maintain.
3. A subroutine that adds to subtotals, prints a detail line, and reads data would most likely be an example of poor cohesion.

Chapter 6, Feedback, p. 155

1. Each page after the first will have headings and one detail line.
2. It will generally be much faster to skip to the new page rather than print blank lines.
3. There are 66 lines, assuming 6 lines to the inch.
4. Detail lines are the lines printed for each iteration of the program. One input record generally produces one detail line. The other lines are heading lines, total lines, etc.

Chapter 6, Feedback, p. 163

1. The field used to determine the timing of the subtotals is called the *control variable*. When the control variable changes (or breaks), it is time to print subtotals.
2. In the detail calculations, add to two fields. In the control break, add to two report totals, and zero out the two subtotal fields.
3. Change the two print images St$ and Rt$ to include an average field, and change the LPRINTs for the subtotals and report totals to include the averages.

```
LPRINT USING ST$; CalSubTot, GroupAvg
LPRINT USING RT$; CalTot, ReportAvg
```

Add the lines to calculate the group average:

```
LET GroupCount = GroupCount + 1
LET GroupAvg = CalSubtot / GroupCount
```

In the subtotal routine, add these lines:

```
LET ReportCount = ReportCount + GroupCount
LET GroupCount = 0
```

Add this line just before printing the report totals:

```
LET GroupAvg = CalTot / ReportCount
```

4. A second control variable (the division) and a division subtotal variable are needed. When the division changes, division subtotals are printed, added into the group subtotals, and zeroed out. When the group number changes, first a division control break is done, then a group control break. At the end of the report, the division subtotals, group subtotals, and report subtotals are printed.

```
Prime read
LOOP while not end of data
        Add to division subtotals
        Print detail line
        Read next data
        If new division
            Print division subtotals
            Add division subtotals to group subtotals
            Let division subtotals = 0
        If new group
            Print group subtotals
            Add group subtotals to report totals
            Let group subtotals = 0
Print report totals
```

Chapter 7, Feedback, p. 181

1.
```
CLS
LOCATE 12,36
PRINT "YOUR NAME"
```

```
2.  'Print a box in the center of the screen
    CLS
    LOCATE 10, 35
    PRINT "**********"
    LOCATE 11, 35
    PRINT "*        *"
    LOCATE 12, 35
    PRINT "*        *"
    LOCATE 13, 35
    PRINT "*        *"
    LOCATE 14, 35
    PRINT "**********"
    ' Now input in the center of the box
    LOCATE 12, 38
    INPUT Number
```

Chapter 7, Feedback, p. 198

1. When using an INPUT$ or INKEY$ function, it may be necessary to make the cursor visible with the LOCATE statement.

2. Hopefully, you thought of several ways. Here are two:

```
PRINT STRING$(40, "=")
PRINT STRING$(40, 61)
```

3. Convert the numeric variable to a string. Then the LEN function can be used. However, the string will include one character for the sign.

```
LET Digits = LEN(STR$(Num)) - 1
```

4. A common use of the VAL function is to convert data from a string variable to a numeric variable after validity checking.

5. INKEY$ does not halt program execution to input characters. It also does not require the ENTER key to be pressed, as does the INPUT statement.

6. Although neither INKEY$ nor INPUT$ require the ENTER key to be pressed, there is an important difference between the two. INPUT$ halts program execution and INKEY$ does not. So INKEY$ would be used when execution is not to be halted.

7. Since INPUT$ *does* halt program execution, it would be used when the input must take place before any further operations occur. INPUT$ is handy in the situation of the message: PRESS ANY KEY TO CONTINUE.

8.
```
'   Read and Print, Right-justified
READ Fruit$
DO UNTIL Fruit$ = "END"
    PRINT TAB(30 - LEN(Fruit$)+1); Fruit$
    READ Fruit$
LOOP
DATA FIG, WATERMELON, PINEAPPLE, PLUM, MANGO, END
```

9. DOG

10.
```
INPUT P$
LET Per = INSTR(P$,".")
PRINT MID$(P$,Per+1)
```

```
11.   INPUT P$
      LET Per = INSTR(P$,".")
      IF Per > 0 THEN
          PRINT MID$(P$,Per+1)
      END IF

12.   LPRINT CHR$(12);        'Advance Paper to Top-of-page

13.   LET Char$ = INPUT$(1)
      DO UNTIL Char$ = "*"
          PRINT Char$;
          LET Char$ = INPUT$(1)
      LOOP
```

Chapter 8, Feedback, p. 233

1. There are two ways to determine whether your printer can print the graphics characters:
   a. Check the printer manual for a reference page that shows the printer's character set. Look for words that say "IBM compatible," or "IBM mode."
   b. Write a little program to print all characters. Use the statement LPRINT CHR$(Num), where Num is varied from 32 to 256. (Printing characters below 32 is not recommended, since several characters may be treated as printer control codes, and cause some printers to lock up, beep, or change character sets, spacing, or margins.)

2. COLOR statements can be used to create a reverse image (black characters on a white background), underline, or blinking characters on a black-and-white monitor.

3. It is not possible to produce smooth curves with text graphics.

Chapter 10, Feedback, p. 263

1. a. Correct
   b. Incorrect. It must be NEXT A.
   c. Two errors here: The FOR statement must have a variable for the index (rather than 4). The NEXT statement is also incorrect. FOR is a reserved word that cannot appear in a NEXT statement.

```
FOR Index = 1 TO 10 STEP 2
NEXT Index
```

   d. Correct
   e. Correct
   f. For this to work, it needs a negative STEP. As it is, the loop will never be entered, since 10 is already greater than 1.

2.
```
' Print the Numbers 3-100
FOR Index = 3 TO 100 STEP 3
    PRINT Index
NEXT Index
```

3.
```
' Print 10 Lines
FOR Count = 1 TO 10
    PRINT "THIS IS A LARK"
NEXT Count
```

4. a.
```
        BICYCLE       150
        TRAIN          65
        BALL          1.5
        NERD          .27
        GAME         6.95
                   223.72
```
    b. 10
        12
        14

    c. * * * * * * *

5.
Loop Iterations	Index after Loop Completion
a. 4	14
b. 10	0
c. 7	6.5
d. 0	5
e. 3	4

Chapter 10, Feedback, p. 267

1.
2	1
2	2
2	3
5	1
5	2
5	3

2. a. * * * * *
        * *
        * * * * * * * * *
        * * * * * *
        *

    b. The extra PRINT is needed to force the next output to another line. Without it, all the stars would appear on one line.

        *

Chapter 10, Feedback, p. 273

1. Integer variables can be used anywhere whole units are being counted (people, accounts, balls, etc.). The index of a FOR/NEXT loop is a good candidate for integer variables.
2. Double precision will hold more digits accurately than single precision.
3. Calculations are quicker with single-precision variables than with double. Also, single-precision variables use half as much storage as double.

Chapter 10, Feedback, p. 285

1. a. 2   e. illegal function call
    b. 2   f. 4
    c. 2   g. 4
    d. 3   h. −1
2. a. 5   c. * * * *
    b. 20   d. YES PLEASE
3. A dummy argument holds the place for an actual argument. At the time the function is executed, the actual argument will take the place of the dummy argument.
4. There is no limit to the number of operations in the expression. The only limit is the 255-character line length.
5. Left as a thought-provoking exercise.

Chapter 11, Feedback, p. 298

1. Valid
2. Valid
3. Valid
4. Invalid. I∗3 is 30, which is too large to be used as a subscript in this array.
5. Valid. The array actually has an element 0.
6. Invalid. Negative subscripts must be indicated in the DIM statement.
7. Valid. The result will be rounded, so this is a reference to A(3).
8. Valid. The resulting subscript will be 0.

Chapter 11, Feedback, p. 299

1.
```
INPUT "ENTER NAME, TYPE 'EOD' TO QUIT ", Aname$
LET Index = 1
DO UNTIL UCASE$(Aname$) = "EOD"
    LET NAM$(Index) = Aname$
    LET Index = Index + 1
    INPUT "ENTER NAME, TYPE 'EOD' TO QUIT ", Aname$
LOOP
```

Or, an alternate approach, which will place EOD into the highest array element:
```
LET Index = 1
INPUT "ENTER NAME, TYPE 'EOD' TO QUIT ", Nam$(Index)
DO UNTIL UCASE$(Nam$(Index)) = "EOD"
    LET Index = Index + 1
    INPUT "ENTER NAME, TYPE 'EOD' TO QUIT ", Nam$(Index)
LOOP
NEXT
```

2.
```
READ Aname$
LET Index = 1
DO UNTIL Aname$ = "EOD"
    LET Nam$(Index) = Aname$
    LET Index = Index + 1
    READ Aname$
LOOP
DATA SAM,JOE,PETE,DAN,MELVIN,EOD
```

Or, an alternate approach, which will place EOD into the highest element:
```
LET Index = 1
READ Nam$(Index)
DO UNTIL Nam$ = "EOD"
    LET Index = Index + 1
    READ Nam$(Index)
LOOP
DATA SAM,JOE,PETE,DAN,MELVIN,EOD
```

Chapter 11, Feedback, p. 314

1.
```
DIM K(20)
FOR Index = 1 TO 20
   LET K(Index) = 100
NEXT Index
```

2.
```
' Divide Each Even Numbered Element By 2
FOR Index = 2 TO 20 STEP 2
   LET K(Index) = K(Index) / 2
NEXT Index
```

```
3.  ' Subtract 1 From Every Element
    FOR Index = 1 TO 20
        LET K(Index) = K(Index) - 1
    NEXT Index

4.  ' Print All 20 Elements, 10 Per Line
    FOR Index = 1 TO 20
        PRINT K(Index);
        IF Index = 10 THEN
            PRINT        'Begin new line
        END IF
    NEXT Index
```

Alternate approach:

```
    ' Print All 20 Elements, 10 Per Line
    FOR Begin = 1 TO 11 STEP 10
        FOR Index = Begin TO Begin + 10
            PRINT K(Index);
        NEXT Index
        PRINT
    NEXT Begin

5.  ' Dimension and Fill a Table
    DIM Goodies(6)
    FOR Index = 1 TO 6
        READ Goodies(Index)
    NEXT Index
    DATA candy, ice cream, popcorn, gum, cookies, gum drops
```

6. In a serial search, every element of the table is checked for a match. In a binary search, the number of elements to search is repeatedly divided in half until a match is found.
7. A binary search should be used when the table is large and can be arranged in sequence.
8. A serial search may be used for small tables or when the most popular elements can be placed at the beginning of the list.

Chapter 12, Feedback, p. 326

```
1.  DIM Grid(3,5)

2.  FOR Col = 1 TO 5
        LET Grid(1,Col) = 1
    NEXT Col

3.  FOR Col = 1 TO 5
        LET Grid(2,Col) = 2
    NEXT Col

4.  FOR Col = 1 TO 5
        LET Grid(3,Col) = Grid(2,Col) + Grid(1,Col)
    NEXT Col

5.  FOR Row = 1 TO 3
        FOR Col = 1 TO 5
            PRINT Grid(Row,Col);
        NEXT Col
        PRINT
    NEXT Row
```

Chapter 13, Feedback, p. 360

1. A disk track is one of the concentric circles on the disk surface used for storing data.
2. A sector is a segment of a track.
3. MS-DOS uses 512 characters per sector.
4. A program file holds executable BASIC statements. A data file holds actual data to be used by a program.
5. a. B: signifies that the file is stored on the diskette in the B drive.
   b. .PRT is the file extension, which is generally used to group programs into like types.
6. a. File
   b. Record
   c. Student name
   d. File

Chapter 13, Feedback, p. 366

1. When the file is read into a program, the fields must be delimited (separated). The commas indicate where one field stops and another starts.
2. The primary function of the OPEN statement is to make the file available for processing. If the file is to be input, it must be found on the diskette. If the program is going to create the file, a new directory entry must be created and space allocated for the new file.
3. The consequence of omitting a CLOSE depends on how the program ends. If an END statement is executed, BASIC will automatically CLOSE the file. If the file is not closed, data will likely be lost at the end of the file.
4. This is a good way to lose a file. The new data will replace the data in the previously existing file.
5. A new directory entry will be created for the new file.

Chapter 13, Feedback, p. 374

1. An error message will be generated.
2. The file buffer is used to temporarily hold the data coming from or going to the diskette. When the data is physically written on the diskette, only whole sectors are written. Data is "saved up," until a full sector can be written. The same is true for reading data from the diskette. An entire sector is read into the buffer. Then the data is actually passed to the program as the INPUT# statements are executed.
3. A file number is in effect only for the duration of the program. The file number is *not* stored with the file. Each program that accesses the file may refer to the file with a different file number.
4. It is not necessary to know the variable names when reading data from a file. The variables may be called by different names when they are read. The concept is similar to the data in DATA statements. Each field is assigned to the next variable in the sequence named.
5. The EOF(n) function evaluates True when the last *good* data is read. The final data may be processed after it is read, before termination of the loop.
6. Sequential files can be opened for INPUT or OUTPUT, but not both at the same time. It is not possible to read a record, make changes in the data, and write it back in the file.

1. The only way BASIC has to find any record in the file is to count the number of bytes from the beginning of the file. If the records were not all the same length, this would not be possible.
2. The record length is specified in the OPEN statement.
3. The field lengths are specified in the TYPE statement.
4. For string variables, the length chosen should be as long as the longest value expected to be in the field. For numeric data, integers require two bytes, long integers and single-precision variables require four bytes, and double-precision variables require eight bytes.
5. The record description provides the structure or layout of the record variable. When a record is written to the disk, the contents of the record variable are output from the program.
6. When a record is read from the disk (GET), the data is placed in the record variable. Then the field names specified in the record description are used to refer to the data.
7.   a.
```
' Read and Print the 4th Record
LET Rec = 4
GET #1, Rec, InventoryRecord
PRINT InventoryRecord.Description, InventoryRecord.Quantity
```
   b.
```
' Create a New Record
INPUT "Item number   ", Rec
INPUT "Description    ", InventoryRecord.Description
INPUT "Quantity       ", InventoryRecord.Quantity
PUT #1, Rec, InventoryRecord
```
   c.
```
' List the File
GET #1,,InventoryRecord
DO UNTIL EOF(1)
    PRINT InventoryRecord.Description, InventoryRecord.Quantity
    GET #1,,InventoryRecord
LOOP
```

Appendix F
Reserved Words in BASIC

These words are reserved by BASIC and cannot be used as variable names. However, reserved words may be imbedded within a variable name. When using the reserved words in their intended fashion, be sure to properly delimit them (with spaces or other special characters required by statement syntax).

Not all of these words are reserved by all versions of Microsoft BASIC, but avoidance of the entire list will provide a measure of compatibility if the program is moved from one version to another.

ABS	DECLARE	INPUT	OR
ACCESS	DEF	INPUT$	OUT
ALIAS	DEFDBL	INSTR	OUTPUT
AND	DEFINT	INT	PAINT
ANY	DEFFN	INTEGER	PALETTE
APPEND	DEFLNG	IOCTL	PCOPY
AS	DEFSEG	IS	PEEK
ASC	DEFSNG	KEY	PEN
ATN	DEFSTR	KILL	PLAY
BASE	DEFUSR	LBOUND	PMAP
BEEP	DIM	LCASE$	POINT
BINARY	DO	LEFT$	POKE
BLOAD	DOUBLE	LEN	POS
BSAVE	DRAW	LET	PRESET
BYVAL	ELSE	LINE	PRINT
CALL	ELSEIF	LIST	PSET
CALLS	END	LOC	PUT
CASE	ENDIF	LOCAL	RANDOM
CDBL	ENVIRON	LOCATE	RANDOMIZE
CDECL	EOF	LOCK	READ
CHAIN	EQV	LOF	REDIM
CHDIR	ERASE	LOG	REM
CHR$	ERDEV	LONG	RESET
CINT	ERL	LOOP	RESTORE
CIRCLE	ERR	LPOS	RESUME
CLEAR	ERROR	LPRINT	RETURN
CLNG	EXIT	LSET	RIGHT$
CLOSE	EXP	LTRIM$	RMDIR
CLS	FIELD	MID$	RND
COLOR	FILEATTR	MKD$	RSET
COM	FILES	MKDIR	RTRIM$
COMMAND$	FIX	MKDMBF$	RUN
COMMON	FNXXXXXX	MKI$	SADD
CONST	FOR	MKL$	SCREEN
COS	FRE	MKS$	SEEK
CSNG	FREEFILE	MKSMBF$	SEG
CSRLIN	FUNCTION	MOD	SELECT
CVD	GET	NAME	SETMEM
CVDMBF	GOSUB	NEXT	SGN
CVI	GOTO	NOT	SHARED
CVL	HEX$	OCT$	SHELL
CVS	IF	OFF	SIN
CVSMBF	IMP	ON	SINGAL
DATA	INKEY$	OPEN	SINGLE
DATE$	INP	OPTION	SLEEP

SOUND	STRING$	TRON	VARSEG
SPACE$	SUB	TYPE	VIEW
SPC	SWAP	UBOUND	WAIT
SQR	SYSTEM	UCASE$	WEND
STATIC	TAB	UEVENT	WHILE
STEP	TAN	UNLOCK	WIDTH
STICK	THEN	UNTIL	WINDOW
STOP	TIMER	USING	WRITE
STR$	TIME$	VAL	XOR
STRIG	TO	VARPTR	
STRING	TROFF	VARPTR$	

Appendix G
Subprograms and Functions

Procedures

QuickBASIC now includes two powerful tools that facilitate well-structured programs. The SUB . . . END SUB can be used to define subprograms, in place of the GOSUB and RETURN; and the new FUNCTION . . . END FUNCTION statements replace the less versatile DEF FN statement. QB refers to both SUBs and FUNCTIONs as **procedures.**

Procedures are far more independent and isolated than the constructs they replace. Although a subroutine may access (and change) any variable in the program, the only variables available to procedures are those that have been explicitly "passed" to them. Also, variables may be defined within a procedure that are available *only* in that procedure. These variables are called **local variables.** (Variables that can be used everywhere, such as all those used in the body of this text, are called **global variables.**)

One of the advantages of programming with procedures is that, on a large project, different programmers may work on different parts of the program without worrying about whether their variable names will conflict with those in other parts of the program. Also, procedures may be written and stored in libraries, and used for many different programs.

Subprograms

A subprogram begins with the keyword SUB, and ends with END SUB. Each subprogram must have a name, which may be from 1 to 40 characters in length.

The SUB Statement—General Form

```
SUB ProcedureName [(ParameterList)] [STATIC]
```

The parameter list is an optional list of the variables you wish to pass from the main program to the subprogram. The variables in the list must be separated by commas. The word STATIC is used for most subprograms. Generally, the only time to omit the STATIC keyword is when a subprogram will call itself (called **recursion**).

The SUB statement—Examples

```
SUB Calculations (Test1, Test2, Test3) STATIC
SUB PrintReport (Nam$, Count) STATIC
SUB PrintTitle STATIC
```

The END SUB Statement—General Form

```
END SUB
```

Calling Subprograms

A subprogram is executed by the CALL statement. The CALL statement must also name the variables to be passed to the procedure.

The CALL Statement—General Form

```
CALL ProcedureName [(parameterlist)]
```

The CALL statement—Examples

```
CALL Calculations (Test1, Test2, Test3)
CALL PrintReport (Nam$, Count)
CALL PrintTitle
```

Passing Variables

In the examples shown, the variable names in the CALL statements exactly match those in the SUB statements. However, the names do not need to match—only the number and type of variables must match. The parameters are passed by position, not by name. That is, the contents of the first variable named in the CALL statement will be placed in the first variable named in the SUB statement. They must be the same type (single-precision, double-precision, integer, or string).

This sample program shows different names used in the CALL and the SUB statements.

Program Listing

```
' **** Program Mainline ****
LET Word$ = "THIS IS A BUNCH OF WORDS"
LET Num1 = 100
LET Num2 = 50

CALL TestSub (Word$, Num1, Num2)

PRINT
PRINT "Printed from the Main Program"
PRINT
PRINT Word$, Num1; Num2
END

' **** Test Procedure ****
SUB TestSub (Sentence$, First, Second) STATIC
    PRINT
    PRINT "Printed from the Procedure"
    PRINT
    PRINT Sentence$, First; Second
END SUB
```

Program Execution

```
Printed from the Procedure

THIS IS A BUNCH OF WORDS   100   50

Printed from the Main Program

THIS IS A BUNCH OF WORDS   100   50
```

Sharing Variables in All Procedures

Another method is available for passing variables to procedures. Variables may be declared as SHARED, which makes them global rather than local. All procedures that are called have access to global variables. This may be advisable for some program variables that must be used in many subprograms. However, making variables global nullifies the structured programming advantage of local variables.

The COMMON and SHARED Statements—General Form

```
COMMON SHARED variable list
```

COMMON and SHARED are two separate statements that are combined here to accomplish our goals. In some other contexts they may be used alone. The variables named in the list are separated by commas.

The COMMON and SHARED Statements—Examples

```
COMMON SHARED Nam$, Amount, Total
COMMON SHARED Miles, Km
COMMON SHARED Nam$, Address$, Phone$
```

Program Example Using Shared Variables

```
' Program To Calculate the Average of Three
' Test Scores
'                   Variables Used:

'          Student$          Name of Student
'          Test1             Score for Test 1
'          Test2             Score for Test 2
'          Test3             Score for Test 3
'          Avg               Test average

'************ Program Mainline ************

COMMON SHARED Student$, Test1, Test2, Test3, Avg

CALL InputData
CALL CalculateAverages
CALL PrintOutput
END

'************** Data Input ***************
SUB InputData STATIC
    INPUT "ENTER STUDENT NAME   ", Student$
    INPUT "SCORE FOR TEST 1     ", Test1
    INPUT "SCORE FOR TEST 2     ", Test2
    INPUT "SCORE FOR TEST 3     ", Test3
END SUB
'************** Calculations **************

SUB CalculateAverages STATIC
    LET Avg = (Test1 + Test2 + Test3) / 3
    LET Avg = INT(Avg + .5)
END SUB

'************** Print Output **************

SUB PrintOutput STATIC
    PRINT
    PRINT "THE AVERAGE FOR "; Student$; " IS"; Avg
END SUB
```

Functions

Functions share many similarities with subprograms, as well as with the DEF FN statement. Functions are defined with FUNCTION . . . END FUNCTION statements. They may pass arguments, but are not invoked with the CALL statement. Instead, functions are used in expressions, such as any BASIC supplied or user-written function (i.e. INT, ABS, LEFT$, VAL).

The FUNCTION and END FUNCTION Statements—General Form

```
FUNCTION FunctionName [(ParameterList)] [STATIC]
    . . .
        FunctionName = . . .
    . . .
END FUNCTION
```

The FUNCTION and END FUNCTION Statements—Examples

```
FUNCTION CountCommas(Check$) STATIC
    CountCommas = . . .
END FUNCTION

FUNCTION Center$(Inp$) STATIC
    Center$ = . . .
END FUNCTION
```

When a function is executed, it returns a value. The name of the function determines the type of value returned—a string name returns a string value; a single-precision numeric name returns a single-precision value. Within the function definition, the function name must be assigned the value to return.

Entering Subprograms and Functions with the Editor

QuickBASIC's smart editor is a big help when entering procedures. To begin a new subprogram or function, type a SUB or FUNCTION statement. The editor opens a new workspace to hold the SUB or FUNCTION. When you want to change from one procedure to another, or to the mainline, press F2. Any procedure or the mainline may be selected from the F2 screen. The editor also takes care of adding the DEFINE SUB and DEFINE FUNCTION statements that must appear in any program using procedures. The statements are added when the file is saved.

Example Program to Demonstrate Subprograms and Functions

```
' ** Data Entry Program To Demonstrate Subprograms And Functions **
'
'   This program has a mainline, 4 subprograms, and two functions.
'
'  The DECLARE SUB and DECLARE FUNCTION statements below were
'     automatically added by the editor, when the program was
'     saved
'
DECLARE SUB DrawFormOnScreen ()
DECLARE FUNCTION Validated! (Amount!)
DECLARE FUNCTION CheckDigit! (Numb$)
DECLARE SUB InputValidData (Idno$, Amt!)
DECLARE SUB ProcessData (ID$, Amount!)
DECLARE SUB TestForFinish (Finished$)

    ***************** Program Mainline *****************
MainLine:
    DO
        CALL DrawFormOnScreen
        CALL InputValidData(ID$, Amount)
        CALL ProcessData(ID$, Amount)
        CALL TestForFinish(Finished$)
    LOOP WHILE Finished$ = "Y"
END
```

```
' ** Subprogram to Draw A Data Entry Form on the Screen *
SUB DrawFormOnScreen STATIC
    CLS
    LOCATE 4, 24
    PRINT "B I G G I E S   I N V E N T O R Y"
    LOCATE 9, 24
    PRINT "ACCOUNT NUMBER"
    LOCATE 12, 24
    PRINT "AMOUNT"
    COLOR 0, 7                          'Reverse Image
    LOCATE 9, 43
    PRINT SPACE$(6)
    LOCATE 12, 43
    PRINT SPACE$(10)
    COLOR 7, 0                          'Back to white on black
END SUB

'  ***** Subprogram to Input And Validate the Data ********
'    Repeatedly Inputs Data Until Valid Data is Entered.
SUB InputValidData (Idno$, Amt) STATIC
    COLOR 0, 7                          'Reverse image
    DO
        LOCATE 9, 43
        PRINT SPACE$(6)                 'Blank out input area
        LOCATE 9, 43
        INPUT "", Idno$
    LOOP UNTIL CheckDigit(Idno$) <> 0
    DO
        LOCATE 12, 43
        PRINT SPACE$(10)                'Blank out input area
        LOCATE 12, 43
        INPUT "", Amt
    LOOP UNTIL Validated(Amt) <> 0
    COLOR 7, 0                          'White on black
END SUB

'  *********** Function to Calculate a Check Digit *****
'    A valid number sets the function name to 1. A number that
'       has too few digits or does not pass the check digit test
'       sets the function name to 0. See chapter 7 (page 198)
'       for a discussion of check digit calculations.
FUNCTION CheckDigit (Numb$) STATIC
    IF LEN(Numb$) < 6 THEN
        LET CheckDigit = 0
    ELSE
        LET D1 = VAL(LEFT$(Numb$, 1))
        LET D2 = VAL(MID$(Numb$, 2, 1))
        LET D3 = VAL(MID$(Numb$, 3, 1))
        LET D4 = VAL(MID$(Numb$, 4, 1))
        LET D5 = VAL(MID$(Numb$, 5, 1))
        LET D6 = VAL(MID$(Numb$, 6, 1))
        LET Check = D1 + D2 * 2 + D3 + D4 * 2 + D5
        LET Check = VAL(RIGHT$(STR$(Check), 1))
        IF Check = D6 THEN
            LET CheckDigit = 1
        ELSE
            LET CheckDigit = 0
        END IF
    END IF
END FUNCTION
```

```
' *** Function to Validate the Numeric Amount Field ***
'      Any amount < 0 or greater than 99999.99 sets the function
'         name to 0, and valid amount sets the function to 1.
FUNCTION Validated (Amount) STATIC
    IF Amount < 0 THEN
       LET Validated = 0
    ELSEIF Amount > 99999.99 THEN
       LET Validated = 0
    ELSE
       LET Validated = 1
    END IF
END FUNCTION


' ******** Stub Module For Processing Data ************
SUB ProcessData (ID$, Amount) STATIC
    'Stub module
END SUB


' ********** Subprogram to Check For More Data *********
'     Passes back only one, uppercase character
SUB TestForFinish (Finished$) STATIC
    LOCATE 24, 10
    INPUT "More data? (Y/N)", Finished$
    LET Finished$ = UCASE$(LEFT$(Finished$, 1))
END SUB
```

Appendix H
Using Special Functions of Printers

Special Printer Functions

Most printers available for use on microcomputers have capabilities beyond straight text printing. Many dot matrix printers have multiple character sets such as italics, condensed printing, or extrawide characters. Features that may often be switched include line length, margins, tabs, underlining, vertical and horizontal spacing, and proportional spacing.

You have already seen how a special, nonprinting character can control the printer. In chapter 6, you learned to send the printer a form-feed character, CHR$(12), to cause the paper to advance to the top of the next page. CHR$(12) is generally accepted as the form-feed. Most other special characters are *not* standard, however. Each printer manufacturer chooses a set of control codes that control the specific functions of that printer.

Some printer manuals clearly demonstrate the method of controlling the special features. Others print tables of codes and leave it to the programmer to figure out. A term often used is "escape sequence." This refers to a sequence of characters, preceded by the Escape character [CHR$(27)—refer to the ASCII code chart in appendix D]. For example, if your printer manual requires an ESC (Escape) and a "Q" to turn on a feature, the statement would be similar to:

```
LPRINT CHR$(27); "Q"
```

The examples that follow are for the Epson/IBM standard. Many other printers emulate this standard. If you do not get good results, consult your printer manual for the correct codes. The examples are intended as a guideline to help you figure out how to use the specific codes for your printer.

```
LPRINT CHR$(27); CHR$(87); CHR$(1) 'Turn on double wide characters
LPRINT "BIG TITLE"
LPRINT CHR$(27); CHR$(87); CHR$(0) 'Turn off double wide characters
LPRINT
LPRINT "REGULAR SIZE"
LPRINT CHR$(15)                     'Turn on condensed mode
LPRINT
LPRINT "DOWNRIGHT SMALL"
LPRINT
LPRINT CHR$(18)                     'Turn off condensed mode
LPRINT "BACK TO NORMAL"; CHR$(27); CHR$(45); CHR$(1);
       "UNDERLINED "; CHR$(27); CHR$(45); CHR$(0);
       "AND NOT UNDERLINED"
```

Program Execution

BIG TITLE

REGULAR SIZE

DOWNRIGHT SMALL

BACK TO NORMAL UNDERLINED AND NOT UNDERLINED

Example Program: Controlling Many Printer Features

```
' Program to Use the Special Functions of the Epson Printer

' May Be Used As A Stand-Alone Program, or Individual
'    Subroutines May Be Included in Programs

'************** Program Mainline **********************
DO
    GOSUB DisplayMenu
    SELECT CASE Choice
        CASE 1
            GOSUB CompressedModeOn
        CASE 2
            GOSUB CompressedModeOff
        CASE 3
            GOSUB DoubleWidthOn
        CASE 4
            GOSUB DoubleWidthOff
        CASE 5
            GOSUB EmphasizedOn
        CASE 6
            GOSUB EmphasizedOff
        CASE 7
            GOSUB SuperscriptOn
        CASE 8
            GOSUB SubscriptOn
        CASE 9
            GOSUB DoubleStrikeOn
        CASE 10
            GOSUB SuperSubDoubleOff
        CASE 11
            GOSUB ItalicOn
        CASE 12
            GOSUB ItalicOff
        CASE 13
            GOSUB ResetLineLength
        CASE 14
            GOSUB SetNumberLines
        CASE 15
            GOSUB AllSpecialFunctionsOff
        CASE 16
            CLS
        CASE ELSE
    END SELECT
LOOP UNTIL Choice = 16
END
```

```
'************ Display Menu And Input Choice **********
DisplayMenu:
   CLS
   PRINT TAB(24); "EPSON PRINTER SPECIAL FUNCTIONS"
   PRINT
   PRINT
   PRINT TAB(15); "1.    Turn on compressed character mode"
   PRINT TAB(15); "2.    Turn off compressed character mode"
   PRINT TAB(15); "3.    Turn on double width printing"
   PRINT TAB(15); "4.    Turn off double width printing"
   PRINT TAB(15); "5.    Turn on emphasized mode"
   PRINT TAB(15); "6.    Turn off emphasized mode"
   PRINT TAB(15); "7.    Turn on superscript mode"
   PRINT TAB(15); "8.    Turn on subscript mode"
   PRINT TAB(15); "9.    Turn on double strike mode"
   PRINT TAB(14); "10.   Turn off superscript, subscript and double strike"
   PRINT TAB(14); "11.   Turn on italic character set"
   PRINT TAB(14); "12.   Turn off italic character set"
   PRINT TAB(14); "13.   Reset line length"
   PRINT TAB(14); "14.   Set number of lines per page"
   PRINT TAB(14); "15.   Turn off all special functions"
   PRINT TAB(14); "16.   Exit Program"
   PRINT
   PRINT
   PRINT TAB(19); "Enter choice (1-16)";
   INPUT Choice
RETURN


'************ Turn On Compressed Mode ****************
CompressedModeOn:
   LPRINT CHR$(15);
RETURN


'************ Turn Off Compressed Mode ***************
CompressedModeOff:
   LPRINT CHR$(18);
RETURN


'************ Turn On Double Width Printing **********
DoubleWidthOn:
   LPRINT CHR$(27); CHR$(87); CHR$(1);
RETURN


'************ Turn Off Double Width Printing *********
DoubleWidthOff:
   LPRINT CHR$(27); CHR$(87); CHR$(0);
RETURN


'************ Turn Emphasized On *********************
EmphasizedOn:
   LPRINT CHR$(27); CHR$(69);
RETURN


'************ Turn Off Emphasized ********************
EmphasizedOff:
   LPRINT CHR$(27); CHR$(70);
RETURN


'************ Turn On Superscript ********************
SuperscriptOn:
   LPRINT CHR$(27); CHR$(83); CHR$(0);
RETURN


'************ Turn On Subscript **********************
SubscriptOn:
   LPRINT CHR$(27); CHR$(83); CHR$(1);
RETURN
```

```
'*************** Turn On Double Strike *******************
DoubleStrikeOn:
   LPRINT CHR$(27); CHR$(72);
RETURN


'**** Turn Off Superscript, Subscript, And Double Strike
SuperSubDoubleOff:
   LPRINT CHR$(27); CHR$(72);
RETURN


'*************** Turn On Italic ************************
ItalicOn:
   LPRINT CHR$(27); CHR$(52);
RETURN


'************* Turn Off Italic ************************
ItalicOff:
   LPRINT CHR$(27); CHR$(53);
RETURN


'************* Reset Line Length ********************
ResetLineLength:
   CLS
   PRINT
   PRINT
   PRINT
   PRINT TAB(15); "RESET LINE LENGTH"
   PRINT
   PRINT TAB(10); "NUMBER OF CHARACTERS FOR LINE LENGTH";
   INPUT Length
   LPRINT CHR$(27); "Q"; CHR$(Length)
RETURN


'************* Set Number Of Lines Per Page ***********
SetNumberLines:
   CLS
   PRINT
   PRINT
   PRINT
   PRINT TAB(15); "HOW MANY LINES PER PAGE";
   INPUT Lines
   PRINT
   INPUT "DO YOU WANT TO SKIP OVER PERFORATION (Y/N)"; Ans$
   INPUT "ALIGN PRINTER FOR FIRST LINE AND PRESS RETURN"; X$
   LPRINT CHR$(27); "C"; CHR$(Lines);
   IF UCASE$(Ans$) = "Y" THEN
       LPRINT CHR$(27); "N"; CHR$(6);
   END IF
RETURN


'************* Turn Off All Special Functions **********
AllSpecialFunctionsOff:
   'Resets all special modes to power up state (including TOF)
   LPRINT CHR$(27); CHR$(64);
RETURN


'************* End of Program ************************
```

Appendix I
Error Trapping

Error Trapping

When errors occur in program execution, a BASIC error message is printed. Common error messages seen by programmers include SYNTAX ERROR and ILLEGAL FUNCTION CALL, which are both caused by misuse of the BASIC language. It goes without saying that all programmer errors must be removed from a program before it is turned over to a user.

There are some errors that may occur when the user runs the program. The user may neglect to switch on the printer, the printer may be out of paper, the door of the diskette reader may be open, or the wrong disk inserted. BASIC also prints error messages for this type of error and halts program execution. A complete list of all possible errors can be found in a QuickBASIC manual or the QB4.5 or QBASIC Help screens under *Run Time Error Codes*. See table I.1 for a partial listing of common errors.

A program can intercept the error conditions, handle the situation, and resume processing. Having the program take care of the error condition (rather than allow BASIC to send the standard system message) is called error trapping. To accomplish the error trapping, two new BASIC statements are needed—ON ERROR and RESUME—and a new function—ERR.

The ON ERROR Statement—General Form

```
ON ERROR GOTO  line label of error routine
```

For error trapping to occur, the ON ERROR statement must be executed before any error condition occurs. Therefore, it is recommended that the ON ERROR statement appear at the beginning of the program. If any error occurs later in the program, the subroutine named on the ON ERROR statement will be executed.

The ON ERROR Statement—Example

```
'********** PROGRAM MAINLINE ***************
ON ERROR GOTO ErrorHandler
...

END
'******** ERROR HANDLING SUBROUTINE *******
ErrorHandler:
```

If any error occurs during program execution (including syntax errors), control will pass to the error handling subroutine. In the subroutine, the error numbers may be checked, messages printed to the user, and a decision may be made to continue processing or to abort the program.

Determining the Cause of the Error with the ERR Function

When an error occurs, the ERR function can be used to determine the error code. The error handling program code can then check the code, print a message, and take appropriate action.

The ERR Function—Examples

```
IF ERR = 27 THEN          'Out of Paper error
   PRINT "Check the printer, and press any key to continue. . ."
   LET Wt$ = INPUT$(1)   'Wait for a keypress
   RESUME
END IF

IF ERR = 71 THEN          'Disk Drive Not Ready error
   PRINT "Check the disk drive"
   PRINT "Press any key to continue. . ."
   LET Wt$ = INPUT$(1)    'Wait for keypress
   RESUME
END IF
```

Table I.1
Common error codes.

Number	Message
1	NEXT without FOR
2	Syntax error
3	RETURN without GOSUB
4	Out of data
5	Illegal function call
6	Overflow (The number computed is too large to fit into the variable type being used.)
9	Subscript out of range
11	Division by zero
19	No RESUME (The error trapping routine has been entered, but it does not contain a RESUME statement.)
24	Device timeout (A hardware error.)
25	Device fault (A hardware error.)
27	Out of Paper (Either the printer is out of paper or not switched on.)
39	CASE ELSE expected
52	Bad file name or number
53	File not found (The file specified does not exist.)
54	Bad file mode
55	File already open

57	Device I/O error
	(An error on an I/O device—some systems return this error for disk drive door open or disk not inserted in drive—see error 71.)
58	File already exists
61	Disk full
62	Input past end of file
63	Bad record number
70	Disk Write Protect
	(An attempt was made to write on a disk that is write-protected.)
71	Disk not ready
	(The disk drive door is open or a diskette is not in the drive—see error 57 above.)
72	Disk media error
76	Path not found

Resuming Program Execution

The RESUME statement is used to continue program execution after an error occurs. The statement appears only in error-handling program code.

The RESUME Statement

```
RESUME
RESUME NEXT
RESUME  line label for continuation
```

The first example (RESUME by itself) will resume execution at the statement that caused the error. The RESUME NEXT will resume execution at the statement immediately following the one that caused the error. The third example, "RESUME line label," will resume execution at the named line.

```
IF ERR = 70 THEN                'Disk Write Protect error
    PRINT "The diskette is write-protected."
    PRINT "Press any key when ready"
    LET Wt$ = INPUT$(1)
    RESUME
END IF
```

What If You Don't Want to RESUME?

Some error conditions can be handled by the program, others cannot. You would not want to check for every possible error condition in your program. The statement

```
ON ERROR GOTO 0
```

turns off error trapping. If there is an error condition that has not been resolved (with a RESUME), BASIC will print the system error message and halt execution.

Any error handling subroutine should include two elements:

1. What to do for specific errors.
   Check error codes
   Print messages
   Perhaps await a keypress
   RESUME
2. What to do for any other error.
   ON ERROR GOTO 0

Example Program: Error Trapping

Program Listing

```
'  *************** Error Trapping Example ************
'  ****************** Program Mainline ***************
ON ERROR GOTO ErrorHandler
'  ******* Generate Some Errors to Test Program *******
OPEN "TESTFILE" FOR INPUT AS #1   'Non-existent file
LPRINT "HELLO PRINTER"            'With printer turned off
END


'  ************* Error Handling Routine **************

ErrorHandler:
    SELECT CASE ERR
        CASE 57, 71
            PRINT "Check diskette drive, and press any key to continue"
            LET Wt$ = INPUT$(1)
            RESUME
        CASE 53
            PRINT "The file needed for this program is not on the disk"
            PRINT "Mount the correct disk, and press any key"
            LET Wt$ = INPUT$(1)
            RESUME
        CASE 27, 24
            PRINT "Check the printer, and press any key to continue"
            LET Wt$ = INPUT$(1)
            RESUME
        CASE ELSE
            ON ERROR GOTO 0
    END SELECT
```

Note for Printer Errors: The error condition 27 (printer out of paper or not ready) may or may not occur, depending on the specific computer system running. Many computers have both hardware and software enhancements that temporarily store output destined for the printer. These *buffers* and *spoolers* send an indication to BASIC that the printed output has been properly received, even though the printer may be switched off. BASIC cannot detect this condition.

Testing the Error Conditions

Any error condition can be "turned on" with the ERROR statement. This statement simulates the error condition and must be placed after the ON ERROR statement.

The ERROR Statement—General Form

```
ERROR  error number
```

The ERROR Statement—Example

```
ERROR 27
```

By placing this statement in a program, the error trap for error number 27 can be tested.

Appendix J
Summary of BASIC Statements and Functions

Statement	Effect
BEEP	Beeps the speaker. Same as PRINT CHR$(7).
CALL subroutine[(arguments)]	Calls a subroutine.
CASE ConstantList CASE ELSE	Used in SELECT CASE structure.
CIRCLE [STEP] (X, Y), radius [,PaletteColor [,StartAngle, EndAngle [,AspectRatio]]]	Draws a circle in medium or high resolution graphics modes.
CLEAR	Reinitializes all program variables and closes files.
CLOSE #filenum	Closes a file.
CLS	Clears the screen.
COLOR [foreground] [,[background] [,border]]	Sets colors in screen mode 0.
COLOR [background] [,[palette]]	Sets color choices in screen mode 1.
COLOR [foreground] [,background]	Sets colors in SCREEN mode 7–10.
COLOR [foreground]	Sets colors in SCREEN mode 11–13.
COMMON variable [, variable2,...]	Passes variables to a chained program.
COMMON SHARED	Defines variables as global.
DATA constant [,constant2,...]	Provides the constants to be read by READ statements.
DATE$ = DateString	Sets the current date.
DECLARE function or sub name (arguments)	Declares a function or subprogram.
DEF FN name(argument(s)) = expression	Defines a function for later execution.
DEF DBL letter [-letter-][,letter[-letter]]	Declares that variables beginning with the named letters will be double-precision.
DEF INT letter [-letter] [,letter [-letter]]	Declares that variables beginning with the named letters will be integer.
DEF LNG letter [-letter] [,letter [-letter]]	Declares that variables with the named letters will be long integer.
DEF SEG [= segment.start]	Defines the beginning of the current segment of memory for subsequent BLOAD, BSAVE, PEEK, or POKE.

DEF SNG letter [-letter] [,letter [-letter]]	Declares that variables beginning with the named letters will be single-precision.
DEF STR letter [-letter] [,letter [-letter]]	Declares that variables beginning with the named letters will be string variables.
DIM array name(number of elements) [,array2(elements),...]	Establishes the number of elements and allocates storage for arrays.
DO [{WHILE|UNTIL} condition]	Begin a loop. (End with the LOOP statement.)
DRAW string	In graphics mode, draws an object using a graphics definition language. (Not covered in this text, consult your manual.)
END	Stops execution of the program and closes all files.
END IF	End of IF block.
END SUB	End of a subprogram.
ERASE arrayname [,arrayname]	Zeroes out arrays.
EXIT {DEF|FOR|FUNCTION|SUB}	Provides an exit from constructs.
FOR loop index = initial value TO terminal value [STEP increment]	Controls execution of a loop. (The NEXT statement indicates the end of the loop.)
FUNCTION name [(paramenters)][STATIC]	Establish a function. (End with END FUNCTION.)
GET #filenum [,recordnumber]	Reads data from a random file. If the record number is not specified, the *next* record is read.
GOSUB linelabel	Begins execution of a subroutine. The RETURN statement returns from the subroutine.
IF condition THEN statement(s) [ELSE statement(s)]	Performs the statement(s) following THEN when the condition evaluates *true*. Performs the statements following the ELSE (if included) when the condition evaluates *false*.

IF condition THEN
   [statement(s)]
[ELSEIF condition THEN
    statement(s)]
[ELSE
    statement(s)]
END IF
	Block IF statement.

INPUT [;] ["prompt";,] variable [,variable2,...]	Inputs data from the keyboard. If a prompt is included, it prints before the input occurs.
INPUT #filenum, variable [,variable2,...]	Reads data from a sequential data file.
KILL "filename"	Deletes a file from disk.
[LET] variable = expression	Evaluates the expression and assigns the result to the variable.
LINE [(XStart, YStart)]—(XEnd, YEnd) [,[ColorAttribute] [,B[F]]]	Draws a line or box in medium or high resolution graphics modes.

LINE INPUT [;] ["prompt";] stringvariable	Inputs all characters (limit 255) typed at the keyboard. Accepts all characters including commas and colons, until ENTER is pressed.
LINE INPUT #filenumber, stringvariable	Reads characters from a disk file until a carriage-return character is encountered (up to 255 characters). All characters including delimiters will be placed into stringvariable.
LOCATE row, column [,cursor]	Places the cursor at the row and column position specified. The optional cursor parameter controls the visibility of the cursor.
LOOP[{WHILE|UNTIL}]condition	Closes a loop that began with DO.
LPRINT [items to print]	Prints data on the printer. Items are separated by commas or semicolons. Without the item list, a blank line is printed.
LPRINT USING "stringliteral"; items to print LPRINT USING stringvariable; items to print	Prints data on the printer, according to the format specified in the string literal or variable.
MID$(stringvariable, start position, number of characters) = stringexpression	Replaces part of a string variable with the string expression.
NAME "old filename" AS "new filename"	Renames a disk file.
NEXT [loop index]	Terminates a FOR...NEXT loop.
ON ERROR GOTO line label	Enables program error trapping and specifies the line label of the error handling routine.
ON numeric expression GOSUB list of line labels	Evaluates the numeric expression and begins execution of the subroutine specified.
ON numeric expression GOTO list of line labels	Evaluates the numeric expression and branches to the corresponding line label.
OPEN mode, #filenum, "filename"	Opens a sequential data file. Mode must be "I" for input files, "O" for output files, or "A" for append.
OPEN "filename" FOR mode AS #filenum	Opens a sequential data file. Mode must be INPUT, OUTPUT, or APPEND.
OPEN "R", #filenum, "filename", reclength	Opens a random data file.
OPEN "filename" [FOR RANDOM] AS #filenum [LEN = reclength]	Opens a random data file.
OPTION BASE number	Sets the minimum value for array subscripts. Must be 0 or 1.
PAINT (X, Y) [[,FillColor] [,BoundaryColor]]	Fills an area on the screen with the selected color, in medium resolution graphics mode.
PALETTE	Assigns colors to attributes.
PLAY string	Plays music specified in string. A special music definition language includes letters for notes, length, tempo, rests, and speed.
POKE MemoryOffset, value	Writes a value (range 0–65535) into the byte specified by offset, in the current memory segment. The current segment is set by DEF SEG.

PRESET (X, Y) [, PaletteColor]	Resets a point in medium or high resolution mode graphics.
PRINT [items to print]	Displays data on the screen. Items to print may be separated by semicolons or commas (with different results).
PRINT #filenumber, variable [, variable2, . . .]	Prints data into a sequential file.
PRINT USING "string literal"; items to print PRINT USING stringvariable; items to print	Displays data on the screen, according to the format specified in the string literal or variable.
PSET (X, Y) [, ColorAttribute]	Draws a point in medium or high resolution mode graphics. Note that color is valid only for medium resolution.
PUT #filenum [,RecordNumber], RecordName	Writes data from a record variable into a random file in the record number named. If the record number is omitted, the record is written in the *next* position.
RANDOMIZE [numeric expression|TIMER]	Reseeds the random number generator. If the expression is omitted, a seed is requested from the keyboard.
READ variable [,variable2,...]	Reads constants from DATA statements into the variable(s) named.
REM remark	Inserts a remark into the program. An alternate format allows substitution of a single quote (') for the word REM.
RESTORE	Resets the DATA pointer to the beginning of the program so that data may be reread.
RESUME RESUME NEXT RESUME linelabel	Resumes execution after error trapping with ON...GOTO.
RETURN	Returns from a subroutine to the statement immediately following the GOSUB.
SCREEN [Mode] [,[Colorburst] [, [ActivePage] [,VisualPage]]]	Sets the screen mode for low, medium, or high resolution modes.
SELECT CASE expression	Begins a CASE structure. (Ends with END SELECT.)
SHARED variable list	Defines variables as global for use in subprograms. Used alone or in COMMON or DIM statements.
SHELL [command string]	Allows execution of DOS commands, programs, and batch files.
SOUND frequency, duration	Generates sound through the speaker. Frequency range 37–32767, duration range .0015–65535.
STOP	Halts program execution. May be resumed with a CONT command.

SUB SubProgramName [(parameters)][STATIC]	Begins a subprogram. (Ends with END SUB.)
SWAP variable1, variable2	Exchanges the contents of the two variables.
TIME$ = string	Sets the current time. Form of string is "hh:mm:ss."
TYPE VariableType	Defines a data structure with one or more elements. (Ends with END TYPE.)
VIEW (V.left, V.top) — (V.right, V.bottom) [,[ColorAttribute] [,boundary]]	Defines a rectangular viewport for drawing graphs in medium or high resolution graphics modes.
VIEW PRINT [TopLine to BottomLine]	Establishes boundaries of a text viewport.
WEND	Terminates a WHILE/WEND loop.
WHILE condition	Begins a program loop. The statements in the loop will be repeated as long as the condition evaluates *true*.
WIDTH [columns][,lines]	Sets the number of columns and lines to display on the screen.
WIDTH "LPT1:", LineLength	Sets the length of the line on the printer.
WINDOW (WLeft, WTop) — (WRight, WBottom)	Redefines the coordinates of the screen or viewport in medium or high resolution graphics. Scales the area to World Coordinates.
WRITE #filenum, variable [,variable2,...]	Writes data in a sequential data file.

BASIC Functions	Function	Returns

Note: All functions that have a $ in the function name return strings. Numeric function names always return numeric values.

Function	Returns
ABS(X)	Absolute value of X.
ASC(X$)	ASCII code number of the first character of X$.
ATN(X)	Arctangent of X (in radians).
CDBL(X)	Double-precision value of X.
CHR$(X)	The character represented by the ASCII code number X.
CINT(X)	X rounded to an integer.
CLNG(X)	X rounded to a long integer.
COS(X)	Cosine of angle X. (X must be in radians.)
CSNG(X)	Single-precision value of X.
CSRLIN	Current row of cursor
CVD(X$)	Double-precision numeric equivalent of an eight-byte string.
CVI(X$)	Integer numeric equivalent of a two-byte string.
CVL(X$)	Long integer equivalent of a two-byte string.
CVS(X$)	Single-precision numeric equivalent of a four-byte string.

DATE$	Retrieves the current date as a ten-character string in the form (mm-dd-yyyy).
EOF(#filenum)	Tests for an end-of-file condition. True at the end of a sequential file.
ERR	Code for error.
EXP(X)	Calculates e to the power of X (where e = 2.71828 . . .).
FIX(X)	Truncated integer portion of X.
HEX$(X)	A string that represents the hexadecimal (base sixteen) value of X.
INKEY$	Returns one character from the keyboard, or a null string if no key has been pressed. Does not suspend program execution.
INPUT$(X)	Returns a string of characters from the keyboard, X characters in length. Suspends program execution.
INSTR([B,] X$,Y$)	Position in X$ where substring Y$ begins. Optional B gives starting search position within X$.
INT(X)	Largest integer less than or equal to X.
LBOUND(array[,n])	Lowest subscript allowable for array. N, if used, specifies which dimension of a multidimensional array.
LCASE$	Lower-case equivalent of X$.
LEFT$(X$,N)	Leftmost N characters of X$.
LEN(X$)	Number of characters in X$.
LOC(#filenumber)	Record number of last record read or written in a random file.
LOF(#filenumber)	Number of bytes in the file specified.
LOG(X)	Natural logarithm of X. (X must be positive.)
LPOS(1)	Current position of the print head within the printer buffer for LPT1.
LTRIM$	X$ with leading spaces removed.
MID$(X$,B [,N])	Substring of X$, beginning in position B for a length of N.
MKD$(D)	Eight-byte string from a double-precision numeric value.
MKI$(I)	Two-byte string from an integer numeric value.
MKL$(L)	Four-byte string from a long integer.
MKS$(S)	Four-byte string from a single-precision numeric value.
NUMERIC expression MOD numeric expression	
	Returns the remainder of a division.

OCT$(X)	A string that represents the octal (base 8) value of X.
PEEK(X)	The byte read from memory location X.
PMAP(coordinate, selection)	Corresponding physical screen coordinate or world coordinate. Coordinate may be X or Y. Selection: 0 = map world coordinate x to screen x 1 = map world coordinate y to screen y 2 = map screen coordinate x to world x 3 = map screen coordinate y to world y
POS(X)	Current horizontal (column) position of the cursor.
RIGHT$(X$,N)	Rightmost N characters of X$.
RND[(X)]	A double-precision random number between 0 and 1.
RTRIM(X$)	X$ with trailing spaces removed.
SGN(X)	Sign of X. 1 = positive; -1 = negative; 0 = zero.
SIN(X)	Sine of angle X. (X must be in radians.)
SPACE$(N)	A string of N spaces.
SPC(N)	N spaces inserted in a PRINT or LPRINT statement.
SQR(X)	Square root of X.
STR$(X)	The string representation of X.
STRING$(N,C$) STRING$(N,X)	A string of length N comprised of the single character C$ or ASCII code number X.
TAB(X)	Print pointer moved to position X on the line. Used in a PRINT or LPRINT statement.
TAN(X)	Tangent of angle X. (X must be in radians.)
TIME$	Retrieve the current time as an eight-character string in the form (hh:mm:ss).
TIMER	Number of seconds elapsed since midnight.
UBOUND(array[,N])	Largest subscript allowable for array. N, if used, specifies which dimension of multi-dimensional array.
UCASE$(X$)	Upper-case equivalent of X$.
USR	Calls an assembly language subroutine.
VAL(X$)	Numeric value of X$.

Appendix K
Converting Programs from Microsoft BASICA or GW-BASIC to QuickBASIC or QBASIC

Compatibility

Programs written in interpreted Microsoft BASIC (BASICA or GW-BASIC) will generally compile and run correctly in QuickBASIC and QBASIC. However, the source program files are stored in a different format on disk, and may require conversion before they can be loaded by QuickBASIC.

A few BASIC statements are no longer legal in QuickBASIC, and a few may behave in a little different manner and may require modification. The statements that cannot be used are those BASIC commands that manipulate the source program. These statements are not legal in QB:

AUTO	LIST	NEW
CONT	LLIST	RENUM
DELETE	LOAD	SAVE
EDIT	MERGE	

These statements may cause problems, as QB requires that they appear at the beginning of the program:

COMMON
DEF *type*
DIM

These statements may require modification:

BLOAD	CHAIN	RESUME
BSAVE	DRAW	RUN
CALL	PLAY	

The BASIC Program Line

Although line length has not changed from the 255-character maximum, several aspects concerning long lines have been changed. The QB editor will not accept Ctrl-Return or Ctrl-J to force the cursor to the next line. However, programs containing those characters that were written for the interpreter will load and run correctly, but the long lines will not display correctly on the screen.

Lines that are longer than 80 characters (including those transferred from the interpreter) will only display the first 80 characters on the screen. The rest of the line may be viewed or edited by placing the cursor on that line, and moving the cursor to the right. Pressing the End key will show the right-most characters of the line.

Loading and Running a Program Created with the Interpreter

QuickBASIC saves programs on disk in a special, compressed format. The interpreter also saves programs in a compressed format. Unfortunately, the two formats are different and incompatible. But both the interpreter and QB will save and reload programs stored in text format, using the ASCII code (American Standard Code for Information Interchange). Also, most editors and word processors can produce text files, which may be called text, ASCII, or non-document format. Since the ASCII format can be used by both versions of BASIC, the program must be loaded in BASICA (or GW-BASIC), and saved in ASCII format. Then QB will be able to retrieve it with the *Open* option on the *File* menu.

Example: This example assumes two diskette drives, A: and B:. A: is used for the diskette holding interpreted BASIC, and then switched to the QuickBASIC diskette at the appropriate point. The diskette in B: holds the program to be transferred.

1. Start interpreted BASIC.
   A>BASICA (or GWBASIC, or BASIC)
2. Load the program you want to transfer.
   LOAD "B:MYPROG"
3. Save the program in ASCII format.
   SAVE "B:MYPROG",A
4. Exit BASIC.
   SYSTEM
5. Remove the BASIC diskette in A: and replace it with the QuickBASIC or QBASIC diskette.
6. Start QuickBASIC.
   A>QB or A>QBASIC
7. For QB 4.0 only, clear the introductory screen with the Enter Key. In QB 4.5 or QBASIC, clear the screen with the Escape Key.
8. Open the *File* menu and select *Open*.
   Alt, F
   Highlight *Open* and press Enter.
9. Type the name of the program, and press Enter.
   B:MYPROG

QB will save programs in ASCII code if requested. Select the *Text* option on the *Save As* dialog box, selected from the *File* menu.

Glossary

Accumulator

A numeric variable used to accumulate a sum such as a total field.

Algorithm

A step-by-step procedure for solving a problem.

Append

To add data to the end of a sequential file.

Argument

The value(s) supplied to a function in order for the function to perform its specified operation.

Arithmetic expression

A numeric value, which may be one variable or constant or a series of constants, variables, functions, and arithmetic operators.

Arithmetic operator

The symbols used for arithmetic operations: $+ \; - \; * \; / \; \wedge$

Array

A group of variables referenced by a single name. To use any one individual variable (element), a subscript must be used.

ASCII

American Standard Code for Information Interchange. The code used by microcomputers to store characters. Each character (letter, digit, special symbol) is represented by a unique number. *See* appendix C.

Background

Each character on the screen is drawn in a box nine dots by nine dots. The dots that form the characters are called foreground, those surrounding the character are the background. *See also* Foreground.

Binary search

A method used to locate a particular value in a sorted array by repeatedly dividing the array in half and discarding the portion that does not contain the value, until a match is found.

Breakpoint

A location in a program where execution should be suspended.

Bubble sort

A method used to sort numeric or alphanumeric data, where adjacent elements are continually compared and swapped until they are in the desired sequence.

Buffer

An area of computer memory set aside to hold a record immediately before it is placed on the disk and immediately after it is read from the disk.

Bug

A program error.

Byte

One character of storage.

Character

A single letter of the alphabet, a numeric digit, or a special symbol (such as $, % *).

Clipping

In graphics mode, any dots specified that would be outside the screen area (or the current viewport) are not plotted.

Cohesion

A measure of how well the statements of a program module are related to one another and the function being performed.

Collating sequence

The order, or precedence, of characters that determines their order for comparing or sorting operations.

Compiler

Software that converts high-level programming languages to the machine code necessary for program execution. The entire program is converted before execution begins. *See* Interpreter.

Computer program

A series of instructions written in a programming language and arranged in a sequence that will cause the computer to solve a particular problem.

Concatenation

Combining two or more strings, thus making a longer string.

Constant

A numeric or character string value that does not change during program execution.

Control break

A point during processing when a special event occurs such as subtotals being printed.

Control variable

The variable used to determine the timing of a control break.

Counter

A numeric variable used to count.

Coupling

A measure of the interdependence of program modules. Modules should be loosely coupled, which is to say that each should stand alone as much as possible.

CP/M

(Control Program/Microcomputers) An operating system for microcomputers written by Digital Research, Inc.

Cursor

Generally a flashing character such as an underline or block that indicates where the next typed character will appear on the screen.

Data element

One variable or field.

Data file

A collection of data records stored on a disk.

Data terminator

A special item of data that indicates the end of the input data. Also called a sentinel or trailer.

Debugging

Finding and correcting the errors in a computer program.

Delimiter

A character such as a comma or semicolon used to separate fields.

Detail line

A line that is displayed for each record processed.

Dialog box

A box that appears on the screen giving information and requiring a response.

Disk Operating System (DOS)

Operating system software that determines how the diskettes are to be formatted and accessed.

Diskette

A floppy disk.

Documentation

Written explanations of the development, design, coding, and operation of a program or system.

Dummy variables

The variables named in a DEF FN statement that establish the relationships to be assigned to the function arguments. Also, a variable used in a location where it is required to use a variable name, but the contents of that variable are of no consequence in the program.

Echo

Display of characters on the screen as they are being keyed.

Empty cell

An unused record position in a random file.

Environment

The interface between the programmer and QuickBASIC. Includes the editor, menus, and dialog boxes.

Error Trapping

The process of intercepting program or hardware errors before they cause the program to abort.

Execution

The actual carrying-out of the program instructions.

E (Exponential) notation

The method of displaying numeric data similar to scientific notation where the exponent and fraction are shown. Generally used for extremely large or extremely small numbers.

Field

A subdivision of a record. One variable.

File

A group of logically related records.

Flag

See Switch.

Floppy disk

A disk made of magnetizable material used to store programs and data for later retrieval.

Flowchart

A pictorial representation of program logic using a set of standard symbols. Used to plan the logic of a program as well as to document a completed program.

Foreground

The actual characters printed or points plotted on the screen. *See* Background.

Function

A prewritten subprogram that performs an operation and furnishes (returns) one value. Many functions are supplied with BASIC, others are written by the programmer. *See* User-defined function.

GIGO

(*Garbage-In Garbage-Out*) A phrase meaning that output can be no more accurate than the input fed into the computer.

Global variable

A variable that is available to all parts of a program.

Hard disk

A multi-surface magnetic disk for storing programs and data. Has faster access than a floppy disk and many times more storage space.

Hierarchy chart

A pictorial representation of the organization of program modules that shows program functions layered in a top-to-bottom, general-to-detail fashion. Used for program planning as well as documentation. Sometimes called a top-down chart.

Hierarchy of operations

A set of rules that determines the order in which arithmetic operations are carried out.

Immediate window

A rectangular area along the lower portion of the editing screen. BASIC instructions typed there will be executed immediately.

Indexed file

A random file that has a separate table of key values called an index. The index is used to look up the record number, given the key value.

Input

The items of data needed by a computer program to perform its operations.

Integer

A whole number.

Interactive

A conversational mode of operation, where there is a dialogue between the program and the operator.

Interpreter

The system software that translates program statements into the corresponding machine instructions for execution. Statements are decoded and executed one statement at a time. *See also* Compiler.

Iteration

One pass or repetition of a loop.

K

Used to indicate the capacity of computer storage, 1K = 1024 characters. Example: 64 K = 65,536 characters of storage.

Line counter

A numeric variable used to count the number of lines printed and determine the timing for a new page.

Literal

A string constant. A series of alphabetic characters, digits, and special symbols enclosed in quotation marks.

Local variable

A variable that is available only in the procedure where it is defined.

Logical operator

AND, OR, and NOT. Can be used in combination with the relational operators to form compound conditions.

Lookup

Find a match for a value in a table. Also called a search.

Loop

A series of repeated program steps.

Mainline

The top level module of a program controlling execution of the other program modules.

Menu

A list of choices displayed to the user.

Modular programming

The process of creating a program by first breaking a problem down into smaller parts, writing subprograms to solve those smaller problems, and combining the subprograms into one functioning unit.

Module

A component of a program designed to perform one task.

MS-DOS

An operating system for microcomputers produced by Microsoft Corp.

Nested loops

Loops contained within other loops.

NULL string

A string containing no characters. An empty string.

Operating system

The control program that supervises computer operations.

Output

The result of program execution displayed on an output device such as the screen or printer.

Page counter

A numeric variable used to count the number of pages and print the page number at the top of each page.

Parallel arrays

Two or more arrays that have elements that correspond to one another.

PC-DOS

The disk operating system used on an IBM-PC.

Pixel

Picture element. One of the individual dots used to form a character or a graphics image.

Precision

A measure of correctness indicating the number of digits that can be held accurately.

Print image

The string used for formatting printed output in a PRINT USING statement.

Procedure

A subprogram or function, defined with SUB or FUNCTION statement.

Processing

The manipulation of data provided as input in order to generate output; includes calculating, summarizing, classifying, sorting, and storing.

Program planning

Developing the program logic necessary to solve the problem before coding is begun. It may be done with a flowchart, hierarchy chart, pseudocode, or other planning methods.

Prompt

A message to the user indicating the desired response.

Pseudocode

English-like statements that describe the logic of a program. Used as a planning tool.

Random data file

A collection of data records organized in such a way as to allow any record to be retrieved or written without disturbing the other records.

Real number

A number that has a fractional part (digits to the right of the decimal point).

Record

A group of related data elements or fields. Generally, the data used for one iteration of a program.

Record key

A control field within a record that identifies that record uniquely. The organizing factor of the file.

Recursion

A subprogram or function that calls itself.

Relational operators

The symbols used for comparisons: $>$, $>=$, $<$, $<=$, $=$, $<>$.

Reserved words

Words that have special meaning to BASIC and cannot be used as variable names. *See* appendix F.

Resolution

A term that is used to define the clarity or sharpness of an image, based on the number of pixels used to form the image. A screen that displays 640 pixels horizontally is said to have higher resolution than one that displays 320 pixels. *See also* Pixel.

Run-time error

A program error that occurs during execution.

Search argument

The item of data that must be matched in a table search.

Sector

One segment of a track on diskette. One sector holds 512 characters.

Sentinel

A special item of data that indicates the end of the input data. Also called a data terminator.

Sequential file

A group of related records organized so that the records must be written or retrieved one after another in sequence. *See* Data file.

Shell sort

A method used to sort numeric or alphanumeric data. The sort algorithm was named for its creator Donald Shell and is more efficient than a bubble sort.

Sort

Arranging the elements of an array into ascending or descending numeric or alphabetic sequence.

String

A variable or constant consisting of letters, digits, or special symbols.

Structured programming

A method of program design, coding, and testing designed to produce programs that are correct, easy to read, and easy to maintain.

Stub

A program module for which the code has not yet been written, designed to allow the program to be tested in its present state.

Subroutine

A program module that is executed by a GOSUB statement and exited with a RETURN.

Subscript

A numeric value identifying a specific element of an array.

Subscripted variable

A variable that has a number in parentheses as a suffix and that can take on different values for each of the numbers in parentheses. *See* array.

Switch

A variable used to indicate a program condition. The only two values assigned to the variable are 1 or 0 for switch ON or OFF. Also called a flag.

Syntax

Rules that must be followed while coding program instructions, similar to grammatical rules for the English language.

Table

An array.

Table lookup or search

A method of locating a particular value in an array by comparing the search argument to each element of the array until a match is found.

Top-down programming

A method of designing a program that first looks at the entire problem, then multiple levels, breaking the problem into smaller and smaller parts. Illustrated with a hierarchy chart.

Trace

Following program execution, line-by-line.

Track

One of the concentric circles on a diskette on which data is stored. A track is divided into sectors.

Trailer

A special item of data that indicates the end of the input data. Also called a data terminator or sentinel.

User

A person who needs and uses the information produced by the computer system. The person who operates the computer.

User interface

The manner of communication between the user and the computer program.

User-defined function

A function that has been constructed by the programmer and coded with a DEF FN statement.

Variable

A storage location in main memory whose contents may change during program execution.

Viewport

A rectangular portion of the screen used to draw an image in medium or high resolution graphics.

VTOC

*V*isual *T*able *Of* *C*ontents. *See* Hierarchy chart.

Watch variable

A program variable whose value is continuously displayed during program execution.

Watch window

A rectangular area that opens across the top of the screen to view watch variables.

Window

A rectangular area of the screen that has been defined for a particular purpose, such as the Immediate Window, the Watch Window, and the Edit Window.

World coordinates

Numbers to plot based on their actual values, rather than on the screen coordinates. Provides a means to draw graphs without converting coordinates from their "real world" values to the dimensions of the screen.

Credits

Index

An Introduction to Visual Basic

Writing Windows Applications

The programs you write with QuickBASIC and QBASIC are text-based programs that run in the DOS environment. You have probably used applications running in the Windows environment, and wondered how you could make your programs look and work like Windows programs. The answer to this question is, "Use Visual Basic."

In chapter 7 you learned to use a combination of Locate, Print, and Input statements to create a good-looking data entry screen (refer to figures 7.1 and 7.3). When entering data, your user must enter the items in sequence, without returning to any field already entered. How much more convenient it is to use a Windows screen, such as the one shown in figure S-1. Using this screen, called a *window* or *form*, the user can tab forward or backward through the fields, click in a field with the mouse, type text, cut, copy, and paste using the Windows clipboard, and click on the Save or Exit button when finished.

Figure S-1
This Visual Basic form replaces the screen created in chapter 7 with Locate, Print, and Input statements (see figures 7.1 and 7.3). The form can be used for data entry running under Windows.

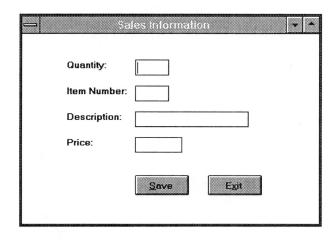

You might think that the programming for such a convenient user interface would be much more complicated than the corresponding QBASIC code, but just the opposite is true. It takes far less code to write this data entry program using Visual Basic than with QBASIC. The key is the power of Visual Basic and Windows.

The Windows Graphical User Interface

Microsoft Windows uses a graphical user interface, or GUI (pronounced *gooey*). The Windows GUI defines how the various elements look and function. The standards include such elements as windows, dialog boxes, menus, command buttons, list boxes, option buttons, check boxes, and scroll bars (see figure S-2).

Figure S-2
A Visual Basic form holding standard Windows elements, such as menus, a list box, a text box, a scroll bar, frames, option buttons, check boxes, and command buttons.

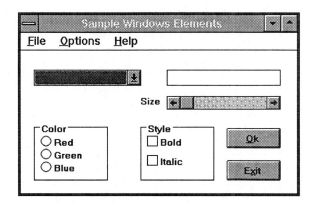

As a Visual Basic programmer, you have a toolbox of these elements available to you, which makes it quite easy to write a program that looks and acts like a standard Windows application. The best part of programming with Visual Basic is that it takes very little Basic code, but it does require a whole new way of looking at programming, called *event driven programming*.

Object Oriented Programming and Event Driven Programming

You may have heard the terms *object oriented programming* (OOP) and *event driven programming*. Microsoft refers to Visual Basic as an event driven programming language, which has many (but not all) elements of an object oriented language. Each release of Visual Basic moves it a little closer to a true object oriented language.

In the event driven model, programs are no longer procedural, with sequential logic. You, as the programmer, do not take control and determine the sequence of execution. Instead, the user can press keys and click on various buttons and boxes in a window. Each of these user actions can cause an *event* to occur, which triggers a Basic procedure that you have written. For example, the user clicks on a command button labeled "Calculate." The clicking causes the button's click event to occur, and the program automatically jumps to a subprogram you have written to do the calculation.

The Object Model

In Visual Basic you will work with objects, which have properties and methods.

Objects

Think of an object as a "thing," or a noun. Examples of objects are forms and controls. Forms are the windows and dialog boxes you place on the screen; controls are the elements you place inside a form, such as text boxes, command buttons, and list boxes.

Properties

Properties tell something about an object, such as its name, color, size, location, or how it will behave. You can think of properties as adjectives that describe objects.

When you refer to a property, you first name the object, then a period, then the property. For example, refer to the Caption property of a form called Form1 as Form1.Caption (say "form1 dot caption").

Methods

Actions associated with objects are called methods. Methods are the verbs of object oriented programming. Some typical methods are Move, Print, Resize, and Clear.

You refer to methods as Object.Method ("object dot method"). For example, Form1.Move moves a form (called Form1), and Image1.Move moves an image control (called Image1).

You will find that methods are similar to QBASIC statements such as Locate and Print. In QBASIC there are two statements for printing (Print and LPrint), depending on whether the output should go to the screen or the printer. In Visual Basic, there is one Print method, which can apply to different objects. Printer.Print sends the output to the printer object; Form1.Print sends output to the form called Form1.

Versions of Visual Basic

There are several versions of Microsoft Visual Basic. Although there is a version that runs under DOS, it is considerably different than the Windows version, and isn't covered here (or many other places). For Windows, there is a Standard Edition and a Professional Edition. Anyone planning to do professional application development, including advanced features of database management, will want the Professional Edition.

There is one more version of VB, the Visual Basic Primer Edition, which was designed specifically for programming students. The Primer Edition has nearly all of the features of the Standard Edition, but it will not allow you to compile your program to an EXE file or print out your project documentation. Unfortunately, due to file size limitations, there is no Help information available in the Primer Edition (which is a serious handicap). If the book you purchased contains a Visual Basic diskette, you have the Primer Edition.

In addition to the various editions of Visual Basic, you must also be aware of the release number. The VB Primer Edition is based on Visual Basic Release 2.0. As this text went to press, Release 3.0 was current, but Release 4.0 was imminent. Everything covered in this text will run on any edition, and on Release 2.0, 3.0, or 4.0. There are minor differences in the menus from one release to the next; those differences will be pointed out where appropriate. If you are unsure which version you are using, open the *Help* menu and choose *About Microsoft Visual Basic*.

Writing Visual Basic Programs

The Three-Step Process

When you write a Visual Basic program, you follow a three-step process.

1. *Define the user interface.*

   In this step, you set up the screens the user will see when running your project. You layout the forms and the controls that appear on the forms. Refer to figure S-1 for an example of a user interface.

   Think of this step as *defining* all of the objects you will use in your project.

2. *Set the properties.*

   When you set the properties of the objects, you give each object a name and define such attributes as the contents of a label, the fontsize of the text, and the words that appear on top of a command button and in the form's title bar.

   You might think of this step as *describing* each of your objects.

3. *Write the Basic code.*

   This is where you write the subprograms that will execute when your program runs. Although you will find some differences between the Basic statements in Visual Basic and QBASIC, they are more alike than different.

   You will find assignment (Let) statements, If...Then...Else, Do/Loop, For/Next, and most of the functions and data types you have used in QBASIC. What is missing, and must be done in different ways, are INPUT and READ/DATA.

   You can think of this third step as defining the *actions* of your program.

The Advantages of Visual Programming

Once you begin designing your programs visually, you will find that it makes the programming process much easier. You begin by laying out the screen; then specify the functions the program must perform. The entire program is written in small subprograms, which makes it easy to test each program function as you write it.

What you will like most about Visual Basic is how quickly you can write "real" Windows applications. With surprisingly few lines of code you can create a powerful program.

Planning a Visual Basic Program

The traditional methods of program planning don't apply when you write an event driven program. When you draw a flowchart or write pseudocode, you specify a sequence of events. By contrast, in an event driven program the user chooses the sequence of events as the program is running. You will still find flowcharts and pseudocode useful when planning a tricky or complicated subprogram, but you will no longer diagram the entire application.

The method that works best for planning a Visual Basic program is to first sketch the user interface. Then, make a list of the functions that must be done for each event. You will see some samples of the planning steps in the example programs that follow.

Visual Basic Projects

Each Visual Basic project consists of at least two files, and usually many more.

1. The .MAK file, called the project file, is a small text file that holds the names of the other files in the project, as well as some information about the VB environment.

2. Each form in your project is saved in a file with .FRM extension. To begin, your projects will have only one form (and therefore one form file). Later, you can expect your projects to have several forms, with one .FRM file for each.

   A form file holds a description of all objects and their properties for the form, as well as the Basic code you have written to respond to the events.

   In Visual Basic, each of these form files is referred to as a *form module*.

3. Optionally, you can have additional files in your project with a .BAS extension. These files hold data declarations and Basic code that can be called from any form. As soon as you begin writing multi-form projects, you will need .BAS files. .BAS files are called *standard code modules*.

4. Custom controls are stored in files with a .VBX extension. If you include controls in your project which are not part of the standard control set, the .VBX file names will be included in the project.

Tip

Before creating any files for your project, first create a new subdirectory. Then save your .MAK file, .FRM files, and .BAS files into the new subdirectory. This will help to insure that you get all of the pieces if you copy or move the project to another disk. It is easy to miss parts of a project unless all files are together in one subdirectory.

The Visual Basic Environment

The Visual Basic environment is where you create and test your programs. Figure S-3 shows the various windows in the Visual Basic environment. Note that each of the windows can be moved, resized, opened, and closed. Your screen may not look like the figure; in all likelihood you will want to customize the placement of the various windows.

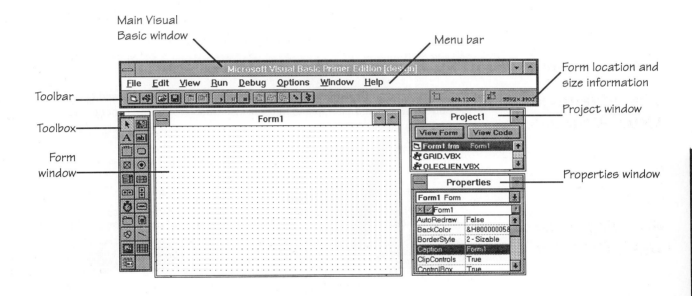

Figure S-3
The Visual Basic environment. Each of the individual windows can be moved, resized, or closed. Windows with a Minimize button (all but the toolbox) may be minimized; the main VB window and the Form window may also be maximized.

The Form Window

The Form window is where you design the forms that will make up your user interface. You can use standard Windows techniques to change the size and location of the form.

The Project Window

The Project window holds the filenames for the files included in your project. The window's title bar holds the name of your .MAK (project) file, which is *Project1* by default, until you save it with a new name.

The Properties Window

You use the Properties window to set the properties for the objects in your project. See "Set Properties," later in this chapter, for instructions on changing properties.

The Toolbox

The toolbox holds the tools you use to place controls on a form. You may have more or different tools in your toolbox, depending on the edition and release of Visual Basic you are using. See figure S-4 for a labeled version of the toolbox.

Figure S-4
The toolbox for the Visual Basic Primer Edition. Your toolbox may have more tools, depending on the edition and release you are using.

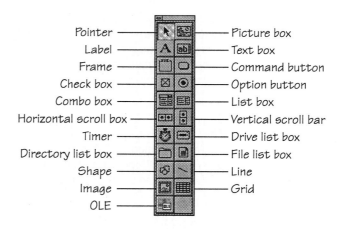

The Main Visual Basic Window

The main Visual Basic window holds the VB menu bar, the toolbar, and the form location and size information.

The Toolbar

You can use the buttons on the toolbar as shortcuts for commonly used operations. Each of the buttons represents a command that can also be selected from a menu. Figure S-5 shows the toolbar buttons.

Figure S-5
The Visual Basic toolbar. Each of these buttons represents a command that you can execute by clicking the button or selecting it from a menu.

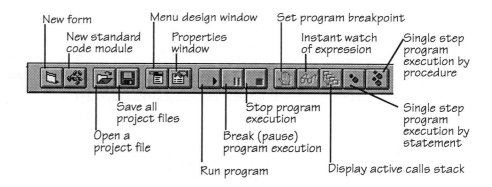

The Form Location and Size Information

The two small diagrams at the right end of the Visual Basic toolbar show the position of the form on the screen, along with the size of the form.

Help

If you are using the Standard Edition or the Professional Edition of Visual Basic (not the Primer Edition), an extensive Help facility is available. Nearly the entire reference manual is built into Help, along with many coding examples.

Design Time, Run Time, and Break Time

Visual Basic has three distinct modes. While you are designing the user interface and writing code, you are in *design time*. When you are testing and running your program, you are in *run time*. If you get a run-time error or pause program execution, you are in *break time*. Notice the title bar notation in figure S-3, indicating that the program is currently in design time.

Supplement

Writing Your First Visual Basic Project

For your first event driven program, you will create a form with three controls (see figure S-6). This simple program will display the message "Hello World" when the user clicks the Push Me command button, and will terminate when the Exit button is clicked.

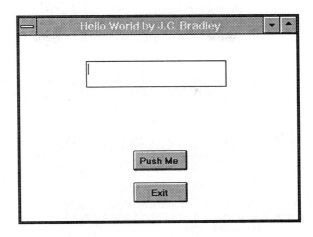

Figure S-6
The Hello World form. The "Hello World" message will appear in the text box when the user clicks on the Push Me command button.

Setup Your Visual Basic Workspace

Before you can begin a project, you must first launch Visual Basic and set up your workspace the way you want it.

Launch Visual Basic

In the Windows Program Manager, open the *Options* menu. If *Minimize on Use* is not checked, click on it to select it (figure S-7). If the *Options* menu is still open, click somewhere off the menu to close it.

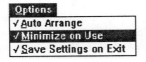

Figure S-7
Open the Windows Program Manager Options menu and make sure Minimize on Use has a check mark, indicating it is selected.

»Step 1: Locate the icon for Microsoft Visual Basic (figure S-8). (You may have to first open a group icon.)

»Step 2: Double-click on the Visual Basic icon.

»Step 3: The Visual Basic program will begin and display the VB environment on the screen (refer to figure S-3).

Figure S-8
To launch Visual Basic, double-click on its icon. Your icon may vary a little, depending on the version you are using.

Set up Your Workspace

»Step 1:   Open the Visual Basic *Options* menu and choose *Environment*. Check each of the options, changing any that do not match (see figure S-9). Click OK when finished.

Tab Stop Width	4
Require Variable Declaration	Yes
Syntax Checking	Yes
Default Save As Format	Text

Figure S-9

Choose Environment from the Options menu, and make sure the Environment options are properly set.

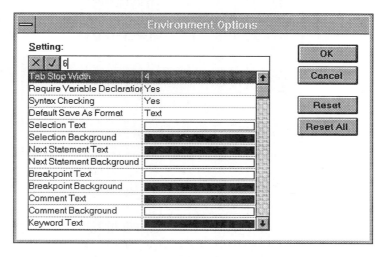

»Step 2:   If the Project window is not displayed, open the *Window* menu and select *Project*. (Note: It's possible for the Project window to be hiding behind the Form window. You may need to move one or the other to see both.)

»Step 3:   If the Properties window is not displayed, open the *Window* menu and select *Properties*. (The Properties window may be hidden behind the Form window. Move or resize the Form window, if necessary.)

»Step 4:   Move and resize the Form window, the Project window, and the Properties window so that all three are visible (figure S-10). (Note: To move a window, point to its title bar, press the mouse button, and drag to a new location. To resize a window, point to its border so that the mouse pointer becomes a two-headed arrow; then press the mouse button and drag the border.)

Figure S-10

Move and resize the windows so that all are visible. (You should see the Program Manager icon at the bottom of the screen.)

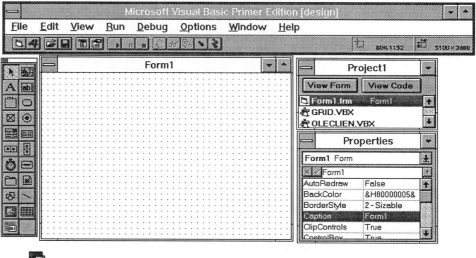

Define the User Interface

Set up the Form

Notice that the new form has all of the standard Windows features: a title bar, control menu bar, maximize and minimize buttons, and a double outline indicating that the form can be resized.

»Step 1: Choose the size and position you want the form to have when the program runs. Resize and/or move it now to select its final location.

Place Controls on the Form

You are going to place three controls on the form: a text box and two command buttons.

»Step 1: Point to the text box tool in the toolbox (figure S-11) and click. Then move the pointer over the form.

»Step 2: Notice that the pointer becomes a cross-hair, and the text box tool looks like it has been pressed, indicating it is the active tool (figure S-11).

»Step 3: Point to the upper-left corner where you want the text box to begin, press the mouse button, and drag the pointer to the opposite corner (figure S-12). When you release the mouse button, the text box and its default contents ("Text1") will appear (figure S-13).

Notice the text box has eight small square handles, indicating that the control is currently selected. While a control is selected, you can delete it, resize it, or move it. Click outside of the control to deselect it.

Figure S-11

When you click on the text box tool in the toolbox, the tool's button is activated and the mouse pointer becomes a cross-hair.

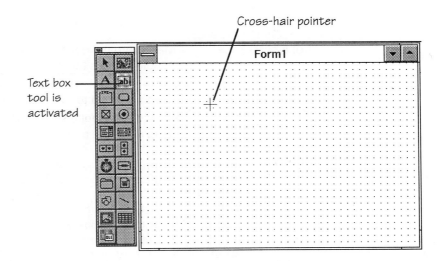

Figure S-12

Drag the mouse pointer diagonally to draw the text box on the form.

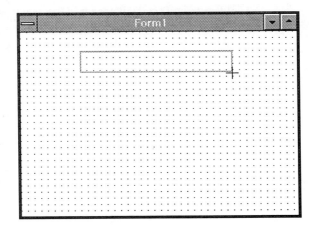

Figure S-13
The newly-created text box
has eight small handles,
indicating that it is selected.
Notice that the contents of the
text box is set to "Text1" by
default.

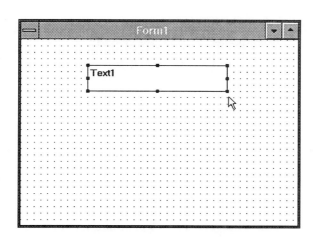

Table S-1

To select a control:	Click on the control.
To delete a control:	First select the control, then press the Delete key on the keyboard.
To move a control:	First select the control, then point inside the control (not on a handle), press the mouse button, and drag it to a new location.
To change the size of a control:	Make sure the control is selected, then point to one of the handles, press the mouse button, and drag the handle.
To change the width of a control:	Drag a side handle.
To change the height of a control:	Drag a bottom or top handle.
To resize a control in two directions:	Drag a corner handle.

»Step 4: Next, you will draw a command button on the form: Click on the Command button tool in the toolbox, position the cross-hair pointer for one corner of the button, and drag to the opposite corner (figure S-14). The new command button should have selection handles.

»Step 5: Create another command button using the alternate method: point to the Command button tool in the toolbox and *double*-click. A new command button of the default size will appear in the center of the form (figure S-15).

»Step 6: While the new command button is still selected, point anywhere inside the button (not on a handle) and drag the button below your first button (figure S-16). As you drag the control, you see only its outline; when you release the mouse button, the control is actually moved to its new location (figure S-17).

»Step 7: Select each control, move and resize the controls as necessary. Make the two buttons the same size and line them up approximately like those in figure S-17.

At this point, you have designed the user interface and are ready to set the properties.

Figure S-14

Select the Command button tool and drag diagonally to create a new command button control.

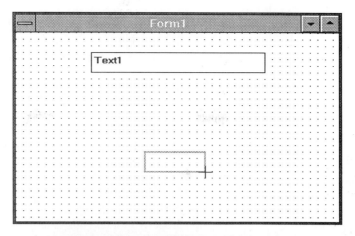

Figure S-15

Place a new command button on the form by double-clicking the Command button tool in the toolbox. The new button appears in the center of the form.

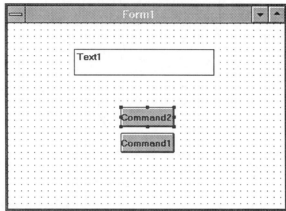

Figure S-16

Drag the new command button (Command2) below Command1. An outline of the control shows you the new location for the control.

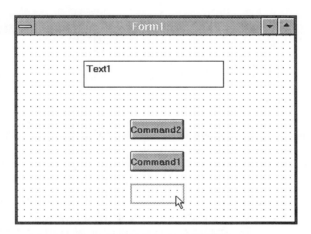

Figure S-17

When you release the mouse button, the control appears in its new location. Resize as necessary.

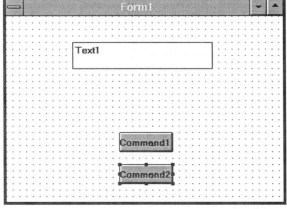

Set Properties

Set the Name and Text Properties for the Text Box

»Step 1: Click on the text box you placed on the form; selection handles will appear. Next, click on the title bar of the Properties window to make it the active window (figure S-18).

Notice that the Object box is showing *Text1* (the name of the object) and *TextBox* (called the *class* of the object).

»Step 2: Scroll the vertical scroll bar of the Properties window until you see the Name property. Click on *Name* and notice that the Settings box shows *Text1*, the default name of the text box (figure S-19).

»Step 3: Type "txtMessage" (without the quotation marks). You will see the new name appear in the Settings box (figure S-20).

»Step 4: Scroll to the Text property and click to select it.

The Text property of a text box determines what will be displayed in the box. Since nothing should display in the box when the program begins, you must delete the value of the Text property (as described in steps 5 and 6).

»Step 5: Double-click on the value in the Settings box (or you can double-click on the Text property line below). "*Text1*" in the Settings box should appear selected (highlighted). See figure S-21.

»Step 6: Press the Delete key to delete the value of the Text property. Notice that the text box on the form now appears empty (figure S-22).

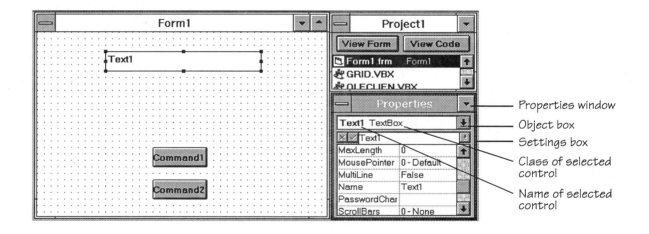

Properties window

Object box

Settings box

Class of selected control

Name of selected control

Figure S-18
The currently selected control is shown in the Properties window.

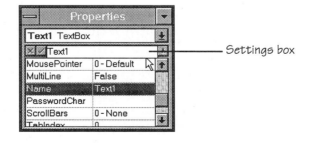

Settings box

Figure S-19
The Properties window. Click on the Name property to see the current value of the property displayed in the Settings box.

Figure S-20
Type "txtMessage" into the Settings box for the Name property.

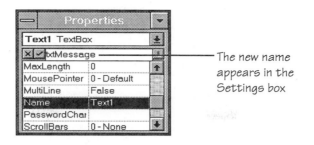

The new name appears in the Settings box

Figure S-21
Double-click in the Settings box to select the entry.

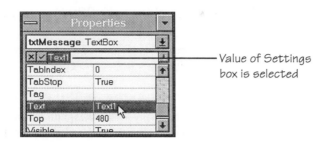

Value of Settings box is selected

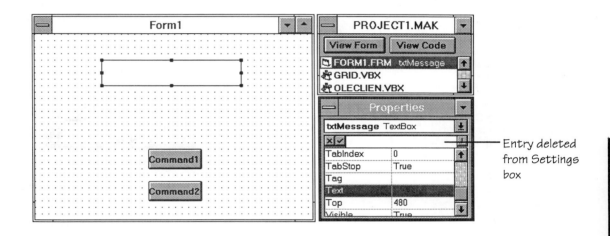

Entry deleted from Settings box

Figure S-22
Delete the value for the Text property from the Settings box. Note that the text box on the form also appears empty.

Tip: Don't confuse the Name property with the Text property. You use the Name property to refer to the control in your Basic code (similar to a variable name). The Text property tells what will be displayed on the form for the user to see (a little like the *contents* of a variable). Since Visual Basic sets both of these properties to the same value by default, it's easy to get them confused.

Set the Name and Caption Properties for the First Command Button

»Step 1: Click on the first command button (Command1) to select it and then look at the Properties window. The Object box should show the name and class of the command button *(Command1 CommandButton).* See figure S-23.

»Step 2: Change the Name property of the command button to "cmdPush" (without the quotation marks).

Although the program would work fine without this step, we prefer to refer to this button by a meaningful name, rather than by Command1, its default name.

»Step 3: Change the Caption property to "Push Me" (without the quotation marks). This changes the words that appear on top of the button.

Figure S-23
The Properties window,
showing *Command1* as the
control and *CommandButton*
as its class.

Set the Name and Caption Properties for the Second Command Button

»Step 1:   Select Command2 and change its Name property to "cmdExit."

»Step 2:   Change the Caption property to "Exit."

Change the Caption Property for the Form

»Step 1:   Click on the form, anywhere except on a control. The Properties window Object box should now show the form as the selected object (*Form1* as the object's name, and *Form* as its class).

»Step 2:   Change the Caption property to "Hello World by *Your Name*" (again, no quotation marks).

The Caption property of a form determines the text to appear in the title bar. Your screen should now look like figure S-24.

Figure S-24
Change the form's Caption
property to set the text that
appears in the form's title bar.

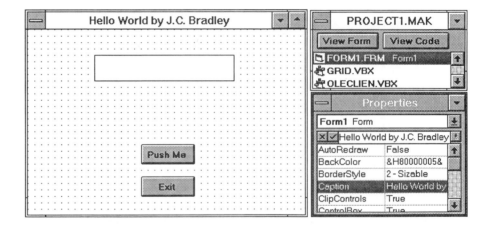

Write Code

Visual Basic Events

While your project is running, the user can do many things, such as move the mouse around, click on either button, move, resize, or close your form's window, or jump to another application. Each action by the user causes an event to occur in your Visual Basic project. Some of the events you care about (like clicking on a command button), and some events you don't care about (like moving the mouse and resizing the window). If you write Basic code for a particular event, then Visual Basic will respond to the event and automatically execute your procedure. Any events for which procedures aren't written are ignored.

Visual Basic Event Procedures

You write code in Visual Basic in *procedures*. A procedure is either a subprogram (beginning with the key word Sub and ending with End Sub), or a function (declared with Function / End Function). Refer to appendix G for more information about writing and calling subprograms and functions. Note: Many programmers refer to subprograms as subroutines, which may be confusing, since GoSub to a line label is also called a subroutine.

Visual Basic automatically names your event procedures. The name consists of the object name, an underscore (_), and the name of the event. For example, the click event for the command button cmdPush will be *cmdPush_Click*. For the sample project you are writing, you will need a cmdPush_Click procedure and a cmdExit_Click procedure.

Code the Click Event for the Push Me Button

»Step 1: Double-click on the Push Me command button. The Visual Basic code window will open, with the first and last lines of your subprogram already in place (figure S-25).

»Step 2: Press the Tab key once to indent, and type this remark:

```
'Display the Hello World message
```

»Step 3: Press Enter, and notice that Visual Basic automatically changes remarks to green (unless you or someone else has changed the color with the environment option).

Follow good coding conventions and indent all lines between Sub and End Sub. Also, always leave a blank line after the remarks at the top of a subprogram.

»Step 4: Press Enter again, press the Tab key once, then type this assignment statement:

```
txtMessage.Text = "Hello World"
```

This is an assignment statement, and it could have contained the optional word *Let*. It assigns the string literal *"Hello World"* to the Text property of the control called txtMessage. Compare your screen to figure S-26.

Figure S-25

The Code window, showing the first and last lines of the subprogram.

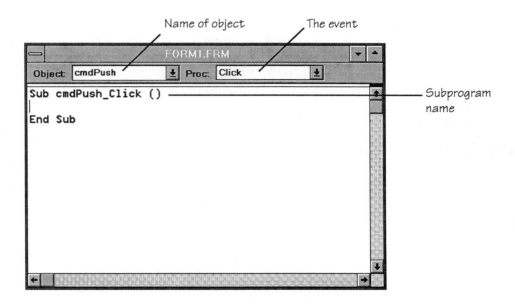

Figure S-26

Type the remark and assignment statement for the cmdPush_Click event. Close the window by double-clicking on its Control Menu bar.

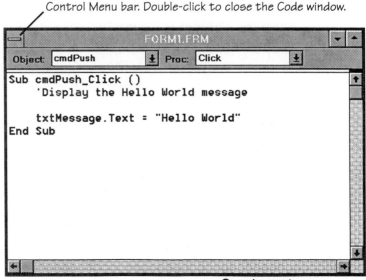

»Step 5: Close the Code window by double-clicking on its control menu bar or by single-clicking and choosing *Close.*

Code the Click Event for the Exit Button

»Step 1: Double-click on the Exit command button to open the Code window for the cmdExit_Click event.

»Step 2: Press Tab once and type this remark:

```
'Exit the project
```

»Step 3: Press Enter twice, Tab once, and type this Basic statement:

```
End
```

»Step 4: Make sure your code looks like figure S-27, then close the Code window.

Figure S-27
Type the remark and End statements for the cmdExit_Click event and then close the window.

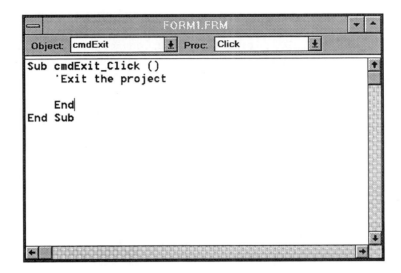

Run the Project

After you have finished writing the code, you are ready to run the project. There are three ways to start running a project:

1. Open the *Run* menu and choose *Start.*
2. Press the Run button on the toolbar.
3. Press F5, the shortcut key for the *Start* command.

Start the Project Running

»Step 1: Choose one of the three methods shown above to start your project running.

Notice that the Visual Basic title bar now indicates that you are in run time, and the grid dots have disappeared from your form (figure S-28). (The grid dots are there to help you align the controls; they can be turned off if you prefer.)

Click the Push Me Button

»Step 1: Click the Push Me button. Your "Hello World" message will appear in the text box (figure S-29).

Click the Exit Button

»Step 1: Click the Exit button. Your project will terminate, and you'll return to Visual Basic design time.

Supplement

Figure S-28

When you run the project, the Visual Basic title bar indicates run time, and the form's grid dots disappear.

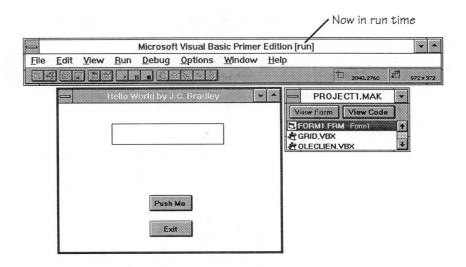

Now in run time

Figure S-29

Click on the Push Me button, and "Hello World" appears in the text box.

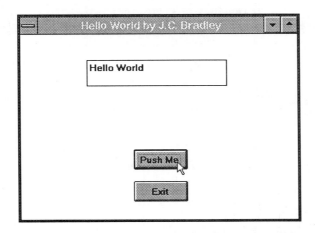

Save the Project

Of course, you must always save your work often. Except for a very small project like this one, you will usually save your work as you go along.

Create a Subdirectory

It's very easy to lose parts of a Visual Basic project and neglect to include all of the files when you copy a project from disk to disk. Therefore, the recommended practice is to always create a new subdirectory before saving your first file.

Note: Due to the way Visual Basic stores its project files, it's difficult to make the program recognize that you have changed the location of a file. Always create your subdirectory first, and save into the subdirectory—do not save somewhere else first, and plan to organize later.

»Step 1: Double-click on the Program Manager icon at the bottom of your screen and then double-click on the Main group icon to open its window.

»Step 2: Locate the File Manager icon and double-click to open its window.

»Step 3: Choose the disk where you want to save your project. If the correct disk is not selected, single-click on its icon to log the disk.

»Step 4: In the directory tree pane (on the left side of the window), click to select the parent directory for your new subdirectory.

»Step 5: Open the *File* menu and choose *Create Directory*. In the Create Directory dialog box, type the new name "demoproj" (without the quotation marks), and press Enter or click OK. Your new subdirectory should appear (figure S-30).

Remember that a subdirectory name may be 1–8 characters in length.

»Step 6: Double-click on the File Manager's control menu box to close the window.

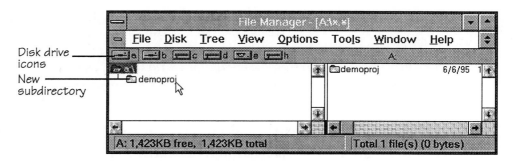

Figure S-30
The File Manager window. Click on the disk drive icon to select the disk you want to use, select the parent directory name in the directory tree pane, and create a new subdirectory.

Save the Form File

»Step 1: Open the Visual Basic *File* menu and choose *Save File As*. This will save the current form.

»Step 2: Check the Drives box and change to the correct drive.

»Step 3: In the Directories list box, double-click on your new subdirectory. The correct path, showing drive and subdirectory, should be showing above the Directories list box.

»Step 4: In the File Name box, type "hello" (without the quotation marks). See figure S-31. Visual Basic will add the correct .FRM extension to the filename.

»Step 5: Press Enter or click OK to save the form file.

Figure S-31
The Save File As dialog box. Select the correct drive and directory, and type the name of the file (without the extension) in the File Name box.

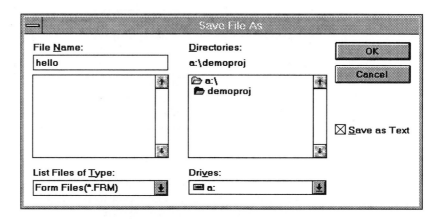

Save the Project File

»Step 1: Open the *File* menu and select *Save Project*. This saves the project (.MAK) file.

»Step 2: Check the drive and directory. They should still be pointing to the correct location.

»Step 3: In the File Name box, type "hello" (without the quotation marks). See figure S-32. This file will be saved as *hello.mak*, since Visual Basic adds the correct file extension.

»Step 4: Press Enter or click OK to save the project file.

Figure S-32
The Save Project As dialog box. Make sure the correct drive and directory are selected, and then type the name of the project file in the File Name box.

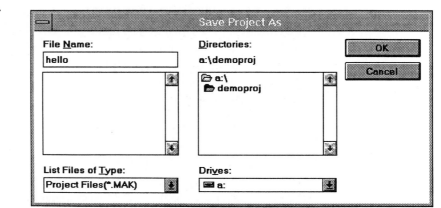

Supplement

Open a Project

Now test your save operation by opening the project from disk.

Open the Project File

»Step 1:   Either click on the Open button on the toolbar or choose *Open Project* from the *File* menu.

»Step 2:   In the Open Project dialog box, check the drive and directory entries. They should still be correctly set.

When you begin a new session you will need to change to your drive and directory before you can open a project.

»Step 3:   You should see your project name, hello.mak, in the file list box (figure S-33). Click on the filename, then click on the OK button (or, if you prefer, you can double-click on the filename).

»Step 4:   If you don't see your form on the screen, check the Project window—it should say *"HELLO.MAK"* in the title bar. Click on the View Form button and your form will appear.

Figure S-33
The Open Project dialog box. Select the correct drive and directory, and find your project name in the file list.

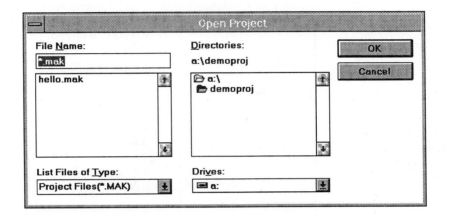

Modify the Project

Now it's time to make some changes to the project. We'll change the size and alignment of the "Hello World" message, and display the message in two different languages. We'll also provide a button that will print the form.

Change the Size and Alignment of the Message

»Step 1:   Click on the text box on your form, which will make selection handles appear.

»Step 2:   Widen the text box on both ends by dragging the handles wider. (Drag the right end farther right, and the left end farther left.)

»Step 3:   With the text box still selected, scroll to the FontSize property and click to select it. The Settings box will show the currently selected size.

Notice the drop-down arrow on the Settings box—the arrow indicates that there is a list of choices.

»Step 4:   Click on the down-pointing arrow to drop down the list of available font sizes (figure S-34). Select 12 point, if it is available. (If it isn't available, choose another number larger than the current setting.)

The numbers for FontSize are shown in points, which is a printers' measurement

system. There are 72 points to an inch.

Figure S-34
Drop down the list of choices for the FontSize property and choose 12 point.

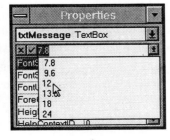

»Step 5:   Select the Alignment property, and again note that there is a drop-down list. Drop down the list and choose *2–Center*.

In order for the Center alignment to work, you must also set the Multiline property to True.

»Step 6:   Select the Multiline property. You can drop down the list to choose True, or just type a "T," which will change the property to True.

Change the Location and Caption of the Push Me Button

Since we plan to display the message in one of two languages, we'll change the caption on the Push Me button to "English," and move the button to allow for a second command button.

»Step 1:   Select the Push Me button and change its Caption property to "English."

»Step 2:   Move the English button to the left to make room for a Spanish button (see figure S-35).

Figure S-35

Move the English button to the left and add a Spanish button.

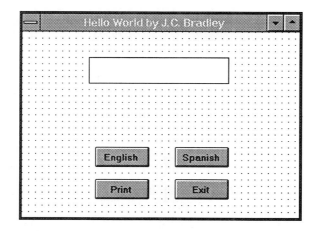

Add a Spanish Button

»Step 1:   Add a new command button. Move and resize it as necessary, referring to figure S-35.

»Step 2:   Change the Caption property of the new button to "Spanish."

»Step 3:   Change the Name property of the new button to "cmdSpanish."

Add an Event Procedure for the Spanish Button

»Step 1:   Double-click on the Spanish button to open the Code window for cmdSpanish_Click.

»Step 2:   Tab once and add a remark:

```
'Display the Hello World message in Spanish
```

»Step 3:   Press Enter twice and Tab once. Then type the following Basic code line:

```
txtMessage.Text = "Hola Mundo"
```

»Step 4:   Close the Code window.

Add a Print Button

»Step 1:   Move the Exit button to the right to make room for the Print button.

»Step 2:   Add a new command button, and move and resize it to match figure S-35.

»Step 3:   Change the Caption property of the new button to "Print."

»Step 4:   Change the Name property of the new button to "cmdPrint."

Add an Event Procedure for the Print Button

To print the form, we will use the PrintForm method, which prints the current form on the printer, without its title bar or borders.

»Step 1: Double-click on the Print button to open the Code window for the cmdPrint_Click event.

»Step 2: Indent and add a remark that tells what you plan to do in the subprogram.

»Step 3: Leave a blank line and indent the following code statement.

```
PrintForm
```

That's all there is to it. The actual format for a method is Object.Method (object dot method). However, we can leave off the object in this case, since it defaults to the current form.

»Step 4: Save your project again. You can use the *Save File* and *Save Project* menu commands, or click on the Save button on the toolbar, which saves both.

»Step 5: Close the code window and run your project again. Try clicking on the English button and the Spanish button. You can click on the Print button any time you wish. (Problems? See "Finding and Fixing Errors" on page S – 23.)

Add General Remarks

Good documentation guidelines require some more remarks in the project. Always begin each procedure with remarks that tell its purpose. In addition, each project file needs identifying remarks at the top. The general declarations section is a good location for these remarks.

»Step 1: Click on the View Code button in the Project window, or double-click on any object, which will open the Code window.

»Step 2: In the Code window, click on the Objects down-pointing arrow to view the list of objects. Notice that every object in your form is listed there.

»Step 3: At the top of the Objects list you will see "*(general)*" (figure S-36). Select this, if it isn't already selected.

Check the entry in the Procedure box (to the right of the Objects box). It should display "*(declarations)*."

This general declarations section of a form module is used to declare variables and arrays that can be used in any procedure of the form. The Option Explicit statement, if it appears, requires that all program variables be defined before use. (Option Explicit is discussed later in this chapter.)

»Step 4: If Option Explicit appears in the Code window, click an insertion point in front of the line, press Enter to create a blank line, and move the insertion point up to the blank line. (If Option Explicit does not appear, that's ok for now.)

Figure S-36
Select *"(general)"* from the drop down Objects list.

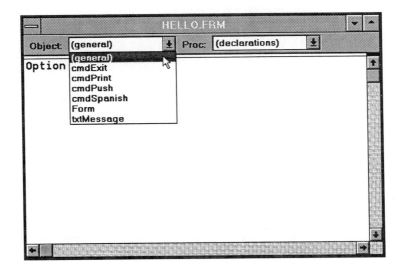

»Step 5: Type your identifying remarks. Recommended minimum: Project Name, Date, Programmer Name, and Project Description. See figure S-37.

»Step 6: Close the Code window.

»Step 7: Save the project again.

Figure S-37
Enter remarks in the general
declarations section of the
form module.

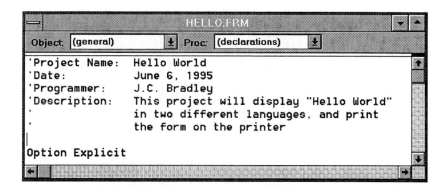

Print the Project Documentation

If you are using the Standard Edition or Professional Edition of Visual Basic, you can print your project documentation. Printing is not available in the Primer Edition.

Select the Printing Options

If you are using the Primer Edition, skip these steps.

»Step 1: Open the *File* menu and choose *Print.* The Print dialog box appears (figure S-38).

»Step 2: Click in the check boxes to select the printing options you want.

Current / All	This refers to the current module (file), or all modules in the project. Since this project has only one module, the two options give the same result.
Form	Print a picture of the form, as it appears at design time.
Form Text	Print a description of every object and its properties.
Form Code	Print all procedures and the general declarations section.

»Step 3: Click OK.

Figure S-38
Select the options you want in
the Print dialog box (not
available in the Primer
Edition).

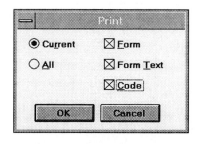

Feedback

1. What are objects and properties? How are they related to each other?
2. What are the three steps for writing Visual Basic projects? Describe in your own words what happens in each of the steps.
3. What is the purpose of these Visual Basic file types: .MAK, .FRM, .BAS, .VBX?
4. When is Visual Basic in design time? run time? break time?
5. What is the purpose of the Name property of a control?
6. What property determines the contents of a text box?
7. What is the purpose of the Caption property of a command button? the Caption property of a form?
8. What is meant by cmdPush_Click? To what does cmdPush refer? To what does Click refer?
9. What is a Visual Basic event? Give some examples of events.
10. What two properties must be set to center text in a text box? What should the value of the properties be?
11. What is the general declarations section of a form module? What belongs there?

Supplement

Finding and Fixing Errors

You may have already seen some errors as you entered the first sample program. Just as in QBASIC, you may get syntax errors, logic errors, and run-time errors.

Syntax Errors

The smart Visual Basic editor finds most syntax errors. It tells you when you break the rules of Basic and when you use an illegal object or property. If you have an Option Explicit statement in your program, it will also tell you when you have used an undefined variable name.

Option Explicit

Requiring variable declaration is one of the big improvements in Visual Basic over QBASIC. Although it's quick and easy to name a new variable on the fly, it's also too easy to misspell a variable name and cause hard-to-detect errors.

If you want VB to check for variable declarations, place an Option Explicit statement in the general declarations section of each module. You can set the environment option *Require Variable Declaration* to *Yes*, which causes VB to automatically place the Option Explicit statement in all new modules created after that point. (It does not add the statement to any existing module.) See "Variables" for more information on declaring variables.

Logic Errors

Logic errors in a Visual Basic project are just like logic errors in a QBASIC program. Your program runs, but it produces incorrect results. Visual Basic has some tools to help track down faulty logic, such as setting breakpoints, displaying intermediate values of variables and expressions, and single stepping program execution.

Run-time Errors

If your project halts during execution, that's a run-time error. Visual Basic goes into break time and highlights the statement causing the problem. If you are able to see the problem and fix it, you can then continue program execution from that location by clicking on the Run button, pressing F5, or choosing *Start* from the *Run* menu. You can restart from the beginning of the program by selecting *Restart* from the *Run* menu, or pressing Shift + F5.

If you need some help finding the error, you can use some of Visual Basic's debugging tools.

Debugging Tools

You can use the buttons on the toolbar or the Debug menu to access Visual Basic's debugging tools. See figure S-39.

Figure S-39
The debugging buttons on the toolbar and the *Debug* menu.

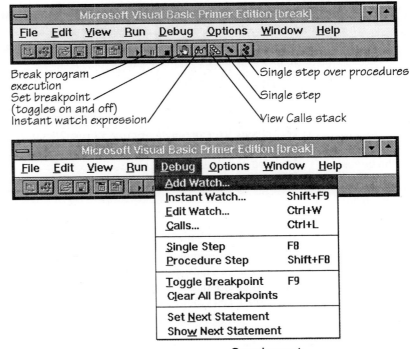

Pausing Execution with the Break Button

You can click on the Break toolbar button to pause execution. This places the project into break time at the current line. The disadvantage of this method is that it is usually preferable to break at a specific point, such as in the middle of a subprogram. To choose the location of the break, set a breakpoint yourself.

Setting Breakpoints

When debugging, you may desire to stop at a particular location in code and watch what happens (which branch of an If...Then...Else, which subprograms were executed, or the value of a variable just before or just after a calculation). To set a breakpoint, display the code, place the cursor on the line before which you want to break, and click on the Set breakpoint button or choose *Toggle breakpoint* from the *Debug* menu. Then start (or restart) program execution. When the program reaches the breakpoint line, it will halt, display the breakpoint line, and go into break time.

Using the Debug Window

When a program is in break mode, there is one additional window—the Debug window. You can use the Debug window to display or change the contents of a variable. The Debug window is similar to the Immediate window in QBASIC. You can enter any single line of code and execute it. For example, to see the current value in a variable called Total, enter Print Total (or the shortcut: ? Total). When you press Enter, the result appears on the next line.

   The Debug window is only available during break time. Since it often is hidden behind a form or the Code window, you may need to display it. To do this, choose *Break* from the *Window* menu or use the shortcut Ctrl + B. You may want to move and resize the window to make it more visible.

Single-stepping Program Execution

Once you are in break time, you can watch the execution of your program, line by line. To select this option, click on the Single Step button on the toolbar, choose *Single Step* from the *Debug* menu, or use the shortcut F8 key. Each time you choose the command, your program will execute the next line of code. You can jump to the Debug window and view (or change) the contents of a variable at any time. If you want to continue with regular execution, choose Start or press F5.

Watch Expressions

If there is a variable, expression, or property you would like to monitor, it's easier to use a Watch variable than to keep printing its value in the Debug window. Highlight the expression in code, then choose *Watch* from the Debug menu. Visual Basic adds the Watch expression to the top of the Debug window, where you can view it in break time. Figure S-40 shows the Debug window with Watch expressions displayed at the top.

Figure S-40

The Debug Window. The title bar holds the name of the form module and the current procedure. Two Watch expressions display their current value, and the value of YesCount is displayed.

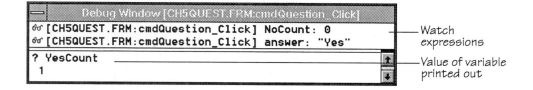

Debug Window [CH5QUEST.FRM:cmdQuestion_Click]

[CH5QUEST.FRM:cmdQuestion_Click] NoCount: 0
[CH5QUEST.FRM:cmdQuestion_Click] answer: "Yes"
? YesCount
1

— Watch expressions
— Value of variable printed out

Instant Watch Expressions

Another useful technique for viewing the current contents of a variable or expression is Instant Watch. This method, like the other debugging tools, is available only in break time. While your program is paused, highlight a variable or expression and choose Instant Watch (from the Debug menu, the toolbar, or Shift + F9). An information box pops up with the current contents of the expression, along with an option to add it as a Watch expression in the Debug window.

Supplement

Visual Basic Help

The Visual Basic Help facility is great! With Help, you really don't need a printed manual, as it allows you to look up any Basic statement, object, property, method, or programming concept. There are many coding examples available, with the added bonus that you can copy and paste the examples into your own project, and even modify them if you wish.

Unfortunately, the Primer Edition of Visual Basic does not have Help available, due to the large size of the Help files.

You can look up any topic in Help by using its Contents list (like a table of contents) or Search (which resembles an index). Also, you can use context-sensitive Help. Select any object on the screen and press F1; VB will automatically display the correct Help page relating the selected object.

Feedback

1. What is the purpose of the Option Explicit statement? How can you have Visual Basic automatically place the statement in all of your modules?
2. What steps would you use to make program execution halt at a particular line and then view the contents of a variable?
3. What is the purpose of the Debug window? When is it available?

Your First Visual Basic Assignment

For your first Visual Basic assignment, you must first complete the Hello World project. Then, add command buttons and event procedures to display the "Hello World" message in two more languages. You may substitute any other languages for those shown. In addition, add a label control to the lower edge of your form, with its Caption property set to your name. (Refer to the "Labels" section following "More Controls.") Use figure S-41 as a guideline, but feel free to modify the user interface to suit yourself (or your instructor).

Make sure to use meaningful names for your new command buttons, following the convention of beginning the name with lowercase "cmd."

"Hello World" in French: Bonjour tout le monde

"Hello World" in Italian: Ciao Mondo

More Controls

There are many more controls available for your use. Additional controls can be found in the Visual Basic toolbox, and they can also be purchased from third parties. In this limited overview, we will discuss only the most commonly-used controls. Refer to figure S-4 for the labeled toolbox controls. Figure S-42 shows some controls on a form.

You can see a complete list of the properties of each of these controls in two ways:

1) Place a control on a form and examine the properties list; and 2) click on a tool or a control and press F1 for context-sensitive Help. VB will display the Help page for that control, which provides a list of the properties and an explanation of their use.

Figure S-41
Make your form look something like this one. Make sure to include a label at the bottom, with its Caption set to your name.

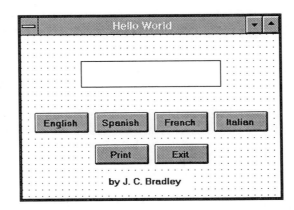

Figure S-42

Examples of labels, a frame,
option buttons, check boxes,
an image control with an icon
as its Picture property, and a
horizontal scroll bar.

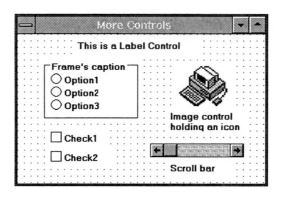

Labels

You use a label any time you have text that you don't want the user to be able to change.
Labels are good for titles, descriptions, directions, and program results. Set the value of the
Caption property to the text you want to appear on the form.

Frames

Frames are used as containers for other controls. Usually, groups of option buttons or check
boxes are placed in frames.

Check Boxes

Check boxes allow the user to select (or deselect) an option. In any group of check boxes,
one or more may be selected. The Value property of a check box is set to 0 if unchecked, 1
if checked, or 2 if grayed.

> Example: If chkBold.Value = 1 Then   'Take some action

Option Buttons

Use option buttons when only one button of a group may be selected. Any option buttons
placed directly on the form (not in a frame) function together as a group. A group of option
buttons inside a frame function together as a group. The best method is to first create a
frame, then create each option button inside the frame. You must be careful to *create* the
button inside the frame; don't create it on the form and drag it inside the frame—it still
belongs to the form's group, not the frame's group.

The Value property of an option button is set to True if selected; False if unselected.

> Example: If optGreen.Value = True Then   'Take some action

Images

An image control is used to hold a picture. You can set its Picture property to a file with an
extension of .BMP, .WMF, .ICO, or .DIB. First place the image control on a form, then
select its Picture property in the Properties window. Notice the Settings box has a new
button holding an ellipses (figure S-43). Click on the button, and the Load Picture dialog
box appears, where you can select a filename (figure S-44). Be aware that there are many
icon files included with Visual Basic; look in the Icons subdirectory under the VB directory.
(Icon files are not available with the Primer Edition.)

If you want the picture to enlarge to fill the image control, set its Stretch property
to True.

Scroll Bars

You can add horizontal scroll bars and vertical scroll bars to your form. Often scroll bars are used to allow the user to select a value over a given range. You, as the programmer, can choose the range (Min and Max) as well as the distance to move when the user clicks on the scroll arrows (SmallChange) and the gray area of the scroll bar (LargeChange). The current setting of the scroll box is stored in the Value property. For example, assume you are using a horizontal scroll bar for entry of an interest rate, which can vary from 5% to 15%. These would be your initial settings:

Property	Setting	
Name	hsbRate	
Min	.05	(Lowest value)
Max	.15	(Highest value)
LargeChange	.05	(Value change for gray area click)
Small Change	.005	(Value change for scroll arrow click)
Value	.05	(Initially set at the minimum value

The scroll bar receives a Change event when the user scrolls. In the hsbRate_Change event, you can check the current value of the scroll bar.

```
IntRate = hsbRate.Value
```

Figure S-43
To change the Picture property of an image control, click on the ellipses button.

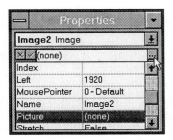

Figure S-44
The Load Picture dialog box. Select the filename of the picture you want to place in the image control.

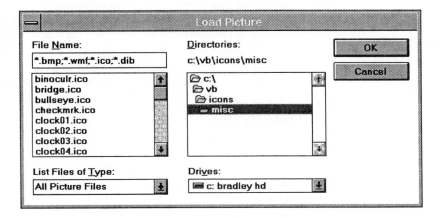

Recommended Naming Conventions for Visual Basic Objects

Name each object with a lowercase prefix, followed by a mixed-case name. Capitalize the first letter of each word in the name.

Object Type	Prefix	Example
Form	frm	frmDataEntry
Command button	cmd	cmdExit
Text box	txt	txtPaymentAmount
Label	lbl	lblTotal
Option button	opt	optBold
Check box	chk	chkPrintSummary
Frame	fra	fraSelection
Horizontal scroll bar	hsb	hsbRate
Vertical scroll bar	vsb	vsbTemperature
Image	img	imgLogo
Picture box	pic	picLandscape
Combo box	cbo	cboBookList
List box	lst	lstIngredients

Feedback

1. You can display program output in a text box or a label. When should you use a text box? a label?
2. How does the behavior of option buttons differ from that of check boxes?
3. If you want two groups of option buttons on a form, how can you make the groups operate independently?
4. Name four or five uses for scroll bars in data entry. (Do not include scrolling a list. List boxes automatically add scroll bars when the list is longer than can be seen at one time.)

Variables

Variables in Visual Basic are just like those in QBASIC, only better. You still have all of the same data types, plus some additional ones. Also, as mentioned earlier, you can (optionally) require that all variables be declared before use. Have you ever spelled variable names differently in two different locations and spent hours trying to find your error? This new option is highly recommended. The time you spend declaring variables is more than made up in decreased debugging time. All of our example programs include the Option Explicit statement in the general declarations section, and Dim statements for variables.

Data Types

In QBASIC you can determine the data type of a variable by adding a character to the end of the name, such as Person$ for string, Count% for integer, and Sum# for double-precision floating point. You can also do this in Visual Basic, but the practice is far less common, because you can declare the type without the suffix (see "Declaring Variables").

Data Type	Use For	Optional Suffix
Integer	Whole numbers in the range -32,768 to 32,767	%
Long	Large whole numbers in the range -2,147,483,648 to 2,147,483,647	&
Single	Single-precision floating point numbers with 6 digits of accuracy	!
Double	Double-precision floating point numbers with 14 digits of accuracy	#
Currency (new)	Decimal fractions	@
String	Alphanumeric data	$
Variant (new)	Chameleon data type that can hold any data of any type	none
User-defined Type	Data structures made up of standard data types	none

Declaring Variables

Use the familiar Dim statement to declare program variables. If you omit the data type, variables will be variants.

Examples:

```
Dim Counter          as Integer
Dim Expenditures     as Currency
Dim Names            as String
Dim Total(1 to 10)   as Long
```

Scope

The scope of a variable determines where it is available. For example, if you declare and use a variable called Counter in a subprogram, it is considered *local* to that subprogram; its name and value are not visible to any other subs. If another subprogram also uses a variable called Counter, it is a different variable, using a different memory location. If you actually need to have the value of Counter available in two different subprograms, you have two choices: 1) you can declare the variable to be common to the module (called a *module-level* variable); or, 2) you can pass the variable to the subprogram. Note: Passing variables to subprograms is covered in appendix G.

To create a module-level variable, place the Dim statement in the general declarations section of a form module. Refer to figures S-36 and S-37 to view the general declarations section.

There is a third level of scope, for projects with multiple forms. If you need to share variables among forms, you need *global variables*. Declare global variables in a standard code module (with a .BAS file extension), using the keyword Global (rather than Dim).

Example declarations in a standard code module:

```
Global MessageCount   as Integer      'global variable
Global GrandTotal     as Currency     'global variable
Dim StatusFlag        as Integer      'module-level variable in
                                      'standard code module
```

It is considered good programming (and more safe programming) to make the scope of variables as narrow as possible. So, first choice is local variables, second choice is module-level variables, and third choice is global variables, which should be used only if absolutely necessary.

Lifetime

The lifetime of a variable is how long it lasts (or *persists*, in programmer parlance). Variables local to a subprogram persist only for that one execution of the sub. Each call to the subprogram gets a new, freshly initialized copy of the variable. If you want to retain the value of a variable for multiple calls, you have two choices: 1) make it a module-level variable; or, 2) make it a *static* variable. A static variable *does* persist for multiple calls; that is, it will hold its value. If you want to create a running total during multiple calls to a subprogram, use a static local variable.

To declare a static variable, use the keyword *Static* in place of *Dim* or *Global*.
Examples:

```
Static RunningTotal    as Currency
Static EventCount      as Integer
```

Program Input

Using Visual Basic you can write powerful interactive projects that require only a fraction of the statements needed in QBASIC. But you must learn to do without some important QBASIC statements, such as Input, Read, and LPrint. The easiest way to input data into your program is to use text box controls. (Of course many other control types also get input from the user, such as check boxes, list boxes, option buttons, command buttons, and scroll bars.)

Using Text Box Controls for Input

In the Hello World project you used a text box control to display program output. Actually, the primary use of a text box is for program input. In figure S-45 there are two text boxes for user input. The user can move from one box to the next, make corrections, even cut and paste if desired, and click the Calculate button when finished. In your program code (in the cmdCalculate_click event procedure), you can use the Text property of each of the text boxes.

Examples:

```
RoomWidth = txtWidth.Text        'Assign Text property to a variable
```

When you want to do calculations with the Text property, you need to make sure it's a numeric value. The quickest and easiest way to do this is to use the Val function.

```
RoomWidth = Val(txtWidth.Text)   'Assign numeric value to a variable
```

You can also perform calculations directly with the Text property:

```
RoomArea = Val(txtLength.Text) * Val(txtWidth.Text)
```

This places the result of the calculation in a variable. You can also place the result directly in a property, such as the Caption property of a label:

```
lblArea.Caption = Val(txtLength.Text) * Val(txtWidth.Text)
```

Clearing Text Boxes and Labels

You can clear out the contents of a text box or label by setting it to an empty string. Use "" (no space between the two quotation marks).

Examples:

```
txtWidth.Text = ""               'Clear the contents

lblArea.Caption = ""             'Clear the contents
```

Resetting the Focus

In Windows programs, one control on the form always has the "focus." You can see the focus change as you use the Tab key to move from control to control. For controls such as command buttons and option buttons, the focus appears as a light dotted line. For text boxes, the insertion point (also called the cursor) appears in the box.

When your program begins, the insertion point is in the first text box you created. (You can change the order by setting the TabIndex property of text boxes.) After you clear text boxes, and want the insertion point to appear in the first text box for data entry, use the SetFocus method. Remember, it's Object.Method, so to set the insertion point in the text box called txtLength, use this statement:

```
txtLength.SetFocus               'Make the insertion point appear here
```

Programming Example:

This example solves the problem from chapter 1: It inputs the length and width of a room, calculates the area, and displays the result. To try this program yourself, select *New Project* from the *File* menu.

The form: See figure S-45

Figure S-45
The form for the room area calculation project.

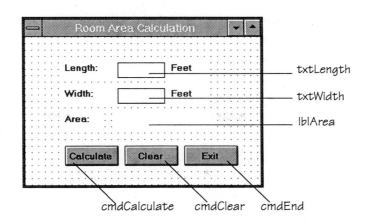

cmdCalculate   cmdClear   cmdEnd

Project Objects:

Object	Property	Setting
Form	Name	frmArea
	Caption	Room Area Calculation
Text box 1	Name	txtLength
	Text	(blank)
Text box 2	Name	txtWidth
	Text	(blank)
Label 1	Caption	Length
Label 2	Caption	Width
Label 3	Caption	Area
Label 4	Caption	Feet
Label 5	Caption	Feet
Label 6	Name	lblArea
	Caption	(blank)
Command button 1	Name	cmdCalculate
	Caption	Calculate
Command button 2	Name	cmdClear
	Caption	Clear
Command button 3	Name	cmdExit
	Caption	Exit

Project Event:

Event	Action
cmdCalculate_Click	Multiply the length by the width
	Display the area with a literal "Square Feet"
cmdClear_Click	Clear the length, width, and area
	Replace the cursor in the top text box
cmdExit_Click	End the program

The project coding:

```
'Room Area Calculation
'June 1995
'by J.C. Bradley
'This project will input the length and width of
' a room and calculate the area
Option Explicit

Sub cmdCalculate_Click ()
    'Calculate the area of a room
    Dim Area        As Single
    Area = Val(txtLength.Text) * Val(txtWidth.Text)
    lblArea.Caption = Area & " Square Feet"
End Sub

Sub cmdClear_Click ()
    'Clear out the previous values
    txtLength.Text = "" 'Empty string
    txtWidth.Text = ""
    lblArea.Caption = ""
    txtLength.SetFocus 'Place the insertion point in the text box
End Sub

Sub cmdExit_Click ()
    'End the program
    End
End Sub
```

Discussion:

Notice that labels that are not referred to in code are not renamed. The only label given a meaningful name is lblArea.

The initial remarks appear in the general declarations section of the form.

Program Output

As was mentioned earlier, Visual Basic does not have an LPrint statement. Technically, it doesn't have a Print statement either—it has a Print method, which can apply to a Form, to the Printer object, or to the Debug window object.

Printing in Visual Basic is more difficult than printing in QBASIC. Visual Basic was designed to run under Windows, a highly interactive environment. It's extremely easy to create forms for interactive programs. You may find the that easiest way to print is to create a nice-looking form and use the PrintForm method. However, this method prints the screen as a graphic, which does not look as good on most printers as text output. (As a side note, most professional programmers using Visual Basic use a separate utility program to format printed reports.)

Printing to the Printer

You can send output to the printer using Printer.Print (Object.Method). Visual Basic sets up a printer object in memory and sends your output there. Then, when your job terminates, or it receives an EndDoc or NewPage method, VB actually sends the contents of the printer object to the printer.

Formatting Lines

Although there is no Print Using, you can use many of the same formatting tools to which you are already accustomed. Commas and semicolons work as expected, as well as the Tab and Spc functions.

Example:

```
Printer.Print Tab(30); "Report Title"; Tab(60); "Page "; PageNumber
```

Printing Blank Lines

In contrast to QBASIC, you can't print a blank line with an empty Print. You must print *something*. You can, however, print an empty string.

```
Printer.Print ""      'Print a blank line
```

Terminating the Page or the Job

The NewPage method sends the current page to the printer and clears the printer object in memory so you can begin a new page. The EndDoc method sends the current page to the printer and terminates the printer job. Note: When your program terminates, VB automatically sends an EndDoc.

Examples:

```
Printer.NewPage        'Send page and begin a new page
Printer.EndDoc         'Send page and terminate print job
```

Formatting Numeric Values

When you want to format numbers for display, either on the printer or on the screen, use the Format function, which in many ways resembles Print Using.

The Format Function —General Form

```
Format[$](expression [ , "format description"] )
```

The optional dollar sign in the function name specifies that the formatted value be a string. Without the dollar sign, the value returned is a variant data type. In most situations the results are the same, but using the dollar sign is slightly more efficient.

"Expression" may be numeric or string, a variable, a literal, or a property.

"Format description" can take one of several forms. Visual Basic has some predefined formats for the most common situations. If you choose one of these formats, you include the format name in quotation marks. You can also create your own format strings, similar to Print Using.

Examples:

```
lblTotal.Caption = Format$(GrandTotal, "Standard")
txtCosts.Text = Format$(Costs, "Currency")
Printer.Print Tab(10); Format$(lblSum.Caption, "Fixed")
Printer.Print Tab(20); Format$(txtRate.Text, "Percent")
Printer.Print Format$(txtWholeNumber.Text, "#,###")
lblRounded.Caption = Format$(BigLongFraction, "#,###.#")
```

Check Help or the Visual Basic manual for more predefined formats. The ones shown here are the most common formats.

Predefined Format	Description
Standard	Two digits to the right of the decimal point, and a comma for thousands, if necessary
Currency	A dollar sign; two digits to the right of the decimal point; a comma for thousands, if necessary; negative numbers in parentheses
Fixed	At least one digit to the left of the decimal point; two digits to the right of the decimal point; no comma for thousands
Percent	Number multiplied by 100 with percent sign on right; two digits to the right of the decimal point

Initialization Steps

Often you need to initialize some items as the project begins. In the example project that follows, the report titles and column headings are printed as an initialization step. As a project begins and the initial form is loaded, a Form_Load event occurs. The event procedure for this event is the ideal location for such initialization. Double-click on the form (not on a control) to view the Form_Load procedure.

See the Form_Load procedure in the following project for an example of printing headings.

Programming Example:

The best way to learn to program in Visual Basic is to do it. If you treat this example as a tutorial, and enter it and run it, you will be on your way to writing Windows applications. Just reading the example is like trying to learn a foreign language or mathematics by reading, so fire up the computer and Visual Basic and *do* the example program.

This program is for the R 'n R Book and Coffee Shop. They need to be able to enter book orders and print a listing, along with a total.

Additionally, they would like the option to display or not display the shop's logo on the screen. (Set the image control's Visible property to True or False.)

Note: When running a Windows application, use the Tab key to move from one text box to the next. The TabIndex property of controls determines the order in which the focus moves. The Enter key activates the default command button—in this case, the OK button.

The form:
See figure S-46.

Figure S-46
The form for the R 'n R Book
Order project

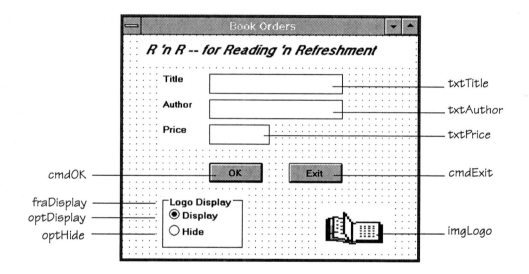

Supplement

Project Objects:

Object	Property	Setting
Form	Name	frmOrders
	Caption	Book Orders
Text box 1	Name	txtTitle
	Text	(blank)
Text box 2	Name	txtAuthor
	Text	(blank)
Text box 3	Name	txtPrice
	Text	(blank)
Label 1	Caption	R 'n R — for Reading 'n Refreshment
	FontSize	12
	ForeColor	(click on ellipses button and select blue)
	FontItalic	True
Label 2	Caption	Title
Label 3	Caption	Author
Label 4	Caption	Price
Command button 1	Name	cmdOK
	Caption	OK
	Default	True (makes dark outline & allows Enter key for selection)
Command button 2	Name	cmdExit
	Caption	Exit
Frame 1	Name	fraDisplay
	Caption	Logo Display
Option button 1	Name	optDisplay
	Caption	Display
	Value	True (makes button selected when program begins)
Option button 2	Name	optHide
	Caption	Hide
Image 1	Name	imgLogo
	Stretch	True
	Picture	(Primer users must find a logo. Others: Click on ellipses button, find VB\ICONS\WRITING\BOOK03)

Project Events:

Event	Actions
cmdOK_Click	Add price to total
	Print a line
	Clear fields on screen
	Reset insertion point
cmdExit_Click	Print report total line
	End the print job
	End the program
imgDisplay_Click	Display the logo
imgHide_Click	Hide the logo

The project coding:

```
'R 'n R Book Orders
'by J.C. Bradley
'June 1995
'This program allows the user to enter book orders on the screen,
' calculates a total, and prints a report on the printer

Option Explicit
Dim BookTotal           As Currency      'Module-level variable

Sub Form_Load ()
    'Print the report headings

    Printer.Print ""                     'Blank line
    Printer.Print ""                     'Blank line
    Printer.Print Tab(30); "R 'n R — Reading 'n Refreshment"
    Printer.Print Tab(40);            ' "Book Order List"
    Printer.Print ""                     'Blank line
    Printer.Print Tab(5); "Title"; Tab(35); "Author"; Tab(75); "Price"
    Printer.Print Tab(5); String$(75, "=")
    Printer.Print ""                     'Blank line
    Printer.Print ""                     'Blank line
End Sub

Sub cmdOK_Click ()
    'Add book price to total, print a line, clear screen
    Dim PriceFormatted As String

    BookTotal = BookTotal + Val(txtPrice.Text)
    PriceFormatted = Format$(txtPrice.Text, "standard")
    Printer.Print Tab(5); txtTitle.Text; Tab(35); txtAuthor.Text;
    Printer.Print Tab(80 - Len(PriceFormatted)); PriceFormatted
    txtTitle.Text = ""                   'Clear out text boxes
    txtAuthor.Text = ""
    txtPrice.Text = ""
    txtTitle.SetFocus                    'Replace insertion point
End Sub

Sub cmdExit_Click ()
    'Print final total and exit

    Printer.Print ""                     'Blank line
    Printer.Print Tab(5); "Total";       'Align total with column above
    Printer.Print Tab(80 - Len(Format$(BookTotal, "Standard"))); Format$(BookTotal, "Standard")
    Printer.EndDoc                       'Terminate printer job
    End
End Sub

Sub optDisplay_Click ()
    'Make the logo visible

    imgLogo.Visible = True
End Sub

Sub optHide_Click ()
    'Make the logo invisible

    imgLogo.Visible = False
End Sub
```

Feedback

1. What is the purpose of the currency data type? Is there any advantage to using currency rather than single or double? (You might refer to "Binary Fractions and Accuracy" in chapter 10.)
2. Can you think of any advantages of using the variant data type? any disadvantages?
3. What is meant by a variable's *scope*? Give examples of each of the three choices for scope in Visual Basic.
4. How do you declare a local variable? a module-level variable? a global variable?
5. Write the VB code to take the contents of a text box called txtName and assign it to a variable called PersonName. Make sure to declare the variable first.
6. Write the VB code to clear the contents of a text box called txtCountry and place the insertion point back in the box.
7. What is the purpose of the EndDoc method? the Print method? the NewPage method?
8. When does the Form_Load event occur? What program steps might go there?
9. In QBASIC, a program that prints a list with multiple detail lines requires a loop. Why is no loop used in the Visual Basic project?

Summary

1. Visual Basic is an event driven language, rather than a procedural language. A program responds to events initiated by the user.
2. In the object model of programming, there are objects which have properties and methods.
3. The three steps to creating a Visual Basic project are: 1) Define the user interface; 2) Set the properties; and 3) Write the Basic code.
4. A Visual Basic project consists of at least a .MAK file and a .FRM file, and may have multiple .FRM files, .BAS files, and .VBX files.
5. The VB environment consists of the Form window, the Project window, the Properties window, the toolbox, the menu bar, and the toolbar.
6. VB has three modes: design time, run time, and break time.
7. Visual Basic code is written in procedures, which are subprograms and functions.
8. Good programming practices require remarks in every procedure and in the general declarations section of a module. All statements between Sub and End Sub should be indented.
9. You can print out a picture of the form; the form text, which is a listing of all objects and their properties; and the form code, which is the Basic statements in the project.
10. The Option Explicit statement, placed at the top of a module, requires that all variables be declared before use. Visual Basic will automatically add Option Explicit to all new modules if the *Options/Environment/Require Variable Declaration* option is set to *Yes*.
11. Visual Basic debugging tools include setting breakpoints, single-stepping program execution, displaying and changing values in the Debug window, and setting Watch expressions.
12. The VB controls covered are text boxes, command buttons, labels, frames, check boxes, option buttons, images, and scroll bars.
13. VB (2.0 and 3.0) has added two new data types: currency and variant.
14. Variables are declared with the Dim, Global, or Static statements.
15. Variables may have a scope of local, module-level, or global.
16. Variables are reinitialized for each call to a subprogram unless declared with the static keyword.
17. Text box controls are used for program input. To calculate with the Text property of a text box, use the Val function to make sure the value is numeric.
18. Clear a text box or a label with an empty string; reset the insertion point in a text box with the SetFocus method.
19. Print output on the printer using Printer.Print. Printer.NewPage sends a page to the printer, and Printer.EndDoc terminates the print job.
20. The Format[$] function can format numbers for display or printing. VB has some predefined formats; you can also create your own print image, similar to Print Using.
21. The Form_Load event occurs as a program begins and the form is loaded. This is a good location for initialization steps.

Programming Exercises

For each of these exercises, design a graphical user interface. Use text boxes for user input and labels for output that you don't want the user to change. (Be aware that labels have a BorderStyle property that you can set to *Single*, which makes a label appear like a text box.)

Consider setting the Default property of one of the command buttons to True, so the user can press Enter after typing text, rather than pick up the mouse to click.

Along the lower edge of each form, include a label with your name so that you will be able to identify any PrintForm output.

Follow good coding guidelines. Include remarks at the top of every procedure; include identifying remarks in the general declaration section; name all objects following the guidelines in this chapter; indent all statements between Sub and End Sub, and follow proper indentation guidelines for If...Then...Else and loops.

1. Calculate the stopping distance for an automobile using the formula in exercise 2.1. Include command buttons for Calculate, Clear, Print, and Exit. (Use PrintForm to print.)

2. Calculate the future value of an investment using the formula in exercise 2.5. Include command buttons for Calculate, Clear, Print, and Exit. (Use PrintForm to print.)

3. Calculate and print a report for piecework employees. Following the payscale shown in exercise 4.1, input each name and number of pieces, display the worker's pay on the screen, and print a report. The report should be similar to the report shown in exercise 4.1, with a title, column headings, and totals. Also include the requirements of exercise 4.2, to include lines for the greatest, least, and average.

   Include command buttons for OK (or Calculate), Clear, and Exit.

4. Write a project that will input sales information and print an invoice. You will follow the general directions in exercise 4.12, but with some modifications.

   Use a check box for the user to select whether or not the item is taxable. In your calculation procedure, check the Value property of the check box:

   ```
   If chkTaxable.Value = 1 Then   'Taxable item, take appropriate action
   ```

   Include command buttons for OK (accept current item, calculate, and print a line); New Customer (complete the previous invoice, clear out the customer name, begin a new invoice); Print Screen (use PrintForm); and Exit (complete the current invoice and quit).

5. Write a Weather Report program using the icons that come with Visual Basic. (Note: If you are using the Primer Edition, you will have to find pictures elsewhere.)

   Design a user interface similar to the one shown on the next page. Place four option buttons inside a frame.

   For the four image controls, set Stretch = True, Visible = False, and the Picture property to one of the icons. The four icons used in the diagram are:

   > VB\ICONS\ELEMENTS\CLOUD.ICO
   > VB\ICONS\ELEMENTS\RAIN.ICO
   > VB\ICONS\ELEMENTS\SNOW.ICO
   > VB\ICONS\ELEMENTS\SUN.ICO

   When the user clicks on an option button, its Click event occurs. In the Click event procedure for each option button, make the correct image visible, the other images invisible, and change the message in the label at the bottom of the screen to something appropriate for the weather. Also include the user's name in the message (taken from the text box above).

   For example, when the user clicks on the Sunny button, you might display a message like:

   ```
   lblMessage.Caption = "The weather looks sunny, " & txtName.Text
   ```

   The Print button should print the form (use PrintForm).

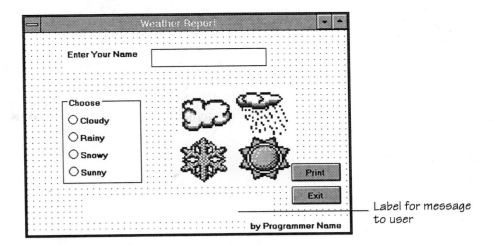

Label for message
to user

6. Write a currency conversion program, using option buttons to select the new currency. Use the four countries shown on the sample form, or any four of your choice. Look up current conversion rates or use the (obsolete) rates shown below.

    Do all currency conversion in the Click event for the Convert button. Use If statements to determine which option button is selected. Then, display the name of the country and the converted amount below the number of dollars.

    ```
    If optJapan.Value = True Then
            ExchangeRate = .011813
            lblCurrency.Caption = "Japan"
    ```

    Format the converted amount to display two digits to the right of the decimal point (but don't include a dollar sign).

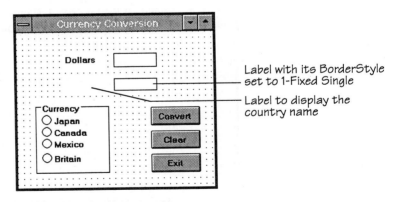

Label with its BorderStyle
set to 1-Fixed Single

Label to display the
country name

The focus must be in the Dollars text box when the program begins; make sure its TabIndex property is set to zero.

Conversion rates (or find current rates in your newspaper):

Japan   .011813
Canada .7271
Mexico .161290
Britain   1.5985

7. Write a program that will change the attributes of a label, depending on the settings of check boxes and a scroll bar. Replace "This is a Test" on the sample form with a message of your choice: your name, a friend's name, your school name, company name, etc. (Keep it short, as you will be increasing the font size considerably.)

Hints about the objects:

large label at top	Make the label quite large and set its Alignment to Center. Examine the properties of labels, and notice particularly the FontSize, FontBold, FontItalic, and FontUnderline.
check boxes	By default, the label will be bold, so set the Value of the Bold check box to 1 (for selected).
horizontal scroll bar	Set its Min = 5, Max = 35, SmallChange = 1, LargeChange = 5. Notice the Value property has been set to 5, the minimum.
Font Size label	Actually there are two labels here: one that says "Font Size," and the other that holds the value selected with the horizontal scroll bar.

Hints about the event procedures:

Click event for check boxes	A Click event occurs each time the state of the check box changes. You must determine whether it was checked (Value = 1) or unchecked (Value = 0). If checked, set the corresponding property of the label to True; if unchecked, set it to False.
Change event for the horizontal scroll bar	Each time the scroll bar is changed, the Change event occurs. At that time, change the Font Size label below the scroll bar, and change the FontSize property of the label. Both should be set to the Value property of the scroll bar.

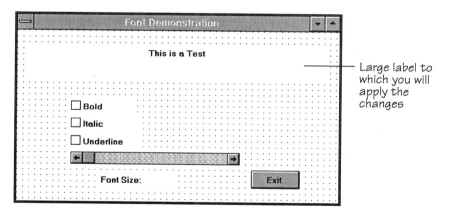

Possible additions: You can also change the color of the label by changing its ForeColor property. Look up the RGB function in Help. For example, to change the label to red, use this statement:

```
lblMessage.ForeColor = RGB(255, 0, 0)
```

8. Write two projects: one to store a table in a small sequential file, and a second to use that table for table lookups.

Project 1: Create a form for data entry of state names and their two-letter abbreviations. Open the file for output in the Form_Load procedure and close it in the Exit procedure. As the user enters a state name and abbreviation, write them into the file. Refer to exercise 11.4 for the list of state names and their two-letter abbreviations.

Project 2: Create a form that allows the user to enter either a state name or abbreviation. When s/he clicks on a Look Up button, look up and display the corresponding value. Make sure to include a Clear button and an Exit button.

You must load the data from your file into the arrays during the Form_Load event procedure.

Note: You can use a random file, if you prefer. However, Type statements must go in a standard code module (a .BAS file), which wasn't covered in this chapter.

Alternative: You could create the sequential file with a text editor, eliminating the first part of the project. Then, just write one project to read the file into arrays and do the lookup.

OPEN "filename" FOR mode AS #filenum	Alternate format. Opens a sequential data file. Mode must be INPUT, OUTPUT, or APPEND.	364
OPEN "R", #filenum, "filename", reclength	Opens a random data file.	386
OPEN "filename" [FOR RANDOM] AS #filenum [LEN = reclength]	Alternate format. Opens a random data file.	386
OPTION BASE number	Sets the minimum value for array subscripts. Must be 0 or 1.	298
PAINT (X, Y) [[,FillColor] [,BoundaryColor]]	Fills an area on the screen with the selected color, in medium resolution graphics mode.	458
PALETTE	Assigns colors to attributes.	471
PLAY string	Plays music specified in string. A special music definition language includes letters for notes, length, tempo, rests, and speed.	232
PRESET (X, Y) [, PaletteColor]	Resets a point in medium or high resolution mode graphics.	449
PRINT [items to print]	Displays data on the screen. Items to print may be separated by semicolons or commas (with different results).	12
PRINT USING "string literal"; items to print PRINT USING stringvariable; items to print	Displays data on the screen, according to the format specified in the string literal or variable.	372
PSET (X, Y) [, ColorAttribute]	Draws a point in medium or high resolution mode graphics. Note that color is valid only for medium resolution.	449
PUT #filenum [,RecordNumber], RecordName	Writes data from a record variable into a random file in the record number named. If the record number is omitted, the record is written in the *next* position.	388
RANDOMIZE [numeric expression|TIMER]	Reseeds the random number generator. If the expression is omitted, a seed is requested from the keyboard.	280
READ variable [,variable2,...]	Reads constants from DATA statements into the variable(s) named.	113
REM remark	Inserts a remark into the program. An alternate format allows substitution of a single quote (') for the word REM.	11
RESTORE	Resets the DATA pointer to the beginning of the program so that data may be reread.	118
RESUME RESUME NEXT RESUME linelabel	Resumes execution after error trapping with ON ERROR...GOTO.	527
RETURN	Returns from a subroutine to the statement immediately following the GOSUB.	17